The Devil in the Holy Water

The Devil in the Holy Water
or the Art of Slander
from Louis XIV to Napoleon

Robert Darnton

PENN

University of Pennsylvania Press
Philadelphia

Published by
University of Pennsylvania Press
Philadelphia, Pennsylvania 19104–4112

Printed in the United States of America on acid-free paper
10 9 8 7 6 5 4 3 2 1

Library of Congress Cataloging-in-Publication Data

Darnton, Robert.
    The devil in the holy water or the art of slander from Louis XIV to Napoleon / Robert Darnton.
        p.   cm.—(Material texts)
    Includes bibliographical references and index.
    ISBN 978-0-8122-4183-9 (alk. paper)
    1. French literature—18th century—History and criticism.   2. Underground literature—
Publishing—France—History—18th century.   3. Libel and slander in literature.   4. Libel and
slander—France—History—18th century.   5. Authors and publishers—France—History—18th
century.   6. Publishers and publishing—France—History—18th century.   7. Law and literature—
France—History—18th century.   8. Literature and society—France—History—18th century.
I. Title.
PQ265.D3675   2009
840.9′005—dc22
                                                                                2009028209

To the memory of Lawrence Stone

Contents

Frontispice du Gazettier Cuirassé.

*Aetna haec impavido vulcania tela ministrat
Aela Gigantaeos Débellatura furores.*

Figure 1. *Le Gazetier cuirassé*, frontispiece to the 1777 edition. (Private copy)

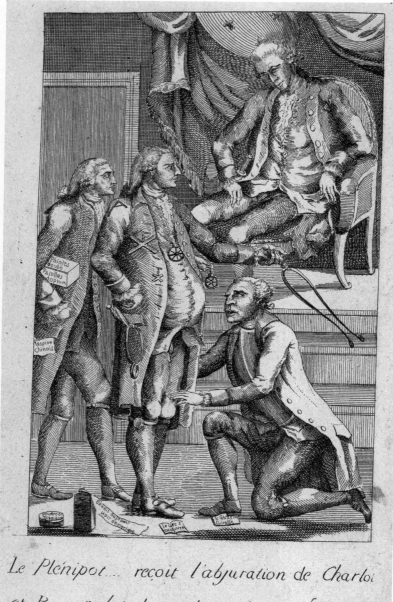

Figure 2. *Le Diable dans un bénitier,* frontispiece. (Private copy)

Figure 3. *La Police de Paris dévoilée*, frontispiece. (Private copy)

P. MANUEL.

Je ne Suis point né délicat,
J'ai l'Ame Sordide et Commune,
J'ai Pillé les Autels et j'ai trahi l'Etat,
Pour accélérer ma Fortune,

Figure 4. *Vie secrète de Pierre Manuel*, print serving as a frontispiece. (Princeton University Library)

Introduction

The four frontispieces reproduced in the preceding pages are evidence of a curious variety of literature, the kind that was most abhorred in early modern Europe and went under the name of libel. The four frontispieces set off the texts of four libels, and the libels connect to tell a story—a tale so full of intrigue and hugger-mugger that it seems too extravagant to be true, although it can be confirmed at every point by documents from the archives of the French police and diplomatic service. Why try to reconstruct it? Aside from its qualities as a detective story, it reveals a great deal about authorship, the book trade, journalism, public opinion, ideology, and revolution in eighteenth-century France. By studying four particularly pungent libels, it is possible to see how the art and politics of slander developed through four regimes—from the reign of Louis XV to that of Louis XVI, the constitutional monarchy of 1789–92, and the Jacobin republic of 1792–94. From these case studies, one can then broaden the investigation to take in the literature of libel in general.

To understand libel it is important to study libelers and the world that they inhabited. They lived in Grub Street, a milieu that was becoming overcrowded after 1750 owing to a population explosion in the republic of letters. By 1789, France had developed a large subculture of indigent authors—672 poets alone, according to one contemporary estimate.[1] Most of them lived down-and-out in Paris, surviving as best they could by hack work and scraps of patronage. When driven to desperation, by either debt or the threat of the Bastille, they tried to escape. They fled to Brussels, Amsterdam, Berlin, Stockholm, St. Petersburg, and other urban centers with Grub Streets of their own. A diaspora of ragged writers sought their fortune wherever they could exploit the fascination for all things French. They tutored, translated, peddled pamphlets, directed plays, dabbled in journalism, speculated in publishing, and spread Parisian fashions in everything from bonnets to books.[2]

The largest colony of all existed in London, which had welcomed French émigrés since the sixteenth century when the first Huguenots sought refuge from persecution. London developed the liveliest Grub Street culture in Europe. It was the site of the *Grub Street Journal* (1730–37) and of the street itself, which ran through the East End and had begun accumulating a population of hack writers in the early seventeenth century. By 1726 when Voltaire arrived as a refugee from the Bastille, the hacks had moved to other addresses and supported themselves in large part from the dogfighting and mudslinging typical of Hanoverian politics.[3] Their Parisian counterparts lived in similar style, scattered in garrets throughout the city. They developed their own genre for slinging mud: the *libelle* (libel), a scandalous account of public affairs and private life among the great figures of the court and capital. The term does not get much use in modern French, but it belonged to common parlance in the book trade of the Ancien Régime, and the authors of such works went down in the files of the police as *libellistes* (libelers).[4]

The colony of French libelers in London had learned to live in the Grub Streets of both capitals. Most of them got their basic training in slander in the literary underground of Paris and emigrated to escape imprisonment, not just in the Bastille but worse—the sordid cells of Bicêtre or Fort l'Evêque or the galleys of Marseille after branding and pillorying in the Place de Grève. Upon their arrival in London, they discovered a world of unbridled pamphleteering and journalism, much of it financed by politicians who paid hack writers to vilify their rivals. Some of the expatriates took up journalism themselves, particularly as contributors to the *Courrier de l'Europe*, a biweekly published in London and reprinted in Boulogne-sur-Mer, which provided the fullest reports about the American Revolution and British politics that were available to French readers during the 1770s and 1780s. Others lived from libels. Thanks to reports supplied by secret informants in Paris and Versailles, they churned out books and pamphlets that slandered everyone from the king and his ministers down to dancing girls and men-about-town. Their works sold openly in England, above all in a bookshop in St. James Street, London, operated by a Genevan expatriate named Boissière. But their main market was in France, where libels became a staple of the underground book trade.[5]

Just how deep and far the underground extended is impossible to say. It certainly penetrated every corner of the kingdom, and it developed into the most vital sector of the publishing industry during the second half of the century. To be published legally, a book had to pass through a gauntlet of censors and bureaucrats attached to the government office in charge of the book trade (Direction de la librairie). By 1789 the government employed nearly two hundred censors to vet manuscripts. They often objected to deficiencies in style and content as well as anything that offended the Church, the state, conventional morality, and the reputation of individuals. Without their written approbation, no book could qualify for a royal privilege, issued by the Chancellory, which conveyed legality and something similar to a copyright. Book

inspectors policed the trade in major cities, confiscating illegal works in cus-
tomshouses and raiding bookshops as occasions arose. The Parisian booksellers' guild (Communauté des libraires et des imprimeurs de Paris) also
exercised police powers, which it used to reinforce its monopoly on privileged
literature.[6]

_The system was less rigid in practice than it appeared to be on paper—
necessarily so, because the printed regulations, about three thousand edicts on
the book trade issued between 1715 and 1789, came so thick and fast that no
bookseller could keep track of the rules of the game even if he intended to
observe them.[7] Inspectors often looked the other way when illegal shipments
entered their territory, and the use of semi-official measures like *permissions
tacites* (agreements to tolerate books that could not receive privileges) opened
up large loopholes in the repressive legislation. Nonetheless, works that challenged orthodox views—including almost the entire Enlightenment—usually
were produced in the printing shops that proliferated outside France's borders
from Amsterdam and The Hague to Brussels, Liège, the Rhineland, Switzerland, and Avignon, which then was papal territory. These publishing houses
also pirated everything that sold well in the legal trade. They developed elaborate networks of smugglers to get the books across France's porous borders
and to distributors who relayed them to booksellers and peddlers everywhere
within the kingdom. By providing hungry readers with a spicy diet of forbidden literature and pirated works, the underground dealers did an enormous
business. They probably transmitted more than half the current literature produced during the eighteenth century—that is, books in all fields of fiction and
nonfiction, aside from professional works, religious publications, and almanacs and chapbooks.[8]

In a previous study, I compiled orders for prohibited literature from
booksellers scattered throughout France and constructed a retrospective best-
seller list. The list included books by Voltaire, Rousseau, and other famous
philosophes along with plenty of pornographic and irreligious works. But a
surprising proportion of the best-sellers were libels—whether slanderous biographies of public personages, inflammatory accounts of contemporary history, or a titillating variety of journalism known as *chroniques scandaleuses.*
Five of the twelve books most in demand—taken from a sample that included
720 titles—belonged to this category. They were *Anecdotes sur Mme la comtesse
du Barry* (1775); *Journal historique de la révolution opérée dans la constitution de
la monarchie française par M. de Maupeou* (1774–76), seven volumes; *L'Arrétin*
(1763), titled *L'Arrétin moderne* in some later editions; *Mémoires de l'abbé Terray, contrôleur-général* (1776), two volumes; and *Mémoires de Louis XV, roi de
France et de Navarre* (1775).[9] Other libels located high on the best-seller list

[handwritten margin notes: "but le rigid in practi"; "Smuggly of illicit books"]

were *L'Observateur anglais, ou correspondance secrète entre Milord All'Eye et Milord All'Ear* (1777–78), ten volumes; *Vie privée de Louis XV, ou principaux événements, particularités et anecdotes de son règne* (1781), four volumes; *Correspondance secrète et familière de M. de Maupeou avec M. de Sor***, conseiller du nouveau parlement* (1771), three volumes; *Les Fastes de Louis XV, de ses ministres, maîtresses, généraux et autres notables personnages de son règne* (1782), two volumes; *Mémoires secrets pour servir à l'histoire de la république des lettres en France* (1777–89), thirty-six volumes; and *Le Gazetier cuirassé, ou anecdotes scandaleuses de la cour de France* (1771).

All these books were anonymous. All were written by obscure hacks. Many were substantial works, which ran to several volumes and gave a disenchanted view of current events and the private lives of "the great" (*les grands*). When I waded into the texts, I found them to be slanderous, tendentious, wicked, indecent, and very good reading: that is why they sold so well. Yet they had never made it into literary history and rarely figured in scholarship on politics and ideology. A lost world was waiting to be explored.

That world looked too vast to be circumnavigated in one book. After publishing some studies of the underground itself—the way it operated and the general character of the literature it purveyed—I decided to investigate the genres that the French lumped together under the denomination of *libelles*. Instead of surveying hundreds of slanderous works and building up an argument, book by book, to general conclusions, I decided to proceed by a close analysis of some representative texts and then to work outward toward a general interpretation of the art and politics of slander. Libels took aim at obvious targets, but they played on the sensitivity of early modern readers in a manner that can seem bewildering today. In fact, some of the texts operate like puzzles. To get their message the reader must crack a code, and once the deciphering is done all sorts of questions arise about the milieu of the authors and the French authorities' attempts to repress them.

Many of the most inflammatory libels from the 1770s and 1780s were produced by the French expatriates in London—"at a hundred leagues from the Bastille," as they put it on the title pages of their tracts. Not only did they slander everyone of any importance in Versailles, but they also grafted blackmail operations onto their literary speculations. The French government responded by sending a series of secret agents to assassinate, kidnap, or buy off the London libelers. Their adventures and misadventures provide a rocambolesque tale that leads directly into the French Revolution. The same kind of literature, developed by many of the same authors, fueled polemics right through the Terror. Its substance changed while its form remained the same.

To understand the interplay of continuity and change, it is necessary to see the polemics of the late eighteenth century from a larger perspective. The long-term history of libeling leads back to the court intrigues of the seventeenth century, the religious wars of the sixteenth century, the power struggles in Renaissance Italy, and the literature of ancient Greece and Rome. Without attempting to recount it in detail, I have tried to show how libelers from the later period drew on techniques developed by early masters such as Aretino and Procopius. Character assassination might seem to be straightforward: dig up some mud and sling it. When studied up close and surveyed over the centuries, however, libels turn out to have peculiar characteristics. They combined basic ingredients, which went under names that sound familiar—"anecdotes," "portraits," "nouvelles" (news)—but actually belonged to rhetorical techniques designed to appeal to early modern readers. Yet all libels had one thing in common: they reduced power struggles to the play of personalities. Whether they vilified royal mistresses or sans-culotte agitators, they avoided complex questions of policy and principle, and they concentrated their fire on the character of their victims. Public affairs therefore appear in libel literature as the product of private lives—sometimes literally, as in the series of "private lives" that extends from *Vie privée de Louis XV* to *Vie privée du général Buonaparte*.

Why devote so much labor and so many pages to such a smutty subject? Almost any book about eighteenth-century France is bound to bear on classic questions about ideology, politics, and the first great revolution of modern times. This book has implications for those questions, but it pursues a different purpose. It is meant to explore a body of literature and the subculture that generated it. I want to understand the lives of libelers, the relation of their publications to their milieu, the way their texts worked (in the use of images and typography as well as rhetoric), the interconnections of libels as a corpus of literature, and, to the extent possible, the reactions of their readers. Libels also figured in political struggles, in the rivalry of court factions before 1789 and of political parties afterward. I will indicate their relevance to political history as occasions arise, but I am not attempting to rewrite that history, and I do not intend to go over familiar subjects such as Jansenism, the parliamentary opposition to the crown, the ideology of absolutism, the state-sponsored reform movement, and the application of Enlightenment ideas to political issues. Instead, I want to strike out in a different direction, one that leads into the problematic area where history and literature shade off into anthropology.[10]

Taken together, the libels communicated an outlook on political authority that can be characterized as folklore or mythology.[11] Although tendentious and inaccurate, it provided a way for the French to make sense of the world

allowing readers to make sense of world around them

around them, not the immediate world of family life and labor but the larger sphere of famous people and great events. The making of meaning, as anthropologists understand it, is a fundamental aspect of the human condition, conveyed primarily by myths and symbols. It took place in many ways in eighteenth-century France, among them by means of telling, hearing, writing, and reading stories. Narratives about the king, his mistresses and ministers, and other public figures lent themselves to a mythical view of the great (*les grands*). As pictured in the literature of libel, *les grands* inhabited a kind of satanic fairyland where they could give full rein to the pursuit of lust and power. In remote settings like the king's apartments in Versailles, the boudoirs of Parisian mansions, and boxes at the opera they behaved like gods, the capricious and malicious deities that had presided over the fate of Greece and Rome. But the fate of France was tied to current events. The rich, the well-born, and the powerful determined the course of affairs that touched the lives of ordinary people, or at least aroused their interest. As the century wore on and disasters accumulated—in war, in peace, and in the marketplace—the demand for information about behavior at the summit of society increased among people near the bottom, those who composed a literate and semi-literate public located for the most part in towns and cities. It could not be satisfied by legal literature, because biographies of public personages, accounts of current events, and most forms of contemporary history were prohibited. For information on such subjects, the French had to rely on whatever they could get from the literary underground—in large part, that is, from libels. They were drawn into an imaginary realm populated by characters who epitomized life among the great—the abbé Dubois, the maréchal de Richelieu, Mme de Pompadour, Mme du Barry, and all the members of the royal family. They came to see the fate of France as a story captured in *Vie privée de Louis XV* and dozens of similar works.

The reduction of complex contingencies to narratives about public figures has proliferated in many times and places. It still exists today. In fact, the personalization of politics has become more insidious than ever, because modern technology makes it possible to spread scandal on a scale undreamt of in the past. Yet today's mass media adhere to a principle worked out in hand-powered printing shops centuries ago: names make news.

Slander has always been a nasty business, but its unsavory character is no reason to consider it unworthy of serious study. By destroying reputations, it helped delegitimize regimes and bring down governments in many times and places. The study of slander in eighteenth-century France is particularly revealing because it shows how a literary current eroded authority under an absolute

→ *what RD thinks slander did*

cont. under
Rev. — devel. from time
but   of L XV

monarchy and became absorbed in a republican political culture, one that reached its extreme point under Robespierre but that carried with it varieties of mudslinging that had been developed under Louis XV. The story therefore begins with one of the most damaging attacks against Louis XV, *Le Gazetier cuirassé* (1771).

PART I

Interlocking Libels

Chapter 1
The Armor-Plated Gazetteer

Faced with the first of the four illustrations presented at the beginning of the book, one might ask a question that belongs at the start of any investigation, according to a formula attributed to Erving Goffman: What is going on here?

The frontispiece appeared opposite the title page of *Le Gazetier cuirassé ou anecdotes scandaleuses de la cour de France*, one of the most shocking and best-selling libels from the Ancien Régime. It shows how a libeler chose to represent himself. He is an armor-plated gazetteer, firing off cannonades in all directions, especially at the menacing figures in the heavens above. Although it stands out as a particularly dramatic image of an eighteenth-century writer, it is difficult to decipher, perhaps intentionally so, because the book was designed to be provocative. It uses two basic devices to catch and hold the attention of readers: it shocks them by slandering the great, and it amuses them by hiding the slander in allusions that have to be puzzled out.

The first edition of *Le Gazetier cuirassé* appeared in 1771, at the height of the greatest political crisis during the reign of Louis XV.[1] The chancellor René Nicolas de Maupeou had reorganized the judicial system by a coup, spectacular enough to be called a "revolution" by contemporaries, which destroyed the political power of the parlements (high courts, which often opposed royal policy) and removed the main obstacles to the exercise of royal power. With the support of the king's mistress, Jeanne Bécu, comtesse du Barry, Maupeou and his fellow ministers, Emmanuel Armand de Vignerot, duc d'Aiguillon, and abbé Joseph Marie Terray, ruled France with an iron hand until the death of the king in 1774. Protests poured out, many of them in the form of libels—so many libels directed at Maupeou that they came to be known collectively as *Maupeouana*. *Le Gazetier cuirassé* stood out as the boldest and most brazen example of this underground literature.

The first edition was a crude piece of printing, done on cheap paper without a frontispiece. Its title page proclaimed its character. It would regale the reader with scandalous anecdotes, and it would blast away at the greatest figures in France from the safety of a location designated by its address: "Printed

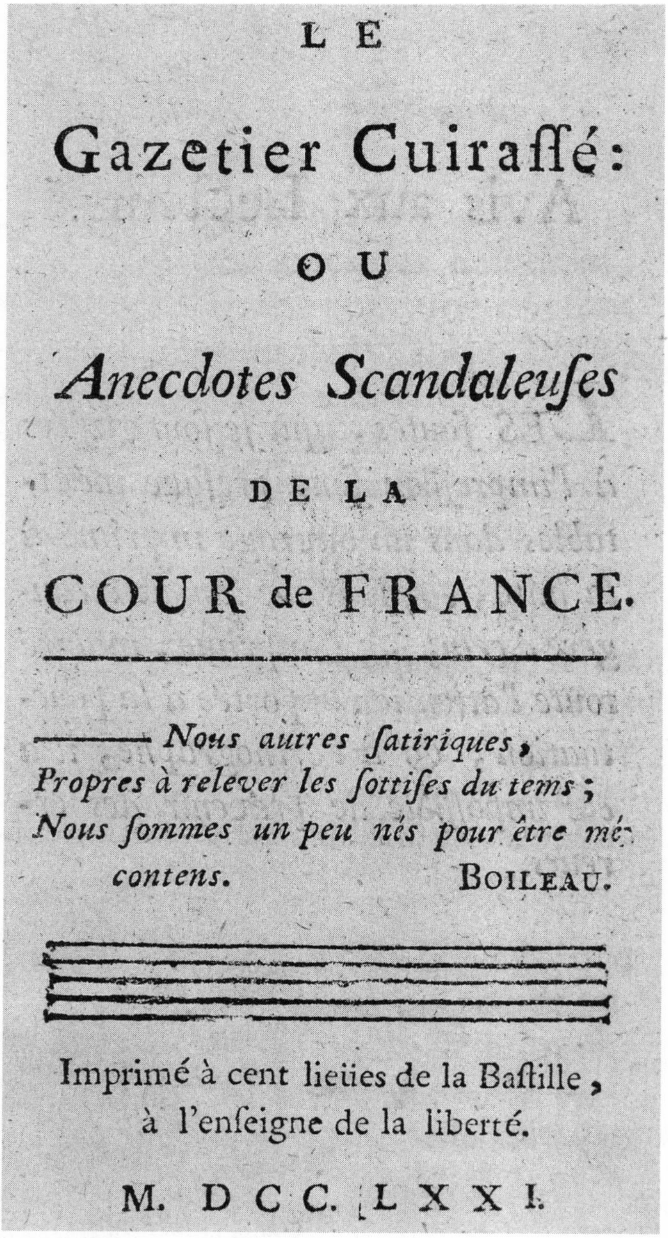

LE

Gazetier Cuiraſſé:

OU

Anecdotes Scandaleuſes

DE LA

COUR de FRANCE.

───────────────────────

──── *Nous autres ſatiriques ,*
Propres à relever les ſottiſes du tems ;
Nous ſommes un peu nés pour être mé-
contens. BOILEAU.

Imprimé à cent lieües de la Baſtille ,
à l'enſeigne de la liberté.

M. D C C. LXXI.

Figure 5. *Le Gazetier cuirassé*, title page to the 1771 edition. (Private copy)

So Eng. considered "free"

at a hundred leagues from the Bastille, at the Sign of Liberty." A subtitle, which was added in the second edition, specified that the anecdotes would convey "news," but news of a peculiar variety: "political," "apocryphal," "secret," "extraordinary," "enigmatic," and "transparent," as well as bawdy, for it would include plenty of material about ladies of small virtue. This kind of journalism seemed to conform to the genre of the *chronique scandaleuse* and it flaunted its seditious character; yet it sounded strangely playful. What did the gazetteer mean by the "confused miscellany about very clear matters" announced in the subtitle? Was he teasing the reader? And why did he adopt such a facetious tone in discussing the desperately serious political crisis that had just engulfed France? There was something puzzling about this gazette.

Smuggled into France, reprinted and pirated several times, *Le Gazetier cuirassé* proved to be such a success, a *succès de scandale*, that by 1777 it had acquired an elaborate frontispiece and some supplementary material revealing the inner workings of the Bastille.[2] The later editions continued to carry the defiant address, which identified France with despotism as symbolized by the Bastille in contrast to England, a hundred leagues away, where printing took place "under the Sign of Liberty."

The title page from the 1777 edition looks archaic to the modern eye. It is smothered in print. The type came from at least eight fonts, including upper- and lowercased italic and roman characters arranged in elaborate combinations. The spacing and use of interlinear leads create complex patterns, so that the reader's gaze dances in and out of the margins and up and down the page in response to the configuration of printed matter. Reading this title page is like contemplating a rococo façade on a building or a painting by Boucher. The design is both playful and provocative, as is the frontispiece on the facing page (see figure 1). It challenges the reader to decipher its details and puzzle out its general meaning.

The Latin caption at the bottom of the frontispiece is the first piece of the puzzle. An educated reader would be able to decode enough of the Latin to see that it celebrated the gazetteer's power to destroy his targets.

Etna provides these volcanic weapons for the stalwart man,
Etna which will defeat the mad fury of the giants.[3]

But a Latin epigram in heptameter verse looked incongruous as a point of entry into a work of unabashed scandalmongering. It seemed to address itself to a reader sophisticated enough to read the Latin and to recognize the myth that it evoked, a story about the titanic rebel Typhon, who tried to storm the kingdom of Zeus by picking up Mount Etna and hurling it at the heavens.

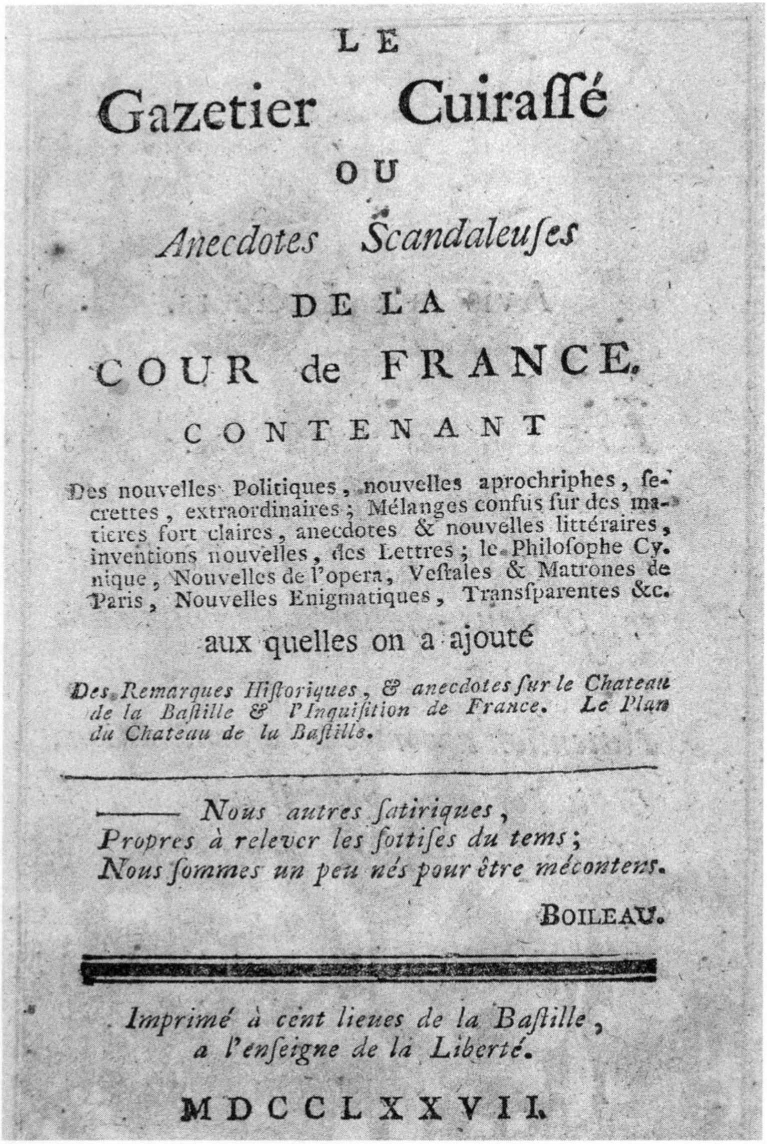

LE
Gazetier Cuiraſſé

OU

Anecdotes Scandaleuſes

DE LA

COUR de FRANCE,

CONTENANT

Des nouvelles Politiques, nouvelles aprochriphes, ſe-
crettes, extraordinaires; Mélanges confus ſur des ma-
tieres fort claires, anecdotes & nouvelles littéraires,
inventions nouvelles, des Lettres; le Philoſophe Cynique, Nouvelles de l'opera, Veſtales & Matrones de
Paris, Nouvelles Enigmatiques, Transſparentes &c.

aux quelles on a ajouté

Des Remarques Hiſtoriques, & anecdotes ſur le Chateau
de la Baſtille & l'Inquiſition de France. Le Plan
du Chateau de la Baſtille.

——— Nous autres ſatiriques,
Propres à relever les ſottiſes du tems;
Nous ſommes un peu nés pour être mécontens.

BOILEAU.

Imprimé à cent lieues de la Baſtille,
a l'enſeigne de la Liberté.

MDCCLXXVII.

Figure 6. *Le Gazetier cuirassé*, title page to the 1777 edition. (Private copy)

Zeus struck back with a volley of thunderbolts, which pinned Typhon under Etna, where he remains to this day, belching up smoke and lava. Despite his anachronistic armor, the gazetteer evidently thought of himself as a hero cast in the mold of the ancients. Instead of identifying himself with the gods, however, he treated them as his adversaries, "giants" who rained down blasts of lightning while he assumed the position of Typhon, firing back volcanic cannonades. He was the hero, the "stalwart man," leading an attack against the evil forces on high.

The initials at the top of the frontispiece show who the villains were, although identifying them requires some additional puzzle solving. If they could decipher the convoluted script and relate it to the most elevated personages in Versailles, eighteenth-century readers would realize that the DB on the upper left stood for du Barry, the SF next to it for Saint-Florentin, and the DM on the right for de Maupeou. In 1771 when the book first appeared, the comtesse du Barry was at the height of her influence as the mistress of Louis XV. Louis Phélypeaux, comte de Saint-Florentin, later duc de La Vrillière, exercised authority over the Bastille and the dispatching of lettres de cachet in his capacity as minister in charge of the Maison du Roi and the Département de Paris. And Chancellor Maupeou had just produced the "revolution" in the power system by destroying the ability of the parlements to constrain the king's authority by refusing to register royal decrees.

The images below the initials identify the three principal villains more explicitly. The picture of the barrel on the left is a rebus, which denotes the king's mistress. (In the eighteenth century, as today, the final letter in *baril* was not pronounced, which gave libelers endless opportunities for puns on du Barry.)[4] A typical, one-paragraph "nouvelle" or newsy anecdote in the text illustrates this standard type of mudslinging: "An equestrian statue of one of our kings [i.e., the statue of Louis XV erected in 1763 in what is now the Place de la Concorde] has been found covered with filth from a barrel which was overturned on top of it, covering it down to its shoulders. The perpetrators of this deed chose a barrel from among those used for the sewage ditches of Paris."[5] Snakes emerge from Saint-Florentin's Medusa-like head and spit out thunderbolts bearing lettres de cachet. The actual cachet or seal shows up clearly as an oval form on the letters, along with the phrase "et plus bas Phélypeaux" ("and lower Phélypeaux")—the standard formula on such documents, which bore the king's signature (often written for him by a secretary) and, at the bottom, the signature of the minister (in this case, Phélypeaux, the family name of the comte de Saint-Florentin) who actually dispatched the arrest warrant.

The head of Maupeou also spits out thunderbolts, as if to indicate his

Figure 7. *Le Gazetier cuirassé*, detail from the frontispiece showing a lettre de cachet. (Private copy)

attempt to obliterate (*foudroyer*) all opposition to his despotic measures. Like Mme du Barry, Saint-Florentin and Maupeou are pilloried throughout the text, along with the duc d'Aiguillon, the abbé Terray, and other key figures in the government. Writing at the most explosive moment of the Maupeou crisis, the libeler meant to dramatize the threat of despotism and his own response to it, for he is the hero of the book. The frontispiece shows him firing off copies of it as though they were cannonballs and grapeshot aimed at the most evil powers of the monarchy.[6]

The self-dramatization extends throughout the front matter of the book, especially in its dedication, which parodies the obsequious style of dedications aimed at patrons.

Dedicatory Epistle
to ME
My dear Person,

Rejoice in your glory without concern for any danger! You will be exposed to it, of course, because of all the enemies of your fatherland. You will sharpen their fury and double their ferocity. But you should know, my dear Person, that in revealing the iniquitous mysteries perpetrated in the dark and secret corners of their conscience, you are avenging the innocent. . . . Make them shudder, those cruel monsters whose existence is so odious and so harmful to humanity. . . .

I know you too well to fear any slackening in your principles. Your resolve is a guarantee that you will never deviate from them. In this opinion, I am, my dear Person,

Your most humble and obedient servant.
Myself

There is no mistaking the political thrust of the book: it is aimed at the leading figures in the French government and the despotism that they are deemed to be perpetrating. But the overblown and self-glorifying rhetoric is undercut by a tone of buffoonery, which shades off into cynicism. Halfway through the text, the author drops the pose of the heroic gazetteer and adopts that of "the cynical philosopher." Then he dishes out endless anecdotes about prostitutes and their aristocratic clients. He describes these stories as "news" and recounts them in short, lapidary paragraphs, somewhat like the news "flashes" of modern tabloid journalism and radio broadcasts. No narrative holds the anecdotes together. They follow pell-mell on the heels of one another without any connecting theme, except the general notion of moral rot eating its way through the top layers of society. Most of them, especially in the section devoted to "news of the Opéra, vestals and matrons of Paris," have no political import. They seem to be meant merely to shock, amuse, or titillate the reader. Many were obviously fictitious—many, but not all and not altogether: the mixture of fact and fiction gave a peculiar flavor to the news that appeared in libels as opposed to the sound but censored reports in the official *Gazette de France*. It was the reader's job to sift the truth from the rumors. The author said so with his usual effrontery in a preface: "I must warn the public that some of the news items that I present as true are for the most probable and that among them some are to be found whose falseness is obvious. I don't take it upon myself to sort them out: it's up to people in high society, who know about truth and lies (from their frequent use of both) to judge and make a choice."

More an enticement than a warning, the preface alerted the readers about what to expect from the book and how to read it. It also cast them in a certain role: they were to think of themselves as sophisticates, "gens du monde," who could sift through gossip for nuggets of truth. *Le Gazetier cuirassé* gave them games to play. Of course, it would provoke plenty of frissons about the horrors of the French government, but it also would provide amusement. It could be enjoyed in the manner of a puzzle, like the word games that were so popular in literary journals at that time. Instead of identifying his victims openly, the anonymous author printed only the first letters of their names followed by ellipsis dots or their titles, which always appeared in italics, and in exposing their private lives, he lifted only part of the veil. It was up to the reader to supply the missing information, pick up hints, decipher allusions, and extract the truth at the core of each anecdote.

The anecdotes would not be effective if they were concocted entirely out of fantasy; libels functioned best when they dealt in half-truths. The libeler often reminded his readers that he drew on a fund of solid information and

then distorted it in the spirit of gamesmanship. After an anecdote about venereal disease transmitted by Mme du Barry to the king, he asserted in a footnote, "This adventure may well not be completely true, but I am assured that
it is not completely false."[7] The book consisted of news, but news with a spin
on it, and by acknowledging that he embroidered on the truth the libeler actually made his message more insidious because he challenged the reader to play
a game that could be won only by puzzling a way through to the hard facts at
the bottom of the stories. Where did he get his facts? The gazetteer did not
reveal his sources, but later libels indicated that he had informants in Versailles. One was said to be a woman named de Courcelles, who possessed such
compromising information that sometimes she would not confide it to the
post and delivered it personally to him in London.[8]

The following examples, all from one page in the first section of the book
titled "Political news," show how this rhetoric operated.

The first bailiff from the old parlement was offered the position of first president in
the new one [i.e., in the subservient court that Maupeou had substituted for the old
Parlement of Paris]; he refused it.

The *Chancel* . . . and the duc *d'Aiguill* . . . dominate the *K* . . . to such an extent
that they have left him free only to sleep with his mistress, pet his dogs, and sign marriage contracts.

The prostitutes of Paris have presented Mme du Barry with so many protests
against the lieutenant of police that he has been forbidden to set foot in any b. . . . . .[9]

The first two anecdotes were not meant to be taken literally, but they illustrated attitudes that had spread throughout the Parisian public: scorn for the
court that Maupeou had created to replace the Parlement of Paris and disgust
at the king's willingness to be manipulated by his ministers. The third anecdote had some basis in fact: Mme du Barry once had been a prostitute.[10] It
spun this information into a story about her sense of solidarity with her former colleagues, which she expressed by forbidding the police to enter any
brothel. A footnote made the point explicit, noting that she had extended her
"grace" to all the whores who once had kept her company.

The book abounds in footnotes. They are keyed to the anecdotes, each of
which occupies a separate paragraph in the text; the makeup of the pages thus
stimulates the reader's eye to move up and down, bouncing from one provocative remark to another. Sometimes the footnotes help the reader decipher the
names and understand the punch lines of the anecdotes, but more often they
add new punch by providing more scandalous material as ambiguous as the
remarks in the text. They even bait the reader by telling jokes against them-

selves. One footnote reads, "Half of this article is true."[11] Which half? It is up to the reader to decide.

Libels in the age of Louis XV were often meant to amuse their readers while slandering their victims. To read them was to play a game. As in the case of romans à clef—another favorite genre, which frequently were libels disguised as novels—the game involved identifying characters whose names were disguised, usually by ellipsis dots. In one edition of *Le Gazetier cuirassé* the footnotes were transferred to the back of the book and labeled "Key to the anecdotes and news items," making the model of the roman à clef specific.[12] The attraction of libels for eighteenth-century readers went beyond the shock effect of scandalmongering. It was also a matter of unlocking enigmas, solving puzzles, decoding rebuses, getting jokes, and cracking riddles.

The riddles presented above were easy to solve. But the guessing game became more difficult as the author led his readers deeper into "behind the scenes secrets, which I will reveal to them by pulling back the curtain."[13] For example: "It is said sotto voce that the countess de *la Mar* . . . , faced with the impossibility of making a prince, had decided to make a little bishop and that she received on that occasion the benediction of the Coadjutor of Reims, who is the most dependable French prelate for this sort of thing next to M. *de Montaz* . . . and prince Louis."[14]

Most readers could be expected to recognize the anticlerical message, which recounted the cuckolding of a count by a prince of the Church, and many would be able to fill in the blanks after the names: the comtesse de la Marck and the archbishop of Lyon, de Montazet. But a footnote extended the irreligious ribaldry further: "The three prelates referred to here are those who come closest to the cardinal de *Bernis*, who took and distilled twelve fresh eggs on twelve distinct occasions within three hours." The reference to the notorious sex life of cardinal Bernis in Rome could not be mistaken, but what exactly was the allusion to the dozen eggs? Perhaps it concerned scandalous behavior like that reported in another libel against Maupeou, *Oeufs rouges*. Perhaps it suggested that Bernis had deflowered a dozen virgins within three hours, setting a record in the sexual annals of the French clergy, although he appeared elsewhere in the text as a homosexual who preferred to copulate with cardinals.[15] Maupeou, in contrast, was said to favor Jesuits, a theme that gave the libeler an occasion to associate buggery with rumors that the government planned to restore the Society of Jesus, which had been dissolved in 1764.[16] The ambiguities and innuendos made the text more titillating, but they sometimes became impossible to disentangle, even in the footnotes that accompanied the anecdotes and ostensibly explained them. Nonetheless, by tacking back and forth between the footnotes and the text and by relating one anecdote to

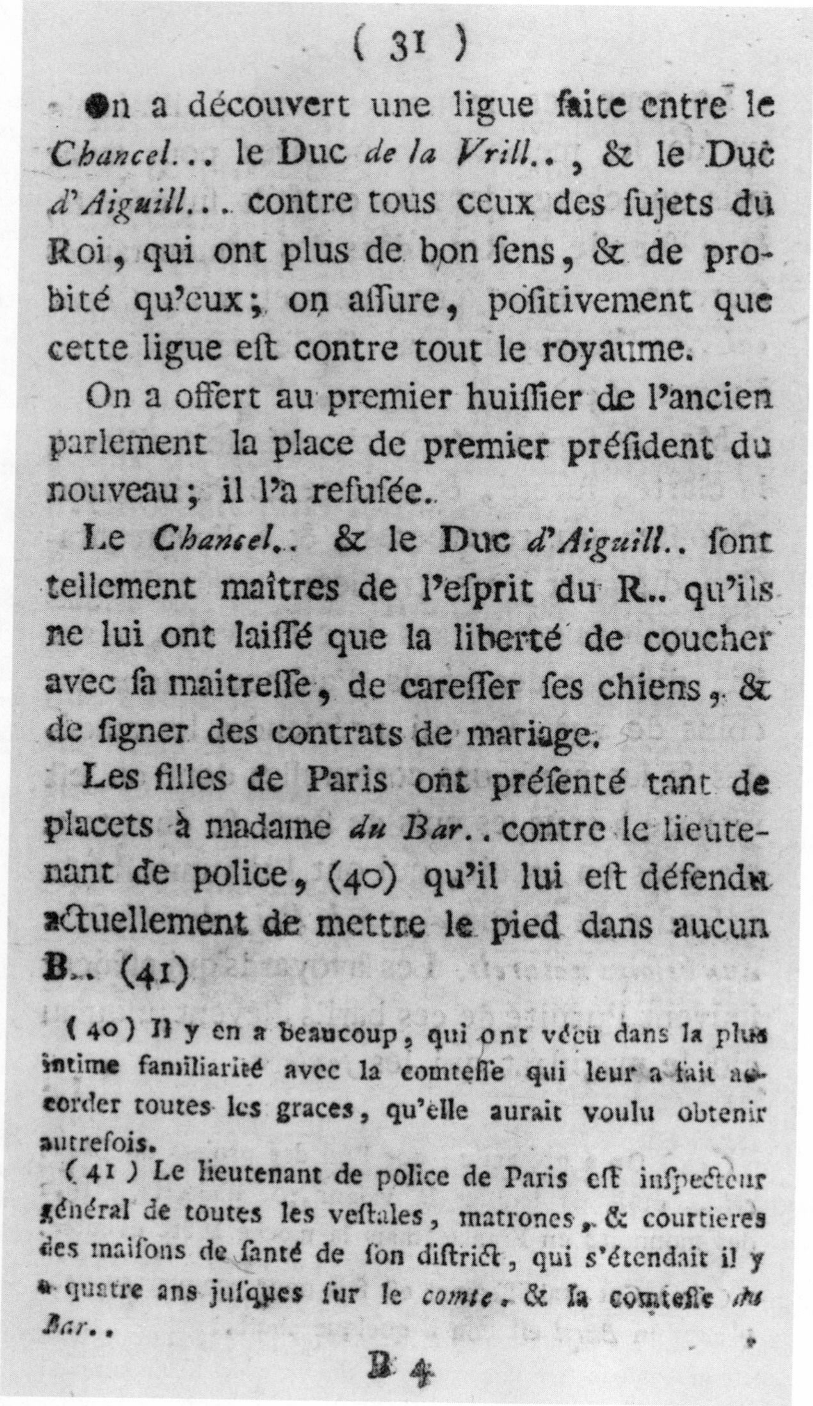

On a découvert une ligue faite entre le *Chancel...* le Duc *de la Vrill..* , & le Duc *d'Aiguill....* contre tous ceux des sujets du Roi, qui ont plus de bon sens, & de probité qu'eux; on assure, positivement que cette ligue est contre tout le royaume.

On a offert au premier huissier de l'ancien parlement la place de premier président du nouveau; il l'a refusée..

Le *Chancel...* & le Duc *d'Aiguill..* sont tellement maîtres de l'esprit du R.. qu'ils ne lui ont laissé que la liberté de coucher avec sa maitresse, de caresser ses chiens, & de signer des contrats de mariage.

Les filles de Paris ont présenté tant de placets à madame *du Bar..* contre le lieutenant de police, (40) qu'il lui est défendu actuellement de mettre le pied dans aucun B... (41)

(40) Il y en a beaucoup, qui ont vécu dans la plus intime familiarité avec la comtesse qui leur a fait accorder toutes les graces, qu'elle aurait voulu obtenir autrefois.

(41) Le lieutenant de police de Paris est inspecteur général de toutes les vestales, matrones, & courtieres des maisons de santé de son district, qui s'étendait il y a quatre ans jusques sur le *comte* & la comtesse *du Bar..*

Figure 8. *Le Gazetier cuirassé*, the makeup of a typical page. (Private copy)

another, eighteenth-century readers probably could get most of the jokes. Those they could not get served as an indication that deeper mysteries remained to be solved. The difficulties increased the pleasure of the game; and as it became more difficult, it gave the readers a sense of penetrating more profoundly into the darkest secrets of the state.

When it exposed the mysteries of statecraft rather than the sex lives of clergymen, the game became seditious, not revolutionary: *Le Gazetier cuirassé* never called for the overthrow of the regime or envisaged the possibility of a fundamental change in the political order. Like many pamphlets before 1789, it denounced ministerial despotism. Mixed in with its jokes and puzzles, it delivered some serious, straightforward attacks on the Maupeou government; but this obvious message should not be dismissed as nothing more than propaganda generated by eighteenth-century court politics.[17] To be sure, the libeler aimed most of his slander at the ministers currently in power, and he showed sympathy for their opponents, the supporters of the exiled duc de Choiseul. But he took an occasional swipe at the Choiseulistes,[18] and he heaped scorn on all the great—peers, generals, judges, courtiers, clergymen, men-about-town, and even men of letters, including Voltaire, d'Alembert, and the entire Académie française. Seen as a whole, the anecdotes fit together like the pieces of a mosaic, conveying a picture of a society corroded by incompetence, immorality, and impotence. The inability of aristocrats to propagate their line provided the libeler with a favorite theme, along with venereal disease transmitted from brothels to the court. Mme du Barry epitomized the line of transmission. As a plebeian wench and former whore who supposedly led the king around by his nose, she embodied the violations of gender and social rank that made Versailles appear as the source of everything offensive to eighteenth-century sensibilities. The scorn for the court extended to the king himself. Dominated by a depraved woman, manipulated by corrupt ministers, and incapable of maintaining France's rank in Europe, Louis XV looked despicable—the antithesis of his predecessor, Louis XIV, the Great. And his successor, the future Louis XVI, could not even procreate an heir.[19]

Although it expressed no sympathy for republicanism, *Le Gazetier cuirassé* demeaned the symbols that had created a sacred aura around French monarchs—the scepter, the throne, the body of the king himself, corrupted by pox and sapped of its virility.[20] At one point the gazetteer even attacked the religious foundation of the monarchy: "The kings of France are challenged to prove their divine origin by showing the contract that the eternal father signed with them."[21] And the later editions contained a supplement exposing the horrors of the Bastille—the isolated cells, thick walls, penetrating cold, terrifying darkness, rats and lizards, foul smells, repulsive food—"that cries out for vengeance before God and men."[22] This protest conformed to a leitmotif that ran through all libel literature: the French monarchy had degenerated into a despotism. It appeared in *Le Gazetier cuirassé* long before works like the *Mémoires sur la Bastille* (1783) by Simon-Nicolas-Henri Linguet had made the Bastille into a myth that expressed everything the French feared and hated about their political system. Yet the radical rhetoric was surrounded by off-color witticisms and jocularity. The mixture seems incongruous to the modern reader. How did eighteenth-century French readers react to it?

We do not know. As in the case of most eighteenth-century works, there is little information about the reception of *Le Gazetier cuirassé* among ordinary readers. But the book's impact can be appreciated from the response of one extraordinary reader: Voltaire. Voltaire's own books had scandalized the reading public throughout Europe. They, too, circulated underground and had been banned and burned. But to Voltaire, they had nothing in common with *Le Gazetier cuirassé*, which horrified him: "A satanic work has just appeared in which everyone, from the monarch to the last citizen, is furiously insulted, in which the most atrocious and absurd calumny spreads a hideous poison over everything that one respects and loves."[23]

Voltaire's response, however, calls for some commentary. Unlike most of the other philosophes, Voltaire supported the Maupeou ministry and welcomed the destruction of the parlements as a victory over the powers of superstition and bigotry that had condemned his books as well as innocent victims of miscarried justice such as Jean Calas. Moreover, Voltaire himself was slandered in *Le Gazetier cuirassé*. The gazetteer mocked him as a sodomite and then added insult to injury by noting that Voltaire had accused Fréron of the same vice.[24] Voltaire often fired epithets like "bugger" at his enemies, perhaps even at Frederick II (a reference to the commander of the "Bulgares" in *Candide* is probably an allusion to Frederick's homosexuality). Can Voltaire, too, be considered a libeler?

Although the question sounds outrageous, there is no denying that Voltaire used slander in his polemical works. During 1759–60 when the philosophes came under attack from every quarter—the Church, the Parlement of Paris, the King's Council, and even the Comédie française, not to mention a host of pamphleteers eager to exploit the repressive mood in Versailles after the attempted assassination of Louis XV by Robert François Damiens—d'Alembert appealed to Voltaire for help. The philosophes in Paris had their backs to the wall, he wrote. Voltaire, as their commander in chief, should come to their rescue with a barrage of pamphlets that he could produce from the safety of his retreat near the Genevan border in Ferney. Voltaire agreed and began to gather ammunition. Dig up dirt about the writers in the enemy camp, he instructed his agents in Paris. Wasn't there some hanky-panky connected with the archbishop of Lyon's intervention in favor of hospital nurses? Which Jesuit in the Collège Louis le Grand was best known for taking liberties with the students? "It is a good thing to expose rogues," wrote Voltaire. He called for "anecdotes"—the essential ingredient of all libels, from his own *Anecdotes sur Fréron* to best-sellers like *Anecdotes sur Mme la comtesse du Barry.*[25] D'Alembert answered with an account of how Abraham Chaumeix contracted venereal disease in the Opéra comique and how abbé Nicolas Trublet seduced his parishioners from the confessional.[26] When he had accumulated enough information of this sort, Voltaire packed it into the salvos of anonymous works that he fired off from Ferney. They helped turn the tide of public opinion in 1760, and he continued to snipe at the enemies of Enlightenment in this fashion until his death in 1778.[27] In fact, Voltaire had churned out libelous works from the beginning of his career: associated (wrongly) with libels against the Regent (especially the poisonous *Philippiques* by François Joseph de La Grange-Chancel), they led to his first stint in the Bastille in 1717. But then libeling can be found everywhere in the literary and political battles of the eighteenth century—and in the *mazarinades* of the seventeenth century, the *Flugschriften* of the Reformation, the *pasquinades* of the Renaissance, and similar genres stretching back into antiquity. It is not that all such literature can be seen as slander but that the libels expressed a pervasive polemical style. Voltaire in Ferney used the same tactics as the libeler who had attacked him. Behind *Le Gazetier cuirassé* lies a vast literature that deserves to be rescued from the oblivion into which it has fallen. One way to begin is with a question: Who was the armor-plated gazetteer?

Chapter 2
The Devil in the Holy Water

Although the armor-plated gazetteer hid behind a curtain of anonymity in *Le Gazetier cuirassé*, he was exposed—and not just exposed but also
libeled—in a subsequent work: *Le Diable dans un bénitier, et la métamorphose
du Gazetier cuirassé en mouche, ou tentative du sieur Receveur, inspecteur de la
police de Paris, chevalier de St. Louis, pour établir à Londres une police à l'instar
de celle de Paris* (1783), or, *The Devil in the Holy Water and the metamorphosis
of the Armor-Plated Gazetteer into a police spy, or the attempt of Mr. Receveur,
a police inspector and [decorated] chevalier of St. Louis, to establish a police force
in London modeled on the one in Paris.* The title summarizes the theme of the
book: the transformation of the armor-plated gazetteer into a police spy
("mouche") during an attempt by an inspector from Paris to set up a secret
branch of the Parisian police in London. The intrepid gazetteer had deserted
to the ranks of the enemy: that was the main scandal revealed in the book,
which also had a frontispiece that expressed its argument in imagery (see figure 2).

In this case, too, the picture required some puzzle solving by the reader.
Its caption, which contains the usual ellipsis dots after the first initials of the
names, explains that it shows the French plenipotentiary in London (the
comte de Moustier) presiding over a ceremony in which "Charlot" renounces
his past and in return receives the cross of St. Andrew from "R. . . . . . .r"
(Receveur, the Parisian police inspector). Charlot is the antihero of the book,
the supreme libeler of the eighteenth century, and the author of *Le Gazetier
cuirassé*: Charles Théveneau de Morande. The scene corresponds to the climactic moment of the narrative, which provides the additional information
needed to decipher the frontispiece.[1] Morande is kneeling at the feet of Receveur, the "grand-master" of a masonic-like Order of Saint Andrew, named for
the X-shaped Saint Andrew's cross on which the police supposedly tortured
their victims. (Receveur wears an emblem of the cross on his jacket above the
handcuffs and instruments of torture dangle from his pocket.) While Morande
pronounces an oath of loyalty as a secret agent of the police, Receveur initiates
him into the order by knighting him with tongs used to hold hot coals against

the feet of prisoners in the Bastille in order to torture them into revealing their accomplices. Moustier presides over the ceremony from a throne-like seat in front of curtains decorated with the Bourbon fleurs-de-lis. On the left, Receveur's assistant, Pierre Ange Goudar, hands Morande the insignia of the order: a medal in the form of a wheel on which prisoners were broken. Goudar, a well-known literary adventurer, figures in the text as a hack writer turned police spy; he is identified in the picture by the title of his best-known work, *L'Espion chinois*, a six-volume *chronique scandaleuse*. (It can be seen on a slip of paper emerging from his pocket, just as Morande's identity is shown by some paper under his foot marked "Le Gazetier cuirassé.") He carries under his arm a box labeled "vials of forgetfullness" and "opium pellets," suggesting that Morande's past will be forgotten now that he has joined the forces of the law.

The title page mirrors this mockery of the French authorities. Like the title page of *Le Gazetier cuirassé*, it consists of a dense field of type. The variety of characters and complex articulation of the spacing serve as a way to induce the reader to pause over details and to enjoy the verbal play piled up line by line. But instead of displaying openly provocative remarks, it teases the reader with paratextual parody. It presents itself as a super-legal work. It carries a fake approbation and privilege, a fake address (the royal printing shop in Paris), a fake dedication (to the marquis de Castries, minister of the navy and one of the characters pilloried in the text), a fake editor (the abbé Jean Louis Aubert, editor of the orthodox *Gazette de France* and censor of the French edition of the *Courrier de l'Europe*, which made him the bête noire of the French expatriate authors of the *Courrier* in London), and a fake author (possibly Arnold Joseph Leroux, a journalist and clandestine printer in the principality of Liège). The devil featured in the title was Receveur, who came to London in 1783 on a secret mission to repress libels and kidnap libelers. His designated victims learned of his plans and lured him into so many fruitless intrigues that in the end he ran around London like a chicken with its head cut off—or, as the French put it, "like a devil in a baptismal font." To a modern reader, the expression might suggest a satanic force undermining sacred institutions. But in the common parlance of the eighteenth century, it denoted frantic but ineffective agitation, as in the popular verse of J.-B.-L. Gresset's *Vert-Vert* (1734).

Bien vite il sut jurer et maugréer
Mieux qu'un vieux diable au fond d'un bénitier.

(Very soon he learned to curse and fume
Better than an old devil in the bottom of a baptismal font.)[2]

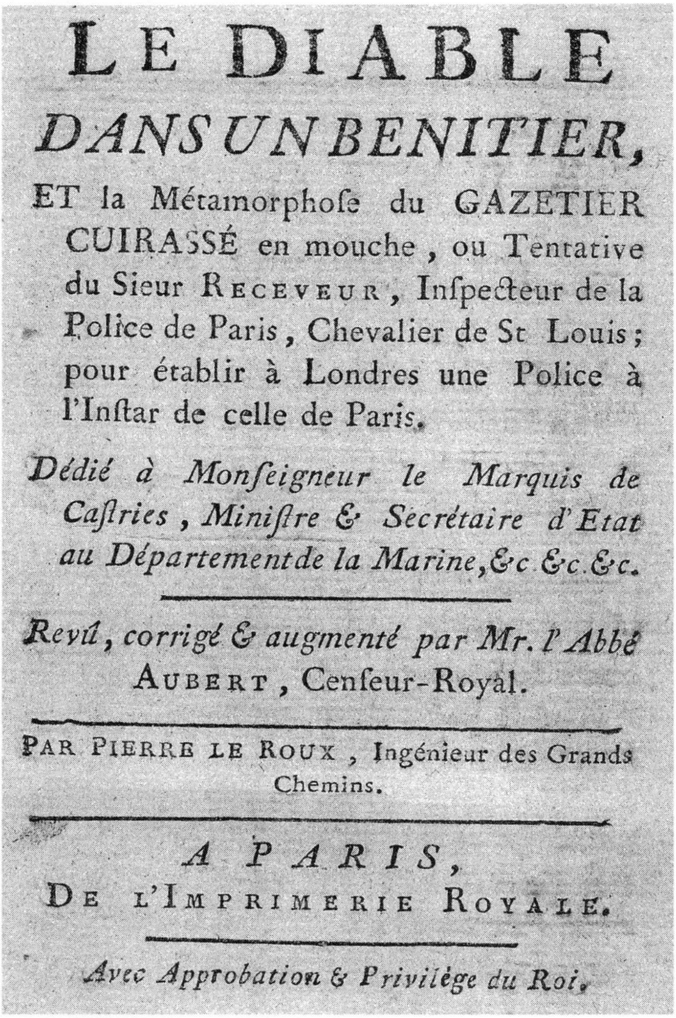

LE DIABLE

DANS UN BENITIER,

ET la Métamorphofe du GAZETIER CUIRASSÉ en mouche , ou Tentative du Sieur RECEVEUR , Infpecteur de la Police de Paris , Chevalier de St Louis ; pour établir à Londres une Police à l'Inftar de celle de Paris.

Dédié à Monfeigneur le Marquis de Caftries , Miniftre & Secrétaire d'Etat au Départementde la Marine,&c &c.&c.

Revû, corrigé & augmenté par Mr. l'Abbé AUBERT , Cenfeur-Royal.

PAR PIERRE LE ROUX , Ingénieur des Grands Chemins.

A PARIS, DE L'IMPRIMERIE ROYALE.

Avec Approbation & Privilège du Roi.

Figure 9. *Le Diable dans un bénitier*, title page. (Private copy)

Receveur may have been irredeemably wicked, but his deviltry was essentially comic, closer to that of Alain-René Lesage's *Le Diable boiteux* than to Milton's Satan. Taken together, the frontispiece and title page promised plenty of shocking revelations, but nothing that smelled of a revolution. Above all they offered a rollicking good read.

The text of the book is as cluttered and complicated as its front matter. It, too, had to be read as a puzzle, not only because its characters were hidden behind ellipsis dots but also because it contained all sorts of hints, allusions, and inside jokes that demanded deciphering and that were accompanied by a great deal of nudging and winking at the readers as if to make them complicit in the plot. The plot itself had some of the characteristics of a roman à clef. One of the surviving copies contains an actual key, penned in at the end by an eighteenth-century reader, who identified the characters according to the dots or dashes after the first initials of their names and noted the pages on which they appeared.

Unlike *Le Gazetier cuirassé, Le Diable dans un bénitier* follows a coherent narrative line, although the story sometimes gets entangled in some confusing chronology. It tells how two villains, Morande and Receveur, joined forces in a common effort to exterminate the production of libels in London. As related by the anonymous author, their biographies represent both sides of Grub Street: Morande, the arch-libeler, personified hack writing, while Receveur, the supreme enemy of the libelers, incarnated the attempt of the police to repress the hacks. Their lives crossed at a point where Grub Street itself was overrun by the back-and-forth traffic of pamphleteers and police: for the libelers often became police spies, and the inspectors sometimes peddled libels. It was the changing of places and turning of coats that made the tale so salty.

Morande first appears in the book in the form of a "portrait." Verbal "portraits," a genre familiar to French readers since the early seventeenth century, stressed the moral as well as the physical traits of characters. They often appeared in libels, much to the consternation of the French authorities, who were especially concerned to protect the reputation of public figures. The narrator of *Le Diable dans un bénitier* introduced Morande directly to the readers, heightening the effect by temporarily abandoning the third-person voice, which prevailed in the rest of the text: "Imagine, readers, a broad, flat face whose features are composed of a livid, mobile fatty matter; haggard and heavy-lidded eyes; a flat nose; broad and open nostrils, which seem to inhale the most brazen air of lasciviousness; . . . a mouth from whose corners there is a constant trickle of livid pus, the true emblem of the poison that it continually spreads about."[3]

This picture, which fits Morande's image in the frontispiece, was followed by a brief biography. Thanks to his natural disposition and his birth in the family of a corrupt Burgundian notary, it explained, Morande got an early start in evil. He enlisted in a cavalry regiment, deserted, drifted into the underworld of gambling dens and brothels in Paris, and soon found himself behind bars in Bicêtre, a prison for particularly disreputable criminals. Upon his release, he put himself beyond the reach of the French police by moving into the demimonde of London. There he lived by pimping for homosexuals and

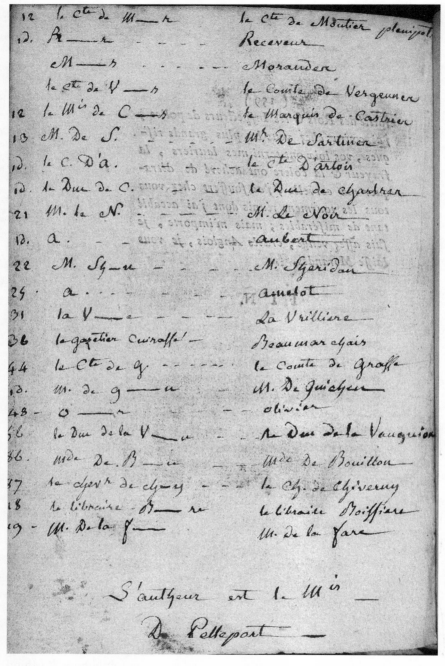

12	le Cte de M——k	le Cte de Moutier plenipot.
12.	R——k	Receveur
	M——h	Morander
	le Cte de V——h	le Comte de Vergennes
12	le Mis de C——h	le Marquis de Castries
13	M. De S.	Mr De Sartinen
12.	le C. D'A.	le Cte D'Artois
12.	le Duc de C.	le Duc de Chartres
21	M. le N.	M. Le Noir
13.	a.	Aubert
22	M. Sh——n	M. Sheridan
25	a.	Amelot
31	la V——	La Vrilliere
36	le gazetier cuirassé	Beaumarchais
44	le Cte de G	le Comte de Grasse
12.	M. de G——n	M. De Guichen
48	O——n	Olivier
56	le Duc de la V——n	le Duc de la Vauguion
86.	Mde De B——n	Mde De Bouillon
87	le chevr de Ch——y	le Ch. De Chiverny
18	le libraire B——re	le libraire Boissiere
19	M. De la F——	M. de la fare

S'autheur est le Mis ——

De Pellepont ——

Figure 10. A manuscript key in a private copy of *Le Diable dans un bénitier*. The column on the left gives the number of the page on which a character appears. The next column contains the disguised version of the character's name, and the column on the right lists the identifications made by the eighteenth-century reader. (Private copy)

then blackmailing them. But he discovered greater possibilities for extortion in France, thanks to correspondents who fed him information about scandalous behavior in Versailles. He strung the anecdotes together in *Le Gazetier cuirassé*, a work of such outrageous slander that the government was willing to pay a fortune to prevent the publication of a sequel, *Mémoires secrets d'une femme publique*, which featured Mme du Barry. It sent Beaumarchais on a secret mission to arrange the payoff: 32,000 livres and an annuity of 4,800 livres. The two rogues proceeded to collaborate as spies, selling their services to the highest bidders, whether French, British, or American, during the American war. Then, while Beaumarchais went on to other intrigues, Morande took up with the Paris police from his headquarters in London. He provided advice, for more extravagant fees, on how to cope with the other French expatriates, who tried to blackmail their way to riches by following his example. Backed by the marquis de Castries in the naval ministry and the comte de Vergennes in the ministry of foreign affairs, the police sent one secret agent after another to silence the libelers by assassination, kidnaping, or bribery. The most important of these missions was led by Receveur in 1783: that is how his career crossed with Morande's, providing the main subject of *Le Diable dans un bénitier*.

The book made Receveur out to be equally satanic but far more sinister, and in sketching his life it provided a great deal of information about the international traffic in libels. From humble origins in the working class of Paris, it recounted, he rose to the height of villainy as the main hit man of the police in their attempts to crush anything resembling the freedom of the press. Although he never mastered reading or writing himself, he showed a precocious disposition toward violence. When only a boy he attached himself to spies and gleefully accompanied the henchmen of the police when they dragged their victims off to prison. He wooed the daughter of the public executioner in hopes of taking up her father's trade, but his own father, an honest coachbuilder with conventional notions of family honor, prevented the union. Receveur therefore joined the army. When stationed abroad he met his first expatriate, whom he lured to Paris and caused to be broken on the wheel for a nonexistent, literary crime. This feat led to a glorious career as an undercover agent of the police: twenty years of espionage, entrapment, lettres de cachet, hangings, and torturing victims in Bicêtre and the Bastille, crowned at the end by a Croix de St. Louis as a reward for service to the king.

Having attained this mastery in the arts of despotism, Receveur—the monstrous Receveur conjured up in *Le Diable dans un bénitier*—embarked on two assignments, which converged in the London mission of 1783. In 1781 he followed the trail of a large collection of unpublished libels—attacks against the princesse de Guémenée, the duchesse de Bouillon, and other grandees, accompanied by prints and threats of blackmail—to Amsterdam. By raiding a printing shop there with the help of the Dutch authorities, he turned up information that led to their source, two men in Paris who collaborated from the opposite sides of Grub Street: pamphleteering on the one side and policing on the other. The pamphleteer was Louis de Launay, an impecunious doctor turned journalist who had taken up libeling after the collapse of the *Gazette anglo-américaine*, which he had edited in Maestricht. (Its proprietor, Samuel Swinton, also published a similar journal, the *Courrier de l'Europe*, which provided a center of activity for the libelers in London.) The police agent was Jean-Claude Jacquet de la Douay, a police inspector in charge of the foreign book trade, who had commissioned one of the libels in order to engineer its confiscation, thereby collecting the blackmail and at the same time impressing his superiors with his assiduousness in enforcing the law. Armed with this information, Receveur hustled back to Paris, arrested both men, and probably tortured them to death in a dungeon. The author of *Le Diable* could only speculate about their fate: de Launay, he believed, had been strangled in the Bastille; he did not know what had become of Jacquet, although he had an explanation for the mystery that surrounded his disappearance. A Third Man, identified only as the "owner" of a cache of the same libels in London, had also collaborated with Jacquet and had warned that he would publish all the material if he learned that Jacquet had come to harm.

In fact, this ominous Third Man (who sounded suspiciously like the anonymous author of *Le Diable*) soon began to issue threats of publication and more demands for blackmail from an address that could not be traced. They were passed on to the French authorities by an expatriate bookseller named Boissière. His shop in St. James Street carried all kinds of French literature, notably libels, and served as a gathering point for the libelers. The situation looked serious enough for the French police to shift the main theater of their operations from the Low Countries to England and to dispatch a succession of undercover agents to investigate. As described in *Le Diable*, these made up a motley crew. Decked out in all sorts of improbable disguises and flummoxed by their inability to speak the language, they never understood the customs of the natives—especially strange institutions like habeas corpus, trial by jury, and the freedom of the press.

First came Louis Valentin Goesman, notorious as Beaumarchais's adversary during his famous trial before the Maupeou court, which had been replaced by the Parlement de Paris when Louis XVI restored the old parlements in 1774. Goesman presented himself in Boissière's bookshop as an Alsatian nobleman, the baron de Thurne, and entered into a series of baroque intrigues, which ultimately resulted in the suppression of one of the works from Jacquet's collection, *Les Amours de Charlot et Toinette* (a pamphlet-poem about the impotence of Louis XVI, the overheated libido of the queen, and a supposed liaison between her and the comte d'Artois, amply illustrated with obscene engravings), for 17,400 livres. As soon as he had bought off that libel, however, Goesman announced that several others were in press. He claimed that he could get them destroyed, thanks to the excellent relations he had established with Boissière. But that would cost a great deal more, and the prospect of endless libels and bottomless expenses made the French authorities decide that they needed another secret agent.

They settled on Alexis d'Anouilh, a police spy who preyed on Parisian low life, and sent him off to investigate Goesman as well as Goesman's libelers. After checking out London's gambling dens and brothels—in recounting his adventures, *Le Diable dans un bénitier* emphasized his attachment to the milieu he frequented in Paris—d'Anouilh made contact with Richard Sheridan, the playwright, who had joined the government as undersecretary of state for foreign affairs and hoped to use his position to fatten his purse. At first it seemed that a well-placed bribe would persuade Sheridan to have an assortment of French expatriates deported as slanderers. But further investigation revealed that the British law of libel did not apply to offenses committed against foreigners. D'Anouilh therefore embarked on a more ambitious project: with Sheridan's help, he would change the law itself—a matter of mobilizing a majority in Parliament and bribery on a much larger scale than he had anticipated. He had already run through the 5,000 louis allotted to him by the naval ministry, which was sponsoring his expedition in collaboration with the Paris police. So he returned to Paris with a request for several thousand more. De Castries, the minister of the navy, listened to d'Anouilh's story—and promptly dispatched him to the Bastille, where Receveur tortured him into confessing that he had kept most of the money for himself.

Whom to send next? Receveur was the obvious choice. True, he did not know a word of English and could barely write French, but he could be trusted. He had already captured dozens of hack writers, and he could investigate d'Anouilh's plots as well as Goesman and the expatriates that Goesman was investigating. Receveur also traveled as a fake baron, accompanied by a retinue of assistants, including Ange Goudar, the author of *L'Espion chinois*, who spoke fluent English and, the police believed, would make an excellent spy. So it was—all of this according to the picaresque narrative in *Le Diable dans un bénitier*—that Receveur, decked out as "le baron de Livermont," set up headquarters in Jermyn Street and launched a campaign to exterminate libels in London.

Receveur's maneuvers, combined with those of Morande, furnished the main subject of *Le Diable dans un bénitier*. The story took so many twists and turns that it is difficult to follow, but it treated the reader to a full account of the tactics employed by the secret police. There were basically three. First, force majeure. Receveur arrived with the tools of his trade: handcuffs, chains, and even, it was said, a carriage with a secret compartment big enough to contain a trussed-up victim. His support staff included a thug named Humbert, who could overpower any author and bundle him off to the Bastille, where torture and interrogation would uncover the whole network of accomplices. But London was full of ragged French writers. Who among them had turned out the latest round of libels? Who was the Third Man in charge of Jacquet's stock of defamatory manuscripts? When Humbert showed up in Grobetty's Tavern, the favorite watering place of the expatriates, they scattered in terror. Soon afterward they distributed a handbill in the streets.

They wrote it in English, but for the benefit of the reading public on the other side of the Channel it appeared in French in *Le Diable dans un bénitier*.

AN ALARM-BELL
Against
FRENCH SPIES
and
A CAUTION,
Especially to Foreigners who do not approve of
being shut up in the *Bastille*.
The brave and free Spirit of Britons is roused against two desperate Gangs of *French Spies*, and their Confederates, some lodged in the City, the other about St. James's, who are continually on the Watch, (Day and Night) furnished with *Gags*, *Hand-cuffs*, and *Daggers*, in order to seize and transport to *Paris*, either *alive* or *murdered*, the Authors or Editors of the three following Pamphlets:
Les Passe-temps d'Antoinette, avec figures.
Les Amours et Avantures du Vizir Vergen***.
Les Petits-Soupers et les Nuits de l'Hôtel-Bouill**.
The two first of which are reported to be now printing in *London*, and the latter printed at *Bouillon* is on Sale in *St. James's Street*, *Haymarket*, and *New-Bond Street*.
For the execution of their diabolical Purpose, two Post-Chaises, constructed for their Design, are prepared, not far from *Duke-Street*, with Boxes inside, made for concealing two or three Men: also fresh Horses at different Places on the Road, and a *French Packet* ready to convey them to France.
*** The Chief of the above SPIES, is that wicked and notorious Fellow R-CEVEUR, (shamefully decorated with the Cross of St. Louis) sent here ten Years ago for the same infamous Business, and then exposed in the Public Papers; now living under a fictitious Title, not an hundred Miles from Jermyn and Bury Street.

This publicity coup put an end to the danger of kidnaping or assassination, because in 1783 London was still seething with hostility toward France and still

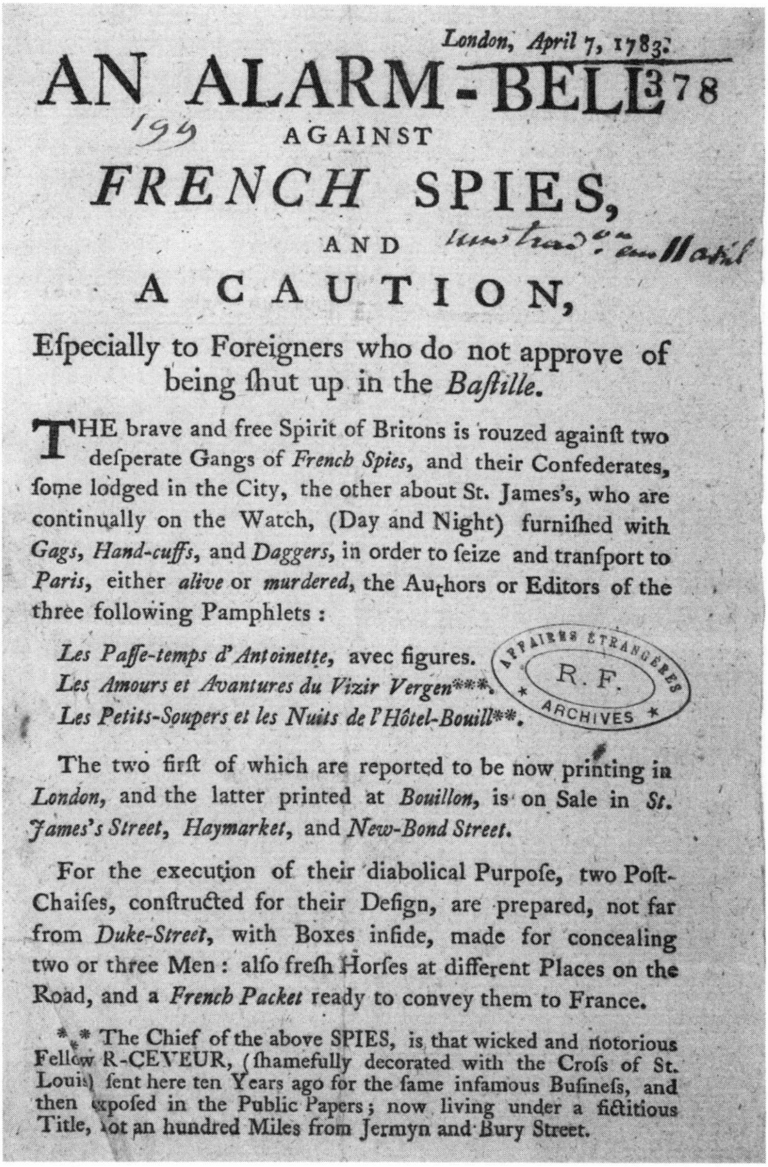

AN ALARM-BELL 378

'99 AGAINST

FRENCH SPIES,

AND *unstrad·· au Matil*

A CAUTION,

Efpecially to Foreigners who do not approve of
being fhut up in the *Baftille*.

THE brave and free Spirit of Britons is rouzed againft two
desperate Gangs of *French Spies*, and their Confederates,
fome lodged in the City, the other about St. James's, who are
continually on the Watch, (Day and Night) furnifhed with
Gags, *Hand-cuffs*, and *Daggers*, in order to feize and tranfport to
Paris, either *alive* or *murdered*, the Authors or Editors of the
three following Pamphlets :

Les *Paffe-temps d'Antoinette*, avec figures.
Les *Amours et Avantures du Vizir Vergen****,
Les *Petits-Soupers et les Nuits de l'Hôtel-Bouill***.

The two firft of which are reported to be now printing in
London, and the latter printed at *Bouillon*, is on Sale in *St.
James's Street*, *Haymarket*, and *New-Bond Street*.

For the execution of their diabolical Purpofe, two Poft-
Chaifes, conftructed for their Defign, are prepared, not far
from *Duke-Street*, with Boxes infide, made for concealing
two or three Men : alfo frefh Horfes at different Places on the
Road, and a *French Packet* ready to convey them to France.

*** The Chief of the above SPIES, is that wicked and notorious
Fellow R-CEVEUR, (fhamefully decorated with the Crofs of St.
Louis) fent here ten Years ago for the fame infamous Bufinefs, and
then expofed in the Public Papers; now living under a fictitious
Title, not an hundred Miles from Jermyn and Bury Street.

Figure 11. A handbill distributed in London by the French libelers warning about the
threat from the Parisian police. From an original copy in a dispatch from the comte de
Moustier, the French plenipotentiary in London, to the comte de Vergennes, the
French foreign minister, dated April 7, 1783. Archives of the French Ministry of Foreign
Affairs, correspondence politique, Angleterre, ms. 539.

capable of exploding in violence as it had done during the Gordon Riots of 1780. As the handbill indicated, Morande had incited a crowd to drive out a detachment of French police, Receveur included, who had tried to kidnap him in 1774.[4] Secret French agents could be executed as spies before September 3, 1783, when the Treaty of Versailles formally put an end to the hostilities between France and Britain. *Le Diable dans un bénitier* noted that one agent, François Henry de La Motte, had been hanged in 1781. In recounting Receveur's mission of 1783, it emphasized that the French police soon faced the danger of being torn to pieces by an indignant crowd of journeymen printers, "solid upholders of the liberty of the press."[5] The handbill therefore forced Receveur to beat a retreat to his apartment in Jermyn Street, and at the same time it provided publicity about three more libels about to be published.

Counseled by Morande and by Moustier in the French embassy, Receveur then fell back on a second line of attack, according to *Le Diable dans un bénitier*. He commissioned an English attorney to prepare a report on the feasibility of charging the libelers with libel in a British court. He also attempted to follow up d'Anouilh's attempts to overcome the legal barriers by intriguing to get a special statute passed by Parliament. But Sheridan would not cooperate, and the report, published in part in *Le Diable dans un bénitier*, only confirmed the sanctity of that peculiarly British institution, the liberty of the press.

The failure to get any cooperation from the British authorities left Receveur with one last option: negotiation. Here the main difficulty derived from the collapse of an earlier round of bargaining over a key libel announced in the handbill: *Les Petits Soupers et les nuits de l'Hôtel Bouill-n: Lettre de milord comte de ****** à milord ****** au sujet des récréations de M. de C-stri-s, ou de la danse de l'ours; anecdote singulière d'un cocher qui s'est pendu à l'hôtel Bouill-n, le 31 décembre 1778 à l'occasion de la danse de l'ours* (*The Intimate Suppers and Nights of the Hôtel Bouill-n: Letter from Lord Count ***** to Lord ***** about the recreations of M. de C-stri-s, or the dance of the bear; a singular anecdote about a coachman who hanged himself in the Hôtel Bouill-n on December 31, 1778 on the occasion of the dance of the bear*), published in 1783. As hinted in its typically provocative subtitle, this work purported to reveal a scandalous affair between the princesse de Bouillon and Charles Eugène Gabriel, marquis de Castries, the minister of the navy. *Le Diable dans un bénitier* recounted the intrigues surrounding the publication of *Les Petits Soupers* and recapitulated its plot in such detail that the text turned into a libel within a libel.

According to the summary of the plot, which corresponded closely to the original, de Castries diverted huge sums from his ministry in order to pay for the princess's gambling debts and then compromised himself in an orgy that involved her servants, notably a coachman who was caught whipping a priest. The priest, a particularly hairy brother from the Théatine Order named Fortuné, had been amusing de Castries and the princess by cavorting naked with an aged chambermaid: hence the reference to "the dance of the bear." The scene took place behind closed doors, but the coachman, who thought he had exclusive access to the maid's bed, found Fortuné in it. In a fit of rage, he set upon Fortuné with his whip, drove him into the street, and raised such a clamor that the night watch intervened. The hubbub made the princess fear that her sex life—a series of debaucheries known only to her partners, her servants, and, as it later turned out, the anonymous libeler—might be exposed before the public. To hush things up, she threatened to dispatch the coachman to the prison of Bicêtre, a fate worse than death, as he saw it. He therefore hanged himself with the cord attached to his whip.

Le Diable dans un bénitier summarized *Les Petits Soupers et les nuits de l'Hôtel Bouillon* in a manner that suggested they came from the same source. It then went on to provide a suspiciously well-informed account of the attempts to use *Les Petits Soupers* for blackmailing the princess. After receiving some threatening letters, it revealed, she prevailed upon de Castries to authorize negotiations with the anonymous libeler through the intermediary of Boissière. The French government was willing to pay 150 louis d'or (3,600 livres tournois) for the suppression of the book, but the author demanded more than it would pay: 175 louis (4,200 livres). So *Les Petits Soupers* went on sale—and could still be bought, the author of *Le Diable* informed his readers, in Boissière's bookshop. Did the same man write both books?

A close study of their texts would confirm that conclusion, but Receveur's detective work, as recounted in *Le Diable*, did not involve literary analysis. He could hardly read French and spoke not a word of English. Therefore, he relied on Morande. As the dean of all libelers, Morande knew every trick and every trickster in the Grub Streets of both capitals. And having been inducted into the secret branch of the Paris police in London, he was willing to share his knowledge. *Le Diable* described him briefing Receveur in the back room of a London tavern, the Dog and Duck.[6] They talked ambushes and lettres de cachet, compared exploits of their villainous pasts (Receveur boasted of having arrested four thousand men, of whom a third had been broken on the wheel), emptied several bottles of wine "at the expense of the ministry for foreign affairs,"[7] as they laughingly put it, fell into each other's arms, and parted fast friends, bound by their common commitment to the cause of suppressing the liberty of the press. Morande, however, retained some secret connections with his old blackmailing business. Instead of taking Receveur to the source of the libels, he led him on wild goose chases—or so the story went in *Le Diable dans un bénitier*, and as will be recounted later, it can be confirmed in all essential details from documents in the French ministry of foreign affairs.

The chases led through a maze of taverns, cafés, and back rooms where Receveur and his men dealt with expatriates of every stripe. Their object was to capture two more libels—*Les Passe-temps d'Antoinette* and *Les Amours du visir de Vergennes*—that came from the stock of the Third Man and that were about to be published in the wake of *Les Petits Soupers de l'Hôtel Bouillon*, according to extortion notes sent to France and passed on to Receveur. In order to trace the notes to their author, Receveur ordered his men to collect samples of handwriting from every suspect they could find. But they went about this task so clumsily that word of it spread throughout the French colony. One of the French adventurers fabricated a letter and sold it to an undercover agent as evidence to be used against another, whom he denounced in the hope of collecting a reward. The other expatriate, however, cleared himself by boldly seeking an audience with Receveur and writing out a letter in a completely different hand. Having gained access to the enemy camp in this manner, he then offered to be the middleman in negotiations to prevent the appearance of yet another libel, which he announced and later concocted by cobbling together material lifted from previous publications.

After several weeks of running after false leads of this kind, Receveur finally walked into Boissière's shop, introduced himself as the baron de Livermont, and asked to enter into pourparlers for the suppression of libels. Boissière, however, was already negotiating with Goesman as the baron de Thurne. Two false barons were more than he could handle. He also refused all invitations to the French embassy for fear of being abducted. So time went by and the Parisian police went round in circles, getting nowhere. By July 1783 a new ambassador, the comte d'Adhémar, had replaced Moustier and recommended abandoning all negotiations with the libelers. They would only provoke the production of more libels, he argued, and in the end Receveur had to agree. Aware at last that Morande had collaborated with the pack of rogues who had led him by the nose, he packed up his kit of torture implements and sailed for France, cursing the land of liberty: "Cursed land, bitch of liberty, people who hate the authority of kings and of police inspectors, I have faced the greatest dangers on your soil; your laws have tarnished my laurels . . . but never mind, I am having adequate revenge, cruel Englishmen, for I am leaving you Morande."[8]

Le Diable dans un bénitier ends on that note. It treats Receveur's mission as an attempt not merely to suppress scandal but also to destroy the freedom of the press. It presents his alliance with Morande as a conspiracy to create a French-type police state in a land of liberty. And it makes the libelers out to be heroes in the general struggle to defend "the rights of humanity," "the rights of man," "the sacred rights of nature," and the principles epitomized by the American Revolution.[9] True, it avoids mentioning most of the libelers by name, and it does not deny that their tracts contained some nasty material or that they played some dirty tricks, even on each other. But the overall radicalism of its message stands out clearly. Like *Le Gazetier cuirassé*, it perpetuated a mythical view of France as a land of despotism, and it went even further than Morande in heaping scorn on "the imbecile Louis XV"[10] as well as his evil ministers and their successors under Louis XVI.

The radical ideology, expressed in occasional bursts of indignation, contrasts curiously, however, with the tone of derision and jest that pervades the book and that also has some affinity with the sardonic rhetoric of *Le Gazetier cuirassé*. *Le Diable dans un bénitier* treats the police as a bunch of clowns. As it describes them, the spies and secret agents stumble over each other in their absurd disguises, bungling all their attempts at villainy. In Paris, it explained, they could simply flash a lettre de cachet and clap their victims in the Bastille. In London they had to cope with alien institutions—a judicial system with juries, a press without censors—among strange people with a bewildering love of liberty. Their ham-fisted efforts to defend the cause of despotism made them look ridiculous, and the ridicule often seemed to be laid on for its own sake, simply to amuse the readers or to shock them. The book slandered some figures, like the princesse de Bouillon, gratuitously, without any connection to the higher principles it espoused. In fact, it hinted at more scandal and more libels waiting to be printed, as if to open up the possibility of a new round of blackmail negotiations. The anonymous author seemed to speak for the "depository" or Third Man in the Jacquet ring of libelers,[11] and the book itself reads like a libel, but one with a new twist; for it made the police themselves—along with higher-ups like Moustier, de Castries, and Vergennes—the object of its scandalmongering. It stripped the veil off their activities and provided readers with a sensational exposé of scoundrels and conspiracies on the police side of Grub Street. It was a libel about libeling, one set squarely in the world of the libelers. It hid their identities, of course, and skewed its narrative so that they appeared as champions of liberty confounding the evil agents of despotism. But it revealed a great deal about their milieu. Of all the ephemeral literature from the Ancien Régime, *Le Diable dans un bénitier* is the richest source of information about the history of slander. In fact, it is so important for a general understanding of libeling that it raises further questions: What were the circumstances of its publication? Who wrote it? Who were the author's associates in the extraordinary colony of French expatriates in London? To answer these questions one must consult the third work concerning the London libelers, *La Police de Paris dévoilée*.

Chapter 3
The Parisian Police Unveiled

As its title announced, _La Police de Paris dévoilée_ (_The Parisian Police Unveiled_) treated the reader to another exposé of evil-doings by the Paris police. Its frontispiece (see figure 3) shows two police agents hustling a handcuffed victim to the Bastille, which looms menacingly in the background. In the foreground, another victim of despotism sleeps in chains on a bedding of straw, as if in a cell of the Bastille, and a Medusa-like murderer prepares to plunge a dagger into the prisoner's breast. The antique dress of the two principal figures suggests their symbolic character: Innocence or Truth is about to be annihilated by Evil or Tyranny, which has pulled off its mask. The unmasking echoes the unveiling depicted at the top: an avenging angel exposes the wickedness below by pulling back a curtain that had kept it hidden and by flooding the scene with light from a torch. The author, Pierre Manuel, probably meant to associate himself with the spread of light, because he placed his name in capital letters under the torchbearer, and he appears throughout the text as a champion of enlightenment in the form of "publicity"—that is, the exposure of despotism by means of the printed word.[1]

This theme stood out in the epigraph printed on the title page: "Publicity is the safeguard of laws and morals," a declaration written in plain French by Manuel himself and a departure from the kind of epigraphs used in most other works, which favored quotations from classical authors. Manuel placed his name prominently under the title and identified himself as "one of the administrators of 1789"—that is, as an elected official of the revolutionary Paris Commune. He also gave the name and address of his publisher, J. B. Garnery, along with the date of publication: "the second year of liberty," or 1790. Everything about the book proclaimed its character as a product of the Revolution. Even the design of the title page broke with the older models from the Ancien Régime. In place of a wordy title and subtitle, loaded with cryptic allusions and elaborate masses of type, it reduced its message to a minimum—short, simple declarations, set off by plenty of blank space. If one were to pick an analogy with painting, the design of the title page summons up David rather than Boucher. And whatever its aesthetic affinities, the politics of the book

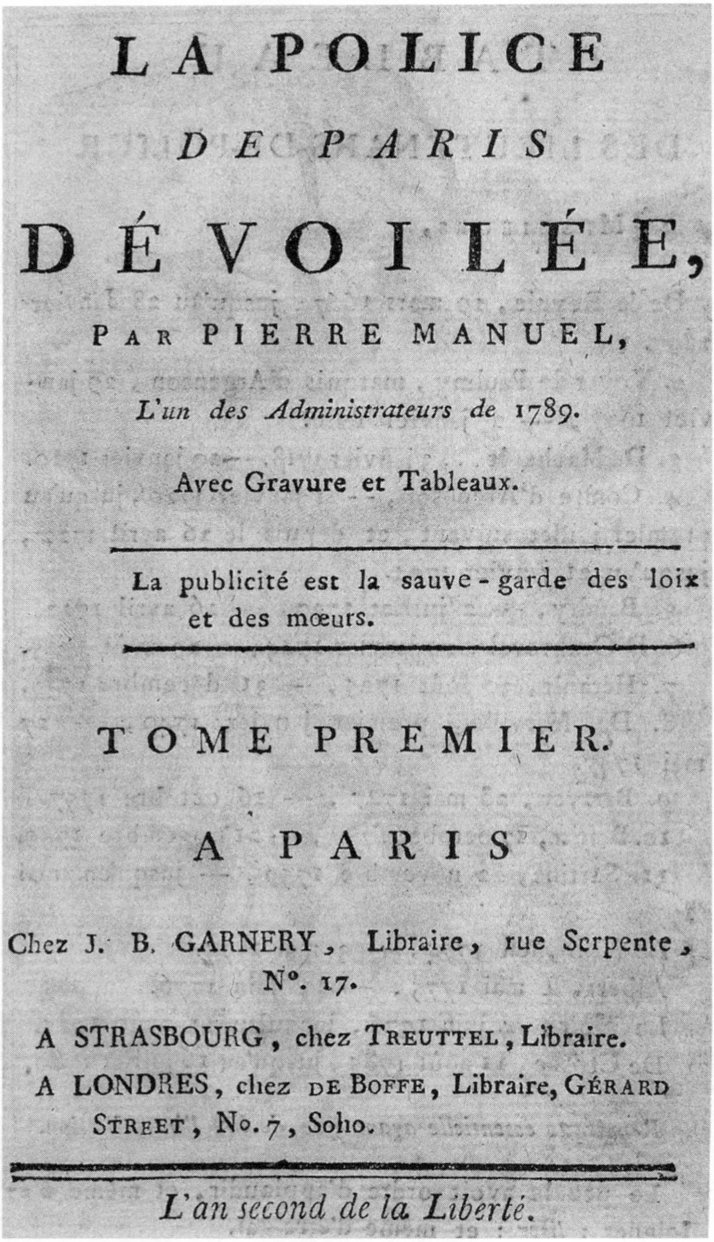

LA POLICE
DE PARIS
DÉVOILÉE,

PAR PIERRE MANUEL,

L'un des Administrateurs de 1789.

Avec Gravure et Tableaux.

La publicité est la sauve-garde des loix
et des mœurs.

TOME PREMIER.

A PARIS

Chez J. B. GARNERY, Libraire, rue Serpente,
N°. 17.

A STRASBOURG, chez TREUTTEL, Libraire.

A LONDRES, chez DE BOFFE, Libraire, GÉRARD
STREET, N°. 7, Soho.

L'an second de la Liberté.

Figure 12. *La Police de Paris dévoilée*, title page. (Private copy)

Connection to event. Support of militants (Jacobins)

stood out clearly from its very first page, a dedication to the members of the Jacobin Club.

Speaking to his brother militants, Manuel explained that he meant to promote liberty under the new regime by revealing how horribly it had been repressed under the old. After his election to the Commune, he had taken charge of the department within the municipal government that oversaw the policing of the book trade. Unlike his predecessors, he insisted, he did not imprison authors and impound books. On the contrary, he did everything possible to promote the freedom of the press, and he used his position to gather material from the archives of the former police in order to publish a full-scale exposé of their abuse of power. Their greatest crimes, perpetrated with the uninhibited use of spies, lettres de cachet, and the Bastille, involved the stifling of public opinion. Manuel therefore devoted a great deal of his two volumes to the arrest of authors and the confiscation of books, sprinkling his narrative with excerpts from the police files. The undercover operation in London provided him with the most sensational material, so he featured it in several sections: "The Policing of Libels," "The Policing of Spies," "The Policing of Prisons," and "The Policing of the Most Remarkable French Refugees in London."

In some respects, therefore, *La Police de Paris dévoilée* was a continuation of *Le Diable dans un bénitier*. It revisited the same episodes, documenting them with archival material that Manuel guaranteed to be accurate, and it revealed their dénouement—a succession of baroque intrigues that led through the entire colony of libelers and ended with the capture of *Le Diable*'s anonymous author. Manuel identified him as Anne-Gédéon Lafitte, marquis de Pelleport and a nasty piece of work, according to the reports compiled by the police. They made him out to be a ne'er-do-well who had been discharged from two regiments and incarcerated several times at the request of his family for "atrocities against honor."[2] After a stint as a teacher in Switzerland, where he married a domestic servant and fathered several children, he decamped for England, abandoning his family. He scraped together a living in London by tutoring and translating until, inspired by Morande's example, he tried to strike it rich by slander and blackmail. His first attempt, *Les Petits Soupers et les nuits de l'Hôtel Bouillon*, failed, exactly as recounted in *Le Diable dans un bénitier*, because he demanded 175 louis for its suppression and the French refused to go over 150. During the negotiations, Pelleport hid behind Boissière, who acted as a middleman and pretended to know nothing about the origins of the libels, although the police suspected he had commissioned them. Next, Pelleport announced, via Boissière, the imminent publication of two even more scandalous works, *Les Passe-temps d'Antoinette* (also referred to as *Les*

Amusements d'Antoinette) and *Les Amours du visir de Vergennes*. Both seemed to be derived from the stock of libels accumulated by Jacquet de la Douay, the police inspector turned underground publisher. Because they slandered the queen and the foreign minister, the government sent its most reliable agent, Receveur, on their trail. He was empowered to kidnap or to bribe their author, and he was assigned to investigate the government's other secret agent, Goesman disguised as the baron de Thurne, who had begun to negotiate with Boissière for the suppression of *Les Passe-temps d'Antoinette* but was making so little headway that the police suspected him of being Boissière's collaborator. Receveur failed to cut through all these intrigues, for the reasons explained in *Le Diable dans un bénitier*, and the result of his failure was *Le Diable* itself— that is, another libel written by Pelleport and sold by Boissière, which exposed all the machinations of the Paris police in London.

The story, like so many others, ended in the Bastille. After procuring the proofs of *Les Petits Soupers et les nuits de l'Hôtel Bouillon*, Morande identified the handwriting on them as Pelleport's and denounced him to the police. They lured him to Boulogne-sur-Mer, captured him, and locked him up in the Bastille on July 11, 1784. On the following day they also imprisoned his close friend, Jacques-Pierre Brissot de Warville, the future leader of the Girondists during the French Revolution. Brissot had joined the expatriates in London, where he tried to found a philosophic club or "Licée" and to support himself by journalism. But his projects threatened to collapse into bankruptcy, and when he traveled to Paris to raise more money the police arrested him on suspicion of collaborating with Pelleport—and perhaps even because Pelleport had incriminated him during an interrogation in the Bastille.

In recounting the fate of the two prisoners, *La Police de Paris dévoilée* made Brissot out to be innocent of any connection with the libel industry. Indeed, he appears as the incarnation of virtue, in contrast to Pelleport and the rest of the reprobates in the French colony of London.[3] That version may be biased, however, because Manuel had developed close ties with Brissot by 1790. They were political allies who followed parallel paths through the Revolution—from the early agitation in Paris to the Girondist period in power and, in the end, to the guillotine.[4] In another book, *La Bastille dévoilée*, which contained excerpts from the dossiers of prisoners in the Bastille, Manuel explained that instead of publishing Brissot's dossier, he had asked Brissot to compose the account of his own *embastillement*. Brissot wrote that he had never had anything to do with the publication of libels: "The true cause of my detention was the zeal with which at all times and in all my writings I have defended the principles that are triumphing today."[5] Pelleport did not receive any such clean bill of health. *La Bastille dévoilée* described him as the chief libeler in

London after Morande's defection to the police: "The record of the interrogations that he underwent could serve as a catalogue of all the pamphlets that
have appeared for the last six years. He was suspected of having composed
all of them."[6] Whatever the extent of the collaboration between them, Brissot
defended himself more effectively than Pelleport did during their interrogations in the Bastille. The police released him after four months, whereas they
kept Pelleport confined for more than four years—until the death of Vergennes, who had issued the order for his arrest, and the appointment of a less
hostile secretary of state in charge of Parisian affairs, Laurent de Villedeuil, in
1788.

La Police de Paris dévoilée concentrated on the police rather than their
victims, but the lives of the libelers, as they appeared in the police files, provided such good copy that Manuel devoted a good deal of space to them. Pelleport and Morande received the fullest biographical notices, but the book
surveyed the entire population of French expatriates, and it included extensive
reports on them by police spies—all transcribed, Manuel insisted, without the
slightest alteration. Whatever their accuracy, the reports give a vivid picture of
the general environment inhabited by the libelers. They even suggest the pattern of a particular subculture: the beginning of *la bohème*.

According to the police spies, the libelers congregated "in slums and cafés
of the lowest sort"—cheap taverns like the table d'hôte at Grobetty's and coffeehouses such as the Café de Stangter and the Café d'Orange, "where all the
French refugees in London gather to declaim against France."[7] The expatriates
naturally gravitated to Boissière's bookshop in St. James Street, where they
could find a full stock of French works, especially the latest libels. The police
file on Boissière indicated that he came from Geneva and had misspent his
youth in the company of international adventurers. While serving as a lackey
in Lubeck, he became involved in a gambling operation, was brought to trial
for theft, but got off for lack of evidence. Then he took up the book trade in
London and turned his shop into a business "whose main trade is to commission libels by starving wretches and then to negotiate for their suppression."[8]
The expatriates also gathered in the offices of *Courrier de l'Europe*, the French-
language journal that specialized in news about British politics and American
affairs. It was published in London by Samuel Swinton, the Scottish entrepreneur who had also founded the short-lived *Gazette anglo-française* of Maestricht, edited by de Launay before he took up libels and disappeared into the
Bastille. The editor of *Courrier de l'Europe* was Antoine Joseph de Serres de La
Tour, who also owned a one-third interest in it. The police put him down in
their files as someone who had "conducted intrigues for twenty years in the
streets of Paris by passing himself off as the son of a battalion commander in

the regiment of Navarre."[9] After becoming involved in a messy bankruptcy, he got a job as a secretary to an administrative official and then ran off to London with his employer's wife.

Several expatriates wrote for the *Courrier*, including Brissot, who had edited the censored edition of it that was published in Boulogne-sur-mer, and Morande, who replaced Serres de La Tour as the editor of the London edition in 1784. Morande, of course, had his own file, which corresponded quite closely to the more tendentious account of his career in *Le Diable dans un bénitier*. The police made him out to be the most notorious and outrageous libeler of London but noted that he had switched sides, renouncing slander and blackmail in order to ingratiate himself with the French authorities. The *Courrier*'s collaborators also included two other adventurers of the same stripe, Perkins MacMahon and John Goy. A defrocked Irish Catholic priest who was born and raised in France, MacMahon had run off with a young woman from his parish in Rouen and lived by writing scandalous accounts of the French court for English newspapers as well as for French journals. Goy left France earlier and spent most of his adult life in England, tutoring and translating for the French embassy. He became subeditor of the *Courrier* but was fired after he slipped some compromising documents to Receveur.

Journalism, especially the French variety published from the relative safety of foreign cities, provided employment, off and on, for other Frenchmen trying to steer clear of the Bastille—and, even more so, the infamous prison of Bicêtre ("escaped prisoner of Bicêtre" was one of the nastier insults in their pamphlets). The best-known of their number was Simon Nicolas Henri Linguet, who moved to London with his *Annales politiques, civiles, et littéraires* after his release from the Bastille in 1782. While trying to keep his journal alive, he published his *Mémoires sur la Bastille* (1783), the most influential of all the books that propagated the view of a monarchy that had degenerated into despotism. Linguet had been treated rather favorably in *Le Diable dans un bénitier*, but he kept his distance from most of the expatriates. The police noted that he did not cut much of a figure in London, and he transferred his base of operations to Brussels in 1785. The other journalists were obscure hacks who divided their lives between garrets and prisons. A sieur Maurice, who had lived from literary odd jobs in Paris—secretarial work and censoring for the police, articles for the *Gazette de France*—had taken refuge in London after being arrested for his involvement in the bankruptcy of the prince de Guémenée. He supported himself primarily, according to the police, by pimping for his wife. A sieur Saint-Flozel, calling himself Lefebvre, had collaborated on the *Journal encyclopédique* of Bouillon and had worked as a secretary in the French embassy in Coblentz until he was fired for "swindles."[10] He then joined forces in London with an abbé Séchamp, who had fled France to avoid arrest for complicity in the murder of a wealthy merchant in Nantes. They tried to launch a philosophical-philanthropic journal like Brissot's *Correspondance universelle sur ce qui intéresse le bonheur de l'homme et de la société* but fell back on the traffic in libels—or so it seemed to the police, who identified Séchamp as one of the intermediaries in the negotiations between Receveur, Boissière, and Pelleport.

Receveur also crossed paths in Grub Street with many other refugees who received brief notices in *La Police de Paris dévoilée*: a flea-bitten baron de Navan, who had deserted his regiment and tried to flog libels both to Receveur and Goesman; a chevalier Joubert, another deserter, who had accompanied Pelleport to London, where he hired himself out to Receveur and then tried to dupe him with some falsified evidence; a sieur Doucet, who had fled from debts in France and a debtor's prison in Ghent and whom Pelleport tried to hire to copy the manuscript of *Les Passe-temps d'Antoinette* so that it could be sold to Receveur in handwriting other than Pelleport's; a chevalier Echelin, a former pimp and police spy in the homosexual underworld of Paris who had spent seven years as an inmate and a spy in Parisian prisons, then took up spying in London, where he offered his services to Receveur but was refused because of his untrustworthiness; a sieur Lamblet, a Swiss who taught languages in London and took up with Pelleport, only to be framed by Pelleport as the author of *Les Passe-temps d'Antoinette*; and a sieur Belson, who pretended to be a doctor under the name de la Boucharderie and became involved in the Goesman-Boissière intrigues while spying for the British as well as the French.

Such was the collection of literary hacks from Pelleport's circle who led the French police on a merry chase through London, according to the documents published in *La Police de Paris dévoilée*. They shaded off into surrounding circles of equally dubious and even more obscure characters. The police "register," as Manuel called it, covered thirty-nine of them in all.[11] It showed how their paths crossed in the Grub Streets of London and how their lives intertwined in an underworld of adventurers who drifted in and out of disaster, accumulating resentment against the regime they had fled. Thus Dom Louis, a monk who had run off with some medallions stolen from his abbey. The police found him churning out seditious literature from a flat in Hampstead. He had produced an anti-Catholic tract, *L'Enfer fermé et le paradis ouvert à tous les hommes*, and was hard at work on a general attack on the French monarchy, *Histoire des rois de France cités au tribunal de la raison*. An ex-Jesuit and ex-convict named Delatouche was a similar case. After his release from a prison in Rennes, he had emigrated to The Hague, where he married a prostitute, and then to London, where he produced a *Courrier de Londres* full of diatribes against France. La Rochette, an expatriate geographer, and Ipreville, an émigré mathematician, also declaimed against everything French but only verbally, as members of "a group of radical agitators who assemble in the shop of Boissière."[12] Beyond the fringe of the "agitators," the police located a collection of outright criminals who were ready to do anything for money. Army deserters, defrocked priests, fraudulent bankrupts, clerks who had run off with cash boxes, fugitives accused of theft and murder, gamblers and swindlers of all varieties, they made quite a rogues gallery, and Manuel probably hoped that their biographies would also make good reading for a public eager to enjoy revelations about the wicked ways of the Old Regime. But did he touch them up to make them sell?

In introducing the police reports, Manuel insisted that he had not changed a word in them.

I found notes about them [the French expatriates in London], which I have reproduced just as I found them. Anyone who is compromised or accused can't complain about me. I am providing them with an opportunity, one they would never have had otherwise, to demand justice or clemency.

The police never had a right to judge a citizen in secrecy, but every citizen must always be ready to account for his life to the French people.[13]

As his defensive tone suggests, Manuel may have worried that his book could be taken as an indictment of the libelers rather than of the police. It might even be considered a libel itself. It had many of the stylistic qualities of the genre: short, sensational anecdotes about prominent personalities; teasing allusions used to allure the reader; famous names half-hidden with ellipsis dots; scandal that seemed to be recounted for its own sake, without any relevance to a general narrative. To be sure, nothing suggests that Manuel modified the documents he quoted. But when he was not citing them directly, he paraphrased them to bring out their shock value. He promised in his preface to reveal the sins of many "*high and mighty noblemen.*" His book exposed them "just as I found them, with their weaknesses, vices, and crimes."[14] And he kept his word.

Large segments of the book consisted of nothing but gossipy anecdotes, compressed into one or two sentences and lined up back-to-back, exactly like the short, sensational news items in *Le Gazetier cuirassé*. The format derived in part from the sources, because the police often reworked the reports of their spies in the form of a gazette, their own version of the manuscript newsletters known as *nouvelles à la main*, which they delivered to Versailles for the amusement of the king and his ministers. But Manuel did not merely reprint the material he extracted from the police archives. He selected and arranged it, just as Morande had done with the news supplied from his own sources. *La Police de Paris dévoilée* contained whole sections devoted to the adventures of priests in brothels (30 pages), prostitution in general (48 pages), gambling dens (14 pages), and assorted vice (144 pages, mainly amusing or shocking anecdotes about depraved aristocrats, dancing girls, and venereal disease). Some typical examples:

The prince de Conti was knocked out of commission by a girl known as the Little F. . . . . He blames it on Guerin, his medical advisor.

Mademoiselle Allar had her portrait painted in the nude by le Noir. Everyone recognizes her.

The duc de . . . surprised his wife in the arms of his son's tutor. She said to him with an impudence worthy of a courtier, "Why weren't you there, Monsieur? When I don't have my esquire, I take the arm of my lackey."[15]

These passages could have come straight out of *Le Gazetier cuirassé*. They corresponded closely in style and content to many of the *chroniques scandaleuses* from the reign of Louis XV. Yet there was a difference. Unlike his predecessors, Manuel exposed scandal from the past. He was separated from his subject matter by a revolution, and he wrote for readers with attitudes and expectations shaped by the great events of 1789. In place of a conventional dedication, he began the book with an open letter to his fellow members in the Jacobin Club, which identified the book's main theme with the primary goal of the Revolution: the purification of civic morality (*moeurs*). It was not enough, he insisted, to produce a new constitution: "France must change its morals just as it changes its laws."[16] The only force that could be mobilized to achieve such an end was public opinion, and it in turn depended on two crucial factors: independent men of letters, who could denounce all forms of corruption, and a free press, which would communicate their views. Every town should appoint a man of letters to promote virtue and repress vice—not by insinuation and irony of the kind that had prevailed among the fashionable authors of the Ancien Régime but by vigorous, open argument. What France needed was truth—that is, virile lessons about civic virtue, which would strengthen the polity in the same way that censors had formed the moral fiber of ancient Greece and Rome: "The great power that shapes morality is *opinion*, and it will never be effective if it is accompanied by soft indulgence. Hypocritical politeness will enervate everyone's character. . . . Lessons! Truths! That is what we owe to ourselves. May frank censure banish cowardly calumny from our fireside gatherings."[17] In place of the ancient agora, the modern censor used the press. But censure was not censorship. Manuel declaimed against all restraints on the printed word and preached the freedom of the press as though he were spreading the gospel of a civil religion.

> But let us say it often, let us say it always: it is especially the liberty of the *press* that will conserve for the people all the benefits of the *revolution*. Printing shops are more useful than parishes; and if the fatherland had apostles the way religion once did, then rich people who don't know what to do with their fortune would hurry to found printing shops just as in past times one founded chapels; and as backers of these benefices, they would see to it that missionaries of philosophy would use them to spread the principles of the *constitution* throughout the land.[18]

Such notions, derived from Rousseau and various strains of civic republicanism, can be found everywhere in the writing of the revolutionaries. The language may ring false to modern ears, but it embodied a rhetoric that pervaded revolutionary politics, from the first sessions of the Estates General to the Convention, and that especially appealed to the members of the Jacobin Club: a rhetoric of denunciation. "It took courage for me to denounce the guilty," Manuel said in his epistle to the Jacobins.[19] Unlike the libelers from the Ancien Régime, who had exposed the vices of the clergy and the court with a light touch, as if to entertain their readers, he presented himself as one who dared to tear away a veil that covered moral rot. There was no hint of humor in his writing. He was not playing games with his readers, not amusing them with wordplay or teasing them with half-hidden allusions. No: he was denouncing moral corruption and doing so openly, as his name on the title page proclaimed. Only by understanding the full extent of the evil under the Ancien Régime could the newly liberated citizens of France protect themselves from enslavement in the future: counterrevolution thrived on corruption, and despotism would revive at the slightest weakening of *moeurs*.

This argument could justify any amount of muckraking, and it must be said that Manuel came up with a great deal of muck when he raked through the archives of the police—not just *La Police de Paris dévoilée* (1790), two volumes, but also *La Bastille dévoilée* (*The Bastille Unveiled*) (1789), eight "livraisons" in four volumes, and *La Chasteté du clergé dévoilée* (*The Chastity of the Clergy Unveiled*) (1790), two volumes. All of these compilations came from the same sources and spread the same message: for the Revolution to succeed, it must purge the body politic of the immorality inherited from the Ancien Régime. Anyone who doubted that conclusion need only consult the documents published throughout the series. Each volume drew on papers captured after the collapse of the Bastille; each exposed scandals; and each did so in the same manner, conveyed by the same metaphors. Manuel spent the first two years of the Revolution unveiling, unmasking, and stripping away curtains that had kept horrors hidden until the dawn of a new age of openness.

His greatest find was a cache of letters that Mirabeau had written from the prison of Vincennes and that the police had kept in their archives after permitting them to be read by their addressees. They included some steamy love letters sent by Mirabeau to his mistress, Sophie de Monnier, who had run away with him after deserting her husband and who was languishing in a separate prison, a victim both of passion and of a lettre de cachet. As its title suggested, *Lettres originales de Mirabeau, écrites du donjon de Vincennes pendant les années 1777, 78, 79, et 80, contenant tous les détails sur sa vie privée, ses malheurs, et ses amours avec Sophie Ruffei, marquise de Monnier* (*Original letters of Mirabeau, written from the dungeon of Vincennes during the years 1777, 78, 79, and 80, containing all the details of his private life, his misfortunes, and his love affair with Sophie Ruffei, marquise de Monnier*) (1792), two volumes, could be considered a libel, like the "private lives" from the Ancien Régime. To Mirabeau's mother, who was also his heir after his death in April 1791, the book was a commercial publication that not only libeled him but also violated her rights to his estate. She took Manuel to court, where he defended himself as a patriot intent on fulfilling his duty by denouncing the abuses of the Ancien Régime. He had used the same argument in a "preliminary discourse" to the *Lettres*, and it worked well enough to get the case dismissed. (It was shifted to another court and abandoned after the overthrow of the monarchy on August 10, 1792.)[20]

Whatever their legal status, Manuel's publications—*La Police de Paris dévoilée* and all the rest—raise questions about his revolutionary career. Was he a Jacobin determined to exterminate vice or a hack writer trying to sell books? Did he believe in all the unveiling and unmasking, or did he use it to exploit a new literary market that was created by the Revolution and driven by the demand for sensational revelations about the Ancien Régime? Did his denunciations express genuine engagement in Jacobin politics, or were they a rhetorical device adapted to a new kind of libel, one that suited the political climate created in 1789?

The either/or questions may seem self-evident to those who believe that ideological commitment can be explained by self-interest. But a modern suspicion of careerism may be inadequate to understand a writer swept into the vortex of the French Revolution. Before jumping to conclusions, it would be better to ask a more straightforward question: Who was Pierre Manuel? One answer appeared in the last of the four interrelated libels.

Chapter 4
The Secret Life of Pierre Manuel

Vie secrète de Pierre Manuel (*The Secret Life of Pierre Manuel*) (1793), the last in the string of libels, carries the story of their interlinked texts and images deep into the Revolution. The design of its title page continues the tendency toward simplification and austerity exemplified by *La Police de Paris dévoilée*.

Reduced to five words in heavy black type, the title calls out to the reader like a headline on a broadside: Manuel, one of the best-known deputies in the Convention, has a secret life—probably something sordid, because the Latin epigraph (Virgil, *Aeneid*, Book II, line 65: "From a single crime learn the wickedness of all") begins with a word that would be obvious to any reader, even someone without the slightest Latin: "Criminé." Manuel must have led a secret life of crime. By opening the book, one could gain access to an account of his evil deeds. However, the title page gave conflicting signs. No author's name appeared on it, so the book might be a libel written by an anonymous hack in the hire of Manuel's enemies. And yet the open display of the printer's address at the bottom of the page suggested that it was not an underground publication. Although *Vie secrète de Pierre Manuel* carried no date, it circulated in the summer of 1793, after Robespierre had joined the Committee of Public Safety and his enemies, the Girondins, had either fled or disappeared into prison. As an ally of the Girondins, Manuel was an obvious target of the triumphant, Montagnard left. Could the attack on him represent a new political line being publicized by the new revolutionary government?

The book has a frontispiece of sorts, but instead of appearing in the accustomed place, opposite the title page, the engraving sticks out unexpectedly between pages six and seven (see figure 4). It sets off the preliminary discourse from the main body of the text, which begins on page seven, so there is some logic to its placement. But it looks incongruous—an engraved portrait on heavy paper, inserted between the flimsy leaves of an anonymous, sixty-three-page pamphlet. The reader comes upon it by surprise, first by encountering its blank back side, then, after turning the page, by confronting an image of Manuel looking out from an oval frame with a self-assured air and

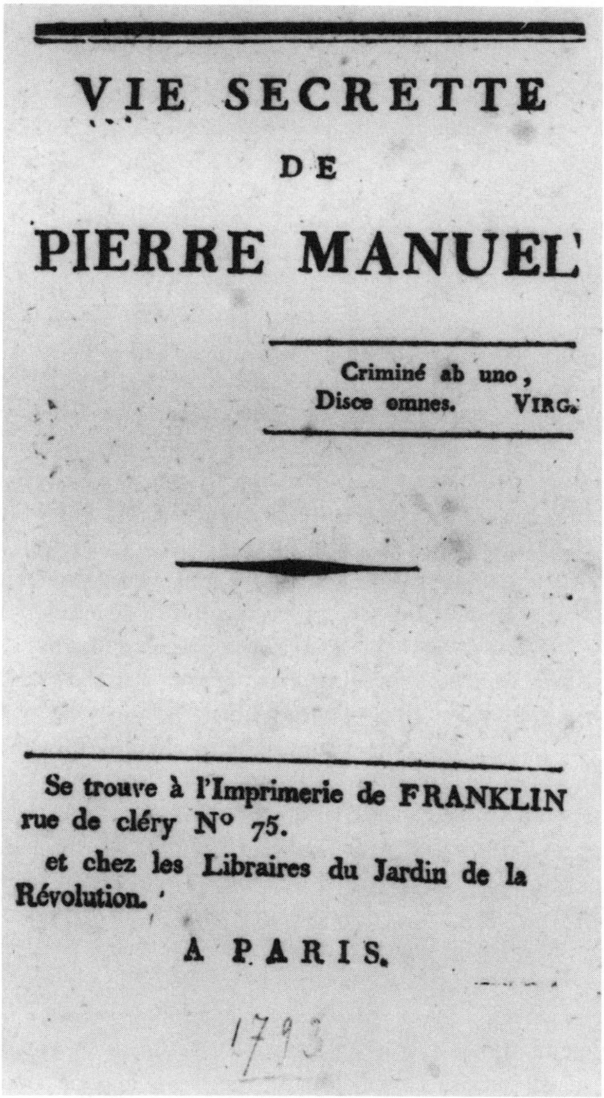

VIE SECRETTE

DE

PIERRE MANUEL

Criminé ab uno ,
Disce omnes.   VIRG.

Se trouve à l'Imprimerie de FRANKLIN
rue de cléry Nº 75.

et chez les Libraires du Jardin de la
Révolution.

À PARIS.

1793

Figure 13. *Vie secrète de Pierre Manuel*, title page. (Princeton University Library)

the sash of a deputy to the National Convention draped across his chest. It is a rather flattering portrait, certainly not a caricature, yet the caption below it reads like the standard stuff of libels.

P. Manuel

I was not born with a delicate disposition,
My soul is sordid and vulgar,
I have pillaged altars and betrayed the state
In order to increase my fortune.

What lay behind these incongruities?

The odd location of the frontispiece corresponded to the shoddy character of the work as a whole. Everything about the book (or pamphlet, depending on how one defines such a publication) suggests that it was cobbled together from cheap material and in haste. The paper is unusually crude—dirty brown in color, uneven in texture, marred by holes and bits of cloth that had resisted the pulverizing process in the paper mill. The text is divided into three parts, which are written in a slapdash manner and fit badly together, as though they had been churned out at high speed by different writers. Part one concentrates on Manuel's early life, part two on his activities in the early stages of the Revolution, and part three on his career as a deputy to the National Convention in 1792–93. But the last part doubles back over the periods covered by the first two and piles up anecdotes without aligning them in a coherent narrative.

The story ends with a general denunciation of its antihero. Having fleeced his constituents, conspired with the counterrevolution, and deserted the Convention, it concludes, Manuel was now living from his ill-gotten gains in a village outside Paris. A footnote on the final page, evidently added at the last minute, announced triumphantly that he had just been arrested: "We have learned a moment ago that Manuel has been arrested at Fontainebleau and taken to the Abbaye. . . . May he serve as an example for anyone audacious enough to imitate him."[1] The arrest occurred on August 20, 1793. Manuel was tried by the Revolutionary Tribunal on November 12 and executed as a counterrevolutionary on November 14. *Vie secrète de Pierre Manuel* was a crude call for the guillotine.

In this respect, it represented a new genre, the Jacobin libel. But it derived from a strain of slanderous literature that had flourished throughout the eighteenth century: hostile biographies, which usually carried titles that began with "Vie privée de . . ." ("Private Life of . . .") or "Vie secrète de . . ." ("Secret Life of . . ."). By uncovering the private lives of public figures, they attempted to destroy reputations and undermine power. In Manuel's case, the anonymous biographer made his intention clear by some heavy-handed moralizing in a "preliminary discourse." It warned its readers that the Revolution had opened the way to power for a new race of hypocrites, one even more perfidious than the priests and courtiers of the Old Regime. Adventurers and intriguers posed as patriots in order to get themselves elected or appointed to the new positions created by the Revolution, and once in place they exploited everything at their command to enrich themselves at the public's expense. Manuel epitomized this species. A sketch of his youth in part one of the text—reinforced by some parting shots at the end of part three—showed how he had struggled to shake off his humble origins and to get ahead under the unfavorable conditions of the Ancien Régime.

Born into a poor haberdasher's family in Montargis (he was actually born in Nemours on December 14, 1753, but he was raised in Montargis), Manuel succeeded well enough in a local school for his parents to send him to a seminary in Sens, hoping that he could become a priest. There he added enough polish to his manners to cut something of a figure as a petit-maître. He shone in the classroom but read philosophical works outside class and learned to have a way with the ladies (all of this according to the *Vie secrète*). His conquests included a daughter of a wealthy bourgeois who found herself pregnant and without prospects for a decent marriage, while Manuel moved on to greater things—that is, to the fleshpots of Paris. At first he ran errands for his father, collecting bills and spending the money on himself. When his income dried up he put on his soutane again, talked his way into the Seminary of Saint Louis, and rose to be an instructor in theology. But he dropped too many Voltairean remarks around the refectory. Expelled and back on the street without a penny, he had to retreat for a while to Montargis, where he was taken in by a sister who had married a certain "Desnoyers, master of billiards and tabacconist."[2] (The anonymous author supplied enough names and concrete detail to establish his authority as an eighteenth-century version of the investigative reporter.) Manuel returned to Paris and put in a brief stint in another religious house, then finally left the Church for what promised to be his true vocation, the book trade.

In its account of this phase in Manuel's career, part one of *Vie secrète* referred only to a "minor job in the book trade," but part three provided some details.[3] In 1785, it recounted, Garnery, a printer and bookseller in the rue Serpente, gave Manuel a room in exchange for some help in the shop. Manuel corrected proof, produced copy for a few "libels,"[4] and distributed material to peddlers. Support from the peddlers, it claimed, provided the initial impulse for his revolutionary career. By promoting his campaign to be elected to represent his district in the Commune, they helped him get a foothold in the municipal administration, where he directed the department in charge of policing the book trade. Instead of repressing unauthorized publications in the manner of the police under the Old Regime, Manuel left the peddlers, book-sellers, and printers free to do as they pleased. In that respect, according to *Vie secrète*, he deserved praise. True to his Enlightenment principles, "he behaved as a true *philosophe*."[5] But then he discovered that he could use his power to line his pockets. His office gave him access to a rich supply of documents from the archives of the police and the Bastille. By sifting through them, he came up with a collection of dossiers about priests who had been caught in broth-els—juicy material of impeccable authenticity, prepared by the police them-selves and ideal to serve up to a public hungry for anecdotes about scandals under the Old Regime. Manuel sold them to a publisher for 1,000 livres per folder—and collected 3,000 livres from Champion de Cicé, archbishop of Bor-deaux, in return for suppressing some of the most compromising material. The result, *La Chasteté du clergé dévoilée*, appeared in two volumes just in time to cream off the anticlerical demand stirred up by the debates over the Civil Constitution of the Clergy in 1790. But it performed no service to the revolu-tionary cause, according to the *Vie secrète*, because the scandalmongering cor-rupted the morals of the young instead of inspiring them with ideals of republican austerity. In short, Manuel raked muck like a libeler from the Old Regime—to make money.

After this lesson in the use of public office for private gain, Manuel never turned back, according to the *Vie secrète*. The narrative of his misdeeds became entangled in repetitions and confused chronology, probably, as mentioned, because the text was thrown together at top speed; but its main point was clear. Having learned the art of slander before 1789, Manuel continued to prac-tice it throughout the Revolution. The papers of the police furnished him with material for limitless "unveiling"—in *La Bastille dévoilée* and *La Police de Paris dévoilée* as well as *La Chasteté du clergé dévoilée*. *Vie secrète* referred to these multivolume compilations only in a general way, in order to emphasize the motive behind them all: Manuel did not publish scandalous material from the archives of the Ancien Régime from a patriotic desire to promote the Revolu-tion; he exploited the Revolution to make his fortune. *Vie secrète* claimed that he sold one compilation to Garnery for 12,000 livres and then supplemented that income by blackmailing persons who did not want their police records to appear in print.

Manuel's greatest coup was *Lettres originales de Mirabeau, écrites du don-jon de Vincennes pendant les années 1777, 78, 79 et 80, contenant tous les détails sur sa vie privée, ses malheurs, et ses amours avec Sophie Ruffei, marquise de*

Monnier. Although he trumpeted his role in this publication as an act of patriotism—more unveiling of abuses from the Ancien Régime—*Vie secrète de Pierre Manuel* condemned it as a commercial speculation. By the time of his death while serving as president of the National Assembly in 1791, Mirabeau stood out in the public eye as the boldest and most visible leader of the Revolution. His love letters to Sophie Monnier provided sensational copy, and Manuel made the most of their market value by lifting them from the archives and publishing them with Garnery in January 1792. According to the account of this incident in *Vie secrète*, they brought in a huge amount of money, and the court case that resulted produced a bonus in the form of favorable publicity. The judge, a reactionary attached to the royalist cause, attempted to condemn Manuel as an agitator, but Manuel defended himself so eloquently that he nearly provoked a riot and got the case dismissed. Now famous as a champion of the people and installed as the public prosecutor (*procureur*) of the Commune, he participated in the overthrow of the monarchy on August 10, 1792, and stood out as one of the most prominent Jacobins elected to the Convention.

Up to this point, *Vie secrète* had provided a relatively favorable account of Manuel's political career. True, he had demonstrated a deplorable love for lucre, but he had always aligned himself with the common people and had promoted the program of the left. Part three of *Vie secrète* showed how the contradiction between his private life and his public life led to the inevitable disaster: Manuel gave in to corruption and went over to the counterrevolution. When he entered the Convention, he sat with the right, voted with the Girondists, and proved suspiciously sympathetic to the cause of the king. During the king's trial, he attempted to rig the voting procedure in a way that would save Louis's life. After he failed, he walked out of the Convention, abandoning his public responsibilities in order to enjoy his ill-gotten gains in private. He had amassed a fortune, not only through his publishing ventures but also by helping himself to luxury goods that had been confiscated by the Republic or donated to it by patriots. By the time he withdrew to Montargis, his outrageous conduct had even alienated his townsmen. They nearly killed him in a riot that took place in March 1793. He had gone into hiding as *Vie secrète* went to press, but his arrest occurred just in time for the insertion of the footnote that announced the end of the story: Manuel was in prison, waiting for the inevitable, ultimate punishment, an example of how the Revolution would go wrong if the wrong sort were allowed to take it over.

The story, of course, was Jacobin propaganda. It adhered to the Robespierrist line about the necessity of virtue in a republic, and it expressed the tendency of the left to deal with its enemies by denunciation, pending the guillotine. The address on its title page—"à l'Imprimerie de Franklin, rue de Cléry no. 75"—is the same as that of similar libels from this stage of the Revolution, the year II (1793–94): *Vie secrète et politique de Brissot* (Imprimerie de Franklin, An II, reprinted in the same year as *Vie privée et politique de Brissot*); *Vie de L.-P.-J. Capet, ci-devant duc d'Orléans* (Imprimerie de Franklin, An II); and *Vie privée et politique de J.-R. Hébert* (Imprimerie de Franklin, An II). The Franklin printing shop was located just a few doors down the rue de Cléry from the printer who produced *Vie privée de l'ex-Capucin François Chabot et de Gaspard Chaumette* (rue de Cléry no. 15, An II). The common titles and addresses suggest a campaign on the part of the Robespierrists to win over public opinion during a crucial phase of the Terror when they were trying to consolidate their hold on power. Evidently they did not consider it enough to eliminate their opponents—whether on the right (Brissot, Manuel, and Orléans) or the left (Hébert, Chabot, and Chaumette)—by the guillotine; they needed to destroy reputations as well. So they dug up dirt about private lives and scattered it through "vies privées," using the same printers and the same model, one derived from the hack writing of the Ancien Régime.

The continuity should not be surprising because all libels slandered their victims in the same way, despite the variations in their tone and context. Whether in a spirit of mockery or indignation, they always stripped off the veil that hid someone's private life and exposed some scandal connected with public affairs. The differences in the four libels discussed thus far correspond to stages in the evolution of a large body of literature. *Le Gazetier cuirassé* marked the culmination of a flood of slander aimed at Louis XV and the leading figures of his reign. For all its radical language, it addressed its readers in a playful mode, which combined defamation with amusement in a style derived from the scandalmongering of the seventeenth century. This ludic quality carried over into *Le Diable dans un bénitier*, which made the police themselves the object of its mockery and revealed the story of their attempts to wipe out slander during the reign of Louis XVI. *La Police de Paris dévoilée* brought the story into the revolutionary era but shifted into a minor key. Righteous indignation now propelled the narrative, although plenty of sensational details remained to whet the appetite of the prurient or thrill-seeking reader. By the time of *Vie secrète de Pierre Manuel*, sensationalism had given way to denunciation, and slander served as propaganda for the Terror.

The succession of libels also conveyed successive images of Grub Street authors. Each work linked up with its predecessors, and each reinforced the self-referential quality that ran through the whole chain, from Morande's dramatization of himself as the intrepid gazetteer to Pelleport's send-up of the police from the perspective of their enemies, and Manuel's self-glorification as the patriot who unmasked the whole business—only to be unmasked himself in the deadliest of the *vies privées*. But did the line end there?

Chapter 5
The End of the Line

Who wrote *Vie secrète de Pierre Manuel*? The catalogue of the Bibliothèque nationale de France, following the *Dictionnaire des ouvrages anonymes* of A.-A. Barbier, attributes it and three of the other Jacobin "private lives" to a certain Pierre Turbat.[1] But neither source, nor any of the numerous bibliographies devoted to the Revolution, cites any evidence for that attribution or any information about Turbat.

If he really wrote all the works that appear after his name in the catalogue of the Bibliothèque nationale de France, Turbat covered a great deal of the ideological spectrum, changing position with every shift of the wind. He followed the violent Robespierrism of his libels from 1793–94 (assuming he was their author) with a fiercely anti-Robespierrist journal, *Petite feuille de Paris*, in 1794–95. There, for the first time, his name appeared in print. He identified himself as P. Turbat, a native of La Charité-sur-Loire, and he described his nature as "a lively, independent character with a burning love for the liberty of my country."[2] This love of liberty did not prevent him, however, from adhering to all the twists and turns of the Thermidorean reaction in politics. By 1798 he had crossed the line that divided reaction from royalism. In *Procès de Louis XVI* (1798) he narrated the trial and execution of the king in a way that made Louis look like a martyr, and he supplemented the story with documents he extracted from the archives of the Revolutionary Tribunal, very much as Manuel had published excerpts from the papers of the Bastille.

Manuel himself appeared in Turbat's last publication, which covered the same ground but this time as an ultra-royalist work by a "friend of the Throne," *Les Tuileries, le Temple, le Tribunal révolutionnaire et la Conciergerie, sous la tyrannie de la Convention* (1814). Turbat described Manuel scornfully as "a man who pretended to be a philosopher and who wrote the ostentatious letter to the king that began with the words: 'Sire, I do not like kings.' "[3] Manuel had placed that defiant remark at the beginning of an open letter to Louis XVI in 1792, causing quite a stir. But in 1814 it sounded like an echo from a past that was already assuming the character of a myth. Turbat quoted it in the course of a sentimental account of the king's last days and added another remark attributed to Manuel, which struck the same note. According to Turbat, Manuel visited Louis XVI in the prison of the Temple soon after the abolition of the monarchy on September 21, 1792, and provided the following description of their encounter: "I thought I should inform him about the foundation of the republic. 'You are no longer king,' I told him. 'Here is a nice opportunity to become a good citizen.' He did not seem to me to be affected. ... I told him of our conquests ... and I announced to him 'the fall of kings as near as that of the leaves.' "[4]

A dramatic scene, but did it ever take place? Did Turbat write the works attributed to him? Who in fact was he? At this point the evidence runs out and the trail of libels disappears into the shifting ideological sands of the nineteenth century.

Chapter 6
Bibliography and Iconography

Although *Vie secrète de Pierre Manuel* drew on the techniques of slander developed in the genre of "private lives" or "secret lives" from the Ancien Régime, it belonged to the political culture of the Revolution. It mixed words and images in ways that were designed to appeal to Jacobins and that look foreign to modern readers. To sort them out it is necessary to reconsider the text from the viewpoint of bibliography and iconography.

A book's frontispiece naturally belongs at its front, no matter how primitive it may be. The misplaced frontispiece in the libel against Manuel therefore needs to be explained, and the best explanation involves a brief detour into bibliographical analysis. By way of a reminder to nonbibliographers, it should be said that early modern books were composed of sheets, and each sheet contained several pages of text arranged so that they could be folded into gatherings—one fold (with four pages) in books of the folio format, two folds (eight pages) for quartos, and three folds (sixteen pages) for octavos. The gatherings, identified by signatures such as A, B, and so on through the printer's alphabet of twenty-three letters, were stitched together and cut so that the pages could be read in consecutive order. *Vie secrète de Pierre Manuel* is an octavo composed of half-sheets. (The vertical chain lines in the paper indicate the octavo format, which was common for casual publications of this kind.) Each gathering therefore consists of four leaves or eight pages (instead of eight leaves or sixteen pages), and the signatures run without interruption from A to H, leaving no extra paper. The bibliographical description of the book—8°: A⁴–H⁴— corresponds to its extremely simple structure: eight half-sheets stitched together with no extraneous matter—except the print of Manuel.

Normally, books and pamphlets contained preliminary leaves, which were used for front matter such as the title page, half-title, dedication, and table of contents, and the main sequence of signatures usually began with the start of the text. This is not the case with *Vie secrète de Pierre Manuel*. It has no preliminaries. Its title page functions as its cover and is the first page in the first of the eight gatherings that make up the book. Because the book lacks a half-title or covering of any kind, the frontispiece could not be inserted in the customary position—following a preliminary leaf and facing the title page. Instead it was glued like a cancel between the last two leaves of the first gathering. In this way, the printer saved paper but sacrificed elegance. The slipshod character of the work suggests that he did not worry about typographical niceties. He turned out a hack job at high speed.

But why should such a book have a frontispiece or any illustrations at all? It may seem strange, since frontispieces usually occurred in more elegant publications. But cheap prints of all sorts—caricatures, broadsides, canards, posters, and engravings of current events—flooded the streets of Paris during the Revolution. They were churned out by shops in the rue Saint Jacques, hung up for sale along the quays, displayed prominently in bookstores, hawked by peddlers, and plastered on walls everywhere in the city. Many of them were portraits of revolutionary leaders. The public, hungry for information about political events, wanted to know what the new race of politicians looked like and what sort of private lives they had led before they appeared on the public scene. A print went perfectly with a "private life," and a public figure like Manuel left a trail of images behind him as he rose through the ranks of the Revolution's leaders.

By following that trail, one can turn up a good deal of information about Manuel and the way he appeared in the public eye. Although he never achieved the fame of a Marat or a Danton and is hardly remembered today except among a few specialists in the history of the French Revolution,[1] he counted among the best-known deputies when the National Convention first met on September 21, 1792, and began to cope with a staggering agenda of problems: the fate of Louis XVI, the creation of a new republic, the defense of the country against the invading armies of Austria and Prussia, and the increasing hostility of the sans-culotte movement in Paris, which had erupted in the horrific massacres of September 2–6.

Manuel owed his election to support from the Parisian militants. Although *Vie secrète de Pierre Manuel* gave a tendentious account of his biography, it got most of the facts right. After struggling without much success to make a living and a name for himself as a man of letters before 1789, he found a new career in the officialdom created by the Revolution in Paris—first as an outspoken champion of the Third Estate in his local electoral district, then as its representative in the Paris Commune, and by 1790 as an administrator in the office of the mayor responsible for the policing of the book trade. Thanks to support from the Jacobin Club, where he became known for his outspoken oratory, he was elected as public prosecutor (*procureur*) of the Commune on December 2, 1791. From that post, he gained notoriety by writing his open letter to the king, the one mentioned by Pierre Turbat that began "Sire, I do not like kings" and went on to recommend that Louis XVI entrust the education of the dauphin to the popular, Rousseauistic author Bernardin de Saint-Pierre. Manuel was suspended from his functions for complicity in the insurrection of June 20, 1792, when a hostile crowd invaded the Tuileries Palace and forced the king to drink to the health of the nation. But he was reinstated in time to participate in the overthrow of the monarchy on August 10. For the next six weeks he rode the wave of sans-culotte power that swept everything before it until it engulfed all Paris in the massacres of September. Although he intervened to save some lives, he stood by the most radical leaders of the Commune—including Robespierre, Collot d'Herbois, and Billaud-Varennes—during the massacres and therefore stood out as a champion of the people during the elections to the Convention. When he took a seat with the radical Parisian delegation on September 21, his portrait was being hawked in the streets along with those of other prominent deputies.

The provenance of these prints cannot be traced, but the images of Manuel that circulated at street level probably were derived, by means of engravings and copies of copies, from a portrait that hangs today in the Musée historique of Versailles. It, too, has an uncertain past. Manuel may well have commissioned it himself, probably sometime in the spring or summer of 1792. By then he had emerged as one of the most popular politicians in Paris, and according to one particularly shrewd observer he had a touch of vanity.

In her *Considérations sur les principaux événements de la Révolution française* (1818), Mme de Staël includes a sketch of Manuel in an account of how she survived the September Massacres. During the last days of August as rumors of the impending catastrophe began to circulate, she considered herself safe. Her husband, the baron de Staël-Holstein, who was the Swedish ambassador, had left Paris, but the Swedish embassy, where she remained, was not a likely target of the crowd. Two of her closest friends, however, had been imprisoned for suspected aristocratic sympathies, and by the beginning of September 1792 the sans-culottes were calling for a slaughter of the prisoners. Rumors had spread about a counterrevolutionary conspiracy that might erupt at any moment from the prisons and spread carnage on the home front while the enemy invaded from abroad. France had declared war on Austria on April 20, confident that its armies would sweep to victory. Instead, the French offensive became stalled; Lafayette, France's most famous general, deserted to the enemy; and the Austrians with their Prussian allies picked off the key fortresses on the French border. They swept past Verdun, and nothing seemed capable of stopping them before they fell on Paris and slaughtered everyone who resisted. The Brunswick Manifesto, issued by the commander of the Austro-Prussian armies on July 25, threatened the sans-culottes with this fate. They responded by calling for a countermassacre, which would eliminate the danger in the prisons so that they then could face the invasion in an ultimate fight to the death. The streets filled with rioters, the air with wild talk. Treachery, slaughter, an uprising to purge the earth of counterrevolution—anything seemed possible.

The situation looked so desperate, as Mme de Staël observed it, that nothing could save her friends except the last-minute intervention by someone with some hold on power. But who? She scoured a list of all the members of the Commune, hoping to find a rescuer. Her eye hit upon the name of Manuel. It called up a vague memory: Wasn't he one of those obscure writers who had struggled to break out of the lower ranks of the republic of letters on the eve of the Revolution? He had published the correspondence of Mirabeau with a preface that had demonstrated a desire for recognition, if not much talent. Perhaps he could be moved by someone who had directed a salon at the summit of the literary world before 1789.

A request for an audience led to a meeting in Manuel's study at seven o'clock—"a rather democratic hour"—on the morning of September 1. While she waited for the public prosecutor to appear, the baroness studied her surroundings: "and I saw his portrait, made for him and placed on his own desk; that made me hope that he might at least be vulnerable to an appeal to his vanity."[2] Not every sans-culotte leader defended the cause of the people from a desk with his own portrait perched in front of him. Once softened up by Mme de Staël, Manuel did not let his plebeian connections prevent him from coming to the aid of some aristocrats. He behaved generously, even heroically, according to Mme de Staël's reconstruction of events. He ordered her friends released, and on the following day he saved Mme de Staël herself. While attempting to escape from Paris in a coach drawn by six horses and mounted by lackeys in livery—an attempt to awe the sans-culottes, which backfired—she was surrounded by a crowd and carried off for interrogation in the Hôtel de Ville. There she encountered Manuel once again. He was receiving reports from the scenes of the slaughter and dispatching emissaries to try to stem it, but he spared a minute from the bloody business to direct her to his office. There she sat for seven hours, watching from the window as the massacrers, covered with blood, reported to the Commune. That night Manuel accompanied her back to her residence in his own vehicle. When groups of sans-culottes stopped them, he called out "Public Prosecutor of the Commune" and they gave way. With the help of a new passport that he arranged to have delivered, she escaped the next day to the safety of Switzerland.

The portrait studied so anxiously by Mme de Staël almost certainly is the one that now hangs in the Musée de Versailles, the only painting of Manuel known to exist. Seen in its current setting, it appears impressive: Manuel sits upright and looks out squarely at the viewer in a dignified pose. It is a highly finished pastel by one of the masters from the Ancien Régime who had rallied to the Revolution, Joseph Ducreux. Despite some important commissions before 1789 (the duc de Choiseul had sent him to Vienna to produce the first official portrait of Marie-Antoinette after her betrothal to the future Louis XVI), Ducreux had failed to be admitted to the Royal Academy of Painting and Sculpture. Like Jacques-Louis David, a close friend of his, he became an ardent Jacobin. He welcomed the transformation of cultural institutions produced by the Revolution, and he painted its foremost leaders, including Mirabeau, Barnave, Saint-Just, and Robespierre. His portrait put Manuel in good, Jacobin company.

The collections of prints in the Bibliothèque nationale de France contain eight portraits of Manuel, all of them copperplate engravings or aquatints.[3] Most have no clues as to their origin, but one is inscribed "Ducreux pinxt P.M. Alix Sculptr," meaning Alix had engraved it after Ducreux's painting. Its caption reads:

P. MANUEL

Public Prosecutor of the Commune of Paris in 1792;
Deputy to the Convention in the First Year of the French Republic;
Author of *L'Année française* in 4 volumes;
of the *Coup d'oeil philosophique sur Saint-Louis*;
of *La Police dévoilée*;
Editor of the *Lettres de Mirabeau*
At the author's residence, rue Christine no. 2

As the caption indicates, the engraving provided favorable publicity for Manuel soon after his election to the Convention. It presents him as a man of letters turned public servant, listing his most reputable works as if they constituted a pedigree (it passed over his more dubious publications in silence). The engraving may also have been meant to bring in some money, because the caption specified that it could be bought from Manuel at his home address. And it has a family resemblance to the other prints, which could have been copied from it or adapted with minor changes from the Ducreux painting.

Despite their similarity, however, the other prints of Manuel belonged to different contexts and transmitted different messages. One was produced after his death; we know this because it gives the date of his execution. Another is the same as the frontispiece in *Vie secrète*, but it has no caption and has been trimmed in such a way that one cannot tell anything about its provenance: it could have been clipped out of the book, or, as seems more likely, it could

Figure 14. Portrait of Manuel by Joseph Ducreux. (Etablissement du musée et du domaine de Versailles)

have circulated independently like other popular prints. Two other portraits probably date from the early days of the Convention and were sold from book-shops and peddler's packs like all the ephemera of 1792–93. The first, a litho-graph by Auguste Bry, simply said it was for sale in the bookshop of Rosselin, Quai Voltaire. The second carried a caption that identified Manuel in a neutral

P. MANUEL,

*Procureur de la Commune de Paris en 1792;
Député à la Convention; l'An Premier de la
République Française.*

*Auteur de l'Année Française en 4 Volumes; du Coup d'Œil philosophique sur St Louis;
de la Police Devoilée; éditeur des Lettres de Mirabeau.*

A Paris, chez l'Auteur, rue Christine, N.º 2.

Figure 15. Print of Manuel. (Bibliothèque nationale de France, Département des estampes, D203608)

P. MANUEL

Procureur de la Commune de Paris en 1792.
Député à la Convention Nationale; l'An I.ᵉʳ de la Répub.ᵉ Française.

A Paris chez Basset, Rue S.ᵗ Jacques au coin de celle des Mathurins.

Figure 16. Print of Manuel. (Bibliothèque nationale de France, Département des estampes, 203610)

manner and gave its source as the print shop of Basset at the corner of the rue Saint Jacques and the rue des Mathurins.

A caricature from February 1790 shows that shop. The Basset hound on the sign above the door is a rebus evoking Paul-André Basset, one of the most important producers and dealers of prints from the late eighteenth century.[4] He made a fortune by adjusting his output of images to shifts in the political temperature. In the 1780s he produced panegyrics to Louis XVI; in the 1790s he adhered to the Jacobin line; and after 1800 he celebrated Bonaparte. In this

Le Joli Moine
Profitant de l'occasion

Figure 17. A satirical print about the secularization of monastic orders. (Bibliothèque nationale de France, Collection Vinck 3362)

case, he depicted his own shop in the background of a scene that served as a bawdy commentary on the secularization of the monasteries: two monks are being shaved and outfitted for civilian life; the one in the foreground, a stereotypical, oversexed man of the cloth, is cavorting with his female barber.

Inside the shop, a saleswoman sits behind the counter with prints piled in front of her. Other prints are displayed outside the door, and a peddler is leaving the shop loaded down with prints to be hawked in the streets. The caricature that dangles from the peddler's pack is one of the best-known prints from 1789: it protests against the exploitation of the Third Estate by showing a prelate and a nobleman riding on the back of a bent-over peasant. To make the message clear, its caption is written out in the form of a note pinned to the pack: "It must be hoped that this game will finish soon."

The images of Manuel circulated in this kind of a setting, and, like Basset's print, they conveyed ideological messages. One caricature, a royalist print from December 1792, casts Manuel in the company of the radical republicans

Figure 18. Detail showing Basset's shop. (Bibliothèque nationale de France, Collection Vinck 3362)

A FAUT ESPERER Q'EU JEU LA FINIRA BEN TOT.

l'duteur en Campagne Ap. 1789.

Figure 19. Print protesting the exploitation of the peasantry. (Bibliothèque nationale de France, Collection Vinck 2793)

who had led the attacks on Louis XVI. While a motley crew of agitators tries to save the nation—represented as an ice sculpture that is melting under rays projected by a Bourbon sun—he flounders ignominiously on a manure pile at the center of the picture, accompanied by his notorious "Sire, I do not like kings." The journalists around him—Brissot, Carra, Gorsas, Fauchet, Desmoulins, and Audouin—belong to different factions of the left that dominated the Convention when it first met.

The left fell apart, however, in the great debate about the king's fate in January 1793. Manuel typified their wavering. Although he did not hesitate to declare the king guilty of treason, he could not bring himself to vote for Louis's immediate execution. He walked out of the Convention as soon as the death penalty was pronounced, then resigned and withdrew to his hometown of Montargis. By March he had acquired such a reputation as a moderate—that is, in Jacobin terms, a Girondist and a counterrevolutionary—that he was nearly killed in a local riot. He went into hiding in the outskirts of Paris but was hunted down after the overthrow of the Girondists on May 31 and was executed on November 14 as one of their co-conspirators.

The dramatic swings in Manuel's revolutionary career provided the main theme of the last print, a large folio sheet that may have been peddled in the streets as a broadside but has survived in book form as one "tableau" in the *Collection complète des tableaux historiques de la Révolution française* (Paris, 1798–1802). This magnificent, three-volume folio collection of engravings offered a view of the Revolution from the perspective of the Napoleonic Consulate—a view that affirmed the fundamental changes produced in 1789–92 while condemning the excesses of 1793–94. Volume II contained portraits of the sixty persons who, in the judgment of the anonymous editors, had played the most important roles in the Revolution. Each portrait occupied one page and was composed of three parts: a shoulder-length engraving of the individual, a picture of some event in which he was involved, and an engraved text or "historical discourse containing the private and political life of the individual being depicted." By combining the text with the pictures, each tableau provided a "portrait" in the fullest sense of the word, one that flushed out the imagery with a biographical sketch of the kind that had flourished in French literature since Jean de La Bruyère and Madeleine de Scudéry.

Many of the mini-biographies, including Manuel's, also had some affinity with libels, as the introduction made clear by emphasizing their treatment of the subject's "private life." The engravings and word pictures went together, very much as they had done in underground classics from the Ancien Régime such as the *Vie privée de Louis XV*. The last and most elaborate portrait of Manuel therefore shows how several elements had coalesced in a retrospective

Figure 20. A royalist caricature of 1792, depicting Manuel at the center of a group of radicals. (Bibliothèque nationale de France, Département des estampes, Collection Vinck 4364)

view of the Revolution that was hardening into an orthodoxy at the time of Bonaparte's seizure of power.

The portrait in the circular frame resembles the other prints of Manuel and could have been derived from the Ducreux pastel. The picture below it shows Manuel being attacked by a crowd of hostile Jacobins during the riot in Montargis of March 1793. A tiny inscription under the picture identified it as the work of Jean Duplessi-Bertaux, painted and engraved by him in the Year VIII (1799–1800). Like Ducreux, Duplessi-Bertaux had won some important commissions under the Ancien Régime but never made it into the Royal Academy of Painting and Sculpture. He, too, followed David's lead into revolutionary cultural politics. He became an ardent Jacobin and turned out paintings and engravings of revolutionary events right up to 1800. Many of the engravings were published in the 1802 edition of *Tableaux historiques de la Révolution française*, which celebrated him as "the CALLOT of our time." In depicting violence, they echo the etchings about the atrocities of war produced by Jacques Callot in the 1630s, but they also have a monumental quality and a classical coolness that evoke ancient bas-reliefs. Their choice of subjects suggests sympathy for the basic gains of the Revolution combined with repugnance at the Terror, or what they referred to as "Maratism." That position, a kind of moderate Jacobinism that suited the early years of the Consulate, came through clearly in the texts engraved beneath Duplessi-Bertaux's tableaux.

The biographical sketch of Manuel portrayed him as inconsistent and insincere, an opportunist who threw himself into the radical movement of the Paris sections only to renounce it after it had swept him into eminence. Here is Manuel's "private and public life," in synopsis, as it was presented to the public for the last time.

If anyone during the Revolution exhibited a capacity for coming up with revolutionary conceptions at one time and a vacillating conduct at another, it was certainly Manuel. It is hard to know what to make of such a strangely contradictory character, considering his public declaration of hatred for kings and the regrets he expressed for the condemnation of the last king of the French, his intimate connections with the partisans of Maratism and his brave opposition to the activities of that party, and his love of philosophy and humanity contrasted with the part he played in the execrable massacres of September 2 and 3. It is generally believed that he only declared himself to be a partisan of Marat in order to get elected to the Convention and that in the end he was ashamed of the excesses he had committed.

From a humble birth, he became a schoolmaster. Then he made a name for himself by publishing his *De la police dévoilée*. By flattering the common people and proclaiming himself an enemy of kings, he managed to get himself named as public prosecutor of the Commune. He was still in office during the uprising of August 10 and claimed responsibility for the success of that day. He was present in the same

Figure 21. Portrait and biographical sketch of Manuel from *Tableaux historiques de la Révolution française*. (Bibliothèque nationale de France, D 203603)

capacity when the murdering took place in the prisons on September 2. He admitted this himself, because during his interrogation [before the Revolutionary Tribunal] he said that he had seen two corpses still palpitating there. It seems that he did little to stop those atrocities, because they continued to take place. After that he was selected as a deputy to the Convention. But from the very beginning he broke with all his colleagues from the Parisian deputation. He joined the party of the Gironde and became one of the most ardent enemies of the Jacobins.

During the trial of the last king, Manuel, who was one of the Convention's secretaries responsible for tabulating the votes, was accused of having mishandled the roll and of being decidedly partial in his behavior. A few days later he resigned and withdrew to Montargis, his hometown. There he was soon hunted down by the agents of the Maratists and the Orléanists and was assaulted by a gang of madmen, who left him for dead. A while later he was arrested and brought before the Revolutionary Tribunal, which sent him to the scaffold.[5]

As the images reproduced in this chapter make clear, the frontispiece of *Vie secrète de Pierre Manuel* (see figure 4) belonged to the genre of popular prints hawked in the streets of Paris during the revolutionary decade. Such prints could not be sold openly under the Ancien Régime because the Parisian police generally managed to curb the satirical bent of the artists and printmakers of the rue Saint Jacques. Despite clandestine production and foreign imports, France never developed a visual political culture comparable to the caricaturing that flourished openly in the London of Hogarth, Gilray, and Rowlandson. But after the fall of the Bastille, the rue Saint Jacques exploded with activity; peddlers did a roaring business in prints as well as pamphlets and supplied a public eager to see the faces of the men whose "private lives" were exposed in print. As their slipshod quality attests, these illustrated booklets were designed to appeal to ordinary readers. Unlike fine engravings, which commonly sold for 10 livres, cheap prints often cost 10 sous (there were 20 sous to a livre), about the same as a medium-size pamphlet or half the price of a short book.[6] A skilled worker like a locksmith or a printer made 40–50 sous a day; he could afford to part with 30 sous for a "private life" with a frontispiece, though not easily, and he might prefer to read it in a tavern or a political club.

Of course, images were sometimes attached to texts in the underground literature of the Ancien Régime. A few libels carried frontispieces that combined sober portraits with slanderous epigraphs exactly as in *Vie secrète de Pierre Manuel*. *Anecdotes sur Mme la comtesse du Barry* (1775), the supreme best-seller in this genre, pictured the royal mistress opposite the title page as if it had captured the true image as well as the inside story of its antiheroine. Underneath the quite attractive portrait, the caption read:

Without wit, without talent, from the midst of infamy,
She was elevated to the throne.
Never against an enemy cabale
Did she conspire;
And unmindful of ambition's warning signals,
A puppet of intriguers, she reigned by nothing other than her charms.

Vie secrète de Pierre Manuel conformed to this well-established model. The continuity in technique—a matter of contrasting words and pictures—linked the propaganda of the Terror to the pamphleteering against Louis XV.

But when the printers assembled the ingredients of *Vie secrète de Pierre Manuel*, they found it impossible to place the frontispiece opposite the title page without adding another half-sheet. Therefore, they inserted it at a convenient place in the first gathering. In the rush to cobble together an attack on a prominent Girondin, the master printer in the Imprimerie de Franklin, rue de Cléry no. 75, may not have had time to commission a new engraving. Instead of investing in an original work, he probably drew on the stock of prints that were available in the nearby shops of the rue Saint Jacques, shops like that of Paul-André Basset, who had produced the engraving of Manuel that had been hawked in the streets several months earlier. The engravers could have touched up an old plate and added the slanderous epitaph, which undercuts the image in the same manner as does the verse engraved under the frontispiece of Mme du Barry.

One can only guess at the exact nature of the production process. But whatever procedure they followed, the printers combined the visual material with a biographical text in a way that would have been familiar to their clients. Many of the other slanderous attacks on revolutionary politicians did the same. I have identified thirty-eight such libels. Most of them carry titles that begin with "vie privée" or "vie secrète," and fourteen contain portraits, usually in the form of frontispieces with derogatory captions. *Vie secrète de Pierre Manuel* was a typical example of a general genre: the revolutionary libel.

The iconographic dimension of this literature hardly seems surprising. Readers wanted to see what such persons looked like, to read their countenances for clues to their character. Thanks to the visual as well as the textual portraits, they could compare the outer with the inner man and enjoy the frisson of seeing villainy stripped bare. Or, if they sympathized with the victims, they could resist the textual argument and look for redeeming features in a slandered politician exposed to the public's scorn. Either way, the message was carried by visual and verbal metaphors of unveiling and unmasking. Manuel himself had done more than any other libeler to exploit this rhetorical register in *La Police de Paris dévoilée* and his other works. In *Vie secrète de Pierre Manuel* he fell victim to the devices that he had perfected.

MADAME LA COMTESSE
DU BARRY.

Sans esprit, sans talens, du sein de l'infamie
Jusques au trône on la porta :
Contre une Cabale ennemie
Jamais elle ne complotta :
Et de l'ambition ignorant les allarmes,
Jouet des intriguans, regna par ses seuls charmes.

Figure 22. *Anecdotes sur Mme la comtesse du Barry*, frontispiece. (Private copy)

J.^{ME} PETION.

En deux mots voici mon histoire;
dans Paris j'étois Adoré;
tout y rétentissoit de mon nom, de magloire
Aujourd'hui j'y Suis Abhorré.

Figure 23. Portrait in *Vie politique de Jérôme Pétion*. (Bibliothèque nationale de France, L27n.16130)

JAC. P. BRISSOT,

Députe du Département de Paris, à l'Assemblée Législative, en 1791,
et à la Convention Nationale, en 1792.

Cet auteur si fameux, qui de la comédie
Atteignit le vrai but, fit de si beaux portraits,
Un siecle avant le mien, devina mon génie,
Il composa Tartuffe et rendit tous mes traits.

Figure 24. Portrait of Brissot, probably from a print peddled separately in the streets, inserted as a frontispiece in *Vie privée et politique de Brissot.* Other copies of this work do not include the print, which probably was inserted in this copy from the stock of engravings hawked in the street. (Private copy)

Not a happy ending—and perhaps not a satisfactory conclusion either for the argument might be vulnerable to a fundamental objection. It seems reasonable to assume that the libels were designed in a way that was meant to elicit particular reactions on the part of their readers, but how can one know how the readers read them?

Chapter 7
Reading

The problem of reader reception has no easy solution. How to get inside the minds of people who tried to make sense of the printed word more than two centuries ago? They left almost no record of their reactions. Occasionally one comes across some remarks scribbled in a margin, an entry in a diary, a paragraph in a commonplace book, a reference in a letter, a report by a bookseller, a note by a police spy, a description in a work of fiction, or an essay by a contemporary fascinated by the spread of reading as a social phenomenon. But how to compose this fragmentary evidence into an accurate general picture? How to investigate all the varieties of reading practices, which could have varied endlessly? How to distinguish the response to libels as opposed to other kinds of writing and to extrapolate from the responses of individuals to the formation of the collective attitude that, for lack of a better phrase, we call public opinion? The difficulties seem so insurmountable that one is tempted to abandon the attempt altogether and to restrict the research to the texts themselves. Instead of dealing with real people, the argument could be limited to the imaginary characters conjured up by some literary critics—the "implicit readers" that texts seem to address and the types of reading that books seem to assume.[1]

But hypercritical skepticism about evidence can be paralyzing. Why not take account of the few documents that have survived in order to see whether they yield at least some tentative conclusions? Here, for example, is a report by a police spy about the reading of libels in a Parisian café, chez Maugis, rue Saint Séverin, probably in 1729.

From nine in the morning until late at night it [the café chez Maugis] is the gathering place of lawyers, attorneys, booksellers and news mongers [*nouvellistes*], who exhibit and read all sorts of defamatory libels. People speak openly there about all sorts of affairs—of the state, of finance, and of foreign relations—and the reports are verified by the booksellers who have correspondents in England, Holland, and Geneva.[2]

Paris had at least 380 cafés by this time. If libels triggered such talk in 1729, how many discussions had they provoked by 1789, when Parisians traded gossip in at least 800 cafés and 2,000 other drinking establishments?[3] According to one description of the agitation produced by an antigovernment tract in 1788, waiters in the cafés of the Palais-Royal made a "fortune" by renting it out, and readers memorized entire passages so that they could declaim them in front of anyone who had failed to get a copy.[4]

Cafés functioned as nerve centers for transmitting messages through the body politic of eighteenth-century Paris. They provided news as well as coffee, news in the form of gossip and gazettes, both legal journals and manuscript *chroniques scandaleuses*. The information they diffused also could be picked up at other key points in the urban landscape—bridges (particularly the Pont Neuf), marketplaces (especially at the Place Maubert), quays (notably the Quai des Augustins), law courts (above all the Cour de Mai of the Parlement de Paris), and public gardens (those outside the Luxembourg and Tuileries palaces). Book peddlers and *bouquinistes* plied their wares in all these places, which served as nodal points in a vast communication system. Throughout the system written messages, whether in print or in manuscript, were amplified by talk. Reading and conversation went together, particularly at the favorite gathering point of *nouvellistes*: the bookshops, cafés, and garden of the Palais-Royal.[5]

The Palais-Royal belonged to the duc d'Orléans, notorious in the 1770s and 1780s for his readiness to collaborate in agitation that undermined the crown. After a fire in 1773, he enclosed its garden in an enormous arcade backed by shops and apartments, including some of the liveliest cafés in the city (the Café du Caveau, the Café de Foy, and, outside the garden, the Café de la Régence on the Place du Palais-Royal). He allowed Parisians to stroll through the garden, speaking as freely as they liked on any topic they chose. They could buy illegal books in the shops under the arcade, stop off in the cafés for refreshment and gossip, take their pick from an endless flow of prostitutes, or try their luck in gambling dens. Most of these activities were illegal, but the police could not repress them without first asking permission from the governor of the palace, because under the juridical system of the Ancien Régime the Palais-Royal constituted a "privileged space" (*lieu privilégié*) subject to the duke's authority as a prince of the royal blood. It was in the Palais-Royal that Diderot let his thoughts fly free—"Mes pensées, ce sont mes catins" ("my thoughts are my strumpets")[6]—and engaged in conversation with the freethinking nephew of Rameau. It was from the Palais-Royal, perched on top of a café table, that Camille Desmoulins summoned Parisians to take arms and triggered the storming of the Bastille.

Although they could not arrest at will the suspicious characters who congregated in the Palais-Royal, the police kept them under surveillance. Many

Figure 25. *Nouvellistes* gossiping and reading in a café of the Palais-Royal.
(Bibliothèque nationale de France)

dossiers in the police archives mention booksellers who dealt in forbidden literature, but only a few refer to their customers. In December 1774, for example, Pierre-Antoine-Auguste Goupil, an inspector of the book trade (and a shady character himself, who will figure in later chapters of this book), received an order from the lieutenant general of police to find the author, printer, and distributors of a libel titled *Lettre de M. l'abbé Terray, ex-contrôleur-général, à M. Turgot, ministre des finances.* Goupil immediately dispatched a spy to sniff around the Palais-Royal. The spy found the *Lettre* for sale in two boutiques and managed to buy two copies from the principal source: the shop of the demoiselle La Marche in a passage that led from the Palais-Royal to the rue de Richelieu. According to Goupil's reports, the *Lettre* attracted quite a crowd to the shop, which was merely an outdoor stall, and its slanderous text set tongues wagging: "People flock to her shop as if they were going to a new play, and that creates a sensation. Besides, this brochure gives rise to talk about the persons who are compromised in it; and although it is quite badly written, the salty, wicked remarks scattered through it make it sold and read."[7] La Marche told Goupil's man that a sequel would soon be published. Her provisions would arrive before those of the other boutiques, and she promised to set aside

Figure 26. Conversation over newspapers in the gardens of the Palais-Royal. The figure on the left is reading the *Courrier de l'Europe*, a French newspaper published in London, which was the most important source of information about the American Revolution and British politics available in France. (Bibliothèque nationale de France)

a half-dozen copies for him. Encouraged by his interest in this kind of literature, she then ventured some compromising sales talk.

She asked him [Goupil's spy] if he knew *Vie de Mme du Barry*. "Naturally," he
answered; "why?" "It's because I still have several copies of 200 that I received from
Flanders two weeks ago." "Do you have this new item?" she then asked in a bantering
tone. "It's the *Bréviaire des chanoines de Rouen*, and it comes from that town." And
immediately she pulled out from underneath her stall the book that I am enclosing
here and for which she charged 2 livres 8 sous. As you can see, Monsieur, it's a compilation of indecencies likely to corrupt morals."[8]

Five days later Goupil burst into La Marche's apartment, a modest flat on
the sixth floor over a tobacconist's shop, looking for her secret stock. He collected some more political pamphlets and pornography, then marched her off
to the Bastille. In interrogating her Goupil learned that her real name was Louise Manichel. She was a native Parisian, thirty-eight years old, and had always
lived by peddling books, like her father, mother, and sister. They had no
authorization to do so, nor had the other *bouquinistes* of the Palais-Royal, Les-
prit, Morin, and Guyot, who also kept copies of the *Lettre de M. l'abbé Terray*
under their counters. They all sold the same wares, La Marche assured Goupil.
She would gladly inform him of her competitors' commerce, and while serving
as a spy, she would supply him with copies of all the latest illegal works, just
as she had done for his predecessor, inspector Joseph d'Hémery, if only he
would release her from the Bastille. But Goupil had strict instructions to trace
her supply line to its source. The path led to la femme Mequignon, a *bouqui-
niste* in the Cour de Mai of the Parlement, who kept a secret stock of the *Lettre
de M. l'abbé Terray*—and kept the stock secret from her husband, who had an
annoying habit of demanding a cut in her profits. Mme Mequignon drew her
provisions from Abraham Lucas, a bookseller in Rouen, and he got his from
Jacques Manoury, a bookseller in Caen who had directed the whole enterprise.
It took Goupil weeks of traveling, arrests, and interrogations to unravel the
production and distribution network. Along the way, he ran up an impressive
expense account for meals in country inns and acquired an excellent education
in the ways of the literary underground—one he would later put to use when
he joined it. But he never identified the printer or the author of the *Lettre*,
and, unfortunately for the historian of reading, he never wrote any more
reports about the crowds that gathered at the various bookstalls and the way
they read snatches of the book to each other, discoursing excitedly about the
secret lives of the great.[9]

That is all one can learn from an unusually rich run of dossiers in the
police archives, but it can be confirmed by a description of the *bouquinistes* in

Tableau de Paris by Louis-Sébastien Mercier. According to Mercier they sold everything, "even the book that was recently prohibited; but they are careful not to put it on display; they show it to you behind the boards of their shop: this monkey business gives them a claim to a few extra pennies."[10] Some of the *bouquinistes* secretly spied for the police, exactly as La Marche offered to do for Goupil: "Among these retailers stationed in passages leading to public promenades, there are spies who serve two purposes: to recognize people placed under surveillance and to denounce anyone who offers them an illicit brochure or who inquires, too eagerly, about one of those libels that, more often than not, have imaginary titles." The customers crowded around the stalls and in the shops to talk as well as read: "You see groups of them who stick to the sales counter as if drawn there by a magnet. They pester the bookseller, who has removed all chairs in order to make them remain standing; but they stay there nonetheless, for hour after hour, propped up against books, continuously leafing through pamphlets and holding forth about the merits and potential impact of works that they have barely glanced at."[11]

Mercier's descriptions of daily life in pre-revolutionary Paris should not be taken literally because he often touched them up to make them more colorful, and he did not hesitate to infuse them with his own opinions. But he had a good ear for casual conversation as well as a sharp eye for the way life was lived at street level. He devoted one whole book, *Les Entretiens du Palais-Royal* (1786), to reports of conversations in the Palais-Royal. Although it does not reproduce talk with the accuracy of a stenographic record, it conveys the way people struck up conversations, the topics they discussed, and the general tone of their encounters. As Mercier presented it, the Palais-Royal created a setting where strangers felt free to accost one another and to discuss anything on their minds. They jumped rapidly from subject to subject, changed conversational partners from one moment to another, and drifted in and out of groups where the most voluble could hold forth for hours. They especially liked to gossip about the great personages of the government and court; so their conversations were often touched off by reading the libels available in the boutiques.[12]

A calumny that appeared in print was more likely to be believed, Mercier maintained, than one diffused by word of mouth. To be sure, reasonable persons ("les hommes sensés") would not be taken in by crude defamation, but they formed a small minority: "They are but a handful in comparison with the gossips, the reprobates, the fools, who believe in calumnies as if they were articles of faith, especially when they are printed."[13] Libelers invented much of what they wrote, yet their writing resonated among a broad public, and they could strike it rich by slandering the great. Mercier claimed that he once had met one of them in Holland. The libeler had made a fortune by collecting anecdotes from informers in France and reworking them as the books and pamphlets that fueled the discussions in the Palais-Royal.

We turn out calumnies [the libeler recounted], and no one . . . keeps up a correspondence as extensive as ours. Courts, cities, families, cloisters are our tributaries. All you need is an imagination given to wickedness, and by making up stories, which attribute vice to one person and ridicule to another, you can earn as much as you want. . . . Even the most devout persons secretly read our libels, although to escape damnation, they piously believe only half of what they see.[14]

Although Mercier attributed great powers of persuasion to libelers, he did not claim that they could manipulate public opinion at will. On the contrary, he noted that the reactions of readers varied, owing to the different degrees of gullibility among individuals and the different subcultures of the Parisian population. A news report might astound market women in the Place Maubert and impress artisans in the faubourg Saint Jacques while arousing nothing but skepticism among the sophisticates of the faubourg Saint Honoré. A pamphlet could touch off quite different discussions in the Luxembourg Gardens as opposed to the Jardin du Roi, the Tuileries, and the boulevards. But credulity prevailed everywhere, especially in the Palais-Royal, the greatest ganglion in the nervous system of the city. Everyone there discussed the news ("nouvelles"). They might take up a strong position on some public question—from reports about ministerial intrigues and foreign affairs to shipwrecks and the weather—at one moment and then retract it an instant later. No matter: they would continue endlessly to comment with conviction about the latest, hottest topic. Mercier described them poring over pamphlets and gazettes, taking in every syllable of print, then leaping into the general discussion, sure of their facts and determined to dominate the debate. They might wait for a lull in the hubbub so that they could steer the talk in a new direction. Then, swimming with the current, they could go on for hours. From time to time they would dash into a café, where they could consult pamphlets and gazettes for new provisions of information. Once reinforced, they would plunge into the talk again, and at the end of the day they would return to their families and harangue their wives and children, a captive audience at the dinner table, who would listen with amazement to revelations about life among the great—exalted persons in exotic places whose very names sounded so strange as to be almost frightening.[15]

This "nouvellomanie" (mania for news) involved a great deal of editorializing. The public readings and debates led to verdicts about everything and everyone.

The impatience of certain *nouvellistes* often degenerates into a frenzy. Their entire existence is devoted to running around public promenades in order to pick up and repeat everything that is said, everything that is printed. And by their rush to believe everything, the most naïve conjectures turn into realities before their eyes. The court, the city, republics, kingdoms, the entire universe is their domain; and they are never more in their element than when they issue pronouncements on ministers, generals of the army, and even sovereigns.[16]

It was from the admixture of reading and talking, much of it stirred up by *nouvellistes* of different stripes, that public opinion took shape. Like many eighteenth-century philosophers, Mercier placed faith in the power of the printing press to keep the public informed and ultimately to make the truth prevail. But he did not envisage public opinion as a process of sifting through competing views so that by means of criticism and reflection a rational consensus would emerge. In place of this standard, Enlightenment view, he described public opinion as a cacophony that swirled through the streets and bubbled up in key sites, such as the Palais-Royal: "It is there that fantasies become realities, that one imagines alliances, fabricates treaties, ousts ministers, and makes sovereigns live or die."[17] Neither rational nor accurate, public opinion nevertheless operated as a force. In fact, it could sweep through Paris like a violent storm, and the eye of the hurricane was located in the Palais-Royal. From the frenzied discussions in the garden and boutiques, all that was needed was one great leap to the top of Desmoulins's café table and Paris would storm off to the Bastille—or so one might conclude from reading Mercier.[18]

But that scenario is much too simple. Although libels fired imaginations and contributed to the collective horror of despotism that mobilized Parisians in 1789, there were other sources of agitation, and there were other kinds of reading. Instead of imagining a straight line of causality—from libeling to reading to public opinion and revolutionary action—it would be more accurate to envisage a broad spectrum of ways in which readers absorbed the printed word. Revolutionary indignation can be taken to represent one extreme; innocent amusement, another—that is, a casual, apolitical kind of reading, which also deserves consideration.

Reading for amusement took many forms, including the kind that is most familiar today: the consumption of light fiction, above all novels. But the French also amused themselves with varieties of reading that are now nearly extinct. One variety, which suggests a good deal about their approach to libels, was reading as puzzle solving. The puzzles came in many formats—handwritten notes, journal articles, printed broadsides, and full-scale books. Some combined words with images, as in the frontispiece to *Le Gazetier cuira-*

ssé. The most elaborate were rebuses, a favorite genre in the eighteenth century.[19]

Other puzzles belonged to the genre of light verse and witticisms known as *pièces fugitives*. They appeared everywhere in literary reviews such as the *Mercure de France*, the most popular periodical under the Ancien Régime. By 1779, when the press baron Charles-Joseph Panckoucke had taken over the *Mercure* and combined its literary section with a political supplement, it had grown to 48 pages an issue; it came out once a week; and it reached 7,000 subscribers plus many thousands of additional readers. (The subscriptions grew throughout the 1780s and attained a high point of 15,000 in 1789.)[20] Large parts of the *Mercure* were designed to be read in a specific manner, one that combined amusement with deciphering. To "get" them, the reader had to solve a puzzle—very much as in the case of the frontispieces and texts of *Le Gazetier cuirassé* and *Le Diable dans un bénitier*. The common French expression "trouver le mot de l'énigme" ("find the word of the riddle," a rough equivalent to "connect the dots" used figuratively in English) referred to this experience, for every issue of the *Mercure* included an *énigme* that had to be solved in a certain way. Only one answer was admissible; any other would have to be dismissed as a misreading. For example, the *énigme* printed in the *Mercure* of April 3, 1784, went as follows:

ENIGME

Je puis avec huit pieds offenser le prochain;
Supprimez le second, je sers un Capucin.

(With my eight feet I can give offense;
Eliminate the second and I am useful to a Capuchin.)

The answer appeared in the issue of the following week: *scandale*. The word had eight letters, and if the second letter was eliminated it became *sandale*. No other reading was possible. The cadence and rhyme added to the wit of the puzzle, making it a successful "jeu d'esprit" or word game of the sort that was extremely popular under the Ancien Régime.

The same issue also carried a *charade*.

CHARADE

Privez de mon premier et transis par le froid,
Les malheureux allaient périr tous de misère,
Lorsque de mon second le chef et digne Père
Sut terminer mon tout et calmer leur effroi.

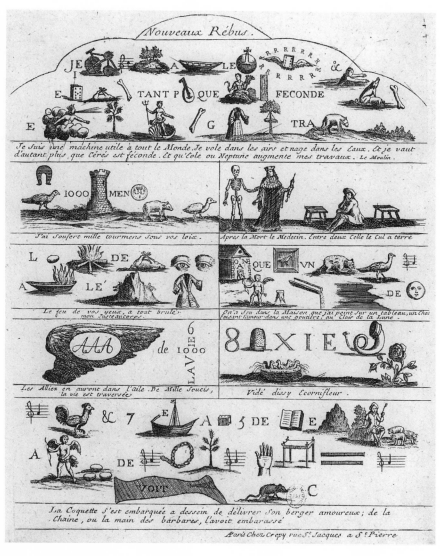

Figure 27. A typical eighteenth-century rebus. (Bibliothèque nationale de France)

(Deprived of my first and frozen to the bone,
The unfortunate were all about to die of misery,
When the leader and worthy Father of my second
Was able to put an end to my all and to calm their terror.)

The answer, which also appeared in the next issue, showed that the author had cleverly played on memories of the terrible winter of 1783–84 and at the same time had paid tribute to the king, who had responded to the extraordinary cold by distributing food to the poor. In this case the numbers referred to syllables rather than to letters. The first was *sou* or penny; the second, *France*; and the "all" was *sou-France*—that is, *souffrance*, or suffering.

Immediately after these two puzzles in the issue of April 3, 1784, came a *logogryphe*, a popular word game that has no equivalent in English but could be described as a super-anagram. Readers were to pick up hints from the verse in order to compose a series of words, all of which, when rearranged anagrammatically, were contained in the single word that was the answer to the riddle.

LOGOGRYPHE

Je suis un être affreux, horrible, extravagant,
Que l'amour et le jeu produisent trop souvent.
J'ai neuf pieds; cube ou rond, à tes yeux je présente
Un seul nom; une chose ou chagrine ou riante;
Un légume; un bon fruit; le contraire de mieux;
Le plus grand bien du pauvre et de l'ambitieux;
Ce que l'oiseau désire enfermé dans sa cage;
Ce qu'éprouve un beau front sur le déclin de l'âge;
L'ouvrage d'un insecte, et l'un des demi-Dieux;
Et l'instant désiré par les amants heureux.

(I am a dreadful, horrible, extravagant being,
Which love and gambling produce too often.
I have nine feet; as a cube or round, I have in your view
But a single name; a woeful or a happy thing;
A vegetable; a good fruit; the opposite of better;
The greatest good of the poor and the ambitious man;
That which is desired by the bird shut in its cage;
That which disfigures a handsome forehead in old age;
The work of an insect, and one of the demigods;
And the moment desired by happy lovers.)

The next issue revealed the answer: *désespoir*. Words could be composed in the manner of an anagram from its nine letters, according to the clues given in each line. They were in successive order: *dé* (*à coudre et à jouer*) (thimble and die for gambling, the same word in French); *idée* (idea); *pois* (peas); *poire* (pear); *pire* (worse); *espoir* (hope); *essor* (flight); *ride* (wrinkle); *soie* (silk); *Persée* (Perseus); and *soir* (evening).

By 1750 every issue of the *Mercure* included a *charade*, an *énigme*, and a *logogryphe* along with a great many other guessing games, almost always in verse, in a section titled *Pièces fugitives*. They appeared under many names: *épigramme, épitaphe, épithalame, étrennes, bouts rimés, question, fable, parodie, anecdote, allégorie, portrait, boutade, bon mot, placet, brunette, chansonette*. Some names also applied to other kinds of writing, which might not include puzzles. But the profusion of names and genres suggests that puzzle solving was a common variety of reading, and it seemed to have no purpose other than amusement and the exercise of wit.

Nearly all the other literary reviews featured the same kind of light verse meant to entertain readers by offering them games to play. Readers often sent in verse puzzles to the periodicals or scribbled them on scraps of paper, which they carried in their pockets and produced in cafés to amuse friends and onlookers. The scraps were traded and collected. Several collections, scrapbooks with scribbled notes pasted on the leaves or registers with entries copied out by secretarial hands, have survived in the Bibliothèque historique de la ville de Paris and the Bibliothèque nationale de France.[21] These *pièces fugitives* are exactly like those in the literary reviews, but they circulated freely without passing through censorship; they could refer to specific individuals (not a possibility in a censored journal), and they include some bawdy and political pieces. Most, however, are quite innocent. For example, one collection contained a typical *logogryphe* about an actress whose last name, Mets, lent itself to a pun about the city of Metz in the region known as the Three Bishoprics.

Lecteur, sans vous donner une peine infinie,
Dans votre mémoire cherchez,
Et dans l'un des Trois Evêchés
Vous trouverez le nom d'une actrice jolie.

(Reader, without giving yourself infinite trouble,
Search in your memory,
And in one of the Three Bishoprics
You will find the name of a pretty actress.)[22]

The copyist incorporated the solution to the riddle in the poem's title: "Mademoiselle Mets, Logogryphe."

When they transcribed more difficult puzzles, the copyists usually wrote the solutions in the margins of the scrapbooks. For example, "Les Echos des

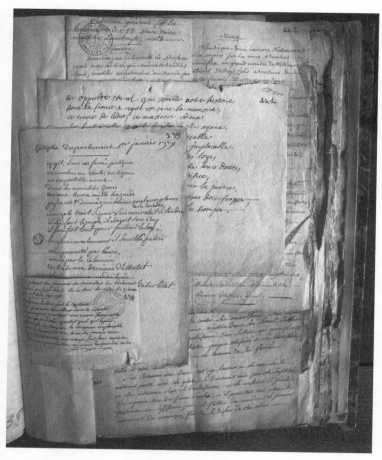

Figure 28. Casual verse pasted into a scrapbook. (Bibliothèque nationale de France)

seigneurs et dames de la cour" made fun of courtiers by using the popular device of an *écho* or word formed from the last syllables in each verse. By listening to the *écho* in the following verse, well-informed readers had all the hints they needed to identify the butt of the joke.

De Vénus et de Bellonne
Egalement favorisé,
Près des belles qu'il empoisonne
Comment est maintenant ce courtisan rusé? . . . usé.

(Of Venus and Bellona
Equally favored,

By the beauties he has poisoned,
How is he now considered, this wily courtier? . . . worn out.)[23]

A note added in the margin identified the target of this verse as the duc de
Richelieu, notorious for his Don Juanism and his military campaigns (hence
the reference to Venus and to Bellona, the Roman goddess of war), which he
continued into his old age. Café wits probably declaimed the fourteen verses
in this poem, pausing after each one in order to challenge their listeners to
identify its subject. The game was slanderous enough but hardly the sort of
thing that would cause a political uproar.

When puzzle poems dealt with current events, they often had sharp
edges, but they rarely inflicted deep wounds. For example, one riddle made
disparaging references to Louis XV and the maréchals de Saxe and de Lowendahl, who led the French conquest of the Austrian Netherlands during the War
of the Austrian Succession (1740–48). Because both marshals were foreigners,
the campaigns caused some murmuring about France's lack of homegrown
commanders. Moreover, the Treaty of Aix-la-Chapelle (1748) required France
to return the conquered territory and to expel Charles Edward Stuart, the
Young Pretender, to whom it had given asylum after supporting his failed
attempt to produce an uprising in Britain in 1745–46. The peace settlement
was therefore perceived by the Parisian public as a humiliation. In entering the
war, Louis had claimed that he had no ambitions to extend his territory, and
in accepting the peace, he pretended to act as a disinterested arbiter. But after
nearly eight years of heavy casualties and taxation, the French felt entitled to
some rewards in the peace treaty. It did not help that the terms of the treaty
were negotiated by another foreigner, the comte de Saint-Séverin, an Ara-
gonese, who represented France in Aix-la-Chapelle. The following poem from
January 1749 appealed to this sentiment of wounded national pride while playing on words and challenging the reader to decode the allusions. The copyist
wrote the answers in the margin.

Louis XV	Celui qui ne voulait rien prendre,
	Celui qui prit tout, pour tout rendre,
Les maréchaux de	Prit deux étrangers pour tout prendre;
Saxe et Lowendahl	
M. le comte de	Prit un étranger pour tout rendre;
Saint-Séverin	
Le Prince Edouard	Prit le Prétendant pour le prendre;
	Prit le Prétendant pour le rendre.
(Louis XV	He who did not want to take anything,
	He who took everything in order to give it back,

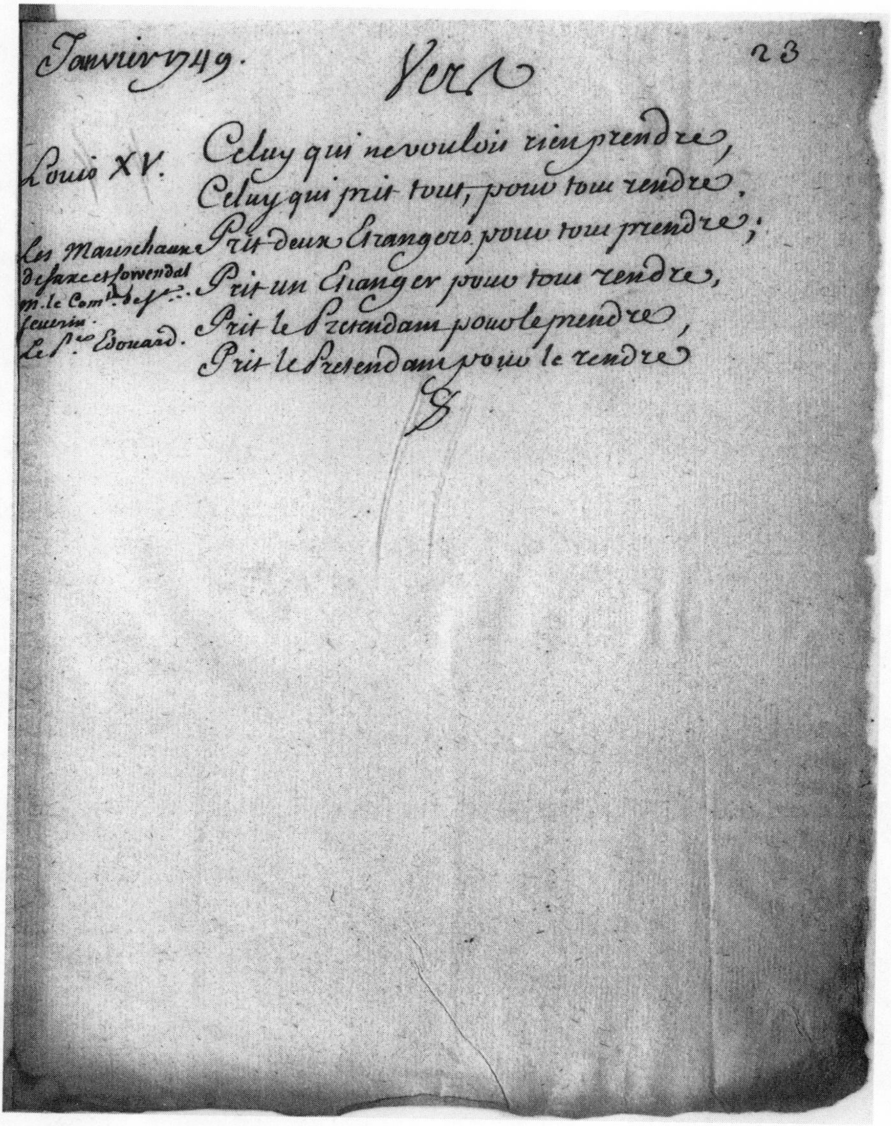

Janvier 1749.   Vers

Louis XV.   Celuy qui ne vouloit rien prendre,
            Celuy qui prit tout, pour tout rendre.
Les Mareschaux Prit deux Etrangers pour tout prendre;
de Saxe et Lowendal
m. le Comte de .. Prit un Etranger pour tout rendre,
seurin .
Le Pce Edouard . Prit le Pretendant pour le prendre,
            Prit le Pretendant pour le rendre,

Figure 29. A political riddle in the form of a poem. (Bibliothèque nationale de France, ms. fr. 12719, p. 23)

Marshals de Saxe and Lowendahl	Took two foreigners to take everything;
	Took a foreigner to give everything back;
the comte de Saint-Séverin	Took the Pretender in order to take him;
Prince Edward [Stuart]	Took the Pretender in order to give him back.)[24]

To solve this riddle readers would have to know a good deal about the recent past; and if they failed to solve it, the solution, once they learned it, could provoke them to see current events with a critical eye. But more often riddles-in-verse provided a triumphal view of events. The French victory at Lawfeldt (July 2, 1747) inspired the following excerpts from a poem of "bouts rimés." The answers, added in the right-hand margin, were to rhyme with the last word in the text to the left, and the copyist also added notes to explain the references.

Le prince Valdeck . . . est échec (b)
On a fait Ligonnier . . . prisonnier (c)
M. de Batiani . . . s'est enfui (d)
Les Anglois sont . . . aux abois.

(Prince Valdeck . . . is defeated (b)
One took Ligonier . . . prisoner (c)
M. de Batiani . . . fled (d)
The English are . . . in a desperate plight.)[25]

The notes explained the references to the allied forces that the French had defeated: Valdeck commanded the Dutch troops; Ligonier, an English commander, was taken prisoner; and Batiani commanded the Austrian troops. Puzzle poems often conformed to this model. Although they circulated outside legal channels, they were as likely to applaud the government as to criticize it.

Given the French love of casual and improvised verse, it hardly seems surprising that such poems provided a running commentary on current events. The political system could tolerate a good deal of this sniping, provided it did not appear in print. But there were limits. The comte de Maurepas, a key minister during the War of the Austrian Succession, was disgraced because he composed or circulated the following poem.

Par vos façons nobles et franches,
Iris, vous enchantez nos coeurs;
Sur nos pas vous semez des fleurs,
Mais ce sont des fleurs blanches

(By your noble and free manner,
Iris, you enchant our hearts;
On our path you strew flowers,
But they are white flowers.)[26]

To the uneducated eye the verse looked like any madrigal about shepherdesses
and pastoral innocence. But an astute and well-informed reader knew that Iris
represented Mme de Pompadour, who had given some white hyacinths to
Maurepas and Louis XV at a private dinner party. "Fleurs blanches" was a pun
referring to menstrual discharge ("flueurs") containing venereal disease. As
soon as the king learned of this riddle, which flew around Versailles and Paris
by word of mouth and in manuscript copies, he dismissed Maurepas and sent
him into exile. Maurepas's fall on April 24, 1749, was the most important political event of the year and therefore touched off still more verse, including the
following *écho*.

La faveur de ton roi, Maurepas, quand tu pars
Dis-nous ce qui t'attire un si cruel revers . . . vers

(Your king's favor, Maurepas, tell us when you leave
What brought upon you such a severe reverse . . . verse)[27]

Occasional verse could occasionally inflict damage on individuals and
perhaps on the political system as a whole. A great deal of discontent welled
up during the mid-century years from which these examples have been taken.
It subsided, then surged again during the last phase of the Jansenist controver-
sies and the Seven Years' War (1756–63), the Maupeou crisis (1770–84), and the
pre-revolution (1787–88). Riddles, puzzles, and word games of all sorts took on
a seditious tone during these critical periods. Hundreds of them can be found
in the *Mémoires secrets pour servir à l'histoire de la république des lettres en
France*, a printed version of a *chronique scandaleuse* or manuscript newsletter
that covered the years 1771 to 1787. But it would be a mistake to attribute too
much influence to this casual verse.[28] For every *logogryphe* aimed at a minister,
there were dozens of others about drinking and wenching. On the whole, this
kind of poetry was meant to amuse readers, nothing more. It had a ludic character, like modern crossword puzzles, and it deserves attention—although it
has never been studied by literary historians—because it illustrates a particular
kind of reading that flourished under the Ancien Régime and can be recap-
tured by replaying the games as they were designed to be played more than
two centuries ago.

Between the shock of libels on the one hand and the amusement of riddles on the other, the spectrum of reading left room for many other sorts of experiences. Did it not include the kind of reading that probably comes to mind first among readers today—namely, the sensation of bending over a book on a table and absorbing its contents silently and alone? Certainly, although the iconographic evidence suggests that readers tended to hold books in their hands, both indoors and outdoors, without propping them on a table; the kinetic element in reading—the feel of the handmade paper, the weight of the volume pressing into the palms—may have been more intense in the eighteenth century than it is now.[29]

Several contemporaries testified to the intensity of reading in isolation; even Mercier invoked it. True, he usually described reading as a social activity that took place in the midst of the hurly-burly of daily life, but he also acclaimed the power of the printed word to cut through social conventions and to penetrate deep into the soul. In various essays he spun fantasies about lives transformed by profound, solitary reading—a young man saved from monasticism by a Voltairean tract, a young woman rescued from adultery by *La Nouvelle Héloïse*, even an heir to the throne won to the cause of the common people by truths transmitted directly to his inner self from books.[30] When he pursued this line of thought, Mercier distinguished three factors: the genius of individual writers, the power of the printing press to diffuse their ideas, and the response to those ideas that ultimately took shape as the judgment of the public.

This view, which fed into the romantic notion of poets as the unacknowledged legislators of the world, was shared by many thoughtful Frenchmen on the eve of the Revolution. The most revealing version of it comes from the *Mémoire sur la liberté de la presse* composed by Chrétien-Guillaume de Lamoignon de Malesherbes in 1788. As director of the book trade from 1750 to 1763, Malesherbes had acquired an unequaled knowledge of how books actually circulated in France, yet his familiarity with the practices of authors, printers, and booksellers—many of them devious and self-serving, even among the greatest philosophes—did not prevent him from believing that truth would inevitably overcome falsehood owing to the power of the printed word. He described the world of print as a vast arena open to everyone. In the clash of competing opinions, clever writers might for a while deceive the public, but sooner or later their errors would be exposed, and truth would triumph. Although he was a dedicated servant of the monarchy, Malesherbes celebrated the printing press as a democratic force: "It is the entire nation that is the judge; and if this supreme judge has been led into error, as often happens, there is always time to bring it back to the truth. . . . In the end, truth prevails."[31] The same ideas, reinforced with a concept of politics as applied math-

Figure 30. *Samuel Johnson,* by Gilbert Stuart, after Sir Joshua Reynolds. Oil on canvas, ca. 1780. (The Donald and Mary Hyde Collection of Dr. Samuel Johnson, Houghton Library, Harvard University)

ematics, provided Condorcet with the material for a philosophy of history. In the darkest moments of the Terror he asserted that reason and justice would ultimately prevail before the tribunal of public opinion, thanks to the combined forces of writing, printing, and reading.[32]

Condorcet clung to this vision of the future with a tenacity that helped him confront the horrors of the present, but it should not be dismissed as a utopian illusion. It corresponded in his eyes to the conditions of intellectual life as they actually existed in eighteenth-century France, and it has a remarkable resemblance to the view of the eighteenth century developed by the modern sociologist Jürgen Habermas. To Habermas, Condorcet's France had all the ingredients of an ideal type: the emergence of a public sphere characterized by rational-critical debate. Reading was the driving force behind this process as Habermas understood it. By poring over books, especially novels, in the privacy of their homes, bourgeois readers developed an individualized subjectivity; and by discussing them in book clubs, subscription libraries, coffeehouses, and salons, they created a reading public—that is, an intersubjective realm where private individuals participated in collective judgments, sharpening their critical faculties in a way that promoted rational debate or, in a word, enlightenment. When the judgments shifted from literary to political issues, the reading public became transformed into a public sphere, ready to subject the state to a rational critique. Public opinion expressed by an informed citizenry challenged an older form of princely sovereignty based on *arcana imperii*, or secrets of state. Reading, reason, and public opinion operated together in democratic fashion—though restricted to the bourgeoisie—very much as Condorcet had understood it; and France was ripe for revolution.[33]

The Condorcet-Habermas thesis helps explain the transformation of the value system that had legitimized the absolute monarchy and the hierarchical order of French society in the seventeenth century. It provides a way of understanding the rational-critical worldview of the deputies from the Third Estate in 1789, who had combined serious reading with solid experience of public affairs in their careers under the Ancien Régime.[34] But it does not correspond to the kind of public opinion that Mercier described in his accounts of the Palais-Royal. Nor does it fit other contemporary descriptions of behavior in cafés, public gardens, and even salons, which did not function as open and egalitarian debating societies. For a theory that makes sense of how opinions took shape in these settings, one can turn to another sociologist, Gabriel Tarde.

Tarde concentrated on two institutions that Habermas identifies with the public sphere: the newspaper and the café. As Tarde understood them, they worked together to produce the phenomena that Habermas described—intersubjective consciousness and public opinion—but they did so in a differ-

drift from Habermas

ent manner. Parisians gathered in cafés and satisfied their appetite for
information by consulting newspapers. Although they read different accounts
of events, they developed a common sense of exposure to a body of information that other readers were absorbing at the same time and in the same fashion. Reading also touched off conversations—not rational debate so much as
a casual commentary—which ran throughout the day, mixing polemics with
witticisms and gathering momentum until some general views emerged. These
views eventually seeped into further printed matter and conversations. So
reading and talking reinforced each other, and in the end they produced public
opinion—not a consensus created by critical reasoning but a collective consciousness shot through with contradictions and passions about what was
going on in public life.[35]

Tarde's analysis of public opinion correlates closely with Mercier's reportage. Like Tarde, Mercier described the interplay of reading and talking in cafés,
where the availability of newspapers and pamphlets provided a menu for the
daily diet of gossip: "We found [in the cafés] readers of public papers who
came there for their daily supply of wit."[36] Public readings took place in the
garden as well as in the cafés of the Palais-Royal and in other gardens, always
triggering talk. Thus Mercier's account of a stroll through the gardens of the
Tuileries.

It's an amusing thing, I said to myself, this eagerness with which all Paris burns to get
the news of the day. . . . I had just begun to ruminate on this subject when, without
noticing it, I arrived in the middle of the Tuileries Gardens, where there was a never-
ending clamor.

"He's wrong," said one person. "He's right," said another. What was the fuss
about? Two well-known opponents who dominated the public scene with their debate
about financial affairs.

Everyone had read their pamphlets, studied their calculations, and it was absolutely necessary to take sides. The worst-informed made the most noise. They entered
into the café, came out of it, and in the midst of this agitation, total strangers spoke to
me as if they had always kept my company.

An abbé put on his glasses and read a few pages from a new decree by the parlement; a retired financier cited an operation that took place in his day . . .

If there are no parliamentary debates in France as in England, it must be said that
the French public is a House of Commons.[37]

Which to prefer, the Habermas-Condorcet or the Tarde-Mercier view of
the effect of reading? To put the question so baldly is to give it an either/or
character that cannot do justice to the complexities of social and intellectual
life in the eighteenth century. Each view may be valid in its own fashion, one
as an explanation of the general transformation of attitudes toward public

affairs, the other as an account of how Parisians made sense of daily events. They may have converged and diverged in ways that have yet to be explored. But the exploration should begin with an attempt to find out more about how some of the printed matter discussed in the gardens of the Palais-Royal and the Tuileries was produced. To undertake that task, it is necessary to suspend the analysis of texts and the consideration of theories and to concentrate on a more conventional variety of history: the study of diplomatic archives and the papers of the police.

PART II

Politics and Police Work

Chapter 8
Slander and Politics

Seen as a succession of texts, the four libels discussed in Chapters 1 through 4 tell a story that fits together nicely, its parts linked in a narrative that extends from the court of Louis XV to the Terror of Robespierre. But was it true? The very notion of historical truth may seem dubious today, when historians take cues from literary critics[1] and history sometimes looks more like a verbal construct made with tropes than a solid edifice built from facts. To search for the facts behind the narrative of the libels may be a misguided undertaking, but they are there, nonetheless: not self-evident, "hard" facts that can be extracted from archives as if they were nuggets of reality but evidence embedded in documents that can be made to make sense.

The documents come from the most familiar, worked-over sources of old-fashioned history: diplomatic correspondence and police archives. Yet they abound with information about literary affairs. The behind-the-text story of the London libelers can be pieced together from letters at the Quai d'Orsay, and the letters confirm the most extravagant details of the libels. While the diplomats cleared their way, the Parisian police mounted an elaborate underground operation to drive the French authors from their lairs in London's Grub Street. As detective stories go, it would be hard to beat the police reports and ambassadorial dispatches that traveled in the diplomatic pouch.

To get an overview of the subject, however, one should begin with the personal papers of Jean-Charles-Pierre Lenoir, lieutenant general of police in Paris from August 1774 to May 1775 and from June 1776 to August 1785.[2] By 1770, the lieutenant general was one of the most powerful officials in France—virtually the equivalent of a modern minister of the interior. While looking after Paris's food supply, hygiene, roads, lighting, safety, and many other aspects of municipal administration, he kept a sharp eye on the circulation of information, whether by rumor, songs, manuscript news sheets, pamphlets, or books. He had a large budget, twelve million livres, and a huge staff—commissioners, inspectors, and subordinates who hired hundreds of secret informers. The spies often denounced authors and peddlers of forbidden books. And they reported regularly on *bruits publics* (public noises) or gossip about public affairs that they picked up wherever Parisians gathered—in cafés, taverns, public gardens, marketplaces, bookshops, and brothels. The lieutenant general presided over this vast information network like an inscrutable, all-knowing god—or so it seemed to Louis-Sébastien Mercier, a writer who knew Paris better than anyone, except the lieutenant general himself.

If this magistrate wanted to communicate to the philosopher everything he knows, everything he learns about, everything he sees, and also inform him of certain secret things about which he [the lieutenant general] alone is pretty well apprised, then nothing would be so interesting and instructive as the philosopher's account of it all. The philosopher would astonish all of his colleagues. But this magistrate is like the Grand Penitentiary: he hears everything and reports nothing.[3]

When Lenoir sat down to write his memoirs, therefore, he could have revealed a great deal about information and how it spread through society on the eve of the Revolution. Unfortunately, he never finished. His incomplete manuscript now sits in three boxes in the municipal library of Orléans, a jumble of notes, memos, and drafts of essays that never saw the light of day. Imperfect as it is, however, the scribbling and jotting provide clues about the way the French authorities viewed the media of their day and attempted to control them. Lenoir's papers also include the richest insider's account of the policing of libels. But before turning to them, it is important to question their reliability. Lenoir had fled from France in the first wave of émigrés after the fall of the Bastille. He wrote at various times between his arrival in Switzerland in 1790 and his death in 1807. Did the trauma of revolution and emigration make him inclined to distort his description of the world he had lost?

Everything about Lenoir's career suggests he was a diligent, intelligent, and responsible official, the kind of high-level administrator who understood his job and its place in the power system of the Ancien Régime. Born in 1732 into a family that had made a fortune in the silk trade under Louis XIV and then began to rise through the status hierarchy in the nobility of the robe, he followed the conventional route to success: schooling in the collège of Louis-le-Grand and the law faculty in the University of Paris; various functions in the offices of the Châtelet court in Paris, where his father had been a *lieutenant particulier*; appointment as a *maître des requêtes*, a key position for promotion to high administrative posts (he proved his effectiveness as a servant to the crown by confronting hostile judges in the parlements of Rennes and Aix-en-Provence during the Maupeou crisis); and the reward of an intendancy, which was immediately followed in August 1774 by his elevation to the top job in the police of Paris. As his notes make clear, Lenoir had a thorough understanding of how gears meshed in the machinery of the power system, and he tried to avoid being caught in them. He knew his way around the patronage networks in Versailles; and therefore he cultivated protectors—especially the comte de Maurepas, effectively prime minister after the young Louis XVI ascended the throne in 1774; A.-R.-J.-G.-G. Sartine, the previous lieutenant general of police who served as minister of the navy from 1774 to 1780; and Charles-Alexandre de Calonne, finance minister from 1783 to 1787. Lenoir also took care to avoid conflict with ministers from hostile factions, though not always successfully. A falling out with Turgot during the bread riots known as the Guerre des Farines (Flour War) led to Lenoir's dismissal in May 1775, but Turgot's own fall made it possible for Lenoir to resume his office in June 1776. He continued as lieutenant general until August 1785, when he became a *conseiller ordinaire* in the Conseil d'Etat, the top administrative council of the kingdom.

During this period, which coincided with the American war and the greatest activity of the libelers in London, Lenoir learned that he could not police the book trade without being drawn into power struggles in the court. Ministers were always worried that an illicit publication could damage their reputation, impair their access to the king, or ruin their ability to mobilize support outside Versailles by appealing to public opinion. Some showed more concern about libels than others, but none, except Maurepas, was truly indifferent to the way he appeared before the public, according to Lenoir. In drafts of his memoirs, he discussed each of Louis XVI's ministers in turn, noting incidents when scandal and slander turned into serious matters of politics. Incomplete as they are, therefore, the Lenoir manuscripts provide a rich view of media politics at a moment when the press was beginning to emerge as a crucial force in history.[4]

But can they be believed? Not only did Lenoir discuss the publishing industry from the perspective of the police, but he also had strong reasons to present it negatively because he, too, was a victim of slander. The first attacks on him took place in 1787, and they proliferated throughout the early years of the Revolution, when radical journalists and politicians outdid each other in denouncing the police of the Ancien Régime. Lenoir found himself cast as a bogeyman in the revolutionary mythology about despots who delighted in arresting innocent victims by lettres de cachet and torturing them in the Bastille.[5] The man who once had been responsible for suppressing libels therefore found himself a target of them. He could hardly be expected to show any sympathy for libelers when he discussed them in his memoirs. He despised them and hack writers in general as "excréments de la littérature."[6]

Yet Lenoir's account of slanderous literature in the France of Louis XVI is actually quite nuanced. Instead of dismissing libels as the ephemeral work of impecunious hacks, he treated them as a basic ingredient in the political system of the Ancien Régime. The police had to take them seriously, he explained, because they could disrupt public order in two ways: they were used as weapons in the endless power struggles of court politics, and they fueled a phenomenon that was gathering force outside Versailles: public opinion.

It seemed to Lenoir in retrospect that the decisive moment in the government's ability to control print and public opinion came with the great crisis of 1770–74, when the chancellor, R.-N.-C.-A. de Maupeou, destroyed the political power of the parlements by reorganizing the entire judicial system of the kingdom: "In 1770 there was a flood of books and libels at the time of the suppression of the parlements. This long crisis, this revolution, produced a license that could not be stopped or punished."[7] The tracts, known collectively as "Maupeouana,"[8] heaped scorn on the government, pilloried its members, and condemned its policies for transforming the monarchy into a despotism.

By the time Lenoir became lieutenant general of police in August 1774, the new king, Louis XVI, had dismissed the Maupeou ministry and set about restoring the parlements. But the anti-Maupeou propaganda continued to reverberate through the kingdom. It was followed by another wave of publications, including best-sellers such as *Anecdotes sur Mme la comtesse du Barry* (1775) and *Vie privée de Louis XV* (1781), which continued the attack on despotism in a more sensational mode by directing their fire against the late king himself as well as his mistresses and ministers. Lenoir attempted to investigate the source of this literature but could not get beyond a few peddlers and booksellers—except in one case. In 1779 an abbé named Jabineau was arrested for smuggling illegal books into Paris. The police also suspected him of having collaborated in the libels against the government during the Maupeou ministry. Maurepas instructed Lenoir to try to discover the identity of the authors of the slanderous three-volume anthology entitled *Maupeouana* while interrogating Jabineau in the Bastille. Jabineau declared himself willing to cooperate, but he could not come up with an adequate answer. He explained that so many people had contributed to the compilation that it could not be attributed to anyone in particular. However, he did name the authors who were known to him. They included some of the best and brightest in France's political and intellectual elite: C.-G. de Lamoignon de Malesherbes, the former administrator in charge of the book trade; A.-T. Hue de Miromesnil, the powerful first president of the Parlement of Rouen; dom P.-L. Lièble, a learned librarian of Saint-Germain-des-Prés; and several eminent lawyers, such as A.-L. Séguier, G.-Y.-B. Target, and André Blonde. Twenty secret presses churned out editions of the work, Jabineau explained, and they were subsidized by financiers, magistrates in the parlements, and even princes and peers. The whole operation was organized with such secrecy that no one knew how far it extended. When Lenoir reported this information to Maurepas, Maurepas trumped it by revealing that he, too, had been one of the contributors.[9]

Libels often originated from persons located at the top of the power structure, Lenoir explained. Ministers leaked information or commissioned pamphlets to undermine each other. As an example, he cited a clandestine campaign of libels to drive Miromesnil from office after he had left the parlement of Rouen to become Keeper of the Seals (that is, effectively minister of justice) in 1774. Maurepas's death in 1781 had left Miromesnil without a strong ally in the government, and some magistrates from the Parlement of Paris, notably C.-F. Lamoignon de Basville, hoped to replace him. But Louis XVI summoned Lenoir to Versailles, directed him to take all possible measures to repress the libels, and with other courtiers present reaffirmed his confidence in Miromesnil. That was enough to stop the slander, Lenoir wrote. A few days later, a magistrate turned in the complete edition of a recently printed libel, and Miromesnil remained in office—until he was finally ousted by Lamoignon after another round of intrigues in 1787.[10]

Jacques Necker, director of royal finances from 1777 to 1781, lost his hold on power during a similar skirmish over scandalous pamphlets. Lenoir described him as particularly sensitive to public opinion, eager to use it to promote his policies, and determined to wipe out any publications that made him look bad. When his enemies attacked him by libels in 1781, he demanded that Lenoir take vigorous action. Lenoir confiscated one pamphlet and imprisoned its printer, but Necker wanted to make an example of its author, Antoine Bourboulon, a well-connected official in the household of the comte d'Artois. That was asking too much, Lenoir objected. He could arrest printers and booksellers, but he could not take action against such a respectable person without authorization by an order from the king. Necker exploded in anger, threatening to arm himself with lettres de cachet and to pack all his enemies off to the prison of Bicêtre, a much nastier place than the Bastille. This incident, skillfully exploited by Maurepas in private sessions with the king (or so Lenoir believed), precipitated Necker's dismissal on May 19, 1781.[11]

According to Lenoir, Necker also subsidized secret presses to turn out propaganda in his favor. He intervened to get an underground printer named Sauson released from the Bastille and set him up in a shop that belonged to the finance ministry. But Sauson took advantage of Necker's protection to produce a sideline of scandalous works; and after the police caught him running off an edition of *Thérèse philosophe*, an obscene philosophical novel, he went back to the Bastille.[12] Necker's rival, Charles-Alexandre de Calonne, wrote a whole string of libels against him—*Lettres de Caraccioli, Les Pourquoi, Les Quand,* and *Crispin à la cour*—Lenoir revealed.[13] Still more libels against prominent figures in Versailles were produced later in the 1780s by sharp-witted writers like Beaumarchais and Chamfort, in collaboration with dissident courtiers such as the marquis de Montesquiou and the chevalier de Créquy.[14]

Lenoir did not characterize all this slander as seditious. On the contrary, he treated it as part of the nasty chatter that had belonged to the power struggles in Versailles since the beginning of the century, and he associated it with his own principal protector, the comte de Maurepas, whom he described at several points in the memoirs as the epitome of an older, more insouciant style of court politics. Maurepas had been a secretary of state in charge of the Maison du Roi from 1718 to 1749 and secretary of the navy from 1723 to 1749. He had maintained his hold on power throughout that long period by developing a sharp eye for intrigue and by ingratiating himself with the king. Thanks to secret reports provided every week by the lieutenant general of police, Maurepas regaled the young Louis XV with endless anecdotes about priests trapped in brothels and courtiers caught with their culottes down. He especially delighted in the *bons mots*, verse, and songs that well-informed wits improvised to standard tunes and that provided a running commentary on current events. Scandalous frivolity of this sort was part of the game that was always being played at court, and it also belonged to everyday life in Paris, as Lenoir understood it.

Bons mots and panegyrics, songs and satire, have always characterized the Frenchman and especially the Parisian. Nothing circulates faster than a witticism and a good, biting epigram, especially when the satire is aimed at an important personage, a distinguished figure or a man in power. . . . M. de Maurepas used to recite the poems against him with great gaiety in his circle of intimates. He said it was and would always be an amusement and that the circulation of such verse occupied the large number of Parisians with time on their hands who wanted to take on an air of importance. He liked to quote Chancellor Pontchartrain who said after being attacked by a cutting satire, "The more you clamp down on such attacks, the stronger they will be."[15]

Yet scandalmongering could destroy political careers. Maurepas learned that lesson in April 1749, when Louis XV dismissed him from the government and sent him into exile because he had been compromised by the poem, cited in the previous chapter, that mocked Mme de Pompadour for giving the king venereal disease. As it was composed to the tune of a popular song, the poem was taken up by street singers and spread everywhere in Paris. Although apparently trivial in itself, this incident produced a decisive shift in the balance of power among the factions in Versailles.[16]

When Maurepas returned to power in 1774 as the dominant figure in the government of the newly crowned Louis XVI, he continued to amuse himself with political witticisms, but he changed his mind about their innocuousness after he learned about the libels being manufactured in London. The turning point in his policy, according to Lenoir, came when the foreign service informed him about *Les Amours de Charlot et Toinette*, the obscene satire that mocked Louis XVI for being unable to produce an heir and for being cuckolded by his brother, the comte d'Artois.

M. de Maurepas, who until then had been indifferent about the epigrams and songs made against him, M. de Maurepas, who used to be amused at all the libels and scandalous anecdotes that were composed and printed with impunity, was informed that some writers had formed a speculation among themselves, that they had created a correspondence network through which those located in Paris sent the latest gossip along with titles and other material to those in The Hague and London, who wrote it all up, had it printed, and sent it back to France in small quantities carried by foreign travelers. A secretary in the embassy in England informed him that an abominable libel entitled *Les Amours de Charlot et d'Antoinette* [sic] soon would be smuggled into France.[17]

At that point, according to Lenoir, Maurepas threw his weight behind the campaign to wipe out libels. The official who took the lead in the repressive measures was the foreign minister, the comte de Vergennes, who dominated the government after Maurepas's death on November 9, 1781. Both ministers worked closely with Lenoir, who kept printers, booksellers, and peddlers under strict surveillance in Paris. But despite all his secret informers, Lenoir found it impossible to follow the production line all the way upstream to its sources.

Men from the court had the scandalous works printed or protected the printing of them. The Parisian police could only get to the retailers and peddlers who sold them. The peddlers were imprisoned in the Bastille, but this punishment had little effect on that class of poor, greedy wretches who often did not know who were the true authors and printers. . . . During the years preceding the Revolution, the law was especially powerless as a weapon against anti-government libels.[18]

The threat from libels became increasingly serious, as Lenoir saw it, because the defamation took a particularly nasty turn in the early 1780s. Instead of spreading gossip about royal mistresses, an old sport that had amused Europeans for centuries, it concentrated on Louis XVI's supposed impotence and Marie-Antoinette's alleged infidelity.[19] Lenoir worried about the effect of such false information, because he noticed a change in the way Parisians behaved toward the queen. She had been quite popular among Parisians at the beginning of the reign, he wrote in one draft of the memoirs. When she visited the city, they greeted her spontaneously with cries of "vive

la Reine." After mid-1781, however, he could not raise any cheers even by distributing money to the crowd.[20] Rumors circulated that she was siphoning off
huge sums from the royal treasury and shipping them to her family in Vienna.
Lenoir traced this calumny to manuscript newsletters produced by two courtiers attached to the households of the king and queen; but he failed to arrest
them, because they fled after being tipped off by another insider in Versailles—
probably one of Vergennes's clerks, he suspected.[21] Other scandalous stories
followed, including one about a secret rendezvous between Marie-Antoinette
and a lover, which spread because she arrived in a rented coach at a ball in the
Opera after her own coach had broken down en route.[22] The worst blow to
the prestige of the crown came when the cardinal de Rohan was arrested on
August 15, 1785, under suspicion of trying to win the queen's favor by presenting her with a diamond necklace. Lenoir retired as lieutenant general four days
before the scandal broke, but he referred to the Diamond Necklace Affair and
the rumors accompanying it—wild talk about the cardinal cuckolding the
king—as a point of no return in Parisians' respect for the monarchy. He even
put it down as an "event that might have been one of the causes of the Revolution."[23]

Lenoir did not venture any extended discussion of causality, but he identified one factor that proved decisive in the rise and fall of ministries, if not in
the collapse of the monarchy itself. That was public opinion. He stressed that
Necker, Calonne, and Calonne's successor, E.-C. de Loménie de Brienne, all
paid great attention to what was being said about themselves by the Parisian
public. And they were right to do so, he reflected, because public opinion
could bring down ministers during the last years of the Ancien Régime. Thus
Calonne's fall during the Assembly of Notables—the meeting of dignitaries
that he called in order to win support for his program to save the crown from
bankruptcy—in April 1787: "Before the end of this assembly, whose members
he had chosen himself, opinion rose up against him. His reputation was
attacked; he was denounced, inculpated, and destroyed in public opinion."[24]
The same force overcame Brienne in August 1788: "Public opinion had completely turned against him."[25] Lenoir was no sociologist. He did not explain
what he meant by the public, nor did he analyze the ways in which gossip
hardened into collective judgment. But he noted the tendency of Parisians to
be skeptical about information from official sources and to give credence to
slander: "Parisians had more of a propensity to believe in hostile gossip and
in the libels that circulated secretly than they did in the facts that were printed
and published by the order or with the permission of the government."[26]
Looking back at the collapse of the Ancien Régime, he saw a complicated mix

of causal elements—ministerial intrigues, contradictory policies, indecisive-ness by the king—but he attributed particular importance to the struggle over information. It existed at many levels, from garrets in Paris to antechambers in Versailles, but it could make or break a government. That was why the police took slander seriously.

Chapter 9
The Book Police at Work

While ministers worried about the effect of libels from the heights of Versailles, the police struggled to suppress them at street level. Police investigation involved every stage in the production and diffusion of a scandalous publication—its origin, usually at some nodal point in a network of oral communication; the drafting of a text, often in a flea-ridden flophouse (*chambre garnie*); the printing of the manuscript, either at a clandestine press in Paris or, more likely, in a shop located at a safe distance ("at a hundred leagues from the Bastille" or "at Philadelphia" as the title pages proclaimed); the distribution of the printed matter through an underground system of wagon drivers, warehouse keepers, and smugglers; and finally, its sale by all manner of book dealers, *bouquinistes*, and peddlers.

As Lenoir observed, the police could not take action against well-protected courtiers. They concentrated on more vulnerable targets farther down the chain of production and diffusion, especially writers and under-the-cloak dealers in the world of Grub Street. That world linked together garrets and backrooms of bookstores throughout the major cities of western Europe. To pursue their quarry, therefore, the Paris police had to follow leads that wound through Amsterdam, Brussels, Liège, and other centers of the libeler diaspora, especially London, which had the greatest colony of all. Much of this territory was familiar to the agents of the police, because they belonged to the same world. Some, like Joseph d'Hémery, the redoubtable *inspecteur de la librairie* who took charge of policing books and authors from 1748 to 1773, were dedicated professionals who worked effectively and even showed considerable appreciation of literature. (D'Hémery's personal files showed that he admired talented writers, notably Montesquieu and Voltaire, and that he scorned poets who could not manage correct versification.)[1] But d'Hémery's successors were shady characters who played both sides of Grub Street. Lenoir, who knew them well, described them as worse than the authors and printers they pursued. In his memoirs, he particularly mentioned two, Pierre-Antoine-Auguste Goupil and Jean-Claude Jacquet de la Douay. Their careers took them through all the cities where libels were produced and ultimately led to the heart of the libel trade in London.

It should be emphasized again that "police" in the eighteenth century meant something very different from what it does today. Not only did police inspectors handle all sorts of tasks that now would belong to municipal administration, but like many officials from the Ancien Régime, they owned their offices; so they could not be disciplined with the severity that accompanies a modern chain of command. D'Hémery, for example, began his career as a policeman on January 16, 1741, by purchasing the office of "exempt en la compagnie du lieutenant criminel de robe-courte au Châtelet"—a long-winded title that meant he had joined the law-enforcement officers attached to the Parisian court of the Châtelet. He gained a promotion seven years later by purchasing the office of "lieutenant" in the same company. It cost him a tidy sum, ten thousand livres, and he bought it from his father-in-law—a way of transmitting assets typical of the Ancien Régime. The offices had income—and eventually pensions—attached to them, and d'Hémery expanded their scope by accumulating functions that had been scattered among other officers, although they served a common purpose: the surveillance of the book trade. His main commission, acquired in 1748, was to enforce the general regulations that governed the trade—an assignment that brought him fifty livres for every offender he put in prison. To this he added other "inspections," which mainly concerned the attempt of the state, through the Direction de la librairie (Administration of the Book Trade) under the chancellor and keeper of the seals, to repress pirated and prohibited books: the inspection of book shipments that arrived by boat from Rouen; the inspection of the bales of books that wagon drivers delivered to the Parisian customs and that were impounded in the syndical chamber of the Parisian booksellers' guild; and the inspection, by means of unannounced visits, of all the printing shops and bookstores in the city. D'Hémery cobbled together these separate assignments little by little until they formed a specialized branch of the police. Having acquired the title of *inspecteur de la librairie* (inspector of the book trade) in 1748, he continued to extend his authority over the book trade for the next twenty-five years so that when he sold his inspectorship to his successor in 1773, he had shaped a large, professional zone of activity within the royal administration. His papers—thousands of letters, memorandums, and reports—show a serious, systematic public servant at work, modernizing the Bourbon monarchy's attempts to police the printed word.[2]

D'Hémery's successor, Pierre-Antoine-Auguste Goupil, was a man of a different kidney. Before Goupil took office, d'Hémery explained the mission to him in a typical memorandum, which reads like a short treatise on the science of policing books (see the text of the memorandum in the electronic supplement to this book). D'Hémery outlined the inspector's main functions under ten rubrics and then explained each of them in a set of supplementary essays. Goupil should inspect every type foundry in the city at least twice a year, keeping a record of everything they produced, from the boldest *gros romain* to the daintiest *petit texte*. He also should keep track of scriveners (*écrivains publics*): by collecting samples of their handwriting, he would be able to follow the trail of compromising copy. Printing shops should be inspected once every three months, bookstores once a year, in order to verify that every work being produced and sold corresponded to the records of privileges and permissions kept in the Direction de la librairie. Peddlers required special attention, because nine out of ten illegal works passed through their hands. Goupil should hire some of them as informers in order to unearth clandestine printing operations, and he should be suspicious of everyone, including authors, especially those who looked down-at-the-heel: "The greatest attention should be paid to such people: having nothing to lose, they will risk everything and show no respect for anything at all." Once he had accumulated enough evidence, Goupil could arrest suspects. But he should follow the proper procedures. He would need to receive a special order—normally a lettre de cachet—from the lieutenant general. Then, accompanied by a constable, he should force his way into the author's lodging or the shop of the printer or bookseller. He should search the premises thoroughly, confiscating all manuscripts, printed sheets, and other papers. He should describe everything he finds in a formal report. And finally, all documents duly drafted, signed, and sealed, he should march the suspect off to prison.[3]

Goupil went about his duties with a different spirit. His way of delivering a lettre de cachet can be appreciated from an episode that Jacques-Pierre Brissot described in his memoirs. It took place in 1777 when Brissot, a young man trying to write his way out of Grub Street, had published a libel that had slandered a prominent leader of a Parisian salon and that resulted in a lettre de cachet for his arrest. Goupil turned up in Brissot's garret and announced the bad news in the politest possible terms.

You have made a silly blunder. Although it does not deserve such a severe punishment, one has been obliged to issue a lettre de cachet. As it will be formally presented for your arrest tomorrow, be sure to decamp today. But, in order for me to seem to have fulfilled my duty, leave behind one or two sheets from the manuscript of that brochure. I will pretend that I found them in your room, and I will produce them as proof of my zeal to execute my orders.[4]

Why such solicitude? According to Brissot, Goupil wanted to enlist him in writing slanderous works that Goupil could pretend to confiscate and then secretly sell with the help of his wife. By playing this double game, Goupil tried to win enough approval from his superiors to advance his career while making extra money on the side. Brissot refused to collaborate, but he was replaced by another hack writer, who also followed a path that led from Grub Street to the Jacobin Club: François-Martin Poultier d'Elmotte.

D'Elmotte (or Poultier, as he called himself during the radical phase of the Revolution, when a name with a handle sounded suspiciously aristocratic) belonged to the race of literary adventurers who passed in and out of the Bastille while improvising careers around whatever opportunities that arose. He found employment at various times as a soldier, a secretary, a journalist, a pamphleteer, an actor, a police spy, and a monk before throwing himself into the Revolution, where he swam with the tide and kept his head above water through the Terror, the Directory, and the Empire.[5]

According to the few scraps that survive from d'Elmotte's dossier in the papers of the Bastille, he was imprisoned on March 9, 1778, for writing pamphlets that Goupil used "for his intrigues."[6] The account of d'Elmotte's *embastillement* published in the third installment of *La Bastille dévoilée* in 1789 confirmed that he had been arrested for collaborating with Goupil, but it did not reveal the nature of his work. D'Elmotte himself provided those details in a letter published in *La Bastille dévoilée*'s sixth installment in 1790, as well as in the radical weekly journal *Révolutions de Paris*.[7] He explained that his contact with Goupil went back to an earlier stint in prison, when he had been arrested for writing pamphlets about peculation and sex in high places. He also contributed articles to foreign journals that made the French authorities look bad, and he dabbled in the illegal book trade. So he could expect to spend a long time behind bars. But after only nine days Goupil appeared in his cell, exuding sympathy and goodwill, and announced his release. They were really comrades, Goupil explained, because they both had served in the gendarmerie; and they should become friends. Goupil would be delighted to share his table and even to arrange for d'Elmotte to succeed him as inspector of the book trade, for he expected to move up to a more lucrative office in the postal service. While waiting for that happy ending to take place, he merely asked that d'Elmotte assist him in his literary activities. Goupil himself did not have a wide knowledge of literature, he confessed, and he particularly needed someone to supply him with "nouveautés"[8]—that is, all the latest scandalous publications about eminent persons in the court and capital—or in other words, libels.

"Nouveautés," it transpired, were at the heart of Goupil's "intrigues."

They penetrated France from printing shops in Amsterdam, Brussels, Liège, and various places in the Rhineland. Goupil traveled on missions to these cities, ostensibly to root out the production at its source but in fact to make secret deals with the printers. He arranged with them to confiscate shipments, turned in some of the books to his superiors to demonstrate his effectiveness as an agent of repression, and secretly sold the rest. He even commissioned hack writers to produce new libels and negotiated their printing so as to engineer further confiscations. On one trip to Holland and the Austrian Netherlands, according to *La Bastille dévoilée*, he set out to impound a particularly nasty attack on Marie-Antoinette that was rumored to be in press. He discovered that no such work existed; so he had one written and printed, returned in triumph with the entire edition, and received a hero's welcome. The queen declared herself willing to reward him with her protection, and from then on he set his sights on a post higher up in the French administration.[9]

By this time Goupil's wife, whom the police described as both cunning and attractive, had managed to ingratiate herself with the princesse de Lamballe, the favorite companion of Marie-Antoinette. Already in the late 1770s scurrilous accounts of the queen's sex life, which included descriptions of lesbian orgies with her favorite, were beginning to appear in manuscript scandal sheets and printed libels. Goupil funneled the libels to his wife, who passed them on to the princesse de Lamballe, who then revealed their existence to the queen. Horrified that such calumny should be circulating and grateful to Goupil for bringing it to her attention, the princess proposed to reward him with an appointment in the postal service—he hoped to replace Rigoley d'Oigny in the *cabinet noir* (black office) where experts steamed open letters in order to extract secret information—and she also planned to promote his wife to the influential position of reader to the queen.[10]

To shuffle patronage in this manner required the intervention of ministers, so at this point Goupil's plot became entangled in court politics. According to d'Elmotte's account of the intrigues, which can be confirmed for the most part by the papers of Lenoir, A.-J. Amelot de Chaillou, the secretary of state in charge of the king's household, suspected A.-R.-J.-G.-G. de Sartine, the minister of the navy, of conspiring to oust him from his office. Amelot even thought he had detected a conspiracy by Sartine and his protégé, Lenoir, to overthrow the entire ministry by persuading the king to restore the duc de Choiseul as the head of the government. In order to acquire incriminating evidence, Amelot enlisted Goupil to spy on Sartine and Lenoir, using all the tricks of his trade. He was to chat up secretaries in the minister's office, squeeze information from valets de chambre, and bribe lackeys. But he needed someone who could wield a sharp pen: hence his desire for the collaboration of d'Elmotte. Goupil would provide the dirt, and d'Elmotte would incorporate it in a secret memorandum, inventing details as needed. Then Goupil would submit the memorandum to Maurepas, who was the real power broker in the government, and they would all surge ahead in the power games played at Versailles: while Maurepas threw Sartine and Lenoir out of office, Amelot would consolidate his hold on the king's household (it included the influential Department of Paris and control of the Parisian police), Goupil would win the lucrative position in the post office, and d'Elmotte would replace him as inspector of the book trade.

As conspiracies went, this one looked almost too baroque to be believed, and d'Elmotte refused to cooperate—or so he said in his version of the affair. But as he described it retrospectively in 1790, his refusal was motivated primarily by a secret arrangement that he had worked out with Lenoir. The lieutenant general permitted him to peddle illegal books, provided that they were not too extreme and also (but d'Elmotte left this implicit in his account of the affair) that he would furnish information about what was circulating underground. Goupil, too, relied on him for fresh information and supplies of libels. So instead of getting him in trouble, d'Elmotte's under-the-cloak business won him protectors. A hack writer-cum-book peddler could hardly have enjoyed happier relations with the police.[11]

D'Elmotte was therefore taken completely by surprise when, as he was about to call on Goupil on March 9, 1778, a police inspector stopped him in the street, presented a lettre de cachet, and took him off to the Bastille. Eight days passed while he sat in his cell, trying to puzzle out what had made his protections come unstuck. When at last he was taken to be interrogated, Lenoir appeared, looking pained. Why, Lenoir asked, had d'Elmotte shown such ingratitude? While the police had turned a blind eye to his underground book business, he had collaborated in a conspiracy to destroy Lenoir and to overthrow the government. D'Elmotte, of course, denied everything. Whether or not he was deeply implicated in Goupil's conspiracy remains unclear. But once Lenoir informed him about Goupil's arrest, he willingly provided as much evidence as he could without compromising himself. He explained his side of the story in a memorandum that Lenoir passed on to Maurepas, and after Maurepas declared himself satisfied, d'Elmotte was released. Goupil's wife, who had been taken to the Bastille on the same day, remained there for seven months and then spent further time confined in the prison-like Couvent de la Madeleine at La Flèche. Goupil himself, who had been shut up in the dungeon of Vincennes while the others went to the Bastille, survived in his cell for three months, his health deteriorating drastically, until he died there, "poisoned or drowned," according to d'Elmotte.[12]

Extravagant as it sounds, d'Elmotte's account of the conspiracy can be corroborated for the most part by an essay Lenoir drafted for inclusion in his memoirs. Lenoir confirmed that d'Elmotte had worked for the police while serving as Goupil's assistant ("commis"), but he indicated that the assistance included the composition of the denunciation that Goupil sent to Maurepas. In it, d'Elmotte even claimed that he and Mme Goupil, who somehow found themselves enclosed in a closet in Lenoir's headquarters, had overheard Sartine and Lenoir discussing their plan to take over the government. But while Goupil fabricated this story to destroy Lenoir, Lenoir received a counterdenunciation from someone intent on destroying Goupil. This person, a chevalier de Saint Louis whom Lenoir did not name, warned Lenoir about Goupil's treachery. Lenoir passed the message on to Maurepas and Amelot. They had just received Goupil's denunciation and therefore decided to get to the bottom of all the plots and counterplots by arresting Goupil, his wife, and d'Elmotte and by interrogating them separately so as to compare different versions of the story. D'Elmotte's version proved to be convincing. He was therefore released while the police worked on the Goupils, who turned on each other with mutual accusations about a long string of crimes involving speculations on libels.[13]

In the end, Goupil realized his game was up. He was suffering from a lung disease, which began to look fatal after several weeks of confinement in the damp dungeon of Vincennes, so he decided to make a general confession to Lenoir. As a boy, he said, he had been driven from his home by his father, who refused to acknowledge his paternity. He took to banditry on the highways; then, at age fifteen, he was shut up in the infamous prison of Bicêtre. In order to get released, he enlisted as a soldier, deserted, and reenlisted, this time in the military branch of the police (*la maréchaussée*), where at last he found some protectors. They recommended him to Sartine, who was then lieutenant general of police. Sartine agreed to take him on as an inspector, and Goupil could afford to purchase the office because he had just married and could dispose of his wife's dowry. Once possessed of some autonomous authority, he immediately abused it. He admitted to all sorts of skullduggery, especially in the policing of libels, which he used as a way to line his pockets while advancing his career. Having got his hands on the manuscript about the relations of the queen with the princesse de Lamballe, he had part of it printed and delivered it to the princess as evidence that he had confiscated the entire edition. He burned it, along with the manuscript, in her presence; and as a reward, she promised to intervene to get him the job in the postal service and to have his wife appointed as reader to the queen.

Having unbosomed himself of his crimes, Goupil told Lenoir that before he died he wanted to see his father. Lenoir contacted the father, a respectable tradesman in Paris, but the old man replied that he had not seen Goupil for twenty-five years and never wanted to see him again. He had cursed his son with a formal malediction, he said. In fact, he did not believe that Goupil was his son at all, for he had eight other children, all of them upstanding subjects of the king, and the only way he could explain Goupil's aberrant depravity was by positing that an accident had occurred soon after his birth: the real Goupil baby must have been exchanged by mistake for another one while in the care of the wet nurse—not an impossibility, considering the way babies were shipped out and passed around in the wet-nursing industry of the Ancien Régime.[14] The father consented nonetheless to a visit in Vincennes. But there was no deathbed reconciliation, and Goupil died in his cell two months later.[15]

Although Lenoir recounted Goupil's story in his usual manner—dead flat and without literary frills—it has the feel of fiction. One can imagine it worked up as a sentimental novel: something by Restif de la Bretonne with illustrations by Greuze. It may therefore look suspicious as an introduction to the policing of libels. But it can be pinned down by enough documentation—fragments from memoirs, police archives, even the contemporary underground newsletter known as *Mémoires secrets pour servir à l'histoire de la république des lettres en France*—to be taken as testimony to the way the literary police, or at least some of them, actually did their job. Duplicity and treachery were built into the system. There was too much money trailing after the libels for most inspectors to keep their hands clean, and cleanliness in handling the king's affairs was hardly common under the Ancien Régime where bribes—referred to euphemistically as *épices* (spice) and *pots de vin* (jugs of wine)—cleared the way for careers throughout the administration and judicial system. It may seem strange, nonetheless, that the police should have been infected by the criminality embodied by Goupil, while dedicated professionals like d'Hémery had earned it a reputation as the most progressive law-enforcing agency in Europe.[16]

Goupil and d'Hémery do indeed represent opposite tendencies within the same system, but Goupil's abuse of the system can be explained by something more than sheer roguishness or whatever may have happened at the wet nurse. The police administration of the Ancien Régime, advanced as it was in comparison to that of other countries, was no modern civil service. Men rose through the ranks by means of patronage and pull, and at the higher levels they had to buy their offices. But the combined effect of protection and venality did not mean that conduct counted for nothing. When Goupil first appeared before his superiors, he looked like a promising young man. His name as it turns up in their records is accompanied by reports of a job well done. His first "inspections"—whether clearing the streets of unauthorized peddlers or accompanying prisoners to the Bastille—seem to have been carried out diligently. Lieutenant general Sartine, his superior in the early 1770s, wrote a fairly positive recommendation for him to his future mother-in-law, who sought information about his character. It was only after his marriage and the purchase of his office, which brought him a decent but not an oversized salary of three thousand livres a year, that Goupil took advantage of the opportunity for large-scale peculation.[17]

The police system made such opportunities available, but it did not resemble the horror stories perpetuated by the libels and by sensational best-sellers like Linguet's *Mémoires sur la Bastille* and Mirabeau's *Des lettres de cachet et des prisons d'état*. Police officers and libelers alike had to make their way through contradictions and complexities. They inhabited an imperfect and a very human world, which should not be confused with the caricatures in the literature that it both repressed and reproduced. It is important to keep a balanced view of the Ancien Régime in mind while following the subsequent account of the book police at work, because Goupil was succeeded by a character who outdid him in turning the system against itself.

Chapter 10
A Double Agent and His Authors

On December 21, 1781, an unidentified man burst into the Café du caveau and announced in great excitement: "Messieurs, I have some big news, and I'm certain of it. Yesterday Jacquet was executed in the Bastille as guilty of the crime of lèse majesté . .. and as author of the libel against the queen."[1]

According to a contemporary report, this flash of news produced "general consternation." It spread from the café, whose location in the Palais-Royal made it a favorite gathering place for *nouvellistes* (gossips who specialized in news), through the oral communication networks of the city. Jacquet did not need to be identified. Everyone in the café knew he was a police inspector assigned to hunt down libels. That he himself had produced a libel against the queen and then had been dispatched by his colleagues inside the Bastille—that was the sort of news that produced a sensation at café tables and then traveled at top speed through all the media of the time. It passed from word of mouth (*nouvelles de bouche*) into clandestine, handwritten newsletters (*nouvelles à la main*), and finally into print, where it can be followed in the underground publication known as *Mémoires secrets pour servir à l'histoire de la république des lettres en France.*

Such news could not appear in official journals like the *Gazette de France* nor in unofficial periodicals like the *Journal de Leyde*, which were produced outside France but permitted to circulate inside the kingdom with the approval (and frequent censorship) of the French authorities. The events that set tongues wagging were banished from the legal press of the Ancien Régime. They circulated everywhere through illegal channels of communication, but in doing so they often got distorted. Jacquet had not been executed. He was sitting in a cell in the Bastille, but he had indeed been locked up for producing libels: that was sensational enough as an item of news, and one can pick up some of the sensations it aroused by following its coverage in the *Mémoires secrets.* (Beaumarchais)

The immediate context for the reports about Jacquet consisted in the circulation of some nasty *noëls* in December 1781. Every year during the Christmas season, French wits improvised satirical songs about current events. These *noëls* spread a spicy commentary about the misdoings of the great, and they caught on easily among ordinary folk because they were composed to tunes that everyone knew.[2] On the eve of Christmas in 1781, Parisians were singing about a subject that went far beyond the bounds of acceptable satire, according to the *Mémoires secrets*. The *noëls* were full of "sacrilegious calumnies"—such horrible things that they could not be mentioned, even in an underground newsletter. The anonymous authors of the *Mémoires secrets* merely observed that they had become "the subject of all the talk and of abhorrence in all of Paris."[3]

At this time rumors about the king's supposed impotence and the queen's supposed infidelities were considered too shocking to be consigned to writing. But the reports about Jacquet indicated that he had published a libel containing the same sacrilegious material that had infected the *noëls*. The escalation from word of mouth to print meant that the authorities had to confront a major problem, and Jacquet's arrest showed that part of the problem arose from insubordination within their own ranks. A police inspector turned libeler! It was extraordinary, and the *Mémoires secrets* announced its determination to get to the bottom of "this dark affair which is so difficult to unravel."[4]

Conscious of the difficulty of sifting fact from fantasy in a world where public discussion about the private life of the sovereign was forbidden, the *Mémoires secrets* restricted its coverage to what it considered the most reliable reports. Jacquet was known as a "bad subject," that much was clear. He worked for the police and specialized in the surveillance of the book trade. That assignment often took him to England and the Low Countries, where he had become familiar with the libel industry by frequenting dubious characters like Théveneau de Morande. Some months before his arrest he had been dispatched to London by Maurepas to buy up the entire edition of a particularly outrageous libel, but when he returned he said that some copies had escaped him. He therefore needed to make another trip and to spend another small fortune to purchase the remaining copies. This sounded suspicious enough for the police to search his luggage when he arrived back in Paris for the second time. Along with the printed works, they found the original manuscript, written out in his own hand.[5]

The information about Jacquet was as scandalous as the books he was supposed to suppress, so the authors of the *Mémoires secrets* continued to follow the story. On January 14, 1782, they corrected their earlier account: Jacquet had not been executed; he was still in the Bastille and had been implicated in other criminal activities. On January 26, they published the title of the libel, *Vie d'Antoinette*, and the names of two accomplices who had been arrested with Jacquet: a bankrupt bookseller named Costard and Michel-Louis de Marcenay, "a man of the world and a bad subject." Two days later, they finally produced some information about Jacquet himself provided by a correspondent in Besançon, his hometown. Jean-Claude Jacquet de la Douay came from a wealthy, well-connected family in the Franche-Comté. After studying law, he had taken up a position as an attorney in the *bailliage* court of Lons-le-Saunier and seemed destined for a distinguished career in the parlement of Besançon, where he had several relatives. But, people said, he was not content with life in the provinces. He left to pursue his fortune in Paris; and if he got in trouble there, nobody would be surprised, because back in Besançon he was known as a "bad subject"[6]—an epithet that pursued suspicious characters like a dog biting at their heels.

A letter from Brussels, published on February 7, revealed that Jacquet had organized an extensive publishing business, which turned out libels from the Low Countries as well as from England. The French police had recently captured several of his collaborators in a raid in Brussels, and people there were stunned to learn that someone in Jacquet's position—a fully commissioned inspector of the foreign book trade (*inspecteur de la librairie étrangère*)—should have printed, peddled, and even written libels himself, along with a whole team of fellow criminals. That seemed to settle the case, except for some final details that arrived from Besançon in November 1782. A correspondent there reported that Jacquet had left a wife and young daughter, who were now living on a small estate near Lons-le-Saunier. As soon as she heard of his arrest, his wife had rushed to Paris in order to beg for clemency, because he had been condemned to death, or so people believed in Besançon. As far as they were concerned, he deserved to be hanged, but they believed his sentence had been commuted to life imprisonment. They could only feel pity for his wife, who came from a good family and had brought him a considerable dowry, which he had squandered.[7]

The *Mémoires secrets* rarely followed a story in such detail. It had devoted two short articles to Goupil's arrest, but its coverage of Jacquet showed that his affair had become a phenomenon of another order, an event that figured prominently in the media of the day—oral, written, and printed—even though in principle it belonged to the secret realm of reason of state. By 1780 libels and the attempts to repress them had emerged in the open as a matter of public opinion. The public exposure of their secret activities added another dimension to the work of the book police.

So much for the way the affair appeared before the public. But what had actually happened? In order to disentangle its complexities, one must consult two sources, the papers of the lieutenant general of police Jean-Charles-Pierre

Lenoir and the police records that Pierre Manuel published in 1789–90, *La Police de Paris dévoilée* and *La Bastille dévoilée*, which can be supplemented by some manuscripts from the archives of the Bastille.[8] Lenoir described Jacquet as a "double agent," who had perfected his talent for duplicity on secret missions for several ministers.[9] Maurepas and Vergennes gave him a special commission to ferret out libels against the French court that were published in London and The Hague. They worried especially about London, because in 1779 they had agreed to pay an extravagant sum—8,000 louis (192,000 livres)—to buy up the entire edition of a particularly nasty attack on the queen by an extortionist in the London colony of French refugees. The anonymous author negotiated through a French bookseller (almost certainly Boissière who kept a shop in St. James Street), and the French foreign ministry enlisted the aid of Lord North, the head of the British government. In the end, a case containing a complete run of printed sheets and engravings, sealed with the arms of North and accompanied by an armed guard, arrived in the Bastille, where it remained under lock and key until the Revolution. But the word soon spread. Inspired by this example, all sorts of adventurers flocked to the London smut factory—Lenoir referred to it as a single "fabrique" but indicated that its operations were scattered throughout London and the Low Countries—in order to manufacture more infamy.[10]

Jacquet's assignment was to put them out of business. His first trip took him to Amsterdam and The Hague, where expatriate French authors and Dutch presses were doing a brisk trade in libels. He returned with a disappointing harvest of off-color anecdotes and songs, which Maurepas dismissed as garbage. Although Jacquet was supposed to concert his activities with the French embassy in The Hague, it reported that it had never seen him and that prospectuses for slanderous works continued to proliferate. Meanwhile, a letter arrived from Charles Théveneau de Morande, the libeler who had turned police spy, saying that Jacquet had been spotted in London, where he had arranged for the publication of manuscripts that he had brought with him from Paris.

This information sounded troubling enough for Lenoir, after consulting with Maurepas, to assign one of his most trusted inspectors to investigate. Although he did not mention this veteran by name, Lenoir's account of the affair indicates that the man he chose was Receveur, the antihero of *Le Diable dans un bénitier*. Receveur had plenty of experience in spying on spies and capturing libelers. When Jacquet left on a second mission to London in 1781, Receveur trailed him, coordinated his investigation with the French embassy, collaborated with Morande, and confirmed Lenoir's suspicions: Jacquet was running an underground publishing business. He commissioned hack writers in Paris to produce the copy; he had it printed in London and Holland; and he hired smugglers to get the books into Paris.

One of the smugglers denounced Jacquet after a quarrel. Meanwhile, the French post office intercepted incriminating letters that two of Jacquet's authors, Michel-Louis de Marcenay and Louis-Claude-César de Launay, had addressed to him. Lenoir therefore had all the evidence he needed to aim a decisive blow at Jacquet's entire operation, including his authors and distributors. On October 30, 1781, as the *Mémoires secrets* reported, the police locked up four prisoners in the Bastille: Jacquet; Marcenay; another writer, abbé Théophile-Imarigeon Duvernet; and the bookseller Costard, who worked for Jacquet as a copyist. Lenoir and his men interrogated the prisoners separately for many days without breaking their resistance. But at last Marcenay cracked. He had written two libels on subjects assigned to him by Jacquet, he confessed. Lenoir then pitted him against the others in a series of "confrontations"— dramatic scenes in which the interrogators brought prisoners together and goaded them into making mutual incriminations. They eventually wrung a confession out of Duvernet, who said he had written a libel against Maurepas for Jacquet and named some of Jacquet's other authors. Jacquet refused to talk and then faked insanity, a ruse that worked well enough for him to get transferred for two years to the asylum in Charenton. As a reward for their testimony, Marcenay and Duvernet were released from the Bastille after relatively short terms, but Jacquet returned there in November 1783 for an indefinite period of confinement. Lenoir ended his account of the affair at that point, but the police bust of October 30, 1781, continued to send repercussions through the world of the libelers because it had opened up leads that Receveur and other secret agents pursued for the next three years.[11]

The saddest dossier produced by their investigations concerns a writer that Jacquet recruited in Amsterdam, Louis-Claude-César, chevalier de Launay. He had embarked on a seemingly successful career as a doctor in Avignon and even became a royal censor for medical books. But by 1780 for reasons that remain unclear, he found himself in Paris and penniless. Hoping to write his way out of poverty, he accepted a position as a one-man author and editor of the *Gazette anglo-française* published in Maestricht by Samuel Swinton, a Scottish speculator and would-be press baron who also owned the *Courrier de l'Europe*, the French paper in London that employed many of the libelers. The *Gazette* failed to make money. Swinton and de Launay quarreled. Swinton abandoned the journal, and de Launay tried to continue it but soon gave up for lack of funds. Now destitute, he made his way to Amsterdam and started writing libels, some of them for Jacquet. When this new wave of defamation reached the streets of Paris, Lenoir dispatched Receveur to trace it to its source, which seemed to be somewhere in the Low Countries. In Amsterdam, aided by French diplomats and Dutch authorities, Receveur raided a printing shop and got the printers to talk. They revealed that the copy had come from de Launay, who by then had returned to Paris. Receveur hurried back and carried him off to the Bastille on September 4, 1782. Sixteen days later, de Launay was found dead in his cell.[12]

The death of de Launay following that of Goupil fed the growing mythology about dark secrets hidden in dungeons and torture chambers.[13] *La Bastille dévoilée* reported that an autopsy had turned up no evidence of foul play, but it left room for suspicion of a "violent death"; and *Le Diable dans un bénitier*, which also recounted the affair, asserted flatly that de Launay had been strangled by Receveur. Despite the scrambled character of the documentation, there is no reason to suspect the police of abusing their prisoners. They continued to haul in libelers, however, and their catch reveals a good deal about the conditions of life in Grub Street.[14]

De Launay and the two libelers arrested with Jacquet illustrate a common tendency among Parisian hack writers: downward social mobility. All three had received good educations and had set out on promising careers—de Launay in medicine, Duvernet in the church, and Marcenay in the royal administration. Just what made the first two deviate from the conventional paths to advancement remains unclear, but Marcenay stumbled in a way that shows how careers could go wrong. According to *La Bastille dévoilée*, he did himself out of a good job in the finance ministry by a practical joke that showed a lack of respect for one of his superiors. He printed and distributed a notice that his boss had just been buried. The boss did not think it funny—by this time the French administration was turning into a "bureaucracy," a term first used in 1764—and Marcenay found himself out on the street. Desperate for work, he took up pamphleteering and emigrated to Holland, where he produced copy for the French-language presses, met Jacquet, and signed on as a libeler.[15]

The other hacks in Jacquet's stable of authors also fell back on writing as a way to put bread on the table when they were hungry. The genre that paid best, as Jacquet proved by recruiting them, was libeling. He furnished the subject matter and the pay; they wrote the texts. Some of the copy also came from Jacquet himself. According to *La Bastille dévoilée*, he occasionally wrote short essays, which he submitted to Lenoir as "extracts" from full-fledged libels which, he claimed, were about to be printed in London or Amsterdam under titles such as *La Vie du prince ****, *Le Portefeuille de ****, *Les Aventures de Mme de Polig****, *Le Ministre de Vergennes*, and *Le Cri de la France contre M. de Maurepas*. Thanks to his contacts in the literary underground, Jacquet assured Lenoir, he could persuade the authors to suppress the complete editions of these works, provided that the police came up with an adequate payoff, which usually varied from 500 to 1,000 louis—that is, from 12,000 to 24,000 livres. (The booty in blackmailing was usually quoted in louis, a more elegant denomination than livres, just as important transactions in England took place in guineas as opposed to pounds.) Most of these books never existed. But by faking and bluffing, Jacquet acquired enough capital to mount a genuine publishing business. His writers and printers turned out a great many libels, although it is impossible to determine who wrote what in this body of literature, which has largely disappeared.[16]

Fortunately, one example, which shows how the business operated, can be traced through the police archives and into the shelves of libraries today: *Les Joueurs et M. Dusaulx*, an anonymous, sixty-page attack on prominent Parisians who compromised themselves in illicit gambling and prostitution. It was written, printed, and published in Brussels by three of Jacquet's collaborators, who formed a branch of their own within his larger enterprise. Jacquet supplied them with information, and apparently assigned one of his Parisian authors, the abbé Duvernet, to provide help as needed. But Brussels was the heart of the operation. Its leader was Jean-Baptiste Imbert de Villebon, a French businessman who had fled to Brussels to escape prosecution for fraudulent bankruptcy. Most of his business involved the trade in illegal books—producing them, selling them, and spying on them for the French police. Some of the books came from the pen of his brother, François-Guillaume Imbert de Boudeaux, a defrocked Benedictine monk who took up libeling as a way to support himself in Paris after he left the monastery. Imbert de Boudeaux's best-known work, *La Chronique scandaleuse* (first published in 1783, supposedly in "Paris, from a corner where one can see everything," expanded to four volumes in an edition of 1785 and to five in 1791), epitomized the scandalmongering that surrounded public figures during the last years of Louis XVI's reign. He specialized in spicy anecdotes which circulated in manuscript newsletters and ultimately appeared in illegal journals such as the *Correspondance littéraire secrète* published by Louis-François Mettra in Neuwied. The Imbert brothers also worked with Antoine La Coste de Mézières, a former army officer who had fallen into a Grub Street existence in Paris and Brussels, where he supplied copy for the underground press. *Les Joueurs* was one of a half-dozen works that this team turned out in 1780–81.[17]

Read out of context, it seems to be an exposé of gambling dens in Paris, thinly disguised as a narrative about two gentlemen from the provinces who were cheated out of their fortunes by underworld characters and tell their sad stories to Jean Dusaulx, an eminent philosophical author of a treatise against gambling, *Lettre et réflexions sur la fureur du jeu* (1775). The narrator adopts a high-minded perspective toward his subject. He moralizes indignantly about vice preying on virtue and defends the principles of Enlightenment against the forces of obscurantism. But in condemning depravity, he provides a voyeuristic account of it. He reveals how prostitutes, decked out as ladies, pick up innocent victims at Parisian theaters, entice them into brothels disguised as salons, ply them with spiked drink, and lead them to gaming tables, where they throw away their families' fortunes, helped to their downfall by professional cheats. The narrative takes the reader from one gambling den to another—the Palais-Royal, the Luxembourg Palace, the Venetian embassy—splicing the descriptions with biographical sketches of the underworld characters who recruit the women of pleasure, cut the cards, keep the bank, and pay the kickbacks to the police. It therefore reads in places like *Le Gazetier cuirassé*, which covered some of the same subjects and which it cites at one point.[18] The scabrous anecdotes follow each other pell-mell, without much connection to the narrative, as if they were related for their own sake.

Thus a typical vignette about a whore, Liennette Dufrêne, daughter of a shoemaker and a flower seller in Lyon, which the narrator inserts gratuitously into the text. After being sold as a child to the son of a banker on the rue des Trois Carreaux for sixty livres, he explains (precise details of this kind figure throughout most libels, giving them an air of authenticity), Liennette made her way through brothels in Montpellier and Bordeaux and finally graduated to Paris, "where everything is put up for sale."

A merchant in the rue Aux Fers took her in and did add to her fortune. He was succeeded by a duke, an avaricious man, notorious for his impudence and lasciviousness. . . . Owing to this avarice or his impotence, Liennette left him and fell back on daily stints in the Tuileries Gardens, in gutters and hovels, and on picking up customers in the vaudeville shows along the boulevards. One evening while doing her rounds, she hooked a servant of the duc de la Vrillière; on another, she took up with a valet of the comte d'Estaing. Inspired by the accounts of their valets, the masters came to see this Phryne. She [later] persuaded the duc de la Vrillière that she was carrying a child by him. She made this impotent wretch think he was a Hercules and saddled his duchy with three children, who, like Liennette, never had a clue as to the identity of their real father. Using the need to support this brood as a pretext, she received permission to go into gambling; and M. Lenoir, who now is serving as God's instrument at the head of the police, gave her permission to set up an establishment. Now Liennette goes around proclaiming, "I have lived with the duc de la Vrillière, and behold, here is his child." She cuts quite a figure with the ladies of her estate and now keeps her gambling den and brothel in the rue de Richelieu.[19]

Despite its moralizing and its ostensible story line, therefore, *Les Joueurs* had most of the features of a *chronique scandaleuse*. But there was more to it than an attempt to exploit the market for scandalous literature. The reference to the duc de la Vrillière, the minister in charge of the Bastille and a bête noire of the libelers, expressed the political message of the text. *Les Joueurs* denounced the police and their superiors in Versailles as the secret power that ran the gambling industry. Every day, it recounted, the bankers of the gambling dens drew their cash from a central treasury run by a police officer named Gombaud, and every night they returned the money to him along with a portion of the day's take. The chain of protections led from Gombaud to Lenoir, la Vrillière, and Maurepas at the very summit of the government. All along the line, the politicians and police helped themselves to the whores as well as the money. The only person in this world who resisted corruption was Dusaulx, the philosophe who had exposed its threat to civic virtue. *Les Joueurs* presented itself as a supplement to his work—he expounded the philosophic principles, it uncovered the abuses—and celebrated him as an incorruptible man of letters who had rejected an attempt to buy him off by Lenoir with a declaration of independence: "I cultivate the world of letters. As I know how to proportion my needs to my revenue, the little I have is sufficient; and I prefer the public good to my own interest."[20]

This profession of faith may have represented the authors' ideal of authorship, but they lived in a real world where appetites had to be satisfied and money made. Their police records show that they designed the book so that it could be used for blackmailing. The names of their potential victims stand out in italics in the text: la Vrillière, minister of the king's household responsible for the Department of Paris (hence his authority over the Bastille); Sartine, minister of the navy and former lieutenant general of police; d'Aligre, first president of the Parlement of Paris; Séguier, attorney general to the parlement; an assortment of courtiers—the duc de Duras, the duc de Mazarin, the marquis de Fleury; and many others, including the proprietors of the gambling houses. How the libelers divided the labor is unclear. It seems that Jacquet initiated the enterprise from Paris, where Duvernet helped him gather information. Imbert de Boudeaux, who lived in a room rented from a secondhand clothes dealer in Paris, and Mézières, who had moved from Paris to Brussels, probably collaborated on drafting the text. Imbert de Villebon oversaw the printing and distribution in Brussels. Everyone involved was arrested during the police crackdown on Jacquet's ring in December 1781 and January 1782. When interrogated in the Bastille, they confessed enough to reveal how a typical blackmail operation was conducted, even though this one ended in failure.

After the completion of the text, they produced a printed prospectus, which they mailed to their intended victims with a cover letter demanding certain sums in exchange for suppressing certain passages. According to the testi-

mony of one collaborator, probably Duvernet, Jacquet directed this phase of
the speculation: "He is familiar with the use of anonymous letters to extract
money from people that he wants to intimidate. I remember having heard him
say, 'We could get a great deal from Sartine, from Montbarrey, and even from
the first president [of the Parlement de Paris], although he is a miser, if we
produced a good tract against them. As to Séguier, he's not worth the trouble.
He hasn't got a penny.' "[21] Mézières hoped to extract payment from five of the
proprietors of the gambling houses, but they refused to be intimidated, and
none of the prospectuses elicited a response. Imbert de Villebon then
instructed his brother in Paris to propose turning over the entire edition to
Lenoir in exchange for a reward. By that time, however, a few copies had
seeped into the market. In the end, therefore, the libelers abandoned their
attempts at blackmail and settled for selling the book for whatever it could
fetch in the underground trade.[22]

Les Joueurs was only a small part of the large business conducted by Jacquet. But the larger the business grew, the more vulnerable it became to a fundamental weakness: it operated on the principle of honor among thieves. It
finally broke down at a crucial stage in the distribution system—the point at
which libels had to be smuggled into Paris. Jacquet's chief smuggler, a bookseller in Versailles named André, received shipments from printing shops in
London and the Low Countries; stocked them in secret warehouses (the palace
itself included all sorts of hidden chambers crammed with forbidden books);
and forwarded them to peddlers in the city by means of various maneuvers
(the most common was to bribe footmen to hide bundles in the coaches of
persons important enough to be exempt from inspection at the city's customs
barrier). In return, André collected a cut in the profits. But how could he know
he was receiving his fair share? He suspected foul play, because Jacquet began
to rely on another technique of getting the books into Paris. Reporting to Lenoir while on a foreign mission, he would announce that he had confiscated a
load of libels and was bringing them back with him to Paris. He could then
pass through the inspection points without difficulty, deposit some of the copies in the Bastille as testimony to his zeal in repressing seditious slander, and
sell the rest on the sly.

In the autumn of 1781, André discovered that Jacquet had imported a
large stock of a half-dozen libels in this manner. They included slanderous
attacks against Maurepas, the duc de Chartres, the comte d'Artois, and Necker,
along with the book that the police most wanted to suppress, *La Vie de la reine*.
Furious at having been deceived by the kind of double dealing that Jacquet
had used against the police, André denounced him to Lenoir—and in return
was rewarded with a commission to double deal himself because, according to

La Bastille dévoilée, he signed on as one of Lenoir's spies while continuing his illicit book business.[23]

While exposing Jacquet's operation, André revealed the names of his collaborators in Brussels. Lenoir dispatched the redoubtable Receveur to hunt them down, and Receveur managed to have both Imbert brothers and Mézières incarcerated in a local jail at the end of 1781. True, he had no authority to do so, but he enlisted the help of some Walloon officials who were eager to accommodate the superpower that had invaded their country regularly for the last hundred years. They kept the prisoners under lock and key in Brussels while Receveur arranged for their transfer to France. The trio entered the Bastille on January 7, 1782, and spent the next weeks undergoing intensive interrogation. Receveur also brought back incriminating evidence in the form of books, which he confiscated in Brussels and Leiden and deposited in a storeroom of the Bastille: *Essai sur la vie de Marie-Antoinette d'Autriche, reine de France, Les Joueurs et M. Dusaulx*, and two pamphlets against Necker.[24]

The transcripts of the interrogations, quoted at length in *La Bastille dévoilée*, show that the police knew they were dealing with seasoned professionals and that their main concern was to turn up evidence about the defamation of the queen.[25] Many titles or versions of the same title recurred during the interrogations: *La Vie de la reine, La Vie privée de la reine, La Vie de Marie-Antoinette*, and *Essai sur la vie de la reine*. Although it is impossible to reconstruct the publishing history of this work, it seems to have gone through several metamorphoses, both in manuscript and in print, before a definitive edition of it appeared in 1789 as *Essais historiques sur la vie de Marie-Antoinette d'Autriche, reine de France: Pour servir à l'histoire de cette princesse*.[26] As part of the speculation that led to his quarrel with André (as well as evidence of his effectiveness in suppressing libels), Jacquet had delivered a portion of his edition of *La Vie de la reine* to the Bastille. The police therefore knew that his authors were producing texts so slanderous as to constitute a crime of "lèse majesté," as they called it in the records of the interrogations. The slander featured the nastiest and most far-fetched stories about the king's supposed impotence, his cuckolding, the queen's orgies with a long series of lovers including the king's brother, the comte d'Artois, and his cousin, the duc de Chartres, and the illegitimacy of her offspring, which it recounted in a particularly graphic chapter (illustrated in some editions) about the birth of her first child.

Faced with such a serious charge, the three prisoners did their best to minimize their role in the affair. Imbert de Villebon tried to establish his innocence by claiming that any seemingly suspicious activity on his part was really a cover for his service as a secret agent of the Paris police. He explained in his interrogation that he had agreed to spy on illicit publishing in Brussels and, he insisted, that he had done his job well. True, he had received money for his services, but he never dreamed of commissioning works in order to engineer their confiscation or to collect blackmail. He had informed Lenoir of more than forty libels that were being written or printed, including the unspeakable attack on the queen. In fact, he had tried to prevent the publication of *La Vie de la reine* by offering three thousand livres for its manuscript through one of his contacts in the literary underground. Unfortunately, the possessor of the manuscript had held out for four thousand livres, and so it eventually appeared in print. Jacquet had bought up the complete edition in London, along with several other libels—or, at least, so he claimed: he had recounted this version of the story when he met with Imbert while passing through Brussels on his way back to Paris from London. According to another version, which seemed more likely to Imbert, Jacquet had pocketed most of the money that the police had provided for the purchase of the edition and then had sold a great many of the copies on the sly. In fact, Imbert believed that Jacquet had never been to London at all but had had the edition printed in Holland after acquiring the manuscript from a discontented courtier in Versailles.

This testimony represented an attempt to shift all of the guilt to Jacquet, but unfortunately for Imbert, the police had extracted some counterevidence from Mézières. He admitted that he had written two libels, *Confession générale de madame la comtesse du Barry* and *La Diligence, ou Conversation libre entre trois gens pas trop sots*, at Imbert's instigation. Although the career of Mme du Barry had provided libelers with their best material for the previous ten years, it remained a crime under Louis XVI to defame the memory of Louis XV, and *La Diligence* included some of the most outrageous allegations about Marie-Antoinette from the *La Vie de la reine*. So the interrogators bore down hard on Mézières.

Asked how he could have brought himself to compose two such horrible works which attack the sacred persons of their majesties, the entire royal family, princes, princesses of the court, ministers, magistrates, and persons occupying the highest rank and dignities?

Replied that he did so at the instigation of sieur Imbert de Villebonne, who promised that he would arrange for the sale of these manuscripts to M. le comte de Maurepas.[27]

In his own interrogation, Imbert had firmly denied commissioning Mézières to write any libels. He had claimed, on the contrary, that he had warned Mézières not to produce anything disrespectful of the king and queen, because such work would be considered a crime of lèse majesté. But Mézières would not listen. Desperate to make some money, he had replied "that until now he had used every possible means of support in order to survive, that this one was the last that remained, and that he wanted to make the most use of it, no matter what the cost."[28]

Mézières's situation in the Grub Street of Brussels may indeed have been desperate, but it was worse in the Bastille. In the face of relentless questioning—and tempted, no doubt, by an offer of clemency if he would talk—he finally broke down and revealed the full extent of the Brussels operation. Imbert had mounted a libel business modeled on Jacquet's. He had furnished Mézières with recent libels and *nouvelles à la main* along with information about the themes in *La Vie de la reine* so that he could cobble together fresh copy. Taking advantage of his role as a police spy, Imbert had planned to produce Mézières's manuscript as evidence that new libels were about to be published and then to collect a reward for their suppression. As seen from Brussels, the police in Paris could be made to cooperate in all sorts of extortion schemes, thanks to limitless sums funneled to them from the government.

There were limits, however. Imbert de Villebon negotiated with Lenoir through his brother, who was well-known to the Parisian police. They had arrested the brother in 1772 for contributing to clandestine newsletters. When they searched his room, they found a large collection of irreligious books, which he had assembled, he claimed, in order to write a defense of Christianity.[29] His later publications, including *La Chronique scandaleuse*, suggest that his views were less than orthodox, but the police were mainly concerned with his activities in the underground book trade. They permitted him to sell some illegal works under the cloak, provided that he clear everything with them and keep them informed of his sources. He therefore spied for the police in Paris just as his brother did in Brussels and was well-placed to relay his brother's propositions to Lenoir. Two of the proposals for suppressing libels that they submitted in November 1781 concerned a supposed attack on the marquis de Castries, who was then secretary of the navy, and another pamphlet about the queen's sex life, titled *Soirées de la reine*. By this time, however, Lenoir had begun to suspect the Imbert brothers of inventing titles of books in order to have them written and printed if he came up with enough money to buy them out. His suspicions were confirmed by André's denunciation of their undercover activities. Instead of sending money, therefore, he sent Receveur, who arrested them along with Mézières. (Imbert de Boudeaux had traveled to Brussels at that time in order to concert plans with the other two.) And when they tried to parry Lenoir's questions during their interrogations in the Bastille, he learned that they had indeed been bluffing: neither of the two libels existed.

But *La Vie de la reine* did. When he arrested the Imbert brothers, Receveur had impounded some correspondence showing that Imbert de Villebon had offered to supply it to two of the most notorious dealers in the illegal book trade, Dufour of Maestricht and Mettra of Neuwied. Villebon answered lamely in his interrogation that he had only dangled the offer as a ruse to find out whether the two booksellers had already received similar proposals from other sources. Imbert de Boudeaux did not defend himself more effectively in his own interrogation. Receveur had confiscated some compromising anecdotes about dignitaries that he planned to publish in Mettra's *Correspondance littéraire secrète*. In his defense, Boudeaux could only assure his interrogators that he had merely jotted down some gossip picked up in Brussels and that he would never publish anything of the sort without first clearing it with Lenoir.

Whether or not they got to the bottom of the Imberts' bag of tricks, the police came up with enough evidence to conclude that Jacquet's collaborators, like Jacquet himself, had played a double game. Just as he had used his office in the police to organize an illegal publishing business, they had exploited their positions as police spies to mount collateral speculations. It may seem odd from a modern perspective that the system should have given rise to so much embezzlement and espionage. But as already explained, state employees in the eighteenth century did not think and behave like modern civil servants—at least not the kind that exist in some countries. (After the collapse of communism in 1989, it became clear that apparatchiks could be entrepreneurs who used the state to develop empires of their own. If Jacquet and company can be compared with anyone today, it would be with the subaltern agents of autocratic regimes.) The Ancien Régime belonged to a category of its own, situated somewhere between the absolutism of early modern monarchies and the bureaucracy of modern states. Its police abused their powers in ways peculiar to the system that employed them. Those who owned their offices used them to fatten their purses, and they easily found collaborators among those who owned next to nothing—indigent authors and marginal book dealers. Grub Street teemed with police spies because it provided a setting where the early modern media—rumors, songs, newsletters, pamphlets, books—took root and spread. Its inhabitants produced the works that the police most wanted to repress, above all, libels. And repression led to collaboration. The police naturally recruited spies from among the hacks, *nouvellistes*, and peddlers whom they encountered on their daily rounds—and when an inspector crossed to the other side of Grub Street in order to mount an illegal speculation of his own, he hired collaborators from the same milieu.

Spying was an important aspect of police work. Lenoir had hundreds, perhaps even thousands, of spies at his service in Paris. Some were full-time employees who wrote daily reports about conversations in cafés and markets.

Others provided occasional information in return for small payments or various favors. A few turned informer to win release from the Bastille and to continue peddling books or writing pamphlets under the "protection" of the police. Shocking as that may seem today, the collusion of the police and hack writers was built into the structure of literary life in the eighteenth century, and the Bastille functioned as a linchpin of the system. The police did not use it as if it were a modern penitentiary, nor did they hold modern notions of punishment by lengthy prison terms. When they imprisoned Mézières and the Imbert brothers, they were dealing with a sector of the book trade that they knew intimately; and having learned all they could from the interrogations, they did not keep the prisoners locked up for a long time. They released Mézières after five months, a typical period of internment, and the Imberts after only two months—presumably so they could resume their role as spies.

Jacquet was a special case. As Lenoir later observed, he never confessed but instead pretended to be mad. When he returned to the Bastille in November 1783 after a year in the asylum of Charenton, he continued to cover up his activities. The few scraps that remain in the archives from his original dossier suggest that he gave way to a growing sense of despair. Never, he wrote in notes to his jailers, had a human being suffered as much as he. His health was ruined. He could not move one leg. He was tormented by headaches, deafness, and chills. He begged for more water, warmer clothing, a better blanket—and news of his family, for he had heard nothing from his wife, and he had four children (not one child, as the *Mémoires secrets* had reported). In a typical note he described himself as "an unfortunate creature perishing behind thick walls, someone for whom the sun will never again shine, a father of four children who are ruined because of his misdeeds and whom he will never see again, a man who begs you in the name of everything that can touch your soul to tell him if his wife is still alive and what the fate is of his children."[30] Prisoners' letters often contained such lamentations, written in the hope of winning some relief from their misery, but Jacquet had reason to believe that he would remain in prison until he died. He could not appeal for clemency to Lenoir, he knew, because Lenoir refused to receive his letters. So he stayed in the Bastille. He stayed and stayed—until July 9, 1789, when he was released and exiled to his native Franche-Comté. He therefore came within five days of being liberated by the French Revolution.

Jacquet reappeared in Paris sometime during the second half of 1789. By then the Bastille was being dismantled and its archives were being published by Pierre Manuel. Manuel needed an assistant who knew his way around the papers of the police and could help in the delicate task of weeding out material that might compromise some leaders of the Revolution. Who could be better suited for this job than Jacquet? In 1792 Manuel was brought to trial for misappropriating some of the archives—the letters that Mirabeau had written from the prison of Vincennes and that his heirs claimed as their property. In his defense, he argued successfully that the papers belonged to the French people and that he had performed a patriotic duty by making them available to the people through publication. In some instances, he explained, he had given former prisoners the dossiers that concerned them. Jacquet was such a case. Manuel testified that he had given "M. Jacquet, police inspector, the dossier concerning him and that on several other occasions, as the need arose, he had asked him to do research."[31]

From police inspector to double agent, underground publisher, prisoner in the Bastille, and research assistant in the editing of the Bastille papers— Jacquet's career spanned the whole range of activities that connected libeling under the Ancien Régime with propaganda in the Revolution.

Chapter 11

Secret Missions

As Jacquet's case demonstrates, the operations of the police could not be contained within the walls of the Bastille; and when they were picked up by the media of the day, they threatened to compound any damage that the libels might produce. Jacquet's misadventures provided café gossips and news-sheet chroniclers with material that was every bit as sensational as the misdeeds of courtiers. In fact, the two types of scandal seemed to complement each other. A corrupt and arbitrary police force worked hand in hand with a decadent and despotic government—that was the main theme of libels like *Le Diable dans un bénitier*. The French authorities therefore faced a double problem: they needed to stifle the production of libels and to do so in a way that would avoid causing further scandal. Ministers like Maurepas and Vergennes took this problem seriously. It became a major concern in French foreign affairs, because the most outspoken libelers operated outside the kingdom. The result was a series of secret missions designed to exterminate the libel industry at its very core: the colony of French expatriates in London.

London had provided an ideal site for manufacturing libels long before Jacquet made it the center of his operations. Thanks to the English Channel, it offered better protection than Brussels or Amsterdam against raids of the kind that Receveur had engineered in order to capture de Launay, Mézières, and the Imbert brothers. Moreover, the long-term hostility of the British to France left them unconcerned about books that slandered Frenchmen, and they gloried in the British tradition of freedom of the press, which went back to the expiration of the Licensing Act in 1695. To be sure, the press often proved to be more free in principle than in practice. Authors and publishers who offended powerful persons could be condemned in court for the crime of seditious libel. But libels flourished in the Walpole era, and they proliferated even more in the 1760s and 1770s during the agitation over John Wilkes and the American Revolution. French visitors could hardly believe the virulence of the British press when they explored the coffeehouses and bookshops of London. And they had only to step inside the shop of Boissière in St. James Street to find the works of a French libeler who outdid the English in scandalmongering: Charles Théveneau de Morande.[1]

Morande's first libel, *Le Gazetier cuirassé*, made him a rich man, the envy of every author who had left France to seek his fortune beyond the range of the Bastille. The *Mémoires secrets* reported that it had earned him a vast sum: 1,000 English guineas or about 24,000 French livres.[2] Thanks to its success, according to some notes by inspector d'Hémery, Morande lived in luxury and drove about London in a coach. Moreover, he had written a sequel, *Mémoires secrets d'une femme publique, ou essai sur les aventures de Madame la comtesse Dub***, depuis son berceau jusqu'au lit d'honneur*, which was likely to make him much richer.[3] Instead of releasing this book directly on the market, Morande prepared its way by advanced publicity. He spread the word that it would be a full-scale, tell-all biography of Mme du Barry in four volumes, complete with illustrations. At this time, early in April 1774, Mme du Barry still occupied a prominent position in Versailles as the official mistress of Louis XV. She had been roughed up badly in *Le Gazetier cuirassé*, but the new book promised to be far worse, according to rumors that reached the *Mémoires secrets*: "It is a satanic compilation. *Le Gazetier cuirassé* is like rose water in comparison with this new masterpiece."[4]

Morande had actually put the rumor mill in motion, because he meant to raise more money than ever by means of a new strategy, one that later inspired the machinations of Jacquet: extortion. In notes passed through intermediaries, he offered to destroy the entire edition for a large sum in cash and an annual pension, which would revert to his wife at his death. (D'Hémery had reported that when he fell on hard times in London, Morande could not pay his rent and had married the daughter of his landlord in order to escape debtor's prison.) The French authorities responded by sending a delegation of undercover agents, ostensibly to negotiate but in fact to kidnap Morande and carry him back to the Bastille, where he could be made to reveal the sources of his information—libels were effective, the police believed, because they contained at least a minimum of accurate information, and Morande seemed to have some well-informed sources.[5]

In fact, Morande's sources functioned so effectively that they tipped him off about the plot. Therefore, when the French agents arrived in London, he received them as if they were bona fide representatives of the foreign ministry; agreed to enter into negotiations, provided that they each advance him 30 louis (720 livres) as a token of their earnestness; and having pocketed the money, raised a hue and cry about an assassination attempt. Henchmen of the French police had infiltrated London! They were trying to murder an innocent author who had sought refuge in a country that respected the freedom of the press!

This well-prepared call for help produced a near riot among Morande's supporters—primarily a crowd of heavy-fisted journeymen printers who had no love for Frenchmen or the police. The half-dozen unmasked agents ran for their lives. One of them, the ubiquitous Receveur, was reportedly dunked in the Thames and driven nearly mad with fright. Morande then continued to prepare his manuscript for the press and went about town reading copies of letters he had sent to Chancellor Maupeou and other grandees in Versailles warning them that they soon would be buried under ignominy.[6]

Such at least was the version of the story diffused by the Parisian newsletters and printed in subsequent libels. It probably was fairly accurate, because it coincides closely with the information available from the police reports and the archives of the Ministry of Foreign Affairs. In any case, the farce played out in London made the government look still worse in Paris, and it left the French authorities in an awkward position. Having failed to abduct Morande, they needed to buy him off. But who could execute such a delicate task, overcoming Morande's justifiable suspicions while keeping everything buried in secrecy? To the makers of strategy in Versailles, there was one man who seemed perfect for this mission, one man who stood out above all others, a man of irresistible charm who was also a master of baroque plots: Pierre-Augustin Caron de Beaumarchais. Songster, musician, vaudevillian, dramatist, speculator, pamphleteer, and publisher among many other things, Beaumarchais was the next of the secret agents that the government dispatched to negotiate with the London libelers. He sailed for England at the height of his fame, but he left under a cloud, owing to the very imbroglio that had made him famous, the Goesman Affair.[7]

Louis-Valentin Goesman (or Goëzman or Goetzmann; the spelling of his name varied considerably, and his name kept changing later in his life, when he adopted a series of aliases) was a judge in the docile new parlement that Maupeou had created to replace the Parlement of Paris in 1771. To its opponents, the Maupeou court epitomized the despotism that the chancellor was inflicting on France by destroying its independent judiciary. To Beaumarchais, the court was the site where his fate would be determined. He had become entangled in a dangerously complex trial with the comte de La Blache; and if he lost his case, he would be ruined. But he could not win the case without being able to argue his side of it in a private interview with the rapporteur or magistrate designated to recommend a decision to the full court. Goesman was the rapporteur, and he refused to meet with Beaumarchais—until, after various maneuvers, Beaumarchais presented his wife with 100 louis (2,400 livres) and a watch garnished with diamonds worth another 100 louis plus a supplementary gift of 15 louis for Goesman's secretary. Mme Goesman agreed to return the bribe if the parlement ruled against Beaumarchais. It did, and the gifts were returned, except for the 15 louis, which Mme Goesman kept for herself. Beaumarchais demanded to have them back; she denied that she had kept them; and her husband retaliated by accusing Beaumarchais of calumny, which led to a second trial, more spectacular than the first.

Acting as his own lawyer, Beaumarchais defended himself in four *mémoires*, or legal briefs, one more eloquent, hilarious, and persuasive than the other. Like most judicial *mémoires*, they were printed and circulated publicly without being subjected to censorship. But unlike the others, they were literary masterpieces, as brilliant as Beaumarchais's plays. They went through many editions, captivating the public and covering the Maupeou parlement with ridicule and contempt. The parlement, embodied in the corrupt and fatuous person of Goesman, therefore stood condemned before "the tribunal of public opinion," a phrase that was coming into common use at this time.[8] In an ineffective attempt to restore its credit, it expelled Goesman. But it also punished Beaumarchais by subjecting him to a sentence of *blâme*—that is, a moral sanction, which deprived him of his civic rights. He had won acclaim as a hero, the champion of the popular resistance to the Maupeou government; but without the legal power to reverse his misfortunes, notably in an appeal against the judgment in the La Blache case, his future looked bleak. What would become of him next?

A secret agent of the government. Mme du Barry and Louis XV had been captivated like everyone else by Beaumarchais's *mémoires*. The king did not vacillate in his support of the Maupeou ministry, but in foreign relations he pursued policies of his own, known to initiates as "the king's secret," which he hid from most of the diplomats in the Ministry of Foreign Affairs. Morande's threats were the kind of thing that belonged to the domain of the king's secret, and Beaumarchais was the kind of man to cope with them—a nondiplomat, talented at intrigues, and likely to appeal to Morande because of his literary renown. Thanks to the intervention of an intermediary at court, Beaumarchais was sounded out about the possibility of a secret mission to silence Morande. He seized it instantly. If he succeeded, he knew that he could get the sentence of *blâme* reversed, and opportunities for other missions might open up for him. Soon after losing his case before the court and winning it before the public, Beaumarchais was matching wits with Morande.

Morande had learned to beware of Frenchmen bearing gifts. After escaping from Receveur and the other agents sent to kidnap him, he seemed intent on selling the *Mémoires secrets d'une femme publique* through the usual channels of the underground book trade. He had completed the printing, packed the copies into crates, and was ready to ship them off to dealers everywhere in Europe when Beaumarchais arrived in London. How Beaumarchais talked himself into Morande's presence cannot be determined, because this episode is one of the most obscure in Beaumarchais's biography. But the two men had much in common: a love of adventure, hatred of the Maupeou regime, and a wicked way with their pens. Morande was as enthralled with Beaumarchais's *mémoires* as all their other readers, and like so many others, he found Beaumarchais irresistible when he met him in person: "He is an adorable man. And I see that he does not play around with the truth," he confided to a correspondent. "He writes so beautifully that it makes me want to hang myself. Voltaire never came close to him as a stylist."[9]

Charm and literary talent did the job—not that Morande put up much resistance to making a fortune by blackmail. He agreed to suspend the shipments of the libel, all three thousand freshly printed copies, and gave Beaumarchais a copy to submit for inspection by the French authorities. Back in Versailles, Beaumarchais received authorization from Louis XV and the foreign minister to reach a final settlement. Back again in London, he now spoke as an agent of the king, thinly disguised as the chevalier de Ronac (an anagram of Caron, his family name, which probably fooled no one, but incognitos went with the job). After some bargaining, "Ronac" and Morande agreed on the sum: 32,000 livres in cash and the annuity of 4,000 livres. At an extraordinary ceremony on the outskirts of the city with Beaumarchais as a witness, Morande burned the entire edition in a lime kiln—all but one copy, which he tore in half, keeping one part and giving the other to Beaumarchais as evidence that the book had physically existed. Beaumarchais returned in triumph to France, but a few days before he could collect his reward and free himself from his legal embroilments, Louis XV died. Louis XVI soon restored the old parlements, and Beaumarchais, exonerated from the persecutions of the Maupeou era, went on to other adventures. His exploits as the chevalier de Ronac left Morande a wealthy man, aware now that he could do better by collaborating with the French authorities than by defying them. As Beaumarchais put it, he was a "poacher . . . who would make a good gamekeeper"—that is, in fact, a police spy.[10] But he also was an example to inspire the other French refugees in London, men with an equal need for money and an equally vicious way with words.

The new reign brought new opportunities for the libelers. Their favorite themes from the days of Louis XV—royal orgies and corrupt courtesans—did not apply to Louis XVI, but the young king and queen offered them another kind of target. Possibly impaired by a genital malformation (but this aspect of royal history is clouded with uncertainty), the future Louis XVI could not consummate his marriage until seven years after his wedding. Word soon spread that he was impotent; that Marie-Antoinette, driven by sexual frustration and a perverse appetite, took many lovers, women as well as men; and that the children born to her were illegitimate. These were the subjects favored by Jacquet and the scribblers in his hire. They worked over endless variations on the theme of the main libel for which Jacquet was imprisoned, *La Vie de la reine*, and they cranked out works defaming ministers, courtiers, and grandees of all sorts. Imbert de Villebon had alerted the police to forty such libels, and he came across only those that surfaced in Brussels, which was but one of the tributaries fed from the main source in London. *Le Diable dans un bénitier* identified that source with a "dépositaire" of Jacquet's manuscripts—a kind of Third Man who may have masterminded the libeling or may have been invented to throw the police off the track.[11] Whether or not Jacquet had really left behind a whole arsenal of libels, London had a large population of hungry French authors who were eager to produce more. They had Morande's example to follow and their own sources in France to supply them with fresh information. So the new ministers of Louis XVI, especially the comte de Vergennes, minister of foreign affairs, found the threat of libels to be greater than ever after Morande had been bought off and Louis XV buried. They also felt less capable of coping with it, because by 1777 the American Revolution had produced a new surge of hostility between France and Britain, which led to war in May 1778. Unable to intervene directly or to expect any help from the British, the French government found itself reduced to paying blackmail and keeping the libelers under surveillance by means of secret agents.

The agent it chose to succeed Beaumarchais was none other than his archenemy, Goesman. How this twist of fortune came to pass is impossible to say, but the archives of the foreign ministry show that by November 1780 Goesman had settled in London and was corresponding secretly with the most powerful men in Versailles. Although Beaumarchais had made a fool of him, Goesman was no idiot. The son of a bailiff in Landser, Alsace, he had studied law at the University of Strasbourg and had risen to a top position in the Alsatian judiciary (*conseiller* in the Conseil souverain d'Alsace), when, like so many talented provincials, he succumbed to the lure of Paris. He sold his office, squandered the proceeds in various projects, and by 1770 found himself trying to live in the style of a Parisian *parlementaire* without the corresponding income. He then attempted to write his way out of debt. With the help of contacts in Versailles and publishers in Switzerland he arranged to launch a *Journal diplomatique*, but it never got beyond the stage of a prospectus whose printing costs he never managed to pay. Some popular tracts on questions of public law and history did not do much better. But the excitement generated by the battle between the government and the parlements suggested that there was money to be made in a two-volume *Tableau historique, politique et juri-dique de la monarchie française*, which would explain the background to the conflict. This book never appeared because Goesman could not pay for the printing bill of volume one and failed to come up with the copy for volume two. The prospectus, however, showed that his main themes—the monarchy did not derive its authority from any ancient contract with the people; it enjoyed unlimited sovereignty; and the parlements had no legitimate claim to represent the subjects of the king—provided the kind of historical and constitutional arguments that Maupeou needed while destroying the old Parlement of Paris and creating the new one.[12]

This service, reinforced by well-placed patronage (some of it apparently from the duc d'Aiguillon), seems to have convinced Maupeou to make Goesman a councillor in his parlement. While working through a heavy caseload, Goesman managed to rent a townhouse and fill it with furniture, but he still had difficulty paying his bills. His salary did not amount to much, he claimed, and did not arrive on time. Bribes like Beaumarchais's seemed to go with the job. But Beaumarchais turned the bribery issue into a scandal that drove Goesman from office. The bill collectors then became more threatening. Goesman changed his name to "de Thurne." He moved into a furnished room, then into a succession of rooms, always one step ahead of the bailiffs. While hiding in the garrets, he turned out pamphlets—on the origins of the peerage, on the coronation of kings, on the juridical aspects of political issues—all of them anonymous and published in Holland and Switzerland. Because he now knew his way around the book trade, he sold his *Tableau historique* to a second publisher under another title. This trick worked well enough for him to copy the text by hand and to sell it, or to arrange for its publication in exchange for a share of the sales, two more times under two more titles. It finally appeared, anonymously, in 1777 as *Histoire politique du gouvernement français, ou les quatres âges de la monarchie française*, which was supposed to run to four volumes but never got beyond volume one. In short, Goesman fell into a Grub Street existence much like that of the libelers with whom he later dealt in London.[13]

Through it all, however, he maintained a façade of respectability. He was a handsome man with an imposing manner and a talent for turning a phrase. After tracking him down in Paris, one of his Swiss publishers found it impossible not to be impressed: "At last I've got hold of M. Goesman. What a man! A very handsome face, a golden tongue, and no gold in his purse."[14] Somehow from his hiding places Goesman managed to maintain contact with people in power. He had ingratiated himself in 1771 with the duc d'Aiguillon, foreign minister at that time, and in 1780 he won the confidence of Sartine, the former lieutenant general of police who had become minister of the navy and wanted to plant a spy in London who could send reports on the strategy behind the movements of the British fleet. It was a dangerous assignment, but it also was a way to escape from crippling debts. Sartine, backed by Maurepas, promised Goesman 200 louis (4,800 livres) to pay off his creditors, 4,000 livres to establish himself credibly as an Alsatian baron on a visit to London, and 12,000 a year as salary. Goesman settled in London in November 1780. During a short trip back to Paris in October 1781, he was ordered to send his secret reports to Vergennes, the foreign minister, instead of Sartine. From then until the end of his mission in July 1783, Goesman corresponded regularly with Vergennes. In his letters he struck the pose of a statesman, wise in the ways of the world, who could detect the deeper currents in events and penetrate the secret maneuvers in cabinets of the great. He also kept asking for money.[15]

Read today in the elegant setting of the Quai d'Orsay, the correspondence has a flavor of intrigue that suits the rococo style of eighteenth-century diplomacy. Goesman used two aliases—one, the baron de Thurne, for everyday activities; the other, the baron de Lerchenberg, for dealings with the French embassy in London, where he also appeared incognito. He sent his letters to Vergennes through two Parisian intermediaries located in the rue de Richelieu, one named Baudouin and the other Guillaume Larcher. When he dealt with especially sensitive subjects, he used a code: sometimes in numbers (a = 18, b = 4, etc.) and sometimes in words, most of them lofty and literary.

Poems, stanzas	explanations
Elegies	fleets, squadrons
Trial	war
Decent farmers	the Americans
The poor philosopher	the king of England
Prometheus	Franklin
Bad farmers	the administration
The good father	Adams[16]

Baudouin and Larcher forwarded the replies from Vergennes, but they never mentioned him by name and they paraphrased his messages in their own words. In this way the correspondence could pass through the normal mail as if it concerned only private individuals, and Goesman could address the foreign minister indirectly without using the formalities dictated by protocol. Vergennes probably agreed to this arrangement because he badly needed information about British affairs during the American war. After breaking diplomatic relations with Britain, France kept only a chargé d'affaires—at first, Gérard de Rayneval, later the comte de Moustier—in its London embassy, and he remained isolated. Goesman, disguised as a visiting Alsatian baron, could send reports about parliamentary debates, ministerial intrigues, and every-thing he picked up in coffeehouses. He received good pay for his services, but he took risks: another of Vergennes's informers, François Henry de La Motte, had been hanged as a spy in July 1781.

Goesman sent two or three dispatches a month, commenting at length on current events and predicting their outcome—always wrongly. Having been introduced by the bookseller Boissière to a valet of the Earl of Shelburne, he pretended to have inside information about the government formed by Shel-burne in July 1782. By the end of that year, when Vergennes was arranging the details of the peace settlement, Goesman foresaw nothing but war. He had spotted two suspicious Spaniards in a London boardinghouse who seemed intent on engineering a diplomatic revolution: Spain would switch allegiance from France to Britain; it would be rewarded with Gibraltar; and the two countries would then embark on a new campaign to win America back for George III. The Treaty of Versailles, signed on September 3, 1783, finally put paid to that absurd idea. By then Shelburne had been out of office for five months, never to return, despite Goesman's continued assurances that he would resume power at any moment. Goesman's false prophecies finally exhausted the patience of Vergennes, who complained about him in a letter to Baudouin: "He reads things hidden in the bottom of hearts and doesn't see events that take place beneath his eyes. . . . His prophecies have not been borne out by a single event."[17] The foreign minister continued to send money, how-ever, because Goesman had shifted his attention to a more urgent task, one that had obsessed Vergennes from the beginning of their correspondence: the suppression of libels.

Shortly after his arrival in London in November 1780, Goesman, like so many other travelers from France, stopped by Boissière's bookshop in St. James Street. It did not take long for Boissière to realize that the "baron de Thurne" was no ordinary tourist, because they soon were talking shop about the illegal book trade. As Goesman later recounted in his reports to Vergennes, he set out to capture Boissière's confidence in order to get information about libels. Boissière probably guessed at the game he was playing and was eager to join it, for a Frenchman with a pronounced interest in libels could always open up possibilities for fresh speculations. Having learned to read through dis-guises as the servant of a confidence man (a gambler named Matousky) and to cheat at the gaming tables of Lubeck, where he narrowly escaped hanging, this Genevan adventurer turned lackey turned gambler turned bookseller may well have felt some affinity with the fake Alsatian baron. In any case, Boissière and Goesman spent much of the next two years negotiating deals to stifle libels.[18]

As Goesman later explained in a memorandum on his undercover activities, the first book that Boissière mentioned to him was *Les Amours de Charlot et Toinette*, an obscene account of the queen's orgies with various lovers, principally the king's brother Charles, comte d'Artois, referred to sardonically as "Charlot." It was written in mock heroic verse and illustrated with plates that showed doctors examining the flaccid royal penis and the queen copulating with Artois. Boissière denied, of course, that he had any interest in this publication. He merely acted as an acquaintance of the author, whom he had promised not to name—and as a man of honor, he never broke a promise. But as a friend of Goesman, he also felt duty bound to convey a warning that the book would soon appear, though it could be cut off completely if the French government would come up with an appropriate sum. Goesman passed the message on to Vergennes; Vergennes arranged for the transfer of the money; and Goesman paid it to Boissière: 17,400 livres and a bill of exchange for 50 louis (another 1,200 livres). In return, Boissière handed over the entire edition with a receipt for the payment, duly signed and sealed and dated July 31, 1781.

I the undersigned both in my own name and as standing in for the proprietor of a work in French verse entitled *Les Amours de Charlot et Toinette*, with illustrations, together with the plates of the aforesaid prints, acknowledge that M. de Thurne has paid me for the entire edition of this work, the prints and the plates, the sum of seventeen thousand, four hundred livres in the currency of France, with a bill of exchange for fifty louis, payable by myself at Ostend on the thirtieth of the next month, promising on my word as a man of honor and subject to a penalty of damages with interest, that neither I nor the proprietor will ever cause a copy of this work to appear, as it has been sold only under the condition of its suppression. In faith of which I have signed the present document on which I have placed my seal. Done in London this 31 July 1781.

Boissière[19]

How then to get the booty back to Paris? Goesman needed to deliver the books to Lenoir as evidence that he had in fact captured the entire edition, but he feared that they might be confiscated in the British customs. Therefore he hired a fishing boat and smuggled the load of printed sheets across the Channel to Ostend, where orders awaited him so that he could pass undisturbed through the French customs to Paris. He delivered it triumphantly to Lenoir, who had it shut up in a special storeroom in the Bastille. The shipment appeared a few years later in an inventory of all the libels that Lenoir had sent to the Bastille: "*Les Amours de Charlot et Antoinette* [sic]. The complete edition. In verse and with engravings that are very insulting to the K."[20]

After returning to London and resuming his reports, Goesman always referred to this affair in the most heroic manner. He had braved dangers and overcome forbidding difficulties in order to protect the honor of his king. That was the only goal of his mission. In order to accomplish it, however, he was forced to run up debts. And at the same time, he kept discovering that more libels were about to be published by the despicable and disloyal French expatriates in London. He felt confident that he could get them destroyed, thanks to his excellent relations with Boissière. But it would cost still more to do so. In fact, the main theme in his self-congratulatory dispatches to Vergennes could be boiled down to one refrain: Send money.

Instead, as recounted in *Le Diable dans un bénitier,* Vergennes sent another agent, Alexis d'Anouilh, a spy employed by the Paris police and the naval ministry, who claimed that he could get to the heart of the problem by bribing his way into the British power structure. He had access, he said, to Richard Sheridan, the playwright, who had become an undersecretary of state for foreign affairs in 1782. Sheridan's speculation on the Covent Garden Opera had saddled him with a heavy load of debt. If encouraged by an adequate gift of louis d'or, Sheridan might persuade the British government to run the French libelers out of the country, a gesture that would have the added benefit of improving relations with France now that the American war was coming to an end. D'Anouilh knew at least enough about England—it rained a great deal there—to adopt an appropriate disguise: he traveled as an umbrella merchant. But after arriving he discovered that the English had odd notions about the liberty of the press, parliamentary government, and the appropriate size of a bribe to an undersecretary of state. Sheridan could not be had by the five thousand louis that had been allotted to d'Anouilh by the marquis de Castries, minister of the navy—or by what remained of them because d'Anouilh appropriated a great many louis for his own expenses. He therefore returned to Paris with a request for more money. De Castries responded by shipping him off to the Bastille.[21]

When interrogated, d'Anouilh failed to account for most of the money he claimed to have spent. Lenoir considered the case serious enough to require further investigation in London. But whom to send next? At this point, he called upon Receveur. Although Receveur could not speak English and his one venture to London as part of the delegation sent to kidnap Morande in 1774 had ended in disaster, he had one great advantage: he could be trusted. He had already captured so many hack writers and booksellers that he had been rewarded with the cross of Saint Louis, a distinction reserved for outstanding service to the crown. Receveur set off with a lieutenant named Barbier sometime toward the end of 1782. When he reached Calais, he decided to send Barbier ahead—perhaps, as recounted in *Le Diable dans un bénitier,* because Receveur had nearly been lynched in 1774 and he stood in danger of being hanged as a spy now that France and Britain were at war. Barbier sought out Morande, who by this time had switched from libeling to spying, and together they uncovered enough of the trail that d'Anouilh had left behind to conclude that he had never made any headway with Sheridan and had squandered his expense account on women and horses. Armed with this information, Receveur reported back to Lenoir. Lenoir finally got d'Anouilh to confess that he had hidden most of the money in order to keep it for himself. And once the police recovered it, they released him.

The need for another mission to London had not disappeared, however, because Goesman sounded an alert about a new attack on the queen, and word arrived of an additional attempt at blackmail—this one aimed at the duchesse de Bouillon by a libeler working once again through Boissière. Boissière's relations with Goesman, and Goesman's requests for money, added a further complication. Lenoir, Vergennes, and de Castries agreed on the necessity for a new man in London. But who was he to be? The obvious choice again was Receveur. He could investigate Goesman as well as the expatriates Goesman was investigating, and he could be trusted to buy off Boissière's libelers as needed. Because peace was imminent, he no longer ran a risk of being hanged, although he had to have a disguise, of course. Lenoir made him another baron, le baron de Livermont, and dispatched him to London in March 1783.

Chapter 12

Hugger-Mugger

When decked out as the baron de Livermont, Receveur traveled in style. According to his expense account, published in glorious detail in *La Police de Paris dévoilée*, he took a coach to Calais accompanied by a servant (170 livres 5 sols), crossed the Channel comfortably (a surprisingly cheap journey: 33 livres 10 sous), settled into an apartment in Jermyn Street, an elegant address close to the French embassy (376 livres 19 sous for a stay of 10 weeks), and had a suit made so that he could appear appropriately dressed for the part he was to play (224 livres.)[1] Aside from his domestic servant, he had two assistants supplied by the Paris police. The first, a tough named Humber, was designated to serve as a body guard or a kidnaper, as the occasion demanded. (Receveur still feared being lynched by a crowd or hanged as a spy if he were unmasked.) The second, Ange Goudar, a veteran libeler turned police spy, was to act as a translator and guide in order to help Receveur find his way through the world of London's Grub Street. Goudar knew it well, having retreated to London at various times in the 1750s and 1760s when he got into difficulty with the police in Paris.[2]

At this point, the story can be picked up and followed in detail from the archives of the ministry of foreign affairs. Vergennes, Lenoir, and the French diplomats in London—Gérard de Rayneval from November 1782 to February 1783, the comte de Moustier from February 1783 to May 1783, and the comte d'Adhémar thereafter—exchanged letters nearly every day, sometimes twice a day. Receveur's mission was the climax of their campaign "to annihilate the race of libelers," as they put it in their dispatches.[3] His efforts to hunt hack writers through the taverns and coffeehouses of London show how seriously the French government took libelers and the literature they produced.

Receveur had a general assignment: to discover who the libelers were and how they could be exterminated. But his immediate goal was to prevent the publication of two libels: *La Naissance du dauphin dévoilée*, another version of the queen's sex life, this time featuring her relations with her favorite, the duchesse de Polignac, and *Les Petits Soupers et les nuits de l'Hôtel Bouillon*, an account of orgies organized by the duchesse de Bouillon, which included the marquis de Castries, minister of the navy. The first appears to have been a sequel to *Les Amours de Charlot et Toinette*. Like the earlier work, it was written in verse and illustrated with obscene engravings, and it also included a selection of the nastiest *noëls* about the queen. Goesman had warned Vergennes about it early in February 1783, stressing his determination as a loyal subject of Louis XVI to prevent the publication of such an atrocity, "which compromises so terribly the glory of my masters."[4] Only a few weeks earlier he had sent the manuscript of another libel, *Réflexions politiques, physiques et morales sur la situation actuelle de la France et de ses finances*, which contained "spicy details" about sex in Versailles as well as hostile comments on the government's policies, and Vergennes apparently had agreed to buy it off.[5] So many libels, one on the heels of the other and all accompanied by demands for money, indicated that the situation was getting out of hand. Instead of commissioning Goesman to purchase the suppression of *La Naissance du dauphin*, therefore, Vergennes merely ordered him to keep an eye on the preparations for its publication. He then turned to Lenoir.

In concerting strategy with Vergennes, Lenoir warned that Goesman could not be trusted. Aside from his suspicious requests for money, he was a hothead who might make a bolt for Versailles and deliver copies of the engravings to the duchesse de Polignac. If he did so, he could ingratiate himself with a powerful protector, but Vergennes might then have to cope with a crisis in the entourage of the queen. The safest course would be to keep Goesman at bay and to send Receveur in his place to negotiate with the libelers. As a tried-and-true agent of the police who had recently gone into retirement, Receveur had no special need of money. He had proven his valor in such enterprises by capturing Jacquet, and if necessary, he could be trusted to buy off the libelers at the best price, while at the same time investigating their relations with Goesman.[6] Vergennes agreed completely. By return messenger he authorized Lenoir to dispatch Receveur to London and stressed that his mission should be kept secret from Goesman. He also instructed Moustier in London to provide Receveur with all necessary support and to send the most delicate information by private letters, which would be kept confidential unlike his formal dispatches, which Vergennes read to the King's Council, normally in the presence of the king himself.[7]

Such was the origin of Receveur's mission to London. While Vergennes and Lenoir prepared it, Goesman continued to send warnings about the latest libels against the queen, accompanied by protests about his own devotion to the crown: "I would be devastated if this affair went wrong and if I saw the august persons of my masters displayed openly before the public." He wanted to handle the negotiations himself and could not understand why he had been told to limit his role to surveillance. If they failed to prevent *La Naissance du dauphin dévoilée* from appearing, he warned, they might in the future be blamed by the dauphin for permitting doubts about his legitimacy to be expressed in public. Judging from some dark hints dropped by Boissière, his intermediary in all dealings with the libelers, Goesman believed that the whole business resulted from a court intrigue—one that could catapult Vergennes from office, though he left the foreign minister to make that reflection himself.[8]

Although *La Naissance du dauphin dévoilée* was the principal object of Receveur's mission, *Les Petits Soupers et les nuits de l'Hôtel Bouillon* also required urgent attention. On December 7, 1782, the duchesse de Bouillon had received a printed prospectus for it along with a letter demanding a blackmail payment. She alerted the police; Lenoir informed Vergennes; and Vergennes agreed to pay for the suppression of both libels. In his instructions to Receveur, Lenoir authorized him to spend up to 200 guineas to prevent the publication of *La Naissance du dauphin dévoilée* and up to 150 guineas for the same purpose in the case of *Les Petits Soupers*. (As an English guinea was then worth slightly more than a French louis d'or, or 24 livres, these were quite large sums—the equivalent of ten years' wages for a semi-skilled laborer in order to suppress *La Naissance du dauphin dévoilée* alone.) If the libelers negotiating through Boissière were to demand more, Receveur was to get clearance from Paris to go beyond that limit. The final contract should contain a penalty clause that would commit the libelers to pay back three times the money they had received in case any copy of the books should ever appear.[9]

Immediately after arriving in London on March 13, 1783, Receveur reported to Moustier in order to concert strategy and to set up lines of communication with France. He especially needed to be briefed about the customs of the natives, Moustier explained in a letter to Vergennes, because London was strange territory when seen from the perspective of a Parisian police inspector. Ministers could not simply issue orders to arrest a writer, no matter how impudently he had attacked them. Everything had to be done according to the letter of the law, and the law did not favor the government. The example of John Wilkes proved that a demagogue could publish the most outrageous things about the king himself and get off scot-free. Moreover, the current ministry, led by Lord Shelburne, could not be counted on for help, because it might collapse at any moment: the English had a curious habit of overthrowing governments by outvoting them in Parliament. In fact, the only feasible way to hunt down the libelers was to enlist one of their own kind, someone with inside knowledge of who they were and how they operated. Moustier had recently made contact with just the man they needed, a man with a very black past but a very strong desire to cleanse his name by cooperating with the embassy: Charles Théveneau de Morande. That name, however, filled Receveur with horror. He explained that of all people, Morande was the one he most wanted to avoid. They were old enemies. Receveur had participated in the abortive attempt to kidnap Morande nine years earlier and was lucky to have escaped from it alive. Nonetheless, Moustier insisted, they had to find some means to suppress the hideous libel aimed against the queen, and he could sound Morande out about the possibility of collaborating secretly with a Parisian police agent. As a cover, they could say that Receveur had come to offer confidential advice to the British government about a plan to organize the London police according to the Parisian model. Morande had already submitted such a plan to his contacts in the Shelburne ministry, and his eagerness to win a pardon from Vergennes might make him willing to overlook the earlier conflict with Receveur.[10]

The archenemies met and made peace on March 17. Morande promised to guide Receveur around London, furnishing details about all the French expatriates and their hiding places. According to the messages sent through the diplomatic pouch, it was agreed that Receveur would send regular reports to Lenoir, while Moustier corresponded with Vergennes. Vergennes and Lenoir could then combine operations in France, and the French embassy in London would cooperate with the Parisian police in a strategy that involved three lines of attack: (1) they would try to find some way to get the French libelers condemned in British courts; (2) they would accumulate information about the libelers in a long-term campaign to destroy their trade, primarily by making examples of the worst offenders; and (3) they would begin negotiations to buy off the libels that were about to be published. The letters exchanged between London and Paris at this time never mentioned plots to kidnap or assassinate the libelers, although Moustier expressed his desire to have them hanged or sent to the galleys, and his successor, Adhémar, did not rule out the use of force. But no matter what their tactics, the undercover agents kept running into obstacles. One theme stood out increasingly in the letters sent from London: it was not easy to police French literature in England.[11]

Conspicuously absent from this plan was the key player in the earlier attempts to suppress the libels: Goesman alias de Thurne. Not only was Receveur's mission kept secret from him, but he became an object of investigation himself. Moustier suspected from the outset that he was playing each side against the other,[12] and this suspicion hardened into a conviction as Morande gained influence in the French embassy. Morande had provided inside information about the libel trade since 1774, when he had made a fortune by abandoning it. Moustier consulted him frequently and found him so helpful as to warrant absolution for the sins of his past. When Adhémar succeeded Moustier as ambassador, he concurred with this view. Morande won him over in the first of many clandestine consultations and soon was back on the French payroll as an undercover agent, supplying the foreign ministry with the information about British shipping and politics that it had earlier sought from Goesman. Meanwhile, he undercut Goesman's position by denouncing his relations with Boissière. As Morande described it, Boissière's operation was a publishing business compounded by a blackmail racket. Boissière directed a stable of authors, set them to work on themes of his choosing, supplied them with essential information, negotiated for them in the blackmailing, and extracted the best terms by refusing to deal with anyone except Goesman. In return, Goesman took a cut in the profits, and his handlers in the rue de Richelieu probably did the same.[13]

Although this view prevailed in the French embassy, Receveur and his men never came up with enough evidence to confirm it. Guided by directions from Morande, they combed through all "the slums and tawdry cafés" in literary London.[14] They collected samples of handwriting for comparison with the blackmail notes. They staked out tables at Grobetty's, Strangter's, and the Café d'Orange, where the libelers liked to gather. In the end, they identified thirty-nine suspicious Frenchmen whose dossiers eventually came to rest in the police archives at the Bastille. But Receveur failed to extract anything from his most promising suspect, an Irish priest named Landis, who had collaborated and then quarreled with Goesman. An adventurer who called himself the "baron de Navan" (London was full of fake French barons) proved to be equally disappointing, despite some dubious dealings with Goesman. That Goesman had made contact with such characters was not incriminating in itself, because he supposedly had been investigating the same milieu for the same purpose—to identify the authors hidden behind Boissière. Moreover, the undercover agents who succeeded him never got further than he did. Instead, they only sent alarm signals coursing through the colony of French expatriates; and the rumors soon reached Goesman.[15]

On April 4 he sent a distraught letter to Vergennes. He had learned that a police inspector was trying to buy off the libelers behind his back—an inspector working with Morande! Yet Morande had extorted hundreds of louis d'or from the French government by libeling, while he, Goesman, had loyally done everything in his power to prevent the libels from appearing. He could not fathom the reason for this strange change in his treatment. But if he had fallen out of favor, Vergennes should be under no illusion about the role of Boissière. Boissière did not produce books; he merely sold them. Although he had access to the authors of the libels, he acted only as a middleman. He had confidence in Goesman, as the successful negotiations over *Les Amours de Charlot et Toinette* had demonstrated, but he would not trust any new negotiator, especially not anyone sent by the Parisian police. In short, there was no way for the police to reach the libelers, except through Boissière, and there was no way for the French government to deal with Boissière, except through Goesman.

Meanwhile, Receveur's attempts to flush the libelers from their hiding places spread consternation among them, too. They feared kidnaping or some other assault like the attempt on Morande in 1774, and they defended themselves in the same way—by exposing the French agents to the potential fury of a London crowd. On April 7 they printed the broadside "An Alarm Bell Against French Spies" and distributed hundreds of copies in the streets.[16] As explained in Chapter 2, this coup uncovered Receveur's disguise, revealed the nature of his mission, and called on Londoners to rise up against the threat of French despotism on the home front, while at the same time it announced the imminent publication of three more libels.

Receveur reported that after this exposure, he feared for his life.[17] The threat of lynching probably was even greater than in 1774, for by 1783 the American Revolution had radicalized street sentiments in favor of liberty, the Anglo-French war had fanned the Londoners' hatred for France, and the combustibility of London crowds, evident since the Wilkite agitation of the 1760s, had been confirmed by the Gordon Riots of 1780. In fact, no riot broke out, but Receveur retreated for a while to the safety of his headquarters in Jermyn Street, and Moustier fretted that he, too, had been compromised.

Moustier's reaction, expounded in a long letter to Vergennes of April 11, showed that Receveur's mission was foundering. Goesman now knew all about it and had actually tried to frighten Receveur into returning to France by warning him of the threat to his life. Goesman had also passed on information that *La Naissance du dauphin dévoilée* really existed. He had seen a copy of an early draft in Boissière's shop. It contained material from previous libels, which was to be reworked and published with prints run off from some old plates. Moreover, new libels were already being prepared. Boissière had a whole gang of writers at his disposal in what he referred to grandly as a "literary society," and these hacks could continue endlessly to recycle horrible stories about the king and queen. To buy them off would only encourage them to produce more, yet there seemed to be no alternative—and no way even to succeed in submitting to extortion, except through Goesman and Boissière. Receveur's investigation had gone nowhere. He and Moustier felt baffled. In fact their task, as they now saw it, looked "impossible."

Some of this discouragement derived from failure in the second line of attack against the libelers: the attempt to have them condemned in English courts. Moustier had applied this strategy primarily in his campaign against *Les Petits Soupers et les nuits de l'Hôtel Bouillon*, which offered the best target for civil or criminal prosecution. By mid-March it had appeared in print, so legal action might be brought in the name of the injured party, the duchesse de Bouillon. But could British law be invoked by a non-British subject? This was the sticking point in a series of memoirs that Moustier commissioned from the best legal talent he could find in London. The first opinion he received, from Lord Barrington, warned that the case would never hold up in a London court because the offense had taken place in England and the duchess lived in France, outside the range of English law.[18] Moustier then set two lawyers to work, looking for a legal way around this difficulty. The first, Thomas Evans, sent a lengthy memorandum, which went over every aspect of the affair and concluded that nothing could be accomplished in a civil lawsuit. He recommended a policy of "silent contempt," which, as the French saw it, seemed thoroughly British and completely unacceptable.[19] The second, Edward Bearcroft, concentrated on the crime of extortion and came to the same conclusion concerning the possibilities of a criminal prosecution.[20] All this English legalese, sent in the original and translated more or less well by Vergennes's staff, probably sounded strange in the foreign office at Versailles. Morande tried his hand at making sense of the situation in a memorandum that explained the background of the case: by commissioning obscene works from impoverished hacks—"miserable wretches who will do anything to escape hunger and need"—Boissière had organized a blackmail racket and therefore could be prosecuted as a criminal.[21]

But how exactly could this be done? The clearest interpretation of the problem actually came from Goesman, who was a man of the law himself and knew how to make English jurisprudence intelligible to French diplomats. In a memorandum of his own, he explained that in England a criminal prosecution for libel had first to go to what the natives called a "grand juré," which would vote on something known as an "indictment." If the vote went against the accused, the case would be tried before a "petit juré," which would make the final decision as to guilt or innocence. The trial could generate a great deal of damaging publicity because it would take place in public, the plaintiff would have to appear in person, and the procedure would involve the testimony of witnesses along with debate about some nasty pieces of evidence. Public figures in England preferred to let libels run their course rather than to be exposed to such an ordeal, compounded by reports in the press. The only feasible option for the duchesse de Bouillon was a civil suit in which she might be able to have herself represented by someone else charged with her power of attorney.[22]

Although this conclusion seemed convincing in London, it looked less attractive from the perspective of Versailles. The duchesse de Bouillon belonged to one of the greatest families in France. From a distinguished German family herself, she had married the only surviving son of the sixth duke, who was also prince de Turenne and a maréchal de camp. Her husband, the seventh duke, was a physical wreck, incapable of procreating. She lived separately from him in the Hôtel Bouillon in Paris and was known to have taken a series of lovers, who were raked over mercilessly, along with the decrepit duke, in *Les Petits Soupers et les nuits de l'Hôtel Bouillon*. Vergennes was determined to prevent such a work from circulating in France. Not only had the duchess demanded its suppression, but rumors connected with its publication in England could damage the delicate network of names and dignities that composed a power system in France. Perhaps, however, the accusation of libel could be attached to someone with no dignity at all. While describing the orgies in the Hôtel Bouillon, *Les Petits Soupers* made fun of the duchess's chambermaid, an old woman named Bours, who supposedly cavorted in the nude with a hairy monk in an exhibitionistic performance before the duchess, which the libeler dubbed "the dance of the bear." As presented in the libel, the dance added an element of plebeian hilarity to the pleasures enjoyed by the duchess and her lovers, including the marquis de Castries, who was also involved in the campaign to exterminate the libelers in his capacity as minister of the navy.[23] If the complaint of slander could be made in the name of the demoiselle Bours, perhaps the case could be settled without sullying the name of the duchesse de Bouillon.

Lenoir proposed this strategy to the duchesse de Bouillon at the end of March. Despite her anxiety about the whole affair, he informed Vergennes, she agreed to have demoiselle Bours sign a "procuration," giving power of attorney to have the case prosecuted in her absence in an English court. With Vergennes's approval, Moustier called in another lawyer to set the case in motion—and received another cold dash of legal advice: the "procuration" would not work; to prosecute the case, demoiselle Bours would have to take up residence in England. But if they could take Boissière to court, they might overwhelm him with enough legal expenses to drive him out of business. Vergennes and Lenoir reassessed the situation a month later, after Moustier's lawyer had done more work on the possibility of a civil suit. The chambermaid option now looked unfeasible to them. English law simply did not provide adequate protection against slander. So, they decided, it had to be changed—by an act of Parliament.[24]

The idea of the French foreign minister and the Parisian police chief combining to improve England's legal system may seem odd, but it had hovered in the background of Vergennes's policies for nearly a year. D'Anouilh had persuaded him in mid-1782 that a majority of British MPs could be brought around to vote for the reforms desired by France if enough palms were greased. In view of the venality in the unreformed Parliament, this notion was not preposterous.[25] And now that peace had been restored, Vergennes could hope for more cooperation from the British, especially as the new government installed in April 1783 included pro-French ministers like Charles James Fox and seemed ready to lend a sympathetic ear. The French embassy in London therefore abandoned its plans for a lawsuit and came up with a "Proposal for a Bill to remedy the license of libels in England." The proposed statute would make English residents liable for slanderous attacks against foreigners, and the English version of the five-page text explained in a footnote that it was aimed squarely at "Boissière, a French book seller in St. James's Street, the known agent of every distressed adventurer."[26] Moustier raised this possibility with Fox early in May, just before ending his tour as the French chargé d'affaires. Fox claimed that English law provided all that was needed to get the libelers behind bars, where they belonged, but he did not grasp the complexity of the legal situation, according to Moustier's report of their conversation. So Moustier enlightened him with a little lecture on British jurisprudence and the superior ways of law enforcement in France.

M. Fox is not much of a jurist, but I am not unhappy with the fact that he is inclined to believe that it is necessary to take legal action and to make an example [of some individuals]. I merely told him that I wanted a bill ad hoc and that the common law did not suffice for me. . . . It would be a good thing if a [statutory] law existed, if only to obviate the necessity of buying off these horrors at a high price. . . . The race of French libelers here is extraordinarily impudent. It will always be very important that the sale of these works in France should be punished by the galleys and their composition by hanging.[27]

To hunt down libels in London was a tedious business, Moustier complained. It had more than doubled his workload. But by the end of May he had returned to France and Adhémar had taken his place, not as a chargé d'affaires but rather as a full-fledged ambassador with his own ideas about how to deal with libelers. Adhémar did not reject the notion of extracting a French-styled bill from Parliament. On the contrary, he pursued it, and Vergennes continued to favor the idea. But by November he and Vergennes had decided it was unworkable. A proposed bill had to be made public and debated in Parliament, Adhémar explained in his last dispatch on the subject, and the public, or rather "the rabble," would not stand for it.[28]

There remained one final means of suppressing the libels: bribery. Receveur was authorized to buy off the authors of *La Naissance du dauphin dévoilée* and *Les Petits Soupers et les nuits de l'Hôtel Bouillon* as soon as he arrived in London. But he quickly discovered that he could not purchase the non-publication of a slanderous book as easily as he had bought his new English suit of clothes. The libelers refused to be lured from their hiding places behind Boissière, and Receveur's attempts to make contact with them embroiled him in endless intrigues, some designed merely to trip him up, for the libelers did not know whether he had come to negotiate or to assassinate. Although it is difficult to discover exactly what happened, it seems that he eventually managed to enter into some negotiations and that the libelers came up with prices. In his final report to Lenoir, written in June after his return to Paris, Receveur summarized their demands as follows:

700 louis: *La Naissance du dauphin,* the *noëls* and the prints announced by sieur Goesman, who should know the author. Plus

Les Passe-temps d'Antoinette et *Les Amours du vizir Vergennes* by the author of the *Petits Soupers.*

600 louis: *Les Rois de France régénérés par les princesses de la maison d'Autriche* with prints, by Lafitte de Pelleport[29]

These prices went far beyond those that Receveur had been authorized to pay. They involved several works that had not existed before he set out for London or that might not exist at all, because they could be nothing more than projects dangled in front of the French in the hope of eliciting more money. By demanding so much, the libelers had overplayed their hand. To learn how they had played it, one must go back to Receveur's first encounters with them in March 1783.

Receveur got possession of some material—manuscripts, proofs, or sample copies—provided by the libelers, although he never managed to negotiate directly with them. Moustier forwarded it to Paris, along with explanations about the difficulty of entering into pourparlers: "We have to deal with rogues retrenched behind the English constitution."[30] The exact nature of these texts is difficult to determine because Moustier did not identify them by title, and, in any case, the libelers frequently changed the titles of their works as they recycled their copy and revised their tactics.[31] But some version of the libels had to reach Vergennes in Versailles so that he could inspect them before agreeing to pay for their suppression. He refused to consider paying anything for *Les Amours du vizir Vergennes*, because he scorned the slander directed against himself.[32] But he found *Les Petits Soupers et les nuits de l'Hôtel Bouillon* poisonous enough, after reading it, to confirm his decision to pay for its destruction, and he sent additional funds to reinforce Receveur's efforts to keep it and other such works off the market.[33] Lenoir had a similar reaction when he read the texts. Although hardened by the reports he received every day about every variety of vice in Paris, he felt profoundly shocked by the libels: "I shall never get over the indignation that I felt at all the horrors I saw [in them]."[34] The French authorities were therefore willing to be blackmailed, but did they succeed?

According to the well-informed account in *La Police de Paris dévoilée*, the bidding for *Les Petits Soupers et les nuits de l'Hôtel Bouillon* broke down after Boissière refused an offer of 150 louis.[35] Whether Receveur felt unauthorized to go beyond that limit or the additional funds from Vergennes failed to arrive on time, Boissière proved that the demand for 175 louis was no bluff, because he put the book on sale. Receveur eventually bought six copies, which he sent to Lenoir.[36] And the broadside, "An Alarm-Bell Against French Spies," provided excellent publicity for it while exposing Receveur's secret mission. *Les Petits Soupers* could be bought at Boissière's bookshop and two other outlets in London, the broadside proclaimed. But what of the other two works it mentioned, *Les Passe-temps d'Antoinette* and *Les Amours du vizir de Vergennes*? By announcing that they were currently being printed in London, it sent an implicit warning that they, too, would soon be published if Receveur did not come up with enough money to suppress them. The publication of *Les Petits Soupers* proved that the libelers meant business. In retrospect, it looks like a strategic move in a game of bidding and bluffing. Certainly the libelers were playing for high stakes—seven hundred louis for a set of three libels, *La Naissance du Dauphin dévoilée*, *Les Passe-temps d'Antoinette*, and *Les Amours du vizir de Vergennes*, according to a report by Receveur.[37] Although their threatened attack on Vergennes got nowhere and never was printed, their projects for slandering the queen continued to be taken seriously in Versailles. In directing the game plan from the ministry of foreign affairs, however, Vergennes faced a problem: he could not easily distinguish threats from feints—genuine works in progress from mere titles invented to see whether they would elicit a response. When he dispatched Receveur to London, he made the suppression of *La Naissance du dauphin dévoilée* the top priority of the mission. Goesman saw a preliminary draft of it, along with a set of illustrations, in Boissière's shop in April: so it really existed.[38] But it seemed to disappear in the profusion of works that cropped up under various titles in the letters exchanged during the next two months: *Les Passe-temps d'Antoinette, Amuse-ments d'Antoinette, Soirées de la reine*, and *Les Rois de France régénérés par les princesses de la maison d'Autriche*. Of these, *Les Passe-temps* looked like the most serious project. It could have been a reworked version of material intended for *La Naissance du dauphin dévoilée* or a new libel, announced before it was written, in order to capitalize on the French government's eager-ness to suppress the earlier libels. But whatever the real as opposed to the feigned threats of the libelers, the government never succeeded in buying what they offered.[39]

Not, however, for lack of trying. Receveur's letters read like a series of lamentations about his inability to make contact with the libelers. After seven weeks of investigation, he sent a long report about all the French expatriates he had been able to unearth, pointing out the likeliest suspects. But Vergennes found it disappointing, and Lenoir spotted several false leads, including one that involved a supposed libeler who was actually a straw man invented by another.[40] Meanwhile, Goesman continued to send missives arguing for a strategy that undercut Receveur's. After the publication of "An Alarm-Bell," he insisted, every Frenchman in London had been alerted to the secret mission of the French police. Some of them tried to take advantage of the situation by announcing new libels that did not exist and by leading the French agents down all sorts of blind alleys. Boissière—a scoundrel, to be sure, but the only person who had access to the true libelers—would never deal with Receveur. In fact, he feared that Receveur would kidnap or assassinate him. He carried a pistol during the day and kept an armed guard in his bedroom at night. Goes-man was the only person whom he would trust, thanks to the confidence built up between them during their earlier transactions. As a token of this confi-dence, Boissière had just given him an "objet majeur," one so important that Goesman did not want to mention it by name and would only deliver it in person to the foreign minister in Versailles. The conclusion was clear: Vergen-nes should summon Receveur back to Paris and leave the whole business in Goesman's capable hands.[41]

By mid-May, this argument began to sound convincing. Receveur was foundering; it seemed that Goesman might turn out to be loyal after all; and it looked as though the two fake barons would collide while pursuing cross-purposes in London. The collision took place on May 18. As Receveur described it in a long report on his activities, he had felt increasingly frustrated by his inability to make contact with the libelers.[42] In France, he explained, you simply armed yourself with an order of the king, broke into an apartment, and arrested an author, and if you found enough evidence, you got him con-demned. In England, they tied up everything in legalities. In fact, a work that was obviously libelous in France would not pass as a libel in an English court. What, under such conditions, could a French inspector do? Receveur had tried everything. The French expatriates, a swarm of poisonous "insects," had unmasked him and led him by the nose in a chase after books that might be imaginary and writers who might be straw men. Fed up at last with being forced to play the fool, he had provoked a confrontation with Goesman on the evening of May 18. By collaborating behind his back with Boissière, Goesman had deflected all of Receveur's attempts to enter into negotiations with the libelers. So Receveur demanded that Goesman take him to Boissière's shop or face the consequences of refusing. Intimidated by this threat, Goesman agreed. But on the following day, he returned and made a furious scene: How did Receveur dare to challenge his devotion to the crown? He would seek justice by appealing over the head of the police to the king himself. Far from bending before this tirade, Receveur stood firm and forced Goesman to take him immediately to Boissière.

Another confrontation followed, this time in the bookshop. Boissière, "trembling all over," claimed that he knew nothing about the libels. What! Receveur replied (all this according to his report, written partly in dialogue), you deny that you showed Goesman, who is standing here as a witness, the text and plates of a horrible attack on the queen of France and that you authorized him to inform the French government that two other such works were about to appear? "I don't say that," Boissière replied, his eyes fixed on the ground. "Well, then," Receveur shot back. "If you want to sell these horrors to me, I will buy them, ipso facto. I have money." But Boissière claimed that he had no libels at his disposal and refused to say anything more. Receveur then repaired to the French embassy, where he persuaded Moustier to order Goesman to make one last attempt to extract a response from Boissière: Would he or would he not sell the libels? Goesman obeyed and returned with Boissière's final answer: "Monsieur, I have nothing more to say. Even if I wanted to [talk], I would not be able to. I haven't seen the authors, and I am not attempting to see them." In the face of such stonewalling, Receveur decided there was nothing more to do except return to Paris.

Receveur submitted this report not to Moustier, who had just gone back to France himself, but to his successor, Adhémar, who was a diplomat of a different stripe. Harsh and haughty, he did not want to have anything to do with undercover agents from the Paris police and hack writers from the French colony in London. The only way to treat this "rabble," he wrote in one of his first dispatches to Vergennes, was to despise and ignore them.[43] Vergennes, however, reminded him that the most important objective was to prevent scandalous works from reaching French readers; so Adhémar continued the campaign against the libelers, though without much conviction. Rather than deal with Boissière, who by now had been frightened out of the picture, he tried to trap the libelers into lawsuits in the London courts; but that strategy failed, as already explained. Meanwhile, Receveur went back to Paris, complaining in more letters and memos that the strategy of bribery also would not work. Lenoir and Vergennes were surprised that he had returned without their authorization, but he claimed that Adhémar had given him leave. Adhémar, now worried about exceeding his own orders, insisted that he had done no such thing and that Receveur wanted to get out of England as quickly as possible because he was incapable of accomplishing anything at all: "His trip was totally useless."[44] The recriminations continued to accumulate in the papers of the foreign ministry, but they added nothing to modify the conclusion that had long been clear: Receveur's mission was a colossal failure. After submitting an expense account that came to 8,380 livres, he went back into retirement. The account did not include an additional 780 livres, which represented the value of a snuffbox that had been stolen from him in London, probably by some quick-fingered libeler. But he hoped to receive compensation from that last indignity: "The magistrate is requested to take it into consideration."[45]

Receveur's disappearance left the field open for Goesman. After the collapse of the negotiations with Boissière, he devoted most of his letters to reestablishing his credibility as a loyal agent and reiterating his requests for money. His fondest desire, he kept insisting, was to pay off the debts he had accumulated in London and return to France. The mysterious "major object" that he had announced turned out to be an illuminated copy of *Les Amours de Charlot et Toinette*, which had remained in the hands of Boissière and which Goesman turned over to the French embassy. The recovery of this volume may have reaffirmed Vergennes's faith in Goesman's integrity, but it hardly reinforced the notion that the libelers could be trusted, for Boissière had promised that every last copy of that libel had been destroyed. Once assured that "this odious obscenity"[46] had safely arrived in France, Vergennes granted permission for Goesman to return and agreed to pay off his debts, which amounted to many thousands of livres in addition to the sums that had already been forwarded to him by the middlemen in the rue de Richelieu—a total of 18,296 livres. By the end of August, Goesman had settled in Versailles and was lobbying for more money. At that point, he seems to have fallen back again on hack writing. What he did during the next ten years remains unclear, but he got into more trouble during the Revolution. On July 25, 1794, in one of the last "batches" of the Great Terror, he was guillotined, along with a truly great writer, André Chénier.[47]

With Goesman gone in the summer of 1783, Morande took over as the main counselor on libeling in the French embassy. He managed to ingratiate himself with Adhémar during an extraordinary private interview, where he confessed all his sins, insisted that his own libels had never offended any "sacred beings" but only ordinary individuals, swore that he could provide important information to the crown, and pleaded for forgiveness, tears streaming down his cheek. Adhémar was impressed: "This is no ordinary sort of man. He is clever and knowledgeable about local conditions. . . . He is hated by his former comrades and is suspect in the eyes of their gang."[48] With Vergennes's approval, Morande then regained the good graces of the French foreign ministry and served it as a spy for the next five years while at the same time taking over the editorship of the *Courrier de l'Europe*. In London, however, he continued to be known as a libeler and was even held up to ridicule in a caricature of the English variety.

By 1784, therefore, the situation in London had been transformed. Moustier, Receveur, and Goesman had disappeared. Boissière had been frightened into the background. Adhémar, who was directing policy from the French embassy, had no inclination to bargain with the libelers, and Morande, who was advising him, had every reason to denounce them. The libelers did not stop libeling, of course. But they had no opposite number with whom to play their old games. In frustration, they produced a libel against the government's attempts to stamp out libeling: *Le Diable dans un bénitier*. It was a diabolical work by the most talented libeler of them all: Anne Gédéon Lafitte, marquis de Pelleport.

THE FRENCH LAWYER *in London*.

THE BODY SOUL & MIND OF THE GAZETIER CUIRASSE

Figure 31. An English caricature of Morande. (Yale University Library)

Chapter 13
Entrapment

Anne-Gédéon Lafitte, marquis de Pelleport, was a scoundrel, all the sources agree. He was a bad hat, a blackguard, a thoroughly wicked ne'er-do-well, and a very talented writer. But who can judge character at a distance of more than two centuries? It may be best to renounce any attempt to see inside his soul and to quote his dossier from the archives of the police.

He is the son of a gentleman attached to Monsieur [the king's brother, the comte de Provence]. . . . He was expelled from two regiments, Beauce and Isle-de-France, in which he served in India. At the demand of his family, he was imprisoned four or five times by order of the king for dishonorable atrocities. He got married in Switzerland, where he wandered about for two years. . . . He is a graduate of the Ecole militaire—not the best it has turned out. He has two brothers who were trained there, too, and who like him received unpleasant discharges from the regiments in which they had been placed.[1]

In short, Pelleport was a déclassé. Born into an aristocratic family, he had sunk into the ranks of the libelers after an unsuccessful career in the army and enough dishonorable conduct to have done time in prison at the request of his parents.

Some material culled from other sources fills out the picture.[2] According to police reports summarized in *La Bastille dévoilée* and the memoirs of his close friend, Jacques-Pierre Brissot, Pelleport was born in Stenay, a small town near Verdun, in 1754. Although his family belonged to the ancient aristocracy of the sword, it had very little money, and what little he hoped to inherit disappeared after his mother died and his father married the widow of a local innkeeper, who would have nothing to do with her itinerant stepson. Pelleport's first travels took him as far as Mauritius and perhaps Pondicherry with two regiments of troops assigned to protect French outposts in India. Exactly when or why he was dishonorably discharged cannot be determined, but by the mid-1770s he had become a student at the Ecole militaire in Paris. Like many young provincials, including Brissot whom he got to know at this time, he succumbed to the attraction of the world of letters. The cult of the writer—the militant philosophe and the novelist who could move millions with a stroke of their pens—came to a climax in 1778 when Voltaire and Rousseau died at the height of their fame. In 1779 Pelleport left Paris, abandoning the prospect of a military career, and set off for the Switzerland of Voltaire and Rousseau, where he hoped to find employment in one of the publishing houses that had produced their works. He traveled to Geneva, Yverdon, and Neuchâtel, but managed only to seduce a chambermaid to the wife of Pierre-Alexandre DuPeyrou, Rousseau's Swiss protector. They eventually married and settled in the Jura mountain town of Le Locle. Pelleport worked there for two years as a tutor in the household of a manufacturer, and his wife bore him two children. He abandoned his family sometime in 1782. By 1783, after a brief stint of employment in The Hague, he was in London, living miserably from tutoring, journalism, libels, and attempts at blackmail.

The marks left by this experience on Pelleport's inner life cannot be known, but they can be surmised from an autobiographical novel, *Les Bohémiens*, which he published in 1790 and which described every phase of his career. He appears in the narrative as a young man with a noble pedigree and an empty purse. Hoping to capitalize on his name, he seeks out a family friend in Versailles. But he finds it impossible to break into the world of patronage and privilege. Disgusted by the system and his own attempt to exploit it, he resolves to become an adventurer.

A ray from the sun of justice penetrated into my heart, made liberty bloom within it, . . . and the shackles of society collapsed at my feet. I said farewell to fortune, and I began to exist . . . I said I will roam the earth, and the barriers of servitude gave way before me. In vain do the despot and his guards police the borders of their empire. I slipped away, like a beaver from a hunter.[3]

Where did Pelleport find his inspiration? From a drifter like himself: Jean-Jacques Rousseau: "And thou who dared to wish equality restored on earth, virtuous citizen of despicable Geneva, thou who dared to expose to men the secret of their tyrants, receive the incense that I will burn on your altar, and from the height of the empyrean guide my steps and my sentiments."[4]

Of course, invocations to Rousseau can be found everywhere in the late eighteenth century, and Pelleport undercut this rhetorical outburst in later sections of the novel, which are shamelessly obscene. But there is a note of authenticity in his prayer to Jean-Jacques. Eighteenth-century Rousseauism was a complicated phenomenon. It appealed to aristocrats as well as obscure provincials, and it was broad and deep enough to inspire the introspection of a libeler trying to make sense of his place in the world.

Pelleport mentioned other sources of inspiration in his bildungsroman:

Don Quixote, the book that opened his eyes to the glories of literature, followed by Ovid, Virgil, and Horace. The hero of the novel, an obviously fictionalized version of Pelleport, enjoyed a happy childhood in Stenay until his mother died, his nasty stepmother took over the house, and he was sent off to school. There he learned to love the classics, thanks to an abbé who befriended him and taught ancient literature in a spirit of pure paganism. That experience also turned into a lesson about literature and liberty, because jealous colleagues denounced the abbé to the school's director for spreading unorthodox ideas about revolutionary Romans. (As Pelleport put it, they persuaded the director, an ignoramus, that Brutus and Cassius were "rebels who conspired against the king in some Parisian garret.")[5] The abbé was dismissed; and as he took to the road, he left a few Latin books with his favorite student as a goodbye gift. Soon afterward the hero of the novel was on the road himself, drifting from regiment to regiment, serving for a while in India, returning to the Ecole militaire, picking up jobs in Switzerland, and landing in London in the company of other dropouts like Morande, Brissot, and the journalists of the *Courrier de l'Europe*. Every stop in this fictional itinerary corresponded to a stage in Pelleport's life. And the way he assimilated it all is suggested by the tone of the narrative, which shifts from satire and ribaldry to outbursts against social injustice and passages of lyrical poetry. The chief libeler of London had a formidable literary talent. But what exactly did he write?

Pelleport appeared only gradually in the sights of the Parisian police as they attempted to track down the publication of libels. At first they could not see beyond the bookshop of Boissière and the blizzard of titles he announced. But eventually they came to suspect Pelleport of having a hand in virtually everything turned out by the French expatriates during the early 1780s.[6] It is still difficult to determine the full extent of his publications because he never attached his name to anything. Moreover, he plagiarized shamelessly or cobbled together texts from many sources in a manner typical of libelers, and in order to attribute works to him one must rely in part on recognizing quirks in his style—a tendency to interrupt narrative passages with long digressions, to scatter bits of poetry and dialogue through his prose, and to step out of a third-person narration in the manner of Laurence Sterne by addressing the reader in the first person. Considering all the available evidence, it seems certain that he wrote *Les Petits Soupers et les nuits de l'Hôtel Bouillon* and *Le Diable dans un bénitier*; he may have written *Les Amours de Charlot et Toinette*; he probably wrote *La Naissance du dauphin dévoilée*; and he at least sketched outlines for its sequels, *Les Passe-temps d'Antoinette*, *Les Rois de France régénérés par les princesses de la maison d'Autriche*, and *Les Amours du vizir de Vergennes*, though they probably were not published. Contrary to Morande's biographer,

I believe that Pelleport, not Morande, wrote *La Gazette noire par un homme qui n'est pas blanc* (1784), though in fact he probably composed only the first forty-eight pages and lifted most of the rest from other libels.[7] He also wrote all or most of a similar libel, *Le Chroniqueur désoeuvré, ou l'espion du boulevard du Temple* (1783), where he dropped a clue about his authorship.[8] He published a short volume of satirical poetry, *Le Boulevard des Chartreux* (1779). He translated *Letters on Political Liberty* (1782), a radical tract by the English philosopher David Williams. And he topped off his oeuvre with his two-volume novel, *Les Bohémiens* (1790).

Fortunately, the attributions involve something more than guesswork, because Pelleport slipped many autobiographical references into his texts. *Les Bohémiens* is an autobiography disguised as a picaresque tale, and many of its details can be confirmed by other evidence, including the papers of the Bastille.[9] The transcript of Pelleport's interrogation in the Bastille following his arrest in 1784 has disappeared, but Brissot's interrogation survives, and it contains clues to many of Pelleport's activities in London. Having been arrested for collaborating with Pelleport, Brissot convinced the police that he had not contributed to any of Pelleport's works, and he provided information about several of them that had escaped the attention of their agents in London. They included *Compte rendu au peuple anglais de ce qui se passe chez la nation française, contenant toutes les anecdotes secrètes et scandaleuses de la cour de France et de ses ministres*, a libel that Pelleport apparently wrote, published, and supplied to an underground bookseller in Bar-le-Duc; *Le Diable dans un ballon*, a translation of an English libel; and *Lettres sur la liberté politique*, the translation of David Williams's political tract. Of these, only the *Lettres sur la liberté politique* has survived. The police confiscated a copy of it and were horrified to find that it was "full of sarcasm and insults against the French government."[10] The offensive passages all occurred in extensive notes, which Pelleport added to the text and which contained characteristic references to his own life as well as imprecations against political despotism and social inequality in France.[11] Brissot also told the police that Pelleport had started to translate Catherine Macaulay's radical, eight-volume *History of England* but abandoned the task. Eight volumes might have been more than Pelleport could handle, but his intention to translate such a work shows that he did not limit himself to frothy, scandalous literature. He was interested in history and political theory, and he produced a considerable oeuvre, most of which has been hidden or lost.

The police uncovered only a small part of it. In fact when they began their investigation of libelers in London, they concentrated on other suspects and took little notice of Pelleport. He thrust himself into the midst of their detective work by a letter addressed to Vergennes and delivered to the French embassy. It began with some purple prose.

Little Chelsea
12 April 1783
Monseigneur,

 In taking leave of my country, I have not left behind my French heart nor the sincere attachment to the royal family which is as it were innate in every gentleman. . . . An occasion has arisen for me to bear witness to my attachment to the king, my master, and to everything that most intimately concerns him, and I eagerly seize it.

Pelleport went on to explain that he had learned of Receveur's mission to suppress the horrible libels that sullied the honor of the king. It so happened that by chance he had come into contact with the author of the particularly execrable brochure titled *Les Passe-temps d'Antoinette* and also *Les Rois de France régénérés par les princesses de la maison d'Autriche*. If Vergennes promised to keep everything absolutely secret, he could help Receveur come to terms with the author. Of course, Pelleport would not become involved in negotiations with such a miserable "scoundrel" (the "scoundrel," of course, was Pelleport himself) and would not accept a penny for his services. He merely wanted to discharge his duty and to leave things in Receveur's hands. As to the libelers in general, he advised the government to treat them with scorn. To buy them off would only encourage them to produce more atrocities: "If you give bread to dogs, they will come back to your door. If you give them some swift kicks, they won't come back. But it is difficult to deliver kicks in this country."[12]

 What to make of such an epistle? Was Pelleport a genuine gentleman offering service to his king? An eccentric attempting to get involved in some intrigue? An adventurer hoping to inject himself into Receveur's mission in order to tap some of the money sloshing about? Or even the author of the libels that he proposed to help eradicate? The correspondence between London and Versailles shows the French authorities trying to make sense of this strange figure who promised to resolve their problems and signed himself with a flourish at the end of his letter as Lafitte de Pelleport.[13]

 After forwarding the letter to Vergennes, Moustier learned that Pelleport had also sent letters to the vicomte de Polignac in Switzerland and to the duchesse de Polignac in Versailles, promising to suppress the libels but this time for a price. It therefore looked to Moustier as though Pelleport had written the libels himself, probably with some help from one of his friends: "le sieur Brissot de Warville, personnage suspect."[14] But Vergennes thought Pelleport's offer worth pursuing, though with a good deal of caution. He instructed Moustier to cooperate with Pelleport and to promise him safe-conduct back to France—where he would be protected from his parents, who still wanted him imprisoned by lettre de cachet—if he succeeded in suppressing the libels.[15] For his part, Lenoir counseled against placing any trust in Pelleport, but he gave Brissot a clean bill of health.[16] And Goesman also offered advice. Worried no doubt about the appearance of another rival in the struggle to take charge of the negotiations with the libelers, he dismissed Pelleport's initiative as an attempt to insert himself into the general scramble for money and influence with the foreign ministry.[17]

While these different diagnoses circulated in the ministry of foreign affairs, Receveur made contact with Pelleport. They skirmished for two weeks over arrangements for the suppression of *Les Passe-temps d'Antoinette*, and eventually discussed prices. Pelleport promised that he could get the job done for seven hundred louis. Receveur refused to part with any money until he had received a copy of the manuscript, proofs, and the copper plates for the illustrations. Pelleport then responded with so many tricky maneuvers that Receveur decided that he was not dealing in good faith, unlike Boissière, a reliable middleman, if a corrupt one. Receveur therefore shifted his attention back to the bookseller, trying to persuade him to negotiate. It is difficult to define Boissière's role at this point. He probably had negotiated for Pelleport earlier but declined to do so now because he considered it too dangerous. To conduct business with the most notorious henchman of the Parisian police was to expose oneself to kidnaping or assassination. Whatever his reason, Boissière refused to cooperate, and Receveur became so disgusted with the whole business that he left England without having purchased any libels at all.[18]

The disappearance of Receveur followed by that of Goesman left Pelleport with no target for his efforts at extortion. He responded by publishing the supreme libel of his career, *Le Diable dans un bénitier*, which skewered everyone in the enemy camp—mainly Receveur and Morande but also their lieutenants, Goudar and Humber, their superiors, Moustier and Castries, and at the top of the chain of command, Vergennes, whom he described as the prime mover of a supremely despotic government. *Le Diable dans un bénitier* hardly concealed Pelleport's authorship, and it made him look like a player who swept all the pieces off the board in a fit of rage when about to lose a game.[19] He certainly had lost as badly as had Receveur. In the case of *Les Petits Soupers et les nuits de l'Hôtel Bouillon*, he had spoiled the opportunity for extortion by publishing the book before settling on terms for its suppression. And in the case of *Les Passe-temps d'Antoinette*, he had failed to make any headway at all in the negotiations. Yet Receveur had arrived with hundreds of louis d'or to buy the libels off. The conclusion was obvious: Pelleport had no talent for blackmailing—unlike Morande, who knew how to collect extortion and to change sides at the right moment. But Pelleport could write. As a libel about libeling, *Le Diable* was a tour de force—funny, wicked, and impassioned in its denunciation of the French police state.

If read against the background of the correspondence in the ministry of foreign affairs, *Le Diable dans un bénitier* suddenly comes to life, or takes on a liveliness that would have escaped uninformed readers in the eighteenth century. Much of the book must have seemed impenetrable to them. Pelleport filled his text with allusions, digressions, and inside jokes that could only be understood by those who knew their way around the world of the London libelers.[20] But every detail—aside from some dialogue that is obviously invented and some exaggeration in the descriptions of Receveur and Morande—corresponds exactly to material in the dispatches between Versailles and London. Pelleport reveals Morande's secret proposal for the reorganization of the London police, Moustier's consultations with the London lawyers, the plan to bring the chambermaid of the duchesse de Bouillon to London, and Goesman's behind-the-scenes collaboration with Boissière. He even includes a reference to the theft of Receveur's snuffbox. If considered as an early version of what is now known as investigative reporting, *Le Diable* was a remarkable accomplishment. It accurately exposed a major operation by the secret police of Paris, one that showed how power was concentrated and exercised throughout an entire system of government.

Moreover, the book could be read in the manner of a roman à clef. As already explained, the names of its characters were disguised in such a way as to challenge the reader to play a guessing game, and the guesses made by one eighteenth-century reader appear in notes at the end of one copy. He or she had no difficulty in identifying the main characters—Morande, Receveur, Moustier, Vergennes, Lenoir, and Boissière—but got others wrong. Goesman appears in the notes as "Guichen," the Gazetier cuirassé unaccountably as "Beaumarchais." The most intriguing mistake concerns a character identified as "M. de la Fare." This character appears in the text as "M. de la F. . . ." and also as "M. de la F—e."[21] In eighteenth-century books, the number of dots after the first letter in a semi-hidden name often corresponded to the number of letters that the name contained. In this case, the five-letter name beginning with F and ending with e must be Fitte—a reference to la Fitte (or Lafitte, as it sometimes appeared) de Pelleport. That is, Pelleport wrote himself into his text.

He had to do so in order to provide a complete version of the story. M. de la F. . . . plays an important part in it. He writes to Vergennes, receives Vergennes's clearance to deal with the libelers, and inserts himself into the negotiations exactly as Pelleport did. He also resembles Pelleport, for he is described as the well-born son of a gentleman who had connections with the French court. Moreover, he is the only sympathetic character in the book. Although presented with a touch of irony about his extravagant behavior, M. de la F. . . . makes monkeys of the police and even gives Moustier a dressing-down. He first appears as follows: "But by a happenstance that proved fatal for these honest gentlemen [the secret agents of the Paris police], into the café walked a M. de la F . . . ., the greatest madcap of all men and the greatest enemy of spies and other henchmen of despotism. He made no secret of the horror inspired in him by these gentlemen."[22] M. de la F. . . . is impudent, impetuous, even slightly mad ("fou").[23] In a typical stunt, he sent an anonymous letter to Lenoir saying that Receveur had been arrested as a spy and was about to be hanged at Tyburn. He also mocked Receveur and his agents by writing "An Alarm-Bell," the broadside that exposed their underground activities.[24] *Le Diable dans un bénitier* certainly qualified as a libel, but it also served as a way to tweak the nose of the police while casting its anonymous author as the hero who engineered their humiliation.

One can only speculate about Pelleport's motives in publishing such a book. They could have included an element of *dépit* and the desire to make money by exploiting the market for shocking revelations about the police, a theme that fascinated French readers at that time thanks to the recent success of *Mémoire sur la Bastille* by Simon-Nicolas-Henri Linguet, another expatriate among Pelleport's acquaintances in London.[25] But the text of *Le Diable dans un bénitier* hints at another purpose. It describes M. de la F. . . . as a friend of the Third Man or trusted agent ("dépositaire") of the scandalous material about the queen that Jacquet had collected. In fact, it suggests that M. de la F. . . . actually was the agent himself, and it indicates his readiness to tap the stock of anecdotes at his disposal in its account of his negotiations with Receveur. In order to provide evidence that new libels were about to be published, it relates, M. de la F. . . . wrote up some of Jacquet's material and showed it to Receveur as proof that the announcement of *Les Passe-temps d'Antoinette* in "An Alarm-Bell" was no bluff.[26] That message reinforced a conclusion conveyed by the book as a whole: the libelers had not been bought off by Receveur, so they had accumulated plenty of unpublished material about depravity in Versailles. There was more to come, and it would be available soon—unless the French government sent another agent to purchase its suppression.

Whether or not Vergennes and his staff picked up this hint from *Le Diable dans un bénitier*, they were horrified at its appearance. Not only did it reveal the secret missions of the police, it made them look like fools. Morande was furious, Moustier horrified, Vergennes appalled, and Adhémar ready to abduct Pelleport by force.[27] Vergennes rejected that suggestion, not because of any unwillingness to resort to violence but rather because he feared the effect it would produce on public opinion: "A secret abduction in a land of liberty would produce such publicity among us as to make it impractical and to prevent the salutary result of the example that we would hope to set."[28] Morande found a man willing to do the job: the baron de Narvan, an army veteran and a notorious brawler who had fled to the expatriate colony in London after a series of incidents in at least seven French regiments. But Adhémar ordered him to steer clear of all such activities while they came up with a better plan.[29]

They finally did so in the spring of 1784. During the winter, Pelleport traveled secretly to France in order to attempt to collect his share of the paternal estate following the death of his father in late 1783. Thinking that he would inherit twenty thousand livres, he invested that sum, before he collected it, in a speculation on champagne. He concocted a get-rich-quick plan to sell French luxury goods in a London shop, which he would establish with Antoine Joseph de Serres de La Tour, the editor of *Courrier de l'Europe*. Although he was planning to give up his editorship, La Tour had doubts about the feasibility of such an undertaking and never committed himself to it. But nothing would stop Pelleport. Using the expected inheritance as credit, he paid for the champagne with promissory notes and soon a shipment was on its way to London. It got as far as Boulogne-sur-Mer, when Pelleport's financing came undone. His stepmother had concocted a plot of the kind that would soon become standard in Balzacian fiction. Before he died, she had persuaded her husband to transfer his estate to herself and the children that she had had by him; as a consequence Pelleport had nothing to inherit. He also had no cash to pay for the final leg of the champagne's transport. In fact, he could not pay for his own passage across the Channel, to say nothing of the promissory notes. In great distress, he persuaded Brissot's mother-in-law, the widow of a wealthy merchant in Boulogne, to loan him some money, and he arrived back in London early in 1784, more desperate than ever to fight off destitution.[30]

As soon as Pelleport made it to London, he launched an even more extravagant scheme. He decided to produce another French newspaper about Anglo-American affairs, one that would cut into the market of the *Courrier de l'Europe* after La Tour ceased to be its editor in 1784. Pelleport planned to call it the *Mercure d'Angleterre* and to print it in Boulogne-sur-Mer, where he had somehow disposed of the stranded champagne. On the face of it, this was a mad undertaking, because the French authorities could shut the operation down at any moment. However, Samuel Swinton, the publisher of the *Courrier de l'Europe*, produced a French edition of his journal from a printing shop he had set up in Boulogne. Unlike the London edition, it had to pass through the French censorship.[31] But it was an enormous success, owing to the demand for information about the American Revolution and British politics in France.[32] Pelleport hoped to tap the same market while editing the journal from a safe distance in London, and somehow he won (or believed he had won) a promise from Swinton to collaborate in the endeavor. In order to set up shop, he had to make a quick trip to Boulogne—another risky undertaking but a feasible one, according to advice he received from Swinton. Swinton even promised to let Pelleport use his presses in Boulogne, a strange offer on the face of it, but Swinton said that he planned to invest in the enterprise and to substitute it for the French edition of the *Courrier*.[33] Pelleport also received backing from another member of the French colony in London, a certain Buard de Sennemar, who offered to accompany him to Boulogne. The two set off on June 30, 1784.

The business trip turned into an ambush. As soon as Pelleport set foot in Boulogne the police collared him, and on July 11, he was sitting in a cell of the Bastille. Adhémar had engineered this operation from London. On June 22, in a private letter to Vergennes, he expressed confidence that it would succeed. Buard was the perfect man for the job: "He is a man who is very mild and very perfidious, who has captured the confidence of this criminal author."[34] The collaboration of Swinton was assured, and Pelleport did not have the slightest idea of the trap they had set for him. He only knew about the bait: his own journal to be published in Boulogne with Swinton's support. On July 1 Adhémar wrote triumphantly that Pelleport and Buard had just set sail. Swinton, who wanted to ingratiate himself with the French, had behaved beautifully. He had even advanced twelve guineas to promote the plan, and Morande, too, had done yeoman's service. They all deserved rewards from the secret treasury of the foreign ministry. In fact, it was a good idea in general to win over such characters with bribes: "It is necessary to entice this species with a little money and to compensate them, not for the good that they do but for the bad that they don't do."

Buard returned to London at the beginning of September and promptly put in for an advance of 70 guineas on the 150 guineas Adhémar had promised him. Adhémar had financed the journey from funds at his own disposal, which, he assured Vergennes, he would be careful not to mention in the quarterly accounts he sent to Versailles. He wanted to compensate Swinton and to keep Buard on the payroll as a spy because Buard had contacts in the British foreign ministry who were ready to provide information for 60 louis a month.[35] Morande collected 100 louis for his part in the affair and went on to a lucrative career, both as another spy for Adhémar and as a new editor for Swinton on the *Courrier de l'Europe*.[36] Meanwhile, Pelleport sat in the Bastille, trying to make sense of it all.

Chapter 14
The View from Versailles

The entrapment of Pelleport was a big event in the eyes of the Parisian police, but it leaves a question hanging: Why did the government take the affair so seriously? Vergennes, Lenoir, and others in authority obviously wanted to prevent important personages from being offended by slanderous works, but they treated the campaign against the libelers as a major affair of state. In fact, it gave rise to a running debate about principles as well as strategy and tactics. By following the debate as it evolved in the correspondence of the foreign ministry, one can see deeper into slander as an issue that worried men in power under the Ancien Régime.

Everyone connected with Versailles agreed about the monstrosity of the libels. The diplomatic dispatches resounded with expressions like "filth," "horrors," "infamies," and "abominations."[1] But the discussion of how to deal with the libelers provoked some disagreement. Out of the continual exchange of letters, two basic positions can be distinguished: active intervention, a policy that committed the government to sponsoring secret agents, paying blackmail, and resorting to violence; and passive contempt (or scorn ["mépris"], a term that cropped up often in the debate), a policy of discouraging the libelers by refusing to deal with them.

The activists dominated policy during the comte de Vergennes's tenure as foreign minister (1774–87). According to a memorandum prepared for Vergennes by Gérard de Rayneval, a veteran diplomat who had served as plenipotentiary in London for a few months in 1782, the libelers should be exterminated, because they had committed the most serious of crimes, "lèse majesté": "This is a race of despicable persons, who do not deserve any attention in themselves; but they cause real harm to society, because they destroy the respect that people owe their sovereigns. Considering them solely from this point of view, it is crucial for all governments to destroy them."[2] Libel in the form of lèse majesté, as Rayneval understood it, took place in the realm of public opinion. It was a crime perpetrated through the press, and it deserved to be punished everywhere, in England as well as in France, even though the English enjoyed liberties protected by a peculiar constitution.

A nation may by its constitution have the right to censure its sovereign. The English nation has this right, but it does not have a right to defame him, to talk about him with impunity, using all the atrocities that an unhinged imagination can produce.... Nations owe mutual respect to one another. This principle is sacred in France, and the English themselves recognize its utility. If they adopted it, however, they fear that they would harm their national liberty. But is this liberty made for an infamous slanderer? Can one consider as a member of society, as a citizen, a vile calumniator, a starving wretch, who, merely in order to support his miserable existence, attacks the sacred person of a sovereign?

Despite his indignation against the libelers, Rayneval tried to develop an argument that could appeal to the English. He used terms like constitution, citizen, and liberty in a way that had an English ring, because the French wanted to persuade the British government to cooperate in the campaign to exterminate libels. In order to do so, Rayneval needed to reconcile the English notion of liberty of the press with the French demand for repression—no easy feat, especially as he let the argument draw him into a discussion of liberty as he had seen it operate in London. His conclusion, although not very coherent, shows how a top French diplomat construed alien notions picked up across the Channel.

One may safely ask: how would the punishment of a libeler infringe English liberty? In England the liberty of the press is seen as a necessity, as a derivative of civil liberty. It is considered the most effective brake that can be used against the authority of the king and his ministers.

One does not contest that way of thinking, but one may assert that the maintenance of the English constitution has nothing to do with [the toleration of] a deluge of abuse against foreign sovereigns and governments that is produced by English presses.

Firmness was required. Only by severe measures against the press could the British government make London cease to be "the source of all the filth about all crowned heads that is printed there every day."

Although the French diplomats never got the British government to take action against the press, they continued to debate the issue among themselves. When the comte de Moustier, who succeeded Rayneval as plenipotentiary in London, learned from his English lawyers that the only recourse against the slander was "silent contempt," he warned Vergennes that the libelers would take refuge behind the English constitution. But he refused to advocate a policy of passive scorn. The stakes were too high, the libels too effective in France: "I would certainly wish that they aroused no more interest in France than they do here and that they had no more effect on readers or on their victims, but the opposite is true, and so it is necessary to take strong measures against peddlers. If some of them were given a sound whipping at the pillory, they would soon give up the under-the-cloak trade."[3]

But flogging peddlers in Paris would not stop writers from producing libels in London. How to get at the root of the problem? As Moustier saw it, it ultimately came down to a matter of the demand from French readers—"the avidity of our French for these infamous productions."[4] Up to a point, demand could be stifled. Moustier favored all sorts of violence on the home front—hanging, flogging, the galleys. But books had a way of seeping into markets, no matter what the state might do to keep them out. It was therefore crucial to take action at the production end of the system in England while repressing distribution in France. Moustier devoted a great deal of time and energy to this effort, but in the end he came up only with a stopgap: bribery. Nonetheless, he continued to recommend active intervention and to oppose a policy of passivity right up until the end of his term in London. "Scorn" might be effective in England, where the public was inured to slander, he wrote to Vergennes, but it would never do in France: "I certainly would resist giving advice to follow the example of English disdain."[5]

"Scorn," however, was exactly what the comte d'Adhémar advocated when he succeeded Moustier in May 1783. It had a lot to be said for it as a policy because blackmail payments encouraged the libelers instead of dissuading them, and more aggressive measures such as kidnaping or court action had proved to be impossible. Moreover, Adhémar wanted to rid the embassy of the dubious characters that it had attracted under Moustier. As already mentioned, he had an exalted notion of his importance as France's first full-fledged ambassador to the Court of Saint James after the end of the American war, and he expressed complete disdain not only for the libelers but also for the agents sent to suppress them. He encouraged Receveur to pack up and told Vergennes that he wanted to have nothing more to do with such lowlifes.[6] Then he prepared to take more drastic action—even to appeal over Vergennes's head. Having learned that the duc de Polignac planned to advise the queen to show nothing but "scorn" for the libels against her, he decided to recommend the same policy to the king and planned to do so in a personal letter.[7] To write directly to Louis XVI about such a sensitive subject was audacious enough in itself, but it also represented a reversal of the policy pursued by Vergennes.

Fortunately for him, Adhémar had informed Vergennes of his intention. The foreign minister immediately replied with a warning.

It is a delicate matter to tell a husband that one dares to suspect and to accuse his wife, even though there is no ground for either suspicion. I share your general view of libels,

Monsieur. I think they warrant only the fullest scorn, and that is the only sentiment that I would feel if any appeared against me. But I do not feel the same indifference when they concern an august personage and when the atrocity is compounded by illustrations accompanying the work. You will say perhaps that such infamy is not sought after [on the marketplace.] But it finds a ready market in this country, and no matter what precautions we may take, we have never been able to prevent it from entering.[8]

Although Vergennes couched the warning in diplomatic language, he made its meaning clear. Adhémar should not take it upon himself to redirect policy on such an important matter, and the matter was indeed important; Adhémar knew very well "what an impression such a publication could make."

As soon as he received this rebuke, Adhémar replied with two letters written on the same day, backing and filling and covering himself with excuses. He did not really intend to write to the king; he had not ordered Receveur back to France; he did not deny the importance of libels—far from it, he acknowledged that they involved "great interests," and he had favored "scorn" only because it was counterproductive to pay blackmail. Vergennes had been misled by Receveur's report on his mission, which Adhémar dismissed as a shoddy attempt to shift the blame onto others for a botched job. The Parisian police and their seedy henchmen had made the French embassy a laughing-stock, but Vergennes could count on Adhémar to carry out his policies.[9]

Adhémar made good on this promise throughout the rest of his ambassa-dorship. Although he continued to use "scorn" in his dispatches about the libelers, he switched to a policy of pursuing them. He tried to goad the British government into action and got at least some verbal support from Fox. He persevered in the attempts at prosecution in the courts, though they never came to anything. And finally he laid the trap that led to Pelleport's arrest, working with Morande, whom he had earlier despised.[10] Adhémar ultimately proved to be more aggressive than Vergennes in hunting down libelers. Although they continued to manufacture slander, he claimed that he had ruined their business. And in the end, he congratulated himself for his success in applying the opposite of the policy that he had advocated in the beginning.[11]

The policy debate conducted in the privacy of diplomatic dispatches does not prove that the French statesmen foresaw the Revolution or perceived a serious threat to the monarchy in the libels produced by the French expatri-ates. For the most part, the diplomats seem to have been appalled at the pros-pect of private lives being exposed in public and of the public having information about affairs of state. Vergennes, who intervened actively in the book trade, refused to permit the publication of any work about current poli-tics: "The discussion of political matters is at the very least useless for the pub-lic, and it has not been [tolerated] up till now in France."[12] He and his subordinates subscribed to the notion of "arcane imperii" or "the king's secret"—that is, the belief that foreign affairs and politics were the king's business and should not be subjected to public inspection. Their persecution of libels expressed their general horror of "publicité," as they called it.[13] Yet they were concerned about the way the public reacted to events. Vergennes was especially anxious about the public's response to the peace settlement at the end of the American war.[14] Diplomats took account of public opinion, even though they deprecated it.

They also worried about their own skin. Moustier and Adhémar trembled at the prospect of losing Vergennes's protection when they thought they had displeased him, and Vergennes may well have had apprehensions about the favor of the king. Far from pursuing a consistent line in state affairs, Louis XVI frequently changed ministers and reversed policies. Power remained grounded in court factions, but instead of being channeled through royal mistresses, it now coalesced around key ministers and the queen herself. Vergennes depended on backing from the comte de Maurepas, the dominant minister of Louis XVI until his death in 1781, and on support from Marie-Antoinette, along with that of her favorite, the duchesse de Polignac. Complaints from the duchess and from lesser figures like the duchesse de Bouillon could begin to unravel the system of protections that underlay Vergennes's position in the Council of State. Not that a rumor could unseat a minister, but loose talk might upset the delicate balance of power in Versailles. Vergennes was wary of disruptions coming from outside the system, as in Adhémar's proposal to forego the normal channels of communication in order to inform the king directly about the libels against the queen. Goesman represented a similar threat. Although he had been recruited as a secret agent, he was an unreliable adventurer who announced at one point that he would personally deliver a sample libel to Mme de Polignac. Much as he distrusted him, Vergennes took seriously Goesman's warning that the libels originated from "a court intrigue."[15] Lenoir confirmed that diagnosis; and when he directed the earlier efforts to exterminate the libels produced by Jacquet, he learned that their ultimate source was a discontented courtier.[16] Libeling was an ingredient of the politics practiced in Versailles, a matter of power struggles linked to patronage and clientism, as they had existed for more than a century.[17]

Yet one can detect a new note of concern in the discussion of the libels—or actually two notes, one clear, the other muffled. When Rayneval, Versailles's expert on all things English, drafted his memorandum on the libelers, he referred to liberty, rights, and constitutional guarantees. He could not avoid that language, although he had some trouble adapting it to French institutions because he needed an argument that would persuade the British government to support the campaign against the French expatriates. No such difficulty inhibited the libelers. They gleefully invoked the English constitution, freedom of the press, and trial by jury while denouncing the French police state. Pelleport made those principles the main theme of his introduction to *Le Diable dans un bénitier*, whose opening sentence reads like a manifesto against despotism: "Despotism, which is irritated and driven to despair by the slightest impediment [to its operation], cannot bear to contemplate the idea of liberty." He even used similar language in his blackmail note about *Les Passe-temps d'Antoinette*.[18] English notions could be translated effectively into French, whether they appeared in philosophical treatises or in libels. Of course, French philosophers had developed their own way of articulating the same concepts. The libelers made the most of the ideas available to them in both cultures. Their works spread a message that threatened the ideological foundation and not just the personal reputations of the powers in Versailles.

The discussion of the libels also conveyed something else, a vague but palpable sense of an ever-present danger. It can be detected in the warning signals sent by Goesman, even though one must make allowances for their self-serving character: "Anything that compromises the glory of sovereigns must not be scorned."[19] "Scorn" was not an adequate defense against this threat. Vergennes did not cut off relations with Goesman, despite his discontent with Goesman's dispatches, because he shared that apprehension and wanted information about anything that could damage respect for the crown. When he rejected Adhémar's arguments for a policy of "mépris," the foreign minister sent a warning of his own: "You are well aware of the malignity of our era and of how easily the most absurd fables are accepted."[20] Fables and their reception—that was the crux of the matter. The libels perpetuated a mythological view of the monarchy, and their tales were producing an effect among the general public. Vergennes could not measure the effect, but he sensed its presence. Outside Versailles, a new phenomenon was gathering force—inchoate, vaguely felt, but present in the deliberations of statesmen as well as in the ineffable reality which, for lack of a better word, we call climate of opinion.

Chapter 15

The Devil in the Bastille

Although Pelleport had cast Receveur, the Parisian police inspector, as the devil in the holy water, the devil in the eyes of the police was Pelleport himself. Having lured him back to France and locked him up in the Bastille, they meant to keep him there. Bastille prisoners—"Bastillants," they called themselves—were not tried and did not receive sentences. They remained in their cells until it pleased a minister to release them. Most prison terms lasted three or four months. Pelleport's lasted four years, from July 11, 1784, until October 3, 1788. He believed at the time that he would spend the rest of his life in the fortress; he was discharged only because his old enemy, Vergennes, had died and because the new ministers were occupied with urgent new questions, like the preparations for the Estates General. They had little interest in punishing a writer for crimes that looked less threatening, if they were remembered at all, than the violence in the streets.[1]

At street level, however, the Bastille occupied a central place in the perception of events.[2] Although it contained only seven prisoners on July 14, 1789, it loomed large in the picture of the Ancien Régime perpetrated through underground literature, especially by libels. From *Le Gazetier cuirassé* to *Le Diable dans un bénitier* and dozens of similar works, the libelers had accompanied their slander of individuals with denunciations of the Bastille, lettres de cachet, police brutality, interrogation by torture, and all the other abuses that, they claimed, made the Bourbon monarchy look like an "Oriental despotism." Before he entered the Bastille, Pelleport had emphasized those themes more than any other libeler.[3] Afterward, he learned to measure the difference between literature and life, and the experience left its mark on the last of his literary works.

Pelleport never suffered any physical violence, but for four years he sat in a cell, abducted and imprisoned, without any formal judicial process, by virtue of a lettre de cachet. Of course, he was not the first author to undergo such treatment—far from it. Writers had been shut up regularly in the Bastille since the seventeenth century, and they often evoked their suffering in their writing. The author as martyr in the cause of freedom of the press was a favorite subject of the century's favorite authors, beginning with Voltaire. Two of the most popular authors in the 1780s, Linguet and Mirabeau, dramatized it by publishing accounts of their own experience as victims of lettres de cachet. Pelleport could have done the same.[4]

But he did not. He had access to plenty of paper, quills, and ink during his four years in the Bastille, and he spent a great deal of the time writing. So he could have produced something similar to Linguet's *Mémoire sur la Bastille.* Instead, he wrote a novel, *Les Bohémiens*, a picaresque account of life on the road among a ragged troupe of authors.[5] The novel did not attack the police, except in some incidental remarks. It satirized their victims, including Linguet himself and Pelleport's bosom friend, Jacques-Pierre Brissot, along with all the London libelers. In fact, it provides the most vivid picture available anywhere of hack writers and their condition on the eve of the French Revolution. And it is written with such verve that it reads in places like *Jacques le fataliste, Candide, Tristram Shandy, Le Compère Mathieu,* and *Justine.* Yet it has been completely forgotten. Only a half-dozen copies exist today, none of them in Paris. *Les Bohémiens* may not be a masterpiece—no more than *Le Chef-d'oeuvre d'un inconnu* by Thémiseul de Saint Hyacinthe, a popular work in the eighteenth century—but it deserves to be rescued from oblivion, not only for its revelations about the lives of the libelers but also because it is a very good read— good enough, certainly, to deserve at least a minor place in the history of literature.[6]

To understand Pelleport's fictional account of the underworld of letters, it is necessary to know what happened to him in the Bastille. The documentation is distressingly incomplete, but enough has survived for one to form some idea of his experience and to reconstruct his relations with the antihero of his novel, Jacques-Pierre Brissot. The police arrested Brissot the day after they locked up Pelleport. At that time, the two young writers were close friends, although they could hardly have been more different in temperament and background. Pelleport was a marquis from the ancient, feudal nobility, Brissot the thirteenth child of a pastry cook. Pelleport was dissolute, cynical, and witty; Brissot, serious, hardworking, and humorless. While Pelleport served as an officer in India, Brissot labored as a law clerk. With the help of a small inheritance, he bought a cheap law degree from the University of Rheims (it sold its degrees after giving perfunctory examinations) but then abandoned the law in order to devote himself to writing and, he hoped, a career as a successor to Voltaire and d'Alembert. Although he eventually produced a shelf-full of tracts on subjects like the injustices of the criminal law system and the wonders of America, he began by churning out hack pamphlets and living the life of Grub Street. As already mentioned, he had to flee Paris in 1777 to escape arrest for slandering a lady known for her respectable role in a salon. In 1778 he began to work as a journalist by correcting proof for the French edition of the *Courrier de l'Europe* put out in Boulogne-sur-Mer. There he met his future wife, Félicité, and her mother, Marie-Cathérine Clery Dupont, the widow of a merchant—two persons who also would figure prominently in *Les Bohémiens*. When Brissot returned to Paris in 1779, Mme Dupont recommended him to a family friend, Edme Mentelle, a professor of geography at the Ecole militaire in Paris. Brissot became a regular member of Mentelle's literary circle, hoping to win recognition as an up-and-coming philosophe. Here it was that he formed his friendship with Pelleport, a former student of Mentelle's who also was setting out to make his mark in the Republic of Letters.[7]

The paths of the two friends parted in 1779, when Pelleport left for Switzerland, but they came together again in 1782, when Brissot arrived in London. They saw each other frequently and kept the same company among the contributors to the *Courrier de l'Europe*. When Receveur began to track libelers in 1783, he put Pelleport and Brissot down together as the most outspoken "anti-Français" in the expatriate colony.[8] He and the comte de Moustier believed that they were the coauthors of several works, including *Le Passe-temps d'Antoinette* and *Les Amours du vizir de Vergennes*. But Lenoir cleared Brissot of suspicion, and there is no reason to believe that Brissot wrote any of the libels.[9] He devoted himself to journalistic tracts about law reform and to the founding of a literary society called the Licée de Londres, which never got off the ground, although it absorbed most of the money that had been provided by a backer named Desforges de Hurecourt. Brissot had gone to Paris in order to raise more funds for the Licée when he was arrested on July 12, 1784.

The police had ways of getting what they wanted from their prisoners. Usually they wanted information, enough to track down accomplices and to determine guilt; for despite the mythology attached to the Bastille, the police showed a genuine concern for justice—justice emanating directly from the throne rather than through the courts. They took pains to determine the facts of each case; kept careful records of interrogations, signed by the prisoners as testimony to their accuracy; and as far as I can tell after reading dozens of dossiers, never relied on torture, a procedure normally reserved for cases that went before a criminal court.[10] But the police knew how to apply pressure without using violence. They generally let a prisoner stew in a cell for several days before informing him of his offense. Meanwhile, they accumulated evidence, both from papers seized at the time of the arrest and from other prisoners or other raids in the domiciles of suspected accomplices. When they interrogated a prisoner, they let this information out in calculated doses, using some to provoke incriminating replies and holding back the rest in order to trap him in inconsistencies. Cases involving two prisoners gave the interrogators an opportunity to cross-examine each suspect separately, then to bring them together in carefully staged scenes known as "confrontations." Because one prisoner generally tried to shift the guilt onto the other, the police would read the transcripts of the interrogations to both of them and then goad them into mutual incriminations.

Whether the treatment of Pelleport and Brissot conformed to this pattern is impossible to say because the only documents to survive are the transcripts of Brissot's interrogations and some accompanying dossiers. Brissot's close friend and political ally, Pierre Manuel, came upon this material in 1789 when he selected documents from the Bastille archives for publication in *La Bastille dévoilée*. He turned it over to Brissot, "while telling me that nothing from me should remain amidst the filth of the police," as Brissot later recounted in his memoirs.[11] Manuel then invited Brissot to write up his own case for *La Bastille dévoilée*. Brissot obliged with an essay that cleared himself of any connection with libelers and libeling. "The true cause of my detention," he claimed, "was the zeal with which, at all times and in all my writing, I defended the principles that are triumphing today."[12] Manuel reinforced this conclusion with a commentary of his own, which he published in *La Police de Paris dévoilée*. Brissot, he explained, was incapable of slander, for he was the incarnation of virtue, whereas Pelleport, a noxious combination of vice and wit, had made libeling a way of life. Pelleport's interrogation in the Bastille showed that the police suspected him of manufacturing nearly all the slander that came off the presses in London, from *Le Diable dans un bénitier* to *Le Passe-Temps d'Antoinette*.[13]

The actual documents connected with Brissot's imprisonment, which remained in his family for nearly two centuries and only recently arrived in the French national archives, give a somewhat different impression.[14] They confirm Brissot's claim that he did not write any libels, but they show that he had close contact with the libelers, including a murky "pecuniary liaison" with Pelleport. Brissot underwent three interrogations, one on August 3, one on August 21, and one (a follow-up session of the former) on August 22. Both were conducted by Pierre Chénon, a police officer with years of experience in extracting information from Bastille prisoners. Whenever Chénon brought up the subject of Pelleport, Brissot stuck to the same story: their relations were asymmetrical—generosity on Brissot's side, treachery on Pelleport's. After abandoning his family, Brissot explained, Pelleport had tried to support himself in London by teaching French and mathematics but was constantly sinking into debt. Brissot came to his aid by giving him loans and helping him find literary odd jobs—translations and employment with Antoine Joseph de Serres de La Tour on the *Courrier de l'Europe*. But Pelleport could not resist the temptation of the big money to be made by libeling and blackmail, so he entered into negotiations with Receveur, playing off real libels, like *Les Petits Soupers et les nuits de l'Hôtel Bouillon*, against imaginary ones, like *Le Passe-Temps d'Antoinette*, which never existed, except as a project to extract money from the French government.

When Chénon pressed him for details about eight other libels, Brissot denied any knowledge of them. But he had plenty to say about *Le Diable dans un bénitier*. He explained that Morande and Swinton, his two greatest enemies in London, had concocted a story that would make him appear as Pelleport's collaborator in the composition and production of the book. They compelled a journeyman from the printing shop of Edward Cox, where *Le Diable* as well as the *Courrier de l'Europe* were produced, to write a letter claiming that Brissot had supplied scandalous anecdotes for the text and had corrected the proofs, which his brother, Pierre-Louis Brissot de Thivars (commonly called Thivars), had delivered to Cox. Brissot easily refuted that story by observing that Thivars, who came to live with him in London, did not arrive until November 1783, long after *Le Diable* had been published. But he could not deny that he had helped Pelleport with the distribution of the book. He admitted sending single copies to his agents in Ostend, a certain Vingtain, and in Cologne, Louis François Mettra. That was an understatement, as Morande later proved, because on March 30 Brissot had directed Vingtain to forward a whole shipment of *Le Diable* to various dealers, and Vingtain replied on April 3, 1784, that he had sent 125 copies to a bookseller in Brussels and six to a bookseller in Bourges.[15] Moreover, an account statement in the hand of Thivars showed that another 100 copies had been shipped to Mettra in Cologne. And the police had confiscated more compromising material from Brissot's Parisian agent, a businessman named Larrivée.

The Larrivée dossier showed that Brissot had developed extensive relations with Mettra, a notorious book dealer, printer, and underground journalist.[16] Mettra distributed (and apparently reprinted) Brissot's *Journal du Licée de Londres*, and he sent Brissot copies of two journals of his own: the *Correspondance littéraire secrète*, a rather innocuous literary review, and a manuscript newsletter, produced by a team of copyists, which contained hard-core scandal sent to Mettra by a secret correspondent in Versailles. Eager to discover the source of the smut about the queen and other figures in the French court, Chénon tried to lead Brissot into revealing information about Mettra's underground newsletter: Hadn't he used it to furnish "anecdotes" for the libels produced in London, including *Le Diable dans un bénitier*? Brissot replied that he felt nothing but disgust for the newsletter and its "filthy anecdotes." Mettra had sent it to him unsolicited and had asked to receive "secret anecdotes" from London in return. In fact, Mettra had tried to enlist Brissot as his London correspondent. Brissot refused, but he passed on the offer with copies of the newsletter to Pelleport, who subsequently agreed to work for Mettra. Whether the Versailles-Cologne connection was the source of the material in Pelleport's libels, Brissot could not say; nor could he identify any of Mettra's correspondents in Versailles and Paris. But he confirmed that Pelleport was connected with the traffic in anecdotes, which constituted the basic material from which libels were made (on the construction of libels, see Part III) and which produced the *succès de scandale* that the French government wanted to avoid.

Brissot also supplied a good deal of information about Pelleport's other activities, and the police culled still more from the letters they had confiscated. They learned all about Pelleport's failed attempt to collect his inheritance, his speculation on champagne and other luxury goods, his quarrel with Brissot's mother-in-law over the repayment of the loan she had given him, and his plans to create a *Mercure d'Angleterre* modeled on the *Courrier de l'Europe*. Pelleport had tried to entice the backer of Brissot's Licée de Londres, Desforges de Hurecourt, to finance the new journal by withdrawing his funds from the Licée. After May 20, when Brissot left on his journey to Paris, Thivars sent him letters from London warning that Pelleport, a "liar" and an "impostor," was betraying him behind his back. Brissot's wife came to despise Pelleport so thoroughly that she would not let him in their house. And while double-crossing Brissot, Pelleport hatched another plot to escape from all his debts. He had seduced a wealthy English widow, a certain "dame Alfred," and was planning to run off with her to America in case the *Mercure d'Angleterre* foundered.

Brissot had not known the full extent of Pelleport's treachery until the police let the information dribble out in the course of the interrogations. The last two interrogations were a marathon affair, which lasted a full day, with a break for a meal at 2:00, on August 21, 1784, and continued for half of the following day. When he returned to his cell, Brissot realized how thoroughly he had been duped. Soon afterward he wrote a nine-page memorandum on his relations with Pelleport. He repeated his denials of any involvement with libeling and added some new information about Pelleport's complicity in underground journalism. Early in 1784, he explained, Pelleport had shown him a draft of a newsletter that he planned to publish. It was to be full of "spicy anecdotes" supplied by a well-informed correspondent in Versailles, and as a sample of its contents, the draft contained a scandalous account of how Charles-Alexandre de Calonne had intrigued to get himself appointed controller general of finance, using the gift of a little dog to win the support of an influential lady in the court. Every detail summoned up by Brissot illustrated the same theme: Pelleport was a literary hack and a depraved rake. "Such is the monster who has just helped to get his benefactor arrested," Brissot concluded.

If Chénon arranged for a "confrontation" between the two prisoners, he could have read all this testimony to Pelleport; and he probably had collected plenty of material from Pelleport to read to Brissot, who later wrote that he owed his imprisonment to a "denunciation" by Pelleport and his other enemies in London.[17] Whether or not such a scene occurred, the two prisoners certainly betrayed each other. Their case, like many others, showed how friendships fell apart in the Bastille.

Pelleport remained in the Bastille for four years after Brissot's release. It is possible to form some idea of his state of mind during this long imprisonment by consulting the few original papers from his dossier that have survived in the archives of the Bastille. He was granted permission to take occasional walks inside the prison yard in 1784 and to breathe the air from its towers once a week in 1788. He requested shipments of books, including Voltaire's *Le Siècle de Louis XIV*, a work on Prussian military tactics, and a treatise on the harpsichord. There is no record of what he read, but he wrote a synopsis of "the philosophical episodes" in Raynal's *Histoire philosophique de l'établissement et du commerce des Européens dans les deux Indes*.[18] He also wrote letters, mainly to his wife. She and her two sons had managed to survive with the help of relatives in Switzerland while Pelleport wrote libels in London; but when she heard of his imprisonment, she came to Paris to beg for his release. She got nowhere, however, and escaped destitution only through the intervention of the chevalier Pawlet, an Irishman involved in educational projects in Paris, who arranged for her and her children to be supported by an orphanage for the sons of military officers. Mme Pelleport visited her husband three times in 1784, nine times in 1785, twice in 1787, and twice in 1788.[19]

Permission for these one-hour meetings was withdrawn in 1786, evidently because Pelleport had misbehaved in some manner. Judging from a note to a friend named Lambert that was captured by his guards, he had attempted to escape: "I threw the rope down yesterday evening each time that you came, but apparently it did not reach the ground. I am counting on Pierre to leave the door open for me during the night. . . . Be patient, my dear Lambert, and wait for me. I want to be in London as badly as you do."[20] Whatever the reason for the cancellation of his wife's visits, Pelleport begged to have them continued at the end of 1786, citing the military record of his family, "which has served the state and our kings for six centuries" and his own misery: "three years of expiation and the most horrible pain."[21]

After the visits resumed, Pelleport's relations with his wife deteriorated.

Somehow she had managed to persuade the authorities to allot her a meager pension of twenty-five livres a month from the budget of the Bastille, but she found it difficult to survive: "My situation is atrocious," she lamented in a letter to the Bastille's major, the chevalier de l'Osme, who treated Pelleport kindly and was his main intermediary in contacts with the outer world.[22] For his part, Pelleport complained in his own correspondence with the administrators of the Bastille that his wife refused to go to Versailles to lobby on his behalf. He suspected her of conspiring with his enemies to keep him in jail while enjoying life in Paris as the mistress of her benefactor, the chevalier Pawlet.

I have not yet reached a decision about what course to take, whether I will wait for an opportunity to demand justice for the abuse of authority by the sieur de Breteuil [the minister in charge of the Bastille in 1787] or whether I will put a swift end to my life. . . . All I ask is that I should not be torn violently from this dungeon cell, which probably will be my tomb. . . . I could never have believed that M. le chevalier de Pawlet would make my dishonor and the loss of my liberty and my life the price that he charges for his bounty to my family. . . . A man's fate is certainly unhappy when, like a vile plaything of all that is close to him, he resembles a wooden top, which clever children spin around, now one way, now another, by beating it with a whip.[23]

Bastille prisoners often filled their letters with lamentations in the hope of softening their captors' resistance to pleas for their release, but there is no reason to doubt the despair expressed by Pelleport. As the weeks turned into months and the months into years, he had reason to believe that he never would be freed.

He filled much of the time with writing. From the beginning of his imprisonment, he had access to all the writing material he needed.[24] In addition to *Les Bohémiens*, he also composed some poetry, which gave him an outlet for his feelings, as he explained in one of his letters: "The lot of Bastille prisoners is somewhat like that of unhappy Indians and miserable African slaves. . . . It is better to dance to the sound of your chains than to chew in vain on your tether."[25] The verse that survives in his dossier shows him venting his resentment in short, satirical *pièces fugitives* aimed at Bernard-René de Launay, the governor of the Bastille.

Avis au *Journal de Paris* sur un songe que j'ai eu

Laun . . . vient à expirer! quoi! passant, tu frémis.
Ce n'est point une calomnie.
Pour son honneur, moi, je m'en réjouis.
C'est la meilleure action de sa vie.

(Notice to the *Journal de Paris* about a dream I had

Laun . . . just expired! What, passerby, you shudder?
It is not a calumny.
For my part, I rejoice at the honor he acquired.
It is the best act of his life.)

Madrigal sur ce qu'on s'est plaint que l'auteur était méchant

Laun . . . s'est plaint que j'ai l'esprit méchant.
D'un coeur si bon le reproche est touchant.

(Madrigal on the complaint that the author is wicked

Laun . . . complained that I have a wicked turn of mind.
It is a touching reproach from one with such a good heart.)[26]

Pelleport scattered similar verse through his published writing. Most of it had the same tone—biting, sardonic, and disillusioned.

A note of nihilism accompanied the mockery that Pelleport turned on the world. The documentation that surrounds his imprisonment does not provide access to his innermost reflections, but what little can be known suggests that they were dark. He brooded over the denunciations that barred his way to freedom while others, like Brissot, were usually released after a few months. He had scores to settle, not just against Brissot but against nearly everyone whom he had known in London—and especially Morande, "a libeler and slanderer by profession."[27] "It would be a thousand times better for me to have fallen into the hands of the savages in Canada than in those of the slanderers," he wrote to de l'Osme. "Better by far, Monsieur, to perish from the blow of a tomahawk [*tomevack*] than to succumb to the poisoned darts of the venomous insects who have reduced me to a state of desiring death every time that I contemplate what remains of my existence in the dark shadow of my tomb."[28] In his despair, Pelleport seems to have abandoned all belief in higher principles. Such, at least, was the testimony of another London libeler who was captured by the police in 1785, Jean-Claude Fini, alias Hypolite Chamoran. Fini described Pelleport not only as the author of the worst of the libels produced in London but also as a "knave," a "monster," and a "disciple of Diagoras [the atheistic philosopher from the fifth century B.C.], who, when you ask him about the primary cause that rules the universe, replies with an ironic smile and makes the sign of a zero, which he calls his profession of faith."[29]

Whom to believe? How to sift through fragments from the Bastille in order to piece together a picture of a life that shattered there? If indirect evidence be admitted, one can turn to a final source, the life and works of a man who never testified about Pelleport but who shared the Bastille with him: the marquis de Sade.

Sade's imprisonment in the Bastille, from February 29, 1784, to July 2, 1789, coincided almost exactly with Pelleport's: July 11, 1784, to October 3, 1788. Did those four years of cohabitation produce any intellectual exchange? Impossible to say. The two men had a good deal in common. Both were marquis from the old *noblesse d'épée*, both had been imprisoned at the request of their families for misbehavior in their youth, and both wrote obscene novels—at the same time and within close range of each other. Their names appear in close proximity in the records of the Bastille.[30]

Daily life in the Bastille was certainly hard, but it is easily misunderstood, owing to the myths that cloud the reputation of the place—the revolutionaries' nightmare of a house of horrors and the revisionists' pastel-tinted picture of a one-star hotel. Modern notions of imprisonment do not correspond to eighteenth-century practices. The Bastille was a converted fortress, used for the confinement of special prisoners who were usually arrested by lettre de cachet and kept without trial for indefinite periods. For the small minority who remained confined for several years, like Pelleport and Sade, the psychological burden could be terrible, but they were not cut off from all contact with the outside world or even with each other. Prisoners did not share cells— nearly half of the forty-two cells in the fortress were empty throughout the 1780s—but sometimes by special permission they were allowed to mix with one another. The most privileged occasionally had dinner together. They played cards, chess, and even billiards for a while in 1788. They had ample opportunity to read and write, at least when the rules were relaxed during the late eighteenth century. They received plentiful supplies of books, paper, and writing instruments. Some even devised ways of exchanging notes.[31]

The Bastille had a fairly extensive library, and although it did not contain much fiction, the prisoners sometimes wrote their own. Did they have any knowledge of each other's literary activities? The surviving evidence does not provide an answer to that question. One can only affirm that imprisonment and the enforced leisure it produced weighed heavily on some of the prisoners, provoking them to reflect on their lives and to express their thoughts in writing. Despite its thick walls and general gloom, or perhaps because of them, the Bastille functioned as a greenhouse for producing literature. It was in the Bastille that Voltaire began *La Henriade*, that La Beaumelle completed his translation of Tacitus, and that Sade drafted *Les Cent Vingt Journées de Sodome*, *Aline et Valcour*, and the first version of *Justine*. While this strange neighbor was venting his passions through his pen, Pelleport wrote a work that expressed a similar gamut of emotions but with a sharper style and greater literary skill.

Such is my assessment. Others may find *Justine* far superior to *Les Bohém-iens*. But Pelleport's book deserves at least to be known. Having described the circumstances of its production, I would therefore like to discuss the text.

Chapter 16
Bohemians Before Bohemianism

Les Bohémiens opens as Bissot, the fictitious version of Brissot, wakes up in a miserable bed in a garret in Reims. He has just bought his law degree, but that extravagance exhausted his savings, 300 livres, and he finds himself deeply in debt. What to do? The best solution he can hit upon is to become a philosopher instead of a lawyer—that is, to skip town before the bailiffs can clap him into debtors' prison. He justifies this resolution by delivering a "philosophical discourse"[1] to his brother, who serves as his sidekick and has been sleeping beside him. It is the first of many philosophical harangues scattered through the book, and it gives Pelleport an opportunity to parody Brissot's vulgar Rousseauism while slipping in some disparaging references to his origins as the son of a pastry cook in Chartres. In absurdly overblown language, Bissot deplores the inequalities of the social system and then veers off into a tirade against the tyranny of creditors based on his *Théorie des lois criminelles*. As this and many other allusions make clear, Pelleport had a thorough knowledge of Brissot's early writings and of his background and family. The younger brother in the novel, Tifarès, corresponds to Pierre-Louis Brissot de Thivars, the younger brother of Brissot who was known as Thivars and who joined him in London in 1783 to provide assistance on various projects. Pelleport describes Tifarès as a skinny, superstitious simpleton, interested in little more than the next meal. When Bissot, continuing his oration, announces that they must leave Reims in order to return to nature—a Rousseauistic solution to the problem of their inability to pay their bills—and therefore feed on roots and acorns, Tifarès protests that he would prefer to find a job as a kitchen hand. Finally, however, he agrees. He puts on six shirts—his way of transporting his entire wardrobe—and the two set off, Bissot-Brissot and Tifarès-Thivars, a modern version of Don Quixote and Sancho Panza.

Next scene: a primitive road in Champagne. Speaking in his own voice, the narrator-author declaims against the corvée (forced labor in building roads) and the exploitation of the peasants. Then he deposits his heroes in a broken-down inn, where they spend their last pennies on a nasty meal—the occasion for another philosophic harangue, this time a parody of Brissot's *Recherches philosophiques sur le droit de la propriété*—and continue, resigned to sleeping in a ditch. After night descends, a brigand suddenly emerges from the darkness, pointing a rifle. He turns out to be Mordanes (Morande, whose name was often spelled with an *s* at the end), the guard and chief poacher of a band of nomads, who are gathered around a fire, roasting the day's plunder. Instead of disemboweling the strangers, the "Bohémiens" invite them to join the feast. While Tifarès instinctively goes to turn the spit, Bissot treats his hosts to the "reception address"[2] he had delivered at the Académie de Châlons-sur-Marne. The actual speech, given at Châlons on December 15, 1780, concerned proposals for the reform of criminal law. Pelleport's parody of it mixes those ingredients with a declamation against despotism, religious intolerance, and assorted social evils, all served up in the pompous rhetoric of provincial academies. To address a troupe of brigands as noble savages—"wise inhabitants of the forests, illustrious savages"[3]—and then to change gears and treat them as straight-laced provincial academicians is to pile absurdity on absurdity, especially as the purpose of it all is to get a free meal. In the midst of his entangled oratory, Bissot glimpses an even happier outcome. If he can be admitted to the company like a neophyte in an academy, he, too, could live by plundering peasants. The same went for Tifarès, who offers his services in plucking chickens "according to the methods of the *Encyclopédie*."[4] The Bohemians recognize the newcomers as men of their own kidney and let them join the troupe.

At this point, Pelleport suspends the narrative in order to provide background information about the Bohemians. He never explains his use of the word itself, but by the second half of the eighteenth century, *Bohémiens* had come to mean more than the inhabitants of Bohemia or, by extension, Gypsies (Romany). Although not yet attached to the modern notion of bohemianism made popular by Henri Murger's *Les Scènes de la vie de bohème* (1848), the term already connoted drifters who lived by their wits and marginal men of letters.[5] Pelleport's Bohemians share this general characteristic, but each of them has highly individual traits. In fact, Pelleport piles on so much detail in describing the main characters—idiosyncrasies, references to publications, names obviously concocted as anagrams—that the reader soon realizes the novel is a roman à clé, which will require continuous decoding.

The guessing game begins as the president of the troupe, the abbé Séchant, introduces its main members to the newcomers. Séchant and his companion, the abbé Séché—their names evoke the aridity of their philosophy—are caricatured versions of two of the London libelers, the abbé de Séchamp and the baron de Saint-Flocel. According to his police report, Séchamp was a former chaplain of the prince of Zweibrücken who had fled to London after becoming implicated in a plot to embezzle funds from a merchant in Nantes. He took part in Pelleport's blackmail operation while attempting to launch a physiocratic-philanthropic review entitled *Journal des princes*, which was intended to undercut the somewhat similar periodical published by Brissot, *Correspondance universelle sur ce qui intéresse le bonheur de l'homme et de la société*. Saint-Flocel joined him in this venture, having gained experience as a journalist on the *Journal de Bouillon*.[6] Brissot described Saint-Flocel in his memoirs as an "excessively dogmatic economist," and the police put him down in their files as an adventurer who changed names and jobs in order to escape punishment for various swindles.[7] The third principal Bohemian was Lungiet, a burlesque counterpart of Simon Nicolas Henri Linguet, the famous journalist who had joined the colony of French expatriates after being released from the Bastille in 1782.[8] Pelleport could not have expected every reader to identify every character in the book, but he made it clear that the Bohemians wandering through Champagne were actually Frenchmen settled in London and that their main activity, robbing barnyards, corresponded to the slanderous journalism of the libelers.

Pelleport did not name the other members of the troupe, but he suggested that there were at least a dozen of them. The secret agents of the Paris police filed reports on everyone they could identify among the French refugees in London and came up with thirty-nine in all—an extraordinary rogues gallery of hack writers and confidence men.[9] Pelleport probably knew all of them. He certainly had plenty of colorful material on which to draw, but he did not attempt to portray the entire population of French writers in the Grub Streets of London because he aimed a great deal of his satire at variations of French philosophy. He therefore divided the Bohemians into three philosophical sects: "la secte économico-naturellico-monotonique"[10] led by Séché, "la secte des despotico-contradictorio-paradoxico-clabaudeuristes"[11] led by Lungiet, and the "philosophes communico-luxurico-friponistes"[12] led by Mordanes. The first represented physiocracy and the doctrine of natural law; the second, enlightened despotism tinged with reactionary social doctrines; the third, predatory self-interest. Taken with Bissot's utopian Rousseauism, the Bohemians covered a great deal of the ideological spectrum.

There also were camp followers. Pelleport named only two, a mother-daughter combination: Voragine and Félicité. Félicité was Félicité Dupont, the "beautiful neighbor" from Mentelle's circle in Paris who had captivated Brissot in 1779, as he had mentioned in his early letters to Pelleport.[13] They married in 1782 and set up house in London, at 1 Brompton Road, near the offices of the *Courrier de l'Europe*, where Pelleport, a frequent contributor to the *Courrier*, visited them regularly. Félicité's mother, Marie-Catherine Dupont, née

Cléry, was as already mentioned the widow of a merchant in Boulogne-sur-mer. She figures prominently in *Les Bohémiens* as the companion of Séchant and the sexual partner of anyone she could get; for Pelleport portrays her as a hideous, sex-starved hag. (Voragine appears to be an obscene anagram, which can be decoded in various ways, all of them nasty, although it also could be an allusion to Jacobus de Voragine, the thirteenth-century author of the *Golden Legend*, a popular collection of legendary saints' lives.) Pelleport's hostility was connected with their quarrel over his speculation on the shipment of champagne and his reluctance to repay the loan she had given him, but it may have had other grounds, perhaps something she had to do with his imprisonment;[14] for his portrayal of Brissot's wife and mother-in-law was particularly vicious, and he made them the central characters in the pornographic subplot of his novel.

Having introduced the principal Bohemians, the narrator steps out of the story and informs the reader that the troupe contains one last philosopher, the greatest of them all. He challenges the reader to guess this character's identity by deciphering the "hidden meaning"[15] of the description that follows. The philosopher belongs to no sect, subscribes to no religion, combines sensations without distortion in his common sensorium, bears his burdens without complaint, enjoys food and drink, and is a great lover. Who could that be? After a satirical tour of contemporary philosophy in which he debunks every variety of intellectual pretentiousness with a verve worthy of Voltaire, the narrator addresses the reader again: "Oh! I can see, my dear reader, that you are becoming impatient and that you cannot guess who is the hero that corresponds to the faithful portrait I have sketched. But you, young village lass, so frisky and alert, you who have lain more than once, drawn by love, under the vigorous Colin, if you read this book you would cry out loud with pleasure: 'Oh! It's Colin. It's our donkey.'"[16]

The stylistic virtuosity in this section of the book typifies Pelleport's technique. He develops a story line that points the reader in one direction, then interrupts it with a digression that shifts the perspective, and returns to the action—or sometimes to a digression within the digression—in a way that calls everything into question. He employs a perverse Shandean method, teasing and playing with the reader, then administering shocks and surprises. The sardonic philosophizing, which runs through a dozen schools of thought, ends in a eulogy of the donkey who carries the baggage of the troupe. And to deliver the punch line, a second putative reader appears, a not-so-innocent village girl who doubles the shock value of the joke by lauding the donkey's sexual prowess—possibly an allusion to the donkey of Joan of Arc in Voltaire's *La Pucelle*.

From philosophy to bestiality, Pelleport turns the trick with a dexterity that outdoes his neighbor scribbling away in another cell: the marquis de Sade.

The libertine undercurrent appears in the very first sentence of the book, where Bissot is described as awakening at the crack of dawn, when "women of pleasure were shutting their eyelids; . . . gentlewomen and all those pretending to be noble still had six hours of sleep before them; and the pious dames, woken by the lugubrious sound of the church bells, were hurrying off to the first mass."[17] A similar passage introduces the eulogy of the donkey at the beginning of chapter five, but here the narrator strikes another tone. He celebrates sex in a lyrical passage, speaking in his own voice without a trace of irony.

Yes, I remember that happy time when I was lying on a mattress in the arms of Julie. The first rays of dawn came through the curtainless window and pulled me from the arms of sleep. A kiss savored tenderly brought my love back to life. Her heart opened to desire before her eyes opened to the light. I merged with Julie; Julie held me tight in her alabaster arms. We greeted the principle of life in that union engendered by its divine fire, and we made ourselves drunk with pleasure in preparation for the day's work.[18]

It is a scene from Grub Street. The poor author wakes up next to his mistress in a garret, and after making love, his thoughts turn to the tyranny of the rich, the powerful, and the bigoted.

Oh, you who employ sinister fairy tales to poison the few, brief moments that we can consecrate to pleasure, believe me: our prayer [i.e., lovemaking] was more agreeable to the Being of beings than the bad Latin with which you offend His ears. And you who harbor sordid greed within your hearts of bronze, you who grow fat by despoiling your fellow men, you who grow rich by taxing the poor, you tyrants stained by the blood of mankind, you barbarous jail keepers who guard the prison doors and keep a heavy hand on the locks, come, hasten all of you to contemplate Mordanes the philosopher as he begins his day, and may envy corrode the desiccated remnants of your corrupt and fetid hearts.[19]

The chapter then continues with the next adventure of Mordanes and the facetious praise of the donkey, but the passion of its opening paragraph provides a disconcerting overture to the burlesque passages that follow. The narrator himself has cut through the narrative with a cri du coeur that could have come from a cell in the Bastille, as if he were a prisoner railing against his jailors and giving full vent to his anger and longing. The reader naturally asks: Who is the person addressing me in this strange manner, and where does he stand amid the philosophies he derides?

After his eulogy of the donkey, the narrator answers those questions by identifying himself. He does not give his name, but he provides enough information to explain his disenchantment with the dominant values of his time—and all his remarks fit the biography of Pelleport. He was born into a privileged social position, he says, but early experience taught him to despise it. Judging from some scornful remarks about wealthy bourgeois who buy their way into the nobility, he belongs to the ancient nobility of the sword.[20] At one point he hints at an abortive military career as "a young gentleman . . . without wealth."[21] At another, he describes his attempt to get an appointment through an aristocratic family friend at court. In the end, he rejects all forms of patronage and takes to the road, inspired by the example of Rousseau—the real Rousseau, not the vulgar version peddled by Bissot. The narrator dedicates himself to the pursuit of liberty and denounces social injustice in language close to that of Rousseau's *Discours sur l'origine de l'inégalité*. Yet he follows this declaration of faith with more ribaldry. His Rousseauism turns out to be strangely Rabelaisian, miles apart from the gushy enthusiasm of Bissot. Bissot, however, like all the other philosophers, proclaims elevated principles and lives by plundering peasants. The narrator contrasts this hypocrisy unfavorably with the anti-philosophy of the donkey, "nothingism" ("riénisme"), as he calls it, which consists of rejecting all systems of thought while satisfying one's appetite.[22] The pursuit of pleasure, unimpeded by social constraints, stands out amid all the pontificating as the only value worth pursuing. At least in that respect, despite their pretentiousness and hypocrisy, the Bohemians represent something positive. Their president, Séchant, describes them as "a troupe of persons who lack neither appetite nor gaiety" when he introduces them to Bissot. They devote themselves to "free and lovable liberty. . . . It is that which has brought us together from every corner of Europe. We are its preachers, and its cult can be reduced to the principle of not harming one another."[23] The Bohemians share an attitude rather than a philosophy. They take a stance toward the world that already looks like bohemianism.

Even as philosophers the Bohemians seem harmless—all except for one: Mordanes. He is the only member of the troupe who appears truly evil. He does all the plundering, while the others hurl platitudes at each other without inflicting damage. His principal employment, stealing animals from barnyards, serves as a metaphor for Morande's undercover activity: betraying people—defenseless victims like Pelleport—to the police. Mordanes also enjoys inflicting pain for its own sake. The most revealing of his atrocities takes place when he bludgeons two copulating chickens to death. The narrator recounts this incident after a long, lyrical passage celebrating sex. Desire is the vital energy that courses through all nature, he proclaims, and free love is the noblest principle in the natural order: "Enjoy pleasure, enjoy it, and take care never to cause the slightest impediment to the enjoyment of others."[24] As an illustration of this hedonistic Golden Rule, he celebrates the joyful lust of some chickens in a barnyard where Mordanes is prowling, and he invokes "the song of the rooster, who calls to his chickens, chooses the lustiest of them, gives her a free, frank, strong, firm embrace, the kind that we would give, you and I, to our own little chicks, if we weren't inhibited by too much humanity, virtue, modesty, and perhaps something else."[25] But in the midst of the chickens' lovemaking, Mordanes, "barbarous Mordanes," kills them with a brutal blow. He is giving Tifarès a lesson in the art of despoiling peasants. Overcome at first by pity, the basic sentiment of sociability according to Rousseau, Tifarès recoils in horror, then thinks better of it, and smashes the skulls of four ducks in a nearby pond. He has switched his allegiance from Bissot to Mordanes and has learned to be a murderer.[26]

Mordanes's own expression of the universal sex drive is rape. He makes Félicité his target. As the Bohemians resume their march across Champagne, Bissot takes up with Félicité, just as Brissot had done with Félicité Dupont in Paris. They pair off and copulate blissfully. A few days later, while Félicité sits alone contemplating her expected motherhood, Morande jumps her, wrestles her down, and is about to penetrate her, when she devises a trick. By suddenly shifting her posture, she makes him miss his target and sodomize her—her way of protecting Bissot's claim to paternity. It is also Pelleport's way of inflicting injury on his former friend: to ravish the wife is to humiliate the husband. Pelleport goes further: he implies that Félicité enjoyed herself, for Bissot is not much of a lover, he reveals, and the stud-like energy of the rapist releases a libidinal charge in her. She even gets satisfaction from her gymnastic ruse. The chapter sports a cynical slogan: "A mouse who has only one hole is soon caught."[27]

The sexual current that runs through the narrative appears as a fundamental force of nature, which the narrator compares to electricity, friction, fire, and phlogiston.[28] Although neutral in itself, it is relentlessly phallocratic in its effects upon society. While elaborating a discourse on natural law, Séché goes so far as to argue that men should own women as a form of property that can be bought, sold, traded, rented, and inherited.[29] To be sure, this burlesque episode reads more like a satire against the subjugation of women than an argument in favor of it. The narrator constantly presents women as objects of male desire, yet he also attributes an aggressive sexual energy to them, for the same élan vital courses through all forms of life: women are for the taking, and they help themselves to men. While Félicité is being raped, her mother, the insatiable Voragine, overpowers Tifarès. She copulates with many of the other

Bohemians, even, the narrator suggests, with the donkey. Séchand, who is incapable of satisfying her "uterine fury," dreams that she takes on an entire pack of Capuchins.[30]

The monks enter the narrative as if from some libidinal underworld. Ostensibly on a pilgrimage, they wander through the countryside stealing from peasants in the same manner as the Bohemians, who come upon them in the middle of the night. At first the Bohemians take them to be satanic creatures celebrating a witches' sabbath but soon realize that they are fellow spirits given to debauchery. The two troupes join forces and settle down for a feast around a fire. They guzzle and gorge themselves into a stupor, wake up, and start to copulate—in twos and threes, then heaps of bodies piled up and linked together in nearly all the combinations celebrated in the libertine literature of the eighteenth century, Sade included. The polymorphous perversion degenerates into a brawl. Fists fly, noses splatter, blood flows everywhere along with muck and fluids discharged from numerous orifices. The donkey leaps into the fray, braying and flailing about deliriously. It is a Dionysian donnybrook, worthy of the best punch-ups described by Rabelais and Cervantes.[31] As dawn appears, the rioters stop for breakfast. They enjoy another hearty meal together, then go their separate ways. A good time was had by all.

The orgy brings volume one to a climax. Volume two takes the troupe through more adventures interrupted by more burlesque philosophic lectures, but most of it is devoted to a disguised autobiography of Pelleport. He constantly interrupts his narrative with digressions that contain fragments from the story of his own life. They can be identified and pieced together to form a second narrative, and in the last hundred pages of the book, the two stories intersect: Pelleport, in the person of an unnamed, wandering poet, joins the Bohemians as they are camping on the outskirts of his native city, Stenay. He recounts his adventures to them, and as they listen they reappear in his tale under new names and in a new setting: Grub Street, London. The intersection and overlaying of the narratives creates a complex structure, but Pelleport spins the story lines together with a sure hand and a light touch: the last segment of the book carries the earlier bawdiness to a new extreme, as if to say that the human comedy is a farce, an off-colored joke.[32]

The poet strays into the text while the Bohemians are setting up camp and preparing dinner. He has just been released from the Bastille and is about to join his brothers in Stenay (Pelleport's birthplace) but has paused to compose a song. Strumming a guitar, he sings a verse that, as he later explains, represents his true philosophy.

Voler de belle en belle,
A l'amour c'est se montrer fidèle;

Voler de belle en belle,
Aux Dieux c'est ressembler.[33]

(To fly from beauty to beauty
Is to prove faithful to love;
To fly from beauty to beauty
Is to resemble the gods.)

Séchant recognizes a kindred spirit and calls out: "An author!" Taken by surprise, the poet panics. He denies any connection with literature because he fears the strangers may be a detachment of police. Not at all, they assure him: they, too, are authors; the donkey is loaded down with the treatises they are writing. They invite him to dinner, and while Tifarès turns the spit, the poet tells the story of his life, which he offers as an explanation of why he took such fright: "I am attached in a way to the republic of letters, but that is a very dangerous thing to admit these days . . . and to prove that to you, I will tell you the story of my literary history."[34]

He was born in Stenay, he explains, as unfertile territory as any place in France for the flowering of literature. His deceased father, an old-fashioned military officer from the ancient nobility of the sword, could hardly read or write. Neither of his two brothers got much of an education. His two sisters were packed off to convents. But his mother had a chambermaid from Paris who loved novels and read *Don Quixote* to him. It was his downfall. Soon he learned to read himself and memorized all the adventures of the man from La Mancha. Eventually, after twists and turns that correspond to Pelleport's biography, he found himself embarked on a literary career and writing for the *Courrier de l'Europe* in London. He got along well with its editor, Antoine Joseph de Serres de La Tour, but not its publisher, Samuel Swinton. So when news reached him of his father's death, he resigned from the journal and set off for Stenay in the expectation of collecting an inheritance. His stepmother dashed those hopes by manipulating the legal procedures. The hapless poet therefore headed back again, penniless and on foot, to London; but he could not make it beyond Boulogne-sur-Mer, because he could not pay his passage across the Channel. On December 24, 1783, after a Christmas Eve mass, he found himself alone in a church in Boulogne—and a miracle occurred.

Here the narrative takes a different turn. Between the poet's childhood in Stenay and his journalism in London, the well-informed reader could fill in the missing parts of Pelleport's biography by inserting episodes mentioned in other digressions: study at the Ecole militaire in Paris,[35] service with a regiment in India, and several years of married life in Switzerland. But Pelleport had not yet provided a full account of his experience in London—nothing beyond the caricatures of the French expatriates cast as Bohemians. In the last section of the book, he gives those writers new names and relocates them in London's garrets and cafés. He also shifts into a different key: the poet's tale, which had included some serious social criticism,[36] turns into an obscene farce organized around the notion of genital gigantism and the supposed craving of women for big penises.

Following the mass, a beggar appears out of nowhere in the empty church, and the poet gives him the last coin in his purse. It is an act of secular humanitarianism, not Christian charity, as the relentlessly irreligious text makes clear.[37] But it provokes a miracle. The beggar is transformed into the glorious Saint Labre, who rewards the poet by giving him a miraculous belt made out of knotted rope. He instructs the poet to hide the belt under his clothing, leaving an end that he can grasp without being seen through his watch fob. Whenever he needs aid, he should pull on the rope, moving from knot to knot according to the severity of the situation. His nose will grow three inches with each pull. As the saint himself discovered when he trod the earth as a poor, itinerant monk, women will find the big nose irresistible, and they will provide as much succor as needed—or more, depending on the number of knots pulled.

While Pelleport was spinning fantasies in the Bastille, the Catholics of Boulogne were celebrating the real Benoît Joseph Labre as their greatest native son, although he actually was born in the nearby town of Amettes in 1748. From his early childhood, he embraced the most austere form of Catholicism. By the time of his death in Rome on April 16, 1783, he had lived like a saint, mortifying his flesh in pilgrimages and performing miracles—136 certified cures, according to a hagiography published in Italian in 1783 and in French in 1784. Canonization did not come until 1881, but Labre's reputation for saintliness provided Pelleport with perfect material for a sacrilegious satire that would carry his hero across the Channel.[38]

The impieties begin in Boulogne itself and take Brissot's mother-in-law, Voragine, in the first part of the book, as their main target. She reappears as Catau des Arches, a sex-starved widow of a merchant who eagerly coughs up 240 livres to play with the poet's nose as soon as he pulls on Saint Labre's belt and dangles the proboscis in front of her. His purse replenished, he reduces his nose to its normal size by letting out knots from the belt, and sails for London, though not before collecting tribute from several other women, who provide occasions for some well-placed barbs about the hypocrisy and pretentiousness of provincial society.[39]

London, by contrast, appears as a teeming world of adventurers, mountebanks, philosophers, scientists, politicians, agitators, publishers, and journalists. Their names swirl by: Fox; Pitt the younger; Lord North; Paul-Henri Maty, editor of the *New Review*; David Williams, the radical deist; Joseph Priestley, the champion of Enlightenment and science; Jean-Paul Marat, then struggling to make a name for himself as a scientist; James Graham, the inventor of the electric fertility bed; and an assortment of extravagant characters, probably acquaintances of Pelleport disguised under unidentifiable names: a German charlatan named Muller; an English quack called Remben; a certain J.P.D.; Ashley, a balloonist; Katerfiette, an astronomer; Piélatin, a violinist. In the midst of them all, the poet encounters "a troupe of miserable, starving Frenchmen"[40]—the colony of French refugees. They include Brissot, who now appears as "Bissoto de Guerreville" (a play on Brissot's full name, Brissot de Warville), the son-in-law of the widow des Arches, who lives as a dealer in secondhand clothes—that is, as a hack writer who cobbles together works by other authors.[41] The poet mentions the journalists connected with the *Courrier de l'Europe* and some other scribblers, but he reserves most of his scorn for Morande, who resumes his treachery as "the slanderer Thonevet" (an allusion to Morande's full name, Théveneau de Morande).[42] Thonevet slanders the poet, attempts to blackmail him, and denounces him to a secret agent of the Parisian police, exactly as in *Le Diable dans un bénitier*. But no intrigue, however nasty, can undo the poet, thanks to his marvelous nose.

Soon all London is talking about it, betting on it, celebrating it in prose, poetry, and scientific treatises. It provokes such a furious debate in Parliament that the government collapses and new elections are held. "Because I love Fox and liberty,"[43] the poet agrees to reserve his nose for the wives and daughters of candidates committed to the Whigs. While he is campaigning for Fox at Covent Garden, however, disaster strikes. A pickpocket slips his hand into the vital watch fob and disappears with the magic belt. The poet despairs. Reduced to the status of a writer with an ordinary nose, he returns to Boulogne to publish a book with the press that Swinton used for the edition of the *Courrier de l'Europe* marketed in France, exactly as Pelleport did in 1784. In this case, the poet puts the blame for the catastrophe squarely on Thonevet. Out of sheer malice, Thonevet composes several libels, attributes them to the poet, and, with the help of widow des Arches, denounces him to the French authorities, who carry him off to the Bastille. Meanwhile, Bissoto has been trying to collect a new supply of rags (used literary works) in Paris. The police suspect him of collaborating on the libels, so they lock him up, too—not in the Bastille, however, but in the nastier prison of Bicêtre, where he soon dies and therefore disappears from the narrative. After a long and miserable stay in the Bastille, the poet is finally released. While walking away, he hears a crier announcing an appeal from the archbishop for witnesses of Labre's miracles to testify to their authenticity so that Rome can initiate the process of canonization. As the most devoted follower of the saint, the poet decides to go to Rome himself. But first he must visit his brothers in Stenay. That is how he has come to cross paths with the Bohemians. He recommends a tavern to them, promising to join them for supper after he has had a reunion with his brothers. They pack up the donkey, continue on their way, and arrive at the tavern. The sun sets. Supper is cooking . . .

The novel ends there with a wonderfully open, inconclusive flourish. Before parting from the Bohemians, however, the poet offers a reflection that provides a conclusion of sorts to his story: "You see all the misery that I have suffered from my sad experience of literature and how I am disgusted with it. So nothing, I assure you, frightens me so much as to hear myself called an author. I always imagine that I am being pursued by a band of those blood-hounds that men in power station at street corners and city limits in order to prevent reason from entering by contraband."[44]

Les Bohémiens is among other things a book about literature, literature understood broadly as a system of money, power, and prestige. Speaking through his narrator, Pelleport views the system from the perspective of Grub Street. He longs for a patron so that he can strike it rich "without being obliged to found either a lycéo-musée, or a museo-lycée, or an academico-musico-lycée, without writing an anthology of correspondence, a journal, mercury, *courrier, gazetier, gazetin, affiches, petites-affiches, annales, gazettes-bibliothèques*, digest of the aforesaid journals, gazettes, etc. and all the other literary swindles so widely employed in our time."[45] But he has no patron, so he must fall back on all those practices so typical of Grub Street—and another one, too: the composition of libels. In one of his many asides to the reader, he asks: "Have you ever been printed alive, my dear reader? Under pressure from your baker and your tavern-keeper, have you pounded the pavement, in shoes without soles, to the shops where rag-and-bone men, merchants who deal in writing, flog the thoughts of the wretches who are reduced by misfortune to making a living from their imagination?"[46]

At this point, the narrator turns on the reader and accuses him (not her, judging from the context) of living in luxury, thanks to dubious maneuvers within some business or bureaucracy, while the poor author starves. Very well, then, reader, he says: let me tell you what it is like to live as an author who lacks independent resources. He then takes you, the reader, on a tour of the Parisian publishing industry, naming names and evoking characters exactly as they existed in the 1780s. You walk into the office of an important publisher, Charles-Joseph Panckoucke, clutching your portfolio, the narrator explains. Would Monsieur be interested in some verse about a recently deceased great man or perhaps a novel in two volumes (that is, *Les Bohémiens*)? It won't sell,

Panckoucke replies, and waves you to the door: he can't find time to talk with the likes of you; he has to catch up on his correspondence. So you drag your manuscripts to a publisher of the second rank, Nicolas-Augustin Delalain. His daughter greets you politely in the bookshop, but when she learns you are an author, not a customer, she turns you over to her mother, in order to spare papa from wasting his time. *Maman* won't even look at the poems: she has already rejected three dozen batches of verse this morning. And when you offer her your "philosophical novel" (again, *Les Bohémiens*), she falls into a fury and runs you out of the office.[47] The only remaining hope is a dealer at the very bottom of the trade, Edme-Marie-Pierre Desauges, a specialist in hack works and forbidden literature who has already spent two terms in the Bastille. He finds your work excellent, just the thing that he can print and sell through his contacts in Holland. You return to your garret, overjoyed. Your landlord, baker, and tavern-keeper agree to extend more credit. You scribble away, adding last touches to your manuscript, until late at night. When at last you have collapsed in bed, there is a knock at the door. In comes a police inspector accompanied by the dread undercover agent Receveur; out you go straight to the Bastille. While you rot in prison, Desauges, who has had your manuscripts copied after denouncing you to the police, prints your book and sells it through the underground. Your hunger verges on starvation; your health gives out; and when at last you are released, you have no choice but to turn yourself in to the poorhouse and die.[48]

In a similar digression, the narrator picks a quarrel with the reader. I know you are tired of digressions, he says. You want to get back to the narrative. You want action, but I won't give it to you because you should learn something about what went into the book you are holding in your hands. You should acquire some knowledge of the literary marketplace. So here is another digression. Books have plenty of readers but not buyers. The ratio is roughly ten to one. One person may be willing to part with some change for a book, but ten or more borrow it or steal it and pass it around in ever-widening circles: from masters to lackeys, mistresses to chambermaids, parents to children, neighbors to neighbors, and booksellers to subscribers in reading clubs (*cabinets littéraires*)—all at the expense of the author. The situation is hopeless—unless the king were to deliver an edict that would transform the basic conditions of literature. For example, he could issue an *arrêt du conseil d'état* with a long preamble about the importance of authors and a series of articles, beginning with the following:

1. No book may be loaned, except within families and then only as far in the collateral line as first cousins, subject to a penalty of 500 livres to be paid to the author.

2. No servants may pass around their masters' books, subject to a penalty of a year's wages or, failing that, physical punishment: they will be branded on the left ear with the letters P D L for *prêteur de livres* and whipped in front of all the bookshops in the town.

Pending such a measure, the narrator proposes a temporary solution. This very book, the one that you are now reading, must be sold only in a fine binding and at a high price, which is to be maintained for the benefit of its author. The publisher is therefore forbidden to sell it in sheets, boards, or paper coverings. The digression ends with a remark delivered directly at the reader, who is deemed to demand that the narrator get on with the story: "Your impatience is getting out of hand, but before giving in to you, it was only just that I looked after my own interests. Every man for himself. No, I won't be a martyr to some ridiculous selflessness and neglect my own business. I do go on a bit about myself, I admit, but what author forgets himself while writing?"[49]

In fact, of course, the author has inserted himself in the narrative throughout the book.[50] The digressions reinforce that tendency by showing how the author's autobiography bears on the condition of literature in general—and how the reader is complicit in perpetuating that condition.

Did readers actually respond in the way called for by the text? Probably not, because the text had so few readers—next to none, judging by the number of copies that have survived and the lack of reviews and references in contemporary sources.[51] The publication of *Les Bohémiens* was a non-event situated at the heart of the most eventful period of French history. Even if a few copies made it into the hands of readers, they can hardly have provoked much of a reaction. The French in 1790 were creating a brave new world and doing so in deadly earnest. They had no reason to be interested in a satirical account of life in a republic of letters that no longer existed. Pelleport's novel was out of date before its publication. Pelleport himself was out of tune with his times. While his contemporaries threw themselves passionately into the Revolution, he stood apart and looked upon the world from a perspective that combined disenchantment with derision—or "nothingism." Yet he deployed a prodigious talent when he evoked the life of Grub Street under the Ancien Régime. Seen from the twenty-first century, his novel looks extraordinarily modern, and his Bohemians appear as the first full embodiment of bohemianism.

Chapter 17

The Grub Street Route to Revolution

In retrospect, it looks as though all roads from the Ancien Régime led to the Revolution. That, of course, is an illusion. We should resist the temptation to read revolutionary tendencies into everything that happened in France before 1789. But there was one road that issued directly onto the revolutionary upheaval: Grub Street. Over it passed an important segment of the Revolution's leaders—not all of them, to be sure: most were solidly bourgeois, many belonged to the nobility, and those who came from the class of scribblers scattered into different camps, including a few on the far right.[1] To study the Grub Street element in the Revolution is not to follow a straight line of causality but rather to investigate a milieu, one that played an important part in the creation of a new political culture through its mastery of the printed word.

The hack writers from the Ancien Régime found a source of income and an outlet for their energy in the pamphlets and newspapers that flooded the public sphere from 1789 to 1800. Estimates vary, and it is difficult to distinguish between a pamphlet, a periodical pamphlet, and a periodical that resembles a modern newspaper. But the revolution in politics certainly touched off a revolution in print. Paris did not have a daily newspaper until 1777. Only sixty-six French-language periodicals circulated in the entire country, nearly half of them published abroad, before 1789. Then the press exploded. At least 2,600 pamphlets were published between January and the opening of the Estates General on May 5, 1789. Nearly 250 newspapers appeared during the six months after the storming of the Bastille and more than five hundred between July 14, 1789, and the overthrow of the monarchy on August 10, 1792. Never before had there been such a demand for copy.[2]

The Revolution was wordy. It needed men who had a way with words, and it drew many of them from the overcrowded underworld of letters, where they had scraped together a living as best they could under the conditions described by Pelleport: censorship, an oppressive book police, a monopolistic booksellers' guild, and rivalry within the ranks of the writers. Conditions varied, and in some ways they had improved by 1780. Censors had become more permissive; the inspectors of the book trade imprisoned fewer authors in the

Bastille; and new government regulations loosened the grip of the big Parisian publishers on the book trade. But in a country without copyright, royalties, or a high rate of literacy, few authors could live from their pens. Louis-Sébastien Mercier, who knew the world of letters better than anyone, put their number at thirty in 1778.[3] Yet Voltaire, Rousseau, and other famous figures had made authorship enormously attractive—in itself, as a source of prestige and as a calling devoted to a cause: liberty, progress, Enlightenment.[4]

The generation born in mid-century flooded the Republic of Letters with young men intent on becoming the successors to Voltaire and Rousseau. Although statistics in the realm of literature raise all sorts of problems—how to define an author? how to find adequate sources?—I have attempted to estimate the size of the literary population during the second half of the eighteenth century. By 1780 there were about three thousand authors in France, well over twice the number that existed in the 1750s. Most supported themselves from conventional occupations such as medicine and the law, but many scraped together a living by combining odd jobs of a more-or-less literary character. They hired themselves out as secretaries, gave private lessons, corrected proof, compiled anthologies, composed almanacs, churned out pamphlets, scribbled copy for clandestine newsletters, contributed articles to foreign journals, peddled books, and spied for the police. Most of these makeshift occupations, along with libel and blackmail, were taken up at one time or another by the writers who appear in the preceding pages: Morande, Pelleport, Manuel, Turbat, Linguet, de Serres de la Tour, Goesman, Goudar, de Launay, La Coste de Mézières, Poultier d'Elmotte, Imbert de Boudeaux, Duvernet, and others, most of them obscure characters but similar in the lives they led to writers who became famous in the Revolution—Mirabeau, Brissot, Carra, Gorsas, Bonneville, Prudhomme, Louvet de Couvray, Fabre d'Eglantine, Hébert, Chaumette, Collot d'Herbois. To this list one could add men with a literary bent who pursued obscure professional careers until the Revolution opened an avenue to fame: Marat as a philosopher-scientist, Robespierre as an essayist-lawyer, Saint-Just as a poet—to name only three of the most famous. The list might be extended to considerable length, if one had a census of all the writers alive in 1789.

But quantitative arguments have their limits. The garret scribblers can also be understood as a figment of eighteenth-century imaginations. Voltaire had made the hack, derided as "Le Pauvre Diable" (the poor devil), into a literary motif, which he used as a weapon for bashing his enemies, and Mercier made writers in "low literature" a favorite subject of his *Tableau de Paris* (first edition, 1781).[5] Unlike Voltaire, Mercier treated them sympathetically, and in *Le Nouveau Paris* (1798), a sequel published seventeen years later, he observed that the indigent writer from the Ancien Régime had provided a model, or at least a name, for the most radical variety of activist in revolutionary Paris: the sans-culotte. According to Mercier, the term was first used in reference to Nicolas Gibert, a poet so poor that he could not afford to buy breeches and became known as "Gibert le Sans-Culotte." After Gibert died, destitute, in 1780, "Rich people adopted this denomination and used it against all authors who were not elegantly dressed."[6] From marginality in literature to militancy in politics, the expression acquired a broader significance. Mercier went on to note that several poets and playwrights from the Ancien Régime threw themselves into the radical revolution: first and foremost Fabre d'Eglantine and Collot d'Herbois, but also more obscure militants such as Charles-Philippe Ronsin, Paul-Ulrich Dubuisson, and Guillaume-Antoine Nourry known as Grammont.[7]

It would be misleading to conclude that poor devils transmogrified into sans-culottes, either by a sociological line of direct descent or by means of literary conventions in speeches and articles. The sociology of authors and the representation of them in literature are too complex to be reduced to any formula, as is the notion of the sans-culotte itself.[8] To understand how the experience of literature under the Ancien Régime fed into the radical politics of the Revolution, it is best to study actual cases. One of the most revealing examples is the last of the authors in the chain of interlocking libels that began with *Le Gazetier cuirassé*, Pierre Manuel. Unlike the others, he never emigrated to London, although he, too, ran into trouble with the police. His story complements theirs by showing how a life was lived in Grub Street, Paris, and how it led to a career in the Revolution.[9]

On February 3, 1786, the police descended on Manuel's modest apartment in the rue des Deux Écus and carried him off to the Bastille. They were trying to find the author of a pamphlet, *Lettre d'un garde du roi*, on the hottest topic of the day: the Diamond Necklace Affair, a spectacular scandal in which the cardinal de Rohan was arrested for trying to win the favor of the queen by giving her a necklace made of diamonds allegedly worth 1,600,000 livres. Although the queen never had any part in the whole business—it was a confidence game contrived by some adventurers who duped the cardinal in order to run off with the diamonds—it made her look bad, so bad in fact that some gossips added Rohan to the list of her supposed lovers. The affair provided pamphleteers with an irresistible subject and the police with an urgent assignment: while the former churned out publications, the latter hunted them down. The arrest of Manuel belonged to the general attempt to clear the streets of anything connected with "cardinal Collier" (the cardinal of the necklace).[10]

Manuel went through six interrogations, an unusually long gauntlet of questions and confrontations, which shows how seriously the authorities took the affair. In his first session with Louis Thiroux de Crosne, Lenoir's successor as lieutenant general of police, Manuel denied that he had written the *Lettre d'un garde du roi* but admitted that he knew the author. He refused to reveal the author's name, however, because, as the police noted, "It is a matter of principle for him not to compromise anyone." He retreated from this defiant stance in his second interrogation by saying that he actually had written the pamphlet himself but did not consider it illegal. It was nothing more than a topical work designed to satisfy the public's curiosity. In his third interrogation, Manuel reversed himself once more, asserting again that he had not written the pamphlet and would not name the true author. The archives contain no record of Manuel's fourth interrogation, but they show that by then the police had rounded up and grilled six other suspects. These included Edme-Marie-Pierre Desauges, a notorious dealer in forbidden books (and the same Desauges as the character described in *Les Bohémiens*), who said he had obtained his allotment of *Lettre d'un garde du roi* from Manuel; a peddler known as Le Normand, who apparently said the same; and Jean-Augustin Grangé, a seventy-three-year-old printer whom the police suspected of producing it. Grangé, a tough veteran of the printing trade, refused to divulge anything, but the others confessed enough for the police to confound Manuel in his fifth interrogation. At this point, he cracked. He identified the author as a fellow hack, Charles-Joseph Mayer, and the printer as Grangé. The police informed Grangé that Manuel had implicated him, but still the old man refused to talk. Then they engineered "confrontations" between Manuel and Le Normand and between Manuel and Grangé on the same day, March 17. That cleared the way for Manuel to make a full confession about his underground activities in his last interrogation, which took place on March 28. Having extracted all the information they needed, the police released him ten days later. It was a typical *embastillement*, which lasted two months—quite different from the case of Pelleport, who was occupying another cell in the Bastille at the same time.

Seen from the perspective of the police, Manuel looked more like a peddler than an author. Although he identified himself as a "man of letters" in his interrogations, they put him down as one of the many small-time producers and distributors of pamphlets in Paris. In his case, the pamphlet was an inoffensive commentary on the Diamond Necklace Affair, couched in the language of a common soldier. As its full title indicates, the *Lettre d'un garde du roi, pour servir de suite aux Mémoires sur Cagliostro* presented itself as a sequel to the legal memoirs written to defend the notorious adventurer, Giuseppe Balsamo, known as the comte de Cagliostro, who had been imprisoned for masterminding the plot to get the diamonds. Cagliostro's memoirs, like Beaumarchais's twelve years earlier, had captivated the public. Manuel told the police that he and Mayer merely wanted to capitalize on their success: "Their success astonished us. That led to the reflection that a brochure wrapped in blue paper produces more money than a useful book." A "blue" pamphlet was a cheap work stitched inside the heavy blue paper used to wrap cones of sugar, as in the case of the crude chapbooks known as the "bibliothèque bleue." Manuel described the *Lettre d'un garde du roi* as a speculation typical of the trivial literature hawked in the streets of Paris. He and Mayer had agreed to go into it together: Mayer was to write the text, Manuel would supervise its publication, and they would split the profits. The printing—two sheets in-octavo plus a title page and endpaper run off at two thousand copies—cost only four hundred livres. It was a purely commercial affair, Manuel insisted throughout his interrogations: "Replied that the book does not deserve to be called a libel, that he produced it only in order to capitalize on the vogue for the *Mémoires de Cagliostro*, that it was merely a commercial speculation without any malign intention."

Of course, libels, too, were commercial speculations, but everything about the pamphlet confirms Manuel's claim that it had no seditious intent. It provides a casual overview of the Diamond Necklace Affair, written as a dialogue, although it takes the form of a letter. The main character is a plain-spoken soldier, a man of the people who wants to get in his two cents' worth by holding forth on the affair as he sees it. Despite all the fuss, it doesn't amount to much, he says. The cardinal, to be sure, behaved extravagantly, but what else can you expect of a person in such a high rank? Cagliostro is an adventurer, but harmless. None of the other accomplices currently in the Bastille deserves to be taken seriously, although due respect must be shown to the king, who is ordained to rule by God and, moreover, is a good family man, far better than the Holy Roman emperor, a ruler given over to court ceremonies. The soldier knows a thing or two about behavior among the great, because he has seen them up close in his capacity as a palace guard. He understands the need for deference and discipline, even the need for the Bastille. Prisons belong to a well-run state, although he has his doubts about some other aspects of the current order of things, such as the necessity of concentrating so much wealth and power in the hands of the upper clergy. But our soldier is just a younger son from the provinces ("cadet de Gascogne"), and he doesn't make pronouncements on affairs of state. As far as he is concerned, everyone connected with the affair should be released from prison, and the whole thing would blow over.[11]

With the release of Manuel, his case, too, was dismissed, even though the police had turned up a great deal of evidence about his involvement with publications far less innocent than the *Lettre d'un garde du roi*. Most were connected with the comte de Mirabeau. In the course of his tempestuous career before the Revolution, Mirabeau had run off with Marie-Thérèse-Sophie Richard de Ruffey, marquise de Monnier, the young wife of an aged magistrate in the Parlement of Besançon. Captured in Amsterdam in 1777 by an agent of the Paris police (inspector de Bruguières, a colleague and occasional companion of Receveur), they went to separate prisons—Mirabeau to the fortress of Vincennes, Sophie de Monnier to a penitentiary for women in Montmartre. The police permitted them to correspond, though not to keep each other's letters. The correspondence therefore remained in the police archives, where Manuel recovered it and published it after Mirabeau's death in 1791. Although he did not say so at that time, he had arranged for the publication of many of Mirabeau's works in the 1780s, for Mirabeau wrote a great deal, and he needed an agent.

In some respects, Mirabeau can be considered an aristocrat in Grub Street. He lived well, to be sure, usually with a valet and as much luxury as he could command, but he lived beyond his means. Having quarreled with his family, he had no regular source of income and fell back on writing as a way to raise money. In 1782 he managed to extricate himself from Vincennes and to escape from a potential death sentence by clearing himself from a charge of abduction and adultery in a spectacular trial held in Aix. After that he churned out publications on all sorts of subjects—topical pamphlets, pornography, financial tracts, political works, anything that would sell. He often hired hacks to provide the main body of his texts and added a layer of rhetoric to make them more provocative. His name in itself promoted sales, because his adventures made him notorious. Impetuous, passionate, freethinking, and scornful of conventions, he combined qualities that made him irresistible to readers; and the public's fascination grew as his books became more radical, culminating in *Dénonciation de l'agiotage*, a libel that helped bring down the government in 1787. Mirabeau drew on his prison experience in *Des Lettres de cachet et des prisons d'Etat*, a denunciation of despotism that became an underground best-seller, like Linguet's *Mémoire sur la Bastille*. And while in prison, he wrote pornographic works, which gave vent to his overheated imagination in the same manner as the prison novels of Pelleport and de Sade. Of the three aristocratic libertines, only Mirabeau occupied an important place in the public sphere. Whatever one thinks of him as a stylist—he specialized in bombast—he stood out during the 1780s as one of the best-known and best-selling writers in France. But to sell his books he needed help. Nearly all of them were illegal, so someone who knew his way around the underground had to look after their printing and distribution. That someone, at least for a while in 1785 and 1786, was Pierre Manuel.[12]

When the police searched Manuel's apartment before taking him off to the Bastille, they confiscated twenty-one letters from Mirabeau and his mistress at that time, Mme de Nehra, who acted as an intermediary in many of his dealings with Manuel. The letters have disappeared, but short summaries of them in the police report show that Manuel had arranged for the printing of one of Mirabeau's pamphlets on financial affairs, *Lettre du comte de Mirabeau à M. le Couteulx de la Noraye, sur la Banque de Saint-Charles et sur la Caisse d'Escompte* (1785) and that he had acted as Mirabeau's agent in the marketing of at least three other works.[13] One of Mme de Nehra's letters "informs sieur Manuel about a manuscript that she wants to have printed quickly." Another told him that she soon would deliver some more manuscripts, and a third warned him that she suspected him of printing a pirated edition of the *Lettre . . . à M. le Couteulx* behind Mirabeau's back. She was right. The other papers confiscated by the police contain the bill of a printer for a small edition of the *Lettre . . . à M. le Couteulx*, which he had done for Manuel: five hundred copies at a cost of three hundred livres—a reference to the pirated edition. This affair led to a nasty quarrel and the rupture of Manuel's relations with Mirabeau: "The first seven letters say that M. de Mirabeau had lost confidence in him. They even contain some bitter complaints and hard remarks." In Manuel's interrogations, he admitted that he had directed the sale of four of Mirabeau's financial pamphlets and that he had hired Grangé to produce one of them, *Réponse du comte de Mirabeau à l'écrivain des administrateurs de la Compagnie des eaux de Paris* (1785), using income from the sales to pay for the printing bill. Grangé confirmed this in his own interrogation, but he and Manuel only played bit parts in the publishing history of Mirabeau's works. The important books went to large publishing houses located outside France. Mirabeau used Manuel as a middleman for the production of topical pamphlets and probably for small collateral speculations on books that could be run off on clandestine presses in Paris while being printed in large numbers at a safe distance in Switzerland and the Low Countries. Manuel denied any involvement in the printing of the more radical and pornographic works of Mirabeau, but he certainly sold them; the police confiscated a stock of *Ma Conversion* (1783) and its reprint, *Le Libertin de qualité, ou confidences d'un prisonnier au Château de Vincennes* (1784), in Manuel's apartment, and the letters they impounded mentioned sales of *Des Lettres de cachet et des prisons d'Etat* (1782). They certainly uncovered enough evidence to prove that Manuel served as Mirabeau's agent in the literary underground of Paris.

There was nothing unusual about this function. Peddlers and petty book dealers (usually semi-legal retailers known as "marchands de livres" in contrast to official "libraires") often acted as small-scale publishers, though that term seems too grand to describe their microscopic speculations. When they scented an opportunity, they would commission someone like Grangé, whose place among printers was as marginal as theirs among booksellers, to run off a few hundred copies of a pamphlet on the latest topic of public interest. They might share profits and risks or pay for the printing after they had collected enough from the sales. This was the kind of operation to which Manuel referred when he described the *Lettre d'un garde du roi* as a "commercial speculation." The police had often encountered micro-businesses of this sort. They did not pay special attention to Manuel's dealings with Mirabeau because they were intent on hunting down everything connected with the Diamond Necklace Affair. But while interrogating Manuel, they turned up a great deal of information about how he made a living. They discovered that he had contracted to become an apprentice bookseller with Le Jay, a well-known master in the Parisian guild. Manuel, who was thirty-four years old at that time, explained that he had not yet made up his mind to enter the profession in this manner, but he provided plenty of evidence that he already was deeply involved in the book trade, primarily as a peddler.

The police found several notes in Manuel's papers about books and pamphlets that he had sold to individuals—for example, a reference to "the pamphlet of the day" for a certain M. Banquet and a list of titles sent to a comte de Turconi. They impounded a small account book "where one can see that sieur Manuel does a business in all sorts of prohibited books." And they seized documents showing that he supplemented this tiny retail business with more important operations as a middleman: thus "a note about various booksellers, small dealers, and peddlers to whom sieur Manuel has sold a work [unnamed], to one of them a dozen copies, to another two dozens, to others the same amount, more or less." These small dealers plied their trade in the capillary system of book distribution, buying and selling from one another as opportunities arose. Manuel had a few suppliers among foreign wholesalers, including Dufour of Maestricht and Mettra of Neuwied (Mettra moved there after floods from the Rhine had destroyed his printing shop at Deutz near Cologne in 1784). He sent a few shipments to booksellers as far away as Marseille and Nantes. But he operated on a small scale, primarily with peddlers like himself.

Manuel's trade included two other elements that made it different from that of most other peddlers. He sold manuscripts of original works to foreign publishers, and he dealt in manuscript newsletters (*nouvelles à la main*). The police turned up letters from two fairly important publishers, Barde of Geneva and Dujardin of Brussels, refusing a manuscript that Manuel had tried to sell.

Nothing suggests that he had written it himself or that he composed the news-letters. A note from one of the middlemen in the distribution network of the newsletters reported that a certain "Mme de Lembliment desires to subscribe." Another, from Audéard, a bookseller in Geneva, complained about the quality of a newsletter, and Manuel promised to improve his service with "news from another source." One of his sources probably was Mettra, who had been send-ing his manuscript gazette to Brissot and Pelleport in London. Other scraps of evidence in Manuel's dossiers confirm that he scraped together a living by combining various operations—book peddling, a few ventures into clandes-tine publishing, and underground journalism—in a makeshift commerce located well outside the limits of the law (it was illegal under the Ancien Régime to peddle books without official authorization, and Manuel dealt heav-ily in forbidden books). When the law caught up with him, he went broke.

Two months in the Bastille were enough to destroy the trade of a very small dealer. What happened to Manuel immediately after his release from the Bastille on April 7, 1786, cannot be determined, but by 1789 he was reduced to living in a room attached to a printing shop in the rue Serpente, which the printer, Garnery, let him use in exchange for correcting proof, writing the occasional pamphlet, and handling relations with peddlers. Such is the account of his condition in *La Vie secrète de Pierre Manuel*, and there is no reason to doubt its accuracy, despite the polemical character of the work. But what to make of a more troublesome reference to Manuel's source of livelihood around 1780? In a short essay among the drafts of his unpublished memoirs, Lenoir said that Manuel had been a police spy.

The essay describes the underground trade of various peddlers, particu-larly a certain Sauson, who took up peddling after a stint of work as a printer's devil. According to Lenoir, Sauson supplied other peddlers with forbidden books, which he produced on a clandestine press. He was caught and sent to the Bastille but then released at the order of Necker, who used him to produce propaganda about financial operations. Unknown to Necker, Sauson also printed pornography, including an edition of the libertine novel *Thérèse philo-sophe*. His fellow peddlers continued to draw supplies from his secret printing shop, until one of them denounced him. That peddler, according to Lenoir, was Manuel: "Manuel, a writer and a peddler who served at that time as a salaried spy for a police inspector, denounced Sauson, saying that he had seen obscene works being delivered from the printing shop in the rue Mazarin that he [Sauson] secretly operated in a location connected with the hôtel du Con-trôle des finances."[14] A raid by the police confirmed Manuel's denunciation—and a few years later Manuel himself was arrested for distributing the equally obscene *Histoire de dom B*** Portier des Chartreux* along with some buttons adorned by scenes of copulating couples based on the sonnets of Aretino. The duc d'Orléans, who had a taste for such things, intervened to save Manuel from prison at that point, but no one could prevent Manuel from confinement in the Bastille in 1786, when the police cleared the streets of everyone who peddled works related to the Diamond Necklace Affair.[15] By then they were well acquainted with him.

The police employed hundreds of spies, some at regular salaries (30 livres to 150 livres per month in 1770), others for casual favors or incidental payments that varied according to the value of the information they provided.[16] Known as "flies" (*mouches* or *mouchards*, a term derived from the name of Antoine Mouchy, a sixteenth-century spy master of the Inquisition), they buzzed around cafés and public gardens, picking up gossip and reporting on suspicious characters. The police were especially eager to receive information about information—that is, about books, pamphlets, *nouvelles à la main*, songs, and rumors—and even to manipulate it, so they often hired hack writers. If Lenoir is to be believed, their agents included Brissot and Mirabeau: "The famous comte de Mirabeau and Brissot de Warville were employed separately by the police to turn out writing, bulletins, and to disseminate them in the public in order to contradict false stories and anecdotes."[17] But Lenoir's testimony cannot be accepted without questioning. He began writing the drafts of his memoirs in 1790 as a refugee from the Revolution, and he continued to work on them until at least 1802, when he returned to France. His memory may have clouded over, and he may have wanted to blacken the names of the revolutionaries who had driven him out of France. Yet he knew Manuel's milieu intimately, and there is no evidence that he lied. On the contrary, he seems to have been an upright and enlightened administrator. It is impossible to know for sure whether Manuel and his companions spied for the police, but one thing is certain: spying belonged to the many métiers of Grub Street.

Manuel also had some other employment, though no dependable source of income. The only occupation mentioned in the biographical notes about him is tutoring. According to a pamphlet attack on him from 1791, he relieved "the well known mediocrity of his fortune" for a while before the Revolution by giving lessons to the children of the duc de la Trémouille.[18] An article about the Diamond Necklace Affair in the *Mémoires secrets* said that Manuel also had tutored the children of a banker named Tourton. But he lost that position because a hostile priest denounced him for spreading impieties. In order to support himself, he therefore took up peddling books and wrote occasional pamphlets such as the *Lettre d'un garde du corps*. The *Mémoires secrets* had nothing to say about that work, but in reporting Manuel's release from the

Bastille, it gave a favorable review to one of his more substantial books, *Coup-d'oeil philosophique sur le règne de Saint Louis*, which it found agreeably Volta-irean.[19] The *Correspondance littéraire* of Grimm and Meister disagreed. It dismissed the *Coup-d'oeil philosophique* as overblown and incoherent.[20] Those are the only references I can find to Manuel's publications in the pre-revolutionary press. Yet he published quite a lot: at least six books and pamphlets. Does he therefore deserve to be considered a "man of letters"? That, after all, was how he identified himself when he was interrogated in the Bastille.

Before attempting to resolve the question of Manuel's professional identity, it might be useful to summarize what can be established about his life before the Revolution.

Birth: Nemours, December 14, 1753, one of four children in the family of a poor tradesman.

Education: after a local Latin school, training for the priesthood in the seminary of Sens. Apparently he was tonsured—that is, took preliminary vows to enter the clergy—and pursued his studies further in a seminary in Paris before turning against the Church. According to *Vie secrète de Pierre Manuel*, which is well-informed though tendentious, he showed so much promise as a schoolboy that his parents encouraged him to continue his education in the hope that he would become a priest. Instead, he took up Voltairean views, tried to cut a figure as a wit in provincial society, and drifted into the book trade in Paris.

Outlook: difficult to determine, but the shift from Catholicism to an irreligious, Enlightenment view of the world seems likely to have taken place during his youth. His early writings are thoroughly anti-Christian, though they have no trace of the passionate Rousseauism that pervades the works of his friends, notably Brissot and Mercier.

Employment: tutoring, pamphleteering, peddling, and odd jobs of many kinds in the underground book trade.[21]

In short, Manuel's life fit into a pattern typical of his generation. From an obscure, provincial background, he felt the pull of Paris and tried to make his way in the world of letters by enlisting among the followers of the philosophes. But to support himself he had to fall back on all sorts of expedients, many of them illegal or unsavory.

His writings indicate how that experience became expressed in print. Like so many young men who came of age in the 1770s and 1780s, Manuel attempted to publish ambitious works that would make his mark among the successors to Voltaire. In the caption to the engraving of himself that he had made in 1792, he cited two books from his pre-revolutionary career: *Coup-d'oeil philosophique sur le règne de Saint Louis* (1786) and *L'Année française* (1789). The first was the only sustained piece of philosophic writing he ever published, although he did not sustain it for long. In a note at its end, he explained that he originally had meant to produce a large-scale, philosophical history of Saint Louis's reign, but after starting his draft he learned that abbé Louis-Pierre Saint-Martin, a priest with advanced views and a position in the Châtelet court of Paris, also planned to write such a work. Manuel therefore cut short his own treatise—it ends abruptly at page 164—and presented it as an essay, which would provide an overview of the reign as seen with "the torchlight of philosophy."[22] Far from trying to debunk a revered figure of France's past, he stressed that he meant to celebrate Saint Louis as a statesman. The saint therefore appeared as a champion of the common people, an enemy of monasticism, and a crusader for "liberty, that inalienable patrimony of nature."[23] The crusades themselves, however, posed a problem. Manuel solved it by interpreting them as a hideous mistake, which Louis made (at the prompting of Saint Bernard, a villain, who was contrasted with Saladin, a hero) only because he was born too soon to have imbibed the philosophy of the Enlightenment. Nonetheless, the crusader did his best to mitigate the horrors of feudalism and to promote liberty and the rights of man. He could do little, unfortunately, to destroy the power of the clergy, which Manuel, invoking Hume, characterized as the root of all historical evil. But history also showed that superstition was retreating before the advance of reason; thanks to the example set by the philosopher saint, the French could expect progress on all fronts. A more anachronistic view of the Middle Ages could hardly be imagined. But Manuel took care not to challenge any contemporary institutions and to keep his social criticism located safely in the past. According to the *Mémoires secrets*, he submitted his text for approval by the police, and it appeared, with a false address but displaying his name on the title page, without creating a stir. In its review, the *Correspondance littéraire* did not remark on any radical ideas in the text but dismissed it as a mediocre work disfigured by "a continuously declamatory tone, which is often completely unintelligible."[24] Whatever one thinks of that judgment, it is obvious that Manuel's most important book did not make his name as a philosopher.

The other book he cited in his epitaph to himself was merely an anthology of writing by others, abridged and adapted for a general audience. It belonged to the popular genre of almanacs, which the French bought as gifts to be given at the beginning of the year. Almanacs usually included information of all sorts, which readers could consult for edification, instruction, or amusement linked to every day of the calendar. The traditional variety contained the names of the saints associated with each day. Manuel secularized this tradition by substituting the names of civic heroes for the saints, as indicated in his title: *L'Année française, ou vie des hommes qui ont honoré la France ou par leurs talents, ou par leurs services, et surtout par leurs vertus: Pour tous les jours de l'année.* This time the book appeared with an approbation and privilege of the king—that is, as a fully legal work. The censor's approbation, printed at the end, praised it for its sound principles and purpose. Along with Manuel's name, the title page carried the name of its publisher, Nyon l'aîné et fils, a reputable house. The text ran to four nicely printed volumes, and the price, binding included, came to 12 livres, a hefty sum. Everything about the book indicates that it was a commercial speculation, designed to bring in a good deal of money.

Of course, the economic purpose did not invalidate its message, which anticipated the calendars and the cult of virtue developed during the Revolution. Although the title page bore 1789 as the year of publication, the calendar was meant to be used from January 1, 1789, and therefore did not allude to anything after 1788. Manuel gave directions about how to use the book in his preface. Fathers were to gather their children around them and read the day's lesson in a manner that would stimulate an edifying discussion. Teachers were to do the same with their pupils. All readers were to derive inspiration from the examples of virtuous men (women went unmentioned)[25] who had been born or died on the appropriate day. In choosing models of virtue, Manuel would not favor the great, far from it: "Far from me those sovereigns distinguished merely by power or valor! I seek out citizens whose enlightenment, talent, and virtue have brought honor to my fatherland."[26] He would celebrate virtuous workers, peasants oppressed by their lords, and "martyrs of intolerance"[27]—such as himself, for he announced that he had formed the idea for the book while suffering in the Bastille. In view of those declarations, it is somewhat odd to find Colbert, Francis I, and the Dauphin (son of Louis XV) among Manuel's heroes. But he said that he had extracted his material from various dictionaries and collections of funeral eulogies, then rewrote it as needed. Although high-minded in principle, *L'Année française* was in practice a scissors-and-paste job.

The only other work of any importance that Manuel produced before the Revolution was *Essais historiques, critiques, littéraires et philosophiques* (1783), a collection of short, belletristic pieces that he had published in various reviews. All of them belonged to the genres of light literature favored by journals like the *Mercure.* In fact, Manuel had tried to break into the ranks of fashionable poets with some frothy verse of his own, which he managed to get printed in the *Mercure.*

Quand on plaît, on est toujours belle:
Toute la vie est un printemps.
Ne crains rien: l'amour et le temps

Te prendront pour une immortelle;
Peut-être un jour, jaloux de mon bonheur,
Les dieux voudront, ô ma Thémire,
T'arracher de mes bras, et non pas de mon coeur,
Pour te faire changer d'empire.

(When one is pleasing, one is always beautiful:
All life is a springtime.
Fear nothing: love and time
Will take you to be an immortal;
Perhaps one day, jealous of my happiness,
The gods will want, oh my Thémire,
To tear you from my arms, and not from my heart,
In order to make you change the place of your dominion.)[28]

The mixture of gallantry and sentimentality made Manuel look like all the other aspiring poets who sent off *vers de circonstance* to the *Mercure*. Manuel's *Essais* did not include any poetry, but they had the same conventional flavor. They included moralistic musings (*pensées*), oriental tales, reflections on episodes in ancient history, and sentimental stories with messages such as: "The masterpiece of love is the heart of a mother."[29] In several essays Manuel paid tribute to the usual heroes of contemporary literature: d'Alembert, Buffon, Rousseau, and especially Voltaire. In others, he stressed the difficulties of emulating them. Fathers, mothers, do not let your children succumb to the temptations of literature, he warned. Young men today dream of winning glory in the Republic of Letters. They write poems, epigrams, essays, all kinds of *pièces de circonstance*, which they send off to literary reviews in the hope of getting a start in "the career of letters."[30] But they soon discover that Paris is flooded with ambitious youths just like themselves. Before long, they learn that literature will not provide them with a living. If fortunate, they may escape from indigence by some form of employment such as tutoring. But then they must face additional humiliation, for their employer is likely to treat them as dirt and to be incapable of understanding their efforts to make a child into a citizen. Those remarks probably referred to Manuel's experience as a tutor in the household of the banker Tourton. But whether autobiographical or not, they reveal his view of literature at a moment when he was struggling to make his name in it. The *Essais* belonged to the struggle. They were designed to exhibit his talent in the very genres he mentioned when describing the efforts of his contemporaries to win recognition as writers. Far from causing any scandal, they appeared with the approval of the government and then disappeared, unnoticed and unreviewed, in the flood of trivial publications by other writers who also were attempting to extricate themselves from the bottom ranks of the Republic of Letters.

The frustrations of young authors and the danger of overcrowding in the literary world struck several of Manuel's contemporaries as an important phenomenon.[31] The most revealing variation on that theme was *Le Petit Almanach de nos grands hommes* (1788) by Antoine Rivarol, probably with some collaboration by L.-P.-Q. de Richebourg, marquis de Champcenetz. Instead of bewailing the lot of obscure writers, Rivarol made fun of them. Other works celebrated the most famous men of letters, he explained; he would dedicate his *Petit Almanach* to the most unknown. He combed through anthologies and literary reviews, extracting the names of all the poets and essayists from the bottom of Parnassus who aspired to rise to the top. Then he overwhelmed them with satirical praise. By absurdly inflated eulogies, he exposed hundreds of hacks and revealed a whole landscape of "Lilliputians," climbing over one another in a general scramble for literary glory. He placed Manuel in the midst of the crowd and dispatched him with one sentence.

MANUEL: an amiable and fluent Muse who could turn out anything but prefers to attain immortality by taking the dainty route through madrigals and epigrams.[32]

Instead of retreating into silence and waiting for the derision to dissipate, Manuel replied with an anonymous libel. Although he attempted to parry Rivarol's satire with some raillery of his own, he relied for the most part on a rhetoric of indignation: "According to you, M. Manuel would be capable of an epic poem because he composes madrigals—he, who with more philosophy than fortune, labors in obscurity on useful works! You denounce him as a maker of epigrams! But no such gall has ever poisoned his soul!"[33]

While defending his own dignity, Manuel claimed to speak for all writers who devoted themselves to the public good; he particularly deplored Rivarol's mockery of the Musée, a literary club, where anyone could gain admittance and find a hearing for his poetry in opposition to the academies that were reserved for the elite.[34] But after occupying this high moral ground, Manuel descended into the pit and began hurling insults. He accused Rivarol of being a fraudulent count and Champcenetz of being both a fake marquis and a homosexual. They replied with a counterattack, written in the form of a letter by a supposed member of the Musée. It celebrated *Le Petit Almanach de nos grands hommes* as a "Saint Bartholomew's Massacre of the literary rabble," poured more scorn on Manuel as a typical member of that milieu, mocked his claim to cut a figure in the Musée, and derided his "pretension to be a success in salons or suppers."[35]

The polemics expressed the nastiness of life at the bottom of the Republic of Letters, where literature was still a subject of slander just a few months before the storming of the Bastille. Do they also expose a contradiction between Manuel's claim to a noble calling as a man of letters and his shabby existence in the literary underground? Perhaps. But contradictions were built into literature as it was experienced by men like Manuel. To preach the gospel of human rights while peddling libels was to live through those contradictions, not simply to hide the sordid pursuit of profit behind a false front of idealism. Manuel probably believed in the principles he preached. His position among "the literary rabble" may have reinforced his commitment to Enlightenment convictions instead of undermining them. Of course, the state of his soul in 1789 can only be a matter of speculation. No one can know it, but at the same time no one should assume that ideological engagement is incompatible with self-interest or that failure leads inevitably to cynicism. A person who hits bottom need not lose faith in high ideals. On the contrary, by coping with hard realities far down in the social order, he or she may become determined to remake reality throughout the entire system—or at least to rally to that cause at a time of revolution. Grub Street may have looked like a dead end to Manuel throughout most of the 1780s, but by July 14, 1789, it had led to a new beginning.

Chapter 18
Slander into Terror

After July 14, 1789, the Bastille was dismantled as a building and reconstructed as a symbol in the retrospective view of France that came to be known as the Ancien Régime. Pierre Manuel contributed more to this symbolic reordering than anyone else. He made a career out of publishing books that exposed the horrors that had been hidden in the ancient fortress, and he used those publications to promote an additional career as a political activist. From words to actions, the course of his life from 1789 to 1793 illustrates the making and unmaking of a revolutionary and, to some extent, of the Revolution itself.[1]

Manuel tried to pass himself off in some of his revolutionary polemics as a conqueror of the Bastille. But he produced no evidence for that claim and eventually dropped it, falling back on his role as a Bastille martyr—that is, as a victim of despotism who had suffered for his selflessness in defending the cause of the people.[2] Anyone who could establish his status as a Bastillant (former prisoner) enjoyed a great advantage in the scramble for offices and influence that took place after July 14, 1789. But political careers could not be fashioned from reputation alone. Manuel had to overcome many disadvantages. He had no immediate family, no profession, no fortune, and no permanent address. The only place that could serve him as a springboard into revolutionary politics was Garnery's printing shop, where he corrected proof and dispensed pamphlets to peddlers in return for a free room.

Manuel wrote pamphlets himself, although they are difficult to identify in the waves of anonymous printed matter that flooded the streets of Paris after August 1788, when the king agreed to call the Estates General. One of them, *Lettre d'un citoyen à un frondeur sur les affaires présentes*, published during the last months of 1788, expresses some of the standard radical positions. It contains fierce attacks on the nobility, feudal dues, and the parlements, along with a defense of Necker, a tribute to the king, and a call for men of letters to lead the people in preparing for the new order.[3] But pamphleteering was not enough to win Manuel a place among the revolutionary leaders. His greatest asset was actually the network of contacts he had built up among the city's peddlers while operating as a peddler himself. According to the *Vie secrète de Pierre Manuel*, they helped launch his political career.

> In 1785 he was employed by Garnery. He earned enough to support himself there, occupying a free room by way of his yearly compensation. He was required only to produce some sheets, some libels for the printing shop, where he made himself useful by correcting proof. . . . His first protectors [in 1789] were the peddlers who turned up each day to supply themselves with the newspapers that Garnery printed. Manuel handed these out to them with an ingratiating manner. He flattered this boisterous species and won their support, which led to a position in a division of the police concerned with the book trade and printing.[4]

Of course nothing in the *Vie secrète*—or indeed in any of the polemical material which is the main source of information about Manuel's revolutionary career—can be taken at face value. But its reference to his immersion in the world of peddlers can be confirmed by his interrogation in the Bastille in 1786 and by a tribute to them that he wrote in 1789 or 1790: "This army of peddlers, which invades streets and crossroads from the Quai des Augustins, seems to force the populace to become familiar with and to discuss all the operations of a government that no longer can keep anything secret. These thousand-strong voices of renown have been useful for breathing life into the public spirit which alone is capable of overthrowing the time-honored edifice of abuse."[5]

The peddlers probably campaigned for Manuel in this manner when he entered Parisian politics, although there is no information about exactly how he got his start. The next piece of evidence merely shows him as an orator demanding energetic action at the lowest and smallest unit of the new political structure that was being pieced together in the summer of 1789. He spoke as a "commissioner" or member of the executive committee in his neighborhood district, one of the sixty constituencies that were created for the elections to the Estates General and that continued to function after the elections as semi-autonomous entities in the revolutionary reorganization of Paris. Each district provided its own battalion to the National Guard and sent representatives to the Paris Commune (known at first as the "provisional municipality"), which governed the city in conjunction with the new mayor, Jean Sylvain Bailly. From district to Commune to national Convention—those were the rungs of the ladder on which Manuel would rise from 1789 through 1792, helped along the way by sonorous speeches in the Jacobin Club.

The earliest among his speeches that have survived in print took place on August 30, 1789, at a meeting of the Districts réunis du Val-de-Grace et de

Saint-Jacques. Manuel harangued the other militants of his neighborhood about the danger of a decline in revolutionary ardor after the great events of the early summer. The district had not supplied enough soldiers for its battalion, he complained, and some of the citizens had betrayed a distressing prejudice against actors, who were being excluded from civic life, despite their qualities as patriots.[6] Manuel's own patriotism sounded unimpeachable, and the District acknowledged it by sending him as its representative to the provisional Commune. Soon after he arrived in the Hôtel de Ville, he managed to take on another position: "administrator in the department of police." In this quality, he assumed special responsibility for overseeing the book trade.[7]

From peddling books to policing them, the transformation of Manuel's situation corresponded to the sense of a world-turned-upside-down, which gripped many Frenchmen during the extraordinary summer of 1789. In his own account of his new function, Manuel emphasized that he dedicated himself to one supreme goal: the liberty of the press. He therefore did everything in his power to remove the institutional debris from the Ancien Régime that encumbered the Revolution's journalists. He also took care to inform the public of his dedication by writing letters to the journals that had sprung up everywhere in 1789 and were edited in large part by his former companions in Grub Street. For good measure, he went on to publish a collection of the letters, along with some of his orations. They provided a vivid picture of Manuel at work, sweeping out the Augean stables of the old police.

In one letter Manuel replies to a request for permission to publish a book. Permission denied, he proclaims: to permit a publication is to admit tacitly that it could be prohibited, so he will issue no permissions; the press is now free. In another, he answers a warning sent from Metz that a shipment of Raynal's *Histoire philosophique et politique des établissements et du commerce des européens dans les deux Indes*, which had been banned and burned in 1781, was on its way to Paris, where it might be confiscated in the Chambre syndicale (inspection office) run by the members of the Parisian booksellers' guild. Let it come, Manuel announces. The press is free, and the guild should be abolished. In a third, an open letter addressed to a royal censor, he demands the censor's resignation, because the press is free. Anyone can now publish anything, even trashy pamphlets and libels, for it is more important to protect liberty than to defend the reputation of individuals. In an open letter to Brissot, his friend and editor of *Le Patriote français*, Manuel says that he himself has been the object of attacks, but he will let his enemies malign him. The press is free, and he is too busy protecting its freedom to reply in kind. In an open letter to Desmoulins, his fellow Jacobin and editor of *Les Révolutions de*

France et de Brabant, he declares that his greatest responsibility in overseeing the police is to keep the press free. The press is a weapon wielded by men of letters, and "it is men of letters . . . who make revolutions."[8]

Manuel's letters provide a good example of revolutionary rhetoric in 1789, but they failed to clarify a complex situation. Article XI of the Declaration of the Rights of Man and of the Citizen asserted that the press was free, subject, however, to "provisions to be set by the law." What might those provisions be? No one in the National Assembly argued in favor of abolishing all restraints on the printed word. But the deputies never agreed on any definition of the line that separated liberty from impermissible expressions of calumny, sedition, blasphemy, and indecency. They also failed to produce a law on intellectual property, although the collapse of the system for granting royal privileges created a need for some modern form of copyright.

Meanwhile, hundreds of newspapers—papers with real news in them— appeared throughout the kingdom, reporting and discussing events with a boldness that was unthinkable before 1789. The new journalists did not even ask permission to exercise their trade. And the officials who remained in the royal administration—at least provisionally, while the revolutionaries attempted to reorganize it—could not comprehend the changes taking place before their eyes. The director of the book trade, Poitevin de Maissemy, wrote one letter after another to the lieutenant general of police demanding action against scribblers like Brissot and Mirabeau, who launched newspapers even before the storming of the Bastille. On April 14, 1789, he denounced the prospectus of Brissot's *Patriote français* as "the utmost degree of audacity reinforced by impunity" and attempted to stifle it by orders sent out to all inspectors of the book trade and officers of the booksellers' guild.[9] After July 14, nothing could stop the flood of new publications.

But a reaction soon set in, because the propertied classes felt increasingly threatened by the escalation of disorder—the peasant uprisings known as the Great Fear, the municipal revolutions throughout all of urban France, the continuous riots in Paris, and the October Days, when the Parisian crowd invaded Versailles and carried the royal family off to Paris. Outbreaks of violence accompanied by violent language, in speech and in print, produced many demands to curb the press. Revolutionary authorities took repressive measures against journalists and pamphleteers on several occasions in 1790 and 1791, and by 1794 they began closing printing shops on a large scale. Even in 1789, when uninhibited publishing reached its peak, all sorts of obstacles stood in the way of untrammeled liberty. Louis Thiroux de Crosne, the last lieutenant general of police, disappeared two days after the storming of the Bastille, but many officials remained in place—police inspectors, censors, officers of the booksellers' guild, and administrators in the Direction de la librairie (officers who authorized publications and regulated the book trade). Although the parlements were abolished, lower courts continued to function. Bishops could still issue condemnations of books. And even the new mayor of Paris, Jean Sylvain Bailly, expressed an increasing concern for disorder of all kinds. By the summer of 1791 he looked like a downright counterrevolutionary, at least to Jacobins like Manuel.[10]

Manuel never exercised any direct power over the police. Although he identified himself as a "provisional administrator of the police,"[11] he had only a supervisory role derived from his position as a representative in the provisional administration of Paris, and even in that capacity, he remained subordinate to Bailly. Moreover, he did not serve for long. He failed to get reelected to the Commune in the summer of 1790 and left Paris in the autumn for Montargis in order to devote himself to the preparation of *La Police de Paris dévoilée*. What did he do during those ten months of administration? Nothing, he later boasted—that is, nothing to impede the activities of printers and booksellers.[12] He may have helped dismantle some of the institutions left over from the Ancien Régime, but his main activity seems to have been gathering and editing documents from the police files. While Brissot and others published journals, Manuel published books—journalistic books full of sensational detail about abuses of power. In that respect, his revolutionary career can be seen as a continuation of his pre-revolutionary activities and as a response to the difficulty that had dogged him throughout the 1780s: the need to make money.

The Revolution did not lift Manuel out of poverty, at least not during its first two years. Although his financial situation is difficult to document, one source indicates that he had done nothing to improve "the well-known mediocrity of his fortune" before December 2, 1791, when he was elected *procureur* (prosecuting attorney) of the Commune.[13] In order to be elected, he had to qualify as an "active" citizen according to the requirements set by the Constitution of 1791—that is, to have paid taxes worth the equivalent of three days' labor. For Parisians, that amount came to 6 livres in 1790 and 7 livres 7 sous in 1791. One of Manuel's political enemies from the right, Charles-Pierre Bosquillon, claimed in a pamphlet that his election was invalid because he had never made those payments. No record of them existed anywhere, Bosquillon argued, and Manuel had not produced any receipts. Instead, he paid his taxes retrospectively in November 1791 when he stood for election and could draw on money from a political backer. That maneuver also violated the law. Moreover, Manuel's ineligibility could be demonstrated in two other ways: he had never enrolled in a company of the National Guard (only active citizens were admitted in the Guard, and they had to come up with a good deal of money to pay for their uniform), and he had not had a fixed, legal domicile in Paris. Bosquillon claimed that Manuel had moved from place to place, getting lodging wherever he could find it—in the rue Serpente, where Garnery gave him a room in return for work in the printing shop; in the rue des Postes, where he got free lodging from a police employee; and in the rue de l'Oursine, where he pretended to have lived in a proper apartment for at least a year, although he could not prove that he had paid any rent for it and he had spent the twelve months from October 1790 until October 1791 in Montargis. Bosquillon's attack did not dislodge Manuel from office, but it provided a convincing picture of an existence improvised from place to place as opportunities arose during the early stages of the Revolution.[14]

All the available evidence indicates that until December 1791, Manuel supported himself primarily by writing. The Revolution opened up new sources of income for writers, not simply because it freed the press but also because it created a huge demand for information, information about the past as well as the present. Unlike other writers who satisfied the need for news about current events, Manuel produced news about abuses that had been concealed under the Ancien Régime. His position in the administration of the police gave him access to the most sensational dossiers that had been stored under lock and key in the Bastille, and he made the most of it in a succession of sensationalist books: *La Bastille dévoilée* (Paris, 1789–90), four volumes in eight installments; *La Chasteté du clergé dévoilée* ("Rome," 1790), two volumes; *La Police de Paris dévoilée* (Paris, 1790), two volumes; and *Lettres originales de Mirabeau* (Paris, 1792), two volumes. The publishing history of these works is complex and obscure, but as their titles indicate, they fit together in a series. All were anthologies based on archives from the Bastille, and all played on the notion of unveiling hidden secrets. Manuel printed his name prominently on the title pages of *La Police de Paris dévoilée* and *Lettres originales de Mirabeau*. The other two books appeared anonymously, but he did not hide his role as their editor.

La Bastille dévoilée came out in installments designed, as it announced, to satisfy the public's "impatience" to learn the truth about what had happened inside the prison walls: "The taking of the Bastille has just opened up a precious depository [of archives], and we are hurrying to publish what it offers to us. You will find here an anthology of evidence and of examples about the atrocities that ministerial despotism ceaselessly perpetuated. This revelation is of a nature to interest everyone, individuals of every age, sex, and rank."[15] This kind of rhetoric—sales talk couched in the form of a civics lesson—continued through all eight installments, which appeared at intervals throughout 1789 and 1790. Each installment contained a selection from the dossiers of the Bastille prisoners during a specific period. The editors guaranteed the authenticity of the documents, but they often paraphrased them, added comments, and even printed commentaries provided by some of the former prisoners, who used the opportunity to recount the suffering they had endured for the cause of liberty.[16] The resulting work could hardly be expected to conform to the standards of editing established a century later. It was aimed at revolutionary readers and belonged to the outpouring of attacks on the Ancien Régime that took place after July 14, 1789. In fact, it had to compete against similar publications, because the papers of the police were scattered everywhere after the storming of the Bastille, and several authors scrambled to publish collections of them. Jean-Louis Carra, a hack writer turned revolutionary just like Manuel, put out a three-volume set, *Mémoires historiques et authentiques sur la Bastille*, in 1789. He, too, denounced despotism and appealed to the prurience as well as the patriotism of his readers: "May those who read these *Mémoires* identify themselves for a moment with the victims . . . and then leap in their imagination to the voluptuous bed of the favorite prostitute [i.e., Mme du Barry]."[17] There was plenty of demand for such revelations in 1789. *La Bastille dévoilée* developed the best strategy to satisfy it, because instead of being published all at once in a single set of volumes, it came out in a succession of eight pamphlet-like installments. They began with the most recent dossiers, which were most likely to interest readers, and then worked up to the 1780s from 1752. Carra's *Mémoires historiques* stopped at the dossiers from 1775, perhaps because by then *La Bastille dévoilée* had captured most of the market. Whatever their relative success, the two works were remarkably similar. They perpetuated the most powerful myth in the new revolutionary culture by revealing how the Bastille had actually operated as a bulwark of despotism.[18]

The mythological view of the Bastille owed a great deal to the publication of the documents from its archives. Earlier works like Linguet's *Mémoire sur la Bastille* had prepared the way. But *La Bastille dévoilée* contained seemingly irrefutable evidence from the actual dossiers of the prisoners. It even disputed the exaggerations that Linguet had scattered throughout the account of his own *embastillement*.[19] In order to reinforce their claim to authenticity, the editors of *La Bastille dévoilée* announced that they would put the originals of the documents they published on display at the Lycée, a literary society that had succeeded the Musée, where anyone could inspect them. This strategy reinforced the effect of publication by installments, which spread new revelations in successive shock waves and produced a powerful effect, judging from a review in the generally skeptical *Correspondance littéraire*: "This collection is truly remarkable, because it is composed entirely of original documents that were found in the Bastille and that have been deposited in the Lycée, where everyone is free to see them."[20]

The impression of authenticity ("l'effet réel" as it is called by literary critics) also derived from the work of the editors, who assembled the text from disparate ingredients and bathed it in the kind of rhetoric that rang true in 1789. Who were these editors—the persons or person who addressed the reader in the preface to the first installment with remarks such as "We hasten to unveil before all of Europe the secret crimes of that horde of transient tyrants called ministers."[21] "We" changed as the installments evolved. In fact, the editorial comments scattered through the book have a self-referential quality that helps explain its character. The first installment presented itself as the collective work of a group of patriots connected with the Lycée—one of the literary clubs open to the general public in contrast to exclusive institutions like the Académie française and the salons. Their purpose, as they explained in the preface, was to inform their fellow citizens of the abuses of despotism so as to prevent anything like it from ever happening again. They were therefore publishing everything that they had been able to recover from the archives of the Bastille that were scattered about the streets on July 14 and that could be consulted in the Lycée's office next to the Palais-Royal. They also promised to devote the proceeds of the sales to the widows and orphans of the patriots who had died in the storming of the Bastille. By installment four, however, the references to the Lycée were dropped, and the "we" of the anonymous editors turned into "I." In installment six, this first-person editor explained that he had continued the publication "almost alone."[22] He could print only the small portion of the archives that had come into his hands, but his duty as a patriot required him to get them out immediately rather than turn them over to a committee in the Hôtel de Ville that was supposed to publish the bulk of the Bastille papers but had become mired in delays. The rest of the work appears to be a rushed job, cobbled together by a single editor.

That editor was Manuel. He was identified by Brissot in a passage of his memoirs where he recounted his imprisonment in the Bastille (as explained in chapter 14). Soon after the Bastille's fall, Brissot wrote, Manuel gave him his own dossier from its archives; and in return, Brissot wrote the entry about himself that Manuel printed in *La Bastille dévoilée*, emphasizing that his imprisonment resulted from his revolutionary principles rather than from any unsavory connections with the London libelers.[23] Manuel reworked the account of his own *embastillement* even more radically. Instead of printing the five interrogations and all the supporting material that showed how he had actually made his living before 1789, he produced a short paragraph, which merely mentioned his suspected involvement in the *Lettre d'un garde du roi* and the distribution of illegal books. Editing for Manuel did not mean falsifying documents. It meant paraphrasing and selecting them.

The principle of selection stood out strongest in *La Chasteté du clergé dévoilée*, a two-volume compilation of police reports about priests arrested in brothels. Its introduction explained why the public should take notice of the particular variety of unveiling that the book had to offer. Like *La Bastille dévoilée* and *La Police de Paris dévoilée*, it would provide a lesson in patriotism. By revealing how the police trapped their victims and carried them off to the Bastille, it would inspire an undying hatred for tyrants and love for liberty. But it had a special contribution to make, because at this point in the Revolution the French were debating the reorganization of the Church, which the National Assembly finally enacted on July 12, 1790, as the Civil Constitution of the Clergy. *La Chasteté du clergé dévoilée* addressed this issue and especially a recent decree of the National Assembly, passed on February 13, 1790, which released monks from their vows so that they could marry, have families, and become integrated in the general citizenry. Chastity was a violation of nature, the introduction asserted. *La Chasteté du clergé dévoilée* demonstrated this fact by exposing the frequency of arrests of priests in brothels, but it did not do so to hold them up to scorn. On the contrary, it argued, they should be pitied, for they, too, were victims of oppression. Ordinary priests, the curates and friars who appeared in the police files, suffered from the tyranny of the upper clergy, who exploited their inferiors and satisfied their own lust in secret seraglios, where the police inspectors could not reach them.

While fortifying their patriotism, the readers of *La Chasteté du clergé dévoilée* could also treat themselves to some voyeuristic sex: "Everything that corruption can invent, the most immoral and the most indecent, . . . is brought together in this collection,"[24] the introduction promised. The readers of the book would have access to the very reports that the police had furnished to Louis XV, who used them to arouse his jaded appetite. They could put themselves in the king's place and enjoy the descriptions of priests in brothels just as he had done. Or if they preferred more sublime sensations, they could shudder at the spectacle of a society driven to the brink of destruction by its own depravity: "One can enjoy contemplating the rugged shoals on which one was about to be dashed; one can enjoy sounding the depths of the gulf that was ready to swallow us. All of these considerations make everything that has come out of that ancient fortress enormously interesting."[25] To be sure, the reports were written in the wooden language of bailiffs and inspectors, but that only made them more authentic. And they included plenty of details about the practices of whores—their prices, addresses, ages, names, nicknames, and the perversions favored by their clients. A reader who desired information about a particular priest could look him up in an index of names at the end of each volume, which made it easy to identify each man and his favorite form of depravity. Unfortunately, the editor admitted, the text lacked illustrations, but it contained so much graphic detail that "the reader's imagination can act as a substitute."[26] *La Chasteté du clergé dévoilée* had all the characteristics of standard, eighteenth-century pornography, reinforced by the libeler's technique of exposing private lives to public ignominy. It was actually a new kind of libel, one that dressed up old motifs in the latest patriotic drag.

The book's appeal to sexual sensationalism accounts for the fact that it appeared anonymously and with a false address, typical of the anticlerical literature from the Ancien Régime: "Rome, from the Printing Shop for the Propagation of the Faith." There is no firm proof that Manuel wrote it. *Vie secrète de Pierre Manuel* attributed it to him and claimed that it originated from a blackmail operation. Once he got his hands on the police reports, *Vie secrète* recounted, Manuel used them to extort money from clergymen who did not want their dossiers published. He managed to squeeze three thousand livres from Champion de Cicé, archbishop of Bordeaux, and to sell off some of the documents to a Parisian publisher. But he kept back enough to form his own anthology, which he sold to Garnery for twelve thousand livres. This speculation proved that Manuel would do anything to escape from poverty, even if it meant corrupting the morals of revolutionary youth. Such was the conclusion drawn by the anonymous author of *Vie secrète de Pierre Manuel*, but he, too, was a libeler, and his account of this episode was too libelous to be taken as conclusive.[27] The most persuasive evidence about Manuel's authorship of *La Chasteté du clergé dévoilée* is circumstantial. The book fit perfectly into Manuel's series of volumes about "unveiling." They all used the same material and adopted the same technique: they served up scandal with heavy doses of moralizing and patriotic rhetoric. Manuel adopted a similar tone in his speeches to the Jacobin Club—but so did other Jacobins and writers who pitched their message to an audience of revolutionary readers, many of whom were unsophisticated sans-culottes.[28] What to conclude? I think it very likely that Manuel wrote *La Chasteté du clergé dévoilée*, but I cannot prove it.

He openly acknowledged his authorship of the third work in the trilogy of "unveiling," *La Police de Paris dévoilée*. It, too, contained a good deal of scabrous material, including more reports about priests arrested in brothels, but it covered all the activities of the police. It was Manuel's summa, the crowning work in which he tried to bring together all the information that he had accumulated from the papers of the Bastille. He explained in its preface—an open letter to the Jacobin Club, which also served as a dedication—that he had left Paris to devote himself entirely to this supreme, patriotic task. Having served to the end of his term in the Commune, he had withdrawn into the provinces where he had been able to labor without interruption on a book that exposed the full extent of the corruption under the Ancien Régime. Like the censors of the ancients, he had denounced immorality wherever he found it, and he had discovered the greatest amount in the dossiers of aristocrats and clergy. To expose depredation among the great required courage, but he had not flinched. And he had performed his duty by using the modern equivalent of Athens's agora: the printing press, which diffused information, formed public opinion, and therefore ultimately determined the course of events. If the French absorbed his lessons, they would reject any attempt to revive despotism, and they would be prepared to adopt the "republican forms of liberty."[29]

They also would be in for a good read. Manuel's suggestive remarks about depravity in high places indicated that there was quite a spectacle for his readers to enjoy, once he had torn away the veil that kept it hidden. A glance at his table of contents showed what was in store: revelations about spies, prostitutes, gamblers, priests, prisoners, actors, and writers, especially writers who had dared to defy the repressive power of the government. A closer look at the text showed the relative importance of the subjects it treated: gambling dens, fourteen pages; priests in brothels, thirty pages; prostitution in general, forty-eight pages; and assorted vice, 144 pages, mainly anecdotes about depraved aristocrats, dancing girls, and venereal disease. It was in this context that Manuel revealed the attempts by the police to exterminate the libel industry in London. That story had enough shock value to occupy an important place in his book. But most of the material he selected from the police archives consisted of short bulletins like the following:

M. Guérin, the surgeon of the prince de Conti, flushes out game by beating every bush and has presented to his highness a child of thirteen, who is completely fresh. Monseigneur enjoined him to try her and to give a report of it at his morning *lever*.

The chevalier de Choiseul-Meuze is competing with [inspector] Desbrugnières over Miss Roncheray. It's a question of who will have the leftovers from His Majesty. She has the ten thousand livre annuity that comes with the Parc-aux-Cerfs [Louis XV's notorious "harem"]. One of them is already sick [with love] from having seen her.

A good day's work: a Monsieur Berger presented the daughter of a cobbler, a Miss Faisan, to the duc de Grammont at his residence in Pont-aux-Choux on the day before Easter. The duke thought he had found the narrow path to happiness, because it took him three days to penetrate all the way to the Hallelujah. But an apprentice butcher had already passed through that territory.

Prince d'Hesnin forgets his wife; his wife forgets him with the chevalier de Coigny.[30]

As explained in chapter 3, these passages had a strong resemblance to *Le Gazetier cuirassé* and other *chroniques scandaleuses* from the reigns of Louis XV and Louis XVI. Apparently Manuel lifted them from the bulletins that the police supplied to the king, but he published so many anecdotes of this kind that his book acquired the aspect of an off-color anthology rather than an indictment of the Ancien Régime. The implicit voyeurism that ran through it all threatened to undercut the high-minded patriotism with which it was presented. Manuel tried to forestall that effect among his readers by insisting on his repugnance at having to serve up so much muck: "I shall stop. A portfolio swollen with vice is lying before me. My hand pushes it aside. . . . It is not the pleasure of speaking ill that caused me to reveal all the shameful aspects of the human species. It was rather the need to demonstrate the extent of the corruption, the gangrene that was eating away at morality."[31]

Whether Manuel's readers followed that lead in responding to his rhetoric is impossible to say, owing to the lack of documentation. But modern readers should hesitate before taxing early modern writers with inconsistency or hypocrisy. What appears to us as a contradiction—moralizing on the one hand and scandalmongering on the other—was a common practice in the eighteenth century; and there is no reason to believe that Manuel considered it illegitimate to make money by exposing vice. Writers still do so with a good conscience. But consciences in 1789–94 operated within a mental world peculiar to their time, and they fixed on a particular vice—not the making of money per se but the kind of corruption that could infect the body politic. In denouncing the gangrene of morals, Manuel echoed a favorite theme of many revolutionaries, notably Robespierre, "the Incorruptible."

This theme stood out in the last book Manuel published from the police archives: *Lettres originales de Mirabeau, écrites du donjon de Vincennes pendant les années 1777, 78, 79 et 80, contenant tous les détails sur sa vie privée, ses malheurs, et ses amours avec Sophie Ruffei, marquise de Monnier* (Paris, 1792), two volumes. The long subtitle suggested that the book belonged to the scandalous genre of "private lives" that had proliferated before the Revolution, but the main title announced a different kind of work—a collection of documents concerning the best-known leader of the early Revolution, who had died in April 1791 and had been buried like a hero in the Pantheon. True, Mirabeau's reputation had begun to unravel by January 1792, when the *Lettres* appeared. He had been in the pay of the court since May 1790 and had secretly furnished the king with advice about how to fortify the throne since the end of 1789. Although much of the advice was sensible and none of it was followed by Louis XVI, all of it looked counterrevolutionary to the horrified members of the left when Mirabeau's correspondence with the king was discovered after the overthrow of the monarchy on August 10, 1792.

Manuel tried to cope with the difficulties of managing Mirabeau's reputation in his long "preliminary discourse" to the *Lettres*. He began with a blast against those who had raised doubts about the integrity of the great man. They were libelers: "Vile and cowardly calumniators! Is it not enough to have soiled by your libels the entire life of one of the founding fathers of liberty! . . . I am going to annihilate you with [this account of] his sublime qualities."[32] Fortunately, Manuel had been able to save Mirabeau's letters from the archives of the police. He was publishing them as evidence of the despotism that had oppressed free spirits—and equally important, as testimony to a great soul, for they revealed Mirabeau as a man of passion, a lover, who had scribbled notes on every scrap of paper he could find in the depths of the dungeon of Vincennes in order to pour out his passion for Sophie de Monnier, who was suffering in a prison of her own, equally a victim of oppression: "I have collected everything, brought everything together: these shards left by love were precious relics for me, and my heart provided a supplement to what I saw with my eyes. Ah! After the travail of producing the *Red Book* of vice [i.e., *La Police de Paris dévoilée*], I had a need of the memoirs of the hero of Vincennes, in order to refresh my blood stream."[33]

Editing for Manuel was a heroic business; the preliminary discourse made that clear. It did not mention his earlier role as the editor/peddler of the obscene books and topical pamphlets that Mirabeau had written before the Revolution, nor did it take account of their falling out when Mirabeau discovered that Manuel had secretly pirated one of those works. Instead, it presented Manuel as a keeper of the flame. Thanks to his position as an administrator of the police, it explained, he had succeeded in assembling a spectacular collection of letters, which would stand forever as a monument to a great man with a great heart. It then provided some background information about the origins of the letters: Sophie's subjection to a decrepit husband, her abduction by Mirabeau, their brief but blissful love life, their arrest in Amsterdam, their imprisonment by lettre de cachet, and their desperate attempts to remain in contact by correspondence, which the police permitted, provided that the letters be returned after being read for safekeeping in the Bastille. Manuel conceded that during his three years in prison, Mirabeau had written some sex books, *Le Libertin de qualité* and *Erotika Biblion*; but they were excusable, because "it was necessary, in order to be read, to speak the language of the brothel and the market place."[34] More important, Mirabeau also wrote *Des Lettres de cachet et des prisons d'Etat*, which prepared the way for the Revolution. In fact, revolution, the cause of the people, became his dominant passion after he was

15

released from prison. So he did not take up again with Sophie; she committed suicide; and he went on to guide France through the great events that were now liberating all of Europe.

The secret love life of the greatest revolutionary of them all, told in his own words—it was a surefire best-seller, and Manuel did not restrain his sales talk. This book would reveal the supreme love story of the century, he assured his readers. It would bare the heart of a man erupting in volcanic passion and that of his "*Sophie*, the light of his soul." Manuel always referred to the lovers as *Gabriel* and *Sophie* (in italics), a gross incongruity in the light of eighteenth-century usage, but one that suited "the passion that consumed them even in the bottom of the dungeons." Manuel had known Mirabeau, and he could assure the reader, "There was not a fiber in his being that did not express the violence of his love. . . . Who revealed these secrets to me? Reader, I pity you if you cannot discern them, as I have, in the letters of *Gabriel*."[35]

This time, Manuel overstepped the limits of propriety that shaped the response of eighteenth-century readers. One reader—not a typical one, to be sure, but someone especially sensitive to the cultural currents beneath the surface of revolutionary politics—expressed his reaction publicly. In a long letter published in the *Journal de Paris* of February 12, 1792, André Chénier, France's greatest poet, attacked Manuel's preliminary discourse as an example of everything bad about revolutionary writing: inflated rhetoric, self-important pomposity, titillating vulgarity, and bad taste. It typified the style of the hacks and demagogues who had recently gained control of the press, Chénier argued. Manuel belonged to the breed of the "new writers" who had remained trapped in obscurity under the Ancien Régime and seized the opportunity opened by the Revolution to flood the streets with trash. Exactly like Rivarol three years earlier, Chénier pitched his argument at the level of aesthetics but aimed it at a political target. He made the implications of his criticism obvious by associating Manuel with "that swarm of orators from the market places, who parade their patriotism by justifying every ignominy and fomenting every disorder." Manuel's defenders would reply by accusing him of aristocratic sympathies, Chénier acknowledged, and he did not deny the elitism implicit in his defense of good taste: "To be sure, reading such a work [Manuel's preliminary discourse] is repulsive to any well-born soul, and it seems to warn one, by the disgust it inspires, that a gentleman [*honnête homme*] does not write in such a manner." The class-laden character of such language exposed Chénier to retaliation by the sans-culotte left, which had recently elected Manuel as *procureur* of the Commune. But Chénier, unlike Rivarol, was no counterrevolutionary. He supported the goals of the Revolution, or at least the Revolution of 1789, although that did not save him from the guillotine—on July 25, 1794, at the last moment of the Terror and eight months after the execution of Manuel.[36]

Manuel got to the guillotine quicker because he threw himself into the lethal politics of the Parisian revolution and the Jacobin Club. During his first term in the Commune, he gained some notoriety by quarreling with Bailly, the conservative mayor of Paris, but failed to get reelected. He therefore withdrew to Montargis in October 1790 and spent the next nine months working over material that he had taken from the Bastille. By then *La Bastille dévoilée* had already been published, so Manuel concentrated on the other compilations, primarily *La Police de Paris dévoilée*, which Garnery put on sale in July 1791, but also the *Lettres originales de Mirabeau*, which Garnery published six months later. Manuel later claimed that he had labored twelve hours a day for ten months to transcribe the barely legible originals of Mirabeau's letters.[37] That work, along with transcribing, editing, and writing commentaries to all the other papers he had appropriated from the police archives, must have taken up most of his time during the first two years of the Revolution. He got some help from the man who knew the inside story of the literary police better than anyone else, Jean-Claude Jacquet, the police inspector turned libeler who had been released from the Bastille in 1789, and Garnery handled the marketing. Manuel said that Garnery ran off twenty thousand prospectuses for the *Lettres originales de Mirabeau* and eventually printed more than fifty thousand copies. Although Manuel did not provide information about the sales and sharing of profits, it seems clear that this speculation on top of the other three solved his financial problems. The "unveiling" anthologies, which came to ten volumes in all, also contributed to his reputation as a radical. In denouncing the police, they promoted his own role as a fearless patriot—a theme he returned to often in his later publications. "It is in order to enlighten a people who claim to be free that, once free himself, he [Manuel] thought it his duty, without taking account of the enemies he would make, to expose the iniquity of the Paris police," Manuel wrote in a preface to an edition of his own letters published by Garnery in 1792.[38] He promoted his activities as a "citizen-*philosophe*"[39] at every opportunity, both in the Jacobin Club and through letters published in the left-wing press.

The letters demonstrate a knack for seizing the public's attention. They had a provocative tone and tended toward self-dramatization. Manual aimed them at well-known public figures, especially "les grands," prominent personages, who could be called to account, brought down a peg, and lectured about their misdeeds from the perspective of the common man. Manuel adopted this rhetorical stance early in the Revolution, when he published open letters to the queen, the comte d'Artois, the duc de Chartres, the archbishop of Bordeaux, and Bailly, exhorting them to mend their ways. They had grand titles, but, he maintained, his quality as a citizen entitled him to give them a public scolding. The ultimate expression of Manuel's self-promotion as the public's scold came in a letter addressed to Louis XVI, which he read to the Jacobin Club on January 29, 1792.

Sire, I do not like kings. They have done too much harm to the world, as can be seen even by standard histories, which flatter the greatest of them—that is, the conquerors, those who have assassinated entire nations! But since the Constitution, which made me a free man, has made you a king, I must obey you. You have a son. As France no longer belongs to you, he belongs to France, and she should educate him for herself.[40]

Manuel went on to propose that the dauphin be educated by Bernardin de Saint-Pierre, the popular, Rousseauistic philosopher. This outburst made Manuel look ridiculous to sophisticates on the right,[41] but it was just the thing to appeal to a constituency of plainspoken sans-culottes. "Sire, I do not like kings" followed Manuel for the rest of his life. The disparity between the form of address ("Sire") and the defiant egalitarianism of the dressing-down captured the spirit of the Paris Sections as they prepared to overthrow the monarchy.

The Sections, supported by the radicals of the Jacobin Club, swept Manuel into power at this time. On December 2, 1791, he was elected prosecuting attorney of the Commune, a position that gave him a platform for reprimanding reactionaries. While the Commune supported him, however, the Department of Paris, a conservative body with jurisdiction over the entire Parisian area, tried to cut him down to size. The confrontation took place in a trial before the new criminal court of Paris, whose principal magistrate (*juge d'instruction*), Etienne François le Pelletier, sympathized with the department. The question at issue was Manuel's right to publish Mirabeau's letters, which Garnery began to market on a large scale at the end of 1791. Mirabeau's mother, as his sole heir, accused Manuel of stealing her property. The letters had remained safe, sealed and stored in a special "deposit" among the papers of the police, after the storming of the Bastille. According to le Pelletier, Manuel had no authority during his term as an administrator of the police to break the seal, make off with the papers, and publish them for his own profit.

Manuel defended himself against this charge at a public hearing on May 22, 1792. On the face of it, his case looked weak, because it consisted of little more than an oration about the patriotism that had inspired him to publish the letters. Having suffered in the Bastille himself and participated in its conquest, he argued, he knew the importance of collecting every scrap of paper from its archives. Nothing was more precious as evidence about the despotism of the Ancien Régime than Mirabeau's correspondence. Therefore, inspired by dedication to the revolutionary cause, Manuel had assembled every stray letter of Mirabeau's that he could find, both from the debris in the Bastille and from members of the public, who responded to an appeal he published in Brissot's *Patriote français.* Le Pelletier objected that the accusation did not concern stray letters but rather the main deposit, which had survived intact and which Manuel had violated using a key from the headquarters of the police. To appropriate private property in that fashion was the same as stealing.

Not at all, Manuel replied. Everything in the Bastille represented appropriation of a different kind: the plundering and oppression of the French people under the Ancien Régime. The archives of the Bastille were therefore the property of the people. In recovering its sovereignty, the people had repossessed this property, a crucial national treasure, because it provided a record of the nation's suffering under despotism. Manuel considered it his patriotic duty to publish as much as possible of that record. In doing so, he not only informed the public but also awakened it to the danger of despotism in the future. Thanks to his long, hard labor as an editor, the archives had become weapons for mobilizing public opinion, weapons that were just as effective as the rifles seized from the arsenal in the Invalides before the storming of the Bastille.[42] Why then had the court brought this charge against him? Not to protect any supposed property of Mirabeau's mother, Manuel concluded, for Mirabeau's letters belonged to the nation. No, the attempt to stifle him was part of something bigger, a campaign by enemies of the Revolution to prevent patriots like him from standing up against the continued threat of despotism.

The case dragged on for several days and finally disappeared in the confusion that accompanied the overthrow of the monarchy on August 10, 1792. In a decision of May 25, the criminal court transferred the proceedings to a civil court, but they were eventually dropped; Manuel thus won his case before the only tribunal that mattered at that time: the court of public opinion. He printed his interrogation as a pamphlet and resumed his activities as prosecuting attorney of the Commune, now better-known than ever. The Jacobin Club, where he had deposited a copy of the Mirabeau letters as "a proof of my patriotism,"[43] hailed his defense on June 1, 1792, as a victory for the revolutionary cause.

By the summer of 1792, therefore, Manuel had written his way into the front ranks of the Revolution's leadership. But the Revolution never stayed still. Although Manuel's rhetoric had appealed to the left of 1792, it did not necessarily have enough thrust to carry him to the end of 1793, and it raised the difficulty faced by all rhetoricians who arrive in positions of power: would his deeds match his words?

Chapter 19

Words and Deeds

Philosophers often insist on the nature of speech as action. In saying something or writing something, they maintain, we perform an act, which elicits similar responses on the part of our listeners or readers. The interchange of speech-acts therefore belongs to the concrete world of deeds, and it produces effects that can be as powerful as those unleashed in the physical world of matter in motion. Manuel's "Sire, I do not like kings" was a slap in the face of the king and his supporters. It catapulted Manuel to stage center when the monarchy began to topple. His writings also moved him toward the front ranks among the figures calling for the public's attention. As their titles proclaimed, the texts showed Manuel in action, tearing back veils, ripping off masks, exposing horrors. But in 1792 and 1793 he became involved in action of a different kind.

Modern readers may be tempted to dismiss the self-dramatization of Manuel's tracts as rhetoric, but rhetoric was a powerful force in the French Revolution, and Manuel's words produced strong reactions in the public. They established him as a leading radical in the Jacobin Club and won him a following among the sans-culottes of the Parisian Sections. Even hostile readers like Chénier understood Manuel's publications as a bid for power, similar to that of "the orators of the market places."[1] Beaumarchais read him in the same way in the spring of 1792, when they engaged in some polemics. Unlike Chénier, however, Beaumarchais did not fight rhetoric with rhetoric and backed away from a confrontation. As the highly visible prosecuting attorney of the Commune, Manuel already wielded a great deal of political power at that time, while Beaumarchais felt increasingly threatened by writers on the new left. To them, he epitomized the literary elite from the Ancien Régime, who had enjoyed privileges and wealth in the world of the salons and the court. Manuel pursued this line of attack in one of his open letters, where he denounced Beaumarchais as a patrician who had neglected his duty to the nation by failing to pay his taxes. Beaumarchais could have replied with all the polemical skill that he had used to crush Goesman in 1774. Instead, he expressed respect for "a writer of your merit," produced proof of his tax payments, and professed loyalty to the cause of the nation.[2]

Mme de Staël, an equally eminent representative of the old Republic of Letters, adopted the same approach when she appealed to Manuel for help on the eve of the September Massacres.[3] As explained in Chapter 6, she persuaded Manuel to rescue two of her friends from certain death in prison by "playing on his vanity" as a writer turned revolutionary. In the end, he saved Mme de Staël herself. The episode, as she described it in her memoirs, illustrated the sense of a world turned upside down that struck so many witnesses of the Revolution. Under the Ancien Régime, the baroness de Staël had enjoyed an existence at the summit of society, where literary prestige and political power converged, while Manuel had barely scraped together a living in the lower ranks of pamphleteers. In September 1792, their positions were reversed. The powerful leader of the Commune led the helpless baroness to his carriage and whisked her out of danger. When the sans-culottes stopped them in the dead of the night and at the height of the massacring, he cleared a path through the carnage by calling out, "Public Prosecutor of the Commune!"

To command a crowd at a time of such violence was to deploy words with extraordinary power. But words failed at a comparable scene just after the storming of the Bastille, when Pelleport attempted to put them to the same good use. After being released from the Bastille on October 3, 1788, Pelleport sought refuge in his hometown, Stenay. He returned to Paris, probably to make arrangements for the publication of *Les Bohémiens*, on July 13. On July 14, he wandered into the Place de Grève just in time to witness the massacre of the Bastille's governor, Bernard-René de Launay. After storming the fortress, the crowd had seized de Launay, dragged him through the streets, beat him senseless, sliced off his head, and paraded it on the end of a pike. While some of the rioters executed this ghastly business, others prepared to do the same to their second captive, the chevalier Antoine Jérôme de l'Osme, who had served under de Launay as major of the Bastille. De l'Osme had treated Pelleport with a great deal of kindness during the four years of his imprisonment. When Pelleport saw him being dragged to an inevitable death, he tried to stop the crowd.

Manuel related the story in *La Bastille dévoilée*.[4] He probably had heard it from Pelleport himself, for it took place after the fall of the Bastille, so he could not have taken it from the Bastille's archives, and unlike other notices in the book, it has a direct style that suggests the two men were acquainted.[5] According to Manuel's account, Pelleport first called out to the crowd. He had been a prisoner, he shouted. He knew de l'Osme well; he could testify that the man was compassionate, that he had treated all the prisoners humanely. He must be released. Intent on dragging its victim to the nearest lamp post for a lynching, the crowd paid no attention. So Pelleport threw himself into their midst and tried to tear de l'Osme free. Already half dead, de l'Osme said to him, "What are you doing, young man? Get away. You will only sacrifice yourself without saving me." But Pelleport would not be dissuaded. He called out again for the rioters to disperse and pushed some of them away. A man with an ax then felled him by a blow to the neck and prepared to finish him off. But before the second stroke could fall, a soldier on horseback crashed into the crowd, overturning the attacker. Pelleport managed to grab a rifle and to flail about at the next attackers. They finally seized it from him, slashed him with sabers, stabbed him with bayonets, and left him to stagger off and die on a stairway of the Hôtel de Ville. But Pelleport lived to tell the tale, and Manuel published it as testimony to the courage of a man who once had lived from libels.

It would be misleading to present the Revolution as a succession of such scenes. Yet it would be equally inaccurate to construe the events of 1789–1800 as if they were nothing more than the working-out of discourse.[6] The revolutionaries filled the world with words—pamphlets, newspapers, speeches, battle hymns, and declarations carved into monuments—but they also smashed into lives with a brutality that nearly killed Pelleport in 1789 and that put an end to Manuel in 1793. The rawness of revolutionary violence needs to be considered in connection with the wordiness of revolutionary politics. They came together in the life and death of Manuel, especially during the period 1792–93, when the Revolution reached its climax.

Although he never stopped talking and writing, Manuel was swept up in the increasing violence of the streets soon after his election as prosecuting attorney of the Commune on December 2, 1791. By then the constitution created by the National Assembly had been accepted by Louis XVI and put into effect through the elections of September 1791, which returned a new parliamentary body, the Legislative Assembly, to exercise power in conjunction with the king. The Assembly soon became embroiled in a debate over the demands for aggressive action against Austria—and ultimately all the anciens régimes of Europe—from a vociferous faction of left-wing deputies led by Manuel's friend and ally, Jacques-Pierre Brissot. The "Brissotins" got their war in the spring of 1792, but they nearly lost it that summer, owing to the series of reverses that led to the September Massacres. At the same time they gained and lost a hold on power by forming a ministry in March, which the king dismissed in June. Once back in the opposition, they joined forces with the Robespierrist faction of the left—Robespierre had opposed Brissot in some fierce debates about the war in the Jacobin Club—and began flirting with the prospect of creating a republic.

The constitutional monarchy could not be overthrown without violence, however, and the destructive blow would have to be delivered by the sans-culottes. They had developed their own political organization and their own battalions, complete with cannon, in the forty-eight Sections of Paris—the successors to the Districts of 1789, where Manuel had his start in revolutionary politics. The increased cost and scarcity of consumer goods, especially bread, raised the danger of riots, just as it had in July 1789, and the reverses of the war gave the rioters a target: the king, barricaded in the Tuileries Palace, and anyone capable of collaborating with him. Louis had been suspiciously eager to go to war. The collapse of the French offensive made it look as though he were secretly collaborating with the enemy—as, indeed, he was—so that he could use a French defeat to restore the Ancien Régime. Moreover, everything suggested that some generals were in league with him. At the end of June, Lafayette left his army at the front and attempted to stage a coup in Paris. Although it failed, it confirmed the fears of the sans-culottes that a counterrevolution could break out at any moment, and their fears fed on a growing obsession about the danger of conspiracies. When the Legislative Assembly voted down a motion to convict Lafayette of treason, the leaders of the Sections directed their suspicions against the politicians of the Assembly, including some Brissotins who had supported Lafayette and were secretly negotiating with the king to form a new government.

The crisis had been building up for months. Already in March, insurrectionary sentiments were being whipped up by "enragés," populist leaders who demanded price controls and the violent repression of suspected counterrevolutionaries. Radical journalists like Marat and Hébert called for heads to roll. The Cordelier Club, dominated by Danton and Desmoulins, demanded extreme measures. And wild talk burst out everywhere in the Sectional assemblies. Royalists, generals, aristocrats, unpatriotic priests, corrupt politicians, speculators in the grain trade, and traitors of all kinds were conspiring to starve the people and undo the Revolution—this chorus of protests rose from the Sections to the Commune, which became the focal point of the sans-culotte agitation. On June 20, the Section militants invaded the Tuileries but did not go beyond humiliating the king by forcing him to drink to the health of the nation while wearing a sans-culotte-style phrygian cap. That "journée" or political uprising looked like a dress rehearsal for a full-scale revolution within the Revolution. As the moment of reckoning drew nearer, the tensions in Paris grew greater, and Manuel was caught in the middle of them.

His reputation as a militant accelerated throughout the first half of 1792 along with the violence of his rhetoric in the Jacobin Club. Following his "Sire, I do not like kings" in January, he harangued the Jacobins with an open letter to the ministers, threatening to punish them for their perfidy with "the vengeance of the people." In February he demanded that they be forced to draw straws to determine which of them should go to the guillotine. And by July he concentrated on the king as "the cause of all our misfortunes."[7] His triumph in the trial over the Mirabeau letters made him one of the most conspicuous enemies of the conservative Department of Paris and one of the most visible radicals in the Commune. After he confounded his judges on June 1, 1792, the Jacobin Club celebrated him as a champion of the popular cause and elected him as its president.[8] Meanwhile, in his capacity as prosecuting attorney of the Commune, he refrained from doing anything to prevent the sans-culottes from storming into the Tuileries on June 20. Far from attempting to calm the agitation in the Sections, he reaffirmed his support of them and of the links that bound them to the Commune. According to one account, he actually helped orchestrate the June 20 uprising or at least looked on approvingly at the rioters from an outpost in the Tuileries Gardens: "In a light blue outfit, a white embroidered waistcoat, large cravat, shaved and powdered, his face radiant."[9] The Department therefore accused him of failing to maintain order as required by his functions in the municipal government. On July 7, it suspended him and Jérôme Pétion, the mayor of Paris, for dereliction of duty. The Jacobins, led by Robespierre, raised a storm of protest, endorsed Manuel and Pétion as patriots, and demanded their reinstatement. The Jacobin sympathizers in the Legislative Assembly responded by overruling the Department's decision and restored both men to office. So Manuel returned to the Hôtel de Ville on July 23, just in time to participate in the next outbreak of violence, the uprising against the monarchy on August 10.[10]

Unlike the *journée* of June 20, the insurrection of August 10 was a pitched battle in the streets of Paris, which produced hundreds of casualties. It required preparation and a great deal of cooperation between the Sections and the Commune. Manuel worked with Pétion, Danton, and other leaders of the sans-culottes to hold the antiroyalist forces together, and after their victory he helped direct the efforts of the newly constituted Commune to prevent the city from dissolving into chaos. But prices continued to spin out of control and the enemy to advance. The fall of Verdun on September 2 ignited the next explosion, because the fear of counterrevolution and invasion had become so combustible by then that the violence could not be contained. When the massacres broke out, Manuel did what he could to limit them. He intervened to save several people trapped in the prisons, not only Mme de Staël's friends but also his own enemies, Bosquillon and Beaumarchais. He went to the scenes of the killing and attempted to stop it. According to Brissot, "Manuel confronted the pikes, the bayonets, the daggers, in order to make them listen to the voice of humanity and of the law. . . . But he was torn away from this holy mission by some blood-stained hands."[11] After the massacres, Manuel worked with Danton and the provisional government in a continuing effort to restore order while the elections to the Convention were held and the army confronted the Prussians.

Relief finally came when the Prussian invasion was turned back at the battle of Valmy on September 20. It was not a decisive victory, but it proved that the reborn nation could defend itself, and it opened the way for a successful offensive into the Austrian Netherlands during the autumn. Moreover, it freed the Convention from military pressure for the immediate future. Word of Valmy reached the newly elected deputies just as they assembled in Paris. They could therefore concentrate on the most urgent political questions: how to organize the new republican regime and what to do with the king. Louis had sought protection from the Legislative Assembly when the sans-culottes stormed the Tuileries on August 10. It suspended him, leaving the Convention to decide on his fate while he remained incarcerated in the Temple, a stronghold not far from the site where the Bastille had stood.

These events came in such a rush and with so much tumult that individuals got lost in them. It is impossible to follow Manuel's actions closely through the chaos of August and September 1792, but when the Convention convened on September 21, he stood out as a leading member of the Parisian delegation. He had been elected along with Danton, Robespierre, Marat, and other leaders of the left. The notions of left and right, however, had become blurred. They originally derived from the seating pattern of the deputies to the Estates General: those who sat to the left of the president on his podium became identified as radicals; those to his right took on the color of conservatives. But the spectrum kept shifting as events pushed the entire Revolution leftward. New radicals constantly emerged with more extreme demands, and the deputies on the new right often seemed to derive from the old left. Some of the confusion resulted from personal connections within the shifting configurations of parties—or factions, as they might be more accurately described. Although the revolutionaries used the term "parti," they never developed anything like modern parties, with formal organizations, voting discipline, election lists, and platforms. Instead, they identified political groups with the names of individuals: Fayettistes, Brissotins, Rolandistes, Dantonistes, Maratistes, Robespierristes, Hébertistes, and so on. They used others labels, too, derived from sources like the names of clubs (Jacobins vs. Feuillants in the Legislative Assembly) or some salient characteristic (Girondins vs. Montagnards in the

Convention, the former associated with some prominent deputies from the Gironde, the latter identified from their seats high up in the Convention's assembly hall). But the lives of individuals often intersected with events in a decisive manner, and the leading revolutionaries studied the direction of events by observing the stance that rival leaders took during critical moments, such as the vote on the fate of the king.

The personal ingredient in revolutionary politics sometimes proved decisive, because the politicians found it difficult to orient themselves amid the violence and confusion. By attaching tendencies to names, they placed markers in the swirl of events and took sides according to signals exchanged among friends and enemies. Their leaders knew each other well. Robespierre and Desmoulins had been students together in the Collège Louis le Grand. Brissot and Marat became firm friends during the years they spent together in London. Brissot also developed close ties with Pétion, thanks in part to their common childhood in Chartres, and they both formed strong friendships with Manuel. Paths crossed and careers entwined in clubs and associations like the Musée and Lycée of Paris, where second- and third-rate writers sought mutual support during the lean years before 1789. Many of them—Mirabeau, Manuel, Brissot, Clavière, Carra, Gorsas, Mercier—collaborated on books and pamphlets throughout the pre-revolutionary era. That experience reinforced the intensity of the alliances formed after 1789—and also of the hatreds when the friendships fell apart. The convergence of friends who were destined to become enemies stood out strongly at the marriage of Camille Desmoulins and Lucile Duplessis on December 29, 1790. The wedding party included Robespierre, Brissot, Manuel, and Mercier. Each of them at that moment was committed to the common cause, and each soon afterward would take up a new position in the realignment of left and right. The sense of solidarity on the one side and of betrayal on the other made the divisions especially lethal. All except Mercier would fall to the guillotine by 1795—all, including both the bride and groom.

Of course, biography—or prosopography, as collective biography is sometimes called—cannot replace the analysis of events and ideologies, but the study of careers can help explain the way events were experienced and ideologies expressed. The last few months of Manuel's life provide a particularly good example of how the distinction between left and right became confused in 1792. When he took his seat in the Convention, Manuel had long been associated with the most radical members of the Parisian delegation: Robespierre, Danton, Desmoulins, and other leaders of the so-called Montagnards. Yet he also had strong connections with Brissot, Pétion, and other prominent moderates or Girondins. Where would he come down when the line was drawn by the necessity of casting a vote? Would he opt for or against the execution of the king?

Manuel wavered. He produced some strong oratory, but he shrank before the prospect of shedding blood. His experience of the September Massacres seems to have shaken his sense of solidarity with the sans-culottes. In a speech at the Jacobin Club on November 5, he spoke out against the massacres.

We cannot ignore that uprising, when the people acted with a wickedness worthy of a king and desired to carry out a Saint Bartholomew's massacre. Who can claim to know that uprising better than I do? Standing on a pile of corpses, I preached respect for the law. . . . Well, then! I maintain that the entire city took part and that it must face up to the guilt, because anyone who stands by while assassins do their work can be considered their accomplice. What were you doing, you brave Parisians, during those moments of desolation? . . . I am tormented by a question: could it be better to aspire to liberty than to possess it?[12]

Collot d'Herbois, a spokesman of the new left, one that soon would threaten to outflank Robespierre, retorted with a remark that made Manuel look like a counterrevolutionary. To disavow revolutionary violence, he warned, was to turn against the Revolution: "Without September 2, there would be no liberty and no National Convention."[13] Collot himself had been a third-rate playwright and actor before the Revolution, but his Grub Street past did not make him inclined to feel any sympathy for Manuel.[14] On the contrary, he led the Jacobin attack against all forms of moderation, and by the end of 1792 Manuel appeared incurably moderate—or, as the Jacobins put it, "brissotized" ("brissoté").[15] He stopped appearing at the Jacobin Club, and on December 31 it expelled him. He had been branded as a Girondin.

Yet he continued to make inflammatory remarks about aristocrats, priests, and kings in the Convention, which he hailed as "an assembly of *philosophes.*"[16] He declared Louis XVI guilty of usurping the sovereignty of the people, a crime inherent in the very act of sitting on a throne: "We must restore to the people, by a terrible lesson, the rights that it should never have lost. . . . Legislators, hurry to pronounce a sentence that will consummate the Revolution. The agony of kings must not be slow. . . . A king who dies is not one less man."[17] Manuel's tendency to issue provocative declarations had not left him. His outspokenness made him qualified in the eyes of the Convention to be its spokesman when it needed to communicate directly with the king. He therefore visited Louis in the Temple and lectured him in the same manner that he had adopted in his earlier open letters. It was on one of these visits, soon after the proclamation of the republic, that Manuel reportedly informed Louis that he had ceased to be king and that all kings would soon fall, just like the leaves on the trees.[18]

Nonetheless, when it came to the vote on the fate of the king, Manuel could not bring himself to support the leftist demand for the death penalty. There were actually three votes: one on the king's guilt, one on whether the nation should pronounce on his punishment by means of a referendum, and one on whether he should be sent to the guillotine. Like many of the Girondins, Manuel had no difficulty in declaring the king guilty but floundered in confronting the other two questions. In the end, he came out in favor of a referendum and against an execution. He later explained his position to the Revolutionary Tribunal as follows: "I took the side of Thomas Paine by proposing deportation to The United States of America."[19] The Girondins, who then included Paine among their number, had always had a particular sympathy for the American republic. To ship Louis off to America struck many of them as a solution to the problem of what to do with him, but it was neither feasible nor satisfactory to the Montagnard left. Robespierre and Saint-Just argued, just as Manuel had done, that Louis had violated the sovereignty of the people and had become an enemy of the nation simply by virtue of his existence as a king. He therefore deserved to die, irrespective of his treachery in betraying the nation to its foreign enemies. They carried their argument by a majority of one. (This calculation includes the votes of deputies who voted in favor of the death penalty but for the possibility of a reprieve. A subsequent vote on January 17, 1793, defeated the option of a reprieve, 380 to 310.)

The razor-thin character of the vote also proved crucial in cutting off Manuel's last connections with the left. He sat as secretary to the Convention and kept track of the tally. According to some testimony made against him ten months later during his own trial before the Revolutionary Tribunal, he kept two tally sheets, one accurate, one falsified. When the fate of the king became clear, he dropped his handkerchief on top of the accurate sheet, removed it, left his place, and returned, having got rid of the last bit of evidence that would have led to the king's death. That story probably was invented in order to speed Manuel to the guillotine. Considering the careful scrutiny of the voting, a maneuver of that sort would never have worked. But the fact that Manuel could have been accused of such cheating indicates the determination of his former allies to get rid of him. Before they could do so, however, he declared good riddance to them. Immediately after the vote, he walked out of the Convention, resigned his seat, and withdrew to his hometown of Montargis.[20]

Manuel remained in Montargis from late January until sometime in the spring of 1793. According to some reports, he was nearly killed when he tried to intervene in a riot that broke out in March.[21] After that, he went into hiding in the area surrounding Paris. He was finally arrested on August 20 in Fontainebleau. He spent nearly three months in the Parisian prison of the Abbaye before he was summoned to appear before the Revolutionary Tribunal on November 13. By then nearly all of his friends among the Girondins had been executed or had committed suicide. Manuel must have known that he faced certain death, but he replied forcefully to all the accusations directed against him by Fouquier-Tinville, the dreaded public prosecutor. This "interrogation" was very different from the one he had undergone in 1786.

The documents from the two cases lie together in the same box in the Archives nationales. Although Manuel was imprisoned by order of the king and without access to a court in 1786, the thirty-six dossiers from his interrogation in the Bastille demonstrate that the police had conducted an elaborate investigation and took care in marshaling the evidence they had collected. The dossier from 1793 looks paltry in comparison. The evidence against Manuel took the form of "diverse denunciations," according to the official record. A nineteen-year-old saleswoman testified that she had heard Manuel say it was important to save the king's life. A painter-decorator claimed that Manuel had visited some aristocrats in Orléans and was known to have expressed "federalist" or anti-Parisian sympathies in Montargis. An army courier said he had heard Manuel deplore the vote against the king. As in so many trials during the Terror, denunciation was treated as a patriotic duty and hearsay was accepted as an indication of how the accused felt—whether he genuinely supported the Revolution in his heart or whether he hid antirevolutionary sentiments under an artificial veneer of patriotism. Fouqier-Tinville adapted that kind of testimony to standard categories of indictment: Manuel had belonged to "the liberticide faction" of Brissot and he had collaborated in "the conspiracy directed against the unity and the indivisibility of the republic."[22] The concept of the crime and the nature of the judicial procedure conformed to the law governing revolutionary justice voted by the Convention on December 16, 1792. After citing this law and ratifying Fouquier-Tinville's accusation, the jury condemned Manuel to death.

The Revolutionary Tribunal published its decision in a carefully printed, eight-page pamphlet. A second, sloppily produced pamphlet repeated the formal judgment and added some commentary: "According to the present indictment, it remains absolutely certain that the accused is one of those great villains who, for the good of the republic, deserve to perish on the scaffold."[23] This rhetoric brought the case of Manuel back to the world of slander and the narrative developed in *Vie secrète de Pierre Manuel,* the third of the printed attacks against him. A final pamphlet, *Véritable testament de Pierre Manuel,* carried the story back to the chapbook "testaments" and gallows journalism that had proliferated in Paris and London for the previous two centuries. It was a crude job: eight pages, full of typographical errors and misspellings, printed with worn-out type on filthy gray paper. It contained a good deal of street language: "He's a man with a good stomach and a bad heart." Yet it indicated that Manuel had stood up to the Revolutionary Tribunal just as he had confronted the killers of the September Massacres—with a great deal of courage: "He underwent his interrogation with audacity and firmness. . . . He wanted several times to harangue the public and to win its sympathy by a touching appeal to morality. . . . On 25 brumaire, after an interrogation that lasted nearly twelve hours on the 24th, he was executed on the Place de la Révolution. Thus do traitors perish. VIVE LA REPUBLIQUE."[24]

Chapter 20
Postscript, 1802

The Revolution did not slow down after the guillotining of Manuel. It picked up speed, accelerating the death rate as well as the rush of events, until the last of Manuel's friends and enemies had also fallen to the guillotine—Desmoulins, Danton, and Robespierre. After Robespierre's death on July 28, 1794, the Terror was dismantled and the killing abated, but the Revolution continued, as wordy as ever. Journalism revived in 1797, pamphleteering flourished, orators filled the air with words. Even after Bonaparte seized power on November 9, 1799, the French continued to draft constitutions and debate public affairs. As First Consul, Bonaparte began to muzzle the press, and as emperor, he destroyed the remnants of its liberty, using a police force that made everything under the Ancien Régime look mild. Yet the French continued to mutter.

One of them was Pelleport. Exactly what became of him after his near death on July 14, 1789, is impossible to say. But he reappeared in one final dossier of the police files. On November 10, 1802, an inspector arrested him for having "made remarks against the government" at some unnamed place in Paris, probably a café. He was then forty-six and had lived through a great deal of revolution, although the police found it difficult to pin his story down. They thought that he had served in the cavalry and might have been a spy. But for whom? All they could get out of him was that he had emigrated at some point and that he was proud of his aristocratic origins.[1]

Before this incident, Pelleport had made one appearance in the official records of the Revolution. According to *Le Moniteur universel*, which published accounts of debates in the legislature, a special courier from Stenay had burst into an evening session of the Legislative Assembly on February 14, 1792. He handed the presiding officer an urgent message from Pelleport, who protested that he had just been imprisoned by the municipality of Stenay because he seemed "suspect"—that is, counterrevolutionary. Pelleport demanded that the foreign minister, Claude Delessart, intervene to get him released.[2]

Why Delessart? When the Assembly's diplomatic committee looked into the affair, it became clear that he had chosen Pelleport as a secret agent to infiltrate the aristocratic, émigré forces that were preparing to invade France from Coblenz. But Delessart was being attacked at that time by Brissot and other radical deputies for harboring pro-Austrian and counterrevolutionary sympathies. Brissot was the most vociferous member of the diplomatic committee. So when the committee met with Delessart to discuss the affair, Brissot castigated the foreign minister for selecting a "complete aristocrat" to deal with the aristocratic threat. Delessart replied that he could hardly have chosen anyone with well-known revolutionary sympathies for such a mission, and he gave the committee access to diplomatic correspondence that proved Pelleport really was a government agent. The Assembly debated the affair on February 17. Several speakers deplored the use of spies and secrecy, tactics that smacked of the diplomacy practiced under the Ancien Régime. Some warned of the danger of traitors within the ranks. And Brissot hinted darkly that Pelleport could have been an arch-traitor, because the dispatches showed that he was already functioning as an agent in Coblenz in June 1791 at the time of the king's flight to Varennes—that is, he might have been involved in the king's attempt to escape from the Revolution. None of the arguments was conclusive, however. So the Assembly dropped the matter without taking action, and at some later date Pelleport was released from jail.[3]

He made it back to the Rhineland, but in what capacity? One reference from the ministry of foreign affairs suggests that he spied for the French during the summer campaign of 1793, but another, drawn from military memoirs, indicates that he turned coat two years later and fought on the royalist side under the prince de Condé, all the while improvising casual poetry. Fragmentary as it is, the evidence reinforces the notion entertained by Bonaparte's police that Pelleport had a long history of espionage behind him.[4]

The police did not consider it worthy of further investigation. By 1802 Paris was full of characters who had compromised themselves under one government or another in the succession of political systems. Pelleport looked like a relic from the Ancien Régime who had washed up on a park bench or a café after a dozen years of revolution and war. He hardly seemed to be a threat, though he made no effort to hold his tongue in the interrogation. He bragged about his noble pedigree and did not deny the seditious talk imputed to him. But he did not count as a big catch. "He doesn't carry any up-to-date papers on him," the police noted. He had no fixed abode. "He doesn't even seem to have any sure source of support." They released him, and he returned to obscurity. He probably died a few years later in a garret, bad-mouthing the government to the end.[5]

PART III

The Literature of Libel

Basic Ingredients

Chapter 21
The Nature of Libels

To follow a few lives from the Ancien Régime into the Revolution is to tell a story, not to explain the general nature of the changes that swept through eighteenth-century France. The careers of obscure characters like Pelleport and Manuel may be interesting in themselves, but they are important primarily because they provide a way to examine the century from an unusual angle. They have the value of markers. Such people swam with the tide and occasionally against it, yet they were only individuals tossed up by events. Having seen them struggle with events, one must leave them to their fate and turn to questions about the broader currents of their culture.

Answers can't be final in this kind of cultural history, which is better suited to opening up lines of inquiry than to closing with a conclusion. But libels proliferated everywhere in early modern Europe. They still crowd the shelves of research libraries. One can study enough of them to see what literary qualities they have in common, even though literary scholars might bridle at the thought of considering them as literature in any way at all. "What is literature?" is one of those questions like "What is Enlightenment?" that can be debated endlessly.[1] It would be more useful to begin with a more manageable query: What was a libel?

The English word is familiar enough, but its familiarity can be misleading. We have a law of libel that has evolved over the centuries. Courts enforce it, writers violate it, and lawyers specialize in the art of determining where it lies amid the boundaries separating different types of defamation. In England, the law of seditious libel served as a device to limit the freedom of the press after the end of prepublication censorship in 1695. It was applied often enough in the eighteenth century to be something of a deterrent to attacks on the government, but writers found ways around it, especially through the use of "innuendos," which provided an effective defense in criminal courts.[2]

Nothing of the kind existed in France. When French libelers attacked a public figure or anyone important enough to pull strings within the government, they were summarily arrested by virtue of lettres de cachet and clapped in the Bastille or, more often, a nastier prison like Bicêtre and Fort l'Evêque.[3]

The registers of the Bastille show a very high incidence of arrests for writing, printing, or selling *libelles*. Owing to ambiguities in the definition and compilation of offenses, no rigorous statistics can be produced, but a preliminary calculation shows that 135 persons were imprisoned in the Bastille from 1659 to 1789 for crimes connected with *libelles*—far more than those arrested for perpetrating atheism, deism, encyclopedism, libertinism, radical political theory, or other kinds of writing associated with the Enlightenment, whether counted separately or lumped together as a whole.[4] The state took libels seriously; historians should, too. But what were they?

Although the term is not much used in French today, it was a commonplace in the seventeenth and eighteenth centuries.[5] French dictionaries from the Ancien Régime all define it in the same way: "A work that contains abusive language [*injures*], reproaches, or accusations against the honor and the reputation of someone," according to the 1690 edition of Antoine Furetière's *Dictionnaire universel*.[6] This definition also prevails in dictionaries from the nineteenth century, which fill it out with philological and historical information. They trace its derivation to the Latin *libellus*, meaning small book, and provide examples of its usage in French back to Ronsard and in Latin to the age of Augustus.[7] Thanks to their classical education, French readers under the Ancien Régime had assimilated a great deal of quasi-libelous satire—by Lucian, Horace, Juvenal, Suetonius, Petronius, and others. Suetonius's *Vie des douze Césars* circulated widely in Latin after the publication of Isaac Casaubon's edition of 1691, and *Les Galanteries et les débauches de l'Empereur Néron*, available in French from 1694, familiarized the educated public with accounts of private lives that could be read as political libel.

Experts in the classics, especially sixteenth- and seventeenth-century humanists, did not merely edit these works. They attacked each other with such vituperation in their academic disputations as to make libeling look like a variety of scholarship. Their practice was harmless enough when limited to the learned, but it could be dangerous when it spread to their patrons. Philipp Andreas Oldenburger was forced to do penance for some satirical remarks about the love life of a German princeling by eating the two most libelous leaves of his *Constantini Germanici ad Justum Sincerum Epistola politica de Peregrinationibus recte et rite instituendis*—and he got off with nothing more than a public humiliation.[8] The Tudors punished libelers by slitting noses and trimming ears in sixteenth-century England, and in France Charles IX decreed by an edict of January 17, 1561: "We desire that all printers, distributors and sellers of placards and defamatory libels be punished for the first offense with the whip and for the second by execution."[9] The punishments subsequently inflicted on *libellistes* (a term first used in 1640) included two exemplary cases:

in 1689 Le Tellier, the brother of Louis XIV's minister of war, the marquis de Louvois, was shut up for thirty years in the iron cage of Mont St. Michel for *Le Cochon mitré*, an attack on the archbishop of Reims, and in 1694 a bookseller and a binder were hanged for distributing a book about the morganatic marriage of Louis XIV and Madame de Maintenon.[10]

Libeling was certainly dangerous—but primarily if it attacked persons of a certain rank. It was the personal character of the attack, according to contemporaries, that distinguished libels from works that took governments, policies, or other general subjects as their targets. Yet the distinction became blurred in common usage because governments protected the reputations of eminent individuals.[11] No clear demarcation between the public and the private spheres existed among the great under the Ancien Régime in France. By offending a *grand*, a libeler risked severe punishment by the state, and he could not count on any protection from legal procedures in the courts. Malesherbes argued for a lenient policy toward the press during his term as director of the book trade (1750–63). He favored repression only in the case of egregious offenses to religion, the state, or morality. Yet he advocated severe measures against books that caused a fourth kind of offense, "personal satires" or "libels." Their authors, he emphasized, deserved to be punished "by blows from the authorities, immediately, without recourse to the courts"—but only if they slandered "persons of importance."[12]

Pierre Bayle had adopted a similar position sixty-two years earlier. In a "dissertation on defamatory libels" at the end of his *Dictionnaire historique et critique* (1695–97), he condemned libelers for damaging the honor of individuals and argued that they should be severely punished. At the same time, in his usual manner of worrying questions from opposing points of view, he observed that the most effective defense against libels was to ignore them, particularly in the case of slander aimed at sovereigns. Nero, he noted ironically, had shrugged off libels or merely exiled their authors, whereas Augustus had treated them as crimes of lèse majesté, worthy of the death penalty. Bayle found nothing to justify Augustus's policy, and in discussing incidents of seditious libel among the moderns as well as the ancients, he sounded sympathetic to toleration. Yet he warned that if the circumstances were right, libels could provoke uprisings. Their effects could not be predicted, but one thing was certain: "That is that the tongue and the pen of one man alone are sometimes more useful for a cause than an army of 40,000 soldiers."[13]

On the conceptual level, ambiguities arose at the point where satire shaded off into calumny. Voltaire attempted to delineate clear distinctions by differentiating among criticism, satire, and libel. Critics, as he described them, made their arguments gently, without mentioning anyone by name. Satirists scored points by attacking individuals, although they did not impugn their private lives. And libelers tried to destroy the honor of their victims by personal defamation. Whatever the validity of those distinctions, Voltaire weakened their force by turning them against his enemies, particularly abbé Pierre-François Desfontaines and Elie-Catherine Fréron, whom he vilified as libelers, using so much vituperation as to sound like a libeler himself.[14]

When reference works from the eighteenth century ventured beyond definitions into commentary, they, too, blurred distinctions and strayed into ambiguities. The most outspoken account appeared in the Jesuit *Dictionnaire de Trévoux*. Libels might begin as satires meant merely for amusement, it warned, but the common people were credulous. They would believe anything, and the general tendency to run down reputations could produce serious damage when it spread among gentle folk ("honnêtes gens"). Moreover, the damage could be lasting because unsubstantiated stories often found their way into histories. The ancients in their wisdom punished libeling by death, as Augustus had determined by defining it as a crime of lèse majesté. The *Dictionnaire de Trévoux* did not go quite that far, but it called for severe repression of libelers in contemporary France.[15]

By contrast, the *Encyclopédie* of Diderot and d'Alembert came close to arguing for general toleration. The article on *libelle* by the chevalier Louis de Jaucourt began with the conventional definition—broadened, however, to include songs and any kind of written work, whether manuscript or printed, that attacked the honor and reputation of an individual—and then wandered off into a wonderfully inconsistent discussion of the larger issues. After disapproving of libels for the damage they inflict on a person's honor, especially if they appeared in print, Jaucourt took up an argument for the freedom of the press. He approached the subject from the perspective of Montesquieu's *De l'Esprit des lois*. In despotisms, he noted, libels do not exist, because everyone is subjected to the arbitrary will of the sovereign, and no one reads. In a liberal or enlightened monarchy ("monarchie éclairée," a phrase that applied to France), however, libels should be tolerated. The example of England showed that all sorts of personal vituperation could be permitted without inflicting much damage. Instead of repressing libels, the English treated them with scorn ("mépris"—here Jaucourt's argument ran parallel to one side of the debate within the French foreign ministry). The dirt slung by slanderers did not stick to anyone, and by brushing it off, the English maintained something far more valuable: liberty. In more authoritarian monarchies, flattery could prevent the prince from perceiving the rightful course to follow, whereas a libel would alert him to the danger of tyranny: "It is often by means of outspoken license that the lamentations of the oppressed penetrate up to the throne, which has no knowledge of them otherwise." Carried away by his argument, Jaucourt came close to advocating limitless freedom of the press. Then, as if appalled by his own radicalism, he drew back and insisted that he did not really mean to favor defamation. He went on to invoke all sorts of conventional considerations about religion, morality, the interests of the state, and the need to maintain social order. But he could not leave the subject there. He ended with a bold non sequitur: "But in a well-run state, I would not want to repress license by measures that would inevitably destroy all liberty."[16]

Louis-Sébastien Mercier developed a later version of the same argument in a chapter on libels in his *Tableau de Paris*. He, too, advocated an English variety of "scorn" as the best policy because it minimized the damage to reputations while maintaining the liberty of the press. Persecution of libels would only make them more sought after and therefore more credible, he warned. If left alone, they would be dismissed as vicious or mendacious by most readers—except in crucial cases, when a patriotic author dared to expose an abuse of power and readers would believe him, despite the apparently slanderous character of his work. How then were readers to distinguish the truthful from the solely defamatory attacks on individuals? Mercier did not say. He merely defended the need for moderate libels and condemned the most extreme kind, those produced by hacks ("la basse littérature"), whose desperation for money drove them to produce "atrocious and gratuitous accusations against the private life of princes and individuals."[17]

A final source seems to offer a way out of these contradictions and ambiguities because it provides an extensive discussion of the subject under a promising title: *Théorie du libelle* (Amsterdam, 1775). It takes the form of a "philosophical dialogue" between two characters, "M.," a worldly and wealthy philosophe of the Physiocratic school (economists who favored free trade, especially in the agrarian sector), and "P.," an aspiring young writer who has just arrived in Paris from the provinces. P. shares all the ideas of the philosophes, and he is eager to enlist with them. Also, like most new recruits, he needs to make some money. For his part, M. has been looking for a talented writer to defend the philosophes against their most prominent enemy, Simon-Nicolas-Henri Linguet. He therefore has assembled all of Linguet's works, invited P. to read and refute them, and is now expecting P. to arrive with his manuscript.

The dialogue takes place in M.'s fashionable apartment in the Faubourg Saint Germain. M. paces the floor, rubbing his hands: "One more pamphlet . . . and he is done for."[18] P. enters, looking perplexed. M. asks for the libel. P. confesses that he did not write it. He spent the entire night reading through Linguet's books, and they seemed distressingly convincing. M. retorts that he doesn't want to hear any nonsense about the validity of Linguet's arguments. He had hired P. to select passages from Linguet's publications, rearrange them so that they seem to contradict each other, and hold them up to ridicule. P.'s assignment was to misquote Linguet and tear his ideas out of context, not to study them. But what about their truth? P. asks. M., annoyed with such a simpleminded question, explains that the philosophes have no interest in truth. They are trying to dominate public opinion, and they have been doing quite well, thanks to help from the censors and support from the salons. They have learned to manipulate the public in the same way that a gentleman masters a horse in a riding academy, and their most effective technique is to blacken the reputation of their enemies. This outburst opens P.'s eyes as to what is really going on in the polemics of Paris. He may be penniless and naïve, but he will not play that game. M. can hire another character assassin. P. leaves, a convert to Linguet's ideas and an enemy of the fashionable world of *philosophie.*

Far from providing any theory, therefore, the *Théorie du libelle* turned out to be another libel. Its author was Linguet himself, and its villain, "M.," was abbé André Morellet, who had ridiculed Linguet in his *Théorie du paradoxe* (Amsterdam, 1775). Morellet also had pretended to be writing a theoretical work, a study of a new kind of rhetoric based on the use of paradox rather than an attack on any individual. He avoided personal remarks about Linguet, whom he referred to only as "L.," and he restricted himself to quoting contradictory selections from Linguet's works. But he arranged the quotations so artfully that he obviously meant to demolish Linguet's reputation as a serious thinker. Morellet also published his tract anonymously and under a false address, so Linguet had some justification for treating it as a libel. But he counterattacked with so much vehemence that his own tract was condemned as a "libel" by a royal edict of April 2, 1775.[19]

These polemics hardly clarified the theoretical issues connected with the concept of libel, but they revealed something of the way it resonated in the society of the Ancien Régime. Linguet objected to the class-specific character of Morellet's appeal. Like Rousseau before him and Robespierre afterward, he identified wit with the sophisticated world of the Parisian elite: "Defamation seems to be one of those games in high society, one of those remedies against boredom. It is gaily at the dinner table and in private gatherings that one slits the throat of a citizen, that one makes him an object of horror and of public malediction."[20] Morellet cast Linguet in the opposite kind of company. First, he quoted an outburst Linguet had delivered against journalists, "forming the lowest rank in the order of literature, in league with brash defamers . . . hacks employed by booksellers, literary hired assassins, compilers of extracts at so much the sheet."[21] Then he noted that Linguet had become a journalist himself.

When the French diplomats took the measure of Linguet and the other exile writers in London, they, too, saw nothing but venality and vulgarity—the qualities of "the rabble," as Adhémar put it. According to such formulations, there was a certain affinity between literary manner and social manners. Writers at the bottom of the literary world adopted styles and genres that distinguished them from those at the top. Of course, some in the elite had come from modest origins (Morellet was the son of a small-time paper merchant in Lyons), and some among the hacks attempted to write with great refinement (Manuel tried to strike a tone of belletristic elegance in his *Essais historiques, critiques, littéraires et philosophiques,* and Pelleport, an aristocratic *déclassé,* filled *Les Bohémiens* with classical allusions). The opposition between the upper and lower ranks in the republic of letters cannot be reduced to a simple formula. But when authors engaged in polemics, they chose weapons that worked best from the positions they occupied. Morellet, Chénier, and Rivarol skewered their opponents with wit. Linguet, Manuel, and Brissot bludgeoned them with rhetoric. Defamation, as a form of rhetoric, was a favorite weapon of writers in the lower ranks of the republic of letters.

But rhetoric, as Morellet demonstrated in his *Théorie du paradoxe,* came in many varieties, including aggressive wittiness. Was there something specific to the rhetoric of libel? Did libels make up a peculiar genre of literature? The characteristic that set them apart, in contemporary usage as well as in dictionary definitions, was the intention to damage the reputation of an individual. When Parisians complained about libels to the police, they emphasized the personal nature of the offense. "This libel reportedly contains some atrocious and fabricated insults intended to destroy my honor and reputation,"[22] wrote a marquis who demanded immediate action by the lieutenant general. Linguet expressed the same view: "A well-aimed libel can overturn everything, change and dominate opinion, destroy a man irrevocably."[23] Even Jean-Paul Marat, who specialized in denunciation, made the same objection: "Do you want to obliterate an individual who is isolated, without defenses, without support? Then slander him in a libel."[24]

Occasionally, however, libels offended public authorities without attacking individuals. On June 30, 1775, the Parlement of Paris condemned two works as "libels": *Catéchisme du citoyen, ou éléments du droit public français* and *L'Ami des lois.* Neither book maligned any public figure. They were political tracts, which, according to the parlement, "consciously misconstrue the true character of the sovereign power; they make a great effort to weaken the links that unite the people to the monarch." The parlement especially deplored the fact that these works openly discussed the affairs of the government, which formerly were kept hidden under a veil of secrecy—the famous "arcana imperii" of early modern statecraft. A libel, therefore, might concern the secret life of the state as well as the secret life of an individual. Libeling was a matter of making the private public, of unveiling secrets, normally with the intention of damaging a person's reputation but sometimes with the broader aim of exposing the activities of the government.[25]

Given this general consensus about the nature of libels, it seems likely that eighteenth-century Frenchmen could recognize one when they saw one. But libels came in every shape and size. Many were pamphlets of only a few pages—often eight, from a half sheet of cheap paper, which could be printed on both sides, folded, stitched, and cut to form a primitive booklet for a small outlay of capital. Others came in imposing, multivolume editions, carefully printed and bound. Bindings varied, because customers often bought books in sheets and had them bound to suit their own tastes. The typography and design of libels tended to be slapdash, as they usually circulated in the downmarket sector of the book trade. All of them were illegal; none was covered by anything like a copyright. So publishers pirated one another with abandon, and best-sellers went through many editions, most of them cheap—that is, 20–30 sous (the equivalent of a day's labor for an unskilled workman or of three four-pound loaves of bread). But editions could be handsome. *Vie privée de Louis XV*, a popular book reprinted at least three times in the 1780s, contained a dozen engravings scattered through four substantial volumes. If bound in calf with gold-tooled decorations, it could look impressive—as if to say, in all its physicality: "Here is a solid and reputable account of a half-century of history." The *Mémoires secrets pour servir à l'histoire de la république des lettres en France* promised even more extensive coverage. It ran to thirty-six volumes, enough to fill a shelf.

Titles served more effectively than size as indicators. Anything with "secret" or "private" in the title was likely to be a libel, especially if the adjective connected with a noun like "life," "memoirs," or "history." The most common titles from the libel literature of the eighteenth century began with "The Private Life of . . ." or "The Secret Life of . . . ," although some private lives could be innocent biographies meant to flatter, not to injure, their subjects, as in the case of *Vie privée du général Buonaparte*. Libelers liked to present themselves anonymously as spies, drawing on an old tradition of popular, pseudo-Orientalism. *L'Espion chinois* and *L'Espion turc* revealed love affairs along with state affairs to a large public. After masquerading as a Chinese spy, Ange Goudar changed costumes and recycled gossip as *L'Espion français à la cour de Londres*. The French fascination with all things English also provided a vehicle for the very popular *Espion anglais*, whose subtitle looked especially alluring: *Correspondance secrète entre milord All'eye et milord All'ear*. Pseudo-correspondence of all kinds worked well as a cover for gossip sheets: *Lettres iroquoises* and *Lettres chérakéesiennes* exploited a strain of exoticism that came from a thinly fictionalized New World rather than the Orient. From "letters" to "correspondence," "memoirs," and "journal," the titles worked endless variations on the themes of letters discovered in lost portfolios, secrets exchanged through the mail, and confidences confessed to diaries. The fictions were transparent, but they added spice to the promised revelations, and they filled the function of alerting the reader to what could be expected: the exposure of secrets.

Did libels therefore shade off into journalism and even fiction? Certainly: the *Mémoires secrets pour servir à l'histoire de la république des lettres en France*, the *Journal historique de la révolution opérée dans la constitution de la monarchie française par le chancelier de Maupeou*, and the *Correspondance secrète et familière du chancelier de Maupeou avec Sorhouet*—all of them best-sellers—provided journalistic accounts of events while slinging mud at individuals. Libels often presented themselves as journals, gazettes, and chronicles. Some were published versions of the *gazettes à la main* that provided hacks like Imbert de Boudeaux with their basic bread and butter. Imbert also recycled the stories from his manuscript bulletins—and from the work of other authors—into a kind of anthology known as a "chronique scandaleuse." He published a book with that very title, *La Chronique scandaleuse*, which shows how libels anticipated some aspects of the modern yellow press. Readers could enjoy such works as a combination of fact and fiction. Many were designed to be read in the same manner as romans à clef. *Mémoires secrets pour servir à l'histoire de Perse* libeled Louis XV and all the figures of his court whom it presented as pashas and mullahs. It contained an elaborate key and a biographical index so that the reader could identify all the characters. In this respect, it resembled two contemporary works of fiction that also hid attacks on the king and his mistresses with code names attached to keys: *Tanastès* and *Les Amours de Zéokinizul, roi des Kofirans*.[26]

Some of these works covered so much contemporary history that they could be taken seriously as historical narratives spiced up with a little scandal. *Mémoires secrets pour servir à l'histoire de Perse*, which probably was written by Antoine Pecquet, a discontented official from the foreign office, contained a remarkably intelligent and detailed history of France from 1715 to 1744.[27] "History" figures everywhere in the titles—notably in Mirabeau's *Histoire secrète de la cour de Berlin* (1789) but also in more obscure but equally illegal works such as *Histoire secrète des intrigues de la France en diverses cours de l'Europe*

(1713) and *Histoire secrète de Bourgogne* (1782). Because "histoire" meant story as well as history, these works promised to provide potential consumers with a narrative that would combine scandal with information about current events. Moreover, "histoire" could also connote biography; so the histories often fit into the long series of "private lives." Thus *Histoire secrète des premières amours d'Elizabeth, d'Angleterre* (1697), *Histoire secrète de Jean de Bourbon, prince de Carency* (1709), and *Histoire secrète de la reine Zarah et des zaraziens, ou la Duchesse de Marlborough démasquée: Avec la clef pour l'intelligence de cette histoire* (1708). The double meanings and superimposed allusions did not mislead readers; on the contrary, the titles informed them of what to expect in a wide variety of genres.

Unfortunately, the notion of genre does not provide much help as a way of characterizing libels. Consider the works encountered along the line that led from Morande to Manuel. They belonged to many genres: chronicle (*Le Gazetier cuirassé*), poetry (*Les Amours de Charlot et Toinette*), dramatic dialogue (*Les Petits Soupers et les nuits de l'Hôtel Bouillon*), reportage (*Le Diable dans un bénitier*), history (*La Police de Paris dévoilée*), correspondence (*Lettres originales de Mirabeau*), and biography (*Vie secrète de Pierre Manuel*). All these books were understood at the time to be libels, and all conformed to the contemporary definitions of libel, yet they spilled over a half-dozen genres. They belong to the same family and have strong family resemblances, but they lack generic affinity. How then to sort out libels as a body of literature?

Instead of attempting to impose a classification system on such heterogeneous material, I find it more effective to study the qualities that libels have in common. The procedure is inevitably subjective, but it offers a way of understanding the peculiar character of libel literature. After reading through a great many French *libelles* from the seventeenth and eighteenth centuries, I selected some typical texts, broke them down into their constituent elements, and studied the way those elements were combined. Whether long histories or short pamphlets, I found that libels generally used the same building blocks. Their basic unit is a short report about an occurrence, usually of a scandalous nature. The libeler presents it as authentic, although he may dress it up by rhetoric to obtain certain effects—shock, horror, amusement, anger, indignation, or other responses from the readers he implicitly addresses. The French usually referred to these reports as "anecdotes," a word that connoted hidden information rather than hearsay, as it does in current usage. They also called them *nouvelles*, meaning news—that is, factual accounts of events, representations of things that actually happened, something similar to "hard news," as we say today, despite the exaggeration of the language used to describe them. These nuggets of news were the irreducible, minimal material out of which libels were composed. They could be combined in many ways, but in themselves they were short, usually a paragraph consisting of only a few sentences. Here is a typical example from Imbert's *La Chronique scandaleuse* (published in one volume in 1783, expanded to two volumes in 1784, to four volumes in 1785, and reprinted with a new fifth volume in 1791): "One day the duke of * * * surprised his dear spouse in the arms of his son's tutor. The worthy lady said to him with all the impudence of a duchess: 'Why weren't you there, Monsieur. When I do not have my esquire, I take the arm of my lackey.'"[28] The same *nouvelle*, slightly rephrased, appeared in Manuel's *La Police de Paris dévoilée* (1790): "The duke of . . . surprised his wife in the arms of his son's tutor. She said to him with all the impudence of a courtier, 'Why weren't you there, Monsieur? When I don't have my esquire, I take the arm of my lackey.'"[29] Libelers constantly lifted material from one another and from common sources, so there is nothing surprising about the fact that Manuel repeated the same anecdote seven years after Imbert. But he placed it in a different context, surrounding it with stories about the depravity of aristocrats and the abuses of power by ministers. Imbert inserted the anecdote among other amusing incidents, so his libel could be read as a joke book. Its facetious character was apparent from its index, which classified its entries under headings like "bons mots," "funny stories," "caricatures," "cuckolds," "puns," and "pasquinades."

A close reading of all the libels published between 1770 and 1800 would turn up countless cases of anecdotes extracted from one publication and inserted in another. To describe this pilfering as plagiarism would be anachronistic. It was standard practice among the libelers, and it illustrates the way they worked. They quarried material from every source at their command and put them together in whatever way that suited their purpose—as scandalous biographies, seditious histories, *gazettes à la main*, chronicles, pseudo-memoirs, pseudo-correspondences, pamphlets, and potpourris. Information was available everywhere in eighteenth-century Paris. It hovered in the air and could be snatched from conversations or forms of oral exchange described as "bruits publics," "on dits," "bons mots," "Pont-Neufs," and "chansons." When reduced to writing, it crystallized into items of news—"nouvelles" or "anecdotes." Libelers combined these ready-made news items by a process of bricolage. The manner of assemblage affected the meaning, so the same anecdote could look like a joke in one context and an indictment in another. In the case of complex narratives, considerable skill was required to produce the desired effect. A gifted libeler like Pelleport set scenes, mixed dialogue with description, and worked his story into a dramatic denouement. Primitive scribblers like the anonymous author of *Vie secrète de Pierre Manuel* cobbled together disparate segments without worrying about chronology or coherence. The ways of constructing libels varied as much as the genres for which they were adapted; libeling was a supremely flexible medium. But all libels had the same general character and the same basic components. They manipulated the information system of their time by extracting material from a wide variety of sources, reworked it, and reinserted it in a manner designed to create the most damage. Libels were a powerful mode of communication. Governments had reason to fear them, both under the Ancien Régime and at every stage in the Revolution.

Chapter 22

Anecdotes

One word that crops up everywhere in the titles and texts of libels is especially disconcerting for the twenty-first-century reader: anecdotes. To us, it suggests a casual story that is likely to be unreliable, as indicated by the expression "anecdotal evidence." To Europeans in the eighteenth century, it meant nearly the opposite. An anecdote was a solid piece of information but one that had been hidden, that needed to be dug up or uncovered or unveiled. Unlike other kinds of information, therefore, it had a special attraction. It was likely to be scandalous.

The dictionary of the Académie française defined "anecdote" as a "secret occurrence or circumstance [*particularité*] of history, which had been omitted or suppressed by earlier historians." It noted that anecdotes tended to be satirical as well as historical; hence the supreme example of their use: "*The Anecdotal History of Procopius.*"[1] Procopius, the Byzantine historian from the sixth century A.D., developed a new mode of depicting the recent past. In addition to his quasi-official account of the wars waged under the emperor Justinian against the Persians, Vandals, and Goths, he wrote a work—anonymous and circulated posthumously in order to protect him from the wrath of his superiors—which opened a way for all the libeling that followed him. Known as *Anecdota* in Greek, it usually bore the title *Historia Arcana* in Latin and *Secret History* in English. As the titles indicated, Procopius connected the notion of anecdotes with that of a secret history, one that would expose the hidden activities of rulers and the underlying explanations of events. The *Anecdota* presented Justinian, his consort Theodora, his general Belisarius, and other great figures in a way that differed completely from Procopius's war histories. Instead of appearing as conquering heroes and majestic dignitaries, they turned out, when seen up close, to be devious and despicable, and their personal flaws accounted for the lamentable state of the Roman Empire. In attacking them, therefore, Procopius exposed the secret side of statecraft—the "arcane imperii," as it came to be known in early modern Europe.[2]

The Procopian notion of anecdotes particularly appealed to writers and readers in eighteenth-century France, when public affairs were considered the private business of sovereigns or, as the phrase went, "le secret du roi." The article on "anecdotes" in the *Encyclopédie* emphasized this connotation of the term: "Anecdotes, a name that the Greeks gave to things that were made known for the first time to the public. . . . This word is used in literature to signify the secret history of facts that happened in the inner cabinet or courts of princes and in the mysteries of their politics." The *Encyclopédie* cited Procopius as the one writer among the ancients who had perfected anecdotes as a weapon of abuse. Horace, Juvenal, Petronius, and many others had mastered satire, but only Procopius knew how to denigrate the great by exposing their private lives.

Although they did not often refer to Procopius, libelers in the eighteenth century deployed anecdotes as he had done—as a way of revealing the hidden side of history, history understood as an account of the recent past, or current events. Libelers therefore presented themselves as historians. They claimed to recount facts. But they hid under a cover of anonymity, because by revealing the true secrets at the heart of the power system, they risked the Bastille, the galleys, or the gallows. *Anecdotes sur Mme la comtesse du Barry*, the most popular libel of the pre-revolutionary years, made these claims explicit in its preface.

Although this work is a very complete life of Madame la comtesse du Barry, the author has preferred to give it the modest title of *Anecdotes* in order to avoid every suggestion of pretentiousness. In this way he has freed himself from the formal order and stylistic gravity that would have been required in a more imposing introduction. . . . But no one should believe that by laboriously pulling together so much [information], he has thoughtlessly included the large number of fables and absurdities, which are recounted about this famous courtesan. . . . As will be apparent, he cites evidence for everything that he asserts, from her birth until her retirement. In this regard, he has observed the scrupulous rules of an historian.[3]

The anonymous author went on to insist that a rigorous biography of this kind could not be considered a "libel," but he also promised to season his text with "some very spicy . . . details," and he filled it with so much scabrous material about his antiheroine that no one could fail to recognize its libelous character. In pretending not to write a libel, he merely asserted his claim to write the truth. And by entitling his work "anecdotes," he laid claim to write as an historian—a Procopian type of historian, the kind who revealed hidden secrets. His readers could therefore expect to enjoy themselves. Unlike heavy, academic history, the preface emphasized, *Anecdotes sur Mme la comtesse du Barry* would provide amusement along with instruction. It had something for everyone, from the philosophical to the frivolous. It was history that read like a novel.

That, of course, was sales talk. Prefaces often tried to entice readers into texts with this kind of rhetoric, so they cannot be taken literally. But they can be studied for the assumptions implicit in their sales pitch. By promoting their wares in a particular manner, they indicated what they were marketing and what readers could expect to experience. Other devices—titles, subtitles, publishing addresses, forewords, footnotes, appendices, illustrations, overall design—gave off similar signals. The self-presentation of slanderous works reveals a great deal about their character and about the way they were meant to be read.

Libelers never referred to their work as libels, because the expression was too negative and it could undercut their claim to tell the truth. They preferred terms like "history" or "memoirs," mixed liberally with references to "anecdotes" so as to convey an aura of authoritativeness. A sequel to *Anecdotes sur Mme la comtesse du Barry* censured its author for concealing the book's character as a libel by misusing "anecdotes" in its title—and then, having established its own claim to veracity, reworked the same material in an equally libelous manner.[4] *La Chronique scandaleuse* tried to lend credence to its scandalmongering by including the key words "anecdotes" and "secret history" in an elaborate subtitle: *La Chronique scandaleuse, ou Mémoires pour servir à l'histoire de la génération présente, contenant les anecdotes et les pièces fugitives les plus piquantes que l'histoire secrète des sociétés a offertes pendant ces dernières années.* Many libels passed themselves off as the memoirs or correspondence of the persons they slandered. The ostensible editors of these publications wrote prefaces guaranteeing their authenticity and explaining their provenance: they had been purloined by private secretaries or found in secret drawers or discovered in lost portfolios. Such transparent fictions show up everywhere in the legal literature of the Ancien Régime, especially in epistolary novels. Eighteenth-century readers were familiar with them and knew how to make allowances for their artificial character. But the rhetorical packaging of a libel did not necessarily vitiate the information it contained. How accurate were the anecdotes at the heart of the secret histories, scandalous chronicles, and pseudo-memoirs? They could not be measured against some objective criterion, so eighteenth-century readers had to distinguish authenticity from artifice as best they could. But that kind of reading—the ferreting out of hidden truth from contrived narratives, the winnowing of fact from fiction—had become a common practice in seventeenth- and eighteenth-century France. It was familiar to anyone who had read classic authors like La Rochefoucauld, La Fontaine, and La Bruyère and (as explained in Chapter 6) who had trained their perception by working the puzzles and word games in popular journals like the *Mercure de France*, *L'Année littéraire*, and *Le Journal de Paris*. When applied to current events, it lent a special fascination to the deciphering of libels.

Some collections of anecdotes turned this mode of reading to their advantage by adopting a playful tone and flaunting their semi-fictitious character. The self-presentation of *Portefeuille d'un talon rouge contenant des anecdotes galantes et secrètes de la cour de France* (1783) and *Le Portefeuille de madame Gourdan, dite la comtesse, pour servir à l'histoire des moeurs du siècle et principalement de celle de Paris* (1783) was not meant to be taken literally. Instead, these supposed "portfolios" added spice to their contents by pretending to be the correspondence of two unlikely letter writers, an all-knowing courtier and a notorious madame of a Parisian brothel. The same obvious artifice characterized the "spies" who could be found everywhere in libel literature. Few readers could have believed that a Turk had composed *L'Espion turc dans les cours des princes chrétiens* (1742), that a Chinese had written *L'Espion chinois, ou l'envoyé de la cour de Pékin* (1742), or that a louse had narrated *Histoire d'un pou français, ou l'espion d'une nouvelle espèce* (1781). A Frenchman did not need to know much English to doubt the authenticity of Lord All'Eye and Lord All'Ear, who exchanged letters in *L'Espion anglais, ou correspondance secrète entre milord All'Eye et milord All'Ear* (1777). And a great deal of skepticism must have surrounded the identities of the authors of *Lettres iroquoises* (1752), *Lettres cherakéesiennes* (1752), and *Lettres d'un sauvage dépaysé* (1738). Voltaire poked fun at all these works in his *Lettres chinoises, indiennes, et tartares* (1776), his last word on a genre that had flourished since Montesquieu's *Lettres persanes*.

Epistolary satire of this sort was a staple of eighteenth-century literature. Readers did not need to believe in the authenticity of the Persians, Chinese, Iroquois, and other exotic correspondents to accept the veracity of the anecdotes they recounted—or at least to detect a kernel of truth hidden in the obvious fictions. Much of this literature was lighthearted or meant to be taken only half seriously. But secret histories that touched on the "secret du roi," the king's private life, his mistresses and ministers, were another matter. The *Mémoires de l'abbé Terray* (1776) was both fictitious and seditious. And the highly popular *Correspondance secrète et familière de M. de Maupeou avec M. de Sor***, conseiller du nouveau parlement* (1771), although obviously fabricated, probably did more to discredit the Maupeou ministry than any other printed work. Anecdotes could inflict damage, even when they came decked out in the unlikeliest disguises.

The slander aimed at royal mistresses could be especially damaging. Both

Madame de Pompadour and Madame du Barry were attacked in pseudo-memoirs and pseudo-collections of letters that appeared under their names. *Mémoires authentiques de Mme la comtesse du Barry* (1776) and *Lettres originales de Madame la comtesse du Barry* (1779) probably seemed too outrageous to pass as genuine. But the more moderate and more widely diffused *Mémoires de Madame la marquise de Pompadour* (1776) and *Lettres de Madame la marquise de Pompadour* (1776) apparently struck some readers as authentic. In a later edition of the Pompadour letters, their supposed editor, who remained anonymous, noted that readers of the first edition had been troubled by errors in the text. How could Mme de Pompadour have written to the French ambassador in Vienna as the marquis d'Albret when his name was actually d'Aubeterre? And why would she have addressed the prince de Soubise as maréchal in 1757, considering that he did not receive promotion to the rank of marshal until October 1758? The editor replied to these objections as best he could in a note at the beginning of volume 4 by spinning a story about Pompadour's supposed secretary. The secretary, who also remained unnamed, had made off with copies of the letters to Holland, where he had died, leaving them to the executor of his estate, who had sold them him to the editor. The editor confessed that he had made some errors in transcribing the manuscript—not from carelessness, he insisted, but owing to the negligence of the secretary, who had been too lazy to write out names in full and to supply the correct dates. Aside from these minor imperfections, the printed text was an accurate reproduction of an absolutely authentic manuscript. Many readers probably dismissed this defense as a fabrication, but the fact that the ostensible editor tried so hard to patch up the holes in his original version suggests that some readers had believed it.

Occasional references in underground newsletters also indicate that libels were taken seriously, even by sophisticated readers. As already explained, *Les Joueurs et M. Dusaulx* (1780) was a libel contrived to promote a blackmail operation. Its text contained a great deal of fictitious dialogue embedded in a far-fetched narrative by a prostitute with a heart of gold. To a modern reader, it seems completely unconvincing. But to the well-informed author of *Correspondance littéraire secrète*, it rang true: "It's a jumble of wickedness that surpasses the imagination. Swindlers, lackeys, spies, pimps, and brothel keepers are the lovers and backers of these ladies. Men in power are also involved with it all."[5] This example of reader response appeared in an underground newsletter aimed at "those who appreciate the freshest anecdotes."[6] The *nouvelliste* was moved by the anecdotal evidence in *Les Joueurs*—stories about gambling dens that identified culprits by name and provided vivid details about their techniques of cheating and of collaborating with the police—and he did not seem to be put off by the obviously artificial narrative in which they were arranged. In an article on the *Lettres iroquoises*, he sounded equally unperturbed by the use of literary artifice. Without even mentioning its fictitious narrator, he stressed its "amusing anecdotes" and its accurate attacks on public figures.[7] Slander could be inserted anywhere within the conventional genres used by libelers: histories, biographies, chronicles, memoirs, collections of correspondence—it did not matter. If the anecdotes were convincing enough, readers would make allowances for the literary devices that accompanied them.

It must be admitted, however, that we don't know a great deal about how readers made sense of books under the Ancien Régime. Despite a recent flurry of research, the history of reading still involves a great deal of guesswork based on margin notes, diaries, correspondence, and whatever clues can be picked up from the books themselves. But at least we have learned to beware of simplistic interpretations. The message conveyed by a book was not stamped on the mind of a reader in a straightforward manner analogous to the way in which ink became printed on paper. Readers construed the printed word in many ways, which did not correlate closely with social position, geographical location, or rates of literacy. A self-taught peasant, Valentin Jamerey-Duval, mastered a wide range of scientific literature without passing through any educational institution. A daughter of an artisan, Marie-Jeanne Phlipon (the future Mme Roland), devoured a great variety of philosophic works and carried a volume of Plutarch to church as if it were a devotional work before her first communion. Aristocratic ladies, including the queen, took in novels through their ears while being read to at their toilette by their chambermaids.[8] It would be misleading to assume that slanderous literature evoked a standard response. A naïve reader might swallow a libel whole, while a sophisticated reader discounted the rhetorical techniques used to make it look convincing. But no one would dismiss it on the grounds that it relied on anecdotes as evidence. Anecdotes might be tendentious, misleading, or even partly false, but in the eyes of eighteenth-century readers they contained solid bits of information culled from hidden sources.

Even Morande acknowledged their power of persuasion, as he indicated by slipping "anecdotes" into the subtitle of *Le Gazetier cuirassé, ou Anecdotes scandaleuses de la cour de France*.[9] Far from concealing the scandalous character of his work, he flaunted it. He even teased the reader with some obviously fabricated stories, such as a report about a new invention, favored by the government, that could hang one hundred victims at once.[10] But burlesque "news" (*nouvelles*) of this kind was not meant to be taken literally. By lampooning the policies of the Maupeou ministry, such news made a serious point: the government was abusing power; the monarchy was degenerating into despotism. Anecdotes, as Morande used them, were essentially true, no matter how extravagant they looked when dressed up as news. His provocative footnotes—"Half of this article is true"[11]—alerted the reader to the way he was meant to be read. And his habit of interspersing the most outrageous articles with accurate reports—Mme du Barry really had been a prostitute, as he claimed[12]—served the same purpose: to convey a general impression of decadence and despotism. Many libelers used similar devices. They purveyed half-truths, mixed fact with fiction, and exploited the shock value of their stories in a way that worked insidiously on their readers. The readers were not expected to believe everything on the page but rather to come around to the view that the anecdotes, however exaggerated, corresponded at bottom to the actual turn of events: they were hidden history.

Did readers really react in this manner? We don't have enough information to answer that question, but we can hazard a hypothesis: libels provoked a wide range of responses, which varied from naïve credulity to sophisticated skepticism, but they were taken seriously, and they could cause serious damage, both to the reputation of individuals and to the support of the government. Louis Sébastien Mercier probably assessed their effect accurately in the essay on "libels" in his *Tableau de Paris*. Readers rushed to procure them, he explained, in order to enjoy the frisson provided by a good scandal, but they were often disappointed, for libels tended to miss their mark by exaggerating the abuses they denounced. Nonetheless, they frequently contained a grain of truth. In fact, they could be the only way to make the truth known in a system that suppressed the liberty of the press. A wise government would tolerate them, and a wise reader would treat them skeptically, waiting for the sifting of fact and fiction that would lead to a definitive work of history.[13]

But libels frequently presented themselves as histories. By adopting a Procopian strategy, they pretended to provide the secret, inside version of events that could not be found in conventional versions of the past. Moreover, they recounted recent events, which did not come within the range of histories printed with royal privileges and censors' approbations. Contemporary history and biography—two of the most popular genres today—had no place within the legal literature of the Ancien Régime because they dealt with issues that were still sensitive and persons who were still alive. The state had ruled those subjects out-of-bounds, and censors patrolled the boundaries, making sure that no narratives of current events received permission to be published.[14] Insofar as contemporary history existed, it had to circulate outside the law. It took the form of "secret" histories or compilations of anecdotes, and it was left to anonymous hacks, like Pierre Nougaret, who produced *Anecdotes du*

règne de Louis XVI, a typically anonymous, illegal, and mediocre work (editions in 1776, 1777, 1780, and 1791)—one of forty-seven books Nougaret
cranked out before 1789, when he joined the ranks of the revolutionaries and
went on to produce sixty-six more.[15] There was, however, an exception to this
rule: Voltaire.

In 1745, at the height of his career as a courtier, Voltaire was appointed
royal historiographer (*historiographe de France*) at a salary of 2,000 livres a
year. Unlike his predecessors, including Racine and Boileau, who treated the
position as a sinecure, he took it seriously. He set out to write the history of
the War of the Austrian Succession (1741–48) while it was actually taking
place—an astonishing enterprise, which reveals a great deal about the fate of
contemporary history and the importance of anecdotes under the Ancien
Régime.[16] "Here I am, duty bound to write anecdotes," Voltaire wrote to the
comte d'Argental in announcing his appointment as historiographer.[17] To collect anecdotes, as he understood it, was to dig out hidden facts that revealed
the human element in events. He used the term in the Procopian manner, and
he used it often, not only in his correspondence but also in works like *Anecdotes sur le czar Pierre le Grand* (1750), *Anecdotes de Louis XIV* (1750), and the
four chapters entitled "Particularités et anecdotes" in *Le Siècle de Louis XIV*
(1751). He intended his history of the War of the Austrian Succession to be
anecdotal in the best sense of the word—full of inside information but honest
and accurate, an attempt to tell the truth.

Voltaire went about this task systematically. Soon after assuming his position as historiographer, he wrote to the foreign minister, the marquis d'Argenson, who had accompanied the king to the front, requesting "anecdotes"
about military operations. D'Argenson, an old friend, obliged with a vivid,
eyewitness account of the French victory at Fontenoy, written four days after
the battle, which occupied a prominent place in the work that eventually
appeared as *Histoire de la guerre de 1741.*[18] Voltaire fired off letters to other
witnesses and participants, conducted interviews, gained access to state papers,
did everything possible to inform himself about the causes and conduct of the
war, and reconstructed the history of events almost as soon as they occurred.
He did the job so well, in fact, that his success created a problem: Louis XV's
officials had never permitted the publication of an inside account of current
events; they barely tolerated the minimal reports on the war that appeared in
the heavily censored *Gazette de France.* Moreover, the French forces suffered
many defeats and humiliations, especially in the colonies, after Voltaire began
to write. And in the end, they sacrificed the victories they had won by returning all their conquests in the peace treaty of Aix-la-Chapelle, which looked like
a disaster to many Frenchmen. How could the crown permit its official histo-

rian to produce a full account of such events, even if he trimmed it to favor Versailles?

Voltaire knew all along that he would have to deal with this dilemma, but he thought he could manage it by pulling strings in Versailles. He asked the marquis d'Argenson to persuade the king to permit the writing of a history that seemed certain to make France look good. France looked very good indeed in August 1745, when Voltaire received permission. Louis XV had just presided over the great victory at Fontenoy and was poised to impose an equitable peace on all the belligerents. Having sung the king's praise as a warrior in the *Poème de Fontenoy*, Voltaire planned to celebrate him as a statesman, changing register from poetry to history. He promised to submit the manuscript to d'Argenson for approval so the king could be sure it would contain nothing offensive, and it would serve as a refutation of the hostile propaganda produced by French refugees in Holland.[19]

Not that Voltaire planned to write anything like propaganda himself. The more he learned about the war, the more absorbed he became in unraveling its mysteries. While events were bursting all around him, he struggled to sort out their general direction and to follow their repercussions through unintended consequences, miscalculations, and sheer accident. He breathed life into the characters he described and recounted their actions with the sense of drama that he infused into his plays. Above all, he conveyed the experience of battle—the chaos, savagery, suffering, and occasional bravura. But he also distorted things. He gave the duc de Richelieu, his friend and protector, the finest role and the best lines, all of them invented, at the Battle of Fontenoy. He moved Frederick II and the Young Pretender, Charles Edward Stuart, in and out of the narrative according to calculations of what would cause least offense in the French court. He never mentioned any of the royal mistresses and the power struggles that surrounded them or the political and economic background to events. The crisis of the king's illness at Metz in 1744 inspired a vivid description of consternation among the common people in Paris, but its political dimension went unacknowledged. And the Treaty of Aix-la-Chapelle proved too unpalatable to receive an adequate analysis.

None of these difficulties was apparent in 1745, when Voltaire began to draft his narrative. But events took a turn for the worse in 1746. D'Argenson fell from office in January 1747, and the war dragged on for nearly two more years, becoming increasingly costly, bloody, and unpopular. Meanwhile, Voltaire ran into problems in Versailles. He made faux pas, lost the support of some key protectors, withdrew from the court, and finally emigrated to Prussia, which had proven to be a less-than-faithful ally during the fighting. When he arrived at the court of Frederick II in 1750, he brought with him a fairly complete draft of the *Histoire de la guerre de 1741*, although he continued to work on it for several more years. In 1752 he sounded Versailles about the possibility of receiving permission to publish it and received a resolute no. Three years later, to his distress and without his permission, his book appeared in print.

Its publication, like that of so many of his works, involved a succession of imbroglios, betrayals, and denials by Voltaire, who protested that he had nothing to do with the whole business. In this case, he was telling the truth. He had settled near Geneva in 1755 after quarreling with Frederick, and he wanted to regain the good graces of Louis. To publish an account of French affairs against the will of the French king would make it impossible for Voltaire to return to Paris. But a copy of the text had slipped out of his control, and three editions of it appeared by 1756. So the publication of *Histoire de la guerre de 1741* made Voltaire persona non grata in France, even though it had been conceived as a work that would consecrate his role as the king's apologist in Versailles. Voltaire's example demonstrated the impossibility of writing contemporary history from within the legal system even under the most favorable circumstances.

Contemporary history looked suspect to the regime because it shaded off into journalism, a kind of writing that seemed even worse. The government wanted to control all the information connected with the War of the Austrian Succession, but in collecting anecdotes about it, Voltaire was behaving like a "reporter."[20] Anecdotes themselves were a kind of news. They did not have to be libelous, hostile to the government, or offensive in any way, for they functioned as a means of communication, which could be put to many uses. Some Parisians collected anecdotes for the sheer fun of it or to have a record of current events. They filed them in portfolios and copied or pasted them into scrapbooks.[21] Edmond-Jean-François Barbier, a lawyer who generally sympathized with the established order, included all sorts of anecdotes, most of them innocent, in his private journal. Published in 1847 as *Journal historique et anecdotique du règne de Louis XV*, it now serves as one of the greatest sources of information about events and the perception of events in eighteenth-century Paris. Barbier never got into trouble with the authorities because he kept his journal to himself. But the police often intervened when anecdotes spilled into the public sphere, because they tended to damage the reputation of important persons and the respect for the regime. As "secret histories," anecdotes provided Parisians with a daily diet of news, the kind of news that could not be found in newspapers.

Most of this news traveled by word of mouth, but many Frenchmen, especially in the provinces, received their supply of anecdotes from clandestine newsletters (*gazettes à la main* or *nouvelles à la main*), which were drafted by obscure *nouvellistes*, copied by scribes, sold "sous le manteau" in Paris by peddlers, shipped secretly to the provinces, and sometimes printed by enterprising publishers outside France. As explained in the previous chapters, a good deal of mystery still surrounds the way this underground journalism functioned. But one stage of its operation can be studied by taking a closer look at its main ingredient: the anecdotes themselves. Before they made it into gazettes, they traveled in people's pockets, scribbled on scraps of paper. Anecdotes had a physical existence. They were objects that circulated at a crucial stage in the channels of communication that connected verbal exchanges with readings of the printed word. To appreciate their importance, one should study them in all their physicality as autonomous items of news.

Consider again the news about the arrest of Jacquet de la Douay on October 30, 1781.[22] An unknown man rushes into the Café du caveau and announces "some big news." Jacquet, he says, was executed yesterday in the Bastille for producing a libel against the queen. The man runs off, leaving the café abuzz with talk. At first, the news was transmitted by word of mouth, but soon afterward it was taken down by a *nouvelliste* and spread in wider circles through a manuscript gazette. The gazette later appeared in print as the *Mémoires secrets pour servir à l'histoire de la république des lettres en France*, a best-seller, which was reprinted many times during the 1780s. The *Mémoires secrets* also was confiscated regularly. Inspectors of the book trade and customs officers impounded it whenever they had a chance because it contained a great many scurrilous reports about public figures. Therefore, like *L'Espion anglais* and *La Chronique scandaleuse*, it qualified as a libel. It provided the sort of secret history that Parisians could not obtain from legal publications. Yet it also was a kind of journal, sold in the form of a book, which contained reports on many subjects, especially in the realm of art and letters, that had no relevance to statesmen and affairs of state. Whether innocent or slanderous, these news items appeared in chronological order, without headings or any articulation other than dates, throughout the thirty-six volumes of its text. Most of them occupied one paragraph. They were anecdotes, short snippets of printed matter, which corresponded to oral "nouvelles" like the report about Jacquet in the Café du caveau.[23]

A great deal of information converged in cafés. The oldest and most famous café in Paris was Le Procope, a monument to Procopius. The name had only symbolic value—it did not derive from the Byzantine historian but rather from Francesco Procopio Dei Coltelli, who founded the café in 1686— yet it suggested the general function of cafés as nerve centers for the transmission of news. Cafés were places where men (they rarely had women customers) recounted anecdotes and wrote them down. *Nouvellistes* also made use of other public spaces: certain benches in the Tuileries and Luxembourg gardens, the courtyard of the Palais-Royal, gathering places at both ends of the Pont Neuf, and the foyers of theaters. When the police arrested J. P. L. Barth for producing *nouvelles à la main*, which he distributed to twenty subscribers in the provinces, they noted: "It was in theatres, public promenades, and social gatherings that he collected this news."[24] But cafés provided the favorite hang-outs for *nouvellistes*. They were the most important points at which the oral and written modes of communication came together. When the police set off to arrest a certain *nouvelliste* named Foulhioux, for example, they went directly to his table in the Café du caveau, where he collected information every day. He protested that his manuscript gazette was nothing more than "the echo of public noises" (that is, *bruits publics* or rumors), but that was why the police considered him so dangerous.[25] "Public noises" converted into print were just what the government wanted to prevent. Vergennes did everything possible to repress the circulation of this kind of news. "Experience has convinced us that of all classes of writers, the paid *nouvelliste* is the most difficult to restrain," he wrote to the lieutenant general of police. "What prudent man would dare put his faith in the conduct of a newsletter writer [*bulletiniste*] who calculates his profits according to the number of secret anecdotes that he can gather?"[26] The anecdote, as Vergennes indicated, was the basic unit in this information system. In explaining the success of the *Mémoires secrets*—"a considerable branch of the book trade unto itself"—Pierre Manuel characterized it as "a chain of anecdotes that please everyone: the public loves to see the foolishness and the feebleness of princes."[27]

The most important contributor to the *Mémoires secrets* and one of the most influential libelers of the century was Mathieu-François Pidansat de Mairobert. In 1749 the police received reports from its spies that he had been declaiming against the government in the Café Procope and distributing defamatory poems about the king and Mme de Pompadour. They broke into his apartment, a modest place over the shop of a laundress in the rue des Cordeliers, carried him off to the Bastille, and frisked him. His pockets were stuffed with scraps of paper covered with scribbling—his harvest from a day of collecting anecdotes. Whenever he arrived in a café and heard a good item of news, he wrote it down and stored it in his clothing for later use. Sometimes, for the sheer pleasure of distributing news, he slipped these little bulletins into the pockets of a companion or scattered them in public parks where they could be found by Parisians taking a walk. Back in his apartment, he compiled the fragments into a manuscript gazette. When the police searched it, they found sixty-eight separate items—topical poems, reports about intrigues

Figure 32. Scraps of paper with topical verse found by the police while frisking a prisoner in the Bastille. (Bibliothèque de l'Arsenal)

in Versailles, bons mots purveyed at the expense of men about town—waiting to be strung together into a draft of what eventually appeared in print as the *Mémoires secrets*.[28]

They turned up a similar cache of scribbled anecdotes when they arrested Imbert de Boudeaux, the author of *La Chronique scandaleuse* who also composed a *gazette à la main*.[29] And when they arrested Barthélemy-François Moufle d'Angerville, Mairobert's successor as the main contributor to the *Mémoires secrets*, they hauled off seven cartons of "bulletins" to the Bastille.[30]

Bulletins of this kind proliferated at intermediate stages in the process of transmission—that is, after anecdotes first began to circulate through oral exchanges and before they crystallized into printed paragraphs. They typically took the form of handwritten notes, jotted down on scraps of paper, which were copied and passed around wherever people gathered to gossip about public affairs. The notes related an incident, a bon mot, a pasquinade, or a verse of a song. They were self-contained narrative units, usually a paragraph in length, and because they could be strung out or spliced together in endless combinations, they provided the basic material for most libels, whether newsletters, *gazettes scandaleuses*, pseudo-memoirs, fictitious correspondence, biographies, or full-fledged histories. These scraps of paper served as the building blocks from which texts were constructed. They were the smallest and most fundamental ingredient in the entire literature of libel.

To form some idea of how they were combined, one should imagine a hack writer in a garret sitting at a table covered with bits of paper, one or two manuscript newsletters, and an assortment of books. He reworks material from one scrap after another, copies paragraphs from the *gazettes à la main*, lifts episodes from the books—most of which are also libels—and glues the parts together with transitional passages of his own devising. He might add long stretches of original prose. But because the newsletters and many of the books had been composed in the same way, the whole process involved endless recycling of anecdotes.

In order to picture the production of the anecdotes themselves, one should summon up a scene from an eighteenth-century café. Men are gathered around tables, talking idly. A *nouvelliste* arrives and asks, "What's new?" The men regale him with a few anecdotes. He writes one down on a slip of paper, then pulls a handwritten note from his waistcoat pocket. It comes from his own supply of anecdotes, and he reads it aloud, adding rhetorical flourishes to bring out the humor or the scandal. One of the listeners borrows the note in order to make a copy and in exchange produces a similar bulletin, which he had stashed in a pocket or tucked into a sleeve. These scraps of paper were normally too ephemeral to have survived, but a few made it into the archives of the Bastille because the police confiscated them after frisking new prisoners. Many more can be found pasted or copied into eighteenth-century journals, where they keep company with other ephemera, equally important, such as songs.[31]

How did this material become embodied in books? It was the favorite stuff of libels because it could be adapted to so many genres. In the case of *chroniques scandaleuses*, a particularly popular genre in France on the eve of the Revolution, the anecdotes were cobbled together without concern for an overall pattern. But libelous biographies and histories required narrative cohesion. To understand how they were blended into an ambitious narrative, it is best to take a close look at another best-seller, *Vie privée de Louis XV, ou principaux événements, particularités et anecdotes de son règne*, which recounted the life of the king and the history of the realm in four dense volumes.

At first glance the book appears impressive, even if bound only in simple cardboard or vellum. Editions varied, and the work went through at least four of them from 1781 to 1785. They usually ran to about four hundred pages per volume in duodecimo format, and each volume included a large assortment of documents at its end, conveying an impression of historical rigor. As its

Figure 33. William Hogarth, "The Distrest Poet." Although this print does not depict a libeler, it conveys the character of a garret existence. One piece of paper on the floor bears the title "Grub Street Journal." William Hogarth, *The Distressed Poet*, 1736. (Harvard Art Museum, Fogg Art Museum, Gift of William Gray from the collection of Francis Calley Gray, G1822. Photo: Imaging Department © President and Fellows of Harvard College)

subtitle suggested, *Vie privée de Louis XV* pretended to blend history with biography, using anecdotes. A preface, written in the name of the bookseller, ostensibly John Peter Lyton of London, promised to enliven the history with verbal portraits of every important personage accompanied by "very curious anecdotes, which cannot be found anywhere else."[32] No fact of any importance would be omitted, the preface emphasized, so the reader could expect a definitive account of the entire reign accompanied by revelations about the people who made the history happen—the king, his ministers, and his mistresses.

Upon closer inspection, the book looks rather strange. It has no introduction, no table of contents, no index, no chapters, and no headings or subdivisions of any kind. The text flows without interruption, other than the

Figure 34. *Nouvellistes* in a café. (Bibliothèque nationale de France)

documentary appendices, from the first page of volume 1 to the last page of volume 4. The year of the events under discussion usually is printed at the upper outside margin of each page, and sometimes the dates of events appear in the side margins opposite descriptions of them; so readers could orient themselves in the chronology. But the narrative jumps from one subject to another and occasionally doubles back on itself. At one moment you are following a military campaign, at another you learn about intrigues to overthrow a minister or the desperate state of the economy. The lack of transitions, signposts, and articulation of any kind leaves the reader plunged into a stream of text that continues for 1,500 pages.

In this respect, *Vie privée de Louis XV* resembles *Mémoires secrets pour servir à l'histoire de la république des lettres en France*, which went on for thirty-six volumes, recounting one news item after another in chronological order, without connecting passages. The parallel should not be pushed too far, however, because *Vie privée de Louis XV* developed themes at considerable length and it contained a strong, general argument. But it did not integrate the episodes it related into a consistent narrative, and it reads in places like the *Mémoires secrets*. In fact the same man wrote both books, or at least most of them. The anonymous author of *Vie privée* was Barthélemy-François Moufle d'An-

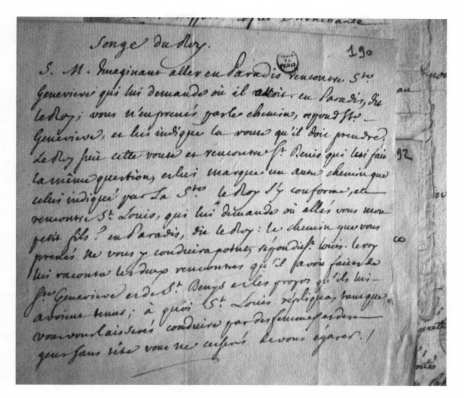

Figure 35. A scrapbook collection of anecdotes, songs, and information about current events. (Bibliothèque nationale de France)

gerville, who studied law, worked for twelve years in the naval ministry, and then lived from his pen—not very successfully, judging from the few sticks of furniture that was all he possessed at his death in 1795. He compiled the last fifteen volumes of the *Mémoires secrets* following the death of Pidansat de Mairobert in 1779, and he distributed the same kind of material—much of it, no doubt, from the seven cartons of "bulletins," which the police returned to him after his release from the Bastille—throughout *Vie privée*. The first book was a *chronique scandaleuse*, the second a history, but each used anecdotes as building blocks.[33]

Not that the two publications were the same—far from it. In *Vie privée de Louis XV*, Moufle adopted the anonymous voice of a narrator, "we," and explained in the first three paragraphs that by deploying anecdotes he would penetrate into the secret history of the kingdom as well as the biography of the king. He began with the first day of Louis XV's rule, September 1, 1715, and he ended on its last day, May 10, 1774. But Louis was only five years old in 1715, and Moufle had little to say about his childhood, except that he was spoiled and poorly educated. The first volume therefore concentrated on great events: the consolidation of power under the Regent, diplomatic successes in maintaining peace, religious quarrels, conflicts between the crown and the Parlement of Paris, and the economic disaster produced by the speculator and political adventurer John Law. This emphasis gave the text some resemblance to modern histories. But all the episodes were recounted in a way that made them look like the result of rivalries among a few individuals, "les grands," who clawed their way to the top by means of court intrigues. History therefore appeared as an endless power struggle among the great, and it could be marked off as a succession of ministries—that is, according to the rise and fall of men who won and lost the favor of the king and who exercised power in his name: at first the Regent, then cardinal de Fleury, and ultimately the mistresses who determined the appointment of the ministers.[34] To convey the process, it was necessary to picture the players and to show them in action. Anecdotes served both purposes. They provided material for portraits of public figures and for descriptions of events. As a result, the text flickered past the reader like a magic lantern show or—if the anachronism be permitted—like news flashes and snapshots, each of which captured an incident or a character. The difficulty consisted in combining them in a way that made a coherent story.

Moufle provided some coherence by adopting a well-defined point of view. Although he remained anonymous, he identified himself as a philosophe, challenged his readers to interpret events from a philosophic perspective, and celebrated the leaders of the Enlightenment whenever the occasion arose.[35] He also described "philosophie" as a force in itself, which began to influence the course of events in the late 1740s, and he produced a clear definition of its character: "By philosophy, we understand the daring to put oneself above all prejudice in matters of doctrine, to listen only to reason, and to practice virtue by following [reason] as it is grounded in our common humanity."[36] In short, Moufle wrote as a partisan of the Enlightenment, and he made it clear that his secular, tolerant, rational views had political implications. He condemned all the parties and lobbies involved in the power struggles, Jansenists as well as Jesuits and the parlements as well as their enemies in the government. In place of these warring interest groups, he defended a single, collective interest—that of the nation. He used terms like "nation" and "fatherland" whenever he described the direction that events ought to take and "despotism" when he deplored their actual course. In the end he prescribed a way to repair the nation's misery: the king should summon the Estates General and entrust a reform program to the representatives of the French people.[37] Moufle's text, composed in 1778 and 1779,[38] conformed closely to the views of the "patriotes" who had opposed Maupeou's authoritarian coup of 1770–74.[39] It also suited the program of the "parti patriotique" that seized the initiative in 1788–89. Poised between two reigns, it looked back on the recent past in a way that prepared for a revolutionary future, even though Moufle, like everyone else in France, could not imagine anything like the Revolution that actually occurred.

There is no mistaking the ideological message that ran through all four volumes of *Vie privée de Louis XV*, but ideology in itself was not enough to hold the story together. How did Moufle make history from the information available to him? From time to time he mentioned a printed source in connection with a particular anecdote. It therefore is possible to track down the sources to see how he selected the material that he combined in his narrative. Then, by reading all the originals alongside Moufle's text, a surprising conclusion emerges: he cribbed nearly everything from other books, most of them libels. *Vie privée de Louis XV* was a collage, a libel patched together from other libels. They, too, were patchworks formed from earlier books or from fragments of information picked up in cafés and lifted from news sheets. They varied, of course, in their character as well as their quality. But nearly all of them were composed from preexisting anecdotes, usually short paragraphs but occasionally a story that would run for a page or two. Libelers did not write free-flowing narratives, filling blank sheets with their own prose. They were scissors-and-paste authors, who cobbled texts together by drawing on a common stock of anecdotes, although they also had some private sources of information. To describe their work as plagiarism would be anachronistic. Moufle made no claim to originality, although he insisted that some of his anecdotes could not be found elsewhere.[40] He pretended instead to be "the first person who has stripped away the veil that hides the entire life of a prince"[41]—that is, to write history in the Procopian manner, selecting anecdotes that would convey the secret life of an antihero. In practice, this method meant that Moufle fashioned his text as if it were a crazy quilt by selecting pieces of ready-made material, cutting and shaping them to fit his fancy, and stitching them together with an ideology peculiar to the "patriots" of the 1770s and 1780s.

To reconstruct the composition of *Vie privée de Louis XV* in its entirety would require several volumes of detailed analysis drawing on a large body of literature, most of it obscure and slanderous, some well-known and innocuous. But it is possible to see how Moufle worked by examining a sizable segment of the whole. I have chosen fifty pages from volume 2, which covers the period 1733–54. Moufle drew most of his material for this volume from four libels: *Mémoires secrets pour servir à l'histoire de Perse* (1745), *Les Amours de*

Zéokinizul, roi des Kofirans (1746), *Lettres de Madame la marquise de Pompadour* (1771), and *Mémoires de Madame la marquise de Pompadour* (1776). But he also plucked anecdotes from Voltaire's *Histoire de la guerre de 1741* (1755), which presents Louis XV in a flattering light; from *Les Fastes de Louis XV*, which is hostile to the king, although too "timid" for Moufle's taste;[42] from *Aux Manes de Louis XV* (1776), another critical libel; and from various journalistic works and pamphlets such as *Journal historique, ou fastes du règne de Louis XV, surnommé le Bien-aimé* (1776) and *L'Avocat national* (1774). His other sources included some manuscript newsletters, which he cited without naming, and word of mouth or, as he called it, "an oral tradition."[43]

Normally Moufle spliced passages from other publications into his text without citing them, but on the occasions when he named his sources, he sometimes criticized them, and he often adjusted the phrasing in ways that show how he worked; thus it is important to take note of the sources themselves. *Mémoires secrets pour servir à l'histoire de Perse*, first published in 1745 and reprinted at least six times by 1769, provided him with the basic narrative of volume 2. It probably was written by Antoine Pecquet, a disaffected official in the ministry of foreign affairs, with help from the group who gathered around Mme de Vieuxmaisons, the wife of a counselor in the Parlement of Paris. Like the salon of Mme Doublet, the circle of Mme de Vieuxmaisons devoted itself to collecting and discussing news, especially anecdotes that made the king look bad and the parlement good. It therefore appeared in a police report of 1748 as "the most dangerous . . . social group" in Paris.[44] Pecquet transformed the gossip from the Vieuxmaisons circle along with information he had acquired in the ministry into a remarkably rich survey of foreign affairs and ministerial intrigues from 1715 to 1745. Although the events ostensibly took place in Asia, a well-informed reader could identify the European counterparts to the eastern countries and the various shahs and mullahs who stood for the potentates in France. Moufle relied heavily on *Mémoires secrets pour servir à l'histoire de Perse*, but he disagreed with its bias in favor of the parlement. He therefore modified its phrasing whenever it glossed over his own favorite themes, such as the "fanaticism" of the parlements' persecution of philosophes and Protestants.[45] And when it did not present Louis XV in a hostile enough light, he touched up the language. For example, he rewrote its description of Mme de Châteauroux's dominance of the king as follows:

The credit of this woman became so great that it was feared that she would succeed completely in governing. *Mémoires secrets* (p. 225)

The credit of the new mistress became so great that it was judged that she would completely govern her royal slave. *Vie privée* (vol. 2, p. 127)

Moufle's second basic source, *Histoire de la guerre de 1741*, presented him with a bias that went in the opposite direction, because Voltaire despised the parlements and made a hero of Louis XV. Having undertaken this work in his capacity as court historian, Voltaire had to eliminate all the elements—the intrigues, power struggles, rise and fall of mistresses and ministers—that might offend the court. But this material occupied a central place in Moufle's account of events. Therefore, in copying Voltaire's text, Moufle toned down the praise for Louis XV and inserted phrases that would prevent any misunderstanding on the part of the reader. In one insert, for example, he wrote that Louis's reign represented "the most absolute despotism joined with the most revolting impunity."[46] Nonetheless, Moufle's formulation of the standard themes of the Enlightenment owed more to Voltaire than to any other philosophe; and when he lifted passages from *Histoire de la guerre de 1741* he faced a further problem: it was so well written that it threatened to take over his own narrative. In the end, Moufle coped with his debt to Voltaire in two ways. First, he acknowledged it: "We will confess once and for all that we are not ashamed to use the ideas and even the wording of this great man when the occasion arises, as we can neither think nor write as well as he."[47] Second, he limited his pilfering to descriptions of military operations and foreign affairs, where Voltaire gave full rein to his talent for depicting action and analyzing events without sounding biased in favor of Versailles. When it came to controversial issues where Voltaire presented French policy in a positive light, Moufle abandoned his text. In his account of the Treaty of Aix-la-Chapelle (1748), for example, Voltaire celebrated Louis's statesmanship as a generous effort to restore order throughout Europe. For Moufle, the peace treaty was a disaster, which ignited the indignation of "the French nation"—a consideration that had no place in Voltaire's vision of history.[48] Voltaire belonged to an older generation that did not relate politics to any notion of national sovereignty. Moufle was a self-conscious patriot who rewrote history for a public that had been radicalized by the resistance to the Maupeou coup of 1771. Despite his Voltairean sympathies, therefore, he made only limited use of Voltaire's account of Louis XV's reign.[49]

The third source, *Les Amours de Zéokinizul, roi des Kofirans*, provided Moufle with material on an aspect of the reign that was conspicuously absent from *Histoire de la guerre de 1741*: the royal sex life and its manipulation by corrupt courtiers. In cutting and pasting, he favored passages that concerned the king's love affairs with the daughters of the marquis de Nesle, and he paid particular attention to the crisis at Metz in August 1744, when Louis was forced to renounce the marquise de Châteauroux. *Les Amours de Zéokinizul* recounted the scene in a dramatic manner, using dialogue and description in a way that made the king look ridiculous. Like *Mémoires secrets pour servir à l'histoire de Perse*, it was a roman à clef, but it was lighter in tone and easier to decode: Zéokinizul was obviously an anagram for Louis Quinze, the Kofirans for the Français. Although several editions of the book contained keys, which identified forty-four to sixty-five characters, the wordplay seemed designed primarily as amusement rather than as a political lesson in the form of a puzzle. The plot moved rapidly from one seduction scene to another, ending with the triumph of Mme de Pompadour. It indicted the king for being led by the nose while his ministers transformed the monarchy into a despotism. But it was a frothy work, similar to the erotic novels of Claude-Prosper Jolyot de Crébillon, who probably was its author and appears on its title page as Krinelbol. Moufle pilfered it unashamedly for boudoir anecdotes, although he disavowed its lighthearted licentiousness.[50]

The same tendency to crib material while pretending to distance himself from it characterized Moufle's use of other works, particularly the libels about Mme de Pompadour. They provided him with the anecdotes he needed for the period that was not covered by the earlier books. He copied them liberally, then minimized his indebtedness with the occasional footnote, such as: "See *Lettres de Madame la marquise de Pompadour, depuis 1746 jusqu'en 1762*, not that we regard them [Pompadour's supposed letters] as authentic, far from it, but at least they are based on facts and anecdotes known to contemporaries."[51] Moufle treated all of his sources in the same manner, cribbing passages and modifying phrasing to suit his purposes. As a way of working, it came down to prying anecdotes from other texts and cobbling them together.

The main difficulty Moufle had to surmount did not concern the selection or the shaping of the basic material but rather the problem of integrating it in a coherent whole. Each source organized its anecdotes in a peculiar pattern, which did not harmonize easily with the others. Moufle blended them as best he could by fitting them into sections of his text where they seemed to be appropriate. He relied on *Mémoires secrets pour servir à l'histoire de Perse* for his general exposition, inserted passages from *Histoire de la guerre de 1741* when he needed descriptions of military campaigns, and cribbed boudoir intrigue from *Amours de Zéokinizul*. To fill in gaps, he lifted bits and pieces scattered through *Journal historique, ou fastes du règne de Louis XV, surnommé le Bien-aimé* (1766), a two-volume chronicle, published with a censor's approbation and a royal privilege, which simply listed events in the order of their occurrence. Occasionally the *Journal historique* added some comments to its chronology. They always favored the regime, and Moufle always eliminated them. He particularly objected to a passage that described the reign of Louis XV as "France's golden century," greater even than the reign of Louis XIV,[52] but he relied heavily on the *Journal historique*, without acknowledging it, for filler. Moufle sometimes added filler of his own, transitional paragraphs or interpretive remarks, which worked like glue, binding disparate passages together. His own prose came to less than ten percent of the text.

The way Moufle assembled the book can be seen from the diagrams reproduced here (figures 36, 37, and 38), which cover fifty pages of *Vie privée de Louis XV* and show the ingredients that went into each page. The hybrid character of the text is actually more complex than figure 38 indicates because Moufle often pieced together separate segments from the same source. For example, most of page 24 of *Vie privée* corresponds exactly to a passage that runs from page 140 to 141 of *Journal historique*, but page 25 contains a mixture of phrases plucked from four different pages of the *Journal*, and page 26 includes a small section of original remarks, which provides a transition to a segment from *Amours de Zéokinizul*, beginning on page 27. The same cutting and stitching occurred everywhere else in the four volumes, which drew on a large number of additional sources, especially the *Mémoires secrets pour servir à l'histoire de la république des lettres en France* and anti-Maupeou publications such as *Journal historique de la révolution opérée dans la constitution de la monarchie française par M. de Maupeou*, *L'Espion anglais*, *Maupeouana*, *Mémoires de l'abbé Terray*, *Anecdotes sur Mme la comtesse du Barry*, and *Lettres originales de Madame la comtesse du Barry*.

Much of this literature had been compiled by Moufle himself and by his collaborator, Pidansat de Mairobert. *Vie privée de Louis XV* was therefore a compilation formed from other compilations, and it provided material for still more compilers. A year after its publication, a two-volume survey of the reign appeared under the title *Les Fastes de Louis XV, de ses ministres, maîtresses, généraux, et autres notables personnages de son règne* ("à Ville-Franche, chez la Veuve Liberté," 1782). This work also looked like an imposing history, but it was a scissors-and-paste job put together in all likelihood by Ange Goudar, the hack writer, *nouvelliste*, and police spy who served as Receveur's lieutenant in the attempt to destroy the French libelers in London. Most of it was lifted from *Vie privée de Louis XV*, but the passages were rearranged, partly rewritten, and supplemented with new material, especially topical songs and bawdy stories, some of them derived from *Le Gazetier cuirassé*. Although it appeared to be a new book, it recycled anecdotes that had been appearing in libels for four decades. The author made no secret of his pilfering, though he claimed to have done a better job of it than the "plagiarist" who had pieced together *Vie privée de Louis XV*: "Like him, we compile; we are privateers; and like many others, we look upon everything good as our legitimate prize."[53] But the authors of libels did not often call each other plagiarists. The concept of plagiarism hardly

Plagiarism: Adapting a Passage

Vie privée de Louis XV, vol. II, p. 31   Les Amours de Zéokinizul, p. 53

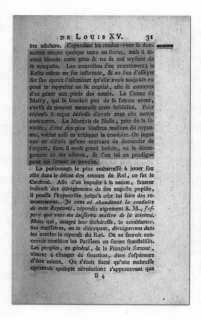

Figure 36. Plagiarism: adapting a passage. The author of *Vie privée de Louis XV* followed *Les Amours de Zéokinizul, roi des Kofirans* closely when he lifted passages, but he modified the phrasing slightly, usually to make the text more succinct. The key to *Les Amours de Zéokinizul* identifies the words in italics. *Suesi* meant *Jésus*, and *Liamil* meant *Mailly*. (Original graphic)

applies to their way of working, for they operated from the assumption that everyone lifted material from everyone else. None of them attached his name to his book. None claimed property rights in what he wrote. They belonged to the anonymous world of hack writing and illegal publishing. Perhaps they should not be described as authors at all.

Whether or not one subscribes to Michel Foucault's notion of the death of the author, it is difficult to think of libelers as authors in the modern sense of the word—that is, as the autonomous creators of original texts. And whether or not one thinks of literature as a kind of discourse in the manner of Roland Barthes or Pierre Bourdieu, it is misleading to conceive of libels as

Plagiarism: Cobbling Passages Together

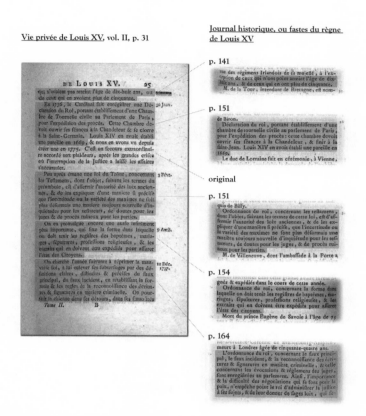

Figure 37. Plagiarism: cobbling passages together. Pages of *Vie privée de Louis XV* often combined paragraphs lifted from different sections of *Journal historique, ou fastes du régne de Louis XV*, a legal publication that provided a chronology of important royal edicts. (Original graphic)

original literary creations. Libelers did not generate texts out of their imaginations. They assembled them from material that already existed, material that itself might be an assemblage of previously existing material. For example, in a description of Louis XV's orgies, *Les Fastes de Louis XV* lifted a passage from *Vie privée de Louis XV*, which had taken it from *Mémoires secrets pour servir à l'histoire de Perse*, which had attributed it to an earlier work, a supposed *Histoire des différentes religions qui se sont introduites dans la Perse*, which cannot be identified. Who was the author of this anecdote? Impossible to say. Its ultimate source may have been some gossip exchanged by courtiers and picked

Plagiarism: The General Pattern

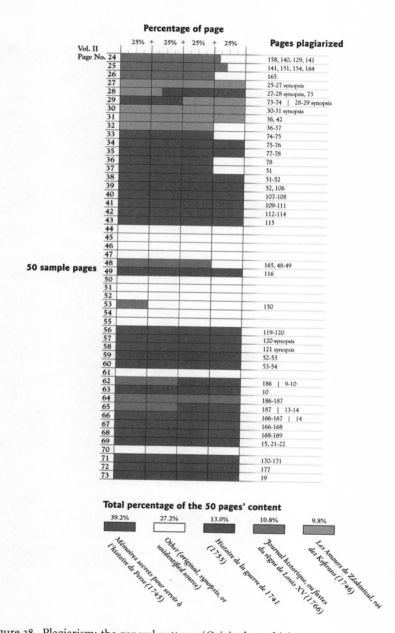

Figure 38. Plagiarism: the general pattern. (Original graphic)

up in a Parisian café, but it reappeared in at least three books, all of them best-sellers.[54] The literature of libel replenished itself continuously in this manner. Libelers dipped into a common stock of anecdotes, added new ingredients, reheated, seasoned, stirred, and served up endless varieties of the same basic recipe.

How did readers digest this brew? The question refuses to go away, even though it cannot be answered satisfactorily. Well-informed readers occasionally noticed the omnipresent plagiarizing, but they did not make much of it, as if it were too common a practice to warrant any commentary. A reviewer in the *Mémoires secrets* panned a particularly slipshod libel, *Le Vol plus haut, ou l'espion des principaux théâtres de la capitale* ("à Memphis, chez Sincère, libraire réfugié au Puits de la Vérité," 1784), by noting that the only well-written sections of its text had been lifted from an assortment of superior libels.[55] No one, however, remarked on the pilfering that went into *Vie privée de Louis XV*. In fact, the *Correspondance littéraire secrète*, a well-informed, clandestine periodical, gave the book a highly favorable review, treating it as a convincing indictment of Louis XV's reign. If the reviewer, who clearly knew his way around the literary underground, failed to notice Moufle's plagiarizing, it seems likely that ordinary readers regarded *Vie privée* as an original work and that they, like him, took its anecdotes seriously.[56] The book certainly sold well, as did the reworked version of it, *Les Fastes de Louis XV*.[57] The anecdotes they recycled circulated everywhere in France—and far beyond France's borders. George Washington possessed an English translation of *Vie privée de Louis XV*. He inscribed his name on the title page but did not underline anything in the text or write any comments in the margins, so it is impossible to know how he reacted as a reader.

The reactions of French readers also remains a matter of guesswork. But if guessing be permitted, I would like to propose a thesis. If we consider our model libel, *Vie privée de Louis XV*, in relation to the literature surrounding it, we can see a pattern in the repetition of anecdotes. All of them describe an incident, which might be trivial in itself but which seems to encapsulate a general theme or to illustrate the basic nature of a character. Each incident has a peculiar twist or ends with a remark that makes it memorable, like a punch line to a joke or a moral attached to a fable. And each appears in several other libels, so the repetition reinforces its memorability. If lifted from their texts and considered next to one another in the way that folklorists abstract tale types from individual narrations, the anecdotes composed a metanarrative, which could have been powerful enough to stamp itself on the collective imagination.

Here, for example, is a string of anecdotes about the king during the early

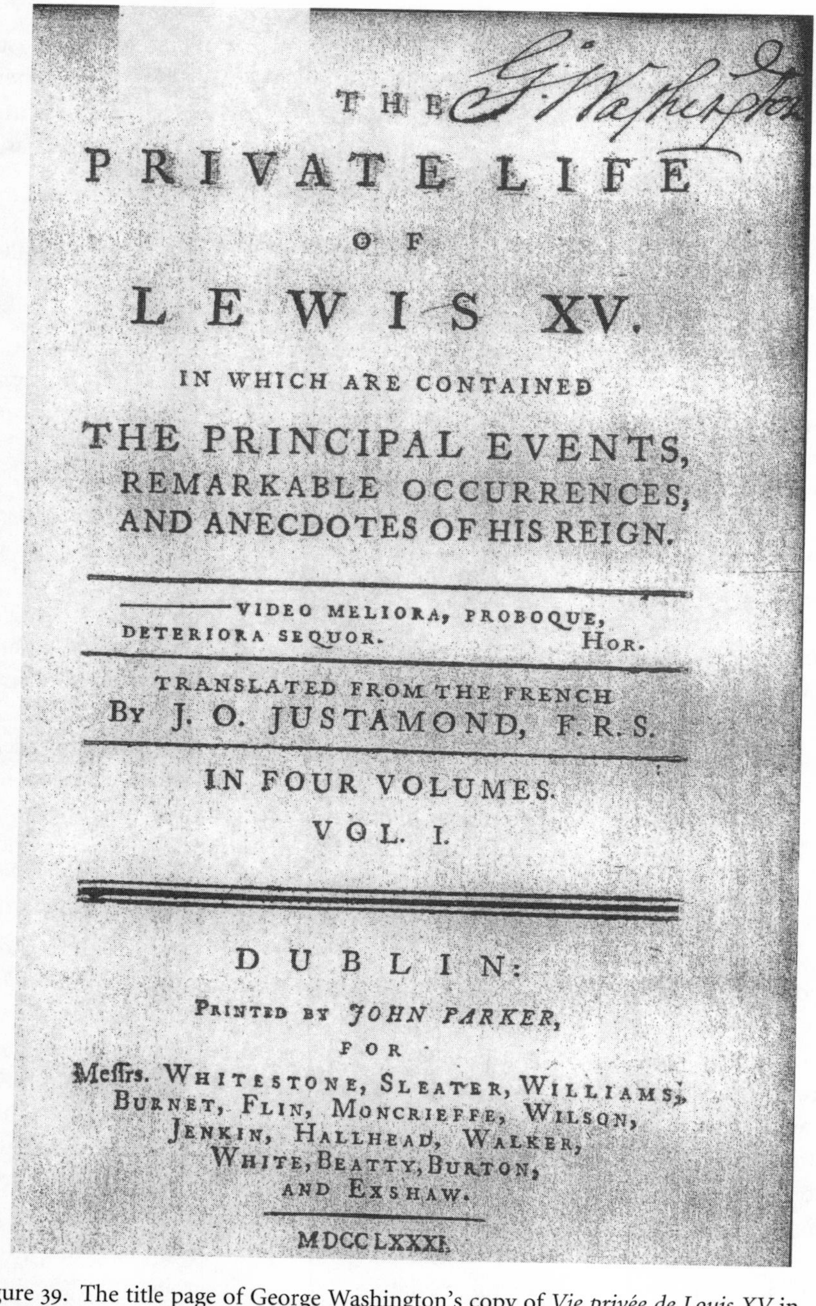

G: Washington

THE
PRIVATE LIFE
OF
LEWIS XV.

IN WHICH ARE CONTAINED

THE PRINCIPAL EVENTS,
REMARKABLE OCCURRENCES,
AND ANECDOTES OF HIS REIGN.

———— VIDEO MELIORA, PROBOQUE,
DETERIORA SEQUOR.   HOR.

TRANSLATED FROM THE FRENCH
By J. O. JUSTAMOND, F.R.S.

IN FOUR VOLUMES.

VOL. I.

DUBLIN:

PRINTED BY *JOHN PARKER,*

FOR

Meſſrs. WHITESTONE, SLEATER, WILLIAMS,
BURNET, FLIN, MONCRIEFFE, WILSON,
JENKIN, HALLHEAD, WALKER,
WHITE, BEATTY, BURTON,
AND EXSHAW.

MDCCLXXXI.

Figure 39. The title page of George Washington's copy of *Vie privée de Louis XV* in translation. (Courtesy of Houghton Library, Harvard College Library. *AC7.Un33P. ZZ1m2)

part of his reign. They are summarized from the versions in *Vie privée de Louis XV* with references to other works, where they appear in similar formulations, usually word for word with the identical quotation at the end.

The king remained infatuated with the queen during the first years of their marriage, but courtiers attempted to acquire influence over him by placing potential mistresses in his path. When confronted by a beauty, however, he refused to give in to temptation, saying, "I find the queen even more beautiful." *Vie privée*, 2: 27; *Amours de Zéokinizul*, 24; *Fastes de Louis XV*, 1: 106.

The cardinal de Fleury consolidated his hold on power by manipulating the sex life of the king. As a first step, he instructed the queen's confessor to exploit her simpleminded piety by warning her that she risked damnation if she continued to have sexual intercourse with the king. She had already borne him an adequate number of children, the confessor warned; further sex was sinful. When Louis joined her in bed one night, she refused his advances. "He swore that he would never again receive such an affront, and he kept his word." *Vie privée*, 2: 28; *Amours de Zéokinizul*, 24–25; *Fastes de Louis XV*, 1: 113.

With Fleury's approval, the duc de Richelieu arranged for the king to take Mme de Mailly, whom they could control, as a mistress. The first rendezvous came to nothing, owing to the timidity of the king. On her second attempt, Mme de Mailly, coached by Richelieu, took the initiative and overcame the king. When she returned from their lovemaking, her clothes in disorder, she said triumphantly to Fleury and Richelieu, "You can see how that lecher has worked me over." *Vie privée*, 2: 30–31; *Amours de Zéokinizul*, 34–36, 42; *Fastes de Louis XV*, 1: 116.

As the king took up the daughters of the marquis de Nesle, one after the other, Fleury tried to defend his own reputation as the king's tutor and the effective head of the government by hypocritically scolding the king for his immorality. Louis replied, "I have abandoned the direction of my kingdom to you. I hope that you will leave me to direct myself." *Vie privée*, 2: 31; *Amours de Zéokinizul*, 37; *Fastes de Louis XV*, 1: 117.

The outbreak of the War of the Austrian Succession caused Fleury to lose his grip on events. He had always tried to promote peace and was so unprepared for war that he did not know whether Prussia would side with France or with Austria. When a confused French envoy arrived in Berlin, Frederick II reassured him saying, "I think that I am going to play your hand for you. If I get any aces, we will share everything." *Vie privée*, 2: 65; *Histoire de la guerre de 1741*, 14; *Fastes de Louis XV*, 1: 138.

While heaping more and more taxes on his impoverished subjects, the king squandered his income on palaces and mistresses, but he was too timid to admit his extravagance to Controller General Orry. He spent 1,200,000 livres to embellish the château de Choisy for Mme de Châteauroux, the last of the mistresses that he chose from the de Nesle sisters. Instead of acknowledging the expense in a discussion of the royal finances with Orry, the king slipped him a note about it afterward. Orry, an accomplished courtier, did not protest against this blow to the solvency of the state. Instead, he remarked at his next meeting with the king, "Sire, I am astonished at the smallness of the sum. I was expecting something larger, and I had put aside 1,500,000 livres in reserve for this purpose." *Vie privée*, 2: 136; *Mémoires secrets pour servir à l'histoire de Perse*, 239.

When the king fell dangerously ill at the front in Metz in 1744, Mme de Châteauroux remained at his beside and the duc de Richelieu prevented anyone from approaching him. Therefore the bishop of Soissons could not gain access to the king in order to warn him of his impending death and to administer extreme unction. The crisis was resolved by the duc de Chartres, second in succession to the throne, who arrived with the bishop in tow and pushed Richelieu aside, saying, "What, a lackey like you is blocking the door to the closest relative of your master!" *Vie privée*, 2: 186; *Amours de Zéokinizul*, 53–54; *Fastes de Louis XV*, 1: 250.

After Louis confessed his sins and renounced Mme de Châteauroux, he miraculously recovered. By this time, the common people in Paris, overcome with consternation, had proclaimed him "Louis the Well Loved." The king's recovery made them delirious with joy. "The king has recovered!" they cried; and the king responded from his sickbed, "Ah! It is so sweet to be loved in this way. And what have I done to deserve it?" *Vie privée*, 2: 188, 191–92; *Histoire de la guerre de 1741*, 108–9; *Fastes de Louis XV*, 1: 249.

But Louis took back Mme de Châteauroux and resumed his immoral way of life. The love of the Parisians turned to disgust. Fishmongers in the marketplaces said, "Since he has taken back his whore, he won't find one more Our Father in the streets of Paris!" *Vie privée*, 2: 207; *Fastes de Louis XV*, 1: 260.

The death of Mme de Châteauroux opened the way for a new royal mistress, Mme d'Etioles, who was later made marquise de Pompadour and gained complete dominance over the king. Although only a bourgeoise, she had been trained for her role as "a piece fit for a king" by her mother. The king came upon her at a masked ball to celebrate the marriage of the dauphin. At his request, she raised her mask long enough to expose her beautiful face, then withdrew into the crowd, artfully dropping her handkerchief behind her. The king seized it, but unable to reach her, threw it in her direction. A general murmur then arose: "The handkerchief has been thrown!" *Vie privée*, 2: 219–20; *Amours de Zéokinizul*, 69; *Fastes de Louis XV*, 1: 264.[58]

It is impossible to know how these anecdotes resonated among readers, but it seems likely that their repetition from edition to edition and from one work to another gave them considerable force. Such phenomena exist today. When Bill Clinton was asked whether he had ever smoked marijuana, he supposedly replied, "Yes, but I did not inhale." To many Americans, that remark summed up the essence of his character and even of his presidency. Key remarks from the libels, usually printed in italics, probably echoed in similar fashion among eighteenth-century Frenchmen. "You can see how that lecher has worked me over" epitomized the undisciplined sexual appetite of the king. "I have abandoned the direction of my kingdom to you" stood for his surrender of his power. "Sire, I am astonished at the smallness of the sum" expressed the royal extravagance and its exploitation by scheming ministers. "Louis the Well Loved" indicated the goodwill that the king could have enjoyed but stupidly squandered. "The handkerchief has been thrown" said that a new chapter in the degradation of the monarchy was about to begin.

Similar buzzwords set off still more buzzing when they became attached to Mme du Barry, Marie-Antoinette, and Louis XVI and then appeared in dozens of subsequent libels. The later anecdotes built on the earlier ones. Far from losing force through repetition, they gained it. Readers knew in advance what to expect, and their anticipation of an anecdote heightened the experience of following it to its conclusion, when the punch line (or so I hypothesize) drove it deeper into the collective consciousness. On a grander, nobler scale, the repetitive storytelling in the *Odyssey* produced a similar effect. Un-Homeric and unheroic as they were, the libels perpetuated a mythology of their own, a negative mythology, which undercut the monarchy of the Ancien Régime at its most vulnerable points.

To arrive so quickly at such a grand conclusion is, however, to stretch the evidence too far. Instead of standing as the final stage of an argument, it would serve better as a hypothesis for further investigation. We may never be able to fathom consciousness, whether collective or individual, as a dimension of history. And we still know very little about the long-term history of slander. But *Vie privée de Louis XV* can at least be taken as a model for the study of other libels, because nearly all the major figures in eighteenth-century France were pilloried in "private lives," "secret anecdotes," and similar publications. By looking more closely at this literature, it should be possible to reach a better understanding of libels in general.

Chapter 23
Portraits

One of the most important passages that Moufle d'Angerville lifted from *Mémoires secrets pour servir à l'histoire de Perse* was a description of Louis XV at age sixteen.

Handsome, well proportioned, a perfectly turned leg, his air noble, his eyes big, his look more soft than proud, brown eyebrows. . . . Hunting was his sole pleasure, either because a secret instinct drew him toward that healthy exercise or because of idleness and the fear of the boredom that already began to poison the most brilliant period of his life. His education having been extremely neglected, for fear of straining his young organs, he did not have a well-furnished mind. . . . He had an invincible repugnance for administrative affairs and could not bear even to hear them talked about. Without the least love of glory, he lacked the energy that in the case of his great-grandfather [Louis XIV] compensated for the deficiency of his education and his ignorance. In a word, his weak character, indolence, and timidity made him liable to be governed by the first person who took hold of him.[1]

This passage conformed to a popular ingredient in early modern literature, which was known as a "portrait." Portraits were verbal pictures inserted at key points in narratives, which supposedly revealed the internal as well as the external nature of a character. They can be found everywhere in the fiction and nonfiction of France, especially during the seventeenth and eighteenth centuries. They made up the most appreciated passages in the works of the most skilled authors, notably La Bruyère and La Rochefoucauld, who could sketch and skewer anyone with a few strokes of the pen. But belletristic portraiture, usually disguised under fictitious names, remained confined for the most part within the limits of acceptable satire. When incorporated into libels, portraits served as a favorite technique of slander. Libelers used them along with anecdotes as a way of organizing full-scale attacks on the reputations of public figures. While the anecdotes advanced the narrative by recounting actions, the portraits filled it out with descriptions of the actors. Both ingredients came from the same sources, caches of information that the libeler had plagiarized, uncovered, or picked up while doing the rounds of cafés.

The information often took the form of a paragraph scribbled on a scrap of paper in the same manner as the anecdotes. *Nouvellistes* and gossipmongers carried these notes around in their pockets, then pulled them out and declaimed them in cafés and public gardens whenever they saw an opportunity to give a public demonstration of their inside knowledge about life among the great. Some of the scrap portraits were collected and pasted or copied into scrapbooks along with witticisms, puzzles, anecdotes, and songs. One such collection contains the following portrait of Louis XV, who at this time had reached the age of thirty-seven.

Character or Portrait of Louis XV July 1747

He has a consistent character, which has never varied. One can win his favor only with difficulty, but if one is sure of oneself, one can be sure of him. The only fault that he never pardons is to have abused his confidence. Once lost, it can be recovered only with great difficulty. He is the same in his love life and never makes up with his mistresses. What is most surprising, he sometimes sacrifices them (1) for the interest of his people. He does not put his heart into the choice of them; and in cases where the merchandise is rather dubious, he accepts them as hand-me-downs from someone else (2) without looking into the matter carefully.[2]

The numbers inserted in the text referred to two notes, which the copyist added so that the reader could identify the allusions.

(1) This is a reference to Mme de Châteauroux when she was sent away from Metz during the king's illness.

(2) This is a reference to Mme de Pompadour, who was given to the king by the duc de Richelieu.

As the notes indicated, portraits had to be read carefully and puzzled out by anyone who wanted to extract their full significance. They also resembled anecdotes in the way they circulated before being incorporated into libels. They belonged to the same strain of Procopian history.

Procopius himself excelled in portraiture. In describing Justinian, he began with physical details, applied with seeming impartiality, and then built up a picture of a moral monster, blacker by far than the Louis XV pictured by the libelers.

His stature was neither too great nor too little, well proportioned and rather inclined to be fat; his face was round and comely; his complexion was fresh. . . . He was crafty and yet easy to be deceived, so that he might be said to be cunning and weak, both together. He never told nor signified anything that was true to any who had business with him, but by the malignity of his nature, he endeavored to circumvent everybody, though he himself was continually exposed to the fallacies of other people. . . . He was inconstant to his friends and inexorable to his enemies. He was equally greedy of blood and of money. He was a great lover of novelty and troubles. He was easily persuaded when any mischief was to be done but obstinate and unmovable to any action that was good. He was excellent at inventing new crimes, but the name of virtue he abhorred.[3]

Whether or not he directly inspired the libelers of the eighteenth century, Procopius represents a tendency that runs through all the literature of libel. From the ancients to the moderns, libelers often suspended their narrative in order to present a portrait of one of the characters in it. The portraits were set pieces inserted into the plot at a point where the character began to play a major role or disappeared from the scene—as if in a play, the actors froze into a tableau vivant and the spotlight fell on one of them while an overhead voice described the inner workings of his soul, or in the way soliloquies interrupt action in Shakespearean tragedies.

Mémoires secrets pour servir à l'histoire de Perse had dozens of portraits scattered in this manner throughout its narrative. All the ministers from abbé Dubois to cardinal Fleury, all the generals through the maréchal de Saxe, all the royal mistresses up to Mme de Pompadour—every major player received a portrait in his or her allotted place. *Vie privée de Louis XV* reproduced most of them and added more, "painted," as its preface promised, with a masterful hand.[4] The verbal portraits were supplemented by actual artwork: fourteen copperplate engravings, which represented the external appearance of the characters and accompanied passages that exposed their inner selves. In principle, therefore, readers could peruse the pictures while following the story and enjoy the book as if they were strolling through a portrait gallery. In fact, however, the engravings were as crude as the stylized illustrations in popular chapbooks. The portrait of Louis XV has a flat, iconic quality, lacking all individuality. The king's features hardly differ from those of the Regent, whose portrait is quite similar, except for his wig, which dates from an earlier era.

The engraving of Mme du Barry in *Vie privée de Louis XV* is the same as the frontispiece of *Anecdotes sur Mme la comtesse du Barry* (see figure 22), a similar work, which also contained the same verbal portraits, word for word. Visually and verbally, libels drew on a common stock of images. The engravers of the rue St. Jacques swapped copperplates just as the authors in the Café du caveau exchanged anecdotes. Libels were down-market products, cobbled together on the cheap; they did not often have illustrations, but when they did, the character of their artwork corresponded to that of their texts.

But the shoddy quality of the pictures leaped to the eye, while the verbal sleight of hand often passed unnoticed. A reviewer of *Vie privée de Louis XV* in an underground newsletter failed to spot its plagiarized passages and praised its depiction of the king, but he condemned the crudeness of the engravings. Readers could expect to enjoy the spicy anecdotes about the royal mistresses, he pointed out, but not the pictures that accompanied them, especially the portrait of Mme de Pompadour, which he found particularly repulsive, as indeed it is.[5] The same reviewer also singled out "the art of making portraits" as the best quality of another libel, *Lettres iroquoises*. It had no illustrations, but it provided plenty of verbal pictures, which it mixed among a rich offering of "amusing anecdotes,"[6] as he also noted with approval. Whether or not they included artwork, libels needed to combine those two basic ingredients, anecdotes and portraits, if they were to satisfy eighteenth-century readers.

That formula may seem odd today, when pictures of public figures appear constantly on television and computer screens, in newspapers and magazines, on billboards and in advertisements. The public of the Ancien Régime lived in a world that had not been saturated with images of the great. Despite the royal iconography promoted by the state, accurate pictures of the king and queen did not come within the visual range of most of their subjects. The finest artists of the realm produced busts and paintings of Louis XV and Louis XVI, but few Frenchmen saw them. Postage stamps did not exist, nor did printed currency. The bas-reliefs on coins conveyed only a stylized, bloodless impression. Prints circulated widely, but they, too, lacked individuality, as in the case of the engravings in *Vie privée de Louis XV*. Louis Sébastien Mercier noted that everyone wanted to picture the king, if only in their imaginations, but that no portraitist could capture the aspect of him that everyone found most fascinating: his character. The king's subjects knew him primarily from whatever rumors might reach them from Versailles, and even the few who observed him at close range could not give an accurate rendition of the inner or even the outer man.[7] Unlike Louis XIV, who put his person on display and had his image multiplied in many forms, Louis XV avoided exposure to the public. He withdrew as much as possible into the private "petits apartements" of his palaces, and after the crisis of 1744—the Metz episode and the resumed liaison with Mme de Châteauroux—he rarely set foot in Paris. He even had a special road built around the city so that he could travel from Versailles to Saint Denis without being exposed to the Parisians. They suffered from an increasing sense of separation from their king, and the more he withdrew from their gaze, the more curious they became to know what he looked like.[8]

That curiosity is difficult to assess at a distance of more than two centuries, but it probably accounted in large part for the success of the libels about the royal family. By studying the verbal portrait of the king in *Vie privée de Louis XV*, French readers learned the color of his eyebrows and the shape of

Mᴱ LA MARQUISE DE POMPADOUR.

Figure 40. Engraving of Mme de Pompadour in *Vie privée de Louis XV*. (Private copy)

his leg, always a crucial aspect of the royal person.[9] More important, they had the impression of seeing into his inner self—his wit, his stock of ideas, his attitudes, his fundamental character. The tone of the portrait conveyed authority, and its favorable touches provided enough relief to make the damning details look convincing. By seeming to strike a restrained, well-informed, and objective view, it communicated an overwhelmingly negative message: Louis would have been a decent person if he had been born into an ordinary family, but he was utterly unsuited to rule over France.[10]

The royal family was a special case, as it still is today in countries like Great Britain. But readers wanted to picture everyone among "the great," and writers obliged with verbal portraits of ministers, generals, prelates, courtiers, and royal mistresses. *Le Gazetier cuirassé* included a portrait gallery of the most notorious courtesans in Paris, and its supposed sequel, *La Gazette noire*, contained a long series of portraits of peers of the realm and tax farmers, stressing their illegitimacy, fraudulent genealogies, and corruption, along with assorted character defects.[11] Other libels served up sketches of criminals like Mandrin, mountebanks like Cagliostro, adventurers like the chevalier d'Eon, and an assortment of necromancers, actors, dancing girls, prostitutes, and men-about-town. Ephemeral literature of this sort could be found everywhere in Paris.[12] It filled the packs of peddlers and piled up high on the stands of *bouquinistes*. A great deal of it probably came and went without leaving a lasting impression. That was Mercier's view, although he emphasized that any libel persecuted by the government was likely to contain "some good truths" that could ultimately shape public opinion.[13]

Now that the private lives of public figures are exposed to relentless coverage in the media, it is difficult for us to appreciate the distinction between the private and the public spheres that existed under the Ancien Régime. The differentiation hardly existed at Versailles, where the king often dined before an audience of onlookers from the general public, and courtiers mixed personal intrigues with affairs of state in their daily diet of gossip. But when the gossip appeared in print and circulated outside the court, the offense was considered a crime. A libel against the king or queen could be a matter of lèse majesté. Outside Versailles, the line between the public and the private had more consistency. By violating it, a libel could be deemed a serious offense, one comparable to assassination in the eyes of the victims. When attacked by a libeler, François Thomas Marie de Baculard d'Arnaud did not consult a lawyer. He went right to the lieutenant general of police: "This scoundrel is a man named Fouilhoux. . . . It is not enough that his retraction be published in the press: I flatter myself that by exercising your well-known sense of justice, you will throw this monster in a prison, marking him with infamy. He is a moral assassin."[14] When Louis-Léon-Félicité, duc de Brancas, comte de Lauragais, residing at the time in London, considered himself libeled by Charles Théveneau de Morande, he, too, did not seek justice in a court. He slapped Morande in the face, forced him to demand pardon on his knees in the street, and demanded that he publish a retraction in the newspapers.[15] Reparation for libel did not necessarily take place by means of lawsuits in eighteenth-century France because honor under the Ancien Régime was attached to rank in a hierarchical order of society. Aristocrats could bring cases before the tribunal of the marshals of France, but more often they resorted to dueling. A duel, however, could not resolve questions of honor between men of unequal status. The drubbing administered to Voltaire by the lackeys of the chevalier de Rohan is the best-known example of how a great aristocrat settled scores with a mere writer. But writers injured honor every time they published a libel. How was the Ancien Régime to deal with them?

Basically, by police action, as illustrated by the attempts to kidnap the libelers of London. The lieutenant general of police often received requests from important people who felt that their honor could only be restored by the arrest of the writer who had besmirched it.[16] Portraits, however, posed a special problem because they were often disguised under fictitious names and distinguished authors frequently inserted them into works of fiction. Dante filled Purgatory and Hell with his enemies in *The Divine Comedy*. Rabelais, Molière, Mlle de Scudéry, Mme de La Fayette, Bussy-Rabutin, La Fontaine, La Rochefoucauld, La Bruyère—nearly all the major writers of early modern France were suspected of slipping slander into their texts. The "portrait" was a literary convention. It fit nicely into novels, especially romans à clef. But romans à clef tended to shade off into libels. How to tell them apart?

This problem tormented royal censors, who frequently complained about the difficulties of detecting hidden references in the texts submitted to them. A censor who approved a work with a portrait that displeased a courtier could get into serious trouble, but he often lacked the insider's knowledge of court life that was necessary to spot the allusion. One censor begged to be excused from vetting a novel because he was not worldly enough to decode it: "I am afraid of the allusions. They are fairly frequent, and I do not dare take responsibility for them. If I had puzzled them out, I might perhaps be free from worry; but as I don't know to whom they refer, I would be most grateful if you would persuade M. de Malesherbes to name another censor. He might be better informed than I."[17] Another censor approved a work with "natural portraits"—his term for straightforward descriptions that seemed to be innocent—but he refused to guarantee that they had no "applications."[18]

The notion of "applications," or hidden allusions to important personages, occurred in several letters sent by censors to their superiors in the book-trade administration.[19] Their in-house memos and correspondence show that they were obsessed by the danger of failing to decipher references to the high and mighty. The reputations of individuals were attached to names, and names among the great had to be protected. One censor feared the wrath of the Noailles family if he permitted a reference to a misdeed committed by one of their ancestors two hundred years earlier.[20] Another dreaded allusions that might be hidden in a saint's life set in the thirteenth century.[21] Censors tended to be relatively obscure clerics and men of letters who did not know their way around the world of the great. Malesherbes, their superior as a member of a great family as well as in his capacity as director of the book-trade administration, described them as a timorous lot who feared offending *les grands*. They could not spot "hidden allusions" in the manuscripts submitted to them, he warned in his *Mémoires sur la librairie* of 1759.[22] So they should not be held responsible for personal insults that escaped their notice. Better to tolerate veiled references of the sort that had appeared in the works of La Bruyère and Molière than to try to repress everything that might give offense. Truly defamatory libels should be punished severely and peremptorily by means of lettres de cachet, but such works would never be submitted to a censor in the first place. Malesherbes did not deny the obligation of the state to defend reputations among the elite. He merely tried to adjust the rules of the game in order to ease the task of his censors, who did not belong to the milieu where reputation had so much importance. In the book trade as in everything else under the Ancien Régime, it was assumed that people were born unequal, that law was based on privilege, and that the privileged should receive special treatment. They alone were important enough to be slandered, but the repression of slander raised enormous difficulties within the administration.

The police faced the same problem. They worried more about the slandering of individuals than about abstract arguments against religious and political orthodoxies. François-Martin Poultier d'Elmotte, the hack writer and peddler who spied for the police, said that he had received the following instructions from lieutenant general Lenoir: "I permit you to deal in books against God, but not against M. de Maurepas; against religion, but not against the government; against the apostles, but not against the ministers; against the saints, but not against the ladies of the court."[23] When the police interrogated an author in the Bastille, they attempted to identify every possible "application" (police jargon for disguised references to public figures) in his books. During his interrogation in 1750, Clément Ignace de Rességuier broke down and admitted that his roman à clef, *Voyage d'Amatonthe*, contained such a libelous portrait of Mme de Pompadour that he deserved to be executed. (He asked only that the deed be done by a sword instead of by hanging, in order to protect the honor of his family, but eventually he was pardoned.) He had been moved, he explained, by "the mad desire to draw portraits. . . . I admit that they are applied in a way that makes them criminal."[24] But the police suspected that he had held back information about many of the "applications." The three worst villains of the book, Amon, Ezon, and Sinon, clearly stood for the maréchal de Belle-Isle, the comte d'Argenson, and the cardinal de Tencin. But could Crysippe be Machault? Ariste, Maurepas? And who the devil were Cydalise, Epaminondas, Zélide, and Iphis? The police spent days poring over the text. They compared it with drafts they had confiscated from Rességuier's garret, scribbled hermeneutical observations in the margins, and pasted elaborate notes next to dubious passages. The copy that they used, now in the Bibliothèque de l'Arsenal, looks as though it had been anatomized by a modern literary critic.[25]

For the authorities of the Ancien Régime, therefore, portraits were problems. For libelers, they were a boon, not only because the public was prepared to pay good money to read books about the great but also because the state was willing to pay even more to suppress them. Literary blackmail has a long history, though one that remains to be written. As a way to make a living from the pen, it began with one of the most talented writers of the Renaissance, Pietro Aretino.

The son of a cobbler in Arezzo, Aretino talked and wrote his way into the circle of Pope Leo X while immersing himself in the lively street culture of early sixteenth-century Rome.[26] Romans kept up a running commentary on current events through jokes, graffiti, songs, and pasquinades—poems attached to a statue known as Pasquino in a square near the Piazza Navona. The pate of Pasquino functioned as a kind of bulletin board. New poems appeared on it every day during critical periods, such as conclaves to elect a new pope. In the hotly contested election of 1522, Pasquino blossomed with sonnets slandering all the candidates, except cardinal Giulio de' Medici, the patron of Aretino. The conclave was supposed to be sealed off from the outside world, but rumors from the street had a way of seeping into it, and the lobbying began long before it met, so Aretino tried to promote the election of Giulio by blackening the names of his opponents. In sonnet after sonnet, nearly fifty in all, each cardinal was branded with a vice: Pucci with whoring, Sion with boozing, Santa Croce with usury, Mantua with buggering boys, and Trani with the most ludicrous flaw of all: domination by his mamma.[27] This strategy failed, although Giulio was elected at the next conclave in 1523. But Aretino's pasquinades produced so much hilarity that copies spread throughout Europe and won him a reputation as a master libeler. He continued to run down reputations by poems, burlesque prophecies, and pseudo-legal judgments (*giudizii*) so offensive that one of his victims, Bishop Giovanni Giberti, nearly succeeded in getting him assassinated. In 1527 Aretino had proved the power of his pen and alienated most powerful grandees of Rome. He therefore sought safety in Rome's rival, the Republic of Venice.

Still patronized by the Medici and supplied with gossip by well-placed informers, Aretino continued from his headquarters in Venice to blacken the names of his enemies and to praise his protectors, but now he relied on the printing press. In 1535 he began to publish his *Ragionamenti*, a sizzling account of Roman mores couched in the form of a dialogue between two prostitutes. From 1538 until his death in 1556, he churned out volumes of his correspondence with the great. By then they had learned to protect their reputations by showering him with gifts. Cosimo de' Medici, Francis I of France, the Holy Roman emperor Charles V, Pope Julius III, and others paid him off so extravagantly that he became famous as the "Scourge of Princes," a title bestowed on him by Ariosto. The *Lettere*, handsomely printed in volumes that circulated through all the courts of Europe, actually contained little libelous material, but Aretino cultivated the notion that he could apply the whip if he chose to do so: "The princes pay me tribute for fear that I will libel them. . . . The greater part of the world's mighty do not fear the anger of the Lord, yet they do fear the fury of my pen."[28] Aretino mastered all the media of his time: word of mouth, letters, manuscript publications, printed books, and pictures, for he had received some training as an artist, and he knew the greatest painters of the late Renaissance, above all Titian, who produced five portraits of him. He had a wicked wit, and he wrote a racy version of the vernacular that cut through the pomposity of the humanists in the Italian courts. He also turned out devotional works and plays. But his reputation rested on the destruction of the reputations of others and on his brazen celebration of sex, above all in the *Sonetti Lussuriosi*, which he wrote to accompany the obscene prints by M. A. Raimondi from Giulio Romano's drawings of sexual positions. At the height of his power, Aretino occupied a magnificent palace on the Grand Canal, lived in a grand style, and even lobbied to get appointed as a cardinal. After his death, he looked out defiantly on subsequent generations from the Titian portraits while his works, condemned by the Congregation of the Index, continued to circulate under the cloak. Abhorred and admired over the centuries, he towers over all hack writers as the greatest of their breed and the supreme example of how to get rich from slander.

Aretino's example also illustrates a paradoxical fact of life in early modern courts: although they operated on the principle of power concentrated in the hands of a ruler, whether an Italian despot or a French monarch, they were vulnerable to the pressure of opinion. The court was a closed world: it excluded everyone outside it, especially the plebes. Yet "public noises" from plebeian sources could upset the balance of power among the great, even in the College of Cardinals, the most hermetically sealed of all patrician bodies. To play the power games at court, grandees needed to protect their names, but their names could be damaged from the outside, by nonplayers who expressed the vox populi, or pretended to do so. If a courtier's reputation was bruised and bruited about by vulgar slanderers, it could command less respect within the corridors of power. Not that any sort of rumor could unseat a favorite. Libelers needed accurate information, and they had to hit targets located at critical points in systems of patronage and protection. But a sharpshooter like Aretino could cause great harm.

This kind of power—the kind that would later be recognized as public opinion—was an important theme of Machiavelli and Castiglione. It differed fundamentally from the power that came out the barrels of guns, the kind that won the battle of Pavia in 1525 and that overwhelmed Rome in 1527. But it, too, was real. Benvenuto Cellini expressed its effectiveness when he described Grand Duke Cosimo de' Medici hiding near Cellini's statue of Perseus, which he had recently commissioned, in order to eavesdrop on the comments of passersby.[29] Magnificence ultimately depended on the admiration of the plebes. One's standing in the court required the protection of one's name. A sniper firing from the outside, even from a miserable garret or a distant country, could inflict terrible damage. The example of Aretino, a cobbler's son established on the Grand Canal, echoed up and down the Grub Streets of Europe for the next three centuries.

By the time it spread through eighteenth-century France, Aretino's reputation had taken on a dark color. The Scourge of Princes appeared as something of a bogeyman, an immoralist in literature comparable to Hobbes and Spinoza in philosophy. But he still commanded respect. An influential biography of him published in 1750 by Bénigne Dujardin, a royal official and man of letters with Voltairean sympathies, emphasized his notoriety as the father of all libelers but did justice to him as a free spirit who defied the authority of the Church. The biography presented Aretino as one of the first writers who made literature his "trade." Because he lived from his pen, it noted, he would write anything for money and readily pandered to the public's taste for scandal. Yet he produced some attacks on clerical abuses that were worthy of approbation by Voltaire.[30]

Voltaire did approve. He referred to Aretino with respect as a writer who held his own among the great by wielding a powerful pen. True, Aretino had merely used satire to make himself rich, but a modern Aretino, someone like

Voltaire himself, could adapt it to a worthy cause: "I am like Aretino. I deal with all crowned heads, except that he tamed them by getting them to pay him off."[31] Voltaire's enemies called him a "modern Aretino" in order to blacken his name,[32] but he used the association with Aretino in a positive way—and so did Frederic II, who employed it as a form of flattery: "Posterity will say that a philosopher who had withdrawn to Ferney . . . made truth shine at the foot of the throne and forced the powerful of the earth to reform abuses. Aretino never did as much."[33]

As authors dared increasingly to criticize the great in the course of the eighteenth century, they developed a concept of modern Aretinism. Despite Voltaire's example, it usually had negative connotations, for there was no way to dispel the sulfurous odor attached to Aretino's name. Pelleport condemned the "aretinism of literature"[34] represented by Morande, even though he wrote in the same vein himself. A scandal sheet entitled *Chronique arétine, ou recherches pour servir à l'histoire des moeurs du dix-huitième siècle* pretended to advance the cause of patriotism on the eve of the Revolution by exposing depravity in the style of Aretino, but it merely consisted of a series of portraits of prostitutes, most of them mini-biographies compressed into two or three paragraphs.[35] Any author who overdid scandalmongering could be castigated as a "modern Aretino." One reviewer applied the epithet to Linguet in order to criticize the mercenary and sensational character of his journalism.[36] Another objected to the "paintbrushes of Aretino" used by Mirabeau to highlight the sex in his libertine works.[37] But the author best known as "the modern Aretino" was Henri-Joseph Dulaurens, a Grub Street hack who brazenly applied the title to himself. Modern Aretinism, as he expressed it, differed from the original variety in one respect: it was progressive and fundamentally Voltairean. Dulaurens could be as obscene as Aretino, or nearly so, but he constantly championed the ideas of the Enlightenment, cited the works of the philosophes, and praised Voltaire above all others. Aretino had mocked the clergy by drawing on a medieval strain of anticlericalism, but he did not challenge Church doctrine. On the contrary, he wrote orthodox theological treatises. Dulaurens turned anticlericalism into a systematic attack on the Catholic Church—its dogmas, its rituals, its relics, its miracles, its saints, its wealth, its power, everything about it that offended an eighteenth-century freethinker, although he drew a line at atheism.

In his two-volume tract, first published in 1763 under the title *L'Arretin* and reprinted several times as *L'Arétin moderne*, he hammered away at this theme so relentlessly that he nearly beat it to death—or so it may seem to a reader today. But his anti-Christian ranting, mixed with bawdy tall tales, possessed plenty of shock value for readers of the eighteenth century. Some chapters contained so many caustic comments about the social order of the Ancien Régime that they took on the tone of the *Ragionamenti*. Sex, Dulaurens argued, was good for society. Honest egoism and pleasure seeking, above all lust, would produce more happiness than the repression, masquerading as virtue, foisted on humanity by the Church. But instead of pursuing this argument to logical conclusions—a line of thought that could have joined Mandeville's thesis about private vices and the public good—he lost it in contradictions and complexities. "I will develop these ideas in another book," he wrote. "A man who works to get bread doesn't have time to perfect his writing."[38] He referred in several places to his poverty and to that of his fellow hacks—those in the rue Taranne, for example, who had to remain in bed while their only pair of stockings was being mended; those who trudged around the provinces on foot, like destitute Savoyards; those in general "who scribble on paper in Paris."[39] Aretinism, he suggested, was a product of Grub Street: "I composed this book, like all my works, at great speed. A man who needs bread doesn't have time to reread his writing. I put Aretino in its title, because that satirical author spared no one in his century. Wiser than he, I respect individuals, and I attack their errors and prejudices."[40]

This formula, however, failed to take account of Aretino's principal mode of attack: highly personalized slander. By sparing individuals, except for a few anti-philosophes, Dulaurens took the teeth out of his Aretinism. Any writer who restricted his satire to general phenomena and threw in some bawdy comments might by this measure pass as a "modern" Aretino. But Aretino's brand of satire did not suit the philosophes in general, and the author who expressed it best was not Dulaurens but Charles Théveneau de Morande, the most notorious of the London libelers. Morande pilloried individuals. He produced caricatures of them, usually with a few quick strokes in the manner of Aretino, and like Aretino he used his verbal portraits to extract money from his victims. He added plenty of social satire and political comment to his slandering, but libel was his bread and butter.[41]

Morande's pedigree as a libeler was obvious to his contemporaries. They called him the "new Aretino" and "the Scourge of Princes."[42] True, he did not write large-scale slanderous portraits like those in *Mémoires secrets pour servir à l'histoire de Perse* and *Vie privée de Louis XV*. He specialized in short thrusts, which went right to the bone, but by doing so he exposed secrets hidden beneath the exteriors that public figures turned to the world. In a section of *Le Gazetier cuirassé* titled "Enigmatical News," he challenged the reader to identify prominent Parisians from descriptions of their vices. One particularly vicious portrait concerned a marquis who tried to hide his homosexuality by accompanying ladies in public after making trysts with men in private.

There is in Paris *a little marquis, one inch under five feet,* who takes a walk every evening in the most suspicious spots of the Tuileries, but who then parades in public with courtesans, who speaks ill of everyone but does not get angry if anyone speaks badly of him (even to his face), who has killed people whom he never saw but has not disturbed the existence of those who wanted to beat him to death. This marquis is held up to scorn wherever he goes, yet he goes to see everyone. If you ask why? It's because he has *an income of fifty thousand écus, a good table, a great deal of effrontery and a little wit.*[43]

When he attacked the most prominent personages, such as the triumvirate of ministers who dominated the government during the last years of Louis XV's reign, Morande piled on nasty details. One "enigma" obviously referred to chancellor Maupeou: "There exists in France a man who is *a little* crazy, *very* knavish, a rogue *without any limits,* black and perfidious *to the last degree,* who plays an *important role,* and passes as a *very enlightened* genius. Who is he? it is asked. And what will happen to him if he fails in his projects?"[44]

Mme du Barry received the worst treatment. Morande inserted a slanderous portrait of her into one long footnote: illegitimate daughter of a monk and a cook, streetwalker at age fifteen, upmarket prostitute a few years later, associate of the fake comte du Barry in a gambling den, wealthy courtesan, royal mistress, countess, and a force for evil in the French government.[45] Similar miniatures appeared everywhere among the scandalous news bulletins that made up most of *Le Gazetier cuirassé.* Other libelers followed his example—or the example of Aretino, which still inspired horror and fascination a century and a half after he had made himself into a model. They wrote in different modes and adopted different genres, but they all combined two basic ingredients: anecdotes and portraits.

To trace the whole history of libel back to two founding fathers, Procopius and Aretino, would be to simplify it out of recognition. Many influences must be taken into account. But the subject is so murky and so vast that some guidelines are necessary if one is ever to sort it out. The best strategy at this stage is to concentrate on the elements that existed everywhere in the literature of libel and to study the ways in which they were combined. They were blended most effectively during the late eighteenth century in a variety of slander that appeared under titles like *vie privée* and *vie secrète.* Before turning to this theme, however, it is important to consider a final ingredient of libel literature, one that existed everywhere, even in the works of Aretino, but that acquired a peculiar flavor in the flow of information between Paris and London—namely, news.

Chapter 24

News

By serving up scandal, libels played on the public's hunger for news. Readers had an insatiable appetite for revelations about the private lives of public figures in the eighteenth century, just as they do today. Then as now, names made news. But news did not always come in newspapers. It usually took the form of a self-contained paragraph, which could be inserted in pamphlets, books, *chroniques scandaleuses*, and other kinds of publications favored by libelers. For all their venality and disingenuousness, libelers prefigured in some ways the modern investigative reporter. They pretended to penetrate into the closed world of the great and to pry open secrets for the delectation of their readers. In fact, they often identified themselves as gazetteers or *nouvellistes*. Morande, the self-appointed "armor-plated gazetteer," epitomized this species, and by following his example, the other French refugees in London made libeling look like reportage. They also learned techniques of slinging mud from English journalists. Their experience is worth considering once more, because it shows how the literature of libel drew on strains of journalism from both sides of the Channel, and by comparing those strains, one can come closer to understanding the nature of news itself as a phenomenon peculiar to the late eighteenth century.

The French expatriates in England felt nothing but scorn for the French press in France. Seen from the perspective of London in the 1770s and 1780s, the newspapers published on the other side of the Channel had no news. Morande mocked the *Gazette de France* in 1771 for limiting its coverage of current events to three topics: the lottery, births in the royal family, and services in the chapel of Versailles.[1] Nineteen years later, Pierre Manuel stressed the same theme.

A people who wants to be instructed cannot be satisfied with the *Gazette de France*. What does it care if the king washed the feet, which weren't even dirty, of some paupers; if the queen took Easter communion with the comte d'Artois; if Monsieur [the older of the king's brothers] deigned to accept [the dedication of] a book that he may well not read; and that the Parlement, in its judicial robes, should have delivered a harangue to the dauphin in diapers?[2]

This assessment was unfair. The weekly *Gazette de France* did read like a court circular, but Paris finally acquired a daily newspaper, *Le Journal de Paris*, in 1777; by then Parisians had access to a wide variety of periodicals, advertising sheets, and French-language journals produced outside the kingdom.

When compared with England, however, France looked like a journalistic wasteland. Londoners had been reading a daily newspaper since 1702. In 1788 London had ten dailies, eight triweeklies, and nine weekly newspapers—more than it has today. Of course, eighteenth-century newspapers, unlike their modern counterparts, contained only four to eight pages, printed at runs of 3,000–5,000 copies. At two-pence halfpenny or three pence a copy, they cost more than half a day's wages of a laborer. But they were available to a broad and highly literate public in barbershops, alehouses, and many of London's five hundred coffeehouses. Newspapers and magazines carried endless material for debate—the political high jinks of John Wilkes, the sex life of Lord Sandwich, the secret marriage of the Prince of Wales, the blockheadedness of George III, the generalship of Washington, sea battles, street riots, the politics of Parliament, and the crimes of Covent Garden. Londoners raked over it endlessly, especially in coffeehouses, where the sharpest wits, known as "paragraph men," did not merely read and discuss the news but also wrote it. When they picked up a juicy item of gossip, they reduced it to a paragraph and submitted it to an editor or printer, who turned it into type and aligned it with other paragraphs in the endless columns of "freshest advices" that composed the city's daily diet of information.[3]

The paragraphs tended to be self-contained items, so there were no extended narratives, as in the modern concept of a news "story," which can fill a column or more. In fact, the paragraphs of news were difficult to distinguish from the paragraph-long advertisements, for there were no headlines or datelines, and the paragraphs were piled on one another without any concern for coherence in their subject matter. Later in the century, when eight-page "chronicles" and "advertisers" appeared, the advertisements were often grouped together on separate pages. Reports about parliamentary debates—tolerated for the first time after 1771—took up a great deal of space, and short essays or letters to the editor occupied large proportions of the columns. Still, the paragraph remained the main unit of news, and it could easily get lost in pages that looked like a sea of small print.

Despite their staid appearance—undifferentiated paragraphs crammed into columns, three or four columns squeezed on a page, four to eight pages composing an issue—some newspapers took on a sensationalist tone in the 1770s. The Reverend Henry Bate, who founded the *Morning Post* in 1772, captured an expanded reading public with a new kind of news—reports about horse races, theatrical performances, crimes, literary squabbles, divorce trials, and the private lives of eminent persons. Bate made news himself because his scandalmongering sometimes led his victims to demand satisfaction "with sword and fist and pistol,"[4] and he demolished them so brutally that he became known in the press as "the Reverend Bruiser" (Bate was chaplain to Lord Lyttleton as well as editor of the *Morning Post*). He went on to found a rival daily, the *Morning Herald*, and declared war on his former newspaper. The *Post* fought back by hiring an editor who could outdo Bate in vilification: the Reverend William Jackson, dubbed as "Dr. Viper" for "the extreme and unexampled virulence of his invectives, . . . [especially] in that species of writing known by the name of paragraphs."[5] The two men of the cloth slugged it out in their paragraphs rather than in person, increasing sales on both sides. Before long, the battles of "the Reverend Bruiser" vs. "Dr. Viper" established the principle that, as already mentioned, still passes as conventional wisdom among journalists: names make news. "Personalities" became standard fare in papers that aimed to entertain their readers rather than merely to inform them about foreign affairs and politics.

The most flamboyant personality in this new era of publicity was John Wilkes, who combined slander with radicalism. As a political maverick, journalist, and notorious libertine, he exploited all the media of his day in a campaign to reform Parliament and to liberate the press from the constraints imposed by the law of seditious libel.[6] Soon after George III ascended the throne in 1760, Wilkes used his *North Briton* to heap scorn on him and his main advisor, Lord Bute, who, Wilkes hinted, was carrying on a love affair with the Queen Mother. When number 45 of the *North Briton* declared that the crown had sunk to "prostitution," the government decided that it had gone too far. It issued general warrants for the arrest of everyone connected with the paper and imprisoned Wilkes in the Tower of London. But Wilkes was also a member of Parliament. When he appeared in court, he claimed parliamentary immunity and went on to denounce general warrants as a threat to the liberty of every freeborn Englishman. He won his case, and in winning it he undercut the legality of general warrants. "Wilkes and liberty" became a rallying cry in waves of protests against the closed and corrupt nature of parliamentary rule. After continued polemics, courtroom battles, and rioting in the streets, Wilkes and his allies won new ground for the freedom of the press. They even established the right to publish accounts of parliamentary proceedings, a practice that Parliament had forbidden since the late seventeenth century. By 1772 they had turned parliamentary politics inside out. The outsiders were not allowed in and Parliament remained in many respects a closed club, but it had opened up to all sorts of demands by the political nation "out of doors," which made itself heard by making the most of a clamorous press.

Sexual scandal compounded the shock effect of the political agitation, particularly in the magazine press. One of the best-known publications, *Town and Country Magazine*, featured exposés of extramarital sex illustrated by silhouettes known as "têtes-à-têtes": on the one side, a rich and powerful man of the world, occasionally a government minister; on the other, a poor but beautiful fallen woman.[7] An even more outspoken magazine, the *New Foundling Hospital for Wit*, regularly combined sex with politics. Its publisher, John Almon, known as "John Vamp," was a radical Wilkite who had been convicted of libel for printing attacks on the government in 1769 and went on to turn his *London Courant* into a hard-hitting scandal sheet. When reworked in magazine format, the scandalmongering made the most of Wilkes's favorite themes: liberty of the press and libertinism. The frontispiece to the *New Foundling Hospital for Wit* of 1769 showed George III blindfolded and being led on a leash attached to his nose by his mother, the princess dowager, who makes an obscene gesture to the Earl of Bute, her supposed lover and the main power behind the government, who lurks behind a tree, signaling his presence by his emblematic boot.

Nothing remotely like such satire could be sold openly in the streets of Paris. Of course, France had an important journalistic tradition of its own. The *Gazette de France*, founded in 1631, originally carried a great many well-informed reports about public affairs, thanks to the talent of its founder, Théophraste Renaudot, and the backing of Richelieu, who used the press like the academies and the arts to reinforce the prestige of the monarchy. When the government collapsed during the Fronde (1648–52), Renaudot remained faithful to Richelieu's successor, Mazarin. So the *Gazette* continued to enjoy royal patronage after Mazarin regained control of the kingdom. But following his death in 1661, the young Louis XIV set out to subordinate everything to the authority of the crown. The dispensing of privileges provided him with one of his principal means of control, one that functioned far more effectively than repression. Privileges could be sold, revoked, divided, and subdivided, and they also brought in revenue. By the end of the seventeenth century, journalism, like most activities connected with the state, had been partitioned into sectors, each of them demarcated by a protective barrier of privilege. The *Gazette de France*, passed on by Renaudot to his heirs, continued to enjoy the exclusive right to report on foreign affairs. *Le Journal des savants*, founded in 1665, won a privilege to cover everything pertaining to scholarship and science. *Le Mercure de France*, founded in 1672 as *Le Mercure gallant*, received belles-lettres, broadly defined, as its domain. These three journals dominated the

Figure 41. A caricature attacking the royal family and the Earl of Bute from the *New Foundling Hospital for Wit.*

periodical press until the end of the Ancien Régime. In principle, no new publication could invade their territory without the king's permission and without
paying them tribute.[8]

In practice, of course, the journalistic landscape became crowded with all
sorts of periodicals. New journals proliferated—in law, medicine, physics,
poetry, and a dozen other domains—and the three privileged journals became
embroiled in endless turf battles, accompanied by intrigues and lobbying in
the corridors of Versailles. Most of the new publications were weekly or
monthly reviews rather than newspapers. Their pagination continued from
issue to issue throughout the year and they contained tables of contents so that
they could be bound and read as books. According to its original privilege, the
Gazette de France enjoyed an exclusive right to publish "the report of things
that have happened"[9]—that is, an account of virtually all events—and it made
the most of its monopoly, although it concentrated heavily on foreign affairs.
By 1752 it was reprinted in thirty-eight cities. But it continued to convey a very
orthodox view of events. From 1762 to 1768 it was actually written from within
the foreign ministry, and its proofs were always submitted to the ministers for
their approval. It usually cost 15 livres a year, the equivalent of two weeks'
wages for a laborer, so it did not penetrate deeply down-market. At the opposite end of the spectrum, advertising sheets, called *annonces*, *affiches*, or *avis*,
sprang up in all the major cities, and they sometimes carried items that could
be considered news.

The foreign French journals wedged into the space between the stately
reviews and the scruffy local advertisers. Although they had to be prudent in
treating France's domestic affairs, they provided extensive coverage of diplomatic and military events. France's involvement in a succession of large-scale
wars from 1740 to 1783 made the public rely increasingly on the excellent
Dutch newspapers, especially the gazettes of Amsterdam, Leiden, and Utrecht.
In 1740 only four foreign journals circulated inside the kingdom. By 1780 there
were fifteen. Their prices remained high (by 1779 the *Gazette de Cologne* cost
36 livres a year in Paris) and their circulation low (normally only a few hundred copies, although the *Gazette de Leyde*, which provided full coverage of the
American war, went from 287 subscribers in 1767 to 2,560 in 1778). They also
ran into continuous difficulties with the foreign ministry and the postal service. Browbeaten by objections from the French ambassador to The Netherlands, the *Gazette d'Utrecht* had to print apologies and retractions—sometimes
using forms supplied by the French ministry—for trivial offenses such as an
irreverent remark about a secondary school in Auxerre. The foreign French
press avoided printing anything that might give offense in Versailles, but it
ultimately succeeded in denting the monopoly of the *Gazette de France*.[10]

Despite the occasional dents, the system of privileged journalism held firm until 1789. In some ways it became more powerful than ever, owing to the monopoly created by Charles-Joseph Panckoucke, France's first press baron.[11] Panckoucke established himself as a bookseller in Paris in 1762 by buying the business of Michel Lambert, an important member of the booksellers' guild who owned the privilege for the *Journal des savants*. Then, piece by piece, he built up a journalistic empire. He acquired two foreign periodicals, the *Journal politique de Bruxelles* and the *Journal de Genève*, along with eight minor French reviews and amalgamated them all in the *Mercure de France*, which he bought in 1778. By 1789, the *Mercure* had become the most widely read and lucrative periodical in France. It had 15,000 subscribers, who paid 30 livres a year (33 livres if they lived outside Paris), and it carried essays by the best-known writers, mostly moderate figures of the late Enlightenment like Jean François de La Harpe and Panckoucke's brother-in-law, Jean-Baptiste Antoine Suard. Although it remained primarily a literary magazine—dedicated to the king, as it proudly announced on its front page—the *Mercure* covered a large range of topics, including politics. But its "political" section concerned little more than uncontroversial reports on foreign affairs. Vergennes, the foreign minister, who wanted to stifle all criticism of the regime, became Panckoucke's greatest patron. Panckoucke also cultivated close relations with nearly everyone in power, especially the lieutenant general of police and the director of the book trade. Thanks to his connections, he received "the exclusive privilege and licenses of the political journals" in June 1778.[12] Of course, this privilege might seem to encroach on that of the *Gazette de France*, but Panckoucke solved that problem nine years later by taking over the *Gazette*. When the Revolution broke, he had acquired a controlling interest in periodical literature by manipulating the two main sources of influence under the Ancien Régime, privilege and patronage.

While the state, reinforced by privileged entrepreneurs, maintained its fundamental control of the press, the demand for unadulterated news continued to grow. It could be satisfied only by marginal characters who operated outside the law, primarily the *nouvellistes* mentioned often in the preceding pages. Like the London paragraph men, they transformed oral reports into short items, usually a paragraph in length. As explained in Chapter 20, these "anecdotes" or "nouvelles" were copied, strung together, and circulated in manuscript newsletters called *nouvelles à la main* or *gazetins*. The newsletters then continued to be copied, transmitted, and sold from one point in a correspondence network to another, functioning as the equivalent of a modern news service.[13]

Nouvelles à la main circulated through all the nerve centers in the information systems that linked the city to the court, the provinces, and subscribers scattered everywhere in Europe. The demand was too great and the subscribers too well connected for the authorities to stamp them out. The police therefore adopted a strategy of imprisoning or exiling the most audacious *nouvellistes* and co-opting the others. They allowed moderate gazetteers to hire copyists and churn out sizable editions of news sheets, provided that everything was vetted in police headquarters. A well-protected *nouvelliste* like the notorious Charles de Fieux, chevalier de Mouhy, who also functioned as a police spy, could claim to have a "privilege" for his *gazetin* and could even enlist the police to repress "pirated" editions.[14] Whenever he stepped out-of-bounds, Mouhy got clapped in the Bastille, and he ultimately disappeared into exile, broken and penniless. But for many years he epitomized the collaboration of hack writers and police inspectors in the Parisian versions of Grub Street. The police even functioned as journalists themselves. By adapting reports from their legions of spies, particularly those connected with brothels and the back-stage intrigues of Parisian theaters, they turned out a *chronique scandaleuse* for the private delectation of Louis XV.[15] François Louis-Claude Marin, general secretary of the book trade under lieutenant general Sartine, edited a manu-script police gazette for four years before leaving the police in 1771 to take over the *Gazette de France*. From an ostensibly clandestine *gazetin* to the super-orthodox *Gazette de France*, the distance was enormous. It showed that the regime could accommodate many varieties of journalism, despite the official intolerance for unofficial news.[16]

By infiltrating the underground, however, the police produced an inevita-ble reaction—a demand for unadulterated news, which a later generation of gazetteers attempted to satisfy by producing *gazetins* that did not pass through police headquarters. The new *nouvellistes* were obscure hacks like François-Guillaume Imbert de Boudeaux, Louis de Launay, François-Martin Poultier d'Elmotte, and others turned up by the police campaigns against libels in the 1770s and 1780s. After compiling a scandal sheet for a few weeks from a Grub Street garret, they usually disappeared into the Bastille or the back alleys of the book trade in Liège, Brussels, Cologne, Amsterdam, Hamburg, or London. A few, however, produced long runs of *nouvelles à la main*. As already explained, Pidansat de Mairobert and Moufle d'Angerville transformed the casual corre-spondence of Mme Doublet into a large-scale news service, whose manuscript bulletins eventually appeared in print as the thirty-six-volume *Mémoires secrets pour servir à l'histoire de la république des lettres en France*. The other key *nouvelliste* of the pre-revolutionary era was Louis François Mettra, of whom more later. Suffice it to say at this point that the legal restrictions on news were offset by clandestine journalists who produced enough copy to keep the public informed, however imperfectly, about the lives of the great and intrigues in the corridors of power. But until 1789, the French did not develop anything like the open, uninhibited press that flourished in England.

What did Frenchmen make of the English variety of journalism when they experienced it firsthand? The colony of French expatriate writers predictably raised a chorus of praise to English liberty and directed it against tyranny in France. They trumpeted this message on their title pages: "printed at a hundred leagues from the Bastille," "at the sign of liberty," "at an island that makes the terra firma tremble." Morande, who used these publishing addresses, referred to his libels as "news," presented himself as a "gazetteer," and celebrated English liberty as opposed to French despotism.[17] The anonymous author of *La Gazette noire* picked up this theme where Morande had left it and took it further: he hailed the liberty of the press in England as the greatest blessing on earth.

Land above all other lands, where man dares to use a right that is inseparable from his being, [the right] to think and to speak in the way that pleases him most, where he dares to open his heart, to untie his tongue, to chatter, to write according to his conscience! Land where tyranny is detested, blasted, combatted, where despotism does not dare to silence the law in favor of some persons and to make use of it in order to slit the throats of others.[18]

There was something infectious about the air of London for the French libelers. They slandered shamelessly, but at the same time they published hymns of praise for the constitutional system that permitted them to do so. In the midst of his blackmail operations, Pelleport penned a tribute to English liberty, which served as the opening salvo of *Le Diable dans un bénitier*. He pictured the French expatriates as perched on a fortress—the British Isles, a bastion of human rights—looking down scornfully on the efforts of the French police to capture them.

Despotism, which is upset and driven to despair by the slightest obstacle, cannot bear to consider the idea of the existence of liberty. For it, the cruelest torture is the spectacle of the happiness among those who have saved themselves by fleeing from its brutal oppression and who enjoy in a neighboring land the sweetness of a government that respects the rights of humanity. It quivers with rage while contemplating its victims sheltered safely from its thunderbolts. It circles endlessly around them and dashes its fangs against the rocks of the fortress from the top of which they look down on it with scorn and pity.[19]

There is no reason to doubt the sincerity of such declarations. Once they arrived in London, the French expatriates discovered a journalistic culture that surpassed anything they had imagined. They became intoxicated with the liberties taken by their English colleagues and set out to imitate them. As a character in one of their libels remarked to its radical narrator, "You scribble away prodigiously, in the English manner."[20]

The same liberties horrified other Frenchmen quartered in London, especially those attached to the French embassy. When French diplomats read the British press, they could hardly believe their eyes. The dispatches of Adhémar to Vergennes expressed shock and indignation at "the criminal license that dishonors this country under the name of liberty. . . . The public newspapers are political libels."[21] The ambassador found the exercise of political liberty by the English equally repugnant. While observing the parliamentary elections of 1784, he reported nothing but brawling, ranting, and plebeian disorder. "Fox and Liberty," the rallying cry of radicals who had chanted "Wilkes and Liberty" twenty years earlier, rang in his ears as nothing more than rabble-rousing.[22] Worse still, the rabble had some influence on government policy, and the rousing came from newspapers: "It is from the gazettes that public opinion is formed here, and public opinion often forces the hand of the cabinet."[23]

Adhémar could not simply read the London newspapers and deplore them at a distance because they did not restrict their slander to British targets. On December 11, 1784, the *Morning Post* carried an item about a love affair in Paris between the duchesse de Polignac, thinly disguised as "Mme P——," and a certain Englishman, "Colonel C——." As the duchess was a well-known favorite of the queen, some of the scandal threatened to rub off on Marie-Antoinette. Two days later the paper accused the queen—clearly indicated but not explicitly named—of having a tryst with a "Mr. W——" and with a French officer in a secret love nest provided by Mme de Polignac in Paris. To the *Morning Post*, which at this time filled its columns with reports of sexual misconduct in the high society of London, the story was irresistible: it showed that shortly after the disastrous war with France, two dashing English officers had wrought a certain kind of revenge on the French king by cuckolding him. To Adhémar, of course, the story was not merely offensive, undiplomatic, and a matter of concern at the highest level of government: it was a case of lèse majesté. But what was he to do? He felt as powerless to muzzle the *Morning Post* as he had been to repress *Le Diable dans un bénitier*. Diplomatic protests, he had learned, would get him nowhere. So after sending copies of the articles with translations to Versailles, he decided to retaliate in kind. He hired a hack of his own to deny the rumors in paragraphs planted in the *Public Advertiser* of December 17 and the *Morning Herald* of December 19.[24] Inevitably, however, this tactic backfired. The *Morning Post* replied with a revelation that the love nest was expanding. "Mme P——" was now believed to be sharing her colonel with "a great lady" (Marie-Antoinette). The English press apparently had an inexhaustible supply of mud to sling at the French monarchy, and Adhémar realized that he could not beat the London journalists at their own game. Therefore he stopped playing, cursed them as "rabble,"[25] and vented his frustrations to Vergennes, who replied in kind: "I cannot imagine that in a civilized country one does not utterly execrate the authors of infamous works as absurd as those which these starving hacks have produced against the queen."[26]

Although relatively unimportant in itself, this episode demonstrates that London newspapers were publishing slander about the sex life of Marie-Antoinette eight months before the Diamond Necklace Affair broke in Paris. It also suggests that the French libelers may have picked up some of the tricks of their trade from English journalists.

Not that they needed to travel to London to learn how to malign the great. France had a long tradition of mudslinging. The biggest explosion of libelous pamphleteering took place during the Fronde (1648–53), a revolt that owed its name to a sling used by street urchins to pelt the authorities. So many of the pamphlets and pasquinades slandered the dominant figure of the government, cardinal Jules Mazarin, that the whole body of literature came to be known as mazarinades. The most notorious of them, *La Mazarinade* by Paul Scarron, apostrophized Mazarin as follows:

Bougre bougrant,
Bougre bougré,
Et bougre au suprême degré,
Bougre au poil, et bougre à la plume,
Bougre en grand et petit volume,
Bougre sodomisant l'état,
Et bougre du plus haut carat . . .

(Buggering bugger,
Buggered bugger,
And bugger to the supreme degree,
Bugger down to the hairs and to the feather
[alternatively: Bugger accurately described and drawn]
Bugger both big and small in volume,
Bugger sodomizing the state
And bugger of the most absolute quality . . .)[27]

No one in the eighteenth century, except Voltaire and François Joseph Lagrange-Chancel, could hurl invective with such deadly aim. The libels against Louis XV and Louis XVI were not new in their scurrility. They were new as news. They belonged to the journalistic culture that had spread through the literary underground in France and that made contact in the 1770s and 1780s with the radical and sensationalist press flourishing openly in England.

The convergence of the two cultural currents can be studied best by taking a last look at the colony of French expatriates in London. Although the documentation is thin, it contains enough information for one to see how the French and English varieties of journalism intersected, at least in some exemplary cases. They came together most strikingly in the *Courrier de l'Europe, gazette anglo-française*, a French-language newspaper published in London, owned by a Scot, Samuel Swinton, edited by a Frenchman, Antoine Joseph de Serres de La Tour, and staffed by many of the expatriates, including Morande, Pelleport, Brissot, Perkins MacMahon, and Poultier d'Elmotte.[28] Like many French newspapers published outside France, the *Courrier* consisted mostly of short items recycled from the local press and destined for readers scattered across Europe. It printed them, one on top of the other in no particular order, under the heading "Paragraphs extracted from English newspapers" and added occasional articles from its own contributors, usually in the form of letters.

In its fifth issue, dated July 12, 1776, the *Courrier* published a letter, ostensibly from a Parisian correspondent, that disparaged the entire French government, heaping scorn in particular on the comte de Maurepas. Vergennes, who had authority over foreign publications in his capacity as foreign minister, promptly banned the *Courrier* from France and cut off its circulation by excluding it from the mail. Ironically, however, he found that he stood to profit from the *Courrier* as a reader himself. He could not read much English, and the *Courrier*'s biweekly digests of the British press provided him with a better supply of information than all the dispatches and translations produced within the ministry of foreign affairs. He especially needed information in 1776, because the American Revolution had touched off a major crisis within the British political system, and France faced the possibility of regaining some of the ground it had lost to Britain since 1740 in the competition to dominate foreign affairs. So when Swinton, using Beaumarchais as an intermediary, apologized for the "bad paragraph," promised to restrain his writers in the future, and offered to let a French censor vet the London edition before it circulated in France, Vergennes reopened the French market to the *Courrier*. By the end of the year, the paper's circulation had risen to 3,000 copies, and in 1777 it reached 6,000, a huge number for the time and an indication of the demand for news about Anglo-American affairs.[29]

This news, according to the paper's prospectus, consisted of "faithful extracts from the fifty-three gazettes that appear every week in London." In fact, La Tour lifted most of his copy from the *Morning Chronicle*, which contained the fullest accounts of parliamentary debates. By the spring of 1778, the debates included all sorts of information about British preparations to go to war with France—more information than a legion of French spies could produce, and all of it available every day in print, thanks to the extraordinary liberty enjoyed by the London press. Respect for this liberty prevented the British government from banning the *Courrier de l'Europe* in Britain, but it tried to prevent issues from reaching France by treating them as illegal exports and seizing them in the customs offices at Dover. Swinton parried this blow by getting permission from Vergennes to reprint smuggled copies of the paper in Boulogne-sur-Mer, where he had rented a house and installed his French mistress and her children. He promised to submit every copy of the French edition to a particularly strict censor, abbé Jean-Louis Aubert, the editor of the *Gazette de France*. And to supervise the printing operation in Boulogne, he hired a young man who was trying, not very successfully, to live from his pen in Paris: Jacques-Pierre Brissot.

As Brissot later recounted in his memoirs, his apprenticeship on the *Courrier de l'Europe* gave him his start in journalism.[30] He corrected proof in Boulogne for a year, adding a few paragraphs of his own and adjusting the copy to the flow of objections that came from Aubert. (By acting as Vergennes's watchdog, Aubert became the bête noire of the *Courrier*'s journalists and therefore was pilloried in *Le Diable dans un bénitier*, which Pelleport mockingly dedicated to him.) At the end of his stint of employment, Brissot made a quick trip to London with Swinton, who introduced him to La Tour and also to "the Reverend Bruiser," Henry Bate. Bate and Swinton had speculated together on the *Morning Herald*. They seem to have shared the same view of journalism as a field of endless opportunity for an entrepreneur quick enough to detect the demand for news. Bate joined Swinton and Brissot on their return trip to Boulogne; Brissot, who had a good command of English, probably absorbed some of their shop talk during the long hours spent together in coaches and aboard the ship. In any case, after coming into a small inheritance, he decided to move to London and set up a shop of his own—a "Lyceum" (*Licée*), which would be a gathering place for men of letters and which would publish another French journal protected by the liberty of the press in Britain. Before launching the *Journal du Licée de Londres*, however, Brissot joined La Tour's staff on the *Courrier de l'Europe*. From February to November 1783 he contributed paragraphs under the rubric "Varieties" for a salary of 2,400 livres. The spectacular growth of the *Courrier* after 1776 made it possible for La Tour to hire several other collaborators from the French expatriates in London, notably Pelleport.[31] By 1784 he had made enough money from the paper to sell his share in it—he had owned one-third and Swinton two-thirds of the original enterprise—and to retire. Swinton asked Brissot to succeed La Tour as editor, but Brissot refused, preferring to produce his own journal. Swinton then hired Morande, who edited the *Courrier* from 1784 to 1791.

The shift in the editorship of the *Courrier* corresponded with the crisis that led to the breakup of the colony of French writers in London. In publishing *Le Diable dans un bénitier*, Pelleport had attacked Morande as an agent of the French police. Morande retaliated by setting the trap that led to the arrest of Pelleport and Brissot in July 1784. Swinton also collaborated in this operation, partly to ingratiate himself further with Vergennes, partly to snuff out competition, for the success of the *Courrier* had inspired projects for other "Anglo-French gazettes." In addition to Brissot's *Journal du Licée de Londres*, these included an abortive attempt by La Tour to produce a new version of the *Courrier* in London; Pelleport's effort to do the same in Boulogne-sur-Mer; and a speculation by two other expatriates, abbé Séchamp, a collaborator of Pelleport's, and Saint-Flocel, a former editor of the *Journal de Bouillon*, to launch a journal modeled on Brissot's.[32] Although none of these schemes ever came to fruition, they showed that a hybrid variety of Anglo-French journalism had taken root in London and that it had considerable appeal for the French writers established there.

The contributors to the *Courrier de l'Europe* absorbed English notions of news by translating English newspapers into French. This process of acculturation took place every day through a demanding routine of reading and writing. To produce eight pages twice a week, each page consisting of two dense columns in quarto format, the *Courrier* journalists had to pore over dozens of newspapers (fifty-three, according to the *Courrier*'s prospectus), extract the items they judged most likely to interest French readers, and transform the alien idiom into readable French. It was hack work, but in performing it, day in and day out, they functioned as cultural intermediaries; and it was through their mediation that the French acquired a great deal of their knowledge about British politics and the American Revolution.

The expatriate authors also familiarized themselves with the ways of the newspaper world in London by means of personal contacts. They probably rubbed shoulders in coffeehouses with all sorts of paragraph men, and they certainly knew publishers like Swinton, booksellers like Boissière, editors like Bate, and printers like E. Cox of 37 Great Queen Street, Lincoln's Inn Fields, who produced the *Journal du Licée de Londres* as well as the *Courrier*. Not that relations were always amicable. When Brissot failed to pay his printing bill, Cox had him thrown into debtor's prison. When Pelleport threatened to become a competitor, Swinton denounced him to the French police. Morande denounced all his colleagues and was especially effective as an undercover agent for the police because he had been assimilated more thoroughly than the other expatriates. He even married an Englishwoman—possibly, as his enemies maintained, because she was the daughter of his landlord and he had no other way to pay his bills when he first arrived in London. Pelleport plotted to escape his own bill collectors, according to police informants, by running off with a wealthy English widow.[33] The French certainly had plenty of contact with the natives.

Thanks to their immersion in Grub Street and in what soon would become Fleet Street, the French expatriates absorbed a great deal of London's scribblerian culture—its hard-hitting journalism, scandalous pamphleteering, and radical politics. They also learned how to translate published versions of it into French. The translating involved much more than finding suitable words in their own language. It was a matter of mediation between cultures, cultures that had enough in common to draw on a similar stock of stories and stereotypes but not enough to avoid constant misunderstandings. The most thoroughly bilingual and bicultural member of the expatriate colony was an Irishman named Perkins MacMahon. He spoke English as his native language but was raised among Jacobite exiles in France. He became a priest, served as a vicar in Rouen, eloped with one of his parishioners, settled in London, worked for La Tour on the *Courrier de l'Europe*, then switched to Bate's *Morning Herald* and took up writing libels about the French court in English.[34] Morande seems to have been nearly as adept in both languages and both varieties of journalism. After becoming editor of the *Courrier* in 1784—all the while continuing his career as a spy—he told the foreign ministry that he sometimes planted paragraphs in the English press in order to be able to translate and publish them in his own journal.[35]

Brissot and his wife—mainly his wife—translated a half-dozen English books.[36] In his memoirs, he expounded the common, eighteenth-century view that translations should not be literal: they should be new creations, he argued, adaptations rather than replicas of the originals, which would convey the spirit of the English texts by reworking them in ways that suited the tastes and needs of French readers. He went on to describe what it would take for a Parisian to write a *Tableau de Londres* comparable to Mercier's *Tableau de Paris*. The foreign author would have to plunge into the world of London's newspapers: "They offer endless caricatures, varied portraits, and curious facts. Here, the most bizarre advertisements; there, the most scandalous anecdotes. Even the political news would offer more than one amusing subject to be portrayed."[37] Anecdotes, portraits, political news—the ingredients were everywhere the same, but to understand the way they set the tone of public life in London, the author would have to learn to decode them by immersing himself in Grub Street: "It is crucial, in a word, to know the sewers of London and their most filthy details."[38] Brissot hastened to add that he did not frequent that milieu. He mixed with the superior sort of writers, he insisted, and he promoted the translation of works by the two who impressed him most: Catharine Macaulay, the radical feminist historian, and David Williams, the radical political philosopher. Because he was too busy with his own journalistic enterprises, he recruited his friend Pelleport to do the job.

During his interrogations in the Bastille, Brissot revealed that he had urged Pelleport to translate Macaulay's eight-volume *History of England from the Accession of James I to That of the Brunswick Line* (London, 1764–83), but it proved to be an unmanageable task. Pelleport preferred shorter, snappier books such as a libel against various public figures in England that he intended to translate under the title *Le Diable dans un ballon.* Apparently it, too, never appeared in print.[39] But Pelleport did complete a translation of David Williams's *Letters on Political Liberty* (London, 1782), and in the process he transformed it into a completely different kind of book. Williams was an austere philosopher. His *Letters* expressed a particularly severe and high-minded variety of British radicalism. They argued for a complete overhaul of the political system, one that would transform the old, unreformed Parliament with its rotten boroughs and corrupt clienteles into a thoroughly democratic institution organized according to the mathematical principles of a new political science. Every adult Englishman should have a vote, Williams argued. Groups of ten voters would elect a representative, who would meet with nine other representatives in a "tything." They would then elect one of their number to represent them in an election at a higher "tything" and so on, until the House of Commons was filled with MPs who would be strictly bound by the will of their constituents. By superimposing elections on one another according to this formula, the British would return to the indirect democracy practiced in the Saxon "Folkmote" before the Normans subjected them to monarchical despotism. Although he deplored "the folly and iniquity of the American War,"[40] Williams did not go so far as to call for the abdication of George III, and he showed no sympathy for the agitation of the Wilkites or street protests by the "populace."[41] Democracy, as he described it, would express the will of the people in perfect tranquility and with mathematical precision, like a finely calibrated machine.

Nothing could be further from the passionate, sardonic, salacious, and convoluted character of Pelleport's writings, yet Pelleport translated the text quite accurately. He vented his own views in the footnotes, which were nearly as long as the main body of the work and which shifted the discussion from England to France. By adopting a burlesque pseudonym as a translator—"the Révérend Père de Roze-Croix, author of the *Boulevard des Chartreux* and many other small works in verse"—on the title page and the preface, he assumed an irreverent voice and prepared the reader for some indecorous commentary.[42] A single copy of *Le Boulevard des Chartreux*, anonymous like everything by Pelleport, has survived in the Bibliothèque municipale of Grenoble. It has the qualities that characterize all of Pelleport's writing—irreligion, ribaldry, parody, and buffoonery, along with protests against oppression and in favor of liberty.

Liberté, *libertas*, vive la liberté,
Plus de cagoterie et point d'austerité.

(Liberty, *libertas*, long live liberty,
No more bigotry and no austerity.)[43]

The footnotes of *Lettres sur la liberté politique* also contain many other personal references—to Pelleport's service in India, for example, to his birthplace, Stenay, to *Le Diable dans un bénitier*, and to his relations with Swinton.[44] At one point he cited Rousseau's "Contrat social,"[45] but instead of pursuing Williams's argument at the level of political theory, he derided and denounced everything about France's system of government. The Bourbons were despots, he said bluntly, and the French had every right to drive them from their throne. Louis XVI might seem to be a decent ruler, but he could turn into a Nero overnight, and Louis XV should have been deposed long ago.

If Louis XV had owed an accounting to the nation . . . , one could have asked him, "What did you do with the enormous treasure that you raised from your subjects from 1753 until the peace of 1763? During all that time, you had neither a fleet nor an army that could make you respected. Why did you take a prostitute from the hands of a tramp and place her nearly as close to the throne as your great-grandfather [Louis XIV] did with the widow of Scarron, during the imbecility that overcame him at the end of his life? . . . Why so many stupid and corrupt controller-generals? Why such vile mistresses? The "whys" could go on forever. . . . Assuredly, if the people, reclaiming its rights as a consequence of the imbecility and the degradation of the monarch, had sent his mistress to the Salpetrière [a prison for prostitutes] and the king to the monks of Saint Denis, the punishment would have been more exemplary than the one that was waiting for the Well Loved in the other world.[46]

This outburst drew on all the major themes of French libel literature since the seventeenth century—extortionate taxes, corrupt ministers, immoral mistresses, incompetence in foreign affairs, the general imbecility of kings, and the debasement of the throne. In a second edition, published sometime soon before the opening of the Estates General, Pelleport called for a revolution: "The Bourbon family imagines that it owns the French nation outright as its property. Its ownership is a fact, preferable to one by right. This will continue until the people, having reflected about its [rights], wants to take back possession of them. We are promised that this event will occur in 1789."[47] After the collapse of the monarchy in 1792, Brissot sponsored a decree of the Convention that made Williams a citizen of the French Republic and invited him to Paris in order to collaborate on the drafting of a republican constitution. But that denouement was unthinkable in 1783, when Pelleport published the first edition of the *Lettres sur la liberté politique* and attempted, not very successfully, to distribute it through Brissot's contacts among booksellers on the Continent.[48] Pelleport's footnotes expressed his anger and helplessness, as an exile in London, before the unlimited power of the Bourbon monarchy: "The king is all; he has brought together all kinds of power; and one thing that should cause fear and trembling for any man who thinks, nothing could prevent him tomorrow from demanding my head for having written this terrible truth, were I crazy enough to return into his territory."[49] A year later he was sitting in the Bastille.

Pelleport's footnotes frenchified Williams's text. They provided a running commentary on it, fleshing out its abstract principles with examples of iniquities on the French side of the Channel. Their tone, alternatingly indignant and irreverent, stood out in contrast to the cool rationalism of Williams's discourse. Pelleport wrote as a libeler on the bottom part of the page, as a translator on the top—or, rather, he made it possible for a further stage of translating to occur in the exchange between the text above and the notes below, in the very act of reading. If understood as a process of cultural adaptation, the translation did not merely exist on the page. It happened in the up-and-down shifting of focus by the reader. It took place in the eye of the beholder.

Of course, many different modes of translation existed alongside Pelleport's. Many other writers learned how to negotiate between the Grub Streets of Paris and London, living from their wits and whatever their pens could produce. The best example may be the man who appeared behind Receveur on the frontispiece of *Le Diable dans un bénitier*, Pierre Ange Goudar.[50]

The police assigned him to serve as Receveur's lieutenant in 1783 because he knew more than anyone else about the underworld of literature in both countries. By then he was seventy-five. His adventures had taken him through garrets and gambling dens nearly everywhere in Europe: from 1744 to 1746 in various courts of Italy; in 1748, Paris; 1750, London; 1752, Portugal; 1753 or 1754, Paris; 1755 and 1762–64, London; later in 1764, Vienna; 1765–66, Venice; 1767,

Naples; 1771, Milan; 1772–73, Venice; 1775–76, Lucca and Florence; 1777, Holland; 1778, England; 1783, Paris and then back with Receveur to London once again, his fourth or fifth sojourn. Why such perpetual motion? Not because of wanderlust. Goudar derived much of his income from gambling and was expelled from one city after another for having too fast a hand at pharaon and biribi. He also sold his services as a spy, mainly for the French foreign ministry, and therefore had to pack his bags and disappear on several occasions. In London he met Sara, a beautiful barmaid, who accompanied him on his tours of gambling dens from 1763 until 1790, a year before his death. He picked up cash along the way by writing and selling books—and peddling Sara, too, as the occasion arose.

Goudar wrote at least seventy-eight original works, although it is difficult to sort out his bibliography because he flogged the same texts under different names and cheated publishers as readily as gamblers. Much of his writing concerned current events, in the form of pamphlets, libels, and *chroniques scandaleuses*. *L'Année politique, contenant l'état présent de l'Europe, ses guerres, ses révolutions, ses sièges, ses batailles, ses négociations, ses traités, etc.* (1759) provided a journalistic account of one year, 1758, during the Seven Years' War. Goudar's best-known work, *L'Espion chinois, ou l'envoyé secret de la cour de Pékin pour examiner l'état présent de l'Europe* (1764), spread scandalous anecdotes over six volumes. A two-volume supplement, *L'Espion français à Londres, ou observations critiques sur l'Angleterre et sur les Anglais* (1780), did not reveal anything about his actual experience as a French spy, despite its alluring title. Instead, it contained essays, loosely modeled on *The Spectator*, about current trends in fashionable London society. Goudar can therefore be considered a freewheeling, freelance journalist, although he never worked for a newspaper. He made it his business to gather information and to sell it, either to the police or to the public. But he is most interesting as one of many adventurers in the age of Enlightenment who constantly crossed boundaries and lived by playing one culture off against another. Like Casanova, whom he got to know well in London, Goudar was a cultural middleman, a chameleon, who changed colors and assumed new roles according to shifts in circumstances. He played the spy both in real life and in literature. Having learned his way around nearly every Grub Street in Europe during a half century of scrambling on the road, he made an ideal guide for Receveur in London. The police knew where to find professionals when they set out to tame the trade in libels. And the lives of other libelers—Morande, Pelleport, Poultier d'Elmotte—fell into the same pattern. Always on the move, crossing borders, dodging lettres de cachet, in and out of prison, they knew how to translate experience from one world to another.

From journalism to libeling and the likes of Ange Goudar, the argument may seem to be getting lost in exotic detail or turning in circles. What precisely is the connection between news and libeling, and why devote attention to the ragged race of journalists who migrated from one Grub Street to another? To clarify things, it seems best to return to the point of departure: the notion of *nouvelles* and the *nouvelliste* mentioned near the beginning of this chapter, Louis François Mettra.

Mettra also did time in Grub Street, although he began life in comfortable circumstances as the son of a merchant banker and art dealer in Paris who traded extensively with clients in Germany.[51] After inheriting his father's business, he went bankrupt, disappeared for several years, and surfaced in 1775 as the editor and publisher of the *Correspondance littéraire secrète*, which was printed in Deutz near Cologne and in Neuwied after 1784. Despite its title, which had the smell of a scandal sheet, the *Correspondance* was mild enough to be permitted to circulate in France, and it continued without interruption from 1775 to 1793, a remarkable run for an ostensibly underground weekly.[52] Mettra also speculated on other periodicals and developed an important trade as a bookseller. But in addition to these quasi-legal activities, he turned out a truly clandestine manuscript gazette based on "bulletins" sent to him by his contacts in Versailles. A team of copyists transcribed items from the bulletins into a news sheet, which Mettra sold by subscription everywhere in Europe. Many of the items in the news sheet found their way into other *nouvelles à la main*, printed gazettes, and even libels, including some produced in London. In short, Mettra operated a kind of news service, and he ran it along lines that connected news with libeling.

To get a closer view of the connection, it is necessary to consult Brissot's dossier from the Bastille. After arresting him, along with Pelleport, in July 1784, the police attempted in their interrogations to discover who had produced the latest crop of libels. The interrogator, commissioner Pierre Chénon, listed eight:

1. *La Naissance du Dauphin*
2. *Les Passetemps d'Antoinette*
3. *Les Rois de France régénérés*
4. *Les Amours du vizir de Vergennes*
5. *Les Petits Soupers de l'Hôtel de Bouillon*
6. *Réflexions sur la Bastille*
7. *La Gazette noire*
8. *Les Rois de France jugés au tribunal de la raison*[53]

Brissot denied that he had anything to do with any of them. He indignantly rejected Chénon's suggestion that he had supplied "the principal anecdotes" used in *Le Diable dans un bénitier*. When pressed, he confessed that he had helped distribute *Le Diable* by sending it to some of his correspondents, but he held to his assertion that he had played no part in the drafting of its text. Chénon had no hard evidence to prove that charge, so he eventually dropped it and pursued a more promising line of questioning: Didn't Brissot's activities in London involve regular contact with Mettra? Brissot had let slip that one copy of *Le Diable* had gone to Mettra in Cologne. By seizing on that opening, Chénon led Brissot to admit that he and Mettra had maintained a commercial correspondence. In fact, Brissot revealed, Mettra reprinted Brissot's *Journal du Licée de Londres* in order to distribute it in Germany, and he had tried to entice Brissot to collaborate in his own journalistic ventures. He sent Brissot both of the news sheets he produced, one printed (that is, the anodyne *Correspondance littéraire secrète*) and one manuscript (the clandestine *gazetin*), while soliciting him to serve as their London correspondent.[54] Above all, Mettra wanted "secret anecdotes," but Brissot refused, protesting that he did not know any. Mettra continued to supply the news sheets nonetheless, until Brissot finally asked him to stop—because, he assured the police, he devoted himself to philosophy and legal theory, and he had no taste for the scandal that Mettra scattered through his copy, "especially the *gazette à la main* from Versailles."[55]

Information about the manuscript gazette was the aspect of underground journalism that the police most wanted to uncover. They knew all about Mettra's activities in Cologne, but they had not been able to identify his main informants—that is, to trace his news back along the chain of transmission to its original source, "anecdotes" relayed in manuscript notes from secret correspondents in Paris and Versailles. Brissot, however, denied all knowledge about the *nouvellistes* at the base of Mettra's news-gathering system. He insisted that he had no use for Mettra's "*gazette à la main*" because "it contains only false news or filthy anecdotes."[56] What then did he do with this trash? Chénon asked. He passed it on to Pelleport, Brissot explained. Pelleport agreed to serve, for a fee, as Brissot's substitute, continued to receive the manuscript gazette, and sent back news as Mettra's London correspondent. Exactly what Pelleport did with the information supplied by Mettra, Brissot could not say—or so he claimed, although the answer was obvious: Pelleport worked it up in libels.

A libeler in London could not inflict much damage in Paris unless he had a reliable supply of information about misdeeds among the great. The anecdotes did not need to be entirely true, but they had to be true enough to injure someone's reputation. That was the principle proclaimed brazenly by Morande in the preface to *Le Gazetier cuirassé*: in his capacity as a gazetteer, he promised to provide news made up of half-truths. He had his informants in Versailles, but he would not serve their reports up raw. By adding spice and ingredients of his own concoction, he would challenge his reader to sift through the anecdotes in order to extract the grain of accurate information at their heart. Morande used "nouvelles" and "anecdotes" as synonyms, as did everyone else in the world of journalists and libelers, although the Londoners sometimes favored the other equivalent term, "paragraph." Morande's libels consisted of nothing more than short anecdotes piled on top of one another like the paragraphs in a London newspaper. This mode of presentation also corresponded to the French genre of the *chronique scandaleuse*. But it did not suit longer libels, which strung out stories that could run to several volumes. In order to see how a kernel of news could grow into a full-sized libel, one can study a final source, *Les Petits Soupers et les nuits de l'Hôtel Bouillon*, the libel that touched off the furious negotiations during Pelleport's attempt to extort blackmail from Receveur in 1783.

The subtitle of the book pointed clearly to its origin: *Letter from Lord Count ****** to Lord ****** about the recreations of M. de C-stri-s, or the dance of the bear; a singular anecdote about a coachman who hanged himself in the Hôtel Bouillon on December 31, 1778 on the occasion of the dance of the bear.*[57] The anecdote in question probably came from a manuscript gazette, either Mettra's or another. It amounted to little in itself—a report of a suicide that could be compressed into a single sentence. But Pelleport blew it up into a ninety-three-page book, using the strange reference to the dance of the bear as a come-on to whet the reader's curiosity. The suicide story merely served as a hook on which to hang a long, rambling exposé of the private life of the princesse de Bouillon. Pelleport recounted it in the manner of a scandalous English tête-à-tête, tipping off the reader about who was sleeping with whom in the fashionable society of Paris.

He set the story in the Paris opera. A visiting English count is admiring the beau monde from a seat in a box before the curtain rises. Curious about the customs of the natives on parade below him, he asks his neighbor to identify them. The neighbor turns out to be a worldly Parisian who knows everything about the secret lives of the great, especially those in the entourage of the princesse de Bouillon. The conversation therefore turns into a *chronique scandaleuse*, exactly as in *La Gazette noire par un homme qui n'est pas blanc*, a sequel to *Le Gazetier cuirassé*, which included a dialogue between an English "milord" and a Parisian sophisticate on the subject of Parisian prostitutes.[58] In the case of *Les Petits Soupers et les nuits de l'Hôtel Bouillon*, the dialogue is reported in a letter written by the count to an English lord: hence the long subtitle. An epistolary form superimposed on a dialogue made for complications, but Pelleport seemed to luxuriate in the rococo complexities of his narrative. He filled it with hints and half-explained allusions, appropriate to the operatic setting. By presenting Parisian scandal as it struck the eye of an English observer, he made the most of the perspective from across the Channel and at the same time drew on a genre of antigovernment pamphleteering represented by a popular libel against the Maupeou ministry, *L'Espion anglais, ou lettre de milord All'Ear à milord All'Eye*. While combining genres in this manner, Pelleport cast the reader in the role of an eavesdropper, as if he (more likely he than she) were seated behind the two sophisticates and could understand their talk as one of their kind. Presumably flattered to be included in such company, the reader had to provide his own gloss on the text, fill in the blanks of the names, and puzzle out the general drift of the story.

The game revealed in the narrative turned out to be deeply decadent, but Pelleport presented it without a hint of moralizing. On the contrary, he recounted all the perversions of the human comedy in the setting of the opera as if they were simply facts of life in high society. After inquiring about the identity of the elegant lady in the loge across from him, the English count is treated to a verbal portrait of the princesse de Bouillon. Old and ugly underneath her makeup, she suffered from a voracious and inexhaustible sexual appetite. As a girl in her father's rustic German duchy, she had taken up with the only lover available, the palace gardener, and had given birth to an illegitimate child. She came to France to wed the prince de Bouillon, but, like his father, he was impotent and therefore depended on cuckoldry to perpetuate the line. The princess complied with one lover after another: the prince de Guéménée, who used her to win the office of royal chamberlain and an apartment in Versailles; the duc de Chartres, who proved too cheap to return her favors with a decent tribute in jewelry; the marquis de Castries, who bought his way to her bed by draining his budget as minister of the navy; and among many others, her favorite, a dubious chevalier known as Jardinié, whose main quality was prowess in bed.

While recounting the princess's love life, the Parisian informant sketched the perversities of everyone in her circle and arrived at last at the orgies involving the dance of the bear and the private suppers (*petits soupers*). After evenings in the opera, he explained, the princess regularly invited a coterie of aristocrats to dine in her Parisian residence, the Hôtel Bouillon. While swilling wine and working up an appetite for sex, they enjoyed a floor show: a hairy monk copulated, standing up, with the princess's aged chambermaid. That was the dance of the bear. Unfortunately, one of the princess's coachmen, who was also carrying on an affair with the chambermaid, discovered her cavorting with the monk, flew into a rage, drove the monk into the street with his whip, and raised such a ruckus that he woke up the whole neighborhood and finished off the night in the custody of the police. Furious that the coachman's recklessness could expose her orgies to all of Paris, the princess threatened to have him shut up forever in the hideous prison of Bicêtre. He could not bear to suffer such a punishment and therefore hanged himself, using his whip as a noose. That was the item of news that served as the base of the book.

Far from expressing any sympathy for the unhappy coachman, Pelleport recounted his death in a tone of cynical amusement.[59] He then produced further accounts of the orgies, which escalated from bawdiness to obscenity, similar in style to some scenes in *Les Bohémiens*. The pornography conveyed a political message, because Pelleport emphasized that the sex was subsidized by the ministry of the navy. To make the implications clear, he noted at the end of the book that the recent defeat of the French fleet at the Battle of the Saints on April 12, 1782, which cost the French twenty million livres in lost ships, could be attributed to Castries's misconduct as naval minister.[60] Along the way Pelleport took swipes at other political figures, including Miromesnil, the Keeper of the Seals, and Lenoir, the lieutenant general of police. And he topped off the attacks on the ministers with a passage that compared the prince and princess of Bouillon to Louis XVI and Marie-Antoinette. Both couples illustrated the same theme: an impotent and incompetent husband dominated by an irresponsible and sex-starved wife.[61]

As French libels went, *Les Petits Soupers et les nuits de l'Hôtel Bouillon* was particularly nasty, but it was no worse than the standard fare in London. Public life in Britain was saturated with libels. As Lord North remarked, "The first thing we lay our hands on in the morning is a libel; the last thing we lay out of our hands in the evening is a libel. Our eyes open upon libels; our eyes close upon libels. In short, libels, lampoons and satires constitute all the writing, printing and reading of our time."[62] This open, hard-hitting, and journalistic style of slander was foreign to the French. It could not be assimilated by French readers until it was translated into an idiom that they could understand. The French expatriates in London had all the necessary qualities, both linguistic and cultural, to function as the translators. They had learned to turn out topical pamphlets, *libelles*, and *nouvelles à la main* in France; and once they crossed the Channel, they mastered the English varieties of journalism. By emigrating from one Grub Street world to another, they emerged as the middlemen who could mediate between similar but separate cultures.

It would be too simple, however, to reduce the cross-Channel traffic in libels to the handful of Frenchmen connected with the *Courrier de l'Europe*. Hack writers and ideological émigrés had moved back and forth between

France and England for generations, if not centuries. Perhaps the first emissary of the new London journalism was John Wilkes himself, who fled from the persecution provoked by his *North Briton* in 1764 and spent two years enjoying the fleshpots of Paris, where he had many friends, including the baron d'Holbach, his schoolmate from the University of Leyden. By 1771, when Morande published *Le Gazetier cuirassé*, French ears had already been tuned to English scandalmongering, at least among the Parisian elite. Pelleport and the other libelers of the 1780s broke open a market that had been breached many years earlier.

Moreover, the cultural distance between Paris and London should not be exaggerated. Some London newspapers were as sober as the *Journal de Paris*, and, as mentioned, the English notion of the paragraph hardly differed from the French concept of the anecdote. French *nouvellistes* can be considered as the equivalent of English paragraph men, and French *chroniques scandaleuses* consisted of short items strung together in the same manner as the paragraphs in the *Morning Chronicle* or *Town and Country*. News itself is a cultural construct, which varies from place to place and time to time, as anyone can see by studying newspapers—the design of their pages, the rhetoric of their articles, the stylization involved in their everyday efforts to convey events in words. Moreover, the history of news cannot be restricted to newspapers, because information about current events and public affairs has always spread through many media—and still is today, as illustrated by the proliferation of blogs. When Aretino pasted handwritten sonnets on the bust of Pasquino in 1522, he was publishing news—a certain kind of news, the kind that consisted of scandal about public figures and that fascinated reading publics everywhere in early modern Europe. What then was distinctive about the scandalous news that arrived in France from England during the second half of the eighteenth century?

Not the scandal in itself. French readers had long been able to find some reports about the misbehavior of the great in *nouvelles à la main*. But they suffered from what was known at the time as "nouvellomanie," a ravenous appetite for news. They could not satisfy it from the censored press, and what little was available from the underground only stimulated their desire for more. In London, however, scandal was flogged openly in the streets. It was a vital ingredient of a news culture that had developed beyond anything imaginable in Paris. Nothing, therefore, was better suited to light up Parisian imaginations than the French libels that arrived from London. They did not differ completely from the older variety of indigenous French libels, but they had a fresh, provocative, journalistic quality that made them especially appealing.

It seems valid to conclude that by the 1780s the libels available in France had developed into a vast body of literature spanning many different genres. Despite their differences, they shared certain characteristics. Whether compressed into short paragraphs or stretched out as voluminous histories, they featured anecdotes, portraits, and news. For purposes of analysis, these three ingredients can be separated, but in actual texts, they merged into each other. An anecdote often took the form of a portrait, which in turn communicated news. The reason for concentrating on a few key features of libels in general is not to reduce them to a single formula but to understand what they had in common. Having characterized them in a general way, it should now be possible to see how they evolved from the slander that flourished under the Ancien Régime to the deadlier kind of character assassination that marked the politics of the Revolution.

PART IV

The Literature of Libel

Private Lives

Chapter 25
Revolutionary Metamorphoses

The French Revolution transformed the world of ordinary French men and women. It reordered space and time, overturned religion, abolished privilege, made all men equal before the law, reorganized family life, created new systems of law and finance, forged a nation out of a jumble of antiquated institutions, replaced the monarch with the people as the source of legitimate authority, and waged war against its enemies everywhere in Europe. The revolutionaries remade their world so thoroughly that by the end of 1789 they looked back on the order they had destroyed only a few months earlier as if it belonged to another era, what they called the "Ancien Régime." Yet no society can wipe out all traces of its earlier existence. Revolutions absorb ingredients that remain from old regimes. No matter how violent and utopian their character, they include elements of continuity embedded in the fabric of institutions and buried in collective consciousness. The simultaneous operation of change and continuity is difficult to follow, because it can be inconspicuous and take many forms. But the close study of one form—in this case, a literary genre—can convey something of the way the French made a new world out of old material.

The genre in question is a particular kind of libel, a slanderous biography, which usually proclaimed its character by a title that began with *The Private Life of . . .* or *The Secret Life of . . .* followed by the name of its victim. A favorite victim in the 1780s and 1790s was the duc de Chartres, who became duc d'Orléans in 1785 and Philippe Egalité in 1792. While his public self changed, the inner man remained the same—that was the most obvious message of five libels: four that attacked Orléans (as I usually will call him for reasons of convenience) in 1784, 1789, 1793, and the Year II (1793–94 in the new revolutionary calendar), and one that defended him in 1790. But the libels reveal a great deal more than variations on a single, slanderous theme. They show how authors adapted rhetorical devices to political circumstances, how they aimed their texts at different kinds of readers, and how libels belonged to the general process of redrawing the line that separated the private from the public sphere during the revolutionary era. Of course, the problems of assessing continuity in change cannot be resolved by studying five texts. After using them as a point of entry into the larger subject, it will be necessary to take a longer view, going back to the seventeenth century, and then to look at some of the most important "private lives" that led from the Ancien Régime into the heart of the Revolution.

Vie privée ou apologie de Très-Sérénissime Prince Monseigneur le duc de Chartres (1784) has all the characteristics of French libels at the peak of their development before the Revolution. It consists of a string of anecdotes interspersed with snatches of songs, epigrams, and pasquinades served up in the manner of a *chronique scandaleuse*. It includes some pornographic episodes worthy of Aretino, whom it explicitly invokes along with the usual disclaimers: the anonymous libeler, adopting the pose of an historian, pretends to reveal such shocking scenes with regret and only because of his duty to promote virtue by exposing vice. Taken together, the parts of the book make up a portrait of one of France's best-known public figures, a prince that the public loved to hate. But hatred is too strong a term. Orléans, or Chartres as he was then known, was a subject of gossip, scandal, derision, and amusement. His misbehavior gave the public a great deal of pleasure. The libel therefore has a light side. It is full of humorous touches, not only from its pervading tone of irony but also by means of jokes and puns.[1] It plays with the reader, beginning with its title page, which is obviously facetious:

PRIVATE LIFE
OR VINDICATION
OF THE MOST SERENE PRINCE
MONSEIGNEUR
THE DUKE
OF CHARTRES,
Against a defamatory libel written in seventeen
hundred and eighty-one; but which did not
appear owing to the threats that we made
to the author to expose him.

By a Society of Friends of the Prince:

OUR LIPS HAVE NEVER BETRAYED THE TRUTH

AT A HUNDRED LEAGUES FROM THE Bastille

M. DCC. LXXXIV.

The long, elaborate phrasing, set off with italics and imposing, uppercase letters of different sizes, brings out the burlesque character of the whole work, which is confirmed by the false address at the bottom, "at a hundred leagues from the Bastille"—the same, provocative address used in *Le Gazetier cuirassé* and other works by the London libelers.

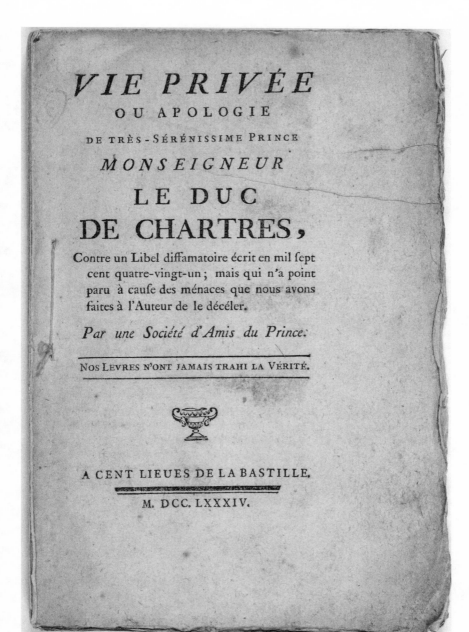

VIE PRIVÉE

OU APOLOGIE

DE TRÈS-SÉRÉNISSIME PRINCE

MONSEIGNEUR

LE DUC

DE CHARTRES,

Contre un Libel diffamatoire écrit en mil sept
cent quatre-vingt-un ; mais qui n'a point
paru à cause des ménaces que nous avons
faites à l'Auteur de le décéler.

Par une Société d'Amis du Prince.

NOS LEVRES N'ONT JAMAIS TRAHI LA VÉRITÉ.

A CENT LIEUES DE LA BASTILLE.

M. DCC. LXXXIV.

Figure 42. Title page of the first of the libels against the duc de Chartres, later duc
d'Orléans and Philippe Egalité. (Private copy)

More facetious front matter follows. A mock dedication sets the tone that prevails throughout the book: a group of friends of the prince, it reveals, has rallied round him to defend his reputation against some infamous allegations—and if the story happens to interest the public, so much the better. A burlesque preliminary discourse provides further hints about the wicked things that are to follow, and the first page of the main text makes clear that it will refute in glorious detail everything that has been said against the duke. The antilibelous libeler goes on to rebut the calumnies so unconvincingly that he confirms the worst of them, winking at the reader knowingly as if to say, "I hope you are enjoying the show."

As in the *Vie privée de Louis XV* and most other libels, the text has no chapters or typographic breaks. Its basic unit is the anecdote, although some of the episodes extend over several paragraphs. Each anecdote is an autonomous story, inserted in the text like an item in an underground newsletter. The narrative jumps from one anecdote to another and strings them out in chronological order for 101 pages. The main episodes can be summarized as follows:

Birth. Orléans père was too occupied with his own concubines to procreate any legitimate offspring. The boy's mother, who could not satisfy her overheated lubricity even with the oversized member of her main lover, the comte de P . . . [Polignac], probably conceived him with one of her coachmen named Lefranc.

Education. The young duke (called duc de Chartres until he inherited his father's title as duc d'Orléans in 1785) learned nothing, except obscenities derived from Aretino and the dirty talk of his mother and the bawds surrounding her.

Early Sexual Experience. Mlle Deschamps, a particularly depraved whore favored by the duke's father, initiated the boy into the bad habits that he soon pursued in every brothel of Paris.

Marriage. Chartres wanted to marry the princesse de Lamballe in order to get his hands on the riches she would inherit from her father, the duc de Penthièvre, and to claim her father's office of Grand-Amiral de France. But her brother, the prince de Lamballe, stood in the way. So Chartres made the prince his companion in debauchery, which led to the young man's death from venereal disease.

Landlord of the Palais-Royal. While continuing to blaze a trail through brothels, Chartres gave way to another base appetite: avarice. In order to increase his already enormous income, he reduced the size of the garden in the Palais-Royal and lined it with shops, which he rented out at excessive prices. All Paris protested with songs and pasquinades about such demeaning conduct for a prince of the royal blood.

The Battle of Ouessant. Although he knew nothing of seamanship, Chartres was determined to be named Grand-Amiral and to win military glory in the war against England. He took command of a warship, which he loaded with wine and the finest delicacies. On July 23, 1778, when the French prepared to do battle with the British off Ouessant on the coast of Brittany, he insisted on commanding his own vessel and then fouled things up so badly that he spoiled the formation of the French fleet. As soon as the British cannons began to sound, he fled in terror below deck. A seasoned officer took over command, while another vessel intervened to take the British fire. The battle was inconclusive, and Chartres won a reputation for cowardice, which was spread far and wide by Parisian wits. Their main theme: the only battlefield in which the prince could hold his own was at the Opera.

Horse Racing and Gambling. Chartres did, however, manage to beat the British at one of their own games, horse racing. He imported the best stallions and jockeys from England and gained a fortune by winning bets, helped by tricks perfected in Perfidious Albion. He also turned the Palais-Royal into a gambling den, where he made still more money, thanks to techniques of cheating taught to him by the slickest card sharks in Paris.

The Mardi Gras of 1778. An argument broke out among the members of the royal family who attended a masked ball at the Opera to celebrate Mardi Gras in 1778. The comte d'Artois, Louis XVI's younger brother, in a drunken fit called Chartres's sister, the duchesse de Bourbon, a whore. Furious, she pulled off his mask. He then smashed her mask and a general tumult broke out, which led to demands for satisfaction on both sides. The duchess expected Chartres to defend her honor in a duel, all the more so as she had recently nursed him back to health after a serious illness. But, a coward to the end, he did nothing.

The Grand Tour. On an English-style grand tour of Italy, Chartres sampled the charms of a famous prostitute in Modena. After a night of wining, dining, and copulating, he tried to sneak off without paying. But before he could escape, the bawd clapped her hands, four thugs appeared, and in fear of a drubbing, Chartres surrendered his purse.

The Diamond Shoe Buckles. At a weak moment when the desire for ostentation overcame his avarice, Chartres commissioned a jeweler to make him a pair of diamond shoe buckles for 34,000 livres. When the jeweler delivered them, he refused to pay, pretending dissatisfaction with their design. Faced with disaster, the jeweler finally agreed to sell the shoe buckles at a loss for 18,000 livres. When Chartres appeared with them in public, a foreign ambassador complimented him on their beauty. Chartres replied that he had tired of the shoe buckles and would part with them for 24,000 livres. The ambassador gladly paid that sum. Then, needing to have the buckles adjusted to fit his own shoes, he took them to the jeweler, who remarked that he had lost so much from the original sale that he wished he had never made them. When the ambassador discovered that Chartres had paid only 18,000 livres, he assured the jeweler that the duke would make up the difference, for a prince of the royal blood would not take advantage of a tradesman. But Chartres refused, asserting that in business a deal was a deal.

The book ends on that note. It has no political message. It merely buries Chartres in ignominy; and whenever it refers to Louis XVI or his ministers, it covers them with praise. In some final remarks, which read like a postscript, the author identified himself as "Mr. Scribler [*sic*]," a member of a group of Londoners who met regularly to discuss public affairs. Thanks to the extraordinary attributes of the three other members, "Mr. Longéars [*sic*]," "Mr. Longsight," and "Mr. Understanding," they received accurate information about all current events. Those names, as many readers would recognize, evoked two of the favorite characters from the pamphlets against the Maupeou ministry in 1771–74, Milord All'eye and Milord All'ear.[2] Mr. Scribler went on to explain that Mr. Longéars had recently died (an allusion to Pelleport's disappearance in the Bastille?). But at a meeting of the three survivors, he had addressed his colleagues from the other world, promising to continue to provide them with bulletins of news—that is with reports about "everything of greatest interest and curiosity that is said and done in the palaces, the royal households, the cabinets, the boudoirs and the alcoves of the court, of the capitol, and of all Europe; in a word, in the most secret and most inaccessible places" (101). In return for this *chronique scandaleuse*, Longéars asked that the members of the group produce a defense of Chartres, which would serve as a deterrent to the infamous libeler who planned to publish an attack on him. The reader could therefore look forward to sequels of the present work, which clearly belonged to the current of scandalous journalism that had flooded the French book market during the previous two decades.

A note in English on the very last page announced that this book could be purchased at the shop of "J. Hodges on London Bridge and W. Reeves, London," as well as at other bookshops in "the greatest cities and towns in Europe" along with three other works: *Le Diable dans un bénitier*, *La Gazette noire*, and *Les Contes couleur de rose*. These references indicated that the *Vie privée ou apologie de Très-Sérénissime Prince Monseigneur le duc de Chartres* was produced within the circle of London libelers who had been attacking public figures in France since the publication of *Le Gazetier cuirassé* in 1771. Its ostensible place of publication—"at a hundred leagues from the Bastille"—identified it with their works, and the reference to "Mr. Scribler" evoked the Grub Street existence of the French expatriates. It might even have been written by Morande, who had become a secret agent of the French government in 1783. By that time, leading members of the French court, especially the king and queen, had developed such an antipathy to Chartres that they may have commissioned Morande to ruin his reputation in the eyes of the public.[3]

One can only speculate about what gave rise to the first of the libels against Orléans. The purpose of the second one, *Vie de Louis-Philippe-Joseph, duc d'Orléans* (1789),[4] is easier to identify. By the time of its publication, Louis-Philippe-Joseph had inherited his father's title of duc d'Orléans and had fomented opposition to the government both in the Parlement of Paris and in the streets of the capital. When the Estates General met in May 1789, he took a seat among the radicals of the nobility. He then favored the cause of the Third Estate and supported all the revolutionary measures with such audacity that many suspected him of plotting to replace Louis XVI either as regent or as king in his own right. The suspicion of an Orléanist plot reached its peak during the uprising of October 5–6, 1789, when a crowd of market women followed by Lafayette and the National Guard marched on Versailles and brought the royal family back to Paris, where it remained as a virtual prisoner in the Palace of the Tuileries. Although no solid evidence linked Orléans to a conspiracy against the crown, the widespread belief that he had engineered the march on Versailles made him think it prudent to accept a mission to London, where he remained until July 1790. The *Vie de Louis-Philippe-Joseph, duc d'Orléans* was written sometime soon after the October Days, the second in the series of violent "journées," which began on July 14 and continued to propel the Revolution to the left until 1795.

The violence was provided by the common people—artisans and shopkeepers reinforced by professional men, especially lawyers—mobilized in the sixty Parisian Districts where the elections to the Estates General had taken place. By mid-October 1789 they had become fiercely suspicious not only of the court but also of the National Assembly, which had followed the king to Paris. The more conservative leaders of the Revolution—especially Bailly as mayor of Paris, Lafayette as head of the National Guard, and Mirabeau as the most conspicuous orator of the National Assembly—tried to contain popular violence. They made provisions for martial law and excluded the poor from the battalions of the National Guard that patrolled the streets to maintain order. Calm did in fact return in 1790, owing primarily to a decline in the price of bread after abundant harvests. High bread prices often triggered rioting when they rose beyond the purchasing power of ordinary consumers, as they had done just before the "journées" of July 14 and October 5–6, 1789. But the Districts remained a threat. They developed neighborhood assemblies and executive committees, where local militants, the future sans-culottes, whipped up hostility to politicians operating at the level of the National Assembly and the municipality of Paris. Always eager to detect conspiracies, the District radicals specialized in denunciations. They took Bailly, Lafayette, and Mirabeau, along with Louis XVI and Marie-Antoinette, as their main targets after October 1789. The *Vie de Louis-Philippe-Joseph, duc d'Orléans* echoed their sentiments. It was essentially a political pamphlet.

Yet it was also a "private life." The first half of its ninety-four-page text recounted the biography of Orléans before the Revolution. It contained nearly all the anecdotes that had appeared in the libel of 1784: Orléans's illegitimate birth, his neglected education, early debauchery, mistreatment of his wife, complicity in the death of the prince de Lamballe, horse racing, gambling, cowardice at Ouessant, and speculation on the redesigned gardens of the Palais-Royal. But it did not follow the earlier libel closely. It modified details and touched them up: thus young Chartres is instructed in sex by a particularly loathsome whore named Montigny rather than the upmarket Mlle Deschamps; Lamballe dies from castration during a desperate operation to save him from syphilis; and venereal disease appears everywhere as a symptom of the moral rot that permeates the aristocracy—and Orléans in particular: "It will be no surprise to learn that by leading the most disorderly and scandalous life, Monseigneur felt his bones calcinated, burned, rotted by the fatal poison that he had inhaled from all the whores he had caressed" (27). Instead of narrating the anecdotes as a series of autonomous episodes, it ran them together in a confused manner and suffused them with prolix moralizing. It contained no lascivious descriptions. In contrast to the bawdiness of 1784, it railed against the evils of sex and hurled insults at everyone it denounced. Its favorite epithets for Orléans were "scoundrel" and "monster," terms that appear throughout the book. The anonymous author also emphasized the evil of conspiracies, which he detected everywhere beneath the surface of events. He cast himself as one of the few vigilant patriots who knew how to detect the secret machinations of the Revolution's enemies. In fact, conspiracy was the central theme of Orléans's biography after 1789: "Well-informed and skeptical people have followed the duc d'Orléans in the insidious labyrinthes of his projects, once they picked up the first thread. They have studied his maneuvers, exposed his steps, and discovered the secrets of his conspiracies" (64–65). Far from employing irony or anything that smacked of humor, it adopted a tone of indignation and outrage. It did not make fun of Orléans; it denounced him.

The rhetoric of denunciation would become standard in 1793–94. What makes the *Vie de Louis-Philippe-Joseph, duc d'Orléans* so extraordinary is that it employs a fully developed version of that rhetoric at such an early point in the Revolution. The author complains that after meeting for six months (that is, from early May until late October 1789, the time at which the text was composed), the Estates General or National Assembly has accomplished virtually nothing. Nothing! The seizing of sovereign power, the abolition of feudalism, the Declaration of the Rights of Man and of the Citizen go unmentioned. Instead of acknowledging any of the great breakthroughs of 1789, the author insists on the one measure, the most important of all, as he puts it, which should have been decreed at first but never was enacted: a law to fix the price of bread permanently at 2 sols per pound. If the common people cannot get bread at the proper price, he warns, they will overthrow the aristocrats conspiring against them in the National Assembly and the Parisian Municipality, too: "If Paris runs out of bread this winter, aristocrats, you had better do something to save your skins. Run away, carry off your fortunes, because the people are outraged at all of your false promises and your dark maneuvering. A third revolution will bring satisfaction for your rank duplicity" (89).

This language evoked the old notion of a famine plot used by the king and the court to subjugate the common people, but it also anticipated the denunciations of the "Enragés" ("wild men") and the Hébertistes (followers of Jacques-René Hébert) who would use the bread issue to foment uprisings among the sans-culottes in the most radical phase of the Revolution. The author did not appeal to the poorest elements in Parisian society, which he described as an unreliable "populace" (64).[5] In fact, he aimed his rhetoric at the middling sort ("honnêtes bourgeois") (85). But he located this public among the common people in the Districts, particularly in the District St. Martin, which seemed to be his home base. He wrote, in short, as a radical embedded in the Revolution at its lowest level. The book itself bore traces of its origin. Badly printed on cheap paper, its sheets assembled in gatherings with disparate colors, its text riddled with misspellings and typographical errors, it looks like a rushed job, dashed off with little concern for phrasing or narrative cohesion.

Why should such a book concentrate its fire on the duc d'Orléans? A succession of conspiracies had nearly undone the Revolution from its beginning, it revealed. Orléans had directed all of them, and now he was plotting to seize power and subjugate the common people by his own version of royal despotism. All the Revolution's leaders were corrupt, all of them—Necker, Sieyès, Mousnier, Mirabeau, Bailly, Lafayette, the lot. They had been bought by Orléans. Recently they had held a secret meeting on one of his estates. Sieyès had harangued them—the author printed his text, furnished by a patriotic friend—on the need to depose the king, who would be hustled off to a monastery while Lafayette escorted Orléans to the Hôtel de Ville and Bailly proclaimed him regent. The conspiracy was leaked before it could be executed. But Orléans had other plots up his sleeve. At one point he had even enlisted Marie-Antoinette—"O execrable woman, your crimes, your outrages are more numerous than the minutes of a year!" (40)—to clear a path for him by getting rid of Louis XVI, an "imbecile monarch" whom she had already made impotent by means of secret potions (40). With the collaboration of her incestuous lover, the comte d'Artois, she would kill off all the heirs to the throne and turn it over to Orléans, who had gained control of her by driving her into debt. This plot, "the most horrible, unimaginable conspiracy" (40), had been aborted by the outbreak of the Revolution, but the Revolution itself was now about to succumb to a new succession of intrigues being combined by the most evil and perfidious of its enemies. It could be saved only by the destruction of the one man who stood for everything it abhorred. The author put the issue squarely to his reader: "Will we always be the deplorable victims of the aristocrats?" (92). It was up to the reader, assumed to be a fellow militant in a Parisian District, to answer that question by taking action.

The *Vie de Louis-Philippe-Joseph, duc d'Orléans*, read at a distance of more than two hundred years, may seem too hysterical and incoherent to be taken seriously. But it is easy, from the safety of the present, to underestimate the passions and phantasms that tormented Parisians in 1789. That was a year when events spun out of control, when ordinary people could barely buy their daily bread, when streets surged with rioters, heads were paraded at the ends of pikes, troops threatened to ram home repression with bayonets, and in the remote realm of politics orators harangued each other furiously, filling the air with strange language and passing resolutions to remake the world. Written in an idiom meant to resonate among the "little people" (*menu peuple*) of Paris, the *Vie de Louis-Philippe-Joseph, duc d'Orléans* was one of the first of many attempts to mobilize the popular element in the Revolution and to turn it against the Revolution's leaders. Orléans made a particularly attractive target because he seemed to embody the most noxious aspects of the old aristocracy along with the most suspect elements of the new political elite. He also had plenty of resources to mount a propaganda campaign of his own. The third libel, *Vie secrète de Louise-Marie-Adélaïde de Bourbon Penthièvre, duchesse d'Orléans, avec ses correspondances politiques* (1790), belonged to this counter-offensive. Read against the *Vie de Louis-Philippe-Joseph, duc d'Orléans*, it shows where the Orléanist camp considered itself vulnerable and how it tried to parry the attacks against the duke.

The title, *Vie secrète de Louise-Marie-Adélaïde de Bourbon Penthièvre, duchesse d'Orléans*, suggests that it belonged to the large corpus of "private" and "secret" lives that slandered their subjects. But some of these works were arguments for the defense. By promising to reveal secret material, they led the reader to expect calumny. They then reversed those expectations and tried to win the reader's sympathy by proving that their hero had been maligned. As biographical narratives, they exposed the private person behind the public self only to reveal a "secret" realm of unadulterated virtue. The *Vie secrète* of d'Orléans's wife made the most of this strategy. It presented her as a devoted spouse and mother, so dedicated to domestic virtue, in fact, that she could be considered a "bonne bourgeoise" (47). Her birth, her education, her youth, her happy marriage, her charitable aid to the poor—everything in her biography bore witness to an exemplary private life. Moreover, from the privacy of the family, she supported the patriotic public activities of the duke. Excerpts (clearly fabricated) from their correspondence during the winter of 1789–90 showed her urging him to ever greater dedication to the Revolution, while he replied from London that he hoped to work wonders on the secret mission that he was coordinating with Mirabeau and Necker. The duchess also maintained good relations with the most illustrious patriots of 1789—Mirabeau, Barnave, Lameth, Pétion, le Chapelier. But like a good wife, she remained in the background: "She hoped that by inspiring her husband with feelings that were more humane, more generous for the sensitive and suffering common people, she was doing a good work that would please God. It is owing to this principle of Christian compassion that she shared the views of her spouse and that she encouraged him to secretly foment the revolution that has taken place" (50).

Not that Orléans's patriotism needed any bolstering. The pamphlet—actually a substantial volume of eighty-three pages—devoted as much space to his virtues as to those of his wife. It refuted nearly all the standard charges in the libels against him, anecdote by anecdote. For example, it celebrated the rebuilding of the Palais-Royal as an instance of the duke's mastery of architecture and solid business sense. He made money from it, to be sure, but he used his wealth to relieve the suffering of the poor during the terrible winter of 1788–89—and besides, what was wrong with a member of the royal family doing business? Unlike the comte d'Artois, who lavished his fortune on self-indulgence and luxuries, Orléans was a progressive prince. He had renounced his title and all of his feudal dues. Living from his own enterprises and happy in the bosom of his family, he was a model patriot. In fact, the duke and duchess pictured in the *Vie secrète* already look like models for the "bourgeois monarchy" that their son, Louis Philippe, would install in France in 1830.

The duc d'Orléans of 1790, bourgeois patriot and man of the people, does not remain confined to the domestic sphere. He is a genuine revolutionary—as the pamphlet puts it, "the father of the people and the antagonist of the princes" (vii). By investing him with this title, it called for him to replace Louis XVI. The Revolution had reached such a critical stage, it argued, that Orléans should be named regent. There was no doubt about his patriotism, because he had secretly backed the revolutionary cause from the very beginning. Now he should assume power. By doing so, he would snuff out the intrigues of Marie-Antoinette, who was siphoning off the public treasure for her brother in Vienna and plotting to seize control of the kingdom. Louis XVI was a nullity.

The queen was about to depose him and rule in her own name, despite the provisions of the Salic Law, which excluded women from the throne. Only heroic action by the duke could save the Revolution at this critical juncture.

In fact, the crisis abated in 1790, when bread regained its normal price, the deputies to the National Assembly concentrated on designing a new constitutional order, and the country celebrated its victory over the Ancien Régime in a wave of patriotic sentiment on July 14, 1790, the first commemorative Bastille Day. The *Vie secrète* failed to exploit the prevailing mood, but it took advantage of the growing resentment against Marie-Antoinette. By tapping the libel literature against the queen, it made the duchess look like her antithesis. It defended the Orléanist cause by celebrating a model couple in contrast to the incompetence and depravity personalized by Louis XVI and Marie-Antoinette. The personalization of politics had become a powerful tendency by this time. The *Vie secrète* shows how it operated in revolutionary polemics and how libels were used to combat libels.

As the Revolution moved into its most violent phase, the violence of the polemics increased. *La Vie et les crimes de Philippe duc d'Orléans* (1793), the fourth of the libels concerning Orléans, illustrates this tendency as it prevailed in the propaganda of the counterrevolutionary right. The text probably was printed in Cologne, as its title page indicated, and it certainly was written by a propagandist for the cause of the émigrés—that is, the aristocrats who had fled France after July 14, 1789, and continued to pour into the Rhineland until well after the collapse of the monarchy on August 10, 1792. Many émigrés hated Orléans even more than they hated the Jacobins, because he, a cousin of Louis XVI and a member of the revolutionary Convention, had cast a crucial vote at the trial of the king, which led to Louis's execution on January 21, 1793.

The fourth libel lifted much of its material from the first, but it adopted a moralistic tone similar to that of the second and third, though from a counterrevolutionary point of view. In structure and style, it differed from the libel of 1789 because it gave a clear, chronological account of Orléans's life. The anecdotes, from the duke's illegitimate birth to his humiliation with the prostitute in Modena and the episode of the diamond shoe buckles, followed one another just as they had done in the text of 1784, but the anonymous author recounted them with indignation rather than irony. Like his predecessor from 1789, he heaped abuse on his antihero, noting with regret that the French language contained nothing stronger than the well-worn epithets "scélérat" (scoundrel) and "monstre" (52). When he arrived at the Revolution, he emphasized the political implications to be drawn from the story of Orléans's private life: "We will show him to be a bad citizen, a traitor to his fatherland, to his king, to the nobility of which he was a member. He will be seen rallying to the flag of the revolt, using bribery, even the mask of virtue and of patriotism, to arrive at his goal, and advancing little by little toward the height of crime, where he finally will become the assassin of his relative, of the most virtuous of kings" (36).

Instead of providing a detailed account of Orléans's role in the political history of the Revolution, the author kept to general remarks about his machinations and corruption. He noted that Orléans had staged the October Days and then conspired in various ways to make the constitutional monarchy unworkable. Curiously, he did not make much of Orléans's part in the crisis that nearly destroyed the monarchy in the summer of 1791. Orléans was suspected of trying to become regent in place of Louis XVI during the turmoil touched off by the king's flight to Varennes on June 20, which came to a climax in the massacre of the Champ de Mars on July 17. But the author skipped over those events and hurried to the crisis that finally brought down the monarchy in 1792. Even then, he did not pay attention to the political intrigues that led to the uprising of August 10, the elections to the Convention, and the September Massacres. He merely indicated that Orléans had a hand in all those disasters, which illustrated the moral of the entire book: private vice led to public calamity. Orléans's vote for the execution of the king was therefore the culmination of a life of crime and an act that precipitated the supreme tragedy for the entire realm. Readers could take consolation from the knowledge that Orléans would soon be punished. He was currently in prison in Marseilles, certain to be assassinated or guillotined. Whatever Orléans's end might be, the author had completed his task: "to bring before the French, in all the blackness of his moral being, the assassin of their king" (100).

Frenchmen, fellow citizens, my brothers, may this tableau arouse in you the most active horror, may it stir up all the faculties of your soul and of your mind. I considered myself duty bound to present him to you, to you the faithful subjects of the most virtuous of kings, in order to increase your aversion to vice and your love for your sovereigns; to you, illustrious *émigrés*, in order to exalt your bravery even more, if that is possible. (100)

There was no doubting the ideology that bound the author to his readers. He invoked the doctrines of the Catholic Church and condemned "modern philosophism" (91) in contrast to the author of the 1789 libel, who appealed to "the divine Jean-Jacques."[6] Yet the two writers shared some of the same ground. Both neglected the close study of revolutionary politics, because they treated events as the product of personalities. For both of them, the "secret life" of the Revolution's leaders ultimately determined its entire course. To produce a portrait of the supreme villain of the Revolution was therefore to expose its inner dynamic, even though they wrote from opposing camps and sought to promote opposite outcomes.

The last of the libels dogged Orléans to his death. In fact, *Vie de L.-P.-J. Capet, ci-devant duc d'Orléans, ou Mémoires pour servir à l'histoire de la Révolution française* (An II) pursued him beyond the grave. A frontispiece opposite the title page noted that he had been guillotined on 17 Brumaire Year II (November 6, 1793), and its caption served as a negative epitaph: "Unfaithful to tyrants and traitor to his fatherland." The text derived heavily from the original libel of 1784. Three-quarters of it repeated the same anecdotes, slightly rearranged and with a few different details (for example, the price of the diamond shoe buckles was inflated to 600,000 livres, and Orléans's avarice was exposed after one diamond had come loose at a ball). When he arrived at the Revolution, the anonymous author foreswore a narrative of events and contented himself with drawing a moral about their outcome: the forces of good and evil had done battle right up to the time of Orléans's death, and now, thanks to the courage of the sans-culottes and the vigilance of the Revolution's leaders, good had triumphed. The Manichaeism at work in the process of history could be seen most clearly from the character of the players: on the one hand, Orléans and his like, "all cheats, sycophants, misers, without genius, without courage"; on the other, "men of genius, genuine, *philosophes*, true children of liberty, who with powerful arms and virile eloquence overthrew the throne, destroyed superstition, and allowed only one altar to remain, that of reason" (55).

The moralizing meant that all salacious detail had to be eliminated from the anecdotes: "Reader, do not expect me to soil this work with the description of the infamous orgies of that man who breathed out perversion from all his pores" (17). The author dealt in epithets, not descriptions—unlike Manuel, who had treated his reader to vivid accounts of immorality under the Ancien Régime. In fact, Manuel was denounced as the co-conspirator of Orléans who had invented the name "Philip Equality" for him as a mask to hide his corrupt and aristocratic character (46). The author went on to congratulate the revolutionary authorities for clamping down on prostitution and limiting luxury. By ridding itself of powdered and bewigged aristocrats, France had strengthened its moral fiber. Moreover, nothing could be more attractive than a village lass with a flower in her hair and a fresh-faced, "vigorous sans-culotte" (32). The author discussed these subjects with his readers in a straightforward, man-to-man manner (his tone seemed to exclude women-of-the-people), as if they understood each other as fellow sans-culottes: "You shudder, honest and virtuous sans-culottes. I must recount to you still more crimes" (19). The intended audience was obvious, but why did the author go to such lengths to condemn a villain who could no longer be a threat? He made his intentions clear in a preface: "Citizen of France, my brother, my comrade, take this and read. You will love even more the happy government procured for you by a propitious fate and the vigor of your arms" (vi). The libel was an attempt to shore up support for the government among the popular forces that had catapulted it into power. It was Robespierrist propaganda, and the Robespierrists resorted to it because they could not be confident of their grip on power.

At every crucial point in its course, the Revolution had lurched leftward by means of insurrections. On July 14, 1789, October 5–6, 1789, August 10, 1792, and May 31–June 2, 1793, the artisans and workers of Paris had provided the violence that made political deadlocks come unstuck. As they saw it, therefore, the "little people" (*le menu peuple, les petites gens*, generally called sans-culottes by mid-1792) were constantly being exploited by the "big" (*les grands, les gros*, those in power, who tended to be known as aristocrats, whatever their birth). By the autumn of 1793, they had learned to be wary of political leaders who used popular violence for their own ends without delivering on promises to satisfy popular demands. The sans-culottes from the forty-eight Parisian Sections, which had replaced the electoral Districts of 1789, overthrew the monarchy by a bloody street battle on August 10, 1792. Their intervention opened the way for a caretaker, "Brissotin" ministry to govern while elections were held for a Convention that would create a new republican order. But once installed in the Convention, the "Brissotin" or "Girondin" politicians did nothing to satisfy the sans-culottes' demands for price controls, energetic measures to win the war, and the repression of suspected counterrevolutionaries. In fact, as conditions deteriorated on every front, the Girondins openly attacked the Sections. The sans-culottes responded on May 31–June 2 by invading the Convention and purging it of the Girondin leaders. But what would guarantee that the Montagnards (Jacobin radicals) who replaced them would be more faithful to the sans-culottes' program?

Throughout the summer of 1793, prices continued to soar and the invading armies threatened once again to descend on the capital, while Girondin sympathizers revolted in the largest provincial cities and the Vendée dissolved in civil war. A Committee of Public Safety composed of the leading Montagnards including Robespierre proved no more effective than the Girondin ministers at mastering the situation. Meanwhile, a new group of radicals, the Hébertistes, whipped up passions in the Sections, demanding a fixed price for bread and summary execution of counterrevolutionaries. Sans-culotte militants stormed the Convention on September 4–5, another potential insurrection, which looked for a while like a replay of May 31–June 2. But the Montagnards managed to placate the sans-culottes by co-opting their leaders and promising vigorous measures to enact their program. The Convention decreed one emergency measure after another: a draconian Law of Suspects (September 17), a General Maximum on prices (September 29), and the centralization of power in the Committee of Public Safety (October 10, followed by more detailed legislation on December 4).

In retrospect, the establishment of the Terror under the dictatorship of the Committee of Public Safety looks like a coherent, premeditated policy. At the time, however, it was improvised in response to shifting circumstances. No one knew whether it would hold together or where it would lead. For several weeks, the Revolutionary Tribunal seemed hesitant to dispatch the prisoners identified most openly with the counterrevolution. Marie-Antoinette and the Girondin leaders were not guillotined until October, and Orléans, who had been arrested on April 5, did not mount the scaffold until November 6. Throughout this period, Robespierre and the eleven other members of the Committee of Public Safety remained apprehensive about being swept from power by new waves of popular violence. The Sections had their own battalions as well as political organizations. Sovereignty as they understood it inhered in them—that is, in the common people, gathered in neighborhood assemblies where they expressed their will directly; it did not belong to the politicians who claimed to speak for the people while striking poses and speechifying on the national stage. By the summer of 1794, the Committee of Public Safety would dismantle the Sections and absorb their leaders into the army and the revolutionary bureaucracy. But at the end of 1793, it was still struggling to keep their support, a matter not only of enacting their program but also of winning them over through propaganda.

The *Vie de L.-P.-J. Capet, ci-devant duc d'Orléans* belonged to this propaganda offensive. It announced on its title page that it had been printed "in Franklin's printing shop, rue de Cléry no. 75." Three other libels that appeared at about the same time bore the same address: *Vie secrète de Pierre Manuel*, *Vie secrète et politique de Brissot*, and *Vie privée et politique de J.-R. Hébert*. Another edition of the *Vie privée* of Hébert carried an additional subtitle: "To serve as a sequel to the Lives of Manuel, Pétion, Brissot et Orléans." And a libel against two other victims of the Terror, *Vie privée de l'ex-Capucin François Chabot et de Gaspard Chaumette*, also claimed to be printed in the rue de Cléry, though at no. 15, not 75. I have not been able to identify the printers who operated at those addresses, but Benjamin Franklin was celebrated as a printer and man-of-the-people by the French revolutionaries at the height of the Terror, so it is not surprising that his name should have been used to legitimate pamphlets intended to defend the Committee of Public Safety by attacking its enemies.

The line of attack followed the party line of the Robespierrists. A postscript at the end of *Vie de L.-P.-J. Capet, ci-devant duc d'Orléans* noted that Robespierre had revealed Orléans's most hideous conspiracy in a recent speech to the Convention: the former duke had plotted to take over the throne in order to surrender it to the Duke of York. This information contradicted a passage in the *Vie de L.-P.-J. Capet, ci-devant duc d'Orléans* that claimed that Orléans had alienated the members of the royal family in England by his loathsome and cowardly behavior during visits to London. However, the Incorruptible had spoken, so the pamphleteer retreated: "It is very natural that the information available to citizen Robespierre should be better than mine, but this cowardice is quite extraordinary, although in conformity with Philip's character" (56). At every point, the pamphlet defended the revolutionary government: "The current regime is a masterpiece of the human spirit" (viii). In fact, it seemed to protest too much, as if compelled to assert the justice of the men behind the Terror. To be sure, it explained to the reader, the "grands" who had dominated previous governments had always been corrupt. They were a distillation of all the worst vices: "lowness, cruelty, debauchery, infamy, and cowardice" (vii). But the present government was based on virtue. Thanks to the vigorous action by the sans-culottes and the unerring vigilance of the Jacobin Club, it had inaugurated a new era in the history of mankind: "Oh, my fellow man who reads this history, think how humanity was debased! Call down blessings on our happy revolution and do not be amazed that noblemen and *grands* should still exist on earth. No, no, the time is not far away when all these chimerical grandeurs will disappear, when all peoples will imitate the august French nation and will respect only liberty and reason" (38–39).

The duke had come a long way. Having provided agreeable scandal to sophisticated readers under the Ancien Régime, he had fueled moral indignation in all camps throughout the early stages of the Revolution; and from beyond the grave he supplied the Robespierrists with the material they needed to assert their authority before the sans-culottes. Although the subject matter remained the same, its meaning kept changing. And whatever it meant, it did not bear out that overused French proverb, "Plus ça change, et plus c'est la même chose."

Chapter 26
Sex and Politics

Sex in high places has always existed. Public personages have private lives. They also have sex lives, which they usually try to keep private. When their sex life leaks into the public, it can become a political problem—but not necessarily, for in some societies a ruler can make use of his virility to impress his subjects or even, if they have an appropriate belief system, to make their crops grow. Owing to the diversity of beliefs, values, and ways of organizing power, the interplay of sex and politics has varied endlessly throughout history. But it has always expressed the assumptions that made it thinkable—and, in particular, an underlying sense of how public life and private life impinge on each other.

The demarcation of public and private spheres under the Ancien Régime in France took place primarily through institutions connected with the king, such as the court, the church, the judiciary, and the police.[1] It made itself known through ceremonies, royal self-display, architecture, music, images, and all the modes of diffusing information. Libels were a minor element in this carefully laid-out cultural topography, but they were important because they disturbed it. They exposed the king's private life before his subjects, dragged court affairs into public view, and treated the public as though it were a participant in the arcane affairs of government, if only as a witness. Not that libels always upset the political players, for the system could absorb a good deal of turbulence. Times varied, and so did the power of calumny. Libels could be shocking, ribald, funny, trivial, sacrilegious, or seditious, but they always bore the mark of their surrounding culture. They appealed to current values and prejudices, drew on familiar rhetorical conventions, put together stories according to standard models, and used language in ways that made sense to their readers. If read for their underlying assumptions, they can reveal a great deal about the world in which they were written. Instead of being dismissed as trash, therefore, libels deserve serious study. They proliferated most extensively under Louis XV and Louis XVI, but at the height of their development, from 1770 to 1790, they continued to use motifs that went back to the sixteenth and seventeenth centuries.

The most famous sexual libel from the era of Louis XIV—and probably the most widely read—was *Histoire amoureuse des Gaules* by Roger de Rabutin, comte de Bussy. Its publishing history illustrates the hazards of making the private public at a time of royal absolutism. Bussy-Rabutin (usually referred to simply as Bussy), a notorious libertine, never meant to publish his novel, a roman à clef about love affairs at the court. He wrote it, he claimed, to amuse himself while exiled to his estate in Burgundy in 1659–60.[2] Later, on various occasions, he read it aloud to small groups of fellow courtiers. One of them, Mme de la Baume, asked him to lend her the manuscript so that she could read it in private. She secretly had it copied; the copies multiplied; and word of the spreading scandal reached the king, who sent Bussy to the Bastille in 1665. After a year of confinement, he was again exiled to his estate. Although permitted to reappear at court in 1687, he remained excluded from public functions until his death in 1693.

Different versions of the manuscript copies inevitably appeared in print. The first edition, which included a key to identify the fictitious names, was published in Liège in 1665 and was reprinted at least eleven times before 1700. In 1666 another version appeared under the title *Histoire amoureuse de France*. It contained the actual names of the characters and some scatological verse, known as "Alleluias," which insulted the king and members of the royal family. It went through at least four editions before the end of the century, and it was followed by other works under titles like *Amours des dames illustres de notre siècle* and *Recueil des histoires galantes*, which buried Bussy's mildly erotic tales in a profusion of sex stories, most of them vulgar and obscene. The best known of these sequels, *La France galante, ou histoires amoureuses de la cour*, published in at least five editions during the 1680s and 1690s, was commonly attributed to Bussy, although he had nothing to do with it. Its text was grafted onto his in later editions; then other "gallant" works were added, until they formed a large anthology of libels about sex at the court of Louis XIV. The expansion of the pseudo-Bussy literature reached a peak in 1754, when a five-volume work appeared under the standard title. By 1789 it had been reprinted several times, and Bussy had acquired a reputation as another Aretino.[3]

Bussy wrote only a tiny fraction of the libels attributed to him. The original version of his book, shorn of all the extraneous growth that it had accumulated, is now recognized as one of the finest works in a century of great literature. What, then, was the nature of his offense? *Histoire amoureuse des Gaules* certainly exposed the sexual peccadilloes of some prominent courtiers, and before recounting their intrigues it exhibited some pitiless portraits of their outer and inner selves. But it was written in fine, chaste French, similar to that of Bussy's cousin, Mme de Sévigné. Moreover, it contained nothing

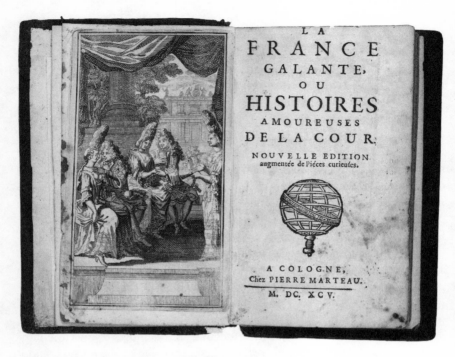

Figure 43. *La France galante*, 1695 edition. (Bibliothèque nationale de France)

irreverent about the king, who enjoyed Bussy's erotic wit (he once asked for a copy of Bussy's *Maximes d'amour* in order to read it with his mistress, Mlle de La Vallière) and supported his election to the Académie française in January 1665. Some of the events discussed in the *Histoire amoureuse* went back to 1649, and were well-known at court. Bussy merely reworked them in a sparkling narrative, which also drew on classical sources such as Petronius's *Satiricon*. And he did not "publish" his account of them; he read it to small groups of like-minded courtiers. Oral performances of that sort fell within the range of acceptable entertainment among the aristocracy. Mme de la Baume stepped over the line of the permissible, the line that divided the private from the public, when she circulated her clandestine copy. At that point, the copying could not be stopped, and Bussy realized he was in serious trouble. As soon as he heard that his manuscript had become "fairly public,"[4] he made inquiries with Mme de la Baume, which led to a violent quarrel. But there was no way to contain the damage. By the time the first printed edition appeared, Bussy was in the Bastille. Gossip, witticism, all sorts of oral virtuosity could be tolerated in the France of Louis XIV, as long as it remained confined within the closed

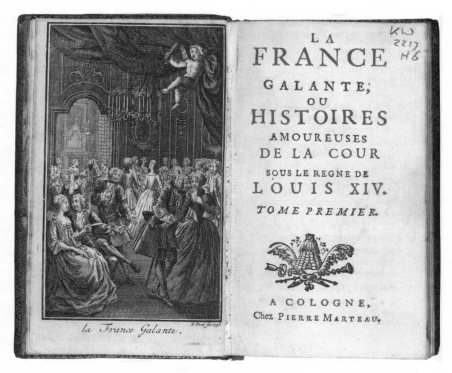

Figure 44. *La France galante,* 1754 edition. (Bibliothèque nationale de France)

world of the court. When it seeped outside, it became a serious matter; and when it was published, either in manuscript or in print, it could turn into an affair of state.

The publication of *Histoire amoureuse des Gaules* implicated Bussy in complex imbroglios, which are difficult to disentangle. Although the evidence is ambiguous, it seems likely that his original text corresponded to the later, fuller, and more scandalous version published as *Histoire amoureuse de France* in 1666.[5] Whether or not he had written the more libelous version, the public attributed it to him and associated him with the increasingly slanderous sequels that continued to appear after 1665. But whatever the degree of calumny, Bussy's crime was basically to have violated the boundary that protected the affairs of the court from the gaze of the great unwashed. No courtier could suffer his or her private life to be exposed in public without feeling humiliated. Mme de Sévigné, the target of some of his deadliest satire, expressed the prevailing attitude: "To be in everyone's hands, to be printed, to be the book that amuses all of the provinces where these things cause irreparable harm, to meet oneself in the libraries . . . [!]"⁶ The greater part of Bussy's crime, though he was not guilty of it, consisted in publication itself.

In comparison to the effrontery of publication, the content of the book was relatively inoffensive. It contains nothing in the way of political comment, yet many of the intrigues took place in the midst of the Fronde. Angélie (the duchesse de Châtillon), one of its two principal antiheroines, nearly becomes implicated in a plot to assassinate Mazarin, is imprisoned by him, loses her husband in one of the battles in the civil war, develops a liaison with the prince de Condé (the chief of the forces that fought the crown during the later stages of the Fronde), and at one point even considers marrying the Stuart Pretender, who would ascend the British throne in 1660 as Charles II. Nearly everyone from every political faction falls in love with her. Yet her only thought is for fame and money, and never does the lovemaking become confused with politics. The only thing that counts in this "histoire amoureuse" is love itself, or rather the game-playing that accompanies it. Lovers spy on each other, intercept letters, bribe their rivals' servants, bluff, cheat, and make fools of themselves—either by looking ridiculous when they lose or by strutting about comically when they win. They care less about sexual conquest than the appearance of it, for they rarely feel passion. They desire little more than to cut an impressive figure at court, to win a reputation for prowess in love, and to avoid humiliation. The narrator, who enters into the action in his own name, humiliates them all. He casts himself as the ultimate seducer and leaves the rest of the players to look ridiculous in the general scramble to exchange partners. Under Bussy's withering gaze, his characters play out roles in an erotic comedy that lacks reference to any value other than self-aggrandizement. Sex exists in this cruel world, but only as a means to an end. It is unlibidinous and utterly apolitical.

La France galante, ostensibly a sequel to Bussy's book, shows how the standard theme of sex-at-the-court became politicized.⁷ It, too, provided sardonic "portraits" of the great and then exhibited them tripping over themselves in the general rush to seduce and cuckold. Like Histoire amoureuse des Gaules, it appeared in a small, duodecimo format, ideal for slipping into a pocket and carrying about until a moment could be seized for surreptitious reading. But it was much fatter than Bussy's dainty book. The edition of 1695 ran to 492 pages of dense type and contained seven novella-like narratives. Louis XIV appears in all of them, sporting an imposing name, "le Grand Alcandre"; but he cuts a sorry figure. In the first tales, which are set in the early phase of his personal reign, he womanizes like everyone else, and the women often make him look foolish. In one tale he is reduced to the role of a servant. One of his mistresses, Mme de Montespan, is about to give birth. The king wants to be present at the event but to keep it secret. Therefore, he has a doctor blindfolded and brought to her hidden bedroom. Unable to know where he is or who has summoned him, the doctor requests some food and wine, and the king, whom he takes to be a commoner, is trapped into waiting on him at table—a comical reversal of roles for a seventeenth-century reader familiar with the king's theatrical style of dining in Versailles. In a later scene, Louis and Mme de Maintenon fall into a quarrel and trade insults as ignoble as those in any lovers' spat. He reminds her of her earlier married life with the deformed poet Pierre Scarron. But she gets the better of him by taunting him with the inadequacies of his own performance in bed. Unlike some of her earlier lovers, she says, he has certain physical failings—and, besides, he smells bad. Throughout all the tales, Louis tries to impose his will on a chaotic court, but he bungles his most authoritarian measures, sends offenders into exile, then unaccountably calls them back, fails to keep track of his own intrigues, and gets stuck with the lesser beauties. Far from ruling as a Sun King, he looks and acts like everyone else, except that his low behavior in an exalted position makes him appear more ridiculous than ordinary mortals.[8]

The last tales in *La France galante* show Louis near the end of his reign, reduced to impotence both as a lover and as a ruler. He has fallen completely under the domination of his last mistress, Mme de Maintenon, who in turn is manipulated by devious Jesuits. Following instructions from the bigoted powers behind the throne, the king attempts to set a tone of austere piety in Versailles, but the young courtiers run wild. Unlike their predecessors in *Histoire amoureuse des Gaules*, they have no interest in gallantry. They prefer perversity. Husbands are ashamed to be known for sleeping with their wives; wives fornicate with their domestic staff; brothers seduce sisters; women chase after men; and the men retreat into homosexuality. The nastiest novella, "La France devenue italienne avec les autres désordres de la cour," takes sodomy as its main theme. It describes a misogynistic secret society of young aristocrats, who drink themselves into a state of brutishness, tie a prostitute to a bed, and blow her up by means of a skyrocket crammed into her private parts. (Despite its obscenity, the text honors the convention of avoiding vulgar words.) Versailles is no Camelot. It is utterly depraved, a world turned upside down, and it communicates its poison to the outside world, which is also dissolving into chaos. Despite its focus on sexual intrigues, therefore, the text transmits a political message: Louis's inability to control his court corresponds to his failure to gain mastery over France and to assert French power in Europe.

This lesson does not merely take the form of an allegory—that is, the familiar notion of the court as a microcosm of the kingdom—and it does not limit itself to general reflections about the moral rot that is consuming society.

The text makes the political points explicit. It condemns the finance minister, Louis Phélypeaux, comte de Pontchartrain, for inflicting unbearable taxes on the poor and even for producing famines by speculating on grain exports. His policies, it claims, will soon reduce the population by a third. As France was undergoing one of the greatest demographic disasters in its history at this time, these remarks were aimed at an open wound. But the text does not dwell on them. Instead, it concentrates on the revocation of the Edict of Nantes (1685), which drove hundreds of thousands of Protestants from the kingdom and touched off a series of rebellions. One tale, "Le Divorce royal, ou guerre civile dans la famille du Grand Alcandre," describes a furious argument between Mme de Maintenon and Mme de Montespan, the mistress she has displaced. They quarrel like fishwives, producing "a little civil war" (460), which runs through the whole court. It corresponds to the civil war raging throughout France. Mme de Montespan wants to help a Huguenot escape to the safety of Geneva, but Mme de Maintenon refuses to open the slightest crack in the tyrannical rule that she and the Jesuits have imposed on the kingdom. In another tale, "Les Amours de Monseigneur le Dauphin avec la comtesse de Rourre," Louis appears as a shadow of his former self, so obsessed with his sins, thanks to the work of the Jesuits, that he cannot sleep at night. Mme de Maintenon helps him fight off attacks of panic by sprinkling holy water around the bedroom.

Nothing could be further from the sophisticated naughtiness of Bussy-Rabutin. *La France galante* transformed his apolitical, erotic novella into an indictment of Louis XIV. It used sexual scandal as a weapon to puncture the cult of the Sun King. And as a political tract, it fit into the propaganda offensive against Louis XIV that was launched by Huguenot exiles in the Netherlands and Geneva. But it is generally attributed to Gatien de Courtilz de Sandras, a literary adventurer who had done time in the Bastille and is best known today as the author of *Mémoires de M. d'Artagnan* (1700), the principal source for *Les Trois Mousquetaires*. As Alexandre Dumas appreciated nearly two centuries later, Courtilz de Sandras knew how to tell a story. He churned out several libels, including *Mémoires de M. L.C.D.R. contenant ce qui s'est passé de plus particulier sous le ministère du cardinal de Richelieu et du cardinal de Mazarin* (1687) and *Vie de Jean-Baptiste de Colbert* (1695), but they were semi-fictitious biographies and novellas rather than journalistic exposés. In this respect, Courtilz de Sandras continued at a vulgar level the kind of narrative developed by Bussy-Rabutin and other important writers such as Madame de Scudéry and Madame de Lafayette. In comparison with their work, the seven "gallant" tales in *La France galante* look crude. But judging by the number of their editions, they captivated seventeenth-century readers—and understandably so, because they wove scandalous details into long narratives, which included character sketches and dialogue along with a great deal of intrigue. Like novels about real people, whether romans à clef, fictitious memoirs, or epistolary exchanges, libels came to occupy an important sector of the book market by the end of the seventeenth century. Their narrative character made them differ from libels derived from *chroniques scandaleuses*, which consisted of little more than a string of anecdotes. Bussy-Rabutin had set in motion a genre of literature that could be called the novella-libel. It inflicted political damage by virtue of its success in telling a tale—a story deemed to be true, or at least based on a foundation of fact, but effective in large part because it was a good read.

Love as an ingredient of libel continued to shape the narratives of other works from the seventeenth century. The two best examples of this extensive literature are *Les Amours d'Anne d'Autriche avec Monsieur le C.D.R., le veritable père de Louis XIV, aujourd'hui roi de France* (1693) and *Les Amours de Madame de Maintenon épouse de Louis XIV roi de France* (1694). Although it was not published until the end of the century, *Les Amours d'Anne d'Autriche* recounted events from its beginning. It described the supposed seduction of Anne of Austria, queen to Louis XIII and mother of Louis XIV, by an obscure foreigner identified only as "C.D.R."[9] By concentrating on this single scandal, it pretended to prove the illegitimacy of Louis XIV's reign, as a long subtitle made clear: *où l'on voit au long comment on s'y prit pour donner un héritier à la couronne, les ressorts qu'on fit jouer pour cela, et enfin tout le dénouement de cette comédie* (in which it is fully shown how one went about providing an heir to the throne, the measures used to engineer it, and finally the denouement of this comedy). In characterizing the text as a play, the subtitle indicated its character; for although it reads like a novel, it is organized in scenes, and its most dramatic sections are written in dialogue.

The first scene shows Cardinal Richelieu, a consummate villain, plotting to tighten his tyranny in France and to prepare the way for a pan-European dictatorship under the pope. Having established his own power by seducing the previous queen, Marie de Medicis, he presumes that it will be easy to engineer the seduction of her successor, Anne of Austria. But at first he attempts to perpetuate his indirect rule by arranging a marriage between his niece and Gaston d'Orléans, brother of Louis XIII and next in line to the throne, because Louis, who is impotent as well as incompetent, has no heir. Gaston replies to this proposal by slapping the cardinal in the face. Swallowing his rage, Richelieu then falls back on a plot worthy of a prince of the Church. He selects C.D.R., who had caught the queen's eye at a ball, to be her lover and instructs Père Joseph, the Capuchin arch-conspirator, to soften her up through the confessional. Joseph gets nowhere, however, because the queen turns out to be unaccountably virtuous. Despite an ardent temperament and the frustration of a twenty-three-year marriage without any sex, she resists all the arguments thrown at her in the climactic scene of the book, when Richelieu and Joseph combine forces in an attempt to overwhelm her with casuistry. They therefore rely on manipulating C.D.R., whom they adorn in splendid clothes and install as the first gentleman of the queen's household. Meanwhile, Richelieu's niece, a confidante of the queen, enlists her in an attempt to foil a supposed plot by Gaston. The niece claims that Gaston is planning to rape her in her bed. If the queen will take her place under the covers, she can testify to Gaston's criminal design. The queen agrees, the cardinal substitutes C.D.R. for Gaston, and the young man does the job. Once embarked on a new life of sexual pleasure, the queen never looks back, and soon—*voilà!*—the future Louis XIV makes his appearance in the world as a bastard.

The story is told with a good deal of art, though it has none of the genius that infuses *Histoire amoureuse des Gaules*. Unlike Bussy, the anonymous narrator avoids the slightest hint of eroticism. When he finally maneuvers the queen into bed with her lover, he abruptly switches the scene: "But here it is necessary for reasons of modesty to draw the curtain and to bring the reader back to the cardinal" (129). Sex for him is entirely subordinated to politics. By demonstrating the illegitimacy of Louis XIV's birth, he contests the legitimacy of his reign: "He was born by means of a fraud; he maintained himself by falsehood and perfidiousness. . . . Infidelity presided over his conception, and it continued to exert its influence in such a way that his life would correspond to his birth and that he would carry the sceptre in the same manner that he had acquired it" (7). This argument had more than metaphorical force, because by the Salic Law, one of the fundamental laws of the kingdom, the French throne could be occupied only by legitimate male heirs. The author also invoked the Bible as authority for the coming punishment of Louis. In an "Avis au lecteur," he sounded like one of the Huguenots who had sought refuge in the Low Countries after the Revocation of the Edict of Nantes, which ended the tolerance of Protestantism in France in 1685. He also celebrated the Revolution of 1688 in England and hailed William III as a hero, whose great character and legitimate claim to rule Britain and the Dutch Republic had been fixed from his birth, a fully legitimate birth in contrast to the disreputable "miniscule semen" (3) that had marred Louis's life from the moment of conception. The true story of Louis XIV's birth, the author emphasized, would confound the libels that the French had published to defend the king during the War of the League of Augsburg (1688–97). *Les Amours d'Anne d'Autriche* was not about love at all. It was a political tract.

Les Amours de Madame de Maintenon, published a year later, resembled *Les Amours d'Anne d'Autriche* in some respects. Both were small duodecimos—the first contained 132 pages of text, the second 90—published under false addresses commonly used for illegal literature: the first appeared "à Cologne, chez Pierre Marteau," the second "à Ville Franche, chez David du Four." They probably belonged to the same propaganda offensive against Louis XIV. But *Les Amours de Madame de Maintenon* differed from its older sister in organization and tone. It was a straightforward biography, and it treated its subject in a light manner, as indicated in a preface, which invited the reader to enjoy a strange spectacle. When she set off on the road that led to the throne, the future mistress of the greatest king in Christendom left from the lowest social position imaginable: "And if you find something ridiculous about that, don't blame this copy; blame the original" (4).

The heroine of *Les Amours de Madame de Maintenon* was born in Martinique to an exiled French convict and a woman of small virtue assigned to him from a boatload of prostitutes expelled from Poitou. At age three, Guillemette, as she was called, left her father's miserable tobacco farm to tend chickens in the barnyard of her godmother. At age six, she accompanied the good woman, who apparently also was a prostitute, to a village back in Poitou, but was left without resources when she turned fifteen and her godmother died. At first Guillemette felt inclined to accept the best chance that was offered her: a proposal of marriage from a one-eyed, hunchbacked peasant. He courted her with cakes and trinkets bought from nearby fairs: "Ha, my dear Guillemette," he said, "I love you dearly; I will be so good to you and will give you such beautiful presents that you will feel forced to feel some love for me" (9). But something told this future mistress of Versailles that she could do better in life. She therefore strung the peasant along while continuing to accept ribbons and needles until a gentlewoman from a nearby château offered to hire her as a servant.

At that point Guillemette began to learn something of the ways of the world, thanks in part to the attention of a local marquis, who sent her sonnets and propositions to join him on his estate. Despite concern about disqualifying herself from the marriage market, Guillemette seized the opportunity to live like a lady and moved in with him. Ten years later, her manners adequately polished, she set off for Paris. As her savings ran out, she considered domestic service once again, but a procuress who also arranged marriages proposed to her in the name of Pierre Scarron, the poet known for his wit as well as his deformities. After toting up pros and cons just as she had done in considering the proposal from the hunchbacked peasant, Guillemette decided that Scarron's wealth outweighed his repulsiveness. He soon relieved her by dying. She then insinuated herself into Versailles, where she became a confidant of Mme de Montespan, the king's mistress. Thanks to her peasant cunning, she replaced Mme de Montespan and began to interfere in affairs of state. Things went swimmingly, until she fell in love with one of her own servants. Père la Chaise, the Jesuit power behind the throne, got wind of the affair and used it to manipulate her. In the end, he replaced the young man in her bed and they ruled the kingdom together, procuring new mistresses for Louis XIV until he gave up on sex as well as governing.

The narrative moves at a fast pace, and the author generally refrains from political comment. He never mentions Louis's wars, taxes, and abuses of authority. Nor does he take Maintenon's biography into its final stage, when she became identified with the oppressive piety and religious persecution at the end of Louis's reign. He lets the story speak for itself—and that is what makes it so effective. By artfully arranging the tale of a royal mistress's rise to power, the author indicts the power system itself. But he does so with a light hand. He maintains a tone of worldly irony, avoids offensive details in the references to sex, and scatters his narrative with snatches of comic dialogue and topical verse. One edition from 1694 ends with a seventeen-page anthology of slightly naughty poems and "énigmes" or verse puzzles in which the reader is invited to guess the subject. They have nothing to do with Louis XIV and the military and demographic catastrophes that engulfed France in one of the darkest periods of its history. *Les Amours de Madame de Maintenon* looks forward to the next century, an age of Pompadour pink, at least as it appeared in the next round of libels.

Libels of all sorts proliferated during the Regency (1715–23), a time noted for libertinism in high society. The satirical verse of young Voltaire, the *Philippiques* of La Grange-Chancel, Montesquieu's *Lettres persanes*, and other works attacked public personages with a verve that outdid nearly everything from the previous century. But the first "private life" that brought the theme of royal sex and politics before the general public was *Les Amours de Zéokinizul, roi des Kofirans*, which did not appear until 1746. (The *Vie privée du cardinal Dubois*, which is discussed in the next chapter and which provides a richly scandalous history of the Regency, was not published until 1789.) As its full title indicated, *Les Amours de Zéokinizul, roi des Kofirans; traduits de l'Arabe du voyageur Krinelbol* drew on the series of libelous "amours" that went back to Bussy-Rabutin. It, too, was a novella-libel as well as a roman à clef, but it disguised the names of the protagonists in a way that shows how it differed from its predecessors. They were obviously anagrams. By figuring so prominently in the title, they invited the reader to play a game. Who was Zéokinizul? A comically exaggerated moniker but one that was difficult to decipher, unless one considered the next anagram, Kofirans, which was closer to the French original: Français. Once identified as king of the French and pronounced aloud, Zéokinizul turned into Louis Quinze. It was a fairly easy brainteaser but difficult enough to entice the reader to venture into the text. The pretense that the book had been translated from an exotic work in Arabic could be dismissed as a literary convention, but who was the translator-author disguised as Krinelbol? No one without an inside knowledge of literary Paris could know. The experts still disagree, but most identify him as Crébillon—that is, Claude-Prosper Jolyot de Crébillon, known as Crébillon fils to distinguish him from his father, the well-known playwright.[10] The text bears all the marks of Crébillon's other works—gaiety, ribaldry, playfulness, anticlericalism, keen psychological observations, and a strong story line.

As in so many eighteenth-century libels, the game-playing took the form of puzzle-solving. Not all the anagrams appeared in the extensive key printed at the end of most editions, and many readers would want to decode the names as they proceeded through the text. Once they had identified Zéokinizul as Louis XV, they would have no trouble spotting Zokitarezoul as Louis XIV and Zeoteirizul as Louis XIII. The context made other identifications obvious: the Kam d'Anserol was the duc d'Orléans, who ruled France as Regent after the death of Louis XIV; and Jeflur was Fleury, who dominated the government soon after the death of the Regent. Louis XV's mistresses among the daughters of the marquis de Nesle could be followed according to their order of succession: Liamil (Madame de Mailly), Leutinemil (Madame de Ventimille), and Lenertoula (Madame de La Tournelle, later Madame de Châteauroux). The military prowess of Vameric made him recognizable as the maréchal de Saxe, although the name could have given some readers trouble (Vameric stood for Maurice, comte de Saxe). The juxtaposition of easy and difficult names made the puzzle more amusing. Pepa was obviously le Pape, but Suesi? (Jésus.) Bileb was the Bible, but Linguelan? (l'Evangile.) Nhir was le Rhin, but Junes? (Unies, for Provinces Unies, the Netherlands.) And Vorompdap (Pompadour) gave pleasure, not because it was hard to puzzle out but because of its sheer absurdity.

The anagrams set the tone of the text. It is meant to amuse the reader, and so its narrative proceeds at a brisk clip. After some quick history, which stresses the freedom of the Krans (Francs) before their subordination to an absolute monarchy, it settles down to an inside account of Louis XV's love life. As already mentioned (see Chapter 20), it takes him through the de Nesle sisters and into the arms of Pompadour. He has to be coached at each stop along the way because he is too timid and inept to be much of a lover. Fleury works out the strategy for the first affair, but he needs the duc de Richelieu (Kelirieu) to handle the tactics. An accomplished seducer in his own right, the duke plays on the king's simplemindedness in order to overcome his inhibitions at betraying the queen, then gives him lessons in winning women. Nevertheless, it takes three trysts to overcome Louis's tongue-tied cowardice, and even then he rises to the occasion only because Madame de Mailly, briefed by Fleury, takes him by storm. From that point on, he expects women to be delivered to him. Richelieu serves as the delivery man, insinuating himself deeper and deeper into the king's confidence, while lining his pockets and undercutting Fleury in the process.

But Pompadour presents a problem. Although ambitious and unhappily married, she is a bourgeoise and therefore, unlike the ladies of the court, reluctant to commit adultery. Richelieu rises to the challenge. He reads her like a book, noting every change in her coloring, every hint of hidden passion in her eyes. He lays traps for her with his libertine version of casuistry: adultery is defined as deceiving a spouse, but her husband has generously agreed to sacrifice her to his sovereign. She won't be violating any marriage vow, because he has already nullified the contract. And the queen's refusal to sleep with the king has effectively invalidated their marriage. Moreover, the leading imams of the realm will tidy up any leftover ethical messiness, because they specialize in adapting religion to special cases. And—this final touch does the trick— Louis has his eye on another candidate, less beautiful but more pliant; so Vorompdap-Pompadour would lose the chance of a lifetime if she failed to act fast. In fact, she should do so for the sake of her husband as well as herself, because he is a notorious omeriseruf (*sous fermier*, a subordinate kind of tax collector notorious for peculation), and the king might well be tempted to make him an example of rigorous royal justice. When she replies with a weak protest about the danger to her reputation, Richelieu overwhelms her with a conclusive argument: "A king on his knees before you, courtiers at your orders, treasures at your disposal, are all of these things to attract scorn? Oh! Stop imagining chimeras in order to combat them; give your consent to make Zeokinizul happy, and I will bring him back to your feet more impassioned than ever" (84).

Once Richelieu has triumphed, the narrative does not pause to describe the king enjoying the spoils of victory, for he is not the victor. The true seducer of Pompadour is Richelieu. He emerges as the most important character in the book after Vorompdap herself. From this point on, Louis nearly disappears from the plot. He has a brief moment of glory at the Battle of Fontenoy, but it clears the way for two final intrigues that bring the book to a close. In the first, Pompadour falls in love with a handsome Englishman captured in the battle. Richelieu reads the passion hidden behind her eyes and attempts to arrange a tryst. But the Englishman, already committed to his true love at home, refuses to cooperate. Although frustrated in her own role as a seductress, Pompadour becomes the effective ruler of France, while Louis tries his hand at a final fling, this time without Richelieu as his go-between. Smitten with the beautiful fiancée of one of his courtiers, he gets rid of the young man by sending him on a mission. She resists the king's advances; her lover sneaks back to woo her; the king has him thrown in prison and is ready to execute him for disobeying orders. But the fiancée implores mercy with such eloquence that Louis grants her request, gives up on womanizing, and resolves to devote himself henceforth to the happiness of his people. The happy ending is not very convincing, but it serves as a way of registering a plea for the king to take his functions seriously at a time when he was barely halfway through his reign.

Crébillon (assuming he is the author) seasons the plot with dialogue and descriptions of the conflicts that take place within the bosom of his characters. Every touch adds to the overall comic effect, and each is done with the deftness deployed in his other novels, notably *Les Egarements du coeur et de l'esprit* (1736), which develops a similar plot about the sexual initiation of a timid, clueless lover. The sex is suggested, not described, and the erotic theme remains subordinate to the novella's bantering tone. Worldly, witty, good-humored, *Les Amours de Zéokinizul* extends the older variety of libertinism into new territory, the broad book market of the mid-eighteenth century. Bussy-Rabutin had restricted his scandalmongering to his fellow courtiers. Crébillon brings the love lives of Louis XV and Mme de Pompadour before the general reading public. He also combines the sex with something new: Enlightenment. He uses familiar devices to make fun of the mollaks (prelates) and faquirs (priests). But he goes beyond old-fashioned anticlericalism by appealing for tolerance, mocking Christian dogma, and attacking the authority of the Church. Many passages could have been written by Voltaire. And a sequel, also presumably by Crébillon, took the irreligion even further. As its title indicated, *L'Asiatique tolérant: Traité à l'usage de Zéokinizul, roi des Kofirans, surnommé le Chéri; Ouvrage traduit de l'Arabe du voyageur Bekrinoll* (1748) concentrated on the Voltairean theme of tolerance. It condemned the persecution of the Huguenots and satirized the bigotry that had taken root under Louis XIV and continued to oppress the French under Louis XV. It flaunted its illegal character with a parodied censors' approbation, signed with the names of philosophes disguised by anagrams, and a parodied royal privilege, signed by "le BON SENS en son conseil." The message was dangerous and deadly serious, but it was conveyed with a light hand and in a spirit of game-playing typical of the early Enlightenment.

Crébillon, or the anonymous narrator, also wove a political message into *Les Amours de Zéokinizul*. He points out that the king is so infatuated with his mistresses that he does not notice that the War of the Austrian Succession has consumed the lives of 100,000 soldiers and seven million *tomans* (livres). Zéokinizul is a *roi fainéant*, a do-nothing king, but also a despot, although he lets his mistresses and ministers exercise power in his name. The historical remarks at the beginning of the book take up a theme made popular during the 1730s by the parlements' resistance to royal edicts—namely, that the king did not possess unlimited power at the beginning of the monarchy and that his authority derived from the consent of the free Frankish people. But royal power gradually increased at the expense of the people's liberty, and under Richelieu, Mazarin, and Louis XIV, the monarchy degenerated into a despotism: "The government, formerly monarchical, became purely despotic" (6).[11] By implication, therefore, the current government of France was illegitimate. It fit into the category of Asiatic despotism, a theme made popular by Montesquieu's *Lettres persanes*, although Crébillon actually set his tale in Africa.

Les Amours de Zéokinizul should not be taken as a revolutionary tract, however. It had none of the anger of later, more radical writing. In its wit and lightness, it breathes the spirit of the Pompadour era, even while taking Pompadour as its target. To see how the darker elements in the theme of despotism came to dominate the literature of libel, it is necessary to follow the tales of royal sex into the second half of the eighteenth century.

Chapter 27
Decadence and Despotism

By 1750 libelers had tied the theme of sex and politics to the coming and going of royal mistresses and ministers. The thematic links could be reworked in endless combinations, and they provided a way to organize a narrative of contemporary history: the king remained a constant—so listless and incompetent that he faded into the background—while the succession of his women determined the entrances and exits of the men who actually shaped events. This formula could be made to fit nearly everything of importance that took place between 1733, when Louis XV first took up with Mme de Mailly, and 1774, when he died. By stringing new anecdotes along the old story line, the libelers reinforced its strength. But no story can be repeated without changing, and after 1750 the tales of royal sex took on a new tone.

The change can be seen by comparing a later libel against Mme de Pompadour with an early one. *L'Histoire de Madame la marquise de Pompadour* (1759) lacks all the light touches of *Les Amours de Zéokinizul, roi des Kofirans* (1746). It is a long, rambling diatribe published anonymously from the safety of London by Marianne Agnès de Fauques. Mlle Fauques had none of the talent of Crébillon fils. She had churned out a half-dozen novels but was known primarily as an adventuress who had extricated herself from a convent in the south of France and lived on the margins of fashionable society in Paris, accumulating lovers and spreading scandal. The police put her down in their files as a dangerous character. She counterfeited letters, betrayed her closest friends, and gave vent to "the hottest and most violent temperament that one has ever seen. . . . There is nothing worse than a creature of this sort who has been a nun. Furthermore, she has a mind as dark as her face. She speaks only of daggers and poisons, and she talks about them casually as if they were matters of no importance."[1] By 1759 Mlle Fauques had followed one of her lovers to London, only to be abandoned and to fall back on teaching French and on writing as a means of support.

L'Histoire de Madame la marquise de Pompadour was an attempt to exploit the demand for information about Louis XV's mistress, then at the height of her power. It begins as a biography, stressing the ignominious origins of its antiheroine and the scramble in Versailles to supply women for the king. But once it places Pompadour in the royal bed, it abandons chronology and serves up one anecdote after another in a text that goes on for 189 pages without divisions into chapters or other distinctive parts. Insofar as it has any organizing principle, it pretends to treat the reader to a view of Pompadour's true character, which it illustrates by revelations about minor episodes at court: she dissipates Louis's boredom at private dinners, which result in sinecures for her unworthy family and palaces for herself; she undercuts the influence of the comte d'Argenson by wrongly attributing a seditious letter to one of his servants; she has the young Dauphin reprimanded for sticking his tongue out at her; she fakes a reconciliation with her absent husband in order to be admitted to Holy Communion and thence to a position in the queen's household; she maintains her hold on the king's sex life by promoting one-night stands with obscure girls in the Parc-aux-cerfs; and, above all, she gains control of all appointments and all policies of the government.[2]

The political message builds on the sexual scandal to convey a picture of unrestrained despotism, which appears all the more reprehensible in that the despot is a woman. Far from expressing any sympathy for her own sex, Mlle Fauques deplores the misplaced gendering of power. Under Pompadour, policy derives "from the ruses of a little woman [*femmelette*] rather than from a brave, male courage" (129). Increased taxes, reversals in foreign policy, and defeats on the battlefield all can be attributed to the incapacity of a woman who believes that she can govern the kingdom in the same way that she rules over her docile lover.[3] In the end, therefore, the whole history of the reign comes down to the domination of an incompetent, ignoble "stateswoman" (*femme d'Etat*).[4] To have revealed the true nature of Pompadour is to have explained the course of current events. The book summarizes this message in its last pages by two "portraits." First, Pompadour at age twenty-three, when she had recently taken over the kingdom: perfect figure, beautiful coloring, and sparkling eyes, which gave off an inner fire. Then:

Today (in 1758), now that she is about thirty-eight years old, it is difficult to make out her real face. Buried under an inch-thick layer of rouge and white powder, it is completely hidden from view. . . . As to her figure, aside from the change that it has undergone from aging, it has become so very thin as a result of her illness that the sight of her is enough to stifle any carnal appetite. Anyone who tried to satisfy himself with such a meatless morsel would be likely to die of hunger. . . . If you combine this sepulchral portrait [of the outer person] with the representation of a heart corroded by deceit, you will have an object worthy only of pity and disdain. Such is the naïve and sincere portrait of the marquise de Pompadour as she appears today in the midst of grandeur, riches, and the pronounced favor of the king that she managed to captivate. (189)

The libels about Louis XV's next official mistress (*maîtresse en titre*), Mme du Barry, were equally nasty but more effective in getting across a basic message: the decadence personified by the king's mistresses bolstered the despotism exercised by his ministers. The two evils were inseparable, and they were mutually reinforcing. By hammering at this theme, the libels from the second half of the eighteenth century made the story of private lives congruent with ideas in political theory. Not that they cited philosophers or developed abstract arguments: far from it, they owed their success to the appeal of their narrative and the punch of the anecdotes that went into it. But vivid details strung out along a strong story line could convey an ideological message, even when they lacked references to ideologues.

Merely by playing with the term "Kofirans," for example, *Les Amours de Zéokinizul* evoked the notion of the French as the Franks—that is, the supposedly freedom-loving Germanic tribe that conquered the Gauls and created the monarchy as an instrument of the people's will. Jansenists and radicals in the Parlement of Paris had linked that mythical view of history to constitutional arguments about the limits of royal power. The arguments fueled politico-religious conflicts throughout the 1730s and 1740s. They exploded again in the 1750s during battles that pitted Jansenists against Jesuits, the parlements against reforming ministers, and the newly vocal partisans of Enlightenment against the defenders of privilege and tradition. By the 1770s, the battle lines had been drawn and redrawn so often that libeling could not be understood apart from its context in the complex ideological landscape.

While the ideologists staked out positions in polemics, political factions scrambled for power in Versailles. Individuals and ideas therefore collided and combined in patterns that would have been familiar to many of the readers of the libels. A narrative that celebrated the fall of Mme de Châteauroux as Louis XV's mistress might be taken as ammunition for the "devout" (*dévot*) party in court. A sympathetic portrait of Mme de Pompadour could reinforce the position of the philosophes and of the pro-Austrian faction that gathered around the duc de Choiseul. And a scandalous anecdote about Mme du Barry could look like propaganda for the parlements against the government as well as the *dévots*. Unfortunately, there is not enough documentation to reconstruct the reception of the libels against the political context that existed at the moment of their publication.[5] But it is possible to characterize the ideological background of libels in general after 1750 by concentrating on their most important theme and on the philosopher who developed it into a central concept of his political theory. The theme was despotism; the philosophe, Montesquieu.[6]

Montesquieu elevated the concept of despotism into a fundamental category of political science. Like Aristotle, he distinguished three basic types of states. But whereas Aristotle had defined them according to the locus of power (monarchies or government by one, aristocracies or government by many, and democracies or government by all), he classified them according to the way in which power operated—that is, the spirit of their laws, which he understood as an ethos generated over long stretches of time by a variety of factors such as climate, religion, customs, and opinion. After careful study of ancient history and of the world around him, he thought it possible to construct a typology that did justice to the dominant ethos (a "principle," "moral cause," or original activating spirit) of different political systems. Hence his three kinds of states, each with its own principle: monarchies, sustained by honor; republics (either aristocratic or democratic), energized by civic virtue; and despotisms, driven by fear.

Far from reducing all states to these ideal types, Montesquieu showed how they shaded off into one another through cyclical processes inherent in history. In a healthy monarchy, the king respected the fundamental laws of the kingdom; his power was transmitted through intermediary bodies like the French parlements; and his subjects obeyed him according to the duties and privileges prescribed by their rank. But if he began to rule by indulging his own arbitrary will, he would sap the institutional constraints on his power; his subjects would increasingly obey him out of fear; and in the end, after a succession of such reigns, the monarch would be transformed into a despot ruling over slaves. His ministers would be slaves themselves—satraps and pashas who gathered around the throne, flattering his appetites and indulging their own. Intrigue and voluptuousness would take the place of honor and service, and the seraglio would become the supreme institution of the state.

Montesquieu's use of Oriental metaphors showed that he drew on a conventional topos, one derived from literature and that he had already exploited in his *Lettres persanes*. But his notion of despotism also grew out of personal experience and reflection. He was horrified by the disasters that overwhelmed France during last years of the reign of Louis XIV, the abuse of power under the Regency, and the threats to the authority of the parlements during the first decades of Louis XV's rule. *De l'Esprit des lois* provided a theoretical basis for the growing sense among the French that their monarchy was degenerating into a despotism. There were other sources as well: parliamentary remonstrances, Jansenist tracts, treatises on constitutional law. The ideological opposition to the crown cannot be reduced to one book. But by placing the problem of despotism at the heart of political theory, *De l'Esprit des lois* supplied exactly what the libels lacked: a full-scale, philosophical perspective on the comings and goings of mistresses and ministers.

Of all the private lives, the one that expressed this perspective most thoroughly was *Vie privée de Louis XV* by Moufle d'Angerville, but the one that sold the best was its sister publication, *Anecdotes sur Mme la comtesse du Barry* (1775) by Pidansat de Mairobert. The two libelers were friends and fellow *nouvellistes* who collaborated on the underground newsletter later published as *Mémoires secrets pour servir à l'histoire de la république des lettres en France*, which they raided frequently for anecdotes. They also drew on the antigovernment tracts of the "patriots" who opposed Maupeou's coup against the parlements. All these publications belonged to a common stock of material produced and recycled by the radicals of the early 1770s. What distinguished *Anecdotes sur Mme la comtesse du Barry* from the others was the way it condensed the general themes of decadence and despotism into a narrative focused sharply on the most notorious of Louis XV's mistresses.[7]

Du Barry's notoriety derived primarily from her dubious past. *Anecdotes sur Mme la comtesse du Barry* made a great deal of her supposed birth at the bottom of society—probably, it argued, as the daughter of a cook and an itinerant monk, although (as it noted with feigned concern for historical rigor) the best-informed authorities still argued over the identity of her father, who might have been a "rat de cave" (one of the much hated inspectors at the bottom of the bureaucracy for collecting taxes). The full force of this sort of calumny may be lost on modern readers, who take lineage less seriously than did readers in the eighteenth century. Under the Ancien Régime, birth determined social rank, and the question of rank had special resonance in the case of royal mistresses. The most celebrated mistresses—Agnès Sorel, Diane de Poitiers, Gabrielle d'Estrées, Louise de la Vallière, the marquise de Montespan, the marquise de Maintenon—all came from the nobility. Far from sullying the throne, they added splendor to it. Kings often selected them from among the finest ladies in their court or had them officially presented to the court in a ceremony that qualified them to be recognized as *maîtresse en titre*—that is, to enjoy official status with the right to give audiences and receive ambassadors. Louis XIV had choreographed life in Versailles so elaborately that it was extremely difficult for an outsider to negotiate a way through the rituals required of an official mistress. Contrary to the account in *Les Amours de Madame de Maintenon*, Mme de Maintenon had no difficulty maintaining the dignity of her position. Far from being a penniless peasant, she was born and educated among aristocrats. True, she fell into poverty, and to escape it, she married a commoner, Pierre Scarron. But after his death she became the governess of Louis XIV's legitimized children, and she had mastered court etiquette long before the king made her his mistress and then his morganatic wife. The first mistresses of Louis XV continued to fit this pattern, but Mme de Pompadour deviated from it. Despite her wit and excellent education, she was irredeemably common, as signaled by her unfortunate maiden name, Jeanne Antoinette Poisson (fish), which gave libelers endless possibilities for puns about fish, fish markets, and fishmongers. Her successor as *maîtresse en titre*, Mme du Barry, brought the downward trajectory in the history of royal mistresses to its lowest point, according to the *Anecdotes*. Du Barry was downright plebeian—in fact, a whore. Her rule in Versailles represented the ultimate stage in the degradation of the French monarchy.

This leitmotif permeates every aspect of *Anecdotes sur Mme la comtesse du Barry*, a large-scale biography that runs to nearly 350 pages in its numerous editions. As in many libels, the text rolls past the reader in a flow of anecdotes uninterrupted by divisions into chapters or distinct narrative sections.[8] Du Barry's five years at court, from April 1769 to May 1774, occupy four-fifths of the book, presumably because they provided most of the "piquant" details that the preface promised to deliver. In fact, they swamp the main story line in so many scandalous episodes that it is difficult to keep the chronology straight. The pages devoted to du Barry's early life hold together better as a narrative. They take her from her first years in a small town in Champagne to Paris, where her mother, then an impoverished widow, sought help from the girl's godfather, a financier who had sponsored her at her baptism as a gesture of noblesse oblige. He provided enough to keep them alive for a few years and to pay for little Manon's education. It never amounted to more than a rudimentary ability to read and to scribble a few words: she still could not spell "comtesse" when the king made her one.

While her mother found work as a cook and later as a domestic servant, Manon blossomed into a teenage beauty. Just who first had her maidenhead is a matter of debate, the narrator explains; and as a conscientious historian, he refuses to pronounce in favor of anyone among the many contenders: an abbé, a colonel, or one of the valets where her mother worked. In any case, Manon took to sex like a duck to water, for she was naughty, pleasure-loving, lighthearted, and endowed with plenty of "tempérament" (natural lust). By age sixteen she had taken a job as a salesgirl in a fashionable boutique, the perfect place for launching a career in gallantry.

Mme Gourdan, proprietor of the fanciest brothel in Paris, spotted Manon's pretty face behind the counter and had no difficulty in recruiting her: the offer of some dresses, trinkets, and pocket money did the job. Properly coached and featured as Mlle Lançon—her name kept changing as she rose through society—the king's future mistress was repeatedly sold as a virgin (thanks to the technology developed by professionals in the sex industry) to Gourdan's best customers: bishops, aristocrats, judges from the parlement, and financiers. Unfortunately, one of the financiers turned out to be her god-

father, who flew into a rage and drove her out of the establishment. Mlle Lançon then took up a career as a kept woman, at first with a clerk, then a
hairdresser, and finally, under the name of Mlle L'Ange, as the mistress of Jean
du Barry, a fake count who ran a gambling house and sold her to his customers on the side. In between lovers she also did tricks, in company with her
mother, as a streetwalker. By the age of twenty, therefore, she had mastered
every refinement known to professionals in the art of love: hence her hold on
the king, for his earlier mistresses had found it difficult to satisfy such an
august bedmate without being overcome with inhibitions. When Louis first
took up with Mlle L'Ange, he confided to the duc d'Ayen that he had never
before enjoyed such pleasures. The duke replied, in one of the bons mots that
was repeated throughout the *beau monde*, "Sire, it's that you have never been
in a brothel" (24).

From the gambling den and the brothel to the throne, the jump was easily
made, thanks to the king's intermediary, his valet, Dominique Guillaume Le
Bel, who procured him girls for one-night stands in the Parc-aux-cerfs, Louis's
famous "harem" (55) in the gardens of Versailles. They came and went at a
rate of one a week, according to the narrator. They had to be cleaned up, per-
fumed, outfitted, and pensioned off at a cost of ten million livres per year, tips
and bribery included. Comte Jean "le roué," as he was known, had collaborated in this business long enough to know that he could play for higher
stakes. He refused to release Mlle L'Ange to Le Bel unless the king, after sampling her, agreed to make her *maîtresse en titre*. Once installed as a permanent
fixture in court, she would serve as a conduit for him to siphon off limitless
sums from the royal treasury.

This strategy worked perfectly. The king could not get enough of Mlle
L'Ange. To provide a somewhat respectable cover, du Barry had her married
off to his brother, "comte Guillaume," a corpulent good-for-nothing known
as "the fat du Barry," who was bought off and exiled. Their sister acted as the
new countess's companion and transmitted directions from "du Barry le
roué," who remained hidden in Paris. Soon he was naming and dismissing
ministers, while milking the treasury of millions. Mme du Barry executed his
orders by weakening the king through sex and drink and then getting him to
sign the desired edicts. Unlike Mme de Pompadour, she had no ambitions of
her own and no interest in politics. She did not even want to accumulate châ-
teaux. Fancy dresses, jewels, and high jinks in the king's private chambers
(*petits appartements*) kept her content.

In itself, the story did not differ fundamentally from the negative biographies among the libels that had preceded it. What set it apart was a detailed
account of court intrigues touched up by anecdotes that illustrated the corrup-

tion and vulgarity that accompanied them. To maintain her hold on the king, the anonymous narrator explained, Mme du Barry had to be formally presented at court—no simple matter, because it required a suitable sponsor and clearance through various factions, including the dauphin and the king's daughters, "Mesdames," who were known for their strict piety and their dedication to the *dévot* party. It might seem incredible that they would accept a creature from the streets of Paris as an ally, but such were the exigencies of court politics. The *dévots* were willing to use the king's mistress to undermine their rivals, the party of the Choiseulistes, who had dominated the government since 1758, when the duc de Choiseul became foreign minister.

As the narrator presented it, Mme du Barry's presentation at court on April 22, 1769, was a major political event, in fact the decisive moment of the entire reign. Choiseul had turned against her, although she had done nothing to offend him. (Thanks to coaching, she treated him and everyone else correctly whenever she appeared in the public sectors of Versailles.) The difficulty came from Choiseul's sister, the duchesse de Grammont, who also wanted to become the royal mistress and went about it so aggressively that the du Barrys, with supporters like the duc de Richelieu, had to campaign against her from self-defense. They won over Choiseul's rivals within the government, Chancellor Maupeou and Controller General Terray. By then, Maupeou was planning to destroy the parlements in order to wipe out all resistance to the power of the crown. Choiseul had always placated the parlements, but in June 1770 the king quashed the trial in the Parlement of Paris of their greatest enemy, the duc d'Aiguillon. Supported by Maupeou and Mme du Barry, d'Aiguillon began plotting to take Choiseul's place in the government. By the end of the year, the intrigues came to a climax, and on December 24, 1770, the king sent Choiseul into exile. Maupeou began to eradicate the parlements in January. D'Aiguillon became foreign minister in June 1771. And from then until the king's death in May 1774, France was governed by a "triumvirate" composed of Maupeou, Terray, and d'Aiguillon, although each of them plotted against the others and all depended on the ultimate source of power, Mme du Barry.

In recounting this "revolution," the narrator made his own position clear: he favored the "patriotes" who opposed the government, and he treated Maupeou's coup as a fatal step into despotism.[9] But he did not explicitly invoke ideological arguments from Montesquieu or the pamphlet literature of the time. Instead of referring to constitutional limits to the power of the crown and historical precedents for restricting it, he left it to the reader to draw those implications and concentrated on a subject more likely to seize the reader's attention: du Barry's role in the midst of court intrigues. He did so by recounting anecdotes. Better than abstract propositions, they brought out the degenerate character of politics and the degradation of the monarchy. A few examples:

Before the fall of the duc de Choiseul and his cousin, the duc de Choiseul-Praslin, who was minister of the navy, Mme du Barry amused herself by seizing two oranges, squeezing them, and tossing them in the air while calling out, "Jump, Choiseul! Jump, Praslin!" (89). (The expression "to jump" [*sauter*] referred to the expulsion of a minister from the government.)

In the privacy of the *petits appartements*, the king liked to amuse himself by brewing coffee. One day, while he was distracted, the coffee boiled over, and Mme du Barry shouted, "Hey, France! Look out! Your coffee is buggering off" (215). ("Eh! La France, prends donc garde, ton café fout le camp." "La France" was the nickname that she used for the king in private, accompanying it with the familiar "tu.")

In order to transact ecclesiastical business, the papal nuncio and the Cardinal de la Roche-Aymon had an audience with the king in Mme du Barry's bedroom. At one point she got out of her bed, stark naked, while requesting the two prelates to pass her slippers to her. Each delivered a slipper to one of her feet and used the opportunity to take furtive glances at the rest of her body (224).

The duc d'Aiguillon wanted to force the marquis de Monteynard from the ministry of war in order to take it over himself. The king was attached to Monteynard, but when Mme du Barry joined forces with d'Aiguillon, he saw that he would not be able to withstand the pressure. "It's inevitable that he will fall," Louis lamented. "The only one who supports him is me" (294).

After the king's death, Mme du Barry was exiled by order of Louis XVI to the Abbaye du Pont-aux-Dames in Brie. In a fit of pique, she exclaimed, "What a beautiful, fucking reign, which begins with a lettre de cachet" (330).

The anecdotes reinforced one another by working over the same themes: the vulgarity of du Barry, the feebleness of the king, the triviality of court intrigues, the baseness of everyone's behavior, and the arbitrary power abused throughout the whole system. By their cumulative effect, they made the monarchy look decadent as well as despotic, and they did so without a great deal of commentary, in a manner typical of libel literature.

Despite the attraction of royal mistresses as a target, libelers also aimed their fire at ministers. The best example of an attack on a prominent politician was also a best-seller, *Mémoires de l'abbé Terray, contrôleur général, contenant sa vie, son administration, ses intrigues et sa chute* (1776).[10] It could be read as a sequel to *Anecdotes sur Mme la comtesse du Barry* because it included some of the same anecdotes, conveyed the same themes, and treated the crisis of

1770–74 from the same point of view: the "patriot" opposition to the government. Yet it differed from the *Anecdotes* in one respect. Instead of concentrating on the sexual subjugation of the king, it gave a detailed account of the politics and power struggles that surrounded him at the level of his ministers.

According to a note by the publisher, the first part of *Mémoires de l'abbé Terray* was written in 1773 by a young lawyer, Jean-Baptiste-Louis Coquereau, who, "inflamed by a patriotic zeal" (iii) and driven to despair by the despotic measures of the triumvirate, committed suicide before he completed the text. Part 1 covers the first 123 pages; part 2 continues the story until Terray's dismissal in 1774, another 127 pages. And a second volume contains an assortment of polemical works from 1768 until 1775. Taken together, the two volumes cover the crisis at the end of Louis XV's reign in great detail. They concentrate heavily on financial affairs and the surrounding struggles for power, and therefore they read like a political tract written from the viewpoint of the "patriots."

The preface of the *Mémoires* insisted that the book should be understood as a history, despite the obviously fictional suggestion in its title that it had been composed by Terray himself as his memoirs. Although the partisans of despotism were likely to denigrate the author as a libeler, the preface explained, he was in fact a historian, a historian of the noblest kind, whose function was "to plead the cause of a nation, and sometimes of all humanity, against powerful ministers, redoubtable potentates, who outrage it, ruin it, degrade it, enslave it, and oppress it under the chains of an intolerable despotism" (v–vi). But libels often tried to legitimize themselves in the eyes of their readers by pretending to be histories. For all its high-flown rhetoric and its commitment to the patriotic cause, *Mémoires de l'abbé Terray* was actually a libel of the most damaging variety, the kind that attempted to destroy a public person by exposing his private life.

Coquereau dispatched with the first part of Terray's biography in one paragraph. Born into an obscure family in a small town near Lyon, young Terray had two assets: cunning and a rich uncle. The uncle, as official doctor to the duc d'Orléans during the Regency, summoned the youth to Paris, had him enter the minor orders of the clergy (as a subdeacon, not a priest), and bought him an office as a clerical councillor in the Parlement of Paris. While rising through the ranks in the parlement, Terray kept a low profile, according to the *Mémoires*. He dressed badly, lived frugally, and won respect as a "patriot" (9) by drafting protests against the fiscal policy of the government. But as soon as his uncle died, leaving him a fortune, he bought a château and took up mistresses—first, the wife of a provincial client, who presided over his sumptuous table and bore him a daughter, then her best friend, who slipped into the abbé's bed at an opportune moment and eventually installed herself as chief of his "seraglio" (209). The *Mémoires* did not treat Terray's sex life at great length because, it claimed, he merely used women to vent his lust while pursuing his political career. Still, it provided the occasional, keyhole view of him copulating. Its scabrous anecdotes pictured him at one point as a rapist, and its inventory of his mistresses included his illegitimate daughter, who provided so much sexual satisfaction that he tried to pass her on to the king, using Mme du Barry as a go-between.

Terray's dominating passion, the *Mémoires* stressed at every point, was not sex but ambition—a raw, indomitable desire for money and power. Having secretly cultivated Chancellor Maupeou, he renounced his opposition to the government, which had been nothing more than feigned patriotism in order to increase his influence in the parlement, and in 1769 he accepted the position of controller general of finances. From that point on, he seized every opportunity to tax the French to death. He drained so much wealth from the exhausted population and he abused his authority so blatantly that he became the most hated figure in the kingdom. In fact, he came to embody the supreme evil of the political system—not royal authority in itself but the degenerate version of it known as ministerial despotism.

The *Mémoires* treated the reader to the inside story of how this transformation took place. Chancellor Maupeou, looking for an opportunity to undercut the dominant power of the duc de Choiseul within the government, tripped up Choiseul's protégé, the controller general Maynon d'Invault, at a tumultuous session of the Conseil d'Etat and prevailed upon the king to replace him with Terray. Then, in order to persuade Terray to accept the appointment, which would expose him to the hostility of the public, Maupeou tempted him with the prospect of enjoying unlimited power: they would work together to destroy the parlements, oust Choiseul, fill the ministries with their protégés, and rule together as masters of the kingdom. Louis XV was such a nullity that he hardly figured as a factor in their calculations.

The execution of this strategy, as recounted in the *Mémoires*, turned into a narrative of all the twists and turns and crooked deals that constituted the political history of France until the death of Louis XV in 1774. Terray spent those five years devising arbitrary measures to tax the country to death. Maupeou eliminated the last vestiges of opposition to the government by creating a new judicial system. And to complete their control of the government, they recruited the duc d'Aiguillon to exercise his tyrannical temperament as minister of foreign affairs. The narrative showed how the triumvirate solidified its power, incident by incident, one intrigue on the heels of another. Then it revealed how fissures opened up. As each of the three operated as a villain in his own domain, promoting his own interests, the power sharing created endless possibilities for treachery. But their coalition held together, because there was a mechanism for arbitrating conflict: Mme du Barry. Although she herself had no interest in governing, her dominance of Louis made it possible for her to intervene whenever the balance of power threatened to tip too far to the advantage of one of the three rogues who enjoyed absolute authority in the name of the king. Therefore, as long as Louis slouched through the last years of his reign, the triumvirate went about its business, grinding down the French.

Terray had the greatest capacity to abuse power in the day-to-day business of despotism because he gained complete control of the king's finances. The *Mémoires* devoted most of its text to an account of his fiscal depredations. It revealed how he increased taxes, siphoned off pensions, bilked royal annuities, fleeced officeholders, exploited the Ferme Générale (a cartel that collected indirect taxes), appropriated assets from the Compagnie des Indes, monopolized the grain trade, and drove the general population into misery. The inside story of Terray's peculation involved constant power struggles, so it ultimately turned into a political narrative, which exposed the last round of wheeling and dealing in the long reign of Louis XV.

In broad outline, the account of political intrigues showed how Terray first aligned himself with Maupeou in order to force Choiseul out of office; then switched his support to d'Aiguillon in an effort to oust Maupeou; continued to shift from one ally to another, hoping to win a cardinal's hat and the ministry of the navy or a position as Keeper of the Seals; and in the end reverted to an alliance with Maupeou by revealing that d'Aiguillon was conspiring to recall the parlement and take over the government. At every critical point, according to the *Mémoires*, Terray shored up his own position by cultivating Mme du Barry. He began his ministry by doubling her pension. At the height of his quarrel with Maupeou he added another 100,000 livres to it. Along the way, he cemented his power by cashing all the notes that she wrote on the court banker, and he topped off his subsidies with the gift of a solid gold *toilette*, so extravagant that it had to be hidden from the gaze of the curious.

By accumulating anecdotes of this sort, the *Mémoires* made its antihero into the supreme villain of a government that it described as the most noxious of the century. Its picture of Terray contradicts the views of many historians, who make him out to be a progressive reformer, intent on attacking vested interests and inequalities, though without subscribing to the laissez-faire ideas of the Physiocrats.[11] The *Mémoires* never entertained any such considerations. It excoriated Terray in language so extreme as to make him seem inhuman: "perfect monster" (223), "political vampire who sucked the blood of all France" (59), "monster guilty of the greatest of all misdeeds, the crime of *lèse-*

Nation, a crime as much greater than that of *lèse-Majesté* as the nation is to its sovereign" (309). Judging from the one review that has survived in the underground periodicals of the time, this caricature seemed convincing to some of Terray's contemporaries.[12] And as the last remark made clear, it had an ideological edge. It conveyed the idea that the rule of the king should be subordinate to the higher authority of the nation and that the nation could not assert its right to determine its destiny without destroying the evil that Terray personified: ministerial despotism.

The slandering of ministers continued right through 1789, gathering ideological intensity. All the important controller generals who succeeded Terray— Turgot, Necker, and Calonne—were dragged through the mud by libelers. This literature generally took the form of political pamphlets, although some of the tracts went on at great length. (*M. de Calonne tout entier* [1788] ran to 370 pages.) But the most interesting libel of the "private life" variety from the last years of the Ancien Régime attacked a minister who had long been dead. *Vie privée du cardinal Dubois, premier ministre, archevêque de Cambrai, etc.* (the address on its title page reads simply "London, 1789") appeared just when the Revolution exploded, yet it pretended to reveal everything about the most notorious politician from the beginning of the century, abbé Guillaume Dubois, prime minister during the Regency of the duc d'Orléans (1715–23).

According to a preface and a note from the publisher, it drew its spectacularly shocking material—all of it guaranteed to be accurate—from a lost manuscript by one of Dubois's secretaries. The editor had merely added some background and supplementary information culled from other private lives. Libels often opened with such claims, which were unlikely to be taken seriously. In fact, *Vie privée du cardinal Dubois* was a hack job, usually attributed to a minor man of letters, Antoine Mongez, who became an ardent revolutionary and eventually a member of the Institut de France.[13] Although it has enough of a central narrative to sustain itself as a biography, it, too, reads like an anthology of anecdotes about the wicked ways of the great. The anecdotes succeed one another in a continuous stream of scandal—389 pages, without chapter breaks or any relief in the form of original ideas. Seen in retrospect, the most intriguing thing about the book is the date of its publication: 1789. Just as the Ancien Régime was collapsing, someone decided to put out a large-scale, slanderous attack on a minister from the Regency, a man who had died sixty-five years earlier. Why?

Internal evidence indicates the text was written in 1783.[14] It makes no reference to the calling of the Estates General or to any events of the Revolution and the pre-Revolution of 1787–88. In all likelihood, the book belonged to the wave of slandering that reached a peak with the activities of the London libelers in 1783, but why did the author choose such an antiquated subject? Perhaps because the anecdotes about Dubois still had enough shock value to make the book sell in the lively market for forbidden literature during the 1780s. The attempts by the state to clamp down on that market, which began in June 1783, may have made the publisher decide to withhold publication until a safer moment.[15] There was little risk in putting out such a work in 1789 and some prospect of making money by exploiting the public's fascination with the evils of the regime that had just been overthrown. *Vie privée du cardinal Dubois* may have been nothing more than a literary speculation. But whatever the reasons behind its publication, its text warrants study as a late example of a libel in the form of a "private life."

It began, like most libels, with the birth of its hero, a subject that lent itself to reflections about the low origins of a personage who would rise to the greatest heights of power. According to the *Vie privée*, Dubois was the son of a provincial apothecary in Brive-la-Gaillarde. He did well enough in the local schools to become an abbé and to win a job as a tutor in the household of a magistrate in Bordeaux. Before long, however, he had got a chambermaid pregnant. The magistrate fired him, and the girl insisted on marriage. After a hurried wedding in Limousin, the couple made their way to Paris, where Dubois lived by giving lessons and his wife disappeared. His lucky break came in 1683, when he was hired as one of the tutors to the duc de Chartres, who would eventually succeed his father as duc d'Orléans. Dubois ingratiated himself with the young duke by initiating him into the pleasures of the flesh. Soon loose women were pouring into the boy's bedroom though back stairs in the Palais-Royal. They never stopped, because the abbé, later cardinal, continued to pimp for the prince until his death. Thus a placard attached to the Eglise de Saint-Honoré where the cardinal was buried.

Rome rougit d'avoir rougi
Le m . . . [maquereau] qui gît ici (22).

(Rome blushes for having bestowed the purple
On the p . . . [pimp] who rests here.)

The text contained many such poems, songs, and witticisms picked up from gossip and *chroniques scandaleuses*. It also peppered its anecdotes with the obscenities for which Dubois was famous, especially b . . . (*bougre*, bugger) and f . . . (*foutre*, fuck), which appeared everywhere as an indication of his loutishness. Thanks to Orléanist patronage, he soon accumulated benefices. He also acquired his first case of venereal disease and produced a second child—this one conceived by a peasant girl in a parish attached to one of his abbeys. Dubois ordered a lackey to act as its putative father at its baptism. Meanwhile, he continued to direct the duke's debauchery in Paris. The text dwelled at length on this inexhaustible subject, although it avoided obscene details. The anecdotes rolled by, one after another, without allowing much respite for the reader. One example can be taken as typical of their tone, as indicated in the following synopsis:

Recruiting fresh flesh for the duke, Dubois came upon an attractive but excessively pious widow. The only possibility of making headway with her was by wooing her himself. He promised her everything, including marriage, and she finally consented. At the banquet following the wedding, he introduced her to the duke. Eventually she retired to a bedroom and waited in the dark for her new husband. Dubois gave the duke directions about how to take his place. On the morning after, the bride woke up, found the duke sleeping next to her, and let out a scream. Dubois came running. She begged him to forgive her, for in the confusion and the dark she had not noticed that somehow she was making love with the wrong man. Her pleas were so earnest that they finally touched the duke, who had a good heart and admitted that they had staged the cuckolding together. In fury and despair, Dubois's bride vowed never to see him again and disappeared into the provinces.

Now a bigamist, Dubois was doubly disqualified to be a clergyman. But the experience had solidified his ties to the duke, who henceforth could refuse him nothing. After he succeeded to his father's title and became ruler of France as regent, the duc d'Orléans needed a reliable lieutenant. Dubois suited him perfectly, not only because they were bonded by their debauchery but also because the abbé owed everything to him. Too obscure to have important connections of his own, Dubois could be trusted to execute Orléans's policy of wresting power from the aristocratic greats and even to handle diplomatic missions. The *Vie privée* did not go deeply into political history, but it provided information about the main events: the creation of the Triple Alliance (at the end of the wars of Louis XIV, France stabilized the peace by aligning itself with its former enemies, Britain and the Netherlands in 1716–17), the failure of the Cellamare conspiracy (in 1718 Orléans stifled a plot, led by the Spanish ambassador, the prince of Cellamare, to oust him from power by placing Philip V of Spain on the French throne), and the collapse of Law's System (the Scottish adventurer John Law put together a state-sponsored financial conglomerate, which imploded spectacularly in 1720).

Dubois played an important part in all these events, but the *Vie privée* described it as little more than a chase after women and money. It treated him as a clown. While recounting his diplomatic missions, it borrowed metaphors from the boulevard theaters: Dubois was a "Harlequin" (140) who raced from one "ridiculous scene" (142) to another. In the Netherlands, he developed a sideline as a pawnbroker. While crossing the Channel, he succumbed to sea-sickness, cursing "like a wagon driver mired in the mud" (145). In England he spent most of his time in bawdy houses. And upon his return to France, he asked that all his pranks be rewarded by nothing less than the archbishopric of Cambrai.

Even the Regent, accustomed to the most extravagant propositions, was dumbfounded: "Are you crazy? You, an archbishop? You are a knave; besides, who would make you a priest?" (226). Dubois had been tonsured as an abbé— that is, he had gone through a preliminary ceremony of shaveling as a first step toward taking holy orders—but he had not been ordained as a priest. Unde-terred, he arranged to rush through the elaborate ceremonies and to take pos-session of one of France's richest benefices in one day. The *Vie privée* reported the widespread joke that it was also the day of his first communion, spoiled only by the fact that Dubois lost his head in the bewildering succession of rites and urinated in his archbishop's robes. He had to overcome a final obstacle, however. Having learned that he had hit the jackpot, his first wife appeared out of nowhere and demanded an audience. Dubois shut her up by bribery and threats, then sent an intendant to destroy the evidence of their marriage in an obscure Limousin village. The intendant staged a fake accident outside the church, requested shelter with the curate, put the curate to sleep with some drugged wine, and tore the incriminating page out of the marriage register.

The *Vie privée* recounted the final stages of Dubois's rise to power in the same fashion. He accumulated seven abbeys, amassed a fortune, got himself named cardinal, and ended as *premier ministre*. Along the way he showed a certain shrewdness, the narrator conceded, but even as a cardinal he remained a buffoon. The *Vie privée* made the point with endless anecdotes, one full-scale "portrait" (103–4), and many excerpts from contemporary ephemera, cob-bling the material together in the manner of a conventional libel. But its stories had no news value in 1789. Why, then, did it go to such lengths to slander a man who had been dead for decades? The simplest answer is that Dubois's biography included so many outrageous episodes that it made a very good read—and still does today, at least in small doses. Dubois incarnated an era that was so notorious for immorality that it generated its own folklore about debauchery in high places. A libeler had merely to tap the enormous repertory of tales about the Regent and his "roués" to come up with a potential best-seller. Historians have rightly dismissed those stories as caricatures, and they have given high marks to the Regent and Dubois as politicians. But the politi-cal folklore warrants attention in itself. It had to be assembled with some art. Fragments appeared in print during the first half of the eighteenth century, but the full historical narrative was not pieced together until the 1780s, when the libelers went to work on it. The *Vie privée de Louis XV* provided a general overview in 1781. But the *Vie privée du cardinal Dubois* gave the first detailed account of the years 1715–23—wildly inaccurate, to be sure, but also, at least in parts, very funny.

The humorous vein in which the text related events conveys a certain tone from the 1780s, the era of *The Marriage of Figaro* and the Diamond Necklace Affair. Of course, no period in history can be reduced to one current in the general atmosphere, but there was a frivolity in the air among the upper classes in the mid-1780s that had some affinity with the lighthearted eroticism of the Regency. The climate changed dramatically in 1789. By then, thunderous declamations against aristocratic depravity—"mauvaises moeurs" (bad morals), according to a favorite expression at that time—had set a new tone in public affairs. But a libel written in 1783, though it lacked moralizing and merely made fun of its subject, could also contribute something to the revolutionary enterprise. The French did not know that they had been living under an "Ancien Régime" until they destroyed it. After July 14, 1789, they needed to come to terms with what it once was. But what exactly was it? They lacked the information and the understanding to answer that question adequately. No historical account produced before 1789 could be trusted afterward, and very few existed, because contemporary history and biography were not permitted under the old system for controlling the press. The French had to learn about their recent past from libels; and their need to learn was particularly acute in 1789, because that was when they faced the necessity of reconstructing the Ancien Régime—not reviving it, of course, but re-creating it as a literary artifact so that the public, the reading public at the heart of the sovereign people, could know what had been overthrown and what might rise again if corruption gained the upper hand. *Vie privée du cardinal Dubois* contributed to that task, although it was not originally intended to do so, and it was succeeded by a far more important contribution, the *Vie privée du maréchal de Richelieu*.

Vie privée du maréchal de Richelieu (1791) brought the long series of libels about the private lives of the great under the Ancien Régime to a fitting climax, because it went over all the territory they had covered and looked back on them from the perspective of the early Revolution. The life of the duke, later marshal de Richelieu, grand-nephew of the famous cardinal, lent itself to this broad treatment. He was born at the end of the seventeenth century (on March 13, 1696) and died (on August 8, 1788) less than a year before the outbreak of the French Revolution. His three marriages took place under three different reigns, the third when he had reached the age of eighty-four. Along the way he participated in many of the great events of the century, as a courtier, soldier, and diplomat, and he seduced dozens of women, the last when he had turned eighty-six and still, as she allegedly reported, made love like a twenty-year-old. So much life, so many women, made Richelieu endlessly interesting to his contemporaries. He had already appeared in many libels, notably as the Iago-like villain who stole the show in *Les Amours de Zéokinizul*. A full-scale life of him was bound to fascinate readers in 1791, not merely for its scandal but also because it would provide a panorama of the Ancien Régime.

The scale of the *Vie privée* was as monumental as its subject—three substantial volumes divided carefully into chapters with digests of the chapters in an elaborate table of contents and more than two hundred pages of supplementary documents, all apparently authentic. Nothing in the corpus of private lives could match it, except *Vie privée de Louis XV*, which covered much of the same ground. The authors remained anonymous, but they dropped hints about what lay behind their enterprise in a preface.[16] They insisted that the text conformed exactly to historical truth based on the papers of Richelieu himself, but they undercut that conventional claim by appealing to the voyeuristic interest of the reader: "It is the hero undressed that will be presented to the public" (1: 2). They promised to deliver "a very spicy narrative" abounding in "curious anecdotes" of the kind that had once amused sophisticates in Parisian salons. *Vie privée du maréchal de Richelieu* was published two years into the Revolution, but it was meant to convey the naughtiness, wit, and laughter still lingering in fashionable circles from the end of the Ancien Régime.

The first chapters introduced the hero as one of the greatest figures in "the annals of gallantry" (1: 41)—that is, they invoked the gallant literature that went back to Bussy-Rabutin or even further, to tales of courtly love from Boccaccio and beyond. Later chapters cited libels from the eighteenth century, including *Vie privée de Louis XV* and *Mémoires secrets pour servir à l'histoire de Perse*, usually to point out inaccuracies. But the pretense of remaining faithful to the historical record did not disguise the basic character of the book. *Vie privée du maréchal Richelieu* was a libel, in fact a kind of summa of libel literature, even though it slandered a dead man. It was composed essentially of anecdotes, although it worked them skillfully into a general narrative, which covered a century and included enough information about wars and politics to help readers keep their bearings.[17] A few examples:

Presented to the court of Louis XIV at the age of fourteen, young Richelieu started chasing skirts like a naughty cherub. (In fact, he may have served as the model for Chérubin in *Le Mariage de Figaro*.) His first conquest came when he snuck into the bed of the duchesse de * * * and hid in a corner under the covers. Already softened up by his outrageous flirting, the lady capitulated after the bundle in the bed turned into a boy, and the boy turned into a lover. (3: 21)

Once old enough to play the part of a man-about-town, Richelieu cultivated a reputation as a seducer. One night he called on three of his mistresses and had his coach stationed outside the house of a fourth so that word would spread about his prowess. He even "cuckolded" the Regent and his principal minister, the Cardinal Dubois, by seducing their many mistresses. One mistress, who pretended to be pious, had put up great resistance to the cardinal. After she finally capitulated, he found her in bed with Richelieu. Instead of turning on his rival, he cursed her: "F . . . ! Madame, why did you give me such a hard time with your virtue and your prudishness and then go whoring with that devil of a man that one finds everywhere?" (1: 225)

Richelieu's most famous coup, which became "the anecdote of all Paris," occurred some years later when he overcame seemingly insurmountable obstacles in order to cuckold a well-known financier, Alexandre-Joseph Le Riche de La Popelinière. La Popelinière had married an actress, Mimi Dancourt, and kept her under close watch by an army of servants in his sumptuous town house. Undaunted, Richelieu rented an adjoining house, had a hole opened through it into Mimi's boudoir, and installed a revolving fireplace, so that they could make love while the master of the house passed the night in his separate bedroom. A disgruntled servant revealed the trick, and La Popelinière packed Mimi off to a convent. But Richelieu did not mind losing her. All that mattered was the feat itself and the glory that it added to his reputation. (2: 34, 93)

The author recounted these anecdotes at considerable length. He filled them out with descriptions of how Richelieu stalked his prey, deciphered facial expressions, modulated his sweet talk, played conflicting emotions off against each other, raised expectations only to frustrate them with periods of feigned indifference, and, when the last defenses had collapsed, closed in for the kill. According to the foreword, the text of volumes 1 and 2 was compiled from Richelieu's papers, but volume 3 was written by the marshal himself. It recounted his early conquests in the first person singular and therefore treated readers to glimpses of his own psychology. Nearly half the volume was devoted to one episode, Richelieu's seduction of two women from the lower-middle class (one was the wife of an artisan who made mirrors, the other a poor widow). They were close friends and lived in the same modest house—hence Richelieu's attraction to them: he wanted to cross class lines and violate the ties of friendship while seducing two beauties under the same roof. That the artisan's wife was extremely devout made the adventure even more enticing. The Richelieu-narrator relates it in great detail. He explains how he played on their vanity, their fascination with the world of the great, their hopes and fears of improving their lot, their contradictory impulses of desire and shame, and finally their authentic sentiment of love. In doing so, he reveals what is driving him. It is not the conquest but the love of the chase, not the prize but the challenge of overcoming the difficulties to win it, and not the women but the aggrandizement of his own ego. We are in the world of *Les Liaisons danger-*

euses. Laclos himself recognized the parallel with his novel. In a review of *Vie privée du maréchal de Richelieu* published on February 8, 1791, he treated the book as both authentic and accurate.

This work of history is as interesting as the best-known novels, and it even outdoes all of those that have been taxed with exaggeration in their depiction of the bad morals in high society. Anyone who reads it will be convinced that the scandalous and atrocious fictions used by authors to expose and condemn the wicked characters of their novels, are actually unequal to reality. . . . It shows that the revolution was just as necessary for the restoration of morality as for liberty.[18]

The author or authors of *Vie privée du maréchal de Richelieu* did not have the talent of Laclos, far from it, but they treated the same themes from the same point of view. Volume 3 was a full-scale novella, the ultimate product in a strain of libel literature that went back to the seventeenth century.

But volumes 1 and 2 contained a great deal more than semi-fictional Don Juanism. They followed Richelieu through every phase of his military career, from his service as an aide-de-camp to maréchal Villars during the War of the Spanish Succession (1700–1714) to his last, disastrous campaign as a marshal in the Seven Years' War (1756–63). Along the way they recounted his diplomatic missions and his involvement in politics—not in detail, for the authors claimed to be biographers who would leave military, diplomatic, and political history to historians. But while they gave seduction stories a prominent place in the chapters devoted to politics, they did not understate Richelieu's importance as a politician. On the contrary, they stressed his commitment to royal absolutism. The king, according to their account of his philosophy, possessed unlimited power, and therefore nothing should limit the power of the king's agents. As *gouverneur* of Guyenne (a largely honorific office, which made him the highest representative of the king in the region around Bordeaux), Richelieu rode roughshod over local sensibilities, dispatched opponents to prison by lettres de cachet, and took special pleasure in suppressing the parlement of Bordeaux during the Maupeou coup. He also wielded arbitrary power in his private affairs, imprisoning servants who displeased him and bullying the police. He was, in fact, a "much feared despot" in his own person (2: 136). And he felt no compunctions about exercising power because he was convinced that it rightly belonged to him as a member of the high aristocracy. Supposedly speaking in his own voice in volume 3, he stressed the necessity of strict hierarchy in the social order.

A king surrounded by an opulent nobility shines to even greater effect by the lustre that the nobles reflect and that is attached to his own representation. A great lord is a link in the chain that originates at the throne and descends by imperceptible degrees toward the common people. He obeys his master [the king] and in turn derives from him the power to make himself obeyed by his own inferiors. He must overawe the people, and wealth is one of the greatest means toward that end. (3: 119)

Nothing could be more politically incorrect than these sentiments in 1791. The authors took care to disavow them[19] and criticized the brutally aristocratic behavior of their hero. Yet the text sometimes hinted at admiration for Richelieu, especially for his bravery on the battlefield: "He never lost his self mastery in situations of the greatest danger, and he derived as much pleasure from a battle as from a rendezvous with pretty ladies" (1: 316). The identification of war and lovemaking pointed to the basic message of the book. Under the Ancien Régime, women were objects of conquest, and the battles for them corresponded to the power plays that ran through all society, from the top down. The play for power took place especially at court. *Vie privée du maréchal de Richelieu* therefore emphasized the marshal's role as a courtier who exercised influence through royal mistresses. After championing Madame de Châteauroux, he pulled strings by manipulating Madame de Pompadour. A quarrel with her eliminated him from the inner circle of decision making for a while, but the advent of Madame du Barry, his protégée, gave him a free hand to determine events. He profited from it by elevating a relative, the duc d'Aiguillon, to the position of foreign secretary and by seconding Maupeou in the crushing of the parlements. By that time, Richelieu had abandoned all ambition to become a minister himself. With the advent of Louis XVI in 1774, he lost his grip on power and contented himself in his old age by ruling despotically over the Comédie italienne, a fiefdom he had acquired in his capacity as first gentleman of the king's bedchamber. One of the last scenes of Richelieu at Versailles showed him at Louis XVI's *coucher*, holding the king's dressing gown and tottering after him helplessly while the king, distracted, walked about the bedroom.

In the end, therefore, the story of Richelieu merged into the history of Versailles, a mixture of endless quarrels over *préséance*, personal jealousies, backbiting, extravagant display, absurd etiquette, debauchery, hypocrisy, pride, indolence, and incompetence, all of it calibrated to the coming and going of royal mistresses and the general law of seduce or be seduced. At the center of the vortex, the king sat on his throne, doing nothing. An "apathetic sultan" (2: 156), he took no interest in anything except hunting and women. Every detail in the book pointed to the same conclusion: France had degenerated into an Asiatic despotism—"Asiatic" because it combined moral depravity with political abuse. By 1791 that theme had been worked over so extensively that it might seem to be worn to death. *Vie privée du maréchal de Richelieu* gave it new life; and the revolutionaries needed to revive it, because they defined the present by reconstructing the past. Richelieu embodied everything that they meant to abolish in 1791, above all the twin evils of decadence and despotism. Yet his secret life proved strangely fascinating, for it expressed the gaiety and good humor of a world they had lost.

Chapter 28
Royal Depravity

Seen from the perspective of the libels that slandered queens and mistresses all the way back to the early seventeenth century, it seems inevitable that Marie-Antoinette would come in for some calumny. But she received far more than her share. The avalanche of defamation that overwhelmed her between 1789 and her execution on October 16, 1793, has no parallel in the history of vilification. A bibliography of all the printed matter that took her as a target before 1794 comes to about 150 items, and some of them excoriate her in language so extreme as to defy belief.[1] Yet they seemed believable to a great many Frenchmen at the time—and that poses a problem.

We may never be able to fathom the obsessions that take hold of entire populations. But without speculating about the pathology of the collective imagination, we can point out some partial explanations of the hatred for the queen. As an Austrian princess, she represented the principal enemy that the French had fought since the sixteenth century. That enmity triggered some visceral emotions in 1792 and 1793, when the Austrian invasion threatened to turn into a massacre of the civilian population. Domestic politics also took on a life-and-death quality as the Revolution radicalized, and therefore the parties of the left could use collaboration with the queen as an accusation to hurl against the parties of the right. No loyal opposition emerged amid the mutual incriminations, because it was impossible at a time of such turbulence to reach any consensus about the basic principles of the political system. Opponents of the government conspired to overthrow it from the left and to undermine it from the right. Moreover, the distinction between left and right—itself an invention of the National Assembly in 1789—kept shifting, because every revolutionary "journée" transformed the political spectrum, changing yesterday's left wingers into today's reactionaries. At the heart of it all, the king betrayed the constitution he had sworn to uphold, and during the early years of the Revolution, when he seemed to play the role of constitutional monarch in good faith, he proved to be so recalcitrant and incompetent that he constantly aroused suspicions. The doubters pointed to "l'Autrichienne" as the power behind the throne. Marie-Antoinette must have been conspiring to sabotage the Revolution and to deliver France into the hands of her brother in Vienna: how else could one explain the continuous disasters that threatened to destroy the new order as soon as it was born?

Conspiratorial explanations belonged to the core of libel literature during the French Revolution, but they could not be fabricated out of nothing. They drew on material produced under the Ancien Régime. The mythology that had grown up around Marie-Antoinette before 1789 provided them with a rich stock of images and themes, and the stockpiling went back to the activities of the double agents in the police and the libelers of London.

Nasty rumors about the queen began to circulate in the mid-1770s. According to the memoirs of her femme de chambre, Jeanne-Louise-Henriette Campan, they resulted in part from Marie-Antoinette's dislike of the burdensome ceremonies in Versailles, including the strict separation of men from women in her entourage. Instead of being surrounded by a convoy of ladies festooned in full dress when she progressed through the palace, she limited her suite to three valets. She replaced female servants with men when she dined. And in her desire to escape from the daily grind of stifling ritual, she arranged for outdoor concerts to be given during summer nights. Although she always remained veiled and seated on a terrace with the royal family during the *Nachtmusik*, rumors spread that she escaped for rendezvous with lovers in the park. Trivial incidents also set tongues wagging. Her coach broke down on one occasion when she was traveling to a masked ball in Paris, and she had to arrive in a rented carriage—a sure sign of a secret tryst, according to the gossips. They designated the comte d'Artois, considered to be the more dashing of the king's two brothers, as her main paramour, but they also fixed on her two favorites, the princesse de Lamballe and the duchesse de Polignac. Louis XVI apparently suffered from phimosis, a condition that rendered him impotent for the first seven years of their marriage. Although a minor operation corrected the problem and Marie-Antoinette gave birth to their first child in 1778, the king—awkward, fat, fond of drinking and of the unregal pastime of locksmithery—was easily caricatured as a cuckold.[2]

The first calumnies, in the form of songs and epigrams, appeared in 1774.[3] By the end of 1778, so many were circulating that a malefactor compiled a whole volume of manuscript copies and left it in the palace so that it would be brought before the king, who reacted with predictable indignation.[4] Full-scale printed libels also began to proliferate in 1778. Morande had shown that a fortune could be made by slandering the great of Versailles at the end of the reign of Louis XV. After he was bought off by the government, his successors among the French expatriates in London, Brussels, Liège, and Amsterdam aimed their fire at Louis XVI and Marie-Antoinette. Some worked for the police who were sent to capture them. The intrigues on both sides of the law led to so many plots and subplots that it might be useful at this point to summarize the ground covered in Part II.

As explained in Chapters 9–12, P.-A.-A. Goupil, a police inspector turned clandestine publisher, produced several works that featured Marie-Antoinette as an adulteress and a lesbian. He received 92,000 livres for confiscating a libel about the queen and the princesse de Lamballe that he wrote himself and had printed in the Low Countries. In March 1778, when he overplayed his hand and became embroiled in court intrigues, he was caught and sent to the Bastille. But the libels continued to appear. In 1779 the government paid 192,000 livres to suppress an attack on the queen by an extortionist in London, and the entire edition, sealed with the arms of Lord North, who had helped in the transaction, was delivered to the Bastille. By then, Jacquet de la Douay had become the special agent of the Parisian police charged with suppressing the production of libels outside France. He outdid Goupil in commissioning them. By the time of his arrest in December 1781, he had produced a whole series of slanderous works about the queen and the leading ministers, some of which also found their way, at great cost, to the storeroom in the Bastille. Meanwhile, Vergennes, the minister of foreign affairs, had dispatched other agents to suppress the increasing output of libels in London, which had become the main center of the mudslinging industry. Goesman, disguised as the baron de Thurne, purchased *Les Amours de Charlot et Toinette* for 18,600 livres on July 31, 1781, and delivered the entire edition, as he claimed, to the Bastille. After his warnings about more libels, accompanied by requests for more money, began to sound suspicious, Vergennes and Lenoir sent Alexis d'Anouilh, another police agent, to investigate. He returned with nothing, except an enormous expense account. So he, too, went to the Bastille, and finally Vergennes and Lenoir called upon Receveur, their trustiest agent, who had gone into retirement after hunting down Jacquet. They dressed him up as another fake baron and sent him off to buy up the latest libels, including *Les Passe-temps d'Antoinette*, and to attempt to suppress the libel industry in general. As it turned out, *Les Passe-temps* never made it into print, at least not under that title, and Receveur never made any headway in his negotiations with Pelleport, who exposed his mission in *Le Diable dans un bénitier*, a libel against the police as well as the ministers behind them. But the continued surveillance of Pelleport finally led to his arrest in 1784, which put an end to most of the libeling in London.

What resulted from all this activity? In *La Police de Paris dévoilée*, Pierre Manuel published an inventory of the confiscated books that Lenoir had consigned to be kept under lock and key in the Bastille, presumably for storage until a decision was taken to have them pulped. They included libels against three ministers and several courtiers as well as the king and queen—fifteen titles in all, of which seven came from Jacquet's operation. The number of volumes came to 3,105 plus entire editions of five works or another 2,500 to 5,000 copies. An employee of the police noted the number of copies on the inventory and added some comments to identify each title. The two most important libels about Marie-Antoinette appeared as follows.

All of the edition *Amours de Charlot et Antoinette.* . . .

Verse and
engravings very
abusive to the Q.

And, from the "works that sieur Jacquet had printed":

534 *Essais sur la vie d'Antoinette* . . . . .

Abominable libel
Against the Q.[5]

By consulting these two works, one can form a good idea of the kind of calumny directed against the queen during the 1780s.

Boissière, the French bookseller in London who served as an intermediary for the anonymous author of *Les Amours de Charlot et Toinette*, signed a contract guaranteeing that he had surrendered every last copy of the book; but as often happened in such cases, a few copies escaped, and a great many circulated from the editions reprinted after 1789.[6] The original edition can easily be distinguished from the reprints, and it has characteristics such as catchwords that mark it as a book printed in London. It hardly counts as a book, however, because it contains only eight pages and two plates, both obscene. The plates correspond to the main theme of the text. One depicts a group of doctors examining the king's limp penis, and it carries a caption saying, "The Consultation. The Faculty [of Medicine] declares him impotent." The other shows Artois about to copulate with the queen, and its caption reads, "Fraternal Generosity. They fabricate an heir."[7]

The text is a long poem full of obscenities undisguised by bowdlerisms or ellipsis dots, except for obvious names such as L . . . for Louis. It begins with a description of Antoinette masturbating. She has no other outlet for her desire, it explains, because the king cannot satisfy her. Having given him a thorough examination, the faculty of medicine has declared him impotent, and the poet does not spare the royal penis in his verse.

On sait bien que le pauvre Sire,
Trois ou quatre fois condamné

Par la salubre faculté,
Pour impuissance très complète
Ne peut satisfaire Antoinette.
De ce malheur bien convaincu,
Attendu que son allumette
N'est pas plus grosse qu'un fétu;
Que toujours molle et toujours croche,
Il n'a de vit que dans la poche;
Qu'au lieu de foutre, il est foutu.

(It is well-known that the poor Sire,
Three or four times condemned
By the salubrious faculty [of medicine],
For complete impotence,
Cannot satisfy Antoinette.
Quite convinced of this misfortune,
Considering that his match-stick
Is no bigger than a straw,
Always limp and always curved,
He has no prick, except in his pocket;
Instead of fucking, he is fucked.)

Enter the comte d'Artois, all ardor and gallantry. He seduces Antoinette in a flash, stripping her not only of her clothes but also of anything that suggests royal majesty. As the poet describes her, she is all palpitating flesh, and she responds to Artois's advances with the artlessness of a shopgirl.

Il baise ses beaux bras, son joli petit con,
Et tantôt une fesse et tantôt un téton:
Il claque doucement sa fesse rebondie,
Cuisse, ventre, nombril, le centre de tout bien;
Le prince baise tout dans sa douce folie.

(He kisses her beautiful arms, her pretty little cunt,
And now a buttock, and now a breast:
He gently slaps her bouncing buttock,
Thigh, belly, belly button, the center of all good;
The prince kisses it all in his sweet passion.)

At the height of the lovemaking, a bell rings and a page appears, then beats a hasty retreat. Disconcerted, they begin all over again, and again the bell rings, exposing them once more to the incredulous gaze of the servant. Antoinette collapses in consternation—and uncovers the cause of the interruptions: in the fury of their passion, they kept rubbing against the ribbon of a bell to call the valet, which had been hidden under a cushion. Every thrust of Artois had acted as a summons for the servant to come running. With the problem solved, the lovers continue, and the poet leaves them copulating happily ever after. He ends his ode with a sybaritic moral.

Quant à moi, si l'on m'asservit
A jouir de grands biens, sans rire, foutre, et plaire,
Afin de me sauver d'une telle misère,
J'aime mieux me couper le vit.
Quand on nous parle de vertu,
C'est souvent par envie;
Car enfin serions-nous en vie,
Si nos pères n'eussent foutu?

(As for me, if I were condemned
To enjoy great wealth without laughing, fucking, and pleasing,
To save myself from such wretchedness,
I'd rather cut off my prick.
When they speak to us of virtue,
It's often from envy,
For after all, would we be alive,
If our fathers hadn't fucked?)[8]

Les Amours de Charlot et Toinette was a slight work. It hardly differed in tone from the bawdiest drinking songs improvised by Pierre Gallet, Charles François Pannard, and the other vaudevillians who gathered in watering places like the Café du caveau. It has the frothiness of Crébillon's *Sopha*, the gimmickry of Diderot's *Bijoux indiscrets*, the naughtiness of Boucher's paintings of Mlle O'Murphy—and not a word about ministers, foreign affairs, or disputes with the parlements. The poem had plenty of shock value, of course. In the eyes of the foreign ministry and the police, it was a crime of lèse majesté. By treating the king as a cuckold and the queen as a sex-starved spouse, it made them look ridiculous—but not threatening. Marie-Antoinette was no more satanic than Mme du Barry—and no more dignified, either. In the light of what was published during the Revolution, *Les Amours de Charlot et Toinette* looks like a bad joke rather than a bomb waiting to explode.

Ten years later, the Marie-Antoinette who appeared in print was a different person. The difference derived in general from the heating up of the political atmosphere and in particular from the Diamond Necklace Affair. Pamphlets, legal memoirs, songs, and epigrams flooded the country after the Cardinal de Rohan's arrest on August 15, 1785. The mildest of them told of a confidence game: some adventurers had convinced Rohan that he could win the queen's good graces if he presented her with a wildly expensive diamond necklace, which they then appropriated. The most extravagant versions of the affair had the cardinal and the queen cuckolding the king, then turning against one another in a vicious quarrel. When the arrest led to a trial before the Parlement of Paris and the crown quashed the trial, sending Rohan into exile, almost anything seemed believable and almost everything in the way of perversion and crime began to be attributed to Marie-Antoinette.

The "private life" that registered this change most fully was *Essais historiques sur la vie de Marie-Antoinette d'Autriche, reine de France, pour servir à l'histoire de cette princesse,* or as the title was phrased in some editions, *Essai sur la vie privée de Marie-Antoinette d'Autriche, reine de France.* It appeared in two parts, both dated 1789. The first part went through ten editions, which varied in length from 58 to 140 pages. The second part, printed separately in some cases and together with the first in others, appeared in six more editions, some of them in two volumes.[9] That so many versions of the same text should have been published in the same year indicates that the publishers responded to an enormous demand. The *Essais historiques* probably reached more readers than any other libel during the French Revolution. It certainly contributed more than any other to the demonization of the queen.

Far from being a revolutionary tract, however, part 1 belonged to the type of slandering developed by the London libelers in the 1770s. Internal evidence shows that it was written between May and October 1781, and an introduction added sometime soon after July 14, 1789, explained that it was found in the Bastille and that it probably was *Les Passe-temps d'Antoinette* (the libel that Receveur had attempted to suppress during his mission to London) published under another title.[10] All the evidence indicates that the text came from the 534 copies of "*Essais sur la vie d'Antoinette*" that Lenoir had locked up in the Bastille with the other libels commissioned by Jacquet de la Douay.

Although the original version of the *Essais historiques* was reprinted many times after the Bastille fell, it contained a great deal of material that did not please the new editors. Therefore, they added eleven pages of notes to correct passages that they considered politically incorrect. Where the old libel attacked the duc d'Orléans, for example, they paid tribute to him as a patriot.[11] By contrast, they added disparaging remarks about Necker, whose conservatism had alienated the left when he rejoined the government after July 14; and they heaped praise on Mirabeau.[12] More fundamentally, they took issue with the general picture of Marie-Antoinette presented in the text of 1781, because it was not nearly black enough to suit them. The editors of 1789 imagined the queen to be deeply depraved, the modern equivalent of the most monstrous female rulers from the distant past: Messalina, the debauched Roman empress, and Frédégonde, the murderous consort of Chilpéric, the Merovingian king in the sixth century. These two, along with many others—Catherine de Médicis,

Brunehilde, Cleopatra—appear often in the later libels against Marie-Antoinette.[13] But instead of citing such appropriate precedents, part 1 of the *Essais historiques*—that is, the older version from 1781—compared the queen with Mme du Barry. The editors protested against this misleading parallel, because Louis XV's mistress, though thoroughly immoral, was, as they saw her and as the pre-revolutionary libels had portrayed her, frivolous and fun-loving. She let herself be manipulated, but she had no interest in politics, whereas Marie-Antoinette not only gave full rein to her vicious appetites but also ran the government and used her power to oppress the people.[14] In fact, the queen's political sins were so great, according to the editors of 1789, that she should be forced from the throne and made to do penance in a dungeon-like cloister.[15]

Although inadequately revolutionary from the perspective of 1789, part 1 of the *Essais historiques sur la vie de Marie-Antoinette* slandered the queen quite effectively in the manner that had prevailed in 1781. It had all the characteristics of a classic libel: anecdotes strung together in chronological order and enlivened by portraits of all the main characters. Moreover, it contained so much gossip about the court that it read in places like a *chronique scandaleuse*. Beginning with Marie-Antoinette's arrival in France in 1768, the narrative recounts her love affairs, one after the other. She copulates with anyone she can get her hands on, though she prefers women; so the comtesse (later duchesse) de Polignac, known as "Madame Jule," ultimately emerges as her principal lover. As in *Les Amours de Charlot et Toinette*, the king appears as an impotent simpleton, eager despite his sexual incapacity to believe that he is the father of the queen's children.[16] But Marie-Antoinette is now presented as a hardened sybarite driven by an inexhaustible libido. She has so many lovers that the court amuses itself by calculating, according to evidence purveyed by various rumors, who could have sired her offspring—her daughter, Marie Thérèse Charlotte, born on December 19, 1778, and the baby (to be named Louis Joseph) not yet born at the time of the writing. Many of the anecdotes concern sexual escapades in the gardens of Versailles during the summer evening concerts. They rarely rise above the level of court scandalmongering, even when they touch on political issues. The fall of Turgot, for example, is recounted as a side effect of a plot to free the queen from the censorious supervision of her straight-laced *dame d'honneur*, the comtesse de Noailles ("Madame Etiquette").

But politics takes a serious turn at one point in the sexual saga as it was construed in 1781. Marie-Antoinette and Madame Jule form a "committee" or "council," which meets in some private rooms of Versailles. They staff it with their lovers and favorites—each receives a slanderous "portrait"—and use it to govern France: "It was in these assemblies that they deliberated on the most important affairs of the ministry. Peace, war, politics, finance, the fall of ministers, and the degree of favor and credit that they could be given—everything was treated and decided as in a final court of appeals; and they called in the king merely for form, in order to have the decisions of this ridiculous assembly ratified."[17] As an example of the committee's power, the text relates the fall of the prince de Montbarrey as minister of war in December 1780 and his replacement by the maréchal de Ségur—a matter of intrigue and favoritism, nothing more. Although unimportant in itself, this incident provokes hostility in the court faction most opposed to the queen, the clientele around the comte de Maurepas. But Marie-Antoinette wins Maurepas over by appealing for his support in her attempt to convince Louis XVI that he had produced her second pregnancy. In the end, therefore, Marie-Antoinette conquers the commanding heights of the political system. Never does the text mention any issues or principles at stake in the back-biting and power brokering. It expresses some sympathy for the suffering of the common people and considerable indignation at the degradation of the monarchy in the eyes of the public.[18] But it draws no conclusions beyond an expression of scorn for the decadence of the court.[19] Of course, decadence provided excellent material for copy. The anonymous author ended his tale by promising to provide a sequel, because "the continuation of the life of our illustrious Marie-Antoinette will doubtless furnish us with ample matter for other volumes of anecdotes."[20]

The sequel, however, published in 1789 as part 2 of *Essais historiques sur la vie de Marie-Antoinette d'Autriche* and as a free-standing volume, incorporates the anecdotes in a fiercely revolutionary account of royal politics.[21] It goes back over Marie-Antoinette's first years at the court, but it now relates them in her own voice, using the first person singular. A note from a supposed editor explains that he has taken her words from a manuscript that somehow fell into his possession, although he neglects to explain why Marie-Antoinette should have drafted such a long and self-incriminating text and how it got into his hands. As a literary device, the first-person narrative is much less effective than that of the *Vie privée du maréchal de Richelieu*, but it has the same purpose: to lure readers into the illusion that they are seeing directly into the narrator's soul. In fact, the text resembles a soliloquy by a villain in a melodrama. Marie-Antoinette exults in her wickedness—"I am a monster execrated by all of nature" (6)—and revels in contemplating the crimes that she plans to commit: "arson, sacrilegion, rape, incest, parricide, profanation" (123).

By this time, the notion of the queen as a monster had been taken up in the prints sold everywhere in the streets. In 1784, when a canard about a monster supposedly captured in Chile was the talk of all Paris, the print makers of the rue Saint Jacques churned out thousands of broadsides to show what it

Figure 45. The Chilean monster pictured in a canard from 1784. (Bibliothèque nationale de France)

looked like. In 1789 they adapted their old designs to a new purpose: the portrayal of Marie-Antoinette.

The most monstrous quality of the evil queen conjured up by the *Essais historiques sur la vie de Marie-Antoinette d'Autriche* was pathological lust. Unlike the relatively innocent Toinette in *Les Amours de Charlot et Toinette*, she always acts as the aggressor, fornicating furiously with everything in her path—men, women, royalty, lackeys, her closest relatives, and any stranger that she can snatch out of the darkness while roaming through the park of Versailles at night. For a steady diet of perversion, she depends on the comte d'Artois and the comtesse (later duchesse) de Polignac. But in relating their orgies, she makes it clear that she seeks a more powerful outlet for her pas-

Figure 46. Marie-Antoinette as a monster in a popular print of 1789.

sions—not merely copulation with everyone she desires but the annihilation
of everyone she hates. Thus her account of copulating as a threesome with
Artois and Polignac: "Our three interlocked bodies composed the most rare
and interesting combinations. Debilitated by our pleasures, exhausted with
fatigue, we took time out only in order to mock the misery of the people and
to drink deeply in the chalice of crime. The brew that filled it served as an
omen that, following the example of Caligula, we soon would drink the blood
of the French people out of their own skulls" (122).

The step from sex to crime carries Marie-Antoinette into deep political
territory. In fact, the sexual motif of the 1789 text serves primarily as a vehicle
for its political message, and the narrative is actually quite chaste. Instead of
dwelling on erotic details, it restricts itself to general remarks and emphasizes
the queen's sexual depravity as evidence of her satanic nature. It echoes themes
from earlier libels, especially the pamphlets against Mme du Barry and

Maupeou, polemics from the Diamond Necklace Affair, and even scandals connected with the maréchal de Richelieu. Marie-Antoinette's misdeeds therefore appear as the culmination of years of political abuse, just as she herself represents the zenith in the line of evil queens that stretches back to Agrippina and Messalina. The narrative also shows how she exercises her malevolent influence from behind the throne. Using a recipe inherited from Catherine de Médicis, she poisons two ministers, Maurepas and Vergennes, and her own son, the dauphin, in order to clear a path to the throne for the comte d'Artois. In the succession of finance ministers, she favors Calonne, because he gives her unlimited access to the royal treasury, and hates Necker for his repulsive honesty. She actually precipitates the Revolution by getting the king to dismiss Necker; and when he falls, she has a whole team of counterrevolutionaries ready to fill the ministry. That plot fails but only because the French people themselves intervene in events by storming the Bastille.

Political conspiracy lies at the heart of the narrative from 1789 in contrast to part 1. Marie-Antoinette uses her orgies with the comte d'Artois to promote a diabolical scheme: she will poison the dauphin; Artois will engineer a coup to get Louis deposed and exiled to a monastery; they will find a way to get rid of Artois's older brother, the comte de Provence; and then they will take over the kingdom, he as regent (at least until they kill her new baby, thereby making Artois king), she as the ultimate source of power. It is, to put it mildly, a rather elaborate plot, so they must recruit conspirators to help them execute it— princes of the blood, prelates, generals, and the most depraved members of the aristocracy. The conspirators attend secret meetings and take oaths to uphold a compact, whose terms Marie-Antoinette quotes in full. Article 2 reads: "The members of this honorable league, having always felt an invincible horror for French blood and desiring to bathe themselves in it, agree to employ the surest means to make it flow in torrents" (115). Besides military force, they will use "calumny, the execrable goddess of crime" (119), along with cloak-and-dagger tactics. The latter includes an attempt by Artois to assassinate the king, which is foiled at the last minute by the comte d'Estaing, one of the few patriots from the aristocracy. On the eve of July 14, the conspirators have sharpened their swords, stocked up on poison, and sent troops to surround Paris. Marie-Antoinette exults in anticipation of the carnage: "Oh, you who read this account, pay close attention to the details of this conspiracy, and you will agree that nowhere on earth is it possible to find a monster as debased as I" (128). But the uprising of the Parisians prevents it all. Artois and the leading aristocrats flee from France, leaving the queen to gnash her teeth in frustration and rage. Nevertheless, she confides to the reader, she will find another way to overthrow the Revolution and to wreak revenge on the Parisians, for they are certain to relax their vigilance once they resume their ordinary activities.

There is nothing subtle about the moral of the story: beware, brave Parisians, of counterrevolutionary conspiracies. The text actually presents Louis XVI in a rather favorable light. Although feeble and ridiculous, he means well. He tries to limit the extravagant expenditure of the queen, and he favors Necker's attempts to put the crown's finances in order. Immediately after July 14, he comes to Paris to express his willingness to rule as a constitutional monarch. It follows—implicitly, because Marie-Antoinette is always deemed to be the narrator—that the French people should support Louis, but only insofar as he cooperates with the National Assembly. The real threat to the Revolution comes from the queen, not the king. She will never stop conspiring, and her plots could break out at any moment.

To get the message across, the author has to resort to awkward devices because he puts it in the mouth of the arch-conspirator herself. She delivers warnings to her readers about her plots to exterminate them, and the audience she addresses is implicitly composed of patriots. "Read and tremble" (9), she tells them, as she begins to describe her wickedness. The narrator-reader relation therefore becomes entangled. "This vile and abject soul of mine will be unveiled to you," she tells the reader. "Now you will be able to read in it as clearly as I can. What a horrible revelation! You had already proscribed my head when these hideous secrets were not yet known to you; what will you do now?" (52). Not only does Marie-Antoinette expose her evil inner self to the reading public, but she calls for her own extinction. It is difficult to believe that anyone could have taken such a discourse seriously. But passions ran high in the streets of Paris in 1789, while the book went through one edition after another. Crude, moralistic, vehement, hyperbolic to the point of sounding hysterical, it represented a new kind of appeal to a new kind of audience—committed revolutionaries, if not yet sans-culottes.

The libels against Marie-Antoinette belong in a class by themselves, owing to the extreme quality of their vituperation, but they also occupied a place at the core of a whole corpus of libels against other members of the royal family. Private lives of Louis XVI, the comte d'Artois, the prince de Condé, the prince de Conti, and the duc d'Orléans all appeared in 1790, and all of them reworked themes from the *Essais historiques sur la vie de Marie-Antoinette*. They were fairly substantial biographies, usually about one hundred pages long, and they conformed to the same model: first a section on the early life of their antihero, which gave an opportunity for the libeler to reveal the true nature of the man behind the public personage, then a series of anecdotes about his misdeeds under the Ancien Régime, and finally a concluding section on his involvement in counterrevolutionary plots. Although they varied in style and content, they always placed the queen at the center of the conspiracies. She appeared as a Jezebel, the king as a clueless cuckold; and the sexual anecdotes provided an occasion for imprecations about the decadence of the aristocracy.

The political situation had changed enough by the end of 1790 for the roles to shift among the principal players. Necker appeared as a villain in most of the "private lives" in this second wave of libels. Orléans did not fit easily into any camp; and the other princes now belonged to groups of émigrés plotting to invade France from abroad and to undermine it from within. The libels usually expressed the views of the far left, and all of them treated politics in the same manner: it could be reduced to a clash of personalities. None of the libels mentioned the Declaration of the Rights of Man and of the Citizen or the abolition of feudalism. They said nothing about the debates in the National Assembly, the restructuring of the state, the Civil Constitution of the Clergy, or any issue of principle. Although they usually paid tribute to the common people for saving the Revolution on July 14, they did not express any clear idea of what the Revolution was. They seemed to assume that its general character could be understood by revealing the characters of the men involved in it. To expose the private life of a prominent individual was to explain the direction of events.

Of course, the king warranted a "private life" of his own, but he did not produce much for his libeler-biographer to work with in the way of anecdotes. Despite its title, *Vie de Louis XVI, revue, corrigée et augmentée de nouvelles anecdotes très intéressantes* (*Life of Louis XVI, reworked, corrected, and augmented by very interesting new anecdotes*) ("London," 1790) looked bland beside the steamy libels about Marie-Antoinette. The author tried to squeeze some interesting prophecy from a horoscope cast at the king's birth, and he filled in the background with the usual stories about the wicked activities at the court of Louis XV. As he described it, Versailles took on the dark colors of Rome under the Borgias or Caligula. Instead of gallantry, it was given over to perfidy, especially in the form of poison plots. Louis XV, the author claimed, had poisoned his own son in order to prevent an assassination attempt. He had escaped poisoning himself only because he refused to take communion on a day when the Jesuits had mixed a fatal potion into the Eucharist. Poison carried off Mme de Pompadour. As a boy, Louis XVI drank a brew spiked with poisonous magots that made him sterile. And after he ascended the throne, poisoners eliminated two of his ministers: Maurepas, who had found Marie-Antoinette and the comte d'Artois in flagrante, and Vergennes, who had discovered the queen's secret subsidies to her brother in Vienna. It was easy to detect the hand behind the later murders: Marie-Antoinette.

But what could be said against Louis XVI himself? He had been distressingly well behaved from early childhood. The hard-pressed libeler, writing as a self-proclaimed "faithful historian" (6), could come up only with stories about hunting incidents, the addiction to making locks, and, later in life, obesity, stupidity, and love of the bottle. To be sure, those characteristics made Louis a perfect target for mockery as a cuckold, but they cast him in a role that was overshadowed by Marie-Antoinette. She stole the show, even in the *Vie de Louis XVI*, which hurried through the events of 1789 in order to reach the following conclusion, which illustrates the crudeness of its reasoning as well as its style: "Antoinette is a whore who swore to do in the French; fat, fat Louis is content. The nation is fattening him in a cage. That's all that is needed: he believes everything and sees nothing. . . . Louis XVI is narrow-minded, but if he had fallen into the hands of a wise and patriotic woman, he would have amounted to something. 'But,' Antoinette said, 'I will arrange things so that I will get rid of my booby and will govern alone' "(103).[22]

Taken together, the libels about the princes of the blood confirmed this view of the king and queen. Each concentrated on its own antihero, but they made the princes look very much alike—dissolute, dumb, unprincipled, and determined to exterminate patriots in order to restore the Ancien Régime. The libels cited each other as well as the *Essais historiques sur la vie de Marie-Antoinette*; they recycled the same anecdotes; and they adopted the same tone, a combination of vituperation and moralizing. Like all the libels built around denunciation, they are difficult for the modern reader to stomach, but that very difficulty serves as a reminder of how thoroughly the Revolution had transformed the style of public discourse. In place of the bawdiness, humor, and sophistication that prevailed before 1789, the libelers of the 1790s sermonized and prophesied. Like their predecessors, they adopted the pose of objective historians or conscientious editors who had come upon a cache of compromising documents, but at the same time—while remaining hidden in anonymity—they trumpeted their own moral superiority to the persons they unmasked, and they insisted on denunciation as a patriotic duty.

The author of *Vie privée de Charles-Philippes* [*sic*] *de France, ci-devant comte d'Artois* ("Turin," 1790),[23] a self-proclaimed "man of letters who has undertaken to write history," announced that his book would teach future generations to abhor crime, thanks to its noble purpose: "to consign to the execration of future centuries the monsters whose sacrilegious existence has been an uninterrupted series of outrages of all kinds and who have wanted to drown in a river of blood the fatherland in which they were born" (3). The author of *Vie politique et privée de Louis-Joseph de Condé* ("Chantilly," 1790) struck the same tone. Writing as "a philosophical historian," he congratulated himself for exposing Condé's depravity in the spirit of revolutionary egalitarianism. An obscure author could now unmask a prince in public because times had changed: "Rank, title, and possessions are merely distinctions imagined for political reasons in order to maintain subordination" (8). He went on to chronicle the adultery of both the prince and princess, and then, in mid-denunciation, he stopped to declare his confidence in his own wife, whose virtue stood out as an indictment of the ladies who made a sport of cuckolding at the top of society. It was an odd comment in the mouth of a libeler, but it illustrated the stance that he took toward his subject. By condemning Condé, he positioned himself on moral high ground; and by moralizing, he made the opposition of virtue and vice serve as an argument for leveling the hierarchical order of the Ancien Régime.

The author of *Vie privée et politique de Louis-François-Joseph de Conti, prince du sang, et sa correspondance avec ses complices fugitifs* ("Turin," 1790) worked over the same themes. After proclaiming his strict impartiality both as an historian and as a *philosophe*, he heaped abuse on Conti. Like the other princes of the royal blood—and Bourbons in general, all of them "execrable monsters" (21)—Conti was made of the same stuff as Nero and Caligula. But he differed from his royal cousins in one respect: he cared only for money. Unlike them, therefore, he had supported the Maupeou government in 1771, when it imposed despotic rule on the kingdom. As a reward, he received millions siphoned off the royal treasury by Terray as controller general of finance. In 1789, however, Conti rallied to the coalition of princes who attempted to destroy the National Assembly; and after their attempted coup misfired, he emigrated to Turin while continuing to conspire with them. He returned to Paris in 1790, took a conspicuous oath of loyalty to the new regime in order to disguise his counterrevolutionary plotting, and now was likely to strike at any moment. The anonymous libeler published letters, which he guaranteed to be authentic, between Conti and the other conspirators. They proved the gravity of the threat and confirmed the libeler's conclusion, addressed to all freedom-loving Frenchmen: "Arm yourselves, arm yourselves" (99).

While conforming to the new tone of revolutionary discourse, the private lives of the princes continued to mix portraits and anecdotes in the manner of the earlier libels. All of them devoted half their text to accounts of debauchery under the Ancien Régime and half to revelations about conspiracies to overthrow the Revolution. In the first half, they sketched the princes' youth by recycling material from pre-revolutionary *chroniques scandaleuses*. For example, they made a great deal of the aforementioned incident in a masked ball, recounted in several earlier libels, when the duchesse de Bourbon interrupted Artois, who was hurrying off to an assignation with a courtesan, and Artois in a fit of anger smashed the duchess's mask. Honor required that her husband, the duc de Bourbon, demand satisfaction, although he was a coward and did so only at the insistence of his father, the prince de Condé. In the end, he and Artois settled scores in a farcical, bloodless duel in the Bois de Boulogne.[24] The libelers also worked over the Diamond Necklace Affair, noting Cardinal Rohan's supposed correspondence with the Empress Maria Theresa, in which he reported on Marie-Antoinette's incestuous adultery.[25] Though stale, these warmed-over anecdotes prepared the way for the main theme of the libels by demonstrating the depravity of the men who were currently conspiring to undo the Revolution.

The accounts of the conspiracies were essentially the same in all the private lives, but the fullest narrative appeared in *Vie privée . . . d'Artois*. It gave a dramatic version of the plot by Artois and his collaborators to murder Louis XVI: a hushed conversation takes place among the conspirators; a valet de chambre overhears it; he informs the comte d'Estaing; d'Estaing races to the king's chamber; they detect footsteps in an adjoining room; d'Estaing flings open the door, exposing Artois; he hands Artois two pistols and challenges him to choose one for a duel: "Your royal highness will not enter the chambers of His Majesty until I am stretched out dead on the parquet" (59); then Artois slinks away. Although a complete fabrication, this anecdote appeared in several libels. The assassination attempt supposedly occurred on July 12, as part of a larger conspiracy to exterminate the incipient revolutionary movement in Paris. Thus more invented dialogue:

The queen: In three days Paris will be a flat plain.
Artois: It may be on Wednesday that we will see the fulfillment of the prediction by a man who remarked, "Some day a father will say to his son: 'Paris was there.'" (62)

As *Vie privée . . . d'Artois* described it, this master plot would be a full-scale, military attack on Paris commanded by the maréchal de Broglie. The libeler came up with plenty of seemingly concrete evidence to prove how close the conspirators had come to wiping out the Revolution. He cited a report from a German soldier who was recruited for the massacre and defected to the patriots, the discovery of four barrels of gunpowder that were to be used to blow up the Estates General, the capture of daggers manufactured especially for the street-to-street battles (a woodcut reinforced the description in the printed text), and captured documents such as a receipt signed by the prince de Lambescq for "three thousand cartridges received at one o'clock in the morning" (70). It was from pseudo-evidence such as this—specific details, indisputable testimony, authentic documents, firsthand reports by tried-and-true patriots—that the conspiratorial mentality took shape. Paris was flooded with "news" of this kind in 1789, and in the countryside, where the Great Fear raged, peasant women swore that they had seen their husbands killed at their feet by brigands who had never existed.[26]

Thanks to the intervention of the common people on July 14, *Vie privée . . . d'Artois* explained, the conspiracy was aborted, Paris was saved, and the princes fled to counterrevolutionary strongholds outside France. But they continued to conspire. The libeler had somehow acquired copies of letters they had sent from Turin and Vienna, and he published them for all the world to see. Artois and Condé had won the king of Spain to their cause, and his troops would soon invade France in coordination with the forces being mobilized by the Habsburgs in northern Italy and Austria. Orléans, pretending to be a patriot on a mission to procure grain in England, would coordinate plans with the British. Therefore, the princes had the Revolution surrounded. Most important of all, they employed agents to destroy it from within the kingdom. Conti, who also adopted the disguise of a convert to patriotism, had returned to France in order to organize a domestic uprising. He had made contact with priests and aristocrats, and he could count on the support of the Revolution's leaders: Necker, Bailly, and Lafayette. All these intrigues could be documented down to the finest details, thanks to the vigilance of patriots like the night watchman in Montargis, who had stopped a suspicious-looking character headed for the Hôtel de Picardie on September 27, 1789. The suspect claimed to be a traveling salesman named Laporte, but he turned out to be a chevalier Tremblay carrying a letter from Artois to Necker. The text, printed in full, proved that Necker was trying to break the back of the revolutionary movement in Paris by forcing the price of bread up to a starvation level and that Lafayette was planning to seize power by a coup with the help of the National Guard. Other letters, also intercepted miraculously by patriots, filled in the details of the plot. In a secret epistle to Condé dated April 8, 1790, Artois exulted that Lafayette was ready to strike, that Necker had just sent four million livres purloined from the treasury, and that he had also given orders to harvest the spring grain while it was still green in order to sabotage the food supply. "Soon we will be completely avenged," he exulted. "All of France will be reduced to ruins, rivers of blood, and corpses" (90).

The conclusion was self-evident. Conspiracies were everywhere: "Every day, every hour, every step that we take in the Revolution reveals new conspiracies to us" (91). In the face of such overwhelming evidence, the libelers exhorted their readers to be ready to take to arms. "Brave Parisians," wrote the author of Condé's private life, beware of the prince and his plots, for he was "a well-known traitor, a criminal guilty of lèze-nation" (88). "Brave Frenchmen," concluded the libeler of Artois, "Do not permit the infamous scoundrel, whose life you now know, to return among you in order to meditate new atrocities" (94). And if the princes dared to set foot on French territory, "Show no pity; tear apart their palpitating entrails so that all the other tyrants of the universe may learn about the terrifying punishment of their like" (96).[27]

The libeling of the royal family had already reached this degree of vehemence by the end of 1790, during the calmest phase of the French Revolution. Between then and 1794 events moved so fast and the Revolution took so many radical turns that the earlier talk about perfidy and conspiracy seemed to be confirmed. To sample the antiroyal libels at the height of the Terror, it is best to examine one last attack on Marie-Antoinette: *Vie privée libertine et scandaleuse de Marie-Antoinette d'Autriche, ci-devant reine des Français* (Paris, 1793). This book combined old and new material in a long and complex summa of antiroyal writing. Although it holds together as a single work, it is a kind of scrapbook, composed of excerpts from old *chroniques scandaleuses*, anecdotes lifted or rewritten from other libels, and accounts of recent events—all of it cobbled together so crudely that the seams show. It consists of four "parts" in three "books" illustrated with twenty-six plates keyed to episodes in the text. The pagination in parts 1 and 2 is continuous; parts 3 and 4 each have separate pagination. Although part 4 was designed as a sequel to the earlier parts and has the same, small, in-18 format, it was a separate publication. It covers the later stages of the Revolution, and its text, published under a slightly different title, includes additional illustrations executed in a different manner. It seems to have been sold both separately and together with the first three parts. The Bibliothèque nationale de France possesses both versions: a copy of part 4 in a crude, cardboard wrapping and a copy of all four parts trimmed and stitched together with gilding and marbled end papers in an elegant, contemporary binding. As physical objects, the two give off strikingly different impressions. One looks like a pamphlet that could have been crammed inside the pocket of a sans-culotte. The other could have fit nicely onto a shelf in the drawing room of a wealthy Jacobin. Such is the effect of packaging on the way a text suggests its social significance.

Whatever the format, the contents of the book posed problems. The text was suitably antiroyalist, but it contained many obscene passages, and virtue was the order of the day in 1793. In a circular announcing a similar work that would be available in his shop in late 1793, a Parisian bookseller warned:[28]

Figure 47. *Vie privée libertine et scandaleuse de Marie-Antoinette d'Autriche* as a luxury object and as a cheap pamphlet. (Bibliothèque nationale de France)

We give advance warning to fathers not to let this work come into the hands of their children. The explicit engravings that accompany it, the equally graphic style in which it is written, could produce disastrous effects, which they would later regret. We have now arrived at a time when severe morality must direct the education of our youth. Therefore, this book should only circulate among mature men, and even then they should be warned that they will not be reading the complete truth but rather strong presumptions about most of the facts that it contains.

The notice might also serve as a warning against the danger of assuming that the French believed everything they read.

The first three parts of *Vie privée libertine et scandaleuse de Marie-Antoinette d'Autriche* certainly recounted episodes that strained belief, notably the deflowering of Marie-Antoinette by her brother: "the introduction of *the Imperial Member* in the *Austrian Canal* brought together the passion of incest, the filthiest pleasures, the hatred of the French, the aversion to the duties of a spouse and mother, in short, everything that lowers humanity to the level of ferocious beasts" (1: 5). The text included the grossest pasquinades from the clandestine newsletters, along with the usual stock of anecdotes: Marie-Antoinette's orgies with the comte d'Artois, the duchesse de Polignac, and the cardinal de Rohan, and all sorts of incidents plagiarized from the earlier libels.[29] To entice the reader, the book opened with a facetious dedication addressed to Marie-Antoinette in the name of Dom-Bougre, the fictional narrator of one of the most pornographic novels from the era of Louis XV. In elegant, ironic language, the libertine monk paid homage to the queen, not for her rank—in his eyes, sex made everyone equal—but rather for her prowess as a voluptuary. To treat equality in 1793 as if it were a joke in an obscene novel from 1745 was to invite the wrath of the guardians of public morality. But Robespierre had not yet established the dictatorship of the Committee of Public Safety, and frivolous touches of this sort did not appear often in *Vie privée libertine et scandaleuse de Marie-Antoinette*. When they did, they looked like vestiges from an older style of libeling, and they were overshadowed by a prevailing tone of moral indignation. The author set that tone when he first introduced Marie-Antoinette. She was not a common mortal but rather the supreme incarnation of evil in a line of wicked queens: "All the villany chronicled by history, the lewdness of the Messalinas joined with the cruelty of the Frédégondes, all the artfulness that our novelists have attributed to their satanic heroines, all are combined in MARIE-ANTOINETTE OF AUSTRIA to a degree of atrocity and refinement unknown on earth before she became connected to the heir to the throne" (1: 4).[30] A copperplate engraving of Marie-Antoinette illustrated this theme. She appeared with her breasts exposed, an assortment of instruments for her evil deeds (a dagger, a dildo, and devices for concocting poison), and an epitaph that summarized the theme of the book.

It is in vain that one searches in one's memory
For the name of abhorred beings.
Nowhere in history can one find
Any who can be compared with her.

This hyperbolic rhetoric echoed the *Essais historiques sur la vie de Marie-Antoinette* of 1789. In fact, the first three parts of *Vie privée libertine et scandaleuse de Marie-Antoinette* were mainly reworked versions of the earlier libel. The author simplified things by abandoning the first person singular, and he interjected some new material along with remarks of his own; but he followed the same sequence of anecdotes and plagiarized entire passages.[31] Part 4 took over the story after 1790, where the *Essais historiques* had left it, and continued it until the imprisonment of Marie-Antoinette in the Temple after the overthrow of the monarchy and the September Massacres of 1792. It continued to chronicle the queen's sexual affairs, but it wove them into an account of politi-

en vain lon cherche en fa memoire
le nom des êtres abhorrés
on n'en trouve point dans l'histoire
qui lui puisse être comparés

Figure 48. The queen and her stock of evil objects in the *Vie privée libertine et scandaleuse de Marie-Antoinette d'Autriche.* (Bibliothèque nationale de France)

cal events—for otherwise, the author explained, "The narration of her life would merely be a licentious novel, which would produce nothing more than a smile among the most indifferent [readers]" (89).

From here on, the narrative was closely tied to accounts of conspiracies. Marie-Antoinette took up lovers, one after the other, as soon as they rose to positions of leadership, and then she manipulated them for her own evil ends. She used Lafayette to try to undermine the work of the National Assembly in 1790 and 1791. He still served her purposes by executing the Massacre of the

Champ de Mars (July 17, 1791), so she continued to fornicate intermittently with him after switching to Barnave, the most influential deputy during the last phase in the drafting of the constitution. When the Legislative Assembly began to meet, she wrapped her tentacles around the comte de Montmorin, who served as foreign minister until October 1791 and continued to influence foreign policy thereafter. As the key figure in the infamous "Austrian Committee," he fit into her plot to provoke a war, which would open the way for her brother, Leopold II (he had succeeded her older brother, Joseph II, to the Austrian throne on February 20, 1790), to invade France and restore the Ancien Régime. The war, declared against Austria on April 20, 1792, provided endless opportunities for treason. In a dream, Marie-Antoinette had a vision of all the evil queens of France, led by Frédégonde, who counseled her on the best techniques of treachery. Thanks to their advice, she went on to plot the September Massacres. She continued to hatch conspiracies while imprisoned in the Temple, even though she lost access to politicians and had to calm her "uterine furies" with dildos. And she was still plotting as the Convention began to deliberate on her fate and that of Louis XVI. At that point the narrative stopped, somewhere in late 1792, leaving the reader faced with an obvious conclusion: the queen deserved the guillotine—and the king, too, for in his simpleminded way, he had let himself be manipulated by her and was equally guilty of treason.

It would be difficult to imagine a cruder explanation for the course of the Revolution, and *Vie privée libertine et scandaleuse de Marie-Antoinette* delivered it in crude language. As evidence, it included an appendix composed of Marie-Antoinette's letters, which had supposedly been discovered in a "small, green portfolio" hidden in a secret drawer of her desk (4: 113). They made the queen speak like a whore. In one letter to Artois, she congratulated him for his prowess at cuckoldry: "You f. . . . . me right onto the bed of my spouse" (4: 120). And in another she described how she had manipulated the king's flaccid penis in order to delude him into believing he had sired an heir. Judging by his language as well as his reasoning, it seems that the author aimed his narrative at an unsophisticated audience. He offered his readers a simple interpretation of every disaster since 1789. They could all be attributed to Marie-Antoinette: "All our past, present, and future calamities have always been and will always be uniquely her work" (3: 134). But even while keeping to the simplest kind of narrative, he found it impossible to avoid the pitfalls thrown up by the complexities of events. In an early version of part 4, he seemed to favor the Girondins—that is, the most moderate faction in the Convention—and he denounced Marat as a monstrous anarchist. In a later version, he or his publisher cut that passage, evidently because the balance of power in the Convention had begun to tip in favor of the radical Mon-tagnards.[32] A libeler could not merely excoriate the queen of evil. He had to take her through a story, and the tale of the French Revolution kept confounding the teller. It refused to remain fixed in simplifications, even in its most extreme, mythological form.

Yet the mythology may have touched the collective imagination in a way that went deeper than journalistic reports about events. In 1789, according to Camille Desmoulins, a four-year-old boy was carried around the gardens of the Palais-Royal on the shoulders of a street porter shouting, "Polignac exiled a hundred leagues from Paris! Condé, the same! Conti, the same! D'Artois, the same! The queen . . . I dare not repeat it."[33] At the same time Arthur Young noted similar reactions while touring through the provinces. He rarely found newspapers, even in important cities, but rumors circulated everywhere. While vainly searching for a newspaper along the route between Strasbourg and Besançon, he witnessed discussions like the following in Colmar on July 24, 1789.

The news at the *table d'hôte* at Colmar curious; that the queen had a plot, nearly on the point of execution, to blow up the National Assembly by a mine, and to march the army instantly to massacre all Paris. A French officer present presumed but to doubt of the truth of it, and was immediately overpowered with numbers of tongues. . . . If the angel Gabriel had descended and taken a chair at table to convince them, it would not have shaken their faith.[34]

Young could not find a single, up-to-date newspaper in Besançon itself: "Well-dressed people are now talking of the news of two or three weeks past, and plainly by their discourse know nothing of what is passing."[35] Information was equally scarce in Dijon, where he arrived on July 30.

I went to search coffeehouses; but will it be credited, that I could find but one in this capital of Burgundy where I could read the newspapers? At a poor little one in the square, I read a paper, after waiting an hour to get it. The people I have found everywhere desirous of reading newspapers, but it is rare that they can gratify themselves. . . . Though they are slow in knowing what has really happened, they are very quick in hearing what is impossible to happen. The current report at present, to which all possible credit is given, is, that the queen has been convicted of a plot to poison the king and Monsieur, and to give the regency to the Count d'Artois; to set fire to Paris, and blow up the Palais-Royal by a mine![36]

In Royat, a village near Clermont-Ferrand, Young himself was nearly imprisoned on August 13, 1789, by a crowd who suspected "that I was an agent of the queen's, who intended to blow the town up with a mine and send all that escaped to the galleys. The care that must have been taken to render the character of that princess detested among the people is incredible; and there seems everywhere to be no absurdities too gross, nor circumstances too impossible for their faith."[37] Information circulated so poorly that people frequently had not heard of events, including the storming of the Bastille, until long after they had occurred,[38] yet they believed everywhere that the queen was plotting to destroy the National Assembly. By whatever osmosis, through talk and through print, the themes of the libels had penetrated deeply into a population located far beyond the range of the daily press.

Marie-Antoinette never appeared as a credible person in the libel literature. She was a phantasm who haunted the imagination of the revolutionaries, whether or not they took the libels literally. She figured everywhere in the revolutionary press—particularly in publications like *Le Père Duchesne* that were aimed at sans-culottes—with the attributes attached to her by the libelers.[39] Part Messalina, part Frédégonde, she kept changing shape according to political circumstances. In the first libels, she appeared in the court of Louis XV like a princess in a bawdy fairy tale, not innocent but merely frustrated by her husband's lack of virility. In the last, she had become transmogrified into a satanic superwoman, the supreme conspirator and ultimate nemesis of the French Revolution.

The libeling did not stop there, however. It had plenty of more down-to-earth tasks to execute, for most of the "private lives" published after 1789 slandered revolutionary leaders, not members of the royal family. The ordinary variety of libels belonged to the hurly-burly of revolutionary politics, although they, too, had a mythical dimension.

Chapter 29

Private Lives and Public Affairs

The Revolution had no sense of humor. It went about remaking the world in deadly earnest. When people got in its way, it denounced them, and it promoted denunciation as a patriotic duty. On the new notes of its paper currency from the Year II (1793–94), it inscribed a slogan:

La loi punit de mort le contrefaiseur
La nation récompense le dénonciateur

(The law punishes the counterfeiter with death
The nation rewards the denunciator)

Revolutionary libels followed suit. Even under the Ancien Régime, slander shaded off into denunciation, for the libeler frequently revealed some misconduct or crime. But the older libels generally settled for besmirching character, and they often did so by making their victims look ridiculous. Laughter was a common weapon in mid-eighteenth-century polemics. As Voltaire put it, "We must get the laughter on our side."[1] Derision inflicted deep wounds on its victims, but it provided amusement for readers who enjoyed the spectacle of a public figure being covered with ridicule. Of course, laughter came in many forms. By 1750, the Rabelaisian belly laugh and other varieties of rib-breaking, thigh-slapping jocularity had given way to smirks and chortles, at least among the elite. Voltaire's sardonic grin, captured in Houdon's sculpture and Jean Huber's sketches, set jaws at a new angle.

The Voltairean smirk had a devastating effect on bigotry under the Ancien Régime, but the revolutionaries hated it. True, they honored the cult of Voltaire and enshrined his ashes in the Pantheon, but they paid tribute to the Voltaire who defended Calas (that is, who led the campaign to reverse the decision of the Parlement of Toulouse that had led to the execution in 1762 of Jean Calas, a Protestant wrongly convicted of murdering his son in order to prevent him from converting to Catholicism) and who denounced injustice, not to the sardonic author of *La Pucelle* and *Le Mondain*. In his speeches to the Jacobins, Robespierre railed against the philosophes and named only one

Figure 49. Jean Huber, sketches of Voltaire. (Voltaire Foundation)

Enlightenment thinker worthy of praise: Jean-Jacques Rousseau, the champion of sentiment. Insofar as the men of 1789 were wits, they generally took sides with the right. Antoine Rivarol and the other contributors to the satirical review *Actes des Apôtres* skewered revolutionary earnestness, while the radicals replied, as best they could, with a few sallies of burlesque mockery in Antoine Joseph Gorsas's *Courrier de Versailles* and the occasional epigram by S.-R. Nicolas de Chamfort. Wit became a sign of counterrevolutionary sympathies under the Terror. Desmoulins hurt his cause when he adopted a satirical tone in *Le Vieux Cordelier*. After he and the other Dantonists disappeared in April 1794, it is difficult to find the slightest trace of a smile in the proceedings of the Jacobin Club, the Commune, and the Convention. Humor did not return until the Thermidorean Reaction gathered momentum, and even then it hid itself for shame. Did Bonaparte ever laugh?[2]

Slander contributed to the occlusion of humor after 1789. By following the literature of libel from the Ancien Régime through the Revolution, one can watch the climate of opinion cloud over. Not that it became black. On the contrary, the utopian energy released in 1789 opened up a bright future for the ordinary run of humanity, whereas the famous "douceur de vivre" of the pre-revolutionary years had remained restricted to the privileged few. It was the tone of public discourse that took on a darker color. The four libels discussed at the beginning of this book illustrate the general nature of the change. In 1771, Morande attacked the Maupeou ministry with pasquinades, puns, epigrams, rebuses, bons mots, dirty jokes, and anything else that would hold it up to laughter. He used devices that had served libelers well since the time of Aretino, and Pelleport did the same. But when Manuel took up where they had left off, the tone changed. A new set of metaphors began to prevail in the texts. Instead of arousing derision, libeling became a matter of unveiling, unmasking, tearing away curtains, and exposing secret lives hidden behind the false fronts turned toward the public. By the time Manuel himself fell victim to this kind of attack, the art of calumny had been transformed. But how typical were the four libels? How did libelers take aim and fire against the new targets provided by the Revolution? And how did the genre of the "private life" adapt to the constantly changing political conditions after 1789?

I have identified forty-two "private lives" published between 1789 and 1800.[3] Although they share the same general characteristics, these libels vary greatly in their physical appearance and their political bias. Some are crude pamphlets only half an octavo sheet or eight pages in length. Several are substantial volumes, although none approaches the long libels against Marie-Antoinette in size and complexity. They advocate counterrevolution as well as radicalization, and they express the views of different political factions right up to Bonaparte's seizure of power. Fourteen include pictures of their antiheroes, usually shoulder-length portraits with hostile captions as in the *Vie secrète de Pierre Manuel*. All are anonymous, but most carry the name and address of a bookseller on their title page, and very few have the fictional addresses—"at the Vatican," "at a hundred leagues from the Bastille"—that belonged to the satirical rhetoric of libels under the Ancien Régime.

A common address in libels with the same political tendency can be taken as evidence of a concerted propaganda campaign rather than a one-off attack against an individual. Four "private lives" of politicians guillotined during the Terror—Orléans, Manuel, Brissot, and Hébert—were produced at the "imprimerie de Franklin, rue de Cléry no. 75." Judging from their rhetoric, they represented an effort of the Committee of Public Safety to bolster its support among the sans-culottes after the executions had taken place. The most intriguing address, "chez Prévost, rue de la Vieille Bouclerie no. 126," appeared in libels printed after the fall of Robespierre that were thoroughly Jacobin in sentiment but hostile to ultrarevolutionary tendencies. Prévost ran a stationery shop, which specialized in schoolbooks, playing cards, and prints meant to be pinned on the wall, including one that was intended to be displayed over a child's bed: "Homage to the Eternel, or the universal prayer of the republican, one sheet of large *carré*, suitable to replace the [religious] images that used to be put near the head of the bed in former times." In a notice at the beginning of a libel against the terrorist Jean-Baptiste Carrier, Prévost announced that he could arrange to get books printed and distributed for authors who wanted to publish independently rather than to rely on booksellers. He worked closely with patriotic peddlers ("citoyens colporteurs"), he explained, and his wife could stitch the sheets.[4] His business seemed to be a mom-and-pop affair, something closer to a tuck shop than a proper bookstore. Thanks to middlemen like Prévost, libels could be produced on the cheap and without passing through the established channels of the book trade.

The cheaper "private lives" seemed to be aimed at an audience of unsophisticated readers and listeners, primarily sans-culottes. They were printed on flimsy paper with worn-out type, and judging by their typographical errors and misspellings, they could not have been read carefully in proof. Many seem to have been dashed off in response to urgent circumstances. A libel that denounced Robespierre soon after his execution situated his birthplace correctly in Arras, then in a later passage placed it in Arles. A libel against François Chabot set a key anecdote in Villefranche, then mistakenly shifted it to Montpellier. The libels distributed by Prévost appeared on dirty sheets, unevenly inked, and set in type from different fonts.

Some of the texts were as primitive as the typography. In Prévost's edition of *Vie sans pareille, politique et scandaleuse du sanguinaire CARRIER*, the anonymous author demonstrated Carrier's evil nature by stringing together "secret anecdotes," which were featured in the subtitle of the book. Little Jean-Baptiste, the author revealed, pulled wings off flies, bashed cats to death, and beat his neighbors' dogs. He roamed through fields enticing lambs with food, then smashed them to death with clubs. He snatched baby birds from nests and pulled their bodies apart with his bare hands. And having tortured all forms of animal life in his village, he turned up abruptly as a full-grown Jacobin in the midst of the French Revolution and began to massacre innocent citizens. The libeler did not explain how Carrier got from deepest Auvergne to a powerful position as an agent of the Committee of Public Safety. Instead, he piled on horrific details about Carrier's atrocities in the mass drownings ("noyades") that he organized to punish counterrevolutionaries at Nantes in

November 1793. To provide emphasis, the libeler punctuated the narrative with epithets like "scoundrel" (*scélérat*) and "monster," the two terms of abuse favored in most of the revolutionary libels. But he especially favored a third: tiger. "Tiger," "devouring tiger," "man-tiger," "barbarous tiger," "bloodthirsty tiger" (13, 18, 19, 29, 58). The repetition of the expletive drummed the point home in a way that reinforced the story line of the anecdotes, and the libeler brought the argument to a climax by providing a "portrait" of Carrier at the end of the pamphlet.

I will display before your eyes his portrait, true to nature, having already traced the picture of his life and his conduct, both private and public. This monster had a large build, all legs and arms; his back was rather curved, his head small, his face long and of a very pronounced character, his eyes small, deep set, and of a tincture that combined blood and bile; his nose was long and aquiline, his look horrible. His coloring was copper brown. He was thin and nervous, and the protuberance of his hips, along with his lack of a belly, made him seem to be cut in two, like a wasp. The harshness of his voice, reinforced by his southern accent, when he was speaking at the podium and somewhat excited, made his speech seem to rise out of some lacerated zone in his bowels, and he pronounced *r*s like a snarling tiger. His physical appearance was the faithful expression of his violent, impetuous, and irascible character. Fury and bloodthirstiness were the basic elements of his temperament. Nature made a mistake in neglecting to give him claws. (60)

Times had changed since Bussy-Rabutin sketched verbal portraits of the ladies in the court of Louis XIV. But there was a particular urgency to the libeling at the time when the private life of Carrier appeared, shortly before November 11, 1794. On that date, Carrier went before the Revolutionary Tribunal to be tried for his crimes. The trial led to his execution on November 16 and marked a turning point in the reaction against the Terror during the chaotic period after the overthrow of Robespierre on 9 Thermidor (July 27). The Thermidoreans needed to steer the reaction in a favorable direction. A pamphlet that made Carrier look like a monster could reassure a sans-culotte audience that the current leaders of the Revolution were eliminating the excesses of the Terror without abandoning the Jacobin program. "Private lives" always conformed to political agendas, no matter how extravagant their language.

They also tended to fit a standard pattern in the way they were organized. They often began with remarks assuring the reader that the author, who was always anonymous, wrote as a patriot determined to unmask traitors and reveal the wicked nature of their inner selves. "Dear reader, my friend," said the author of *Vie politique de Jérôme Pétion* (1793), "it is important, it is necessary for every faithful patriot to know the inner recesses of the human heart. The proof of this lies in the tricks, the ruses, and the other means that Jérôme

Pétion used to lure the people back to the yoke of the tyrant."[5] Next came details about the antihero's background, the more specific, the better, because the libeler needed to produce seemingly factual material in order to establish his authority. The authors of the private lives of Necker, Lafayette, Marat, and Hébert presented themselves to their readers as historians and carefully noted the date and place of birth of the men they libeled. In *Vie publique et privée de M. le marquis de La Fayette* (1791), the anonymous "historian" went out of his way to refute an anecdote in a rival but equally hostile libel, which explained Lafayette's departure for the American Revolution as an attempt to escape the humiliation of being cuckolded. Not true, said the author of *Vie publique et privée*. Like most aristocrats, Lafayette had an arranged marriage, but he volunteered to fight in America for the love of adventure, and he fought bravely, even though he later botched everything as commander of the National Guard in Paris. It was important to get facts right, because "veracity and impartiality are the most indispensable qualities in writing history."[6] By disentangling the true story of Lafayette's youth, the author had been able to see to the bottom of his soul and could provide a correct assessment of his contribution to the French Revolution: he was a traitor who deserved the guillotine.[7]

Nearly all the libelers relied on anecdotes about the childhood of their antihero in order to assert knowledge about his inner self and then to pass judgment on his career as a revolutionary. They often concentrated primarily on the pre-revolutionary career of their man, because their main concern was to defame his character, not to trace his role in events. "Let us see Marat as he leaves his honest parents and follow him" (6), wrote the author of *Vie criminelle et politique de J. P. Marat* (1795), who promised to reveal the inner nature of the public personage. He went on to describe Marat as a mountebank who tramped from fair to fair selling fake cures, a practice that prepared him to pull the wool over the eyes of the sans-culottes when he posed as the Friend of the People. *Vie criminelle et politique* did not give a detailed account of Marat's activities during the Revolution. Instead, it fell back on declamations seasoned with epithets: "It is time to lift the veil that until now had covered the odious and skeletal frame of that bloodthirsty monster and to fix the memory of him" (3).

Most libels passed quickly over the history of the Revolution in this manner, even though their authors claimed to be historians.[8] Sometimes they recounted a particular incident, such as the role of the duc d'Orléans in the October Days or the atrocities of Carrier at Nantes, but they rarely paused over complexities. They said next to nothing about political alignments, offered no analysis of events, and seldom mentioned ideas or principles of any kind except for the opposition of patriotism and counterrevolution or virtue and depravity. By focusing entirely on the character of an individual, they reduced the Revolution to the play of personalities. They favored "portraits" rather than accounts of causality and contingency. The portrait of Robespierre, like that of Carrier, evoked moral qualities by physical description.

Here is a portrait that has been made of this ambitious person. He lived 35 years; his height was five feet two or three inches; his posture rigidly straight; his bearing firm, brisk, and even a little brusque; he often fidgeted with his hands as if by a kind of nervous tick; the same movement could be seen in his shoulders and in his neck, which he shook convulsively to the left and the right; his clothes were elegantly clean and his hair always carefully dressed; his somewhat frowning physiognomy had nothing unusual about it; his coloring was livid, bilious; his eyes dull and lusterless. . . . His speeches—sometimes harmoniously modulated, sometimes harsh and brilliant, and sometimes trivial—were always composed of commonplaces and digressions about *virtue*, *crime*, and *conspiracy*.[9]

Having established Robespierre's inner and outer character, the author did not pause over the momentous events of 1793–94. Instead, he described Robespierre's downfall on 9 Thermidor (July 27, 1794), dispatched him to the guillotine, and closed with an address to the readers: "May this example teach you to have no more idols. . . . Remember that liberty does not exist in men and that, on the contrary, it is men who destroy liberty. Rally around the Convention. . . . Virtue will always be the basis of its operations."[10] "Private lives" often ended on such a hortatory note. They had immediate political purposes, but like folktales, they were stories with morals.

Most private lives conformed to this general model. But they varied enormously, appeared in different contexts, and argued for and against politicians in many different camps. If read as narratives set in successive phases of the Revolution, are their differences outweighed by their common characteristics? A précis of some typical texts, arranged in chronological order, should help one draw conclusions about their general nature.

Vie privée et ministérielle de M. Necker (1790) illustrates character assassination as it was practiced at the beginning of the Revolution. It is a long and rambling pamphlet of eighty pages, written in the spring of 1790, when Necker still dominated the government, and it emphasized the following points about his biography. Birth and education: in a family of Genevan tradesmen. Necker did not excel in school, except for lessons in arithmetic, which fed his dominant passion, the lust for wealth. Early career: clerk for a merchant banker in Paris. He speculated with money pilfered from the cash box and then appropriated 800,000 livres from the estate of an Englishman who died while visiting Paris; so he had accumulated enough capital to begin banking on his own.

Secret debauchery: although married to the daughter of a Genevan pastor, he seduced a young German countess living in Paris. After he had become minister of finance, she threatened to denounce him if he did not return 24,000 livres that he had borrowed from her. He replied by punching her in the stomach and menacing her with a lettre de cachet. By then he had taken up with numerous prostitutes, while always maintaining the demeanor of a stern, Swiss Protestant. His main interest, however, continued to be the accumulation of riches, supplemented by a new passion, the desire for power. Political career: Necker's dexterity as a speculator led to his appointment as finance minister, a post in which he enriched himself at the public's expense and bankrupted the government while cultivating a reputation for integrity. He fattened his fortune by monopolizing and speculating on grain throughout 1789. When the catastrophic price of bread led to riots, he tried to manipulate the crowd in a way that would undermine the National Assembly and make him the de facto ruler of a despotic monarchy. That strategy involved a succession of conspiracies with aristocrats, émigrés, financiers, and false patriots from the first ranks of the Revolution's leaders. They came to a climax in the October Days, which Necker secretly directed from his office in Versailles. Once he had the king under his control in Paris, he began plotting to provoke another famine and to sabotage the constitution being written by the National Assembly. Current outlook: more slaughter in the streets, civil war, and a full-fledged counterrevolution. Moral of the story: beware citizens, this depraved monster is about to strike again; he has mounted a conspiracy to restore the Ancien Régime and make slaves of you all.[11]

Vie publique et privée de Honoré-Gabriel Riquetti, comte de Mirabeau (1791) looks back over the Revolution from a somewhat later phase and a different point of view: it is counterrevolutionary propaganda, which presents all the events between 1789 and 1791 as the result of one man's evil genius. That Mirabeau was indeed a genius, the most extraordinary character of the century, the author readily acknowledges, because by stressing his subject's superhuman villainy, he can explain everything that went wrong in France. It all began with the child's precocious viciousness, illustrated by his attempt as a small boy to poison his father. By the time he had reached middle age, he had been in and out of prison several times, had ruined the lives of his wife and countless mistresses, had swindled everyone who crossed his path, and had taken up the life of a literary hack, supporting himself by pornography and political tracts turned out for anyone willing to subsidize him. Mirabeau's scandalous life provided plenty of material for lascivious details, but the libeler avoided them, preferring instead to convey Mirabeau's degradation before 1789 by anecdotes about his scramble for money—how he stole the watch of his coiffeur, cheated the peddlers of his illegal works, bamboozled his publishers, and dragged his mistresses from one furnished room to another in an endless struggle to escape the bill collectors. The narrative evokes a Grub Street existence, and even describes the first stage of the Revolution as an "insurrection of starving authors for hire" (50), with Mirabeau at their head.

Once the monarchy began to totter, Mirabeau saw his opportunity to strike it rich. After getting elected to the Estates General, he and his publisher Le Jay put out one of the first uncensored newspapers, *Journal des Etats-Généraux*, a "periodical libel" (52) that brought in subscriptions worth 60,000 livres in the first three days. Then he realized that he could make even bigger money by selling himself to the court. He collected a secret salary of 6,000 livres a month on top of a million livres for speeches in favor of the government's fiscal policy. As he fattened his purse, he acquired an appetite for power. The inside story of the October Days, which the libeler recounted at length, proved that Mirabeau had plotted to destroy the monarch who had been paying him off. He considered having Louis XVI murdered while hunting or simply frightened so badly that he would flee the kingdom. In the end, Mirabeau decided to cooperate with Necker in a plot to provoke a civil war by starving the population of Paris. The king could be assassinated with the connivance of Lafayette when the poor marched on Versailles, or if captured, he could be forced to abdicate in favor of a regency under the duc d'Orléans, another accomplice, who would permit Mirabeau to rule from behind the throne. This conspiracy, "the most horrible plot that had ever been contrived" (80), did not quite turn out as planned. The gardes-du-corps saved the king and queen on October 5–6, but the royal family was taken as hostage to Paris, where Mirabeau continued to direct events. As the libeler surveyed the situation in the spring of 1791, things looked worse than ever. The feudal order had been hopelessly overturned, the Paris crowd seemed ready to explode once more, and the last decent members of the National Assembly, the right-wing royalists known as Monarchiens, had fled for their lives. The only glimmer of hope came at the point where the libel ended: on April 2, 1791, Mirabeau died following an orgy with some dancing girls from the opera: "Such was the end of the most extraordinary man that France ever produced, . . . a perfect model of villainy" (105).

Far from treating Brissot as out of the ordinary, the author of *Vie secrète et politique de Brissot* (1793) described him as all too typical of a species that had threatened to undo the Revolution from the beginning: the false patriot. The pattern of Brissot's life, as the libeler sketched it, corresponded to that of many revolutionary leaders. Born into a modest and pious family in Chartres, Brissot tried to shake off his humble origins by passing himself off as a philosopher and attaching an aristocratic-sounding suffix to his name: "de Warville." In fact, his writings were mainly compilations of works by others—and libels, for the author, who claimed to write as a true patriot and to recount nothing but the facts, asserted that Brissot had composed Pelleport's most outrageous tracts, including *Le Diable dans un bénitier*. Having defamed others, Brissot therefore appeared in his own "private life" as an adventurer and a hack who would write anything "in order to have shoes and shirts" (33). The libeler also characterized him as a "financier," though not a very successful one, because his involvement in shady speculations failed to rescue him from indigence. The need for money took Brissot from one dubious form of employment to another. By 1789 he had become a seasoned confidence man, and he treated the Revolution as the ultimate confidence game. In league with fellow spirits like Pierre Manuel, one of his closest collaborators, he cultivated a reputation as a super-patriot. He insinuated himself into the Jacobin Club, then the Legislative Assembly and the Convention, where he used every opportunity to get rich quick. Fortunately, some sharp-eyed Jacobins saw through his disguise, tore off his mask, and exposed him as the leading hypocrite in the ranks of the counterrevolutionaries.[12] The Revolutionary Tribunal would soon reveal the extent of his corruption, but the author had uncovered enough to pronounce on the lesson it taught. Speaking directly to the "citizen reader" (44), he stressed two points: beware of false patriots and support the Convention. Along with *Vie secrète de Pierre Manuel* and *Vie politique de Jérôme Pétion*, *Vie secrète et politique de Brissot* figured as the centerpiece of an attempt by the radical, Montagnard party in the Convention to destroy the Girondins in the eyes of the public late in 1793, during the first phase of the Terror.

    Vie privée et politique de J.-R. Hébert (1794) and *Vie privée de l'ex-Capucin François Chabot* (1794) belonged to the next phase, the spring of 1794, when the Robespierrists purged the extremists ("Hébertistes") on the left and the moderates ("Dantonistes") on the right. Like several other "private lives"— those of Brissot, Pétion, Manuel, Orléans, and Chaumette (I have not turned up a private life of Danton)—they represented an attempt by the Committee of Public Safety to firm up its support among the sans-culottes, who could be presumed to harbor some doubts about the patriotism of the current government after seeing so many prominent patriots guillotined as counterrevolutionaries.

    Half of the life of Hébert consisted of anecdotes about his misdeeds before the Revolution. According to the libeler, he perfected the technique of "false denunciations" (9)—his specialty during the Revolution—in school, where he learned how to blame his friends for his own misdemeanors. Like many provincial youths, he sought his fortune in Paris and soon was reduced to living by expedients, most of them criminal. He found employment as a ticket checker in the Théâtre des Variétés for fifteen months, until he ran off with 3,000 livres from its cash box. Seven months of cohabitation with a prostitute exhausted that sum and left him penniless in the street. He begged shelter from a friend, who took him in, only to be stripped of his possessions when Hébert decamped. Once he had run through this booty, Hébert repeated the same trick, this time with a doctor, who took pity on his undernourished state, fed and housed him, and then was stripped of his most valuable possessions, which Hébert pawned in order to buy some clothes. Having failed to earn an honest living from his pen, Hébert continued to sink deeper and deeper into destitution: "Without a shirt, without shoes, he never left a garret that he rented on a sixth floor except to borrow 24 sols from his friends or to get them by swindling" (13).

Salvation finally came with the Revolution. After persuading a friend to put up some money, Hébert founded *Le Père Duchesne*, a journal full of political commentary written in violent language, which succeeded in large part because of its false denunciations. He married, used his wife's fortune to reissue the journal in his own name, and became a powerful figure in the Commune. By whipping up popular fury about the rising price of food, he attempted to produce a new insurrection, one that would be directed against the Convention and that would plunge France into civil war. As soon as the anarchy in the streets had created conditions favorable for a coup, he planned to seize power and to install a despotic system of government. Fortunately, alert patriots in the Convention discovered the conspiracy. Hébert and his accomplices were condemned by the Revolutionary Tribunal on March 22, 1794. Unmasked and abhorred by the public that he had misled, he spent his last night screaming like a madman in his cell. Then, true to form, he died in a cowardly manner under the guillotine: "Thus did this monster come to an end; thus will all traitors end who still dare to combat the genius of the Republic" (30).

Vie privée de l'ex-Capucin François Chabot showed how the leaders of the Convention triumphed over an equally dangerous movement, which came from the right. Chabot personified it, according to the author, because his life consisted of nothing but intrigues and he never committed himself to the Revolution—or to anything else, except the accumulation of ill-gotten gains. Born into a fairly prosperous family in Milhaud, he did well enough in school to set out on an ecclesiastical career. But underneath his clerical robes he was a libertine. He spent his youth seducing women and stripping them of their wealth. His first victim, a wealthy widow in Villefranche, offered him her purse as well as her body. When he had had enough of both, he abandoned her. She died of a broken heart, leaving him a gold watch in her will. Her servant girl, sent to deliver the watch, ended up in Chabot's bed. After making her pregnant, he persuaded a wagon driver, whom he had corrupted through the confessional, to marry her. This arrangement led to a smuggling business, which Chabot directed under the cover of his priestly functions. Although he cared more for money than for sex, he continued to seduce women as opportunities arose. He made some extra income by tutoring a fifteen-year-old girl. When she became pregnant, he persuaded a surgeon to perform a brutal abortion, then confessed her on her deathbed and pocketed the large sum that an aunt paid to him for officiating at her funeral. He continued to go from one love affair and speculation to another—each the subject of an indignant anecdote—until he was elected to the Legislative Assembly and then to the Convention. The narrator does not explain how Chabot pulled off this trick, abandoning debauchery in the provinces for politics in the capital. Nor does he enter into any details about Chabot's political career, because all that is needed to understand it are the anecdotes about his corruption: "After having sketched the private life of Chabot, we leave it to our readers to judge what the nation could expect from such a corrupt man, who was capable of every political and moral crime, thanks to his addiction to vice and his passion for deception and for riches. . . . Intrigues, guile, vileness, knavery, and especially hypocrisy—he used anything and everything to usurp the reputation of a patriot" (39). Corruption was the main charge brought against the Dantonistes, whose venality made them essentially the same, according to the libeler, as the Hébertistes at the opposite end of the political spectrum. Chabot therefore went to the guillotine with Danton and his followers on April 5, 1794. It was a spectacle that should edify the reader, for it taught a salutary lesson: "Fortunately, virtuous and enlightened men stand out against these monsters, foil their plots, and . . . assure the happiness of France. . . . In vain does intrigue agitate, in vain does calumny hover over the virtuous and enlightened men who defend the sovereignty of the people and see to the execution of the law" (v). The conclusion was clear: support Robespierre and his companions in the Committee of Public Safety.

But a few months later it was Robespierre's turn to be unmasked. *Vie secrète, politique et curieuse de M. J. Maximilien Robespierre* (1794) showed that he was no different from the others. Born to relatively poor parents in Arras, he did well in school and attracted enough local patronage to win a place in the Collège Louis-le-Grand in Paris, then to practice law and try to gain a reputation as a man of letters in his hometown. When the Revolution came, he made a name for himself as a deputy to the National Assembly by denouncing others. But his patriotic posturing merely served as a cover for his ambition, for above all he was a hypocrite bent on seizing power. His opportunity came at last—the author skips over the first four years of the Revolution in one, quick leap—when he began to direct the Terror from the Committee of Public Safety. Every night he prepared a list of his next victims, putting "A" (for absolve) after their names if he meant to spare them and "G" if he intended to send them to the guillotine. Nothing pleased him more than striking terror in the hearts of other deputies by threatening them in speeches to the Convention—or merely by staring intently at them during debates. At last on 9 Thermidor (July 27, 1794), the Convention rose against him. When he attempted to dispatch another set of innocent victims to the guillotine, the deputies shouted him down, exposed his counterrevolutionary plotting, and decreed his arrest. "Robespierre unmasked, grinds his teeth and roars like a tiger that can no longer dismember the prey that has escaped it" (18). The author describes the uprising of Thermidor in some detail, as if he were a journalist reporting on a recent event. As Robespierre's head falls under the guillotine, the rest of the Revolution recedes into the background. It had been a succession of conspiracies, the author explains. One leader had succeeded another, duping the common people by posing as a patriot, then eliminating his opponents and ruling as a despot. Robespierre was the worst of them all. But now at last the Revolution had reached the end of the line of traitors; there was only one option left for the readers of this horrific tale: "Rally around the Convention" (35).

But the line did not end at Thermidor. Libelers went on denouncing conspirators in "private lives," which continued right up to Bonaparte. The later publications did not add anything new to the corpus, except more variations on the interlinked themes of hypocrisy, corruption, and treachery. They continued to pound away with the same epithets and metaphors and to maintain the same tone of moral indignation. In *La Vie de Boissy d'Anglas* (1796?), for example, the libeler addressed his victim, François-Antoine Boissy d'Anglas, a veteran of the Convention and a leading member of the legislative body that replaced it (the Conseil des Cinq-Cents, elected in September 1795), as follows: "Knave, insinuating reptile, you took on all the postures, all the masks that suited the shifts in circumstances! . . . With the blackest, the most atrocious heart you affect an air of gentleness and goodness, and yet you are a true tiger, a famished vulture. When examining you, no matter what the perspective, one is suffused with indignation" (5–6).

By now the genre had been worked over so thoroughly that libelers turned it inside out and produced "private lives" that were positive. A favorable *Vie privée de J. P. Marat* had appeared in 1793, although it was eclipsed by the vituperative *Vie criminelle et politique de J. P. Marat* of 1795. *Vie privée des cinq membres du Directoire* (1795) outdid its predecessors by presenting eulogistic biographies of all the members of the Directory's executive body in a work that read like propaganda for their reelection. François-Martin Poultier d'Elmotte, the libeler who had collaborated with Goupil and had spied for Lenoir before the Revolution, also used a positive "private life" to promote his own career under the Directory, but he added a new wrinkle. In *Les Crimes et forfaits du représentant du peuple Poultier, avec l'acte d'accusation porté contre lui* (1797?), he published an indictment against himself and then triumphantly refuted everything in it while hiding in anonymity. *Vie privée du général Buonaparte* (1798?) appears bland in comparison. It merely celebrated the hero of the Italian campaign of 1797 as the greatest soldier-statesman of all time.

In looking back over the entire corpus of "private lives" published between 1789 and 1800, the element that stands out is their surprising sameness. They attacked politicians from every camp at every phase of the Revolution, yet they all look alike. Of course, the short pamphlets appear cruder than the elaborate biographies, and one can detect differences in style. Yet the libels followed the same basic formula and employed the same rhetorical techniques, most of them derived from the libel literature of the Ancien Régime. They made arguments by stringing together anecdotes. Although the libelers added plenty of commentary to make their points clear, they relied primarily on the narrative power of the anecdotes themselves to get their message across. They also made use of portraits—in frontispieces, in elaborate verbal descriptions, and in the form of character sketches built up throughout the entire work. By constructing portraits, the libelers tried to establish their credibility as experts who could penetrate to the inner man hidden beneath the public figure. They also asserted their authority as historians who recounted facts in an unbiased manner. But the facts they selected were so tendentious and so closely linked to recent events that the libelers actually functioned as journalists, and even in this capacity they did not provide detailed reports about occurrences, except in a few cases, such as accounts of the October Days and the fall of Robespierre. Libels belonged to the news media, but only in a general way, in the manner of pamphlets rather than newspapers. They restricted themselves to background sketches of figures in the public eye, as some news magazines do today, except that they were relentlessly polemical. While pretending to inform readers, they attempted to sway them for or against political factions in response to the pressure of events.

Whatever their bias, the tone and style of the libels were remarkably similar. They used language calculated to arouse indignation in their readers, resorting primarily to violent expressions and hyperbole. The person they attacked was always the blackest villain imaginable; the conspiracies they uncovered were always the most evil plots in history. The libelers also turned up the volume of their rhetoric by calling their victims names. They had a particular fondness for "scoundrel" and "monster," but they also favored animal expletives: vampire, reptile, tiger. And in thundering against the wickedness of their antiheroes, the libelers adopted a stance of moral rectitude. They defended virtue against vice, moralizing incessantly. Their puritanical tone led them to avoid erotic details when railing against sexual misdeeds. In fact, they nearly always emphasized the lust for lucre rather than for women as the dominant passion of the men they libeled—and their subjects were all male, except for Marie-Antoinette. The misogyny and the libidinal undercurrent in the attacks on her put them in a class by themselves. Ordinary "private lives" had little to say about women, except as victims of predatory males. The only woman they mentioned among the leaders of the Revolution was Théroigne de Méricourt, who led the march on Versailles during the October Days, and she appeared as an "amazon," repulsively masculine in her cross-dressing and brutality.[13] As a general rule, libels from the Ancien Régime featured sexual depravity; those from the Revolution, economic corruption. The revolutionary villains almost always pretended to be patriots in order to line their own pockets; and if they did not seek wealth, they lusted for power. To tear the mask off a false patriot was therefore to expose corruption of a particular kind, one that involved famine plots, misappropriation of public funds, and sequestering spoils from victims arrested in the name of the nation. Sexual corruption tended to be titillating, a subject fit for libeling in the era of Louis XV but not for an age of revolutionary regeneration. After 1788, libels struck a note of moral indignation and held it, relentlessly, until 1800. They did not amuse; they denounced, and they treated denunciation as a public duty.

What was their significance? All libels were aggressive. They were meant to inflict damage, and they had clear objectives—to destroy a politician, to denigrate a faction, or to sap sympathy for a political movement. But they also communicated a general view of the Revolution. It always appeared in them as a struggle of good against evil, although the identities of the heroes and villains varied according to the political persuasion of the libelers. Whether seen from the left or the right, the forces of evil had one consistent characteristic: they acted by conspiracies.[14] Far from being peculiar to the sans-culottes, the conspiratorial mentality existed among all participants in the Revolution, from the beginning until Bonaparte's seizure of power and beyond. The libelers gave voice to it by using their two favorite devices: the denunciation of corruption and the unmasking of hypocrites. Their obsession with unmasking—a metaphor that recurs throughout the texts along with unveiling and stripping away curtains—expressed a peculiar view of the revolutionary struggle: despite the mobilization of the masses, it came down to a conflict between individuals. The only "private life" that attacked a collective body, *Vie privée des ecclésiastiques, prélats et autres fonctionnaires publics, qui n'ont point prêté leur serment sur la Constitution civile du clergé* (1791), actually was composed of dozens of individual portraits, all of them featuring the same characteristics: hypocrisy and decadence. In the end, therefore, libeling meant slandering a particular person. The personal character of libels gave them special appeal for a public confused by the complexities of revolutionary politics, and it also made them newsworthy, according to a formula that still exists today: names make news. But news of this kind conveyed a distorted picture of the Revolution because it simplified everything. Parties and programs became identified with individuals, as indicated by labels such as Fayettistes, Brissotins, Rolandistes, Dantonistes, Hébertistes, and Robespierristes. By reducing politics to personalities, libels obscured the fundamental conflicts of principles and interests that ran through the Revolution. That is why they all looked the same.

The personalization of politics did not merely simplify and distort events; it also shifted the balance between the private and the public sphere. To be sure, the concept of the public sphere has been invoked so often by historians that it seems to explain everything and to apply to any place and time from the end of the Middle Ages to the present.[15] But revolutionary libels show how the line that divided the public from the private was erased at a crucial moment in history. When a libeler unmasked a victim after 1789, he did not simply reveal the true man hiding behind the face turned toward the outer world. Nor did he merely oppose the inside to the outside. He destroyed the distinction between them. He made the private public, transforming the intimate aspects of his victim's life into an issue of public debate. To expose the private life behind the public person was to change the character of political discourse and to turn political conflict into a battle of denunciations.

Of course, libels constituted but one, small current in the flood of revolutionary literature. They hardly had the power to transform politics by themselves, and the revolutionaries had plenty of other means of communication at their disposal. In newspaper articles, pamphlets, speeches in political clubs, debates in legislative assemblies, and public ceremonies, they pitched their remarks at a high level of principle and laced their rhetoric with references to Tacitus, Cicero, Montesquieu, and Rousseau. But even Robespierre, the supreme Rousseauist, advocate of ancient virtue, and prophet of the cult of the Supreme Being, dealt primarily in denunciation. To understand that dimension of the Revolution, it is crucial to read the private life of all his victims and of Robespierre himself.[16]

Libels did not determine the course of the French Revolution. They punctuated it, marking it off as a succession of conspiracies and spreading the notion that its failures were the work of false patriots. Unmasking conspirators became a mode of revolutionary action. When it took the form of libeling, it appealed in new language to a new kind of public. By 1793 the libeler addressed his reader as a fellow citizen and sans-culotte. He grabbed the reader, so to speak, by the arm, stopped him in his tracks, and harangued him urgently, indignantly, face-to-face, at a high pitch and in deadly earnest. Gone were the knowing looks and complicit smiles exchanged between writer and reader in an earlier age, when libels were meant to amuse while they went about their basic task of destroying reputations. The long string of "private lives" shows how the Revolution reworked material it inherited from the Ancien Régime. It kept the form and changed the substance, fitting a genre derived from the court of Louis XIV onto a new and unruly body politic.

Conclusion

Slander, libel, defamation, calumny, character assassination, mud-slinging, scandalmongering, bad-mouthing, and billingsgate flourished as never before in eighteenth-century France. Yet vilification has existed in most political systems from antiquity to the present. What is to be learned by concentrating on the French example?

First, one should not dismiss slander as mere background noise, the inevitable accompaniment to conflict in any kind of government. Some states may be able to absorb it with little disruption, but it can inflict serious damage on others. A state built on a cult of personality is likely to be vulnerable to personal attacks, even though it monopolizes other forms of power. Princely courts can be undone by libels that destroy reputations, snap bonds of patronage, and disrupt clienteles. Even a president of a modern republic can lose his hold on power if his campaign managers and public relations experts fail to stifle scandals about his private life.

In the monarchy of the Ancien Régime, where sovereignty was identified with the person of the monarch and was invested with sacred power, the slandering of the king sent shock waves through the whole system. It was a crime of lèse majesté. To be sure, the system could absorb most of the shocks, and there were other, more serious sources of ideological damage: Jansenism, which challenged political authority by mobilizing religious belief; parliamentary obstruction, which undermined the legal basis of Bourbon absolutism; even the Enlightenment, which subjected all authority to rational criticism. As a vehicle of ideology, libel literature did not represent a comparable threat. It contained little in the way of sustained political reasoning, although it could be identified with the interests and ideas of different political factions at different times in the course of the century. Instead of operating at an intellectual level, libels struck below the belt and aimed to produce visceral reactions. They pictured Louis XV as an ordinary mortal—a feckless mediocrity in his youth, a dirty old man at the end of his reign. They made Louis XVI appear both impotent and incompetent, and they caricatured Marie-Antoinette as a moral monster and an agent of the Austrian enemy.

To modern readers these caricatures may seem too extravagant to be taken seriously. But they were designed to play on the sensitivities of readers from the eighteenth century, and they did so successfully enough to alarm the government. Diplomats, ministers, and police chiefs did everything possible, at enormous cost, to stifle the production and distribution of libels. Instead of dismissing slander as beneath contempt—an attitude that prevailed among the elite in England—they worried about its effect on an unsophisticated public. And they probably were right, although there is not enough evidence to sustain a thorough study of reader response.

"Desacralization" works well enough as a way to describe the erosion of the aura of sanctity that had traditionally surrounded the king of France,[1] but it does not do justice to the broader effect of the libels. They attacked everyone of eminence, especially the great of the capital and court. Court figures were particularly vulnerable to slander because they combined government with personal networks of patronage and protection, and they existed in the heavily charged atmosphere of Versailles, where the corridors of power glittered with memories of the Sun King. As in the seventeenth century, power was dispensed by favorites and mistresses; factions clustered around competing royal households; lobbyists plotted in antechambers; and ministers ran the kingdom as long as they could keep hold on the wavering confidence of the king.

Well-placed slander set off power struggles at many points within this system. It had done so everywhere in courts since the dawn of the Renaissance. But France was the most populous and powerful country in eighteenth-century Europe. Its administrators had devised rational schemes to deal with its complex problems, and they drew on a modern bureaucracy (the word itself dates from 1764) to carry them out. Yet they had not developed comparable measures to defend the state against the kind of bad-mouthing and back-stabbing that had shaken the little courts of Italy three centuries earlier. That the pasquinade should have remained so lethal so long after Aretino says a great deal about the uneven evolution of the modern state.

Of course, there was more to slander as a political weapon than word of mouth within the court. By 1750 a large reading public had come into existence in all the urban centers of France, above all in Paris. By 1789, this public had developed an enormous appetite for news, and it derived its basic stock of information about the doings of the great through slander in the form of printed tracts. Although much of the information originated from gossip in Versailles, most of it was reduced to writing by obscure hacks. The population of writers also expanded enormously from 1750 to 1789, filling garrets and spilling into cafés, where gossip was distributed. Desperate for support, the hacks sometimes hired themselves out as hit men to destroy reputations for anyone who would pay. More often, they speculated on their own, exploiting the demand for dirt in the lucrative underground book trade or combining publishing with blackmail. The colony of French libelers in London was but one of many such operations in a network of Grub Streets that extended throughout western Europe.

The London libelers deserve special attention because their activities can be documented in detail, both from their own publications and from the archives of the Parisian police and the French ministry of foreign affairs. The story involves a splendid cast of rogues, one worth examining for its own sake, but it is important for the way it shows how libeling had penetrated into the ranks of the authorities. When police inspectors like Goupil and Jacquet de la Douay organized libelers into publishing ventures of their own, the power system was threatened from within. And when powerful men like Vergennes and Lenoir devoted so much effort to the fight against libels, they confirmed the gravity of the threat.

How threatening was it really? The question cannot be answered definitively, owing to our inability to trace and weigh the impact of reading on public opinion—or even to know what public opinion was and how it gathered force on the eve of the Revolution. Nonetheless, there is enough evidence to indicate the existence of a powerful tide of hostility toward the government in specific sites like the Palais-Royal, where the call went out for the storming of the Bastille. Libels helped mobilize an angry public in Paris and direct the anger at particular targets, such as the two top ministers in 1787–88, Charles-Alexandre de Calonne and Etienne-Charles Loménie de Brienne. Of course, other factors like the price of bread and the threat of uncontrollable taxation also whipped up discontent, but the impact of the libels was not limited to the damage inflicted on one or two individuals. They had a cumulative effect, something I would characterize as the creation of a political myth.

From the beginning of the century to the end, libelers hammered at the same theme: despotism. By attacking ministers, royal mistresses, and the king himself, they built up a picture of a monarchy riddled with the abuse of power. The evil as they presented it was systemic, not merely a side effect of power grabs by a few evil persons. Of course, libels consisted of personal stories, basically revelations about the private lives of public figures, but the concrete details dramatized a general theme. They showed how wicked individuals rose to the top and then gave full vent to their wickedness, unchecked by any institutional restraints. Although this scenario left room for consideration of constitutional issues and normative principles, the libelers avoided theoretical issues. They moralized; they did not philosophize. Readers interested in the philosophical implications of the stories would have to go to books that accompanied the libels in the crates shipped throughout the literary underground. They could consult the works of Rousseau, Mably, d'Holbach, and other philosophes, particularly Montesquieu. Montesquieu had exposed the danger of despotism in the *Lettres persanes*, and he had analyzed it in *De l'Esprit des lois*. Monarchies tended to degenerate into despotisms, he explained. Despotism was a distinct variety of government, one with its own activating principle and general culture. It required no stretch of the imagination to associate the seraglios described by Montesquieu with the Parc-aux-cerfs "harem" featured in many of the libels against Louis XV. But the libelers left their readers to make the connections. They reduced complex questions to the play of personality, and in doing so they showed that personal corruption operated as the driving force behind events—that is, they conveyed a general picture of contemporary history.

In their prefaces, the libelers often identified themselves as historians and described their books as histories, partly to beguile the reader into accepting their claim to objectivity but also because the texts really were histories, *histoires* in both senses of the word in French: they related stories and provided narratives of events. Even "private lives" could be read as histories, notably in the case of *Vie privée de Louis XV*, which provided a detailed, four-volume account of events from 1715 to 1774. Of course, all the narratives were tendentious, and all of them conveyed the same message: France was sinking ever deeper into despotism. They made the recent past look like a succession of corrupt ministers, one worse than the other. The kings themselves were not especially vicious, but they surrendered the kingdom to the vilest of their favorites, usually at the direction of a degenerate mistress or, in the case of Louis XVI, a depraved queen. Therefore, contemporary history could be reduced to variations on a single theme: ministerial despotism.

Although the libels allowed for occasional exceptions to that formula—sometimes they had a good word to say for Turgot, sometimes for Necker—it hardly did justice to the complexities of French history after 1715. But that is the point. Libels eliminated complexity by reducing their narrative to a simple story line; then they worked variations on that line by adding endless detail. In practice, the technique came down to a matter of accumulating anecdotes and stringing them together to form a story. The notion of an "anecdote" differed fundamentally in the eighteenth century from what it is today. It referred to the secret side of history, to events that actually had occurred but had been kept hidden from the public. Anecdotes took the form of information about incidents that would compromise someone in power, and at first they circulated by word of mouth or as items in a clandestine newsletter, usually only a paragraph in length. Paragraphs became the building blocks of libels. Libelers quarried them out of *nouvelles à la main* or letters and transcribed them from oral sources. Whatever their origin, they were treated as hard facts, authentic bits of past experience, which could be pieced together in a story. The libelers could also rearrange the pieces in new narratives, and they often lifted anecdotes from one another's texts. Libels therefore developed family resemblances, like a series of mosaics or frescos from a single school of artists. By 1789 a body of literature had evolved with the same ingredients scattered everywhere, all of them deemed to be true, all of them reinforcing one another in a common picture of the recent past. Of course, there were exceptions—the occasional libel composed of a continuous narrative that flowed smoothly without interruption from anecdotes. But most libels fit into the same general picture or metanarrative. Readers could recognize key episodes and distinguish a basic outline in all the plots, so they had a mental frame in which to sort out new events. Libels fed into a collective worldview.

Now, this claim, I realize, involves some speculation. We cannot reconstruct the world as it was seen by people who died centuries ago. We cannot trace the mental processes that occurred while they were reading. We can only study what evidence remains, scattered in disparate sources and in the texts themselves. But close reading and comparison of the texts reveals some common tendencies. The authors were always addressing their readers, guiding their reactions and directing their way through the narratives. In some cases, they set puzzles, which admitted of only one solution, or they challenged readers to identify the villains of a story in the manner of a roman à clef. Even after arriving at the solution, however, readers could draw whatever conclusions they pleased. There is no getting around the problems posed by the open-ended and varied character of reading. Ultimately, therefore, the argument turns on the nature of the reading matter. If it was widely diffused and conveyed a basic set of themes, one can expect to find some congruence between those themes and the public's understanding of them.

The preceding pages attempt to make that argument. They also extend it into the revolutionary period. At first glance, one might expect libel literature to have disappeared after 1789, since so much of it was geared to sensitivities peculiar to the Ancien Régime—the fascination with word games and wit, for example, and the connection of anecdotes with the inner life of the court. Libels certainly changed during the Revolution. By 1792, their authors had given up appealing to the reader's desire for amusement and had shifted from ridicule to denunciation. The tone of libels became cruder, their rhetoric more moralistic. Yet their form remained essentially the same. They strung together anecdotes, featured portraits, and revealed sensational bits of news just as they had done before the Revolution. They also favored the well-worn metaphors developed in the earlier literature. They stripped back curtains, tore off veils, and ripped away masks in order to reveal the true features of the villains they attacked. And they continued to recount "private lives" just as libels had done under Louis XIV and would continue to do until the accession of Napoleon and beyond, deep into the nineteenth century.

Like their predecessors, the revolutionary libels did not deal in abstract ideas or offer any political analysis. They, too, reduced complex events to the clash of personalities. And as the personalities all had the same flaw—a lust for lucre and a readiness to conspire with counterrevolutionaries under a hypocritical veneer of patriotism—they looked remarkably alike. There was even a sameness to the parties associated with them. Whether Fayettistes, Brissotins, Dantonistes, Hébertistes, or Robespierristes, they were identified by names, not policies; and they did not represent anything beyond the constant danger of collaboration with counterrevolutionary plots.

Although the tendency to personalize politics did not distinguish the revolutionary libels from those of the Ancien Régime, the rhetoric of denunciation gave them a new tone. It was an attempt to appeal to plebeian readers. By 1793 the reading public in Paris contained far more sans-culottes than sophisticates, and the authors who wrote for it took their cues from the bellicose journalism developed by Hébert and Marat. They aimed to arouse indignation and anger, the uncomplicated emotions of *Le Père Duchesne*. Compared with the *Vie privée de Louis XV*, the *Vie secrète de Pierre Manuel* looks crude. It called for blood, and it belonged to the propaganda that hounded Manuel to the guillotine. The lethal character of libels under the Terror sets them apart from the naughty books that amused readers under the Ancien Régime. Yet they had many common characteristics, and the continuity should not be surprising; for revolutions cannot create new worlds out of nothing, despite the utopian energy that drives them. They must build with materials gleaned from the ruins of an old regime. The libelers of the Terror adopted techniques developed by their predecessors under Louis XV, who picked up tricks from Aretino and Procopius. All of them tried to win their case before the public by exposing vice in private life.

It is not an uplifting story. Literary history lacks nobility when seen from below—that is, from Grub Street, where libels were cobbled together like the lives of their authors, from dirt and grit. The dirt may be distasteful, but the grit infused energy into a huge body of literature, one largely forgotten but worthy of study; for it reached readers everywhere, and it helped shape their understanding of the world in which they lived. That world has disappeared, but slander still dogs at the heels of the great. To see how it brought them down in the eighteenth century is not to draw a lesson from the past but rather to understand how authoritarian regimes can be vulnerable to words and how well-placed words can mobilize the mysterious force known as public opinion.

Notes

Introduction

1. Antoine de Rivarol, *Le petit almanach de nos grands hommes* (n.p., 1788). I have tried to calculate the growth of the literary population in eighteenth-century France in two studies: "A Police Inspector Sorts His Files: The Anatomy of the Republic of Letters," in *The Great Cat Massacre and Other Episodes in French Cultural History* (New York, 1984), and "The Facts of Literary Life in Eighteenth-Century France," in *The Political Culture of the Old Regime*, ed. Keith Baker (Oxford, 1987), 261–91. All estimates run into the problems of defining an author and of interpreting imperfect sources. After taking these problems into account, I concluded that France contained at least three thousand authors in 1789, an "author" being someone who had published at least one book.

2. For some revealing case studies, see Aleksandr Stroev, *Les aventuriers des Lumières* (Paris, 1997).

3. See Pat Rogers, *Grub Street: Studies in a Subculture* (London, 1972), and John Brewer, *Party Ideology and Popular Politics at the Accession of George III* (Cambridge, 1976).

4. The French had no equivalent for the English term "Grub Street" in the eighteenth century, but they often talked about "la basse littérature," "la canaille de la littérature," and "les Rousseau du ruisseau"—expressions that show up often in the works of Voltaire, Louis-Sébastien Mercier, and others. There is no full-scale study of this milieu, but I have sketched aspects of it in *The Literary Underground of the Old Regime* (Cambridge, Mass., 1982).

5. The richest source of information about the French expatriates in London is the archives of the French Ministry of Foreign Affairs at the Quai d'Orsay: Correspondance politique: Angleterre, especially mss 540–50. The most important printed sources include the anonymous and tendentious but very revealing *libelle* by Anne-Gédéon Lafitte (or simply Lafite in some versions of his name), marquis de Pelleport (or Pellepore in some versions), *Le Diable dans un bénitier, et la métamorphose du Gazetier cuirassé en mouche . . .* (London, 1784); the police reports published by Pierre-Louis Manuel, *La Police de Paris dévoilée* (Paris, 1790), 2 vols.; Manuel's edited and paraphrased versions of papers from the Bastille, *La Bastille dévoilée, ou recueil de pièces authentiques pour servir à son histoire* (Paris, 1789–90), 8 "livraisons" or volumes, depending on how they are bound; and the superb collection of documents edited by Gunnar von Proschwitz and Mavis von Proschwitz, *Beaumarchais et le "Courier de l'Europe"* (Oxford, 1990), 2 vols. The biography of the most notorious libeler, Charles Théveneau de Morande, by Paul Robiquet, *Théveneau de Morande: Etude sur le XVIIIe siècle* (Paris, 1882), draws on those sources but frequently gets them wrong. It has been superseded by Simon Burrows, *Blackmail, Scandal, and Revolution: London's French Libellistes, 1758–92*

(Manchester, 2006). Burrows dissents from my interpretation of this subject, which I first published as "The High Enlightenment and the Low-Life of Literature in Prerevolutionary France," *Past and Present*, no. 51 (1971), 81–115. For a discussion of these issues, see Haydn Mason, ed., *The Darnton Debate: Books and Revolution in the Eighteenth Century* (Oxford, 1998).

6. The richest source of information about censorship is the reports and memorandums composed by the censors themselves in Bibliothèque nationale de France, Collection Anisson, manuscrits français 22137–52, and the *Mémoires sur la librairie* by Chrétien-Guillaume de Lamoignon de Malesherbes, Director of the Book Trade (Directeur de la librairie, an office in the royal administration under the Chancellory) from 1750 to 1763. See Roger Chartier, ed., *Mémoires sur la librairie: Mémoire sur la liberté de la presse* (1809; Paris, 1994). Among secondary works, see especially Barbara de Negroni, *Lectures interdites: Le travail des censeurs au XVIIIᵉ siècle, 1723–1774*. For a synthesis of the literature on all aspects of the book trade under the Ancien Régime, see Henri-Jean Martin and Roger Chartier, eds., *Histoire de l'édition française: Tome II, Le livre triomphant, 1660–1830* (Paris, 1984).

7. Giles Barber, "French Royal Decrees Concerning the Book Trade, 1700–1789," *Australian Journal of French Studies* 3, no. 3 (1966), 312–30.

8. This is my own estimate, but I admit that I cannot prove it. It is based on a reading of virtually all the documents from the period 1750–89 in the manuscript collections of the Bibliothèque nationale de France and the Bibliothèque de l'Arsenal, as well as the fifty thousand letters by booksellers, publishers, and other persons involved in the book industry in the papers of the Société typographique de Neuchâtel, Bibliothèque publique et universitaire, Neuchâtel, Switzerland. Because the French state could not effectively enforce privileges for books, piracy developed into a major industry, one that far outstripped legal production.

9. Robert Darnton, *The Forbidden Best-Sellers of Pre-Revolutionary France* (New York, 1995), and its companion volume, *The Corpus of Clandestine Literature in France* (New York, 1995). The sampling technique and the problem of bias built into the sources are discussed in these volumes.

10. As exemplary studies, see Roland Barthes, *Mythologies* (Paris, 1957); Clifford Geertz, *Negara: The Theatre State in Nineteenth-Century Bali* (Princeton, N.J., 1980); and Jacob Burckhardt, *The Civilization of the Renaissance in Italy* (New York, 2002).

11. Social scientists have advanced various definitions of myth and folklore. Although the concepts often overlap in common usage, myth tends to connote belief about something transcendental or profoundly significant such as the origin of the world, whereas folklore concerns expressive culture linked to more secular subjects as in the case of riddles or trickster tales. See the essays "Folklore" and "Myth" in *International Encyclopedia of the Social and Behavioral Sciences*, ed. Neil J. Smelser and Paul B. Bates (Amsterdam, 2001), 8: 5711–15, 15: 10273–78. I have used both terms. "Folklore" seems more appropriate to the subject matter of libels, but "myth" conveys their general view of the political system's fundamental nature.

Chapter 1. The Armor-Plated Gazetteer

1. For a masterful survey of the entire reign, see Michel Antoine, *Louis XV* (Paris, 1989). On the crisis of 1770–74, two works from the nineteenth century remain funda-

mental: Jules Flammermont, *Le Chancelier Maupeou et les parlements* (Paris, 1885), and Marcel Marion, *La Bretagne et le duc d'Aiguillon* (Paris, 1898). The ideological polemics ignited by the Maupeou "revolution" are discussed in Durand Echeverria, *The Maupeou Revolution: A Study in the History of Libertarianism, France, 1770–1774* (Baton Rouge, 1985), but that study will be superseded by the forthcoming work of Shanti Marie Singham based on her doctoral dissertation at Princeton University, "'A Conspiracy of Twenty Million Frenchmen': Public Opinion, Patriotism, and the Assault on Absolutism During the Maupeou Years, 1770–1775" (1991).

2. I have identified six editions of *Le Gazetier cuirassé*, two from 1771, one from 1772, one from 1777, one from 1785, and one from 1790, but there probably were several more, most of them pirated. What I take to be the first edition, a poorly printed work on cheap paper from 1771, does not have a frontispiece. A copy of another edition from 1771 in the Bibliothèque nationale de France, Lb38.1270, is printed with greater care and includes the elaborately engraved frontispiece that appears on subsequent editions. The later editions include both the frontispiece and the new material about the Bastille. It is somewhat misleading to refer to "pirated" editions, as the original edition had no copyright, privilege, or claim to legality. The French foreign ministry learned of an edition printed in Geneva and demanded that the Genevan authorities punish the printer. See Theodore Besterman, ed., *The Complete Works of Voltaire: Correspondence and Related Documents* (Banbury, 1975), 38: 197.

3. I would like to thank Denis Feeney for help in translating the Latin.

4. See "Baril" in *Le Grand vocabulaire français* (Paris, 1768), 1: 147: "Le *l* final est muet devant une consonne; mais il se fait sentir devant une voyelle." See also André Martinet and Henriette Walter, *Dictionnaire de la prononciation française dans son usage réel* (Paris, 1973), 129.

5. *Le Gazetier cuirassé ou anecdotes scandaleuses de la cour de France* (1777), 54. A footnote on the same page made the allusion even clearer: "Si ce casque royal avait été *ombragé* de tous les panaches que la comtesse aurait pu y ajouter, le piédestal se serait écroulé à coup sûr." For more punning on *baril*, see p. 32. For reasons of convenience, quotations are taken from the 1777 edition, although the phrasing is the same in the editions of 1771.

6. The work that I take to be the second edition of 1771 contains an "explication du frontispice" on the verso of the title page: "Un homme armé de toutes pièces et assis tranquillement sous la protection de l'artillerie qui l'environne, dissipe la foudre et brise le [*sic*] nuages qui sont sur sa tête à coups de canon. Une tête coiffée en méduse, un baril, et une tête à perruque sont les emblèmes parlants des trois puissances qui ont fait tant de belles choses en France. Les feuilles qui voltigent à travers la foudre au-dessus de l'homme armé sont des lettres de cachet dont il est garanti par la seule fumée de son artillerie, qui les empêche d'arriver jusqu'à lui. Les mortiers auxquels il met le feu sont destinés à porter la vérité sur tous les gens vicieux qu'elle écrase, pour en faire des exemples." This explanation is missing from the later editions, presumably because the readers were meant to decipher it by themselves.

7. *Le Gazetier cuirassé*, 44.

8. *Le Diable dans un bénitier, et la métamorphose du Gazetier cuirassé en mouche, ou tentative du sieur Receveur, inspecteur de la police de Paris, chevalier de St. Louis, pour établir à Londres une police à l'instar de celle de Paris* (Paris, 1783), 37, 79.

9. *Le Gazetier cuirassé*, 31.

10. See Erica-Marie Bénabou, *La Prostitution et la police des moeurs au XVIIIe siècle* (Paris, 1987), 257–59. This solid work of social history cuts through the legends surrounding Mme du Barry and the other women procured for Louis XV, several of whom were prostitutes.

11. *Le Gazetier cuirassé*, 34.

12. Ibid., 123. This copy in the Bibliothèque nationale de France, Réserve, Lb38.1270, apparently comes from the second edition of 1771. The text of the key is the same as that of the footnotes in the other editions. In this edition the main text is followed by two separate sections, *Mélanges confus sur des matières fort claires, par l'auteur du Gazetier cuirassé: Imprimé sous le soleil* and *Le Philosophe cynique, pour servir de suite aux Anecdotes scandaleuses de la cour de France: Imprimé dans une île qui fait trembler la terre ferme.* They appear in the form of supplements with separate pagination and their own keys at the end. In what I take to be the first edition, also published in 1771 (the exact sequence of the editions is difficult to determine), all this material is strung together with continuous pagination and footnotes instead of keys. The facetious titles, addresses, and diverse modes of breaking up the text were apparently meant to capture the reader's attention and to provide amusement.

13. *Le Gazetier cuirassé*, 124.

14. Ibid., 49.

15. Ibid., 172.

16. Ibid., 41, 176.

17. See, for example, "Copie d'une lettre écrite de Paris le 10 juin 1771," ibid., 118–22, and "Epître à un ami," ibid., 75–76, in which the anonymous author congratulated himself for his heroism in opposing tyranny and adopted a sentimental style at odds with his slandering as a self-proclaimed "philosophe cynique."

18. See, for example, the attack on Choiseul's distant cousin, the duc de Praslin, who had served in his government as foreign minister and naval minister. *Le Gazetier cuirassé*, 27.

19. Ibid., 47.

20. By 1771, the libeler noted, the king could no longer copulate successfully, despite the tricks that Mme du Barry had learned in brothels and employed to revive his exhausted libido. Ibid., 54–55, 57. As an example of denigrating the symbols of the monarchy, see p. 171: "On a publié un monitoire pour savoir ce qu'étaient devenus le sceptre et la main de justice d'un des plus grands rois de l'Europe. Après des perquisitions très longues, ils se sont trouvés sur la toilette d'une jolie femme appellée comtesse, qui s'en sert pour amuser son chat."

21. Ibid., 106.

22. Ibid., p. 20 of the supplement at the end titled "Remarques historiques et anecdotes sur le château de la Bastille et l'Inquisition de France."

23. Voltaire, "Quisquis," in *Questions sur l'Encyclopédie par des amateurs* (n.p., 1775), 6: 278. A review of *Le Gazetier cuirassé* in the underground *Mémoires secrets pour servir à l'histoire de la république des lettres en France*, entry dated August 15, 1771, treated the book as an audacious attack on men in power, including the king, but noted that its joking tone and scabrous anecdotes made it "une rapsodie très informe et fort méchante."

24. *Le Gazetier cuirassé*, 174.

25. Voltaire to Jean Le Rond d'Alembert, August 13, 1760, *Complete Works of Voltaire*, 106: 44–45.

26. D'Alembert to Voltaire, September 2, 1760, *Complete Works of Voltaire*, 106: 88.

27. The polemics of 1759–60 marked a crucial turning point in the French Enlightenment. D'Alembert, writing from Paris, castigated Voltaire as the leader of the philosophes for failing to understand the gravity of the threat to their cause. At first Voltaire hesitated, but once convinced of the need to go on the offensive he produced a series of attacks on the anti-philosophes. See all of the letters they exchanged in 1760, especially d'Alembert to Voltaire, May 6, *Complete Works of Voltaire*, 105: 284; d'Alembert to Voltaire, May 26, ibid., 105: 329; Voltaire to d'Alembert, June 10, ibid., 105: 361; d'Alembert to Voltaire, June 16, 1760, ibid., 105: 375; Voltaire to Nicolas Claude Thiriot, July 7, ibid., 105: 443; Voltaire to d'Alembert, July 9, ibid., 105: 449; and Voltaire to Thiriot, September 9, ibid., 106: 108. Most of the attacks were aimed at Voltaire's favorite enemy, Elie Catherine Fréron, editor of *L'Année littéraire*, who actually reacted with a good deal of dignity and treated them as *libelles*. See Fréron to Chrétien Guillaume de Lamoignon de Malesherbes, August 20, 1760, *Complete Works of Voltaire*, 106: 67.

Chapter 2. The Devil in the Holy Water

1. *Le Diable dans un bénitier, et la métamorphose du Gazetier cuirassé en mouche* (1783), 84–85.

2. "Diable," in Pierre Larousse, *Grand Dictionnaire universel du XIXe siècle* (Paris, 1866), and Alain Rey and Sophie Chantreau, *Dictionnaire des expressions et locutions* (Paris, 1989), 406. The text of *Le Diable dans un bénitier* does not explain which character was referred to in the title; the devil could have been Morande. That seems unlikely, however, because the narrative emphasizes the way Receveur was thwarted by his intended victims among the libelers.

3. *Le Diable dans un bénitier*, 36.

4. According to a version of this incident in *Mémoires secrets pour servir à l'histoire de la république des lettres en France* (London, 1777–89), entry for February 5, 1774, the Londoners nearly massacred the secret agents from the Parisian police: "L'exempt Receveur en a eu une telle frayeur qu'il est encore fou." As there are so many mutually incompatible editions of the *Mémoires secrets*, citations to it conventionally appear only with the date of the entry, not with volume and pages.

5. *Le Diable dans un bénitier*, 100.

6. This pub, established in 1723, still exists on Great Russell Street opposite the British Museum.

7. *Le Diable dans un bénitier*, 106.

8. Ibid., 158–59.

9. Ibid., 5–6, 10–11, 52.

10. Ibid., 31, 37, 40.

11. See ibid., 59–60, 119–22.

Chapter 3. The Parisian Police Unveiled

1. The angel-like figure at the top of the frontispiece could be Chronos, though he is not holding an hourglass, which depicts time in the standard iconography of him. I cannot identify the fox-like familiar of the evil figure holding the dagger.

2. Pierre Manuel, *La Police de Paris dévoilée* (Paris, 1790), 2: 235. References to the London libelers are scattered throughout *La Police de Paris dévoilée*. See 1: 38–39, 136–56, 236–75, 2: 28–30, 231–69.

3. Ibid., 2: 28.

4. Brissot and Manuel referred to one another often in their writings. See, for example, J.-P. Brissot *Mémoires (1754–1793)*, ed. Claude Perroud (Paris, 1910) 1: 187, 2: 26, 205–6. By the end of 1792, Manuel was known as a prominent "Brissotin" or "Girondin," and the Jacobin Club accused him of having been "brissotisé." See *La Société des Jacobins: Recueil de documents pour l'histoire du Club des Jacobins de Paris*, ed. Alphonse Aulard (Paris, 1892), 4: 612.

5. *La Bastille dévoilée, ou recueil de pièces authentiques pour servir à son histoire* (Paris, 1789), 8 installments bound in 4 volumes, 3: 78. In various sources, such as the catalogue of the Bibliothèque nationale de France, this work is attributed both to a certain Charpentier and to Manuel. It has all the marks of the other compilations that Manuel produced from the same sources during the French Revolution: *La Police de Paris dévoilée* and *La Chasteté du clergé dévoilée, ou procès-verbaux des séances du clergé chez les filles de Paris, trouvés à la Bastille* (Paris, 1790). The anonymous editor of *La Bastille dévoilée* noted (3: 75) that he was printing the notice on Brissot's imprisonment that he had received from Brissot himself. In his memoirs, Brissot indicated that this editor was Manuel, who had sent him his dossier from the Bastille, "en me disant qu'il ne fallait pas qu'il restât rien de moi dans les ordures de la police." Brissot, *Mémoires*, 2: 23. I conclude that Manuel wrote all or most of *La Bastille dévoilée*, though he might have had some assistance.

6. *La Bastille dévoilée*, 3: 66.

7. *La Police de Paris dévoilée*, 2: 258–59.

8. Ibid., 2: 236. In another report, the police described Boissière's shop as a "conciliabule politique," where the French refugees exchanged outrageous remarks about the French regime (ibid., 2: 246).

9. Ibid., 2: 234. On the *Courrier de l'Europe*, see Gunnar von Proschwitz, "Courrier de l'Europe (1776–1792)," in *Dictionnaire des journaux, 1600–1789*, ed. Jean Sgard (Oxford, 1991), 1: 282–93, and the superb collection of documents and commentary published by Gunnar von Proschwitz and Mavis von Proschwitz, *Beaumarchais et le "Courrier de l'Europe"* (Oxford, 1990).

10. *La Police de Paris dévoilée*, 2: 246.

11. Ibid., 2: 231.

12. Ibid., 2: 247.

13. Ibid., 2: 231–32.

14. Ibid., 1: 6.

15. Ibid., 2: 91, 93, 123.

16. Ibid., 1: 8.

17. Ibid., 1: 7.

18. Ibid., 1: 8–9.

19. Ibid., 1: 6.

20. See Manuel's "Discours préliminaire" in the *Lettres originales de Mirabeau* and his defense at the trial, published as *Interrogatoire de Pierre Manuel, Procureur de la Commune* (1792), Bibliothèque nationale de France Lb39.5939.

Chapter 4. The Secret Life of Pierre Manuel

1. *Vie secrète de Pierre Manuel* (Paris, undated but published in 1793), 63.
2. Ibid., 28.
3. Ibid., 29.
4. Ibid., 47.
5. Ibid., 34.

Chapter 5. The End of the Line

1. See Antoine-Alexandre Barbier, *Dictionnaire des ouvrages anonymes* (Paris, 1879), 4: 964, 983, 1001. Although he had access to some important documents, Barbier often erred in his attributions, and he did not cite his sources. Turbat does not figure in J.-M. Quérard, *Les Supercheries littéraires dévoilées* (Paris, 1869), nor in any of the works on journals and journalists during the eighteenth century. He is mentioned in Maurice Tourneux, *Bibliographie de l'histoire de Paris pendant la Révolution française* (Paris, 1890–1913), 4: 231, but in this case Tourneux derived his attributions from Barbier.

2. *Petite feuille de Paris par Turbat, imprimeur en lettres*, no. 42, 25 frimaire An II (December 15, 1793), 166.

3. *Les Tuileries, le Temple, le Tribunal révolutionnaire et la Conciergerie, sous la tyrannie de la Convention par un ami du trône* (Paris, 1814; anonymous, but by Pierre Turbat according to the catalogue of the Bibliothèque nationale de France), 86.

4. Ibid., 85.

Chapter 6. Bibliography and Iconography

1. Despite his prominent role in the events of 1792–93, there is no biography of Manuel before the publication of Huguette Leloup-Audibert, *Pierre Louis Manuel (1753–1793): Du pouvoir à l'échafaud* (Gien, 2006), which has little information about his early life. The biographical notice in Auguste Kuscinski, *Dictionnaire des conventionnels* (Paris, 1916–19), 2: 427–28, summarizes most of the available information about his life. Some key documents concerning his pre-revolutionary career are in the dossier related to his imprisonment in the Bastille on February 3, 1786: Archives Nationales W295, no. 246; Bibliothèque de l'Arsenal ms. 12460; *La Bastille dévoilée, ou recueil de pièces authentiques pour servir à son histoire* (Paris, 1789–90), 3: 105–6; and Frantz Funck-Brentano, *Les Lettres de cachet à Paris, étude suivie d'une liste des prisonniers de la Bastille (1659–1789)* (Paris, 1903), 415–16. There are also some perceptive remarks on Manuel's life as a hack writer before 1789 in Gudrun Gersmann, *Im Schatten der Bastille: Die Welt der Schriftsteller, Kolporteure und Buchhändler am Vorabend der Französischen Revolution* (Stuttgart, 1993), 146–52. Aside from his own writings, the best sources on Manuel's role in the Revolution are F. A. Aulard, ed., *La Société des Jacobins: Recueil de documents pour l'histoire du Club des Jacobins de Paris* (Paris, 1889–97), 6

vols., and Paul Robiquet, *Le Personnel municipal de Paris pendant la Révolution* (Paris, 1890), 2 vols.

2. Anne Louise Germaine Necker, baronne de Staël-Holstein, *Considérations sur la Révolution française*, ed. Jacques Godechot (1818; Paris, 1983), 283.

3. Bibliothèque nationale de France, Département des estampes, D203602–5, D203608–10, and *Collection complète des tableaux historiques de la Révolution française, en deux volumes* (Paris, 1798). See also *Images de la Révolution française: Catalogue du vidéodisque coproduit par la Bibliothèque nationale et Pergamon Press* (Paris, 1990), 3 vols.

4. Although there is no full-scale study of Basset, the character of his trade can be pieced together from references in Maxime Préaud, Pierre Casselle, Marianne Grivel, and Corinne Le Bitouzé, *Dictionnaire des éditeurs d'estampes à Paris sous l'Ancien Régime* (Paris, 1987), 45–46; Roger Portalis and Henri Béraldi, *Les Graveurs du dix-huitième siècle* (Paris, 1882), 3: 719; and Marcel Roux, *Bibliothèque nationale Département des Estampes: Inventaire du fonds français* (Paris, 1933), 2: 157–58. For general accounts of prints during the eighteenth century, see Pierre-Louis Duchartre and René Saulnier, *L'Imagerie parisienne (L'Imagerie de la rue Saint-Jacques)* (Paris, 1944); Antoine de Baecq, *La Caricature révolutionnaire* (Paris, 1988); Klaus Herding and Rolf Reichardt, *Die Bildpublizistik der Französischen Revolution* (Frankfurt am Main, 1989); Christoph Denelzik-Brüggemann and Rolf Reichardt, *Bildgedächtnis eines welthistorischen Ereignisses: Die Tableaux historiques de la Révolution française* (Göttingen, 2001); and François-Louis Bruel, *Un Siècle d'histoire de France par l'estampe, 1770–1871* (Paris, 1909), 8 vols.

5. *Collection complète des tableaux historiques de la Révolution française* (Paris, 1798–1802), 2: n.p. On the complex publishing history of this work, see Claudette Hould, "Neue Hypothesen zu den französischen Ausgaben der *Tableaux historiques de la Révolution française*," in *Bildgedächtnis eines welthistorischen Ereignisses*, by Denelzik-Brüggemann and Reichardt, 35–84.

6. De Baecq, *La Caricature révolutionnaire*, 27.

Chapter 7. Reading

1. The history of reading has developed into an important field of research. As I understand it, it began in Germany, where the theoretical and empirical problems were addressed in the 1960s. Among the theoreticians, Hans Robert Jauss and Wolfgang Iser demonstrated the potential of a "Rezeptionsästhetik." See Jauss, *Literaturgeschichte als Provokation* (Frankfurt am Main, 1970). Among the empiricists, Rolf Engelsing revealed how much could be discovered about reading practices in his pioneering study of Bremen, published under the somewhat misleading title, *Der Bürger als Leser: Lesergeschichte in Deutschland, 1500–1800* (Stuttgart, 1974). In the course of this research he formulated a thesis about a "reading revolution" in the late eighteenth century, one that involved a shift from "intensive" and repeated reading of a few books to "extensive" reading of all sorts of printed matter. See his "Die Perioden der Lesergeschichte in der Neuzeit: Das statistische Ausmass und die soziokulturelle Bedeutung der Lektüre," *Archiv für Geschichte des Buchwesens* 10 (1969), columns 944–1002. I have criticized that thesis in my own attempt to provide an overview of the subject in "First

Steps Toward a History of Reading," *Australian Journal of French Studies* 23 (1986), 5–30. Roger Chartier accepts it and associates it with Stanley Fish's notion of an "interpretive community" in his essays, notably "Communautés de lecteurs," in *L'Ordre des livres: Lecteurs, auteurs, bibliothèques en Europe entre XIVe et XVIIIe siècle* (Paris, 1992), 13–33. Reinhard Wittmann also subscribes to Engelsing's argument, although he vitiates it by noting that the older mode of "intensive" reading was often mechanical while the modern version of "extensive" reading was often passionate. See his "Une Révolution de la lecture à la fin du XVIIIe siècle?" in *Histoire de la lecture dans le monde occidental,* ed. Guglielmo Cavallo and Roger Chartier (Paris, 1997), 331–64. The essays compiled in the latter provide excellent examples of more recent research. The present chapter picks up the argument where I left it in *The Forbidden Best-Sellers in Pre-Revolutionary France* (New York, 1995), chap. 9.

2. Bibliothèque de l'Arsenal, ms 10170, fol. 4.

3. The figure of 380 cafés comes from Jacques Savary des Bruslons, *Dictionnaire universel de commerce* (1723), as cited in Jean Claude Bologne, *Histoire des cafés et des cafetiers* (Paris, 1993), 102. Louis-Sébastien Mercier claims that Paris had 800 cafés in 1788: *Tableau de Paris* (Amsterdam, 1788), 12: 297. Other estimates set the number of cafés at 1,000 and of cabarets at 3,000 or more by 1789. See Thomas Brennan, *Public Drinking and Popular Culture in Eighteenth-Century Paris* (Princeton, N.J., 1988), 76–89. Brennan notes that cabarets (taverns), unlike cafés, tended to have plebeian clienteles. They were centers of neighborhood sociability, and as far as one can tell from judicial archives, their table talk generally concerned matters of local gossip rather than public affairs.

4. *Lettre à Milord XXX au sujet de M. Bergasse et de ses Observations dans l'affaire de M. Kornmann* (1788), 3. In his *Tableau de Paris,* 5: 57, Mercier noted that at the height of the demand for some works, booksellers occasionally cut them into parts and rented them out by the hour.

5. I have tried to develop an argument about eighteenth-century Paris as an information system in two essays: "The News in Paris: An Early Information Society," *American Historical Review* 105 (February 2000): 1–35, and "Public Opinion and Communication Networks in Eighteenth-Century Paris," in *Opinion,* ed. Peter-Eckhard Knabe (Berlin, 2000), 149–230.

6. This famous remark occurs in the first paragraph of Diderot's *Neveu de Rameau.*

7. Pierre-Antoine-Auguste Goupil to Jean-Charles-Pierre Lenoir, lieutenant général de police, January 18, 1775, in Bibliothèque de l'Arsenal, ms. 12446.

8. Ibid.

9. All the stages of the investigation can be followed from the documents in Bibliothèque de l'Arsenal, ms. 12446. For information on Manoury and his role in the underground book trade, see my *Edition et sédition: L'Univers de la littérature clandestine au XVIIIe siècle* (Paris, 1991), chap. 5.

10. Mercier, *Tableau de Paris,* 12: 93.

11. Ibid., 12: 94–95.

12. Louis-Sébastien Mercier, *Les Entretiens du Palais-Royal* (Paris, 1786). See also Mercier's descriptions of conversations and reading in *Les Entretiens du jardin des Tuileries de Paris* (Paris, 1788). On Mercier as an observer of Paris, see the introduction by Jean-Claude Bonnet and the notes by him and his collaborators in their excellent

edition of *Tableau de Paris*, ed. Jean-Claude Bonnet (Paris, 1994, reprint of the successive editions from 1781–87), 2 vols.

13. Mercier, *Les Entretiens du Palais-Royal*, 105.

14. Ibid., 105–6. See also Mercier's observation about the power of libels on p. 104: "Orgon sort d'une société blanc comme la neige, on lui campe un libelle à sa porte; le voilà plus noir que l'encre même, et demain la ville et les faubourgs qui l'adorent aujourd'hui, le déchireront à belles dents."

15. "Les nouvellistes," ibid., 184–88.

16. Ibid., 185.

17. Ibid., 187.

18. Mercier changed his mind about many things, including the effect of a free press and public opinion, during the Revolution. See his *Le Nouveau Paris* (Paris, 1799; repr. and ed. Jean-Claude Bonnet, Paris, 1994), a sequel to *Tableau de Paris*, especially the chapters "Palais-Egalité, ci-devant Palais-Royal," "Philosophisme," "Esprit public," "Imprimeries," "Consommation de papier," "Libellistes," and "Sans-culottes."

19. Bibliothèque nationale de France, Département des estampes, Collection Hennin no. 8362. The address on this broadside indicates that it was produced by Jean-Baptiste Crépy, "rue Saint-Jacques, à l'image de Saint Pierre." Crépy was an important merchant of popular prints during the second half of the eighteenth century. See Maxime Préaud, Pierre Casselle, Marianne Grivel, and Corinne Le Bitouzé, *Dictionnaire des éditeurs d'estampes à Paris sous l'Ancien Régime* (Paris, 1987), 92–93.

20. *Dictionnaire des journaux, 1600–1789*, ed. Jean Sgard (Oxford, 1991), 2:856–57.

21. Many of the collections are catalogued as "chansonniers" or scrapbooks of street songs, but they contain all sorts of verse and prose in addition to the songs. One of them, ms. C.P. 4312 in the Bibliothèque historique de la ville de Paris, has a table at the end, which refers to its contents (all the entries are in verse) according to the following genres: "épigrammes, rondeaux, odes, épitaphes, épîtres, chansons, contes, huitains, madrigaux, quatrains, bons mots, ballades, frivolets, fables." For other examples, see Bibliothèque historique de la ville de Paris, mss C.P. 4274–79, 4289, 4290–91, and N.A. 229. The most important sources in the Bibliothèque nationale de France are the Chansonnier Clairambault (I mainly studied the volume for 1749, ms. fr. 12719) and the Chansonnier Maurepas (I mainly studied ms. fr. 12650, which covers 1747). Although scholars have concentrated on these last two, well-known *chansonniers*, they have done little research on other forms of collecting, which included many kinds of ephemera. For lack of a better term, I have called them scrapbooks. The closest French expression is *journal*, although that has a connotation close to the English "diary." I know of no equivalent in French for "commonplace book" or of French research similar to the study of commonplace books that is now flourishing in Britain and the United States.

22. *Les Etrennes des acteurs des théâtres de Paris, contenant leurs noms, portraits et caractères* (Paris, 1747), 9, in Bibliothèque nationale de France, Chansonnier Maurepas, ms. fr. 12650, 387–422.

23. Bibliothèque nationale de France, Chansonnier Clairambault, ms. fr. 12719, p. 243.

24. Ibid., ms. fr. 12719, p. 23. See also the satirical riddle about de Saxe and Lowendahl in the Chansonnier Maurepas, ms. fr. 12650, p. 145. It was written as a caption to a print that shows the devil dragging them both to hell. The devil describes

them as follows: "Tous deux vaillants,/ Tous deux prudents,/ Tous deux galants;/ Tous deux paillards,/ Tous deux pillards,/ Tous deux bâtards;/ Tous deux sans foi,/ Tous deux sans loi,/ Tous deux à moi."

25. Chansonnier Maurepas, ms. fr. 12650, p. 155.

26. *Journal et mémoires du marquis d'Argenson*, ed. E. J. B. Rathery (Paris, 1862), 5: 456.

27. Chansonnier Clairambault, ms. fr. 12719, p. 244.

28. Street songs seem to have been more radical and more widely diffused than incidental poetry. See my "Public Opinion and Communication Networks."

29. See Eric Schön, *Der Verlust der Sinnlichkeit oder die Verwandlungen des Lesers: Mentalitätswandel um 1800* (Stuttgart, 1987), a bold but speculative account of the kinetic and sensual elements in reading.

30. Louis Sébastien Mercier, *Histoire d'une jeune luthérienne* (Neuchâtel, 1785), 142–43; *Mon Bonnet de nuit* (Lausanne, 1788), 1: 72; *Tableau de Paris*, 5: 57, 168.

31. Chrétien Guillaume de Lamoignon de Malesherbes, *Mémoires sur la librairie: Mémoire sur la liberté de la presse*, ed. Roger Chartier (1809; Paris, 1994), 226.

32. J.-A.-N. Caritat, marquis de Condorcet, "Huitième époque: Depuis l'invention de l'imprimerie jusqu'au temps où les sciences et la philosophie secouèrent le joug de l'autorité," in *Esquisse d'un tableau historique des progrès de l'esprit humain*, ed. O. H. Prior (1794; Paris, 1933).

33. Jürgen Habermas, *The Structural Transformation of the Public Sphere: An Inquiry into a Category of Bourgeois Society*, tr. Thomas Burger with Frederick Lawrence (Cambridge, Mass., 1989), 49–56. On the reading public and public opinion, see also 23–26, 85–88.

34. See Timothy Tackett, *Becoming a Revolutionary: The Deputies of the French National Assembly and the Emergence of a Revolutionary Culture (1789–1790)* (Princeton, N.J., 1996).

35. Gabriel Tarde, *L'Opinion et la foule* (Paris, 1901). Selections from Tarde's writings are available in English in Terry N. Clark, ed., *Gabriel Tarde on Communication and Social Influence* (Chicago, 1969). Tarde anticipates some of the ideas developed by Benedict Anderson in *Imagined Communities: Reflections on the Origin and Spread of Nationalism* (London, 1983).

36. Mercier, *Les Entretiens du Palais-Royal*, 51. See also p. 67.

37. Mercier, *Les Entretiens du jardin des Tuileries*, 3–5.

Chapter 8. Slander and Politics

1. I should confess that my own understanding of libel literature owes a good deal to the kind of literary criticism represented by Roland Barthes, notably in his *Mythologies* (Paris, 1957).

2. The following account is based on the Lenoir papers in the Bibliothèque municipale d'Orléans, mss. 1421, 1422, and 1423. Georges Lefebvre pronounced them genuine and described them briefly in "Les Papiers de Lenoir," *Annales historiques de la Révolution française*, no. 21 (May–June 1927), 300–301. Since then they have been used in a few studies, of which the most important is Pierre Chevallier, "Les Philosophes et le lieutenant de police Jean-Charles-Pierre Le Noir (1775–1785)," *French Studies* 17 (April

1963), 105–20. I have published extensive extracts from Lenoir's papers in two articles, "Le Lieutenant de police J.-C.-P. Lenoir, la Guerre des Farines et l'approvisionnement de Paris à la veille de la Révolution," *Revue d'histoire moderne et contemporaine* 16 (1969), 611–24, and "The Memoirs of Lenoir, lieutenant de police of Paris, 1774–1785," *English Historical Review* 85 (1970), 532–59. A complete version is now being prepared for publication at the Université d'Orléans, and a selection of Lenoir's essays on libels can be consulted in the electronic supplement to this book. Curiously, Lenoir's papers were not used extensively in the biography of him by Maxime de Sars, *Le Noir, lieutenant de police* (Paris, 1948), and de Sars dismissed the use of them by the police archivist Jacques Peuchet in *Mémoires tirés des archives de la police de Paris, pour servir à l'histoire de la morale et de la police, depuis Louis XIV jusqu'à nos jours* (Paris, 1838), 3: 1–104. Judging from the style and content of the material published by Peuchet, I believe that he had access to some of Lenoir's papers that have since disappeared. In any case, his six-volume work has valuable information about the police under the Ancien Régime.

3. Louis-Sébastien Mercier, *Tableau de Paris* (Amsterdam, 1783), 1: 192–93.

4. See Lenoir's account of his relations with the ministers in Darnton, "The Memoirs of Lenoir."

5. Ibid., 535n1.

6. Draft of an essay titled "Sciences et arts libéraux," Lenoir papers, Bibliothèque municipale d'Orléans, ms. 1422, titre 8.

7. "Sûreté," Lenoir papers, ms. 1422, titre 6.

8. The term was used broadly to designate all the works that attacked the Maupeou ministry, but it also referred specifically to the collection of tracts entitled *Correspondance secrète et familière de M. de Maupeou avec M. de Sor***, conseiller au nouveau parlement*, which was originally published in three volumes in 1771 and reprinted at least twice before 1774 under the title *Maupeouana*.

9. "Sur les écrits clandestins," Lenoir papers, ms. 1423, 263–64.

10. Darnton, "The Memoirs of Lenoir," 542–43.

11. Ibid., 556–57.

12. Notes grouped under the heading "Moufle, Costard, Prudhomme, Godefroy, Desauges, Granger, Neveu, Le Normand, Sauson," Lenoir papers, ms. 1422, titre 6.

13. "De l'administration de l'ancienne police concernant les libelles, les mauvaises satires et chansons, leurs auteurs coupables, délinquants, complices ou adérents," Lenoir papers, ms. 1422, titre 6.

14. Ibid.

15. Ibid.

16. For a detailed account of this episode, see Robert Darnton, "Public Opinion and Communication Networks in Eighteenth-Century Paris," in *Opinion*, ed. Peter-Eckhard Knabe (Berlin, 2000), 149–230.

17. "Mélanges," Lenoir papers, ms. 1423.

18. "Des imprimeurs et libraires, des colporteurs, des censeurs d'ouvrages littéraires," Lenoir papers, ms. 1422, titre 6.

19. "Des Mesures de police contre la médisance et contre la calomnie," Lenoir papers, ms. 1423: "Les moeurs du successeur de Louis Quinze étant inattaquables, le nouveau roi fut inaccessible de ce côté à la calomnie pendant les premières années de son règne, mais on commença en 1778 à le diffamer du côté de sa faiblesse, et les premières calomnies qui furent ourdies contre sa personne ne préludèrent que de très peu de mois ceux de la méchanceté contre la reine."

20. Darnton, "The Memoirs of Lenoir," 545. In a note mixed among his papers, ms. 1423, fol. 338, Lenoir remarked, "Je n'avais fait encore jusques là [1777] en aucune circonstance distribuer de l'argent pour exciter les cris de *vive la reine*. Depuis, j'en ai vainement fait répandre; ce moyen n'a produit que des cris presqu'isolés ou des battements de mains que l'on disait et reconnaissait avoir été payés."

21. Darnton, "The Memoirs of Lenoir," 545–46.

22. Lenoir papers, ms. 1422, titre 2.

23. Darnton, "The Memoirs of Lenoir," 541, 546.

24. "Résidus, notes éparses," Lenoir papers, ms. 1423, fol. 83.

25. Ibid.

26. "Sûreté," Lenoir papers, ms. 1422, titre 6.

Chapter 9. The Book Police at Work

1. See Robert Darnton, *The Great Cat Massacre and Other Episodes in French Cultural History* (New York, 1984), chap. 4.

2. This description of d'Hémery's career and functions is based on long study of his papers, known as the Collection Anisson, in the Bibliothèque nationale de France, ms. fr. 22061–22193. Ernest Coyecque included a brief biography of d'Hémery in the introduction to his superb inventory of the papers, *Inventaire de la Collection Anisson sur l'histoire de l'imprimerie et la librairie principalement à Paris* (Paris, 1900), 2 vols.

3. "Etat des objets relatifs à la librairie dont le sieur Goupil doit être chargé sur la démission du sieur d'Hémery qui en avait le détail ci-devant," Bibliothèque de l'Arsenal, Bastille papers, ms. 10028, fols. 307–10. Another copy is in the Bibliothèque nationale de France, ms. fr. 22053, pièce 44.

4. J.-P. Brissot *Mémoires (1754–1793)*, ed. Claude Perroud (Paris, 1910), 1: 104–5.

5. See the notice on Poultier d'Elmotte by François Moureau in Jean Sgard, ed., *Dictionnaire des journalistes, 1600–1789* (Oxford, 1999), 2: 807–8; the minimal information on Poultier's imprisonment in the Bastille in 1778 in the Bastille papers, Bibliothèque de l'Arsenal, mss. 12478, 12481; Pierre Manuel, ed., *La Bastille dévoilée* (Paris, 1789) 4: 17, 5: 65–68, 6: 9–22; *Les Crimes et forfaits du représentant du peuple Poultier* (Paris, 1794), a libel full of suggestive but unreliable information; and the remarks on Goupil as well as Poultier in the papers of the lieutenant general of police Jean-Charles-Pierre Lenoir, Bibliothèque municipale d'Orléans, ms. 1422, titre 6.

6. Frantz Funck-Brentano, *Les Lettres de cachet à Paris: Etude suivie d'une liste des prisonniers de la Bastille (1659–1789)* (Paris, 1903), 402, and Bastille papers, Bibliothèque de l'Arsenal, ms. 12478.

7. *La Bastille dévoilée*, 5: 65–68, 6: 9–22; *Révolutions de Paris*, no. 29 (January 30, 1790), 33–35; no. 30 (February 6, 1790), 33–38; and no. 31 (February 13, 1790), 35–38. Poultier d'Elmotte's letter spread over these three issues of *Révolutions de Paris* confirmed the account of his imprisonment that he published in *La Bastille dévoilée*, using most of the same language but with some additional detail.

8. *La Bastille dévoilée*, 6: 11–12. The term "nouveautés" when used by booksellers usually meant the most recent publications, but Poultier d'Elmotte used it to refer to recent libels.

9. Ibid., 3: 54–65. See also *Mémoires secrets pour servir à l'histoire de la république*

des lettres en France (London, 1777–89), entries for March 29 and May 11, 1778. In her memoirs, Jeanne-Louise-Henriette Campan, the femme de chambre of Marie-Antoinette, recounted a version of this incident in which Goupil's profit was said to be 72,000 livres for purchasing the libel, which he had written himself, and 24,000 livres as a reward for accomplishing his mission with such dispatch: *Mémoires sur la vie de Marie-Antoinette, reine de France et de Navarre* (Paris, 1876), 119–20.

10. In his letter in *Révolutions de Paris*, no. 30 (February 6, 1790), 33–34, Poultier d'Elmotte said Goupil described his intrigues as follows: "Je suis sur le point d'obtenir, par la faveur de Mme la princesse de Lamballe, un bon de visiteur général des postes. J'entretiens cette éminente protection par le moyen des nouveautés que je lui porte et dont ensuite elle fait part à une personne d'une plus haute importance." He later referred to the princesse de Lamballe "et sa royale commettante" in a manner clearly indicating the queen.

11. In his account of this conspiracy in *Révolutions de Paris*, no. 30 (February 6, 1790), 35, Poultier d'Elmotte stressed his contacts with the suppliers of libels located outside France: "Je cherchai tous les moyens de me procurer les nouveautés qui s'imprimaient chez l'étranger. Pour cela, j'entretins des correspondances très dispendieuses à Londres, en Suisse, à Genève, et en Allemagne."

12. *Révolutions de Paris*, no. 31 (February 13, 1790), 37.

13. Bibliothèque municipale d'Orléans, Lenoir papers, ms. 1422, titre 6: "Goupil, sa femme, Delmotte [*sic*], etc."

14. See Olwen Hufton, *The Poor of Eighteenth-Century France, 1750–1789* (Oxford, 1974).

15. In addition to Lenoir's papers, which are the main source for this chapter's account of Goupil's imprisonment and death, see Pierre Manuel, *La Police de Paris dévoilée* (Paris, 1790), 1: 262–65.

16. As an example of how the Paris police served as a model for other regimes that wanted to modernize their police, see "Mémoire sur l'administration de la police," written for Joseph II and Maria Theresa of Austria in 1776 by a police commissioner named Lemaire that was published by Augustin Gazier in *La Police de Paris en 1770* (Paris, 1879). Lenoir followed Lemaire's memoir when he organized his papers and drafted his memoirs.

17. These remarks are based on documents scattered through a box in the Bibliothèque de l'Arsenal, Bastille papers, ms. 10028. They include Sartine's letter of recommendation about Goupil to Mme Payen, November 9, 1770: "On m'a rendu de lui en différentes occasions un assez bon témoignage. Plusieurs personnes de considération s'y intéressent. Je lui connaît de l'intelligence et de l'activité. Peut-être met-il un peu trop de vivacité dans les affaires dont il est chargé, mais il y a lieu de croire qu'il s'en corrigera avec l'âge et l'expérience, et je ne crois pas, Madame, que ce doive être un obstacle aux arrangements que vous auriez à faire avec lui, s'il vous convient d'ailleurs. Quant à la protection que je peux lui accorder, elle dépendra de la façon dont il se conduira." The box also contains various reports related to arrests conducted by Goupil dating back to November 9, 1768. Goupil received his commission to succeed d'Hémery on November 4, 1773. In an accompanying letter, Sartine instructed him to follow the guidance of d'Hémery. It was the transfer of his office on this occasion that prompted d'Hémery to write the memorandum about his functions mentioned at the beginning of this chapter.

Chapter 10. A Double Agent and His Authors

1. *Mémoires secrets pour servir à l'histoire de la république des lettres en France* (London, 1777–89), entry for December 21, 1781.

2. See *Anecdotes sur Mme la comtesse du Barry* (London, 1775), 251: "On fait assez volontiers sur la fin de l'année des *noëls* où la cour est ordinairement critiquée. On y rappelle les anecdotes les plus scandaleuses du moment, ou galantes ou politiques. . . . Il y a toujours des méchants qui font parvenir ces facéties aux gens intéressés."

3. *Mémoires secrets*, entries for December 15 and 20, 1781.

4. Ibid., December 21, 1781.

5. Ibid.

6. Ibid., January 28, 1782.

7. Ibid., November 2, 1782.

8. In general these sources agree, and they can be confirmed in part by documents from the Ministry of Foreign Affairs. Although Manuel insisted that he did not change a word of the originals and offered to make them available to his contemporaries for inspection, his editing showed an obvious bias; thus, it is important to compare his version of events with documents available from other sources.

9. Bibliothèque municipale d'Orléans, Lenoir papers, ms. 1422, draft notes for an essay titled "Sûreté."

10. Ibid. In *La Police de Paris dévoilée* (Paris, 1790), 1: 37–39, Manuel printed a memoir from the police archives that was drawn up in the form of an inventory listing forbidden books kept under seal in a storeroom of the Bastille. They included: "Toute l'édition d'un ouvrage acheté à Londres. Malle cachetée du Lord North. On pense que c'est un libelle contre la R.[Reine]."

11. There are some apparent slips in Lenoir's account, for example his reference to de Launay as an "abbé" who was arrested at the same time as Jacquet and Marcenay. The Bastille records show that the second author arrested on October 30, 1781, was Duvernet and that de Launay, a doctor turned journalist, was not arrested until September 4, 1782. See Bibliothèque de l'Arsenal, Bastille papers, ms. 12453. I suspect that in drafting his memoirs Lenoir confused Duvernet with de Launay.

12. Bibliothèque de l'Arsenal, Bastille papers, ms. 12453, pièces 61–76. On Swinton and the *Courrier de l'Europe*, see J.-P. Brissot, *Mémoires (1754–1794)*, ed. Claude Perroud (Paris, 1910), 1: 155–79; Gunnar von Proschwitz, "Courrier de l'Europe (1776–1792)," in *Dictionnaire des journaux, 1600–1789*, ed. Jean Sgard (Oxford, 1991), 1: 282–93; and Gunnar von Proschwitz and Mavis von Proschwitz, *Beaumarchais et le "Courrier de l'Europe": Documents inédits ou peu connus* (Oxford, 1990), 1: 100–103, 2: 611–16.

13. See, for example, *Mémoires secrets*, entry for October 11, 1784.

14. Although the summaries of the police archives printed in *La Bastille dévoilée* seem to have kept close to the originals, which are often quoted verbatim, at one point in its account of the de Launay affair *La Bastille dévoilée* lifted some text from *Le Diable dans un bénitier, et la métamorphose du Gazetier cuirassé en mouche* (1783) without acknowledging it: see *La Bastille dévoilée*, 3: 56–57, and *Le Diable dans un bénitier*, 57. But the account in *La Bastille dévoilée* agrees with some of the original documents that have survived in the Bibliothèque de l'Arsenal, Bastille papers, ms. 12453. The latter include some correspondence between de Launay and Swinton and a report by a doc-

tor who had examined de Launay's body and certified that he had died of natural causes.

15. *La Bastille dévoilée*, 3: 39–40.

16. Ibid., 3: 36–39.

17. Ibid., 8: 102–33.

18. *Les Joueurs et M. Dusaulx* (1780), 59.

19. Ibid., 11–12.

20. Ibid., 53.

21. Bibliothèque de l'Arsenal, Bastille papers, ms. 12453, pièce 48. Although this document is unsigned and undated, it accompanies other papers in Duvernet's dossier, so it probably was written in the Bastille by him.

22. In addition to the documents printed in *La Bastille dévoilée*, 8: 102–33, there is information on this affair in Bibliothèque de l'Arsenal, Bastille papers, ms. 12451, fol. 105 and ms. 12453, pièces 37, 45–52.

23. *La Bastille dévoilée*, 3: 37–39, 8: 113, 123.

24. Bibliothèque de l'Arsenal, Bastille papers, ms. 12453, pièces 1–4, 37. The two pamphlets against Necker were titled *Conversations de M. Necker* and *Les Administrations provinciales*. Receveur returned from his mission to Brussels and Leiden with a large load of books: five packages containing the libels mentioned above, which were stored in the Bastille's "dépôt des livres." These books correspond to several listed in an inventory of "Ballots conservés au dépôt de la Bastille sous le cachet de M. Lenoir," which was printed in *La Police de Paris dévoilée*, 1: 39. The list included a special section on "ouvrages que le sieur Jacquet a fait imprimer," which were described as follows:

200 *Réflexions sur les pirateries du sieur Gombault*

300 *Administration provinciale*

79 *Conversation de Mme Necker*

534 *Essais sur la vie d'Antoinette* . . . libelle abominable contre la R.

34 *Les Joueurs de Dussault* [*sic*] . . . libelle contre M. Amelot et autres

500 *Erreurs et désavantages de l'Etat* par Pellisery . . . libelle contre M. Necker

700 *De l'Administration provinciale, in quarto par M. le Trône* . . . ouvrage saisi et retenu par ordre de M. le garde des sceaux et de M. Necker

Of these titles, the second and last probably referred to the same work, an attack on Necker's proposal for provincial administrations: Guillaume-François Le Trosne, *De l'Administration provinciale et de la réforme de l'impôt* (Basel, 1780). I have not identified the *Réflexions sur les pirateries du sieur Gombault*, but it probably was a libel attacking Gombault's role in the policing of gambling related to *Les Joueurs et M. Dusaulx*. The *Conversations de Mme Necker* (not M. Necker, as mentioned in the Bastille papers, ms. 12453, pièce 1) might have been an early edition of *Conversation de Madame Necker avec Madame la princesse de P. . .* (1789). The other attack on Necker was Roche-Antoine de Pellissery, *Erreur et désavantage pour l'Etat de ses emprunts du 7 janvier et du 7 février 1777* (Basel, 1777).

25. The following account is based on the documents in *La Bastille dévoilée*, 3: 36–40, 8: 108–33.

26. For a full discussion of this important libel, see Chapter 27.

27. *La Bastille dévoilée*, 3: 40.

28. Ibid., 8: 118.

29. Bibliothèque de l'Arsenal, Bastille papers, ms. 12400, dossier Imbert de

Boudeaux. The books included works by Voltaire and Rousseau and many atheistic treatises produced by the baron d'Holbach and his associates, notably *Système de la nature, Le Christianisme dévoilé, Recherches sur l'origine du despotisme oriental,* and *Histoire critique de Jésus Christ.* In his interrogation, Imbert claimed to have frequented the circle of the scientist Jean-Jacques Dortous de Mairan, where he had encountered d'Alembert.

30. Bibliothèque de l'Arsenal, Bastille papers, ms. 12453, pièce 14. Jacquet's letters, addressed to the governor of the Bastille and to his main assistant, Antoine Jérôme de l'Osme, are undated. They reveal nothing about his activities as a double agent and contain only pleas to relieve his suffering. Thus ibid., pièce 28: "Jamais mortel n'a souffert autant que moi."

31. As explained in Chapter 17, Manuel did not distort the manuscripts he published, and he made them available for inspection by the public. But he selected them in a way that suited his purposes, and he also summarized some dossiers in his own words. His summary of the material concerning Jacquet in *La Bastille dévoilée,* 3: 36–39, certainly was not flattering, and there is no reason to doubt its accuracy. The same is true of the essay on Jacquet in *La Police de Paris dévoilée,* 1: 256–62.

Chapter 11. Secret Missions

1. The most important work on Morande, the French libelers in London, and their relations with the French authorities is Gunnar von Proschwitz and Mavis von Proschwitz, *Beaumarchais et le "Courier de l'Europe": Documents inédits ou peu connus* (Oxford, 1990), 2 vols. The only biography of Morande is Paul Robiquet, *Théveneau de Morande: Etude sur le XVIIIᵉ siècle* (Paris, 1882), which is superficial and inaccurate but, in my view, characterizes him correctly as an unprincipled literary adventurer. Simon Burrows, in "A Literary Low-Life Reassessed: Charles Théveneau de Morande in London, 1769–1791," *Eighteenth-Century Life* 22 (1998), 76–94, provides a scholarly sketch of Morande's career yet concludes unconvincingly that he was a high-minded patriot, devoted to reform rather than sheer self-interest.

2. *Mémoires secrets pour servir à l'histoire de la république des lettres en France* (London, 1777–89), entry for September 1, 1771.

3. Bibliothèque nationale de France, ms. fr. 22101, pièce 91, note by d'Hémery dated August 10, 1771, on *Le Gazetier cuirassé*: "Cet ouvrage . . . est une satire affreuse contre la France et tous ses ministres et les personnes en place. . . . Le chevalier L. qui m'a prêté ce livre m'a dit qu'il savait de bonne part que l'auteur était un M. le chevalier de Morande, qui avait resté longtemps à Paris jouissant de la plus mauvaise réputation et répandu beaucoup avec la société qu'on appelle de ces Messieurs, qui avait passé en Angleterre, où ayant fait des dettes dans l'auberge où il était logé, avait épousé la fille de la maison pour s'en débarrasser; qu'il avait assuré qu'il avait été lieutenant dans les carabiniers, et qu'enfin depuis qu'il avait fait cet ouvrage il avait un carrosse et faisait beaucoup de dépense. On assure aussi qu'il est lié avec d'Eon [Charles de Beaumont, chevalier d'Eon, the notorious agent of Louis XV's secret diplomacy in London who passed as a woman] et qu'il pourrait bien avoir été de société avec lui pour la composition. Pour moi, je crains bien que M. le comte de Lauragais [Louis Léon Félicité de Brancas, comte de Lauragais, a patron of the arts and wit who spent a great deal of

time in London] y a eu quelque part, car il est impossible que des gens absents de Paris depuis longtemps aient pu être si bien au fait de toutes les nouvelles qu'on raconte. On assure encore que le chevalier de Morande a deux ouvrages du même genre tous prêts à imprimer." On the *Mémoires secrets d'une femme publique*, see also *Anecdotes sur Mme la comtesse du Barry* (London, 1775), 312.

4. *Mémoires secrets*, entry for April 30, 1774. In 1791 when he had returned to France and became embroiled in polemics with Jacques-Pierre Brissot, Morande published his own version of his activities in London during the 1770s and 1780s: *Réplique de Charles Théveneau de Morande à Jacques-Pierre Brissot sur les erreurs, les oublis, les infidélités et les calomnies de sa Réponse* (Paris, 1791), especially pp. 19–22. Despite the polemical bias of this self-apology, Morande's account seems to be quite accurate, and it tallies with information in the archives of the Ministère des affaires étrangères and with the archives of the Parisian police published (and in parts paraphrased) by Pierre Manuel in *La Police de Paris dévoilée* (Paris, 1790), 1: 265–67, 2: 250–53.

5. Bibliothèque nationale de France, ms. fr. 22101, pièce 9, note by d'Hémery dated August 10, 1771.

6. *La Police de Paris dévoilée*, 1: 265–66, 2: 250–53; *Mémoires secrets*, entries for February 5 and 19, April 30, 1774. In his version of the affair, Morande claimed that he had also obtained a warrant for the arrest of the French agents: *Réplique à Brissot*, 20–21. The information in these sources coincides with the account of Morande's activities in *Anecdotes sur Mme la comtesse du Barry*, 310–13, 321–24. The *Anecdotes* contains some passages that also appear in the *Mémoires secrets*, probably because they were written by the same man, Mathieu-François Pidansat de Mairobert. Both works must be read with caution, owing to their tendentious character; but they were well-informed.

7. Of the many studies of Beaumarchais, the old biography by Louis de Loménie, *Beaumarchais et son temps* (Paris, 1856), 2 vols., still provides a sound overview of an extraordinary career, and the latest biography by Maurice Lever is excellent: *Pierre-Augustin Caron de Beaumarchais* (Paris, 1999–2004), 3 vols. Once Beaumarchais's correspondence is published, possibly within the next few years, many aspects of his adventures will become clear. Meanwhile, his relations with Morande can be followed through the rich collection of documents in von Proschwitz and von Proschwitz, *Beaumarchais et le "Courier de l'Europe,"* which is the main source of the following account.

8. According to Lever, Mme du Barry herself used the term: *Pierre-Augustin Caron de Beaumarchais*, 1: 464.

9. Von Proschwitz and von Proschwitz, *Beaumarchais et le "Courier de l'Europe,"* 1: 221.

10. Ibid., 1: 112.

11. *Le Diable dans un bénitier, et la métamorphose du Gazetier cuirassé en mouche* (1784), 58–59.

12. Goesman deserves a full-scale biography. For some basic information, see the biographical sketch under his name (spelled there as Goetzmann) in *Dictionnaire de biographie française*, ed. J. Balteau et al. (Paris, 1933–). Many more details can be gleaned from Goesman's correspondence with the Société typographique de Neuchâtel (STN), thirty-eight letters concerning his publishing projects and his checkered career: Bibliothèque publique et universitaire de Neuchâtel, papers of the STN, ms. 1158. This dossier can be supplemented by information on Goesman in the dossiers of other STN

correspondents, notably Du Terraux, ms. 1146; Bailleux, ms. 1115; and Boullanger, ms. 1126. The following account is based on this material, on Goesman's published works, notably his *Histoire politique du gouvernement français, ou les quatre âges de la monarchie française* (Paris, 1777), of which only the prospectus and volume 1 appeared in print, and on his extensive correspondence with the French foreign ministry in Ministère des affaires étrangères, Correspondance politique, Angleterre, mss. 533–45.

13. Goesman's publishing projects, mentioned in his correspondence with the STN, included a half-dozen works on law, the history of the monarchy, the history of the French peerage, and some anonymous pamphlets on current events. The first volume of his highly orthodox and monarchist *Histoire politique du gouvernement français* was published in 1777 with an approbation and privilege by Jean-Augustin Grangé, a Parisian bookseller and printer. Although it was intended to run to four volumes, the rest of it never appeared. Before this volume came out, Goesman had arranged to publish the same text with the STN as *Tableau historique, politique et juridique de la monarchie française* and with the Société typographique de Lausanne as *Les Fastes de la nation française*. He also sold it to another Parisian publisher, Edme-Jean Le Jay, as *Les Trois Ages de la monarchie française*. After discovering that they both had been swindled, the publishers in Neuchâtel and Lausanne planned to join forces in pirating the 1777 Parisian edition, but they never executed this project. As far as I can determine, the incomplete edition of 1777 was the only version of the book that appeared in print. Goesman tried to sell his manuscript to these publishers, but in the case of the STN edition he commissioned the printing and then tried to shift the printing cost to the STN and to receive compensation in the form of free copies or a share in sales. The STN nearly completed the printing of volume 1 but stopped when it realized that he would not pay his bill, which ran to 2,267 livres. This led to a lawsuit, an out-of-court settlement, and eventually a loss of 1,705 livres by the STN. Despite all the confusion and obfuscation that surrounds it, the history of this speculation demonstrates one conclusion: Goesman tried to get the same work published under four different titles with four different publishers.

14. Samuel Frédéric Ostervald to STN, June 7, 1775, STN papers, ms. 1189.

15. Goesman managed to ingratiate himself into the entourage of Lord Shelburne and Charles James Fox. His letters provide an interesting commentary on British politics while going on at great length about his genius as an observer of them and his need for money. After returning for good to France, he wrote a memoir, dated September 6, 1783, which probably was intended for Vergennes. It summarized his activities and included copies of letters by Sartine and Vergennes authorizing them. Sartine's letter, undated, stressed the need for a spy—"un homme sûr dont le caractère ait subi des épreuves"—and explained his choice: "J'ai jeté les yeux sur le sieur Goesman de Thurne, dont je connais le zèle, l'application, et les études." Ministère des affaires étrangères, Correspondance politique, Angleterre, ms. 544.

16. Goesman to Vergennes, August 15, 1781, Ministère des affaires étrangères, Correspondance politique, Angleterre, ms. 533. Goesman did not use the code in his normal letters, which he sent through Larcher and Baudouin. He reserved it for special dispatches, as he explained in his letter of August 15, 1781: "Pour tromper la vigilance et la curiosité des commis au bureau des postes, il a été convenu qu'on ferait un usage très sobre du chiffre." This letter was printed accurately in *La Police de Paris dévoilée*, 1: 239–40, presumably from a copy sent to the police. The conformity of that version

with the original manuscript is an indication of the accuracy of the documents reproduced in *La Police de Paris dévoilée*.

17. Vergennes to Baudouin, December 12, 1783, Ministère des affaires étrangères, Correspondance politique, Angleterre, ms. 546.

18. On Boissière's shady past, see the police report on him in *La Police de Paris dévoilée*, 2: 236–37, and the subsequent report on Goesman, 2: 237–38, who is described as his "intime ami." In a dispatch to Vergennes of March 31, 1783, the comte de Moustier relayed the following information turned up by the Parisian police in London: "On a découvert que Boissière connaît Matousky. Il a pâli à ce nom. Les indices font présumer qu'il est le voleur de ce joueur." Ministère des affaires étrangères, Correspondance politique, Angleterre, ms. 541.

19. Memoir by Goesman dated September 6, 1783, presumably intended for Vergennes: Ministère des affaires étrangères, Correspondance politique, Angleterre, ms. 544. The memoir was reprinted correctly but with one phrase deleted in *La Police de Paris dévoilée*, 1: 237–38—another indication of the authenticity of the documents in that work.

20. Memoir by Goesman dated September 6, 1783; *La Police de Paris dévoilée*, 1: 38–39.

21. Unfortunately, nothing remains about d'Anouilh's mission in the papers of the Bastille other than the record of his entry on September 3, 1782. See Frantz Funck-Brentano, *Les Lettres de cachet à Paris: Etude suivie d'une liste des prisonniers de la Bastille (1659–1789)* (Paris, 1903), 410. But his activities and the origins of Receveur's mission can be reconstructed from the information in *La Police de Paris dévoilée*, 1: 267–68; *La Bastille dévoilée, ou recueil de pièces authentiques pour servir à son histoire* (Paris, 1789), 3: 51–55; and *Le Diable dans un bénitier*, 14–54. The latter, though well-informed, is so tendentious that it must be read with a good deal of skepticism.

Chapter 12. Hugger-Mugger

1. *La Police de Paris dévoilée* (Paris, 1790), 1: 250–55.

2. On the fascinating career of this literary adventurer, see Jean-Claude Hauc, *Ange Goudar: Un aventurier des Lumières* (Paris, 2004).

3. Moustier to Vergennes, April 11, 1783, Ministère des affaires étrangères, Correspondance politique, Angleterre (cited henceforth as AE), ms. 542.

4. Goesman to Vergennes, February 14, 1783, AE, ms. 540.

5. Goesman to Vergennes, January 3, 1783, AE, ms. 540. Goesman sent a synopsis of this work for Vergennes to inspect, using Baudouin as the intermediary in their secret correspondence. Vergennes later declared himself satisfied with what he saw, so presumably the French government sent a payment to suppress it. The details of this affair are obscure, because much of it was settled at a meeting between Baudouin and Vergennes in Versailles. They also discussed it in their own correspondence, which is full of coded references: they referred to Goesman as "Mr. Smith" and to the libels as "chevaux" to be purchased in Ostend. The correspondence between Baudouin and Vergennes, interspersed with reports from Goesman, includes a dozen letters written during the first two weeks of January 1783. As far as I can tell, the *Réflexions politiques* never appeared in print.

6. Lenoir to Vergennes, February 24, 1783, AE, ms. 541.

7. Vergennes to Lenoir, February 25, 1783, and Vergennes to Moustier, February 26, 1783, AE, ms. 541.

8. Goesman to Vergennes, undated but clearly from late February 1783, AE, ms. 541. Goesman expressed the same sentiments in several other letters, notably those of March 7 and 12, 1783, AE, ms. 541. In the former, he insisted, "Il ne saurait être indifférent de s'exposer de laisser aller à la postérité des estampes qui tendent à déshonorer une reine, à vilipender son auguste époux, et à exciter le ressentiment dans un prince à peine né. C'est que, d'après ce que j'ai aperçu, ceci tient à une intrigue de cour, et si je suis autorisé à faire des propositions, je la dévoilerai." In the latter, he again stressed the danger of a conspiracy in Versailles, though he did not make explicit its potential threat to Vergennes, and he asked for a quick payment of his "pension": "Elle me servira à gagner Boissière de manière que je sois sûrement instruit de tous les pas qui se feront dans la négociation actuelle, à même d'en éclairer et arrêter la conclusion, et de parvenir ainsi à soustraire à la publicité un libelle que la méchanceté présente et future ne manquerait pas d'accueillir. De veiller et de travailler à la gloire de mes maîtres, est le meilleur usage que je puisse faire du revenu, quoique modique, que je tiens d'eux."

9. For Lenoir's instructions, see *La Police de Paris dévoilée*, 1: 241. This text, like the other documents printed in *La Police de Paris dévoilée*, seems reliable. Although it was not preserved in the archives of the foreign ministry, it was followed in *La Police de Paris dévoilée* by a letter from Moustier to Vergennes of March 16, 1783 (AE, ms. 541), which corresponds exactly to the copy saved in the archives of the foreign ministry. Several other documents in both sources are also identical. Some appeared in *La Police de Paris dévoilée* and not in the archives of the ministry of foreign affairs, because Manuel had access to the police archives from which the originals have disappeared. There are more details on the blackmailing of the duchesse de Bouillon in *La Police de Paris dévoilée*, 1: 254, and in a legal memorandum prepared for Moustier by Edward Bancroft, an English lawyer, included in a dispatch from Moustier to Vergennes, April 18, 1783, AE, ms. 542.

10. Moustier to Vergennes, March 16, 1783, AE, ms. 541.

11. See especially Moustier to Vergennes, March 17 and 19, 1783, AE, ms. 541; Moustier to Vergennes, May 6, 1783, AE, ms. 542; and Adhémar to Vergennes, October 4, 1783, AE, ms. 545.

12. Moustier to Vergennes, March 19, 1783, AE, ms. 541: "Le nommé Thurne paraît jouer les deux partis."

13. See especially Moustier to Vergennes, March 23, 1783 (two letters sent on the same date), and March 31, 1783, AE, ms. 541; and Vergennes to Adhémar, July 4, 1783, AE, ms. 543.

14. *La Police de Paris dévoilée*, 2: 259.

15. Receveur's reports were sent directly to Lenoir, so they do not appear in the archives of the ministry of foreign affairs, but Manuel found them in the police archives and published several of them in *La Police de Paris dévoilée*, 2: 231–69.

16. Moustier enclosed a copy of the broadside, which is reproduced in Chapter 2, in a letter to Vergennes of April 11, 1783, AE, ms. 542. He also included a translation and noted that the broadside compromised him as well as Receveur, because the reference to Duke Street would be taken to designate the French embassy. He felt especially appalled by the fact that "les ouvrages abominables que cette race infernale a enfantés y sont annoncés avec l'impudence la plus affectée."

17. Adhémar to Vergennes, June 12, 1783, AE, ms. 542.

18. Moustier to Vergennes March 22, 1783 (AE, ms. 541), which includes a translation of a letter from Barrington.

19. Moustier included the long memorandum in a dispatch to Vergennes of April 7, 1783, AE, ms. 541.

20. Moustier to Vergennes, April 18, 1783, AE, ms. 542.

21. Untitled and undated memorandum by Morande, apparently sent in Moustier's dispatch to Vergennes of April 18, 1783, AE, ms. 542. Morande cited some successful prosecutions for slander that involved Wilkes as a defendant and Burke as a plaintiff.

22. Goesman included a copy of this undated memorandum in a long account of his mission that he sent to Vergennes on September 6, 1783, AE, ms. 544.

23. *Les Petits Soupers et les nuits de l'Hôtel Bouill-n: Lettre de milord comte de ****** à milord ****** au sujet des récréations de M. de C-stri-s ou de la danse de l'ours; anecdote singulière d'un cocher qui s'est pendu à l'Hôtel Bouill-n, le 31 décembre 1778 à l'occasion de la danse de l'ours* (1783), 84–85.

24. On this complex discussion about strategy, see especially Lenoir to Vergennes, April 1 and 7, 1783, AE, ms. 541; Moustier to Vergennes, April 18, 1783, AE, ms. 542; and Lenoir to Vergennes, May 17, 1783, AE, ms. 542.

25. In this respect, the work of Sir Lewis Namier remains authoritative, despite the convincing arguments against it by John Brewer. See Namier, *The Structure of Politics at the Accession of George III*, 2nd ed. (London, 1957), and Brewer, *Party Ideology and Popular Politics at the Accession of George III* (Cambridge, 1976).

26. The text was included in Moustier's dispatch to Vergennes of April 21, 1783, AE, ms. 542. Another copy, dated May 6, 1783 (AE, ms. 542), appears in the archives accompanied by a letter from Vergennes to Lenoir of the same date.

27. Moustier to Vergennes, May 6, 1783, AE, 542.

28. Adhémar to Vergennes, October 27, 1783, AE, ms. 545. See also Adhémar to Vergennes, October 4, 1783, and Vergennes to Adhémar, October 16, 1783, AE, ms. 545.

29. Memorandum to Lenoir by Receveur, June 4, 1783, AE, ms. 542. The memorandum also mentioned a final work, which was then being written by an expatriate who was not connected with the libelers: "Un ouvrage intitulé *Les Rois de France jugés au tribunal de la raison* avec gravures, qui se fait par le moine dom Louis, évadé de l'Abbaye de Saint Denis il y a 18 mois. Cet ouvrage est protégé par Milady Spencer, mais il n'est pas encore question de le vendre."

30. Moustier to Vergennes, March 23, 1783, AE, ms. 541.

31. For example, in his letter to Vergennes of March 23, 1783 (AE, ms. 541), Moustier reported, "Je joindrai la brochure en question [probably *La Naissance du dauphin dévoilée*] à cette lettre. Elle est presq'aussi courte qu'elle est mauvaise, heureusement. Le libraire [Boissière] voudrait qu'on la 'r'habillât', qu'on lui donnât plus de 'piquant.'" And in a letter to Vergennes of April 11, 1783 (AE, ms. 542), which probably refers to *La Naissance du dauphin dévoilée*, he noted how the libelers reworked old material in new publications: "Vous en avez en ce moment, Monseigneur, un exemple frappant. On a supprimé ici des estampes contre la reine; on a étouffé ailleurs un ouvrage horrible contre Sa Majesté. Ne faut-il pas encore employer l'argent pour supprimer un ouvrage qui doit réunir l'un et l'autre de ces infâmes et exécrables projets? Enfin il n'est que trop vrai que Goesman a vu les estampes en question, ainsi que l'ou-

vrage auquel elles doivent être jointes, et que c'est de l'argent que l'on veut pour les supprimer."

32. Vergennes to Adhémar, October 16, 1783, AE, ms. 545.

33. Vergennes to Moustier, April 9, 1783, AE, ms. 541. In a memorandum dated April 23, 1783 (AE, ms. 542), Vergennes noted that he had approved a letter of credit for 400 louis in order to support Receveur's mission.

34. Lenoir to Vergennes, April 21, 1783, AE, ms. 542.

35. *La Police de Paris dévoilée*, 1: 136–37. This account corresponds to the version in *Le Diable dans un bénitier* (1784), 119, which says that *Les Petits Soupers* went on sale after its author refused an offer of 150 louis and held out for 175.

36. *La Police de Paris dévoilée*, 1: 251. In a letter to Vergennes of March 16, 1783 (AE, ms. 541), Moustier reported that *Les Petits Soupers* had just been published: "On dit qu'elle est écrite dans le plus mauvais ton et qu'elle est désagréable à lire. Je le crois facilement d'après le prospectus qu'on m'avait adressé et que j'avais jeté au feu." He must have been referring to a second edition. A copy of *Les Petits Soupers* in the Bibliothèque municipale de Rouen contains a prefatory note that explains it was a second edition, as the police had confiscated a shipment of the first edition (presumably all of it) in an entrepôt outside Paris. This copy carries a false address: "Bouillon, 1783," and it ends on p. 93 with a note saying that the written text had been completed by May 30, 1782. I have not been able to locate any copies of the first edition.

37. "Compte rendu à son excellence Monsieur le comte d'Adhémar, ambassadeur de Sa Majesté Très Chrétienne en Angleterre," dated May 22, 1783 (AE, ms. 542), written by Receveur for Lenoir and submitted to Adhémar. In a letter to Vergennes of May 9, 1783 (AE, ms. 542), Goesman reported that Boissière had told him that the manuscript of *La Naissance du dauphin* was still in his hands, that he would provide a synopsis of *Les Passe-temps d'Antoinette* and of *Les Amours du vizir de Vergennes*, and that he wanted to sell all three libels as a package deal.

38. Goesman to Vergennes, May 9, 1783, AE, ms. 542.

39. Vergennes made it clear in a letter to Adhémar of October 16, 1783 (AE, ms. 545), that the government had never bought off any of the libels pursued by Receveur. In the report on his mission that Receveur wrote from London on May 22, 1783 (AE, ms. 542), he discussed the possibility of suing Boissière and using evidence from Goesman "sur la proposition de lui vendre les horreurs dont lui sieur Goesman a donné avis, qui sont *La Naissance du dauphin dévoilée et les amusements de la reine* représentés en quatre planches avec des notes analogues les plus obscènes et des couplets de noëls qui intéressent l'honneur du roi, de la reine, de M. de Coigny, et de Mme de Polignac, adaptés à des figures plus mordantes et plus saillantes (ce sont les termes du sieur Goesman) que celles des *Amours de Charlot et d'Antoinette*, sur la proposition aussi de lui procurer la vente de deux autres libelles faits à ce qu'il lui a dit, et le fait est vrai, par l'auteur des *Petits Soupers de l'hôtel de Bouillon*, intitulés *Les Passe-temps d'Antoinette* avec figures et *Les Amours du vizir de Vergennes*."

40. See Lenoir to Vergennes, May 4, 1783, and Vergennes to Lenoir, May 6, 1783, AE, ms. 542.

41. Goesman, "Mémoire concernant les libelles," dated May 9, 1783, AE, ms. 542, and Goesman to Vergennes, May 12 and 13, 1783, AE, ms. 542.

42. Receveur, "Compte rendu à son excellence Monsieur le comte d'Adhémar, ambassadeur de Sa Majesté Très Chrétienne en Angleterre," dated May 22, 1783, AE, ms. 542.

43. Adhémar to Vergennes, June 12, 1783, AE, ms. 542.

44. Adhémar to Vergennes, May 27, 1783, AE, ms. 542. Adhémar found it particularly reprehensible that Receveur had returned "sans avoir rempli l'objet de sa mission, mais non sans avoir pris bien des peines et sans avoir compromis le gouvernement par des traites, des offices, des promesses, et toutes sortes de démarches qui n'ont abouti qu'à relever l'insolence d'un tas de drôles qui se sont moqués de l'agent de la police."

45. *La Police de Paris dévoilée*, 1: 255.

46. Vergennes to Adhémar, June 25, 1783, AE, ms. 543.

47. Goesman's activities once he was back in France can be followed by a long series of his letters in the summer of 1783: AE, mss. 544, 545. See also Adhémar's assessment of him in Adhémar's dispatches to Vergennes of June 15 and 25, 1783, AE, mss. 542, 543.

48. Adhémar to Vergennes, June 15, 1783, AE, ms. 542.

Chapter 13. Entrapment

1. Pierre Manuel, *La Police de Paris dévoilée* (Paris, 1790), 2: 235. This report was probably written by Receveur or his lieutenant Ange Goudar during their investigation of the French expatriates in London. Presumably Receveur sent it to Lenoir, and it remained in the police archives until Manuel published them.

2. *La Bastille dévoilée* (Paris, 1789), 3: 66–71; *J.-P. Brissot Mémoires (1754–1793)*, ed. Claude Perroud (Paris, 1910), 1: 303, 318–22, 395–96, 2: 7–8; and my edition of Brissot's correspondence with the Société typographique de Neuchâtel, where Pelleport often appears: *J.-P. Brissot, His Career and Correspondence (1779–1787)* (Oxford, 2001), available on the Web site of the Voltaire Foundation. There also is some important material concerning Pelleport scattered through the Brissot papers in the Archives Nationales, Paris, ms. 446 AP 1–24. Finally, Pelleport inserted a great deal of autobiographical information, which can easily be identified, in two of his anonymous publications: a long novel, *Les Bohémiens* (Paris, 1790), 2 vols., and a picaresque poem, *Le Boulevard des Chartreux* (Grenoble, 1779).

3. *Les Bohémiens*, 1: 63.

4. Ibid., 1: 64.

5. Ibid., 2: 152.

6. In the section on Pelleport's detention in the Bastille, Pierre Manuel noted: "Les divers interrogatoires qu'on lui a fait subir pourraient tenir lieu du catalogue de tous les pamphlets qui ont paru depuis six ans. Il était soupçonné de les avoir tous composés." *La Bastille dévoilée*, 3: 66.

7. Paul Robiquet, *Théveneau de Morande: Etude sur le XVIIIe siècle* (Paris, 1882), 109. Antoine-Alexandre Barbier, *Dictionnaire des ouvrages anonymes* (Paris, 1874), 2: column 526, attributes *La Gazette noire* to Morande, but J.-M. Quérard, *Les Supercheries littéraires dévoilées* (Paris, 1874), 2: 142, tends to think it was written by Pelleport. Morande's contract negotiated with Beaumarchais in 1774 committed him to stop writing libels, and from then on he collaborated with the French authorities. Thus, it seems unlikely that he would have written numerous passages in *La Gazette noire par un homme qui n'est pas blanc; ou oeuvres posthumes du Gazetier cuirassé* ("imprimé à cent lieues de la Bastille, à trois cent lieues des Présides, à cinq cent lieues des Cordons, à

mille lieues de la Sibérie" 1784) that insult Vergennes, Lenoir, Sartine, and even Louis XVI himself. Many passages in the first forty-eight pages of the text, which include radical denunciations of French despotism, have a strong resemblance to those in other works by Pelleport, and parts of the dialogue on pp. 169–203 read like the dialogue in *Les Petits Soupers et les nuits de l'Hôtel Bouillon*, complete with a "milord anglais." I do not believe that Morande ever wrote dialogue.

8. In the preface to the second volume of *Le Chroniqueur désoeuvré, ou l'espion du boulevard du Temple* (London, 1783), 6, the anonymous author teases the reader by offering hints about his identity. He was not Mayeur de Saint-Paul, he wrote, and not Poultier d'Elmotte: "Je me fais appeler M. de P et trois étoiles." If each star stood for a syllable, "de P* * *" could be "de Pelleport," provided that one stretched out the pronunciation to Pel-le-port.

9. In two clearly autobiographical passages of *Les Bohémiens*, 1: 124 and 129, Pelleport identified himself as the author of a poem, *Le Boulevard des Chartreux*. The poem, a secular-minded satire against monasticism, was printed as an anonymous, thirty-one-page pamphlet, *Le Boulevard des Chartreux, poème chrétien* ("à Grenoble, de l'imprimerie de la Grande Chartreuse," 1779), and a copy has survived in the Bibliothèque municipale of Grenoble, section d'études et d'information, 0.8254 Dauphinois. In the preface to his translation of a radical tract by the English philosopher David Williams, *Lettres sur la liberté politique, adressées à un membre de la Chambre des Communes d'Angleterre, sur son élection au nombre des membres d'une association de comté; traduites de l'anglais en français par le R. P. de Roze-Croix, ex-Cordelier*, 2nd ed. (Liège, 1783–89), Pelleport described himself as "le Révérend Père de Roze-Croix, auteur du *Boulevard des Chartreux* et de bien d'autres petits ouvrages en vers." Pelleport also depicted himself as "le très-révérend père de Rose-Croix" [*sic*] in *Les Bohémiens*, 1: 110. He seems to have enjoyed playing games with the reader and scattering clues about his identity throughout his anonymous works.

10. Interrogation of Brissot, August 21, 1784, Archives nationales, Paris, ms. 446 AP2.

11. See, for example, Pelleport's preface and his note on p. 3 of *Lettres sur la liberté politique*: "La famille des Bourbons s'imagine posséder en toute propriété la nation française: elle a une possession de fait, préférable à celle de droit. Cela durera jusqu'à ce que le peuple, ayant réfléchi sur les siens, veuille s'en mettre en possession." Apparently a first edition of the translation was published in 1783. I have been able to locate only a "seconde édition" published in 1789. Pelleport translated the English text quite accurately, but his footnotes are far more angry and extreme than anything in the original, which David Williams published anonymously as *Letters on Political Liberty Addressed to a Member of the English House of Commons on His Being Chosen into the Committee of an Associating County* (London, 1782). Williams, who knew Brissot quite well, advocated a radical reform of Parliament so that the English would recover the political liberty that they supposedly had enjoyed before the Norman conquest. See Brissot to Williams, "Londres, ce vendredi matin" (late 1783), in *J.-P. Brissot: Correspondance et papiers*, ed. Claude Perroud (Paris, 1911), 77.

12. Letter evidently intended for Vergennes (hence the "Monseigneur"), April 12, 1783, in Ministère des affaires étrangères, Correspondance politique, Angleterre (cited henceforth as AE), ms. 542.

13. Pelleport's signature actually read "LaF de Pellepor." His name was spelled in several ways at the time. I have used the most common version: Lafitte de Pelleport.

14. Moustier to Vergennes, April 21, 1783, AE, ms. 542.

15. Vergennes to Moustier, April 24, 1783, AE, ms. 542.

16. Lenoir to Vergennes, May 4, 1783, AE, ms. 542. In forwarding Receveur's reports on all the expatriates in London, Lenoir explained to Vergennes, "Le sieur Brissot d'Warville dont il parle pages 1 et 2, auquel il attribue d'abord beaucoup de menées, de propos, et qu'il paraissait disposé à croire auteur, en partie, des lettres de Pelleport, m'est connu pour avoir composé quelques ouvrages sur les lois criminelles de différents royaumes qu'il a parcourus depuis plusieurs années. Il a été l'année dernière à Bruxelles et dans les Pays-Bas. Il est depuis quatre ou cinq mois à Londres et m'a dit, avant de partir, qu'il allait y prendre, sur la constitution de l'Angleterre, des connaissances capables de le guider dans la suite de ses ouvrages. Je n'ai pas lieu jusqu'à présent, de le croire mauvais sujet ni libelliste, et je pense que le sieur Receveur n'en a une si mauvaise idée que parce qu'il aura su qu'il était connu de Pelleport, Maurice, et autres réfugiés et qu'il le croit réfugié lui-même." In warning Vergennes about Brissot, Moustier had said he thought Brissot once had worked in the ministry of foreign affairs. But Vergennes replied in a letter of April 25, 1783 (AE, ms. 542), that no one in the ministry had known him.

17. Goesman to Vergennes, May 9, 12, and 13, 1783, AE, ms. 542.

18. In his "compte rendu" to Adhémar of May 22, 1783 (AE, ms. 542), Receveur described his dealings with Pelleport over *Les Passe-temps d'Antoinette* at some length and concluded: "Par tous ses mensonges, ses fourberies, son embarrass à m'en communiquer seulement le titre, et par sa réputation, j'ai jugé qu'il était lui-même l'auteur de celui qu'il voulait me vendre (seulement sept cents louis), et j'ai jugé juste, puisqu'il a montré celui qu'il a fait à un particulier nommé Warville [i.e., Brissot], un des écrivassiers du *Courier de l'Europe* aussi anti-français que lui, et qu'il a proposé à un autre réfugié nommé Doucet de le mettre au net." On this episode, see also Brissot's *Mémoires*, 1: 320–21.

19. The London embassy immediately attributed the book to Pelleport and linked it to *Les Petits Soupers et les nuits de l'Hôtel Bouillon*, which he had also published anonymously: Adhémar to Vergennes, October 4, 1783, AE, ms. 545. According to *La Police de Paris dévoilée*, 2: 29, Morande acquired some proofs of *Les Petits Soupers* corrected in Pelleport's hand and forwarded them to France as evidence of his authorship.

20. See, for example, the anecdote about "Philidor," one of the expatriates who mixed with the lowlife in the Café d'Orange, related in *Le Diable*, 145: "Philidor, étant gris, se permit devant les valets qui peuplent ce taudis, des propos indécents sur une personne qu'il doit respecter." Pelleport relates this incident with a good deal of winking at readers who could guess at the identity of Philidor, the person he insulted, and the audience of his remarks, who included one of Receveur's spies. Although anyone could get the general gist of the passage, its saltiness cannot be appreciated without knowing that the anecdote concerns one of Pelleport's drinking companions, an expatriate artist from Lyon named Laboureau. The incident appears as follows in the report on Laboureau in *La Police de Paris dévoilée*, 2: 258–59: "Le sieur Laboureau, orateur né du Café d'Orange où se rassemblent tous les réfugiés français qui viennent déclamer à Londres contre la France. . . . Comme Laboureau est celui des Français qui sont à Londres qui tient le dé le plus souvent dans les taudis et les cafés du bas étage fréquentés par les réfugiés, il n'est pas hors de propos d'observer que c'est un des hommes les plus dangereux qui existent. . . . L'officier français envoyé à Londres en mars 1783 l'a entendu

tenir à une table d'hôte le propos le plus impertinent, en disant avec le sourire du mépris, 'Si j'étais à l'hôtel du *Bougre bon,* par allusion à celui de Bourbon, rue des Petits-champs à Paris, je ferais meilleure chère qu'ici.'"

21. *Le Diable dans un bénitier, ou la métamorphose du Gazetier cuirassé en mouche* ("Paris," no date), 97, 119, 120, 121, 135, 137, 139, 140, 144. The shift from the use of dots to that of a dash begins on p. 135 and probably resulted from a later stage in the composition of the text.

22. Ibid., 97. See also the description on p. 120: "M. de la F. . . . , tout étourdi qu'il est, ne manque pas d'une sorte de pénétration, il crut apercevoir la possibilité de gagner quelques louis, en servant le roi et la reine. On dit qu'il est assez bien né et que son père est attaché au roi."

23. Ibid., 98.

24. Ibid., 99. The most extensive passage about M. de la F. . . .'s activities concerns a private conversation he had in the French embassy with Moustier. According to the version of this incident in *Le Diable dans un bénitier,* 135–44, la F. . . . replied to Moustier's threats to have the libelers hanged with an eloquent defense of civil liberties as they were enshrined in the British constitution.

25. Pelleport paid tribute to Linguet in his letter to Vergennes of April 12, 1783, AE, ms. 542: "J'aime et j'estime M. Linguet. Il est ici comme moi sous la protection des lois." And he cited the example of Linguet's *Mémoire sur la Bastille* in *Le Diable dans un bénitier,* 96.

26. *Le Diable dans un bénitier,* 59–60, 119–21. Curiously, the text indicates that Morande contributed to this work. I cannot explain that remark, except as an attempt by Pelleport to show that Morande had collaborated with the libelers behind Receveur's back. Pelleport hinted that he himself was the "dépositaire" of Jacquet's manuscripts in a suggestive phrase on p. 119: "M. de la F. . . . [. . .] avait des liaisons avec le possesseur des libelles de Jacquet."

27. Adhémar to Vergennes, October 3, 1783, AE, ms. 545; unsigned memorandum to Vergennes by a member of his staff, dated October 14, 1783, AE, ms. 545. In a letter to Vergennes of October 17, 1783 (AE, ms. 545), Moustier complained, "Enfin je trouve bien amer ce fruit posthume de ma mission à Londres qui en a été offert par la vengeance de quelques scélérats, qui me croient l'auteur du refus qui leur a été fait de leur payer la contribution honteuse qu'ils exigaient pour prix de leur silence. La brochure détestable qui circule actuellement n'est que le prélude des horreurs auxquelles se prépare cette bande exécrable. Il est affreux d'alimenter de pareilles espèces. . . . C'est le produit du *Courier de l'Europe,* qui fournit à leur existence."

28. Vergennes to Adhémar, October 16, 1783, AE, ms. 545.

29. Moustier to Vergennes, October 17, 1783, and Adhémar to Vergennes, October 26, 1783, AE, ms. 545. See also *La Police de Paris dévoilée,* 2: 255.

30. The account of Pelleport's embroiled affairs is based on twenty letters to Brissot by a certain Larrivée, Brissot's agent in Paris, in the Brissot papers, Archives Nationales, Paris, ms. 446 AP1.

31. The censor, abbé Jean-Louis Aubert, editor of the official *Gazette de France,* was one of the figures satirized in *Le Diable dans un bénitier,* 73–74. He had cut some letters that Pelleport published in the London edition of the *Courier de l'Europe,* in April 1783, numbers 30–40, revealing Morande's plan to reorganize the London police on the Parisian model. Pelleport referred to this episode in a passage of *Le Diable,* p.

141, which praised the liberties guaranteed by the English constitution in contrast to French despotism. Lenoir also mentioned it in a letter to Vergennes about the London libelers, and Vergennes replied in a letter to Lenoir of May 6, 1783 (AE, ms. 542): "La diatribe sous le nom de Pelleport concernant la police, insérée dans les derniers numéros du *Courier de l'Europe,* ayant été retranchée de cet ouvrage qui se répand en France, il n'y a pas d'autre suite à donner à cette affaire, qui est déjà oubliée." Brissot worked on the French edition of the *Courier de l'Europe* in 1778 and described the censorship of it in his *Mémoires,* 1: 321–22.

32. See Gunnar von Proschwitz, "Courrier de l'Europe (1776–1792)," in *Dictionnaire des journaux, 1600–1789,* ed. Jean Sgard (Oxford, 1991), 1: 282–93.

33. Swinton had attempted to found another such journal when he created the *Gazette anglo-française* under the editorship of de Launay in 1780. In late June 1784 (AE, ms. 549), Adhémar sent Vergennes a printed "Prospectus d'un ouvrage périodique sous le titre de *Journal de la Grande Bretagne.*" It was to be a biweekly publication distributed by two booksellers who carried a great many forbidden French books, Changuion of Amsterdam and Virchaux of Hamburg; it could well have been another version of Pelleport's planned *Mercure.*

34. Adhémar to Vergennes, June 22, 1784, AE, ms. 549.

35. Gérard de Rayneval (substituting for Adhémar, who had returned to France on leave) to Vergennes, October 13, 1784, AE, ms. 550. On the later aspects of this plot, see Adhémar to Vergennes, December 1, 1784, AE, ms. 550.

36. Adhémar to Vergennes, December 7, 1784, and Vergennes to Adhémar, December 17, 1784, AE, ms. 550.

Chapter 14. The View from Versailles

1. These expressions can be found in nearly all the letters, for example, Rayneval to Vergennes, March 1, 1783; Moustier to Vergennes, March 23, 1783, April 11, 1783, and May 6, 1783, in Ministère des affaires étrangères, Correspondance politique, Angleterre (cited henceforth as AE), ms. 541.

2. Untitled memorandum dated "1er mars 1783 (environ)," AE, ms. 541. In the preceding paragraph, Rayneval classified libel against crowned heads with "les crimes de lèse majesté." The quotations in the following paragraphs come from the same memorandum.

3. Moustier to Vergennes, March 23, 1783, AE, ms. 541.

4. Moustier to Vergennes, May 6, 1783, AE, ms. 542.

5. Moustier to Vergennes, April 11, 1783, AE, ms. 542. See the similar remarks in Moustier's dispatch of May 6, 1783, ibid.

6. Adhémar to Vergennes, June 12, 1783, AE, ms. 542: "En général, Monsieur, le ton de l'espionage, les rapports de toutes les espèces, une communication continuelle avec les scélérats qui remplissent Londres ont jeté du ridicule sur notre manière d'être ici. . . . Permettez-moi donc, Monsieur, de débarrasser l'ambassade de tous ces fripons qui l'obsèdent et qui n'ont été que trop employés jusqu'à présent."

7. Adhémar to Vergennes, May 27, 1783, with a copy of Receveur's report on his mission dated May 22, 1783, AE, ms. 542.

8. Vergennes to Adhémar, May 29, 1783, AE, ms. 542. This letter reads like a personal communication rather than an official dispatch. Vergennes rebuked Adhémar gently, while invoking his attachment to him (in another letter he gave him friendly advice about how to improve his dispatches); and Adhémar, sensing a serious faux pas, took the criticism in this fashion: Adhémar to Vergennes, June 12, 1783, AE, ms. 542.

9. Adhémar to Vergennes, June 12, 1783, AE, ms. 542.

10. On Adhémar's aggressive measures against the libelers, see especially his letter to Vergennes of October 4, 1783 (AE, ms. 545), in which he reviews his activities and recommends kidnaping Pelleport.

11. See Adhémar to Vergennes, February 17, 1784, AE, ms. 547: "Vous savez, Monsieur, quels motifs respectables m'ont porté à leur faire la guerre. Je les ai ruinés." In a letter to Vergennes of December 17, 1784 (AE, ms. 550), Adhémar again noted his retreat from an adulterated policy of "mépris."

12. Vergennes to Le Camus de Néville, November 19, 1783, AE, ms. 546. See also Vergennes to Laurent de Villedeuil, November 25, 1784, AE, ms. 550: "Je crois qu'il y a beaucoup d'inconvénients à laisser introduire et distribuer en France tous ces ouvrages où les sujets discutent leurs droits vis-à-vis des souverains."

13. See, for example, Receveur to Adhémar, May 22, 1783, AE, ms. 542; Adhémar to Vergennes, October 4, 1783, AE, ms. 550; and Goesman to Vergennes, March 12, 1783, AE, ms. 541.

14. In a letter of February 12, 1783, AE, ms. 540, Vergennes thanked Baudouin, one of his secret agents in Paris, for communicating "des choses intéressantes sur la manière dont le public de Paris envisage la paix qui se négocie." See also Lenoir's report to Vergennes of November 26, 1783, AE, ms. 546, on the "publication" of the peace treaty through ceremonies performed in the streets of Paris.

15. Goesman to Vergennes, March 12, 1783, AE, ms. 541.

16. Lenoir to Vergennes, March 27, 1783, AE, ms. 541. According to his testimony in the Bastille, reported in *La Bastille dévoilée*, 8: 126, Imbert de Villebon said that the original manuscript of Jacquet's libels against the queen came from a source in the court. Jacquet had confided "qu'il tenait ce manuscrit d'un seigneur de la cour mécontent du roi, lequel seigneur l'avait donné à Jacquet pour le faire imprimer."

17. For an account of politics in Versailles during the reign of Louis XVI, see John Hardman, *French Politics, 1774–1789: From the Accession of Louis XVI to the Fall of the Bastille* (London, 1995).

18. In his letter to Vergennes of April 12, 1783 (AE, ms. 541), in which he offered to deal with the supposed libelers, Pelleport stressed that "Il n'est quant à présent dans la constitution anglaise aucun moyen de les arrêter." In addition to the English constitution, he cited the "droit des gens et de la nature." And he rejected all "actes du pouvoir arbitraire" such as Receveur's supposed plan to kidnap Linguet: "J'aime et j'estime M. Linguet. Il est ici comme moi sous la protection des lois, et tout homme est obligé de faire en son particulier tout ce que lui est possible pour empêcher que ces lois ne soient violées." This is extraordinary language for a blackmail operation. It should not be dismissed as mere rhetoric or cynicism.

19. Goesman to Vergennes, May 16, 1783, AE, ms. 542.

20. Vergennes to Adhémar, May 21, 1783, AE, ms. 542.

Chapter 15. The Devil in the Bastille

1. According to the well-informed account, probably written by Pierre Manuel, in *La Bastille dévoilée, ou recueil de pièces authentiques pour servir à son histoire* (Paris, 1789), 3: 66–69, Pelleport owed his release to the solicitations of his wife, her protector, the chevalier Pawlet, and the compliance of the new minister in charge of the Bastille, Laurent de Villedeuil. See also Manuel, *La Police de Paris dévoilée* (Paris, 1790), 2: 235–36.

2. Two of the best and most recent works in the large literature about the Bastille are Hans-Jürgen Lüsebrink and Rolf Reichardt, *The Bastille: A History of a Symbol of Despotism and Freedom*, trans. Norbert Schürer (Durham, 1997), and Monique Cottret, *La Bastille à prendre: Histoire et mythe de la forteresse royale* (Paris, 1986).

3. A good example of the way he inserted denunciations of despotism into his narrative is chapter 9 of *Le Diable dans un bénitier*, where he describes an imaginary encounter between himself as M. de la F. . . . and the comte de Moustier, France's plenipotentiary in London. In response to Moustier's defense of arbitrary power, M. de la F. . . . confounds him with a harangue in favor of the liberty of the press, trial by jury, and constitutional restraints on the government.

4. Simon-Nicolas-Henri Linguet, *Mémoire sur la Bastille et sur la détention de M. Linguet, écrits par lui-même* (London, 1783), and Honoré-Gabriel Riqueti, comte de Mirabeau, *Des Lettres de cachet et des prisons d'état: Ouvrage posthume, composé en 1778* (Hamburg, 1782). In addition to the works cited above, note 2, see the old but still useful study by J. Delort, *Histoire de la détention des philosophes et des gens de lettres à la Bastille et à Vincennes* (Paris, 1829), 3 vols.

5. Although there is no direct evidence about the circumstances in which Pelleport drafted *Les Bohémiens*, it seems certain that he wrote all or most of the text in the Bastille. He could not have composed such a long and complex novel in the few months that followed his release from the Bastille on October 3, 1788, especially as he was occupied in 1789 with family affairs and trips between Paris and Stenay, as recounted in *La Bastille dévoilée*, 3: 69–70. Moreover, the text does not refer to any events after 1788 or hint at any point about the possibility of a revolution. On the contrary, the narrative is set in a social order that seems oppressive but stable, as if the earthquake of 1789 were unthinkable.

6. As far as I can tell, *Les Bohémiens* (Paris, 1790), 2 vols., has been completely forgotten. It is mentioned under Pelleport's name in various library catalogues, and it receives a passing mention in Fernand Drujon, *Les Livres à clef* (Paris, 1888), 1: column 139, and in Charles Monselet, *Les Oubliés et les dédaignés* (1857; reprint, Paris, 1993), 1: 12. I have found only one discussion of it in the secondary literature, a brief essay by Paul Lacroix, *Bulletin du bibliophile* (Paris, 1851), 408–9. Lacroix aptly described it as follows: "Voilà un admirable, voici un abominable livre. Il mérite d'être placé à côté des romans de Voltaire et de Diderot, pour l'esprit, pour la verve, pour le talent prodigieux qu'on est tout étonné d'y rencontrer; il doit aussi avoir sa place à côté des infamies du marquis de Sade et des grossières obscénités de l'abbé Dulaurens. Dès que ce singulier ouvrage aura éveillé la curiosité des amateurs, il sera certainement très recherché." Lacroix claimed, without citing any sources, that the novel was printed by Charles-Joseph Panckoucke, who destroyed most of the copies after discovering that he was one of the many literary figures satirized in it. Two copies exist in the United

States, in the Library of Congress and in the Boston Public Library, and one in France, in the Bibliothèque municipale of Rouen.

7. See my discussion of the relations between Pelleport and Brissot in Robert Darnton, *J.-P. Brissot: His Career and Correspondence, 1779–1787* (Oxford, 2001), which can be consulted at the Web site of the Voltaire Foundation: http://www.voltaire.ox .ac.uk/.

8. Receveur described both men in this fashion in the report on his activities in London that he submitted to the comte d'Adhémar, the French ambassador who succeeded Moustier in 1783: Receveur to Adhémar, May 22, 1783, in Ministère des affaires étrangères, Correspondance politique, Angleterre (cited henceforth as AE), ms. 542.

9. Moustier to Vergennes, April 21, 1783, AE, ms. 542: "Le sieur Brissot de Warville, personnage suspect, a été dans les bureaux de Mgr. le comte de Vergennes. . . . Le *Passe temps d'Antoinette* et les *Amours du visir* ont, dit-on, été envoyés de France, mais il est plus probable que les auteurs sont Brissot de Warville et Pelleport." Lenoir sent a favorable report on Brissot to Vergennes on May 4, 1783 (AE, ms. 542): "Le sieur Brissot d'Warville . . . m'est connu pour avoir composé quelques ouvrages sur les lois criminelles de différents royaumes qu'il a parcourus depuis plusieurs années. Il a été l'année dernière à Bruxelles et dans les Pays Bas. Il est depuis quatre ou cinq mois à Londres et m'a dit, avant de partir, qu'il allait y prendre, sur la constitution de l'Angleterre, des connaissances capables de le guider dans la suite de ses ouvrages. Je n'ai pas lieu, jusqu'à présent, de le croire mauvais sujet ni libelliste, et je pense que le sieur Receveur n'en a une si mauvaise idée que parce qu'il aura su qu'il était connu de Pelleport, Maurice et autres réfugiés, et qu'il le croit réfugié lui-même." Vergennes confirmed Lenoir's judgment by noting that Brissot had never been employed in the ministry of foreign affairs: Vergennes to Moustier, April 25, 1783, AE, ms. 542.

10. On the legal aspect of interrogations in the Bastille, see Frantz Funck-Brentano, "La Bastille d'après ses archives," *Revue historique* 42 (1890), 61.

11. *J.-P. Brissot Mémoires (1754–1793)*, ed. Claude Perroud (Paris, 1910), 2: 23.

12. *La Bastille dévoilée*, 3: 78.

13. *La Police de Paris dévoilée*, 2: 28: "Brissot de Warville, dont le seul défaut est celui du sévère Caton, la passion de la vertu, . . . ne devait pas être mis sur la même ligne que le marquis de Pelleport, qui avec autant d'esprit et de tempérament n'aima que les femmes et les plaisirs." See also *La Bastille dévoilée*, 3: 66.

14. Brissot papers, Archives nationales, 446 AP2. These documents are the source of the following account. They had not been deposited in the Archives nationales when I first began to work on Brissot, and I was not granted access to them when they first arrived in the archives. Now that I have been able to consult them, I have modified the severe view of Brissot that I expressed in "The Grub Street Style of Revolution: J.-P. Brissot, Police Spy," *Journal of Modern History* 40 (1968), 301–27. The documents make clear that Brissot stood up very well to the interrogations that he underwent in the Bastille and that he did not collaborate on any libels. But they do indicate that he had close contact with libelers and other figures in the literary underground, and they do not bear out the moralistic account of his relations with the French expatriates in London that he later produced: "En m'établissant dans cette île, je m'étais fait une loi d'éviter tous les réfugiés dont la vie n'était pas intacte et dont la liaison, si elle n'eût pas été dangereuse pour moi, eût pu paraître suspecte à des yeux peu éclairés. Cependant j'ai quelquefois laissé venir chez moi des Français dont les erreurs me paraissaient

condamnables; mais j'espérais les ramener à la vertu. La conduite, les opinions, la vie intérieure de l'homme vertueux ont nécessairement de l'influence sur celui dont le coeur n'est pas entièrement gangrené." *J.-P. Brissot Mémoires,* 1: 302–3.

15. Vingtain to Brissot, April 3, 1784, replying to Brissot's letter of March 30, in *J.-P. Brissot: Correspondance et papiers* (Paris, 1912), ed. Claude Perroud, 467. Vingtain's letter was first published by Morande in *Réplique de Charles Théveneau de Morande à Jacques-Pierre Brissot, sur les erreurs, les oublis, les infidélités et les calomnies de sa Réponse* (Paris, 1791), 106–7. As Brissot did not dispute its authenticity during his polemics with Morande in 1791, I accept it as genuine. Bruzard de Mauvelain, a close friend of Brissot's who lived from shady dealings in the underground book trade in Troyes, sent two letters to the Société typographique de Neuchâtel (STN) about Brissot's imprisonment, which he attributed to the compromising connection with Pelleport: "Il a eu un tort de se lier avec un imprudent, et un plus grand encore—celui de se mettre sous la coupe du ministère de France." Bruzard de Mauvelain to STN, August 20, 1784, in Darnton, *J.-P. Brissot,* 349. Mauvelain probably had information from Brissot about the production of libels in London, because he asked the STN to supply him with several of the most extreme works, including "6 *Passe-Temps d'Antoinette* avec figures." Mauvelain to STN, February 15, 1784, Bibliothèque publique et universitaire de Neuchâtel, Papers of the STN, ms. 1179.

16. Larrivée's letters are in the Brissot papers, Archives nationales, 446 AP1. On Mettra, see the essay by Jean-Robert Armogathe and François Moureau in *Dictionnaire des journalistes, 1600–1789,* ed. Jean Sgard (Oxford, 1999), 2: 711–13.

17. *J.-P. Brissot Mémoires,* 2: 8.

18. Undated note by Pelleport among various letters and messages that he asked the administrators of the Bastille to transmit and that they confiscated instead, Bibliothèque de l'Arsenal, Bastille papers, ms. 12454.

19. Records of these visits and other details about Pelleport's confinement appear in the administrative correspondence of the Bastille's officers: Bastille papers, ms. 12517.

20. Undated note, Bastille papers, ms. 12454.

21. Pelleport to the baron de Breteuil, December 16, 1786, in Bastille papers, ms. 12454.

22. Mme Pelleport to de l'Osme, April 1 (probably 1788), Bastille papers, ms. 12 454. One of de l'Osme's relatives had served with Pelleport's brothers in the army, and de l'Osme treated Pelleport in a friendly manner. Pelleport remained grateful to him and tried unsuccessfully to save him from lynching after the storming of the Bastille. *La Bastille dévoilée,* 3: 69–70.

23. Pelleport to François de Rivière de Puget, lieutenant du roi in the Bastille, November 22, 1787, Bastille papers, ms. 12454. In a previous letter to de Puget, undated and in the same dossier, Pelleport wrote that despite his reproaches to his wife, he still felt "beaucoup d'amitié pour elle."

24. In an undated note to the Bastille's governor, the marquis de Launay, de Losne recommended granting the following request from Pelleport: "Je vous prie, Monsieur, de laisser écrire le sieur de Pelleport, de lui donner des livres, plume, encre et papier." A note at the bottom, dated July 11, 1784, indicated that such permission had been given: "Fait comme il est requis." Bastille papers, ms. 12517.

25. Undated note by Pelleport to an unidentified person, Bastille papers, ms. 12454.

26. Undated verse by Pelleport on a scrap of paper under the heading "Mes adieux à Pluton," Bastille papers, ms. 12454. Alfred Bégis claimed that Pelleport got on well with de Launay, who gave him presents of fruit as a reward for music lessons that Pelleport gave to de Launay's daughter. Such favorable treatment could have occurred at some time before Pelleport turned against de Launay. However, Bégis only communicated this observation to Franz Funck-Brentano privately and without providing any documentation: Funck-Brentano, "La Bastille d'après ses archives," 72.

27. Pelleport to de Launay, undated letter, Bastille papers, ms. 12454.

28. Pelleport to de l'Osme, November 16, 1784, Bastille papers, ms. 12454.

29. Jean-Claude Fini (known as Hypolite Chamoran or Chamarand) to de Launay, undated letter (probably mid-1786), Bastille papers, ms. 12454. Chamoran was detained in the Bastille from November 27, 1785, until July 31, 1786. He and his supposed wife, Marie-Barbara Mackai, seem to have been involved with Pelleport in the production of *libelles* and the blackmailing operations in London, but he denied everything and denounced Pelleport vehemently during his stay in the Bastille. He is mentioned briefly in *La Bastille dévoilée*, 3: 101, and in a letter from Morande to the foreign minister, Armand-Marc, comte de Montmorin, April 28, 1788, in Gunnar von Proschwitz and Mavis von Proschwitz, *Beaumarchais et le "Courier de l'Europe": Documents inédits ou peu connus* (Oxford, 1990), 2: 1013.

30. For example, in notes about special requests and permissions granted to prisoners, a clerk recorded that de Sade's wife had sent him a waistcoat and a candle on November 13, 1784, and that Pelleport's wife had visited him on November 19, 1784: Bastille papers, ms. 12 517, fols. 79, 82. Two recent books in the vast literature on de Sade contain detailed accounts of his life in the Bastille: Laurence L. Bongie, *Sade: A Biographical Essay* (Chicago, 1998), and Francine du Plessix Gray, *At Home with the Marquis de Sade: A Life* (New York, 1998). On Sade's writing in the Bastille, see especially Jean-Jacques Pauvert, *Sade Vivant* (Paris, 1989).

31. See Funck-Brentano, "La Bastille d'après ses archives," 38–73, 278–316; Monique Cottret, *La Bastille à prendre: Histoire et mythe de la forteresse royale* (Paris, 1986), 31–33, 129; Claude Quétel, *De Par le Roy: Essai sur les lettres de cachet* (Toulouse, 1981), 48–49; and Joseph Delort, *Histoire de la détention des philosophes et des gens de lettres à la Bastille et à Vincennes* (Paris, 1829; reprint, Geneva, 1967), 3 vols.

Chapter 16. Bohemians Before Bohemianism

1. *Les Bohémiens* (Paris, 1790), 1: 3.

2. Ibid., 1: 33.

3. Ibid., 1: 38.

4. Ibid., 1: 41.

5. The 1762 edition of the *Dictionnaire de l'Académie française* gave the following definition: "BOHÈME, ou BOHÉMIEN, BOHÉMIENNE. Ces mots ne sont point mis ici pour signaler les peuples de cette partie de l'Allemagne qu'on appelle *Bohème*, mais seulement pour désigner une sorte de vagabonds qui courent le pays, disant la bonne aventure et dérobant avec adresse. 'Une troupe de Bohémiens.' On dit familièrement d'une maison où il n'y a ni ordre ni règle, que 'C'est une maison de Bohème.' On dit proverbialement 'Qu'un homme vit comme un Bohème' pour dire qu'il vit comme un

homme qui n'a ni feu ni lieu." One of the earliest references to literary bohemians, *Le Chroniqueur désoeuvré, ou l'espion du boulevard du Temple* (London, 1783), 2: 22, caustically described a boulevard theater, Les Variétés amusantes, as "cet espèce d'antre de Bohémiens."

6. Pierre Manuel, *La Police de Paris dévoilée* (Paris, 1790), 2: 244–47. On Saint-Flocel and the *Journal des Princes*, see *Dictionnaire des journalistes, 1600–1789*, ed. Jean Sgard (Oxford, 1999), 2: 899.

7. J.-P. Brissot, *Mémoires (1754–1793)*, ed. Claude Perroud (Paris, 1910), 1: 329; *La Police de Paris dévoilée*, 2: 246–47.

8. See Darline Gay Levy, *The Ideas and Careers of Simon-Nicolas-Henri Linguet: A Study in Eighteenth-Century French Politics* (Champaign, Ill., 1980), and Daniel Baruch, *Simon Nicolas Linguet ou l'Irrécupérable* (Paris, 1991).

9. *La Police de Paris dévoilée*, 2: 231–69.

10. *Les Bohémiens*, 1: 47.

11. Ibid., 1: 50.

12. Ibid., 1: 51.

13. Brissot to Pelleport, undated letter from 1779 in Robert Darnton, *J.-P. Brissot, His Career and Correspondence, 1779–1787* (Oxford, 2001), 66. Brissot's letters to Pelleport from this period show that they were close friends.

14. See note 39 below.

15. Ibid., 1: 56.

16. Ibid., 1: 60. In a later aside to the reader, the narrator, who in this instance can be identified with the author, seems to subscribe to the donkey's hedonism (2: 63–65).

17. Ibid., 1: 1.

18. Ibid., 1: 53.

19. Ibid., 1: 54–55.

20. Ibid., 1: 65. See also the similar remarks in 1: 75, 181.

21. Ibid., 1: 68.

22. Ibid., 1: 59. "Riénisme" suggests the "zéro" mentioned above that Hypolite Chamoran claimed was Pelleport's "profession de foi."

23. Ibid., 1: 45–46.

24. Ibid., 1: 135.

25. Ibid., 1: 93. See also the similar remarks on 1: 132.

26. Ibid., 1: 136. See also 1: 127 on "la douce pitié, mère de toutes les vertus."

27. Ibid., 2: 113. The rape scene is recounted with false naiveté by Félicité in a journal that the narrator claims he discovered in the "lycée de Londres"—a reference to the philosophic club Brissot attempted to create in London after the model of the Parisian Musée of Mamès-Claude Pahin de la Blancherie (2: 112). In an earlier episode, the narrator presents Félicité as eager to be raped (1: 158).

28. Pelleport had studied science and mathematics and apparently taught both while he was employed as a tutor in Le Locle and London. *Les Bohémiens* includes a long digression about science, inspired in part by contemporary balloon flights and experiments with electricity, which concludes that "le gaz inflammable est le principe universel" (1: 164). Metaphors about phlogiston or inflammable air permeate Pelleport's descriptions of sexual activity. Thus the references to "fluid igné" (1: 192); "étincelles phosphoriques" and "foyer électrique" (1: 195); "flamme" (1: 199); and "feu violent" (1: 214).

29. *Les Bohémiens*, 1: 203–9.

30. Ibid., 1: 210.

31. Pelleport invokes *Don Quixote* at the end of the description of the brawl. *Les Bohémiens*, 1: 214.

32. While maintaining an elevated tone and using classical rhetoric, often in a mock-heroic manner, Pelleport sometimes jolts the reader by interrupting his narrative with *grosses blagues* (dirty jokes). For example, he makes a gratuitous reference to "Beaumont-le-Vicomte, dont le seigneur des accords a troqué le *m* du premier mot contre le *c* du troisième" (2: 128).

33. *Les Bohémiens*, 2: 131.

34. Ibid., 2: 135.

35. An example of the autobiographical allusions that Pelleport scattered through the text is a passing reference to Edme Mentelle, the professor of geography at the Ecole militaire who had befriended him and Brissot, as "Manteau" in *Les Bohémiens*, 2: 141.

36. See the long declamation against the injustices of the social order in 2: 167–77, notably the poet's condemnation of the "ancienne tyrannie du droit féodal" (2: 168).

37. *Les Bohémiens*, 2: 185.

38. The biography of Labre written shortly after his death by his confessor, Giuseppe Loreto Marconi, *Ragguaglio della vita del servo di Dio, Benedetto Labre Francese* (Rome, 1783), was translated into French a year later by Père Elie Hard under the title *Vie de Benoît-Joseph Labre, mort à Rome en odeur de sainteté* (Paris, 1784). See the article on Labre in the *New Catholic Encyclopedia* (New York, 2003), 9: 267.

39. Catau des Arches may be a play on Catherine Dupont. The text heaps scorn on Mme Dupont, stressing her hideous body and frustrated sex life. It claims that she devoured twenty miserable lovers while maintaining a façade of bourgeois respectability in Boulogne. It also suggests that Pelleport held her responsible, with Morande, for his *embastillement*. In 2: 231, the poet refers to collaboration between Mme Dupont (Catau des Arches) and Morande (Thonevet) as follows: "Le calomniateur Thonevet s'était avisé de composer plusieurs atroces libelles et de me les attribuer. Il s'unit, dans le dessein de me perdre, avec la veuve irritée. Ils écrivirent au ministre, et je fus enlevé à midi dans la ville de Boulogne et conduit à la Bastille."

40. *Les Bohémiens*, 2: 227.

41. Brissot republished essays by others in a ten-volume anthology titled *Bibliothèque philosophique du législateur, du politique, du jurisconsulte* (Neuchâtel, 1782–85). In his account of his voyage to London, the poet says he accompanied the youngest of Mme des Arches's four daughters and deposited her in the London residence of "un benêt de gendre, négociant en friperie" (2: 202), whom he later mocks as the "fripier Bissoto de Guerreville" (2: 219). Mme Dupont did indeed have four daughters, and the youngest, Nancy, joined the Brissots in London in 1783. She may well have made the trip in the company of Pelleport, who is mentioned along with her in the correspondence between Brissot and members of the Dupont family. See the three letters from Nancy's brother François Dupont to Brissot, April 22, 1783, May 7, 1783, and May 14, 1783, in *J.-P. Brissot: Correspondance et papiers* (Paris, 1912), ed. Claude Perroud, 52–55. See also Brissot, *Mémoires*, 2: 302, 338.

42. *Les Bohémiens*, 2: 227.

43. Ibid., 2: 226.

44. Ibid., 2: 234.

45. Ibid., 2: 88–89. Among other things, these references evoke Brissot's Lycée de Londres and his journalistic *Correspondance universelle sur ce qui intéresse le bonheur de l'homme et de la société* as well as his *Bibliothèque philosophique du législateur, du politique, du jurisconsulte.* While settling accounts with Brissot, Pelleport presented him—accurately, I would say—as a typical hack writer struggling to survive in the difficult conditions of Grub Street.

46. *Les Bohémiens,* 1: 111.

47. This scene, recounted in 1: 113, takes place in the bookshop of the publisher of the *Almanach des muses,* who at that time was Nicolas-Augustin Delalain. But the text identifies him as "P. . ." so I may have failed to pick up the allusion intended by Pelleport.

48. *Les Bohémiens,* 1: 111–18. This long passage, brimming with concrete details, demonstrates a thorough familiarity with life among the hack writers of Paris, but it also conforms to a genre, the dangers of life as a *littérateur,* which was a favorite theme of well-known writers such as Voltaire and Linguet.

49. *Les Bohémiens,* 2: 76.

50. Gérard Genette and other literary theorists have rightly insisted on distinctions that are apparent throughout *Les Bohémiens,* notably the distinction between the voice of the narrator and that of the author and the distinction between the text as a set of signs and the story as a sequence of events. For an overview of these issues in relation to literary theory, see Gerald Price, *A Dictionary of Narratology* (Lincoln, Neb., 1987), and Mieke Bal, *Narratology: Introduction to the Theory of Narrative* (Toronto, 1985).

51. I have gone through the most important literary reviews and other periodicals from 1790 and have not found a single reference to *Les Bohémiens.*

Chapter 17. The Grub Street Route to Revolution

1. See Edna Lemay, *Dictionnaire des Constituants, 1789–1791* (Paris, 1991), 2 vols., and Timothy Tackett, *Becoming a Revolutionary: The Deputies of the French National Assembly and the Emergence of a Revolutionary Culture (1789–1791)* (Princeton, N.J., 1996).

2. See Jean Sgard, "Postface: Répartition et typologie des titres," in *Dictionnaire des journaux, 1600–1789,* ed. Jean Sgard (Oxford, 1991), 2: 1131–40; Jacques Godechot, "Caractères généraux de la presse révolutionnaire," in *Histoire générale de la presse française,* ed. Claude Bellanger, Jacques Godechot, Pierre Guiral, and Fernand Terrou (Paris, 1969), 1: 428, 434–36; Pierre Rétat, *Les Journaux de 1789: Bibiliographie critique* (Paris, 1988); Hugh Gough, *The Newspaper Press in the French Revolution* (Chicago, 1988); and Jeremy Popkin, *Revolutionary News: The Press in France, 1789–1799* (Durham, N.C., 1990).

3. Louis-Sébastien Mercier, *De la littérature et des littérateurs* (Yverdon, 1778), 39, and "Trente écrivains en France, pas davantage," in his *Tableau de Paris,* ed. Jean-Claude Bonnet (Paris, 1994, reprint of the successive editions from 1781–87), 2: 318–19.

4. The following remarks are meant only as an overview of a complex subject, which I have tried to explore in previous publications, especially "The High Enlighten-

ment and the Low-Life of Literature," *Past and Present: A Journal of Historical Studies*, no. 51 (May 1971), 81–115, and "The Facts of Literary Life in Eighteenth-Century France," in *The Political Culture of the Old Regime*, ed. Keith Baker (Oxford, 1987), 261–91. I think the argument in those works is still valid. But I would like to emphasize three qualifications, which they did not make sufficiently clear. First, the hierarchical nature of the Republic of Letters did not exclude the possibility for talented young men to rise to the top: the career of Marmontel provides a good example of upward social mobility. Second, the growing population of the milieu I describe as Grub Street did not mean that the Republic of Letters was completely polarized between those at the top and those on the bottom; on the contrary, there were many intermediate positions occupied by men (and a few women) who thought of themselves as writers but did not depend on literature for a living. Third, although frustrated ambition embittered many hack writers, it did not in itself turn them into hacks, libelers, or pornographers. They were driven into hack writing by poverty. Poverty was the defining characteristic of Grub Street, not psychological resentment. In my view, Grub Street should be understood sociologically, as an element in what Pierre Bourdieu characterized as "le champ littéraire," and it also existed at the level of collective representations, owing to polemics about the status of various writers.

5. For studies of the literary repercussions of Voltaire's famous poem, "Le Pauvre Diable," see *Le Pauvre Diable: Destins de l'homme de lettres au XVIIIe siècle*, ed. Henri Duranton (Saint-Etienne, 2006). I have attempted to get at the reality behind the literary motif in a study of my own: "The Life of a 'Poor Devil' in the Republic of Letters," in *Essays on the Age of Enlightenment in Honor of Ira O. Wade*, ed. Jean Macary (Geneva, 1977), 39–92. Among the many depictions of poor and marginal writers in Mercier's *Tableau de Paris*, see especially the chapters titled "Auteurs"; "Des demi-auteurs, quarts d'auteur, enfin métis, quarterons, etc."; "La littérature du faubourg Saint-Germain, et celle du faubourg Saint-Honoré"; "Misère des auteurs"; and "Le Musée de Paris."

6. "Sans-culottes," in *Le Nouveau Paris*, ed. Jean-Claude Bonnet (Paris, 1994), 445–49; quotation from p. 446.

7. "Fabre d'Eglantine," in *Le Nouveau Paris*, 450–51.

8. See Haim Burstin, *L'Invention du sans-culotte: Regards sur Paris révolutionnaire* (Paris, 2005).

9. In addition to the sources cited in chapter 5, note 1, see M. Michaud, *Biographie universelle ancienne et moderne* (Paris, 1843–65), 26: 396–97; and Jean Tulard, Jean-François Fayard, and Alfred Fierro, *Histoire et dictionnaire de la Révolution française, 1789–1799* (Paris, 1987), 969.

10. The following account is based on Manuel's interrogation and the accompanying dossiers in Archives nationales, W295, no. 246. Frantz Funck-Brentano used this material in the helpful notice on Manuel's imprisonment in *Les Lettres de cachet à Paris: Etude suivie d'une liste des prisonniers de la Bastille (1659–1789)* (Paris, 1903), 415. Manuel referred briefly to this episode in *La Bastille dévoilée ou recueil de pièces authentiques pour servir à son histoire* (Paris, 1789), 3: 105–6.

11. *Lettre d'un garde du roi, pour servir de suite aux Mémoires sur Cagliostro* (London, 1786), quotation from p. 4. On p. 30 the soldier gives his opinion on the subject of libels: "Un libelle n'est pas un grand délit. . . . Cependant je conçois qu'il serait affreux de tolérer les libellistes. Nos réputations seraient continuellement menacées."

12. Of the many contemporary sources on Mirabeau's involvement in publishing, propaganda, and finance, the most revealing is Etienne Dumont, *Souvenirs sur Mirabeau et sur les deux premières assemblées législatives, ouvrage posthume publié par J. L. Duval* (Paris, 1832). And of the large secondary literature on Mirabeau, the old biography by Louis de Loménie and Charles de Loménie still holds up quite well: *Les Mirabeau: Nouvelles études sur la société française par Louis de Loménie, de l'Académie française, deuxième partie continuée par son fils* (Paris, 1889), 4 vols. Most of the financial side to the literary story can be found in the works of Jean Bouchary, especially *Les Manieurs d'argent à Paris à la fin du XVIIIème siècle* (Paris, 1939), 3 vols. I have discussed the speculations and ghostwriting behind Mirabeau's pamphlets in "Trends in Radical Propaganda on the Eve of the French Revolution (1782–1788)" (D.Phil. diss., Oxford University, 1964), chap. 5 and appendix 3, and I have published a summary of this research as "The Pursuit of Profit: Rousseauism on the Bourse," in *George Washington's False Teeth: An Unconventional Guide to the Eighteenth Century* (New York, 2003), chap. 7.

13. *De la Banque d'Espagne, dite de Saint-Charles: Par le comte de Mirabeau* (n.p., 1785); *Sur les Actions de la Compagnie des eaux de Paris: Par M. le comte de Mirabeau* (London, 1785); *Réponse du comte de Mirabeau à l'écrivain des administrateurs de la Compagnie des eaux de Paris* (Brussels, 1785).

14. Lenoir papers, Bibliothèque municipale d'Orléans, ms. 1422.

15. Ibid.

16. Jacques Peuchet, *Mémoires tirés des archives de la police de Paris, pour servir à l'histoire de la morale et de la police, depuis Louis XIV jusqu'à nos jours* (Paris, 1838), 1: 11, 3: 15–25, and the essay by a police *commissaire* named Le Maire written for the empress Maria Theresa of Austria and published by Augustin Gazier as "La Police de Paris en 1770," in *Mémoires de la Société de l'histoire de Paris et de l'Île de France* (1879), 5: 1–131. Instead of payment, the police often permitted agents recruited from shady milieus to continue in criminal activities—everything from prostitution to peddling illegal books—in return for reporting on others engaged in the same trade. As testimony to the contemporary notion that spies swarmed everywhere in Paris and that their reports made the Parisian lieutenant general of police omniscient, see the chapters titled "Espions," "Les Colporteurs," "Hommes de la police," and "Lieutenant de police" in *Tableau de Paris*, chaps. 59, 60, 61, and 63.

17. Peuchet, *Mémoires*, 3:17. I have found the same passage, phrased slightly differently, in Lenoir's papers, Bibliothèque municipale d'Orléans, ms. 1422.

18. *Résumé pour Charles-Pierre Bosquillon, citoyen actif contre M. Manuel, élu procureur de la Commune de Paris* (Paris, 1791), 11. Michaud's *Biographie universelle*, 26: 396, describes Manuel as a "précepteur des enfants d'un riche financier, qui lui assura une pension. Il vivait dans la capitale de ce revenu et du produit de quelques pamphlets distribués sous le manteau." The *Nouvelle biographie générale* (Paris, 1850), 33: columns 326–29, specifies that he tutored the children of a banker named Tourton. Kuscinski, *Dictionnaire des Conventionnels*, 3: 427, asserts that he was a "précepteur dans plusieurs familles et employé chez le libraire Garnery" and that this threadbare existence left him "pauvre et aigri" when the Revolution broke out.

19. In an article on the *Lettre d'un garde du roi*, entry for February 11, 1786, the *Mémoires secrets pour servir à l'histoire de la république des lettres en France* noted, "Un M. Manuel, . . . qui ayant perdu son état de gouverneur des enfants de M. Tourton par

la sortie violente qu'un certain abbé Royou avait fait contre lui dans l'*Année littéraire*, en le représentant comme un impie, comme un homme abominable, avait été obligé pour ressource de se faire libraire, ou colporteur, a été aussi arrêté." The *Mémoires secrets* referred unsympathetically to Manuel in its entries for February 12 and April 29, but on April 30 it contained a favorable review of his *Coup d'oeil philosophique sur le règne de Saint Louis*, noting in particular his scornful treatment of the crusades. It also referred to him favorably in an article of May 14, which announced his release from the Bastille.

20. *Correspondance littéraire, philosophique et critique par Grimm, Diderot, Meister, etc.*, ed. Maurice Tourneux (Paris, 1879), 14: 392–95.

21. In addition to the sources already cited, some information—suggestive but not reliable—can be gleaned from a few polemical works published during the Revolution, notably *Vie secrète de Pierre Manuel* (a libel but one with some seemingly accurate information about Manuel's early life in Montargis) and *Collection complète des tableaux historiques de la Révolution française* (Paris, 1798), 3: n.p. (a collection of engravings with biographical notices).

22. Pierre Manuel, *Coup-d'oeil philosophique sur le règne de Saint Louis* ("à Damiette, et se trouve à Paris chez les marchands qui vendent les nouveautés," 1788), 5. The date is odd, as the work was reviewed in 1786, and it does not seem to have gone through another edition.

23. Ibid., 44.

24. *Correspondance littéraire*, 14: 394.

25. However, in his *Coup-d'oeil philosophique*, 92–95, Manuel had some things to say in favor of the emancipation of women as well as slaves and Jews.

26. Pierre Manuel, *L'Année française, ou vie des hommes qui ont honoré la France, ou par leurs talents, ou par leurs services, et surtout par leurs vertus: Pour tous les jours de l'année* (Paris, 1789), 2: v.

27. Ibid., 1: ix.

28. Manuel, "Vers à mon amie," *Mercure de France*, March 20, 1784, p. 98.

29. Pierre Manuel, *Essais historiques, critiques, littéraires et philosophiques* (Geneva, 1783), 80.

30. Ibid., 10.

31. This theme appears in many of the works of Mercier, including the *Tableau de Paris*, and of Linguet, notably *L'Aveu sincère, ou lettre à une mère sur les dangers que court la jeunesse en se livrant à un goût trop vif pour la littérature* (London, 1763). It was dramatized in one of the plays by which P. F. N. Fabre d'Eglantine tried and failed to make a name for himself as a writer before the Revolution: *Les Gens de lettres*, performed in 1787 and published in *Mélanges littéraires par une société de gens de lettres* (Paris, 1827).

32. *Le Petit Almanach de nos grands hommes* (n.p., 1788), 120.

33. *Supplément à la nouvelle édition du Petit Almanach des grands hommes, ou lettre à Messieurs de Rivarol et de Champcenets, par un des grands hommes du Petit Almanach* (n.p., 1788), 12. Manuel followed this outburst with one of his poems. Although he published this thirty-one-page pamphlet anonymously, his authorship is easy to detect and was soon exposed by his opponents.

34. Ibid., 5, 9, 30. On the relatively open and democratic character of the Musée as opposed to the salons and academies dominated by the literary elite, see Mercier, *Tableau de Paris*, chaps. 531 and 946.

35. *Lettre d'une muséenne à M. Manuel, auteur du Supplément au Petit Almanach des grands hommes* (n.p., n.d.), quotations from 4 and 8.

Chapter 18. Slander into Terror

1. Manuel's career after 1789 can be traced through his numerous publications, which are listed in the catalogue of the Bibliothèque nationale de France. See especially the collection of his speeches and essays that he published with Garnery in 1792, *Les Lettres de P. Manuel, l'un des administrateurs de 1789, sur la Révolution, recueillies par un ami de la constitution* (Paris, 1792). The attacks on him cover the same ground from the opposite perspective, and they can be supplemented by publications from the two trials that determined his fate: *Interrogatoire de Pierre Manuel, Procureur de la Commune* ([Paris], 1792) and *Jugement rendu par le Tribunal révolutionnaire, établi par la loi du 10 mars 1793, séant à Paris, au Palais, qui . . . condamne Pierre Manuel à la peine de mort, conformément à la loi du 16 décembre 1792* (Paris, 1793). See also the documents connected with his trial before the Revolutionary Tribunal in the Archives nationales, W295, no. 246, pièces 46–54. The many polemical works involving Manuel are cited in Maurice Tourneux, *Bibliographie de l'histoire de Paris pendant la Révolution française* (Paris, 1890–1913), 5 vols., and Manuel's numerous speeches at the Jacobin Club can be followed in F.-A. Aulard, *La Société des Jacobins: Recueil de documents pour l'histoire du Club des Jacobins de Paris* (Paris, 1889–97), 6 vols. Manuel's speeches in the Convention are summarized in its proceedings as reported in *Gazette nationale ou le Moniteur universel* and, more conveniently, *Archives parlementaires de 1787 à 1860*, ed. Mavidal and E. Laurent (Paris, 1897), vols. 52–60. Finally, Manuel's role in the revolutionary politics of Paris can be documented from *Actes de la Commune de Paris pendant la Révolution française*, ed. Sigismond Lacroix (Paris, 1894), première série, vols. 2–3, and deuxième série, vol. 8. Some additional information appears in Paul Robiquet, *Le Personnel municipal de Paris pendant la Révolution* (Paris, 1890), 2 vols.

2. In the *Interrogatoire de Pierre Manuel*, 13–14, Manuel referred to himself as a "vainqueur de la Bastille," but he dropped that claim in his *Lettres de P. Manuel*, where he emphasized his martyrdom as a prisoner (36).

3. *Lettre d'un citoyen à un frondeur, sur les affaires présentes* (ca. 1788). Although this anonymous pamphlet is commonly attributed to Manuel and conforms to his style, its authorship is uncertain.

4. *Vie secrète de Pierre Manuel* (Paris, [1793]), 47–48.

5. *Lettres de P. Manuel*, 98. See also Manuel's tribute to peddlers in *La Bastille dévoilée* (Paris, 1789), 4: 65–66: "Il ne suffisait pas que des écrivains-philosophes composassent des livres, il fallait encore les faire imprimer, les faire colporter, les faire arriver jusqu'à nous, à travers une infinité d'obstacles, à travers une armée d'espions et de délateurs. Un colporteur d'alors a plus fait, à mon avis, pour la révolution, que les citoyens qui viennent d'endosser l'habit bleu, la giberne et le mousquet [that is, members of the National Guard]."

6. *Lettres de P. Manuel*, 71–89.

7. According to the title he used when he identified himself during his trial of 1792, Manuel became "administrateur de la municipalité provisoire au département de la police" and "administrateur de la police provisoire" (*Interrogatoire de Pierre Manuel*,

2–3). As one of several deputies who oversaw the police, he assumed a specialized function as "administrateur particulièrement de la librairie" (6). But that did not mean he exercised direct police power, which was taken over by the office of the new mayor of Paris. The Assemblée générale de la Commune provisoire first met on October 8, 1789, and on the following day it named Manuel along with six others as *conseillers administrateurs* attached to the Département de la police. See Robiquet, *Le Personnel municipal de Paris*, 253–57, and *Actes de la Commune de Paris*, première série, 2: 682, where Manuel is identified as a representative from the district of Val-de-Grâce united with the district of Saint-Jacques du Haut Pas, "38 ans, littérateur."

8. *Lettres de P. Manuel*, 90–91, 95–96, 101–2, 111–12, 121, 141, 204; quotation from p. 111.

9. Manuel quoted de Maissemy's letter in *La Police de Paris dévoilée* (Paris, 1790), 1: 64–65. The original and Maissemy's orders to confiscate the prospectus are in the Collection Anisson-Duperron, Bibliothèque nationale de France, ms. fr. 22070, pièce 78.

10. On the early reaction against the unlimited liberty of the press, see G. Charles Walton, "Policing Public Opinion in the French Revolution" (Ph.D. diss., Princeton University, 2003).

11. *Interrogatoire de Pierre Manuel*, 3. On the title page of *La Police de Paris dévoilée*, Manuel used a simpler term, "L'un des administrateurs de 1789." The different formulas that he used—as mentioned above, note 7—suggest the uncertainty in the demarcation of authority at this time of institutional chaos. Some of Manuel's activities can be followed from decrees of the Paris Commune. See, for example, *Actes de la Commune de Paris*, première série, 2: 550, 4: 682.

12. Even the hostile *Vie secrète de Pierre Manuel*, 34, complimented Manuel for acting as a "véritable philosophe" by doing nothing to limit the liberty of the press.

13. *Résumé pour Charles-Pierre Bosquillon, citoyen actif, contre M. Manuel, élu Procureur de la Commune de Paris* (Paris, 1791), 11.

14. Ibid., especially 9–15. For documents related to the Bosquillon affair, see *Actes de la Commune de Paris*, deuxième série, 8: 517–50.

15. *La Bastille dévoilée*, 1: 1, 2: 137. The "Avertissement" at the beginning of volume 1 explains the circumstances and purpose of the publication. In this and other references, the installments, called "livraisons," are cited as volumes, although they were often bound together.

16. At the beginning of the third installment, an unpaginated notice facing the title page described the entries on the prisoners as "des notes historiques sur ces mêmes prisonniers, fournies ou par des mémoires qu'ils nous ont remis ou par des dépositions qu'ils nous ont faites, ou prises dans des papiers trouvés à la Bastille, dont les originaux sont entre nos mains."

17. *Mémoires historiques et authentiques sur la Bastille* (Paris, 1789), 1: x–xi. Carra made a reference, 1: vi, that clearly indicated his authorship. He did not continue his publication of the Bastille papers beyond volume 3, which ends at 1775.

18. On the history of the Bastille papers and their publication, see Frantz Funck-Brentano, *Catalogue des manuscrits de la Bibliothèque de l'Arsenal* (Paris, 1892), vol. 9, introduction, and Funck-Brentano, *Les Lettres de cachet à Paris: Etude suivie d'une liste des prisonniers de la Bastille (1659–1789)* (Paris, 1903), xlvii–liii. See also François Ravaisson, *Archives de la Bastille* (Paris, 1866–84), 16 vols., although it stops at 1759. Like most

other sources, the catalogue of the Bibliothèque nationale de France attributes *La Bastille dévoilée* to Manuel. Funck-Brentano notes that Manuel collaborated with a certain
Charpentier, although he cites no evidence. I think it is possible that Manuel had one
or more collaborators in the preparation of the first installments, but as explained
below, internal evidence suggests that he had completely taken over the editorship by
installment three.

19. *La Bastille dévoilée*, 4: 3.

20. *Correspondance littéraire, philosophique et critique par Grimm, Diderot, Raynal, Meister, etc.*, ed. Maurice Tourneux (Paris, 1879), 15: 495.

21. *La Bastille dévoilée*, 1: 3.

22. Ibid., 6: 1.

23. *J.-P. Brissot, Mémoires (1754–1793)*, ed. Claude Perroud (Paris, 1910), 2: 23. In
printing Brissot's essay, Manuel included a note that indicated his own role as editor:
"Il a bien voulu se donner la peine de faire son article. Nous l'insérons tel qu'il nous
l'a envoyé." *La Bastille dévoilée*, 3: 75.

24. *La Chasteté du clergé dévoilée, ou procès-verbaux des séances du clergé chez les
filles de Paris, trouvés à la Bastille* ("à Rome, de l'Imprimerie de la Propagande, et se
trouve à Paris, chez les marchands de nouveautés," 1790), 1: x.

25. Ibid., 1: vi.

26. Ibid., 1: 24.

27. *Vie secrète de Pierre Manuel*, 47–48: "Il a vendu pour son profit au libraire
Duplain, passage de la Cour du commerce, tous les procès-verbaux que les commissai-
res de police avaient dressés lors de l'arrestation des différents ecclésiastiques trouvés
au b. . . [bordel] et c'est par le fait de cet intriguant malévole chargé de veiller sur les
moeurs, que la jeunesse curieuse fut corrompue et empoisonnée après la lecture des
anecdotes libertines des prêtres, anecdotes qui auraient dû rester secrètes, mais qu'il
avait vendues moyennant 1000 livres le cahier à Duplain, après s'être fait payer par
Champion de Cicé, alors archevêque de Bordeaux et chancelier, 3000 livres pour tenir
ces aventures secrètes. Il trouvait cet honorable trafic si lucratif qu'il y prit goût. Il
forma une compilation de toutes les pièces dont il était le dépositaire de confiance,
pour en faire un recueil piquant qu'il vendit 12000 livres à Garnery, et après s'être fait
payer encore de ceux qui, croyant reprendre la totalité de leurs pièces, n'en recevaient
que les parties les plus insignifiantes et les moins utiles."

28. Jean-Louis Carra, a hack writer quite similar to Manuel, tried to entice readers with a rhetoric like Manuel's in the introduction to his *Mémoires historiques et
authentiques sur la Bastille*, 1: x: "Que ceux qui lisent ces mémoires s'identifient un
moment avec les infortunés . . . et que de là ils élancent leur imagination indignée sur
le sopha voluptueux de la prostituée favorite [of Louis XV]."

29. *La Police de Paris dévoilée*, 1: 7.

30. Ibid.; quotations from 2: 115, 121, 153, 93.

31. Ibid., 2: 229.

32. *Lettres originales de Mirabeau, écrites du donjon de Vincennes pendant les
années 1777, 78, 79 et 80; contenant tous les détails sur sa vie privée, ses malheurs, et ses
amours avec Sophie Ruffei, marquise de Monnier* (Paris, 1792), 1: viii.

33. Ibid., 1: ix.

34. Ibid., 1: xxxviii.

35. Ibid.; quotations from 1: xv, xvi, xix.

36. Quotations from the reprint of Chénier's article in his *Oeuvres complètes*, ed. Gérard Walter (Paris, 1950), 267–72. While Chénier wrote the longest and strongest condemnation of Manuel's edition of the Mirabeau letters, many other critics reacted negatively. Even *Le Moniteur* (February 14, 1792), which was normally mild in its reviews, condemned the bad taste and equivocal morality of Manuel's preliminary discourse. For references to other reactions and the polemics surrounding the edition, see *Actes de la Commune de Paris*, deuxième série, 8: 551–608.

37. *Interrogatoire de Pierre Manuel*, 9. This pamphlet, a transcription of Manuel's interrogation of May 22, 1792, in the trial concerning the *Lettres originales de Mirabeau*, provides a good deal of information about their publication, and it can be supplemented from the documents collected in *Actes de la Commune de Paris*, deuxième série, 8: 551–608.

38. *Lettres de P. Manuel*, iv. Manuel referred to himself in the third person because he wrote as if he were the anonymous editor of his letters. He completed this thought by splicing in a sentence he had published in *La Police de Paris dévoilée*, 2: 229: "Il fallait bien constater à quel degré en était la corruption, la gangrène des moeurs."

39. Ibid.

40. Aulard, *La Société des Jacobins*, 3: 348. The text is quoted in Auguste Kuscinski, *Dictionnaire des Conventionnels* (Paris, 1916–19), 3: 427.

41. This view was expressed by the royalist cartoon reprinted in Chapter 5 (figure 20).

42. When asked about his appropriation of the archives, Manuel replied as follows, according to the *Interrogatoire de Pierre Manuel*, 7: "A répondu qu'il s'en est emparé les 14 et 15 juillet, dans ce moment où tout ce qu'avait volé le despotisme était à la disposition du peuple qui recouvrait et sa souveraineté et ses propriétés; qu'ils sont devenus dans ses mains les armes de l'opinion publique tout comme les fusils enlevés aux Invalides sont devenus les armes de la liberté; et que cette conquête lui était plus facile qu'à un autre parce que lui-même enfermé à la Bastille, il avait pu sur les lieux connaître les archives de cet enfer des vivants; qu'il a recueilli les lambeaux de lettres et des papiers indéchiffrables; qu'il fallait toute sa patience, tout son opiniâtreté dans le travail pour tirer parti des papiers poudreux qui eûssent effrayé un savant du seizième siècle; et que c'est un bienfait national que d'avoir deviné un trésor là où tant d'autres n'auraient cru voir que des papiers de procureurs." The self-righteousness of Manuel's defense may look tendentious to modern readers, but it should be remembered that similar disputes about access to police archives broke out all over Eastern Europe after the collapse of the Communist regimes in 1989–90.

43. Manuel presented the *Lettres originales de Mirabeau* to the Jacobins in a histrionic manner by placing them under a bust of Mirabeau and exclaiming: "Je dépose ces lettres sous son buste, sous les lauriers mêmes que vous lui avez décernés. . . . La peine qu'il m'a fallu prendre pour les lire, et je ferais mieux de dire pour les deviner, est une preuve de mon patriotisme." He also presented a sample lettre de cachet he had taken from the archives of the Bastille and which the Jacobins voted to have framed for display along with a stone from the Bastille. Aulard, *La Société des Jacobins*, 3: 335. See also the other references to Manuel's trial in sessions of the Jacobins (3: 599, 639).

Chapter 19. Words and Deeds

1. André Chénier, "Observations aux auteurs du *Journal de Paris sur l'éditeur des lettres de Mirabeau*," in Chénier, *Oeuvres complètes*, ed. Gérard Walter (Paris, 1950), 271. Chénier described Manuel as typical of the new order of writers who dominated the revolutionary press: "Ils ne veulent pas voir que, cette partie d'industrie humaine ayant longtemps été comprimée sous des entraves sans nombre, dès que la barrière a été levée, une foule immense a dû se précipiter pour goûter à la hâte le plaisir de tout imprimer; et que nécessairement, le plus grand nombre de ces nouveaux écrivains avait négligé jusque-là de savoir lire et de savoir penser, préliminaires indispensables de l'art d'écrire" (271).

2. Pierre Augustin Caron de Beaumarchais, *Beaumarchais à Monsieur Manuel* (Paris, 1792), 3. It should be noted, however, that Beaumarchais slipped some irony into his flattery, and he did not resist the opportunity to take a swipe at the commercialism behind Manuel's revolutionary publications: "Mais si jamais j'imprime à mon profit les souillures de la police, les lettres d'autrui dérobées, je me condamnerai d'avance aux reproches fondé du procureur syndic actuel de la commune de Paris" (5).

3. As in Chapter 5, the following account is based on Germaine Necker, baronne de Staël-Holstein, *Considérations sur la Révolution française*, ed. Jacques Godechot (1818; Paris, 1983), 283–86.

4. Pierre Manuel, *La Bastille dévoilée* (Paris, 1789), 3: 69–70.

5. In a prefatory note opposite the title page of volume 3, Manuel explained that the entries on some of the Bastille prisoners were based on "des notes historiques sur ces mêmes prisonniers fournies ou par des mémoires ou par des dépositions qu'ils nous ont faites." He may have met Pelleport in the Bastille itself, where they both were prisoners in 1786.

6. This tendency was stimulated especially by François Furet, *Penser la Révolution française* (Paris, 1978). Although I admired Furet and once worked closely with him, I disagree with his emphasis on discourse and the determinant effect of ideas. My own approach to the French Revolution, as should be apparent in this chapter, draws more heavily on social history, and it stresses the contemporary perception of events as well as the contingent character of the events themselves.

7. Speeches in the Jacobin Club of February 5, February 12, and July 18, 1792, in F.-A. Aulard, *La Société des Jacobins: Recueil de documents pour l'histoire du Club des Jacobins de Paris* (Paris, 1897–98), 3: 364, 374, 648.

8. Ibid., 3: 683. Manuel served as vice president and as president of the Jacobins in June 1792, at the high point of his appeal to the left.

9. Paul Robiquet, *Le Personnel municipal de Paris pendant la Révolution* (Paris, 1890), 2: 488.

10. Aulard, *La Société des Jacobins*, 3: 639, 648, 668, 4: 79, 111; Robiquet, *Le Personnel municipal de Paris*, 498.

11. J.-P. Brissot, *Mémoires (1754–1793)*, ed. Claude Perroud (Paris, 1910), 2: 243.

12. Aulard, *La Société des Jacobins*, 4: 460.

13. Ibid.

14. As an example of Collot d'Herbois's hack writing and the politics it expressed when he toured the provinces with a troupe in 1775, see his skit, *Le Bon Angevin, ou l'hommage du coeur, comédie en un acte, mêlée de chants et vaudevilles et suivie d'un*

divertissement, composée en l'honneur de Monsieur, Frère du Roi, Duc d'Anjou (Angers, 1775), 4: "Français! Quelle nation plus heureuse que la vôtre! Votre roi veut être votre père; les princes augustes qui l'entourent veulent être vos frères et vos amis: le plaisir suit aujourd'hui l'obéissance, et le devoir parmi vous conduit à la félicité."

15. Aulard, *La Société des Jacobins*, 4: 612.

16. *Archives parlementaires de 1787 à 1860*, ed. Mavidal and E. Laurent (Paris, 1897), 52: 69.

17. Ibid., 54: 244–45.

18. *Les Tuileries, le Temple, le Tribunal révolutionnaire et la Conciergerie, sous la tyrannie de la Convention* (Paris, 1814), 85. This anonymous, royalist work quoted this remark by Manuel from an issue of the *Journal de Cléry* in 1792. I have not been able to verify it in the original.

19. "Interrogatoire de Manuel, 23 brumaire An II," Archives nationales, ms. W295, no. 246, pièce 46.

20. The fullest account of Manuel's supposed attempt to falsify the tally is a "dénonciation" by Elisabeth Mouttenot femme Vialla dated 24 brumaire Year II in the papers on Manuel's trial, Archives nationales, ms. W295, no. 246, pièce 43. There is also an allusion to this incident in the "Acte d'accusation" by Antoine Quentin Fouquier-Tinville dated 23 brumaire Year II, ibid., pièce 54. Louis Sébastien Mercier also refers to it in *Le Nouveau Paris*, ed. Jean-Claude Bonnet (1798; Paris, 1994), 879.

21. *Archives parlementaires*, 60: 346. See also J.-P. Brissot, *Mémoires*, 2: 227.

22. Fouquier-Tinville, "Acte d'accusation," Archives nationales, ms. W295, no. 246, pièce 54. The various denunciations precede this document, pièces 47–53. A printed version of Fouquier-Tinville's case against Manuel was published with the decree of the Revolutionary Tribunal condemning him to death as *Jugement rendu par le Tribunal révolutionnaire, établi par la loi du 10 mars 1793, séant à Paris, au Palais, qui . . . condamne Pierre Manuel à la peine de mort, conformément à la loi du 16 décembre 1792* (Paris, 24 brumaire, Year II).

23. *Jugement rendu par le ribunal* [sic] *criminel révolutionnaire, établi par la loi du 10 mars 1793, séant à Paris, au Palais, qui . . . condamne à la peine de mort, sur la place de la Révolution, Pierre Manuel* (Paris, n.d.), 4. This phrase did not appear in the official publication with the same title. Both appear in the Bibliothèque nationale de France, L41b.2232.

24. *Véritable testament de Pierre Manuel ci-devant Procureur de la Commune et député à la Convention Nationale, écrit la veille de sa mort, dans la prison de la Conciergerie, suivi de plusieurs morales touchantes qu'il fit au Tribunal révolutionnaire pour gagner le peuple à son avantage* (n.p., n.d.), 2, 8.

Chapter 20. Postscript, 1802

1. This last reference to Pelleport occurs in the daily reports prepared for Bonaparte by the police under Joseph Fouché: "Préfecture de police, 1ère division, 19 brumaire An XI," Archives nationales, ms. F7.3831. It was published by F.-A. Aulard in *Paris sous le Consulat: Recueil de documents pour servir à l'histoire de l'esprit public à Paris* (Paris, 1903–9), 3: 386–87.

2. *Gazette nationale ou le Moniteur universel*, February 16, 1792.

3. Ibid., February 18, 1792.

4. At this point the documentation becomes thin and unreliable. The best source is a short essay, "Lafitte de Pelleport," signed S. Churchill in *L'Intermédiaire des chercheurs et curieux* (October 30, 1904), 50: columns 634–37. It cites an account of the siege of Valenciennes in June and July 1793, where Pelleport may have acted as a secret agent for the French foreign ministry. It also cites *Journal d'un fourrier de l'armée de Condé: Jacques de Thiboult du Puisact, député de l'Orne*, ed. Gérard de Contades (Paris, 1882), which contains a convincing description of Pelleport as a witty soldier-poet in the army of the prince de Condé at Steinstadt in the summer of 1795. In his journal, pp. 63, 65, 69, Thiboult notes that "Lafitte de Pelleport" pleased Condé and other officers with his poems, notably some verse about the duc de Bourbon that he improvised while mounting the guard one morning in July. However, in a note on p. 63, Contades claims that Pelleport left the army in November 1795 to join a sister in Philadelphia. In a later work, *Emigrés et Chouans: Le chevalier de Haussey, Armand de Chateaubriand; Un Chouan à Londres; Les gentilshommes poètes de l'armée de Condé; Puisaye et d'Avaray* (Paris, 1895), 190, Contades asserted that Pelleport died of yellow fever soon after arriving in Philadelphia. That unlikely ending is contradicted by the shorter but more sober essay on Pelleport in the *Biographie universelle ancienne et moderne* (Paris, 1843), 32: 398, which has Pelleport die in Paris around 1810. Two other notices in the *Intermédiaire des chercheurs et curieux* (January 20, 1904), 49: column 79, do not clarify the obscurity surrounding Pelleport's biography. But a great deal more could be pieced together by a close study of his writings, which contain many autobiographical references and can be identified, despite their anonymity, by hints he scattered throughout them.

5. "Préfecture de police, 1ère division, 19 brumaire An XI," Archives nationales, ms. F7.3831.

Chapter 21. The Nature of Libels

1. Many modern discussions of this theme take off from Jean–Paul Sartre's famous essay, "Qu'est-ce que la littérature?" published in *Temps modernes* from February through July 1947, and Roland Barthes, *Le Degré zéro de l'écriture* (Paris, 1965).

2. When private individuals considered themselves libeled, they could take their case to civil courts, but they often refrained from doing so in order to avoid unpleasant publicity. In legal terms, libel involved written defamation and could be prosecuted as a crime or a tort, whereas slander was defamation by speech and limited to tort actions. But no clear boundary separated the two terms in ordinary usage. See C. R. Kropf, "Libel and Satire in the Eighteenth Century," *Eighteenth-Century Studies* 8 (1974–75), 153–68, and Philip Hamburger, "The Development of the Law of Seditious Libel and the Control of the Press," *Stanford Law Review* 37 (1985), 661–765.

3. Of course, persons who considered themselves defamed by a libel could take their case to court, but legal action was not a feasible option for an eminent person who sought redress against an obscure, anonymous hack writer. Court cases about libel generally concerned ordinary individuals in the middle ranks of society. As an example of such a case, see *Mémoires secrets pour servir à l'histoire de la république des lettres en France*, December 30, 1784.

4. I have compiled these statistics from Frantz Funck-Brentano, *Les Lettres de*

cachet à Paris: Etude suivie d'une liste des prisonniers de la Bastille (1659–1789) (Paris, 1903). The largest category of offenses was "Jansénisme," although the term covered all sorts of activities aside from publishing. Undifferentiated "délits de la librairie" was also a large category, but one cannot determine the kinds of publications it covered without consulting the individual dossiers.

5. On libels during the first half of the seventeenth century, see Christian Jouhaud, "Les libelles en France dans le premier XVIIe siècle: Lecteurs, auteurs, commanditaires, historiens," *XVIIe siècle* 49 (1998), 203–17. There is no general study of libels in early modern Europe.

6. I used the 1691 edition: Antoine Furetière, *Dictionnaire universel* (The Hague and Rotterdam, 1691). The phrasing is nearly the same in the entries on *libelle* in the *Dictionnaire de Trévoux* (Trévoux, 1704), and the eighteenth-century editions of the *Dictionnaire de l'Académie française* restrict their definition to two words: "écrit injurieux." Samuel Johnson does not go much further in the entry after "Libel" in his *Dictionary of the English Language*, 4th ed. (Dublin, 1775): "A satire; defamatory writing; a lampoon."

7. See "libelle" in *La Grande Encyclopédie, inventaire raisonné des sciences, des lettres et des arts* (Paris, 1886–1902) and in *Grand Dictionnaire universel du XIXe siècle* (Paris, 1866–70). By the time of Augustus, the Romans used *libellus* to mean defamatory pamphlet. The *Oxford Latin Dictionary*, ed. P. G. W. Glare (Oxford, 1996), 1022, notes its use in the *Annals* of Tacitus: "Augustus was the first to conduct trials on slanderous pamphlets (*famosi libelli*) under the pretext of the law of lèse-majesté (*maiestas*)." For this and other information about libels among the ancients, I am indebted to Christopher Jones and Peter Brown.

8. See the article on him in the *Allgemeine Deutsche Biographie* (Berlin, 1887; reprint, 1970), 24. I am indebted to Martin Muslow for this reference and for general information about humanist disputations.

9. "Libelle," in *Grand dictionnaire universel du XIXe siècle*. Pierre Bayle discussed the edict of 1561, its renewal in 1577, and other measures against libels in his "Dissertation sur les libelles diffamatoires" at the end of his *Dictionnaire historique et critique* (1695–97; Paris, 1820), 15: 160–69.

10. "Libelle," in *Grand dictionnaire universel du XIXe siècle*.

11. For examples of usage, see "libelle" in *Grand Larousse de la langue française* (Paris, 1975); *Le Grand Robert de la langue française* (Paris, 2001); and *Trésor de la langue française: Dictionnaire de la langue du XIXe et du XXe siècle (1789–1960)* (Paris, 1971–94).

12. Chrétien-Guillaume de Lamoignon de Malesherbes, *Mémoires sur la librairie: Mémoire sur la liberté de la presse*, ed. Roger Chartier (original text dates from 1759; Paris, 1994), 101–2. Malesherbes also noted that royal censors were often incapable of spotting veiled, libelous remarks about the great, because the censors did not belong to the elevated world of "gens . . . considérables" (91).

13. Pierre Bayle, "Dissertation sur les libelles diffamatoires," in *Dictionnaire historique et critique* (1695–97; Paris, 1820), 15: 173.

14. Voltaire, "Mémoire sur la satire à l'occasion d'un libelle de l'abbé Desfontaines contre l'auteur," in *Oeuvres complètes de Voltaire* (1739; Paris, 1879), 23: 47–64.

15. "Libelle," in *Dictionnaire de Trévoux*.

16. "Libelle," in *Encyclopédie ou dictionnaire raisonné des sciences, des arts et des métiers* (Paris and Neuchâtel, 1751–72).

17. Louis-Sébastien Mercier, *Tableau de Paris*, ed. Jean-Claude Bonnet (Paris, 1994, reprint of the successive editions from 1781–87), 2: 28. As an example of libeling attached to moneygrubbing, Mercier alluded to the activities of Goupil (2: 27).

18. Simon-Nicolas-Henri Linguet, *Théorie du libelle, ou l'art de calomnier avec fruit, dialogue philosophique pour servir de supplément à la Théorie du paradoxe* (Amsterdam, 1775), 11.

19. Bibliothèque nationale de France, ms. Fr. 22101. The arrêt du Conseil condemned the book as a "libelle . . . contenant d'ailleurs des injures, des déclamations et calomnies contre des personnes dignes de l'estime et de la confiance publique."

20. Linguet, *Théorie du libelle*, 223–24.

21. *Théorie du paradoxe* (Amsterdam, 1775), 128.

22. A letter from the marquis de Favras to the lieutenant general of police quoted in Pierre Manuel, *La Police de Paris dévoilée* (Paris, 1790), 1: 111. See a similar example in ibid., 1: 224.

23. Linguet, *Théorie du libelle*, 9.

24. Jean-Paul Marat, *Offrande à la patrie, ou discours au tiers-état de France* (1789), 25.

25. Bibliothèque nationale de France, ms. Fr. 22101. The edict deplored the tendency of the libels to weaken the monarchy by exposing the inner secrets of its government: "Heureuse la France si ces problèmes politiques fussent toujours demeurés sous le voile dont la prudence de nos pères avait enveloppé tout ce qui concerne le gouvernement et l'administration, pour ne point exciter de fermentation dans les esprits. . . . Les auteurs de ces deux ouvrages ne cherchent qu'à détruire toute subordination dans le corps politique de l'Etat." Malesherbes also castigated polemical writing that challenged the authority of the king but did not defame any individuals as "libelles téméraires." Malesherbes, *Mémoires sur la librairie*, 57.

26. For a more extensive discussion of reading and romans à clef, see my essay, "Mlle Bonafon and the Private Life of Louis XV: Communication Circuits in Eighteenth-Century France," *Representations* (Summer 2004): 102–24.

27. In his edition of *Anecdotes curieuses de la cour de France sous le règne de Louis XV* (Paris, 1908), ciii, xcvii–c, Paul Fould disputes this standard attribution and argues that the *Mémoires secrets pour servir à l'histoire de Perse* (Amsterdam, 1745) was written by François-Vincent Toussaint. He claims that the *Anecdotes curieuses* was an early draft of the *Mémoires secrets*, one written by Toussaint without using the Persian setting to camouflage the names. Fould produces some important evidence, but I do not find it entirely convincing, particularly as Pecquet receives unusually favorable treatment, which sounds like special pleading, in the *Mémoires secrets* (Berlin, 1759 ed.), 94–95.

28. Imbert de Boudeaux, *La Chronique scandaleuse, ou Mémoires pour servir à l'histoire de la génération présente, contenant les anecdotes et les pièces les plus piquantes que l'histoire secrète des sociétés a offertes pendant ces dernières années* (Paris, 1791), 1: 37.

29. *La Police de Paris dévoilée*, 2: 123.

Chapter 22. Anecdotes

1. "Anecdote," in *Dictionnaire de l'Académie française* (1762; reprint, Nîmes, 1778). Samuel Johnson followed the French in advancing his own definition, which had

no suggestion of inaccuracy, false rumors, or unreliable gossip: "1. Something yet unpublished; secret history. 2. It is now used, after the French, for a biographical incident; a minute passage of private life." *A Dictionary of the English Language*, 4th ed. (Dublin, 1775).

2. For a convenient survey of the literature on Procopius, see *Paulys Realencyclopädie der Classischen Altertumswissenschaft* (Stuttgart, 1957), 45: columns 273–599.

3. *Anecdotes sur Mme la comtesse du Barry* (London, 1775), preface (unpaginated). For statistics on the enormous diffusion of this libel, see Robert Darnton, *The Corpus of Clandestine Literature in France, 1769–1789* (New York, 1995), 19–20.

4. *Remarques sur les Anecdotes de Madame la comtesse Dubarri par Madame Sara G...* (London, 1777), 11. The author, probably Ange Goudar writing in the person of his mistress Sarah, reworked the most outrageous anecdotes about Mme du Barry while pretending to be above such things and to despise his rival author as "un assassin littéraire qui tue périodiquement. . . . Chaque ligne est une satire, et chaque page forme un libelle diffamatoire" (84–85). The *Remarques* added a few new anecdotes, although it condemned the original *Anecdotes sur Mme la comtesse du Barry* for doing the same thing: "Comme le sac des anecdotes commençait à se vider, et que l'auteur en avait besoin pour grossir son livre, il a recours aux historiettes accessoires" (127). In fact, the *Remarques* probably was a hack work intended to exploit the success of the libel it supposedly refuted.

5. *Correspondance littéraire secrète* (n.p., n.d.), May 16, 1781.

6. Ibid., November 14, 1781.

7. Ibid., September 21, 1784. The author was reviewing a new fourth volume attached to the original text, which appeared in two volumes in 1752.

8. Testimony about the experience of reading in these cases can be found in Valentin Jamerey-Duval, *Mémoires: Enfance et éducation d'un paysan au XVIIIᵉ siècle*, ed. Jean Marie Goulemot (Paris, 1981); *Mémoires de Madame Roland*, ed. Claude Perroud (Paris, 1905); and Mme Jeanne-Louise-Henriette Campan, *Mémoires sur la vie de Marie-Antoinette, reine de France et de Navarre* (Paris, 1886). See also Jacques-Louis Ménétra, *Journal de ma vie: Jacques-Louis Ménétra, compagnon vitrier au 18ᵉ siècle*, ed. Daniel Roche (Paris, 1982), and Nicolas Edme Restif de la Bretonne, *Monsieur Nicholas; ou, Le coeur humain dévoilé*, ed. J.-J. Pauvert (Paris, 1959).

9. It should be noted, however, that Morande later deprecated *Le Gazetier cuirassé* as a "ramas d'anecdotes." *Réplique de Charles Théveneau Morande à Jacques-Pierre Brissot sur les erreurs, les oublis, les infidélités, et les calomnies de sa Réponse* (Paris, 1791), 19.

10. *Le Gazetier cuirassé, ou Anecdotes scandaleuses de la cour de France* (1777), 100.

11. Ibid., 34.

12. Erica-Marie Benabou, *La Prostitution et la police des moeurs au XVIIIᵉ siècle* (Paris, 1987), 257–59.

13. Louis-Sébastien Mercier, *Tableau de Paris*, ed. Jean-Claude Bonnet (Paris, 1994, reprint of the successive editions from 1781–87), 2: 25–29.

14. A rare example of a historical work that was tolerated by the regime is *Journal historique, ou fastes du règne de Louis XV* (Paris, 1766), but it was little more than a compilation of events, not a narrative, and it excluded anything that might offend the authorities. Paul-Philippe Gudin de La Brenellerie, the author of an innocuous history, *Aux Manes de Louis XV et des grands hommes qui ont vécu sous son règne, ou Essai sur*

les progrès des arts et de l'esprit humain sous le règne de Louis XV (Lausanne, 1777), explained in a preface that he had assumed it could be published legally in France, but after attempting to get it past the censors, he gave up and had it published anonymously abroad. The censors were so timid, he recounted, that they would not permit the slightest remark that might displease an influential person.

15. Nougaret was a fascinating Grub Street character and a rival of Restif de la Bretonne, but as far as I can tell he has never been studied. For a list of his publications, which were extraordinarily varied and profuse right up to his death in 1823, see Alexandre Cioranescu, *Bibliographie de la littérature française du dix-huitième siècle* (Paris, 1969), 2: 1342–45. See also the brief notice on him in *Dictionnaire des journalistes, 1600–1789*, ed. Jean Sgard (Oxford, 1999), 2: 746–47.

16. Historians normally date the beginning of the war from Frederick II's invasion of Silesia in December 1740, but the French often set its beginning at France's involvement in 1741: thus the title of Voltaire's *Histoire de la guerre de 1741*. The following discussion owes a great deal to the scholarly edition of that text by Jacques Maurens, *Histoire de la guerre de 1741* (Paris, 1971), and to the work of René Pomeau, notably *Voltaire en son temps* (Oxford, 1985–94), 5 vols.

17. Voltaire to Charles Augustin Feriol, comte d'Argental, April 5, 1745, *The Complete Works of Voltaire: Correspondence and Related Documents*, ed. Theodore Besterman (Geneva, 1970), 93: 224.

18. René Louis de Voyer de Paulmy, marquis d'Argenson, to Voltaire, May 15, 1745, ibid., 93: 243: "Voici les anecdotes que j'ai remarquées ou que l'on a remarquées pour moi." For similar remarks about anecdotes, see Voltaire to d'Argenson, May 26, 1745, ibid., 93: 255, and Voltaire to comte Otto Christoph von Podewils, May 1, 1745, ibid., 93: 233.

19. Voltaire to d'Argenson, August 17, 1745, ibid., 93: 306. See also Voltaire to d'Argenson, September 30, 1745, ibid., 93: 306, and Voltaire to d'Argental, October 1745 (exact date not given), ibid., 93: 346.

20. René Pomeau, one of the greatest authorities on Voltaire, described him in connection with *Histoire de la guerre de 1741* as a "reporter de génie" and characterized his research as the "contact du journaliste avec le réel." See Pomeau's introduction to Voltaire, *Oeuvres historiques* (Paris, 1978), 15.

21. References to portfolios of anecdotes can be found scattered through many sources, including the libels themselves. For example, a libel against the controller general, abbé Joseph Marie Terray, recounted an incident that confirmed rumors about the government's speculations on the grain trade, and then it observed: "L'anecdote au surplus, pour qu'elle ne fût pas oubliée, fut consignée dans de méchants vers, que les curieux recueillirent toujours dans leur portefeuille, comme très courus alors et complettant le recueil de tant d'autres où les opérations sinistres du contrôleur général étaient consignées." *Mémoires de l'abbé Terrai* ("à la Chancellerie," 1776), 265.

22. See Chapter 9 and the sources cited there.

23. See *The "Mémoires secrets" and the Culture of Publicity in Eighteenth-Century France*, ed. Bernadette Fort and Jeremy Popkin (Oxford, 1998), especially the essay by Pierre Rétat, "L'Anecdote dans les *Mémoires secrets*: Type d'information et mode d'écriture," 61–72.

24. Pierre Manuel, *La Bastille dévoilée, ou recueil de pièces authentiques pour servir à son histoire* (Paris, 1789), 7: 132.

25. Pierre Manuel, *La Police de Paris dévoilée* (Paris, 1790), 1: 218.

26. Ibid., 1: 212.

27. *La Bastille dévoilée*, 8: 50–51.

28. Bastille Papers, ms. 11683, Bibliothèque de l'Arsenal. This large dossier contains a good deal of information on Mairobert, who was described by a police agent (probably Joseph d'Hémery) in a note dated July 2, 1745, as "un jeune homme qui aimait à recueillir les vers courants, qui ne négligeait pas ceux qui étaient malins, les portait dans ces poches, et ne se faisait pas prier pour les réciter ou pour en laisser prendre copie. . . . Ses entretiens ordinaires se tenaient dans les cafés toujours garnis d'espions de police." In petitioning for an administrative post in 1762, Mairobert described himself as "sans fortune et réduit aux talents." He seems to have scraped together a living by various expedients, although he had contacts among the Parisian elite, worked for a while in the naval ministry, and even served as a royal censor. In reporting to the lieutenant general of police about Mairobert's imprisonment on July 2, 1749, commissioner Rochebrune noted that Mairobert's brother, a lawyer, had told the police that Mairobert had ceased to have anything to do with his family and did not want to pursue a career in the law or finance. Instead, he gave himself over to "le fol empressement qu'il avait d'avoir toutes les pièces fugitives et satyriques qui paraissent et de les distribuer par un principe de vanité et pour faire croire qu'il était en relation avec tous les auteurs." See the biographical notice in *Dictionnaire des journalistes*, 2: 787–89.

29. *La Bastille dévoilée*, 8: 19, 129.

30. Ibid., 8: 54.

31. Although I have never encountered a full description of a scene such as this, I have come across many accounts of café gossip and *nouvellistes* declaiming anecdotes. For a more exhaustive treatment of the interaction between oral and written exchanges, see my essay, "Public Opinion and Communication Networks in Eighteenth-Century Paris," *Opinion*, ed. Peter-Eckhard Knabe (Berlin, 2000), 149–230, which has been printed in book form as *Poesie und Polizei: Öffentliche Meinung und Kommunikationsnetzwerke im Paris des 18; Jahrhunderts* (Frankfurt am Main, 1996). Many of the eighteenth-century collections of anecdotal material are known as "chansonniers" because they concentrate on songs, although they often include prose anecdotes, and many scrapbook-type collections of ephemera contain all sorts of anecdotal snippets, sometimes copied neatly, sometimes pasted helter-skelter on pages. Systematic research in these sources would reveal a great deal about the communication of information under the Ancien Régime. There still is much to be gleaned from the collections in the manuscript department of the Bibliothèque nationale de France, notably mss. Fr. 12650, 12719 13659, 13662, 13694–95, 13699–712. The Bibliothèque de l'Arsenal has rich runs of similar documents, e.g., mss. 10029, 10169–70, 10319, 10819, 11544. And some of the richest material is located in the Bibliothèque historique de la ville de Paris, especially mss. 580, 625–36, 648–49, C.P. 4274–79, C.P. 4311–12, and N.A. 229.

32. *Vie privée de Louis XV, ou principaux événements, particularités et anecdotes de son règne* (London, 1781), vii.

33. Moufle was sent to the Bastille twice—in 1750 for collaborating on a libel, *Le Cannevas de la Pâris, ou mémoires pour servir à l'histoire de l'Hôtel de Roulle* (1750), and in 1781 for *Vie privée de Louis XV*. In each case he was released after a few days, no doubt owing to the intervention of protectors. Although he came from a fairly wealthy

family, he seems to have sunken into poverty after he lost his job in the naval ministry in 1760. See *La Bastille dévoilée,* 8: 49–54; the police report on Moufle in Bibliothèque nationale de France, n.a.f., ms. 10782; and *Dictionnaire des journalistes,* 2: 733–35. The *Mémoires secrets* do not cover the period before 1762, so Moufle could not draw on them for the first two volumes of *Vie privée,* which carry the story of the reign up to 1754. The last two volumes contain many passages that appear in the *Mémoires secrets* and in other works Moufle wrote in collaboration with Mairobert, notably *Journal historique de la révolution opérée dans la constitution de la monarchie française par le chancelier de Maupeou* (London, 1774–76), 7 vols. Moufle may have had a hand in three other works normally attributed to Mairobert: *Maupeouana ou correspondence secrète et familière du chancelier de Maupeou avec Sorhouet* (London, 1771), 2 vols.; *L'Observateur anglais ou correspondence secrète entre milord All'eye et milord All'ear* (London, 1777–78), 2 vols.; and *Anecdotes sur Mme la comtesse du Barry.* In fact, Moufle and Mairobert collaborated so extensively that it is impossible to know who wrote what.

34. For Moufle's general comments on history, which he described as a cycle of analogous occurrences, see *Vie privée de Louis XV,* 1: 30.

35. See ibid., 1: 82, 199, as examples of Moufle's technique of casting the reader in the role of a "lecteur philosophe," who should reflect on the general significance of events. When he cited the French philosophes, Moufle favored Voltaire, but he also referred to Montesquieu, Helvétius, and Raynal. Although he never mentioned Rousseau by name, he invoked the concept of a "contrat social" (1: 5).

36. Ibid., 2: 224. See the similar remarks on philosophy: 1: 168, 2: 315, 4: 114, 203–4.

37. See, for example, ibid., 1: 4–5, 2:46, 95, 4: 66, 95, 172, 232.

38. Ibid., 1: 128.

39. See, for example, ibid., 4: 172, 204, 224, 231.

40. Ibid., 1: vii.

41. Ibid., 1: vi.

42. Ibid., 3: 205.

43. Ibid., 1: 1. In other passages Moufle attributed anecdotes to "une relation manuscrite" (3: 116–17, 138) and to "un mémoire manuscrit curieux" (3: 138).

44. Bibliothèque nationale de France, n.a.f., ms. 10783. On the authorship of *Mémoires secrets pour servir à l'histoire de Perse,* see the entry on it in Antoine-Alexandre Barbier, *Dictionnaire des ouvrages anonymes, troisième édition, revue et augmentée par MM. Olivier Barbier, René et Paul Billard* (Paris, 1872–79), 3: 244–46, and the remarks in the previous chapter, note 27. See also the reference to Pecquet in *Vie privée de Louis XV,* 2: 41.

45. Compare *Vie privée de Louis XV,* 2: 14–15, and *Mémoires secrets pour servir à l'histoire de Perse* (Amsterdam, 1745; Berlin, 1759), 100–101.

46. *Vie privée de Louis XV,* 1: 52.

47. Ibid., 2: 62.

48. Ibid., 2: 300.

49. Voltaire later incorporated his *Histoire de la guerre de 1741* in his *Précis du siècle de Louis XV* (1770), which extended the narrative to the end of the 1760s, but the *Précis* was even more incompatible with Moufle's views. So in discussing the later years of the reign, Moufle avoided it and relied on more radical works such as *Anecdotes sur Mme la comtesse du Barry* and *Mémoires de l'abbé Terray.*

50. For example, after copying its account of the king's seduction by Mme de

Mailly, he added a note (*Vie privée de Louis XV*, 2: 30): "Voyez *Les Amours de Zéokini-zul, roi des Kofirans, ouvrage traduit de l'arabe, du voyageur Krinelbol*, un de ces écrits obscurs et licencieux, dont il faut se défier cependant, et que nous n'adoptons qu'au-tant que les faits se rapportent avec les manuscrits plus authentiques que nous avons sous les yeux, ou avec le récit des courtisans contemporains."

51. Ibid., 2: 220. See the similar remark on the equally apocryphal *Mémoires de Madame la marquise de Pompadour*, 2: 359.

52. Ibid., 2: 112, and *Journal historique, ou fastes du règne de Louis XV, surnommé le Bien-aimé* (Paris, 1766), 2: 2.

53. *Les Fastes de Louis XV, de ses ministres, maîtresses, généraux, et autres notables personnages de son règne* ("à Ville-Franche, chez la Veuve Liberté," 1782), xiv. A similar avowal about lifting anecdotes occurs in *Anecdotes du règne de Louis XVI, contenant tout ce qui concerne ce monarque, sa famille et la reine* (1776; Paris, 1791), 1: ix: "J'ai recueilli les anecdotes les plus intéressantes éparses dans plusieurs ouvrages très rares."

54. *Les Fastes de Louis XV*, 1: 122–23; *Vie privée de Louis XV*, 2: 34–35; *Mémoires secrets pour servir à l'histoire de Perse*, 76–78.

55. *Mémoires secrets*, December 19, 1784: "Les bonnes choses qu'on y trouve sont des lambeaux pillés de l'*Espion anglais*, des *Mémoires secrets*, des *Mémoires de l'abbé Terray*, de la *Gazette littéraire de l'Europe*, etc."

56. *Correspondance littéraire secrète*, March 7, 1781. The reviewer identified the author of the book as "M. Mouffle de Georville" (modified but incorrectly to "d'Am-erville" in a follow-up notice of March 14) and noted that he had been imprisoned in the Bastille for his audacity. Despite some criticism, the review was quite favorable: "Le style m'en a paru négligé, mais l'ouvrage n'en est peut-être pas moins curieux. . . . L'histoire des maîtresses de Louis XV se lit aussi avec tous ses détails."

57. I ranked them 32nd and 39th of the 720 forbidden works whose diffusion I studied in *The Corpus of Clandestine Literature*.

58. Other works alluded to the same incidents and followed the same story line but did not recount the anecdotes in full with the punch-line quotations at the end of them. For example, *Mémoires de Louis XV, roi de France et de Navarre* (Rotterdam, 1775) conforms closely in its narrative and its general message to *Vie privée de Louis XV*, but it did not lift material from earlier publications.

Chapter 23. Portraits

1. *Mémoires secrets pour servir à l'histoire de Perse* (Amsterdam, 1745; Berlin, 1759), 31, and *Vie privée de Louis XV, ou principaux événements, particularités et anecdotes de son règne* (London, 1781), 1: 42.

2. Bibliothèque nationale de France, ms. fr. 12650, p. 147.

3. *The Debaucht Court: Or, the Lives of the Emperor Justinian and His Empress Theodora* (London, 1682), 42–45. The anonymous author of this translation identified the work on p. 1 as "The Secret History of Procopius."

4. *Vie privée de Louis XV*, 1: vi.

5. *Correspondance littéraire secrète* (n.p., n.d.), March 1, 1781 (unpaginated).

6. Ibid., September 21, 1784. In a review of *Les Portraits, ou dialogues entre un peintre et un poète*, January 14, 1781, the author also emphasized the importance of ver-

500 Notes to Pages 303–306

bal portraits and quoted some at length. He quoted anecdotes in the same manner, in order to satisfy "les amateurs d'*anecdotes toutes fraîches*" (November 14, 1781).

7. Louis Sébastien Mercier, *Tableau de Paris*, ed. Jean-Claude Bonnet (Paris, 1994, reprint of the successive editions from 1781–87), 1: 154.

8. It is impossible to estimate the number of Frenchmen who saw official portraits of Louis XV. Paintings and busts were copied, and Parisians could see them in the biannual salons (exhibitions in the Louvre), which attracted a large public in the second half of the eighteenth century. See Thomas E. Crow, *Painters and the Public in Eighteenth-Century Paris* (New Haven, Conn., 1985), and Willibal Sauerländer, *Ein Versuch über die Gesichter Houdons* (Munich, 2003). But the diffusion of images of Louis XV seems to have been trivial compared with the propaganda campaigns that spread the iconography attached to Louis XIV. See Louis Marin, *Le Portrait du roi* (Paris, 1981), and Peter Burke, *The Fabrication of Louis XIV* (New Haven, Conn., 1994). On the alienation of Louis XV from the Parisians, see Arlette Farge, *Dire et mal dire: L'opinion publique au XVIIIᵉ siècle* (Paris, 1992).

9. Colin Jones aptly emphasizes legginess as an aspect of the representation of kings, especially Louis XIV, who was admired for his dancing. See his *The Great Nation: France from Louis XV to Napoleon, 1715–99* (New York, 2002), 1–2.

10. The distinction between Louis as a quite amiable, ordinary person and Louis as an incompetent king is a major theme of *Vie privée de Louis XV*, emphasized from the very beginning (1: 2): "Qui de nous n'a pas entendu dire à ses serviteurs, à ses familiers, à ses ministres: 'Que le roi n'est-il né parmi nous! Il serait le particulier le plus aimable, le meilleur mari, le meilleur père, le plus honnête homme de son royaume.'"

11. *Le Gazetier cuirassé, ou Anecdotes scandaleuses de la cour de France* (1771), 126–34, and *La Gazette noire par un homme qui n'est pas blanc, ou oeuvres posthumes du Gazetier cuirassé* (1784), 130–69. Although most of *La Gazette noire* was plagiarized from other libels, I think its first part was written by Pelleport. Its author could not have been Morande, who had renounced libeling and had begun working secretly for the Paris police by 1784.

12. As examples of the frothier variety, see the sketches scattered through *chroniques scandaleuses* such as *Le Chroniqueur désoeuvré, ou l'espion du boulevard du Temple* (London, 1781–83), 2 vols.; *Le Vol plus haut, ou l'espion des principaux théâtres de la capitale* ("Memphis, chez Sincère, réfugié au puits de la vérité," 1784); *Correspondance de Mme Gourdan* (1783); and *Portefeuille d'un talon rouge* (Paris, 178*). *Le Chroniqueur désoeuvré* contains some teasing hints about the identity of its author in the preface to volume 2: "Je me fais appeler M. de P et trois étoiles" (2: 6). If each star in "M. de P * * *" represented a syllable of the author's name, he could have been "de Pel-le-port." The radical tone of the first part of the book corresponds to that in other works by Pelleport, which include similar hints about his identity.

13. Mercier, *Tableau de Paris*, 1: 159.

14. Pierre Manuel, *La Police de Paris dévoilée* (Paris, 1790), 1: 224.

15. *Mémoires secrets*, April 30, 1774.

16. See, for example, *La Police de Paris dévoilée*, 1: 111.

17. Abbé Guiroy to an unspecified official in the Direction de la librairie, October 25, 1751, Bibliothèque nationale de France, Collection Anisson-Duperron, ms. fr. 22137.

18. Report by a censor named Rousselet, October 30, 1751, ibid., ms. fr. 22139.

19. Report by a censor named Simon, February 23, 1752, ibid., ms. Fr. 22139: "Le tout est susceptible d'allégories fines et délicates sous des noms saints, qui peuvent avoir des applications malignes à la cour, raisons pour lesquelles je crois qu'il serait dangereux d'en permettre l'impression dans ce royaume, même avec permission tacite, et ce pour ne point être exposé à des reproches et réprimandes à cause des différentes applications qu'on en peut faire." See also the similar remarks in a report by another censor, Morin, July 31, 1761, ibid., ms. fr. 22150. "Applications" was a term commonly used in reference to hidden allusions to a public figure. See, for example, *Le Gazetier cuirassé*, 92.

20. Undated letter from a censor named de La Haye to Chrétien-Guillaume de Lamoignon de Malesherbes, ibid., ms. fr. 22138.

21. Undated report by a censor named Mercier, ibid., ms. fr. 22152.

22. Chrétien-Guillaume de Lamoignon de Malesherbes, *Mémoires sur la librairie: Mémoire sur la liberté de la presse*, ed. Roger Chartier (original text dates from 1759; Paris, 1994), 101. Malesherbes, who belonged to the world of *les grands* himself, addressed his *Mémoires* to his father, the Chancellor, and made the social inferiority of the censors clear in explaining the need to allow for their limitations in devising a workable policy. See his remarks on the censors on pp. 58, 91–93, 101–2, 206.

23. *La Bastille dévoilée, ou recueil de pièces authentiques pour servir à son histoire* (Paris, 1789), 7: 13. This remark was too ironical to be taken literally, but it illustrated the primary concern of the police: to protect the reputation of important individuals rather than to enforce the respect for general principles.

24. Rességuier letter, apparently to the governor of the Bastille, December 16, 1750, Bibliothèque de l'Arsenal, ms. 11733.

25. Ibid. The pages of the novel are covered with notes by the police and are interspersed with handwritten pages that the police copied from Rességuier's manuscript, which also is included in the dossier. For more details on this and a similar affair—a roman à clef entitled *Tanastès*, which also contained libelous "applications"—see my essay, "Mlle Bonafon and the Private Life of Louis XV: Communication Circuits in Eighteenth-Century France," *Representations* (Summer 2004), 102–24.

26. The following discussion is based on the large literature on Aretino and the Renaissance, notably Bertrand Levergeois, *L'Arétin ou l'insolence du plaisir* (Paris, 1999), and Thomas Caldecott Chubb, *Aretino: Scourge of Princes* (New York, 1940). For discussions of publishing and politics in the late Renaissance, see Brian Richardson, *Printing, Writers and Readers in Renaissance Italy* (Cambridge, 1999), and Laurie Nussdorfer, *Civic Politics in the Rome of Urban VIII* (Princeton, N.J., 1992). On the revealing case of Aretino's would-be successor, Ferrante Pallavicino, see Francesco Urbinati, *Ferrante Pallavicino: Il flagello dei Barbarini* (Rome, 2004); and on the parallel case of "anecdotes" and the secret history of Florence, see Harald Hendrix, "Firenze segreta: L'aneddoto nella prosa storiografica del seicento," in *Studi di teoria e storia letteraria in onore di Pieter de Meijer*, ed. Dina Aristodemo, Costantino Maeder, and Ronald de Rooy (Florence, 1996), 351–62. I am grateful to Harald Hendrix for guidance through this literature.

27. Although Aretino mentioned his name in some of the sonnets, their attribution remains uncertain in several cases. See Vittorio Rossi, *Pasquinate di Pietro Aretino ed anonime per il conclave e l'elezione di Adriano VI* (Palermo and Turin, 1891). I have used the modern edition: *Sonetti lussuriosi e pasquinate* (Rome, 1980).

28. Aretino to Vassallo, December 1552, *The Letters of Pietro Aretino*, ed. Thomas Caldecott Chubb (New Haven, Conn., 1967), 304.

29. *The Autobiography of Benvenuto Cellini*, trans. George Bull (London, 1956), 364–67.

30. Bénigne Dujardin, *La Vie de Pierre Aretin par M. de Boispréaux* (The Hague, 1750). Dujardin used Boispréaux as a pseudonym. He produced a well-informed and balanced interpretation of Aretino's life and works, drawing heavily on the *Lettere*. Aretino appears in the text (iii) as "un homme à qui l'éloge et la satire donnent deux visages. . . . Si j'interroge ses partisans, c'est un poète divin, le fléau des princes, le censeur du monde. Si je consulte ses ennemis, je ne trouve qu'un ignorant, un misérable écrivain dont l'impudence cynique et la causticité seules ont fait le mérite." For references to Aretino's role as a libeler and a hack who made a fortune by scandalmongering, see pp. 2, 32–54, 185, 229–30.

31. Voltaire to René Louis de Voyer de Paulmy, marquis d'Argenson, June 16, 1745, *The Complete Works of Voltaire*, ed. Theodore Besterman (Geneva, 1970), 93: 274. See also Voltaire to the marquis d'Argenson, October 19, 1745, ibid., 93: 312: "Je mets les princes à contribution comme l'Arétin, mais c'est avec des éloges."

32. *Année littéraire* (1786), 7: 234.

33. Frederick II to Voltaire, May 15, 1774, *Complete Works of Voltaire*, 124: 415.

34. Pelleport used this phrase in one of the voluminous notes he added to a tract by David Williams, which he translated as *Lettres sur la liberté politique, adressées à un membre de la Chambre des Communes d'Angleterre sur son élection au nombre des membres d'une association de comté; traduites de l'anglais par le R. P. de Roze-Croix, ex-Cordelier*, 2nd ed. (Liège, 1783–89), 84. In this case, it served as an allusion to the blackmailing operations of Morande.

35. *Chronique arétine, ou recherches pour servir à l'histoire des moeurs du dix-huitième siècle* ("à Caprée," 1789) reprinted in *Chroniques libertines*, ed. Jean Hervez (Paris, 1912), 167–218.

36. *Mémoires secrets*, August 31, 1778: "M. Linguet a d'autant plus de peine à se départir de son rôle d'Arétin moderne, qu'il l'a trouvé très lucrative l'année dernière, et qu'une année de son journal, tous frais faits, lui a rendu 50,000 l. nettes."

37. *Correspondance littéraire secrète*, September 14, 1784. The reviewer also described a pornographic work attributed to Mirabeau as a "manuel de l'Arétin" (September 28, 1784).

38. *L'Arretin* ("à Rome, aux dépens de la Congrégation de l'Index," 1763), 2: 35.

39. Ibid., 1: 95, 145, 148. Dulaurens also indicated the difficulties he faced as a hack writer by quoting Molière at the beginning of his book (1: xvi): "Si l'on peut pardonner l'essor d'un mauvais livre,/ Ce n'est qu'au malheureux qui compose pour vivre."

40. Ibid., 1: xlv.

41. It should be noted, however, that despite his fame as the Scourge of Princes, Aretino probably made more money from flattery and well-placed dedications than from outright blackmail.

42. *La Police de Paris dévoilée*, 1: 266–67.

43. *Le Gazetier cuirassé*, 150. Italics in the original.

44. Ibid., 155. The italics in the original were designed to make the "enigma" look like one of the puzzles in literary reviews such as the *Mercure*. Morande made Maupeou's identity clear in an accompanying footnote.

45. *Le Gazetier cuirassé*, 44–45.

Chapter 24. News

1. *Le Gazetier cuirassé, ou anecdotes scandaleuses de la cour de France* (1777, first ed., 1771), 14.

2. Pierre Manuel, *La Police de Paris dévoilée* (Paris, 1790), 1: 201. Jacques Peuchet, who knew the police of the Ancien Régime from the inside, stressed the same theme: "Le *Mercure* et la *Gazette de France* étaient soumis à la censure, et rien de ce qui pouvait blesser les gens en place n'y était toléré. La sécheresse était le principal caractère de ces feuilles." Peuchet, *Mémoires tirés des archives de la police de Paris, pour servir à l'histoire de la morale et de la police, depuis Louis XIV jusqu'à nos jours* (Paris, 1838), 3: 329. Peuchet described the proliferation of underground *nouvelles à la main* as a consequence of the lack of news in the official press.

3. This and the following discussion of English journalism is based on the rich research of many historians, notably Lucyle Werkmeister, *The London Daily Press, 1772–1792* (Omaha, 1963); Hannah Barker, *Newspapers, Politics, and Public Opinion in Late Eighteenth-Century England* (Oxford, 1998); Jeremy Black, *The English Press, 1621–1861* (Stroud, 2001); and Bob Clarke, *From Grub Street to Fleet Street: An Illustrated History of English Newspapers to 1899* (Aldershot, 2004). Estimates of literacy and readership involve a great deal of speculation. The historians of the London press agree that total sales of newspapers, including triweeklies and weeklies, came to 25,000 copies a day by 1788. If each copy was read by ten persons, a quarter of London's population regularly consulted a newspaper. That estimate may be too high, because many Londoners read more than one paper and many papers circulated widely outside London. However, Clarke (*From Grub Street to Fleet Street*, 15) claims that each copy could have reached forty persons, including the illiterate poor who listened to public readings in taverns and at street corners. Jeremy Black (*The English Press*, 104) estimates that each copy was read by twenty persons, making a total readership of 500,000. The estimate of ten readers per copy comes from a letter by Dennis O'Bryen to Edmund Burke in 1782, quoted by Barker (*Newspapers, Politics, and Public Opinion*, 23), who favors the more modest estimate of 250,000 total readers. Although most Londoners could read—the literacy rate was nearly total among small shopkeepers and craftsmen—few below the middle classes could squander 2 ½ pence or 3 pence a day to purchase their own paper. On paragraph men and paragraphs, see Johann Wilhelm von Archenholz, *A Picture of England* (London, 1789), 65, quoted in John Brewer, *A Sentimental Murder: Love and Madness in the Eighteenth Century* (London, 2004), 40; Barker, *Newspapers, Politics, and Public Opinion*, 44; and *Literary Liberty Considered; in a Letter to Henry Sampson Woodfall* (London, 1774), 16–17. I would like to thank Will Slauter for informing me of this source. As a remarkable study of the transmission of news, I would recommend his "News and Diplomacy in the Age of the American Revolution" (Ph.D. diss., Princeton University, 2007).

4. Werkmeister, *The London Daily Press*, 21.

5. Ibid., 80.

6. See Arthur H. Cash, *John Wilkes: The Scandalous Father of Civil Liberty* (New Haven, Conn., 2006), and John Brewer, *Party Ideology and Popular Politics at the Accession of George III* (Cambridge, 1976).

7. Brewer, *A Sentimental Murder*, chapter 4. See also John Brewer, "Personal Scandal and Politics in Eighteenth-Century England: Secrecy, Intimacy and the Interior

Self in the Public Sphere," in *Media and Political Culture in the Eighteenth Century*, ed. Marie-Christine Skuncke (Stockholm, 2005), 85–106. On the long-term history of scandal literature in England, see Adam Fox, *Oral and Literate Culture in England, 1500–1700* (Oxford, 2000); Alastair Bellany, *The Politics of Court Scandal in Early Modern England: News Culture and the Overbury Affair, 1603–1660* (Cambridge, 2002); Harold Love, *English Clandestine Satire, 1660–1702* (Oxford, 2004); and Anna Clark, *Scandal: The Sexual Politics of the British Constitution* (Princeton, N.J., 2004).

8. This brief survey of the history of French journalism derives from a scholarly tradition that goes back to the excellent work of Eugène Hatin, *Histoire politique et littéraire de la presse en France* (Paris, 1859–61), 8 vols., and Franz Funck-Brentano and Paul Estrée, *Les Nouvellistes* (Paris, 1906). It draws on the more recent synthesis by Claude Bellanger et al., *Histoire générale de la presse française* (Paris, 1969), and it owes a great deal to current research inspired especially by Jean Sgard and Pierre Rétat, *Dictionnaire des journaux, 1600–1789*, ed. Jean Sgard (Oxford, 1991), 2 vols.; *Dictionnaire des journalistes, 1660–1789*, ed. Jean Sgard (Oxford, 1999), 2 vols.; *Les Gazettes européennes de langue française (XVIIᵉ–XVIIIᵉ siècles)*, ed. Henri Duranton, Claude Labrosse, and Pierre Rétat (Saint-Etienne, 1993); *"La Gazette d'Amsterdam": Miroir de l'Europe au XVIIIᵉ siècle*, ed. Pierre Rétat (Oxford, 2001); Gilles Feyel, *L'Annonce et la nouvelle: La presse d'information en France sous l'ancien régime (1630–1788)* (Oxford, 2000); Jack R. Censer, *The French Press in the Age of Enlightenment* (London, 1994); and Jeremy D. Popkin, *News and Politics in the Age of Revolution: Jean Luzac's "Gazette de Leyde"* (Ithaca, N.Y., 1989).

9. *Dictionnaire des journaux*, 1: 446.

10. For an overview of the growth of the press, see *Dictionnaire des journaux*, 2: 1131–40; Censer, *The French Press in the Age of Enlightenment*, 8; and Gilles Feyel, "La Diffusion des gazettes étrangères en France et la révolution postale des années 1750," in *Les Gazettes européennes de langue française*, 81–98.

11. See Suzanne Tucoo-Chala, *Charles-Joseph Panckoucke & la librairie française, 1736–1798* (Pau, 1977).

12. *Dictionnaire des journaux*, 2: 925.

13. Recent research on *nouvelles à la main* and *nouvellistes* has added a great deal to the basic work of Estrée and Funck-Brentano, *Les Nouvellistes*. See especially *De Bonne Main: La communication manuscrite au XVIIIᵉ siècle*, ed. François Moureau (Paris, 1993), and *Répertoire des nouvelles à la main: Dictionnaire de la presse manuscrite clandestine, XVIᵉ–XVIIIᵉ siècle*, ed. François Moureau (Oxford, 1999).

14. In his capacity as a spy, Mouhy provided the police with the fullest account of Mme Doublet's "bureau de nouvelles": see the documents reproduced by Pierre Manuel in *La Police de Paris dévoilée*, 2: 206–7, and the similar material in Jacques Peuchet, *Mémoires tirés des archives de la police*, 3: 329–37. See also the article on Mouhy in *Dictionnaire des journalists*, 2: 735–37, and *Répertoire des nouvelles à la main*, xxiv.

15. *La Police de Paris dévoilée*, 1: 327, 350, 358.

16. On Marin, see *Dictionnaire des journalistes*, 2: 684–85, and *Répertoire des nouvelles à la main*, 313.

17. *Le Gazetier cuirassé*, vi: "Il n'appartient pas à toutes les nations de dire ce qu'elles pensent: la Bastille, le paradis de Mahomet, et la Sibérie sont des arguments trop forts pour qu'on puisse leur rien répliquer. Mais il est un pays sage, où l'esprit peut profiter des libertés du corps et ne rien craindre de ses productions; c'est dans ce

pays où les grands ne sont que les égaux des moindres citoyens, où le prince est le premier observateur des lois, que l'on peut parler sans crainte de toutes les puissances de la terre, que le sage peut juger les extravagances et en rire, en donnant des leçons à l'humanité dont la barbarie d'un pouvoir injuste ne le punira pas." Morande's reference to Mohammed's paradise was a stock allusion to oriental despotism, as he made clear in a footnote (vi): "En France on enferme, en Turquie on étrangle, en Russie on exile dans les deserts; l'un revient à l'autre."

18. *La Gazette noire par un homme qui n'est pas blanc, ou oeuvres posthumes du Gazetier cuirassé* (1784, "imprimé à cent lieues de la Bastille, a trois cent lieues des Présides, à cinq cent lieues des Cordons, à mille lieues de la Sibérie"), 5. Paul Robiquet, in *Théveneau de Morande: Etude sur le XVIIIe siècle* (Paris, 1882), 92–93, 108–9, claims that Morande wrote this radical, anti-French libel, but that seems very unlikely because by 1784 Morande had become a secret agent of the French government. Various allusions—sallies against Capuchins, mockery of Vergennes, praise of Rousseau, the use of facetious dialogue, and Rabelasian touches—suggest that the anonymous author, at least of the first section, was Pelleport. The first section also includes some violent denunciations of French despotism, which sound like passages in Pelleport's *Les Bohémiens* and which invoke abstract political principles, including the normative view of law championed by Pufendorf. The last sections mainly contain bawdy anecdotes plagiarized from various *chroniques scandaleuses*.

19. *Le Diable dans un bénitier, et la metamorphose du Gazetier cuirassé en mouche* (Paris, 1784), 5–6.

20. *La Gazette noire*, 195.

21. Adhémar to Vergennes, October 27, 1783, Ministère des affaires étrangères, Correspondance politique, Angleterre, ms. 545.

22. Adhémar's dispatches to Vergennes in March and April 1784 are full of remarks about street agitation and electioneering. In reading them, one has the impression that a revolution was more likely to break out in London than in Paris.

23. Adhémar to Vergennes, December 7, 1784, Ministère des affaires étrangères, Correspondance politique, Angleterre, ms. 550.

24. Adhémar to Vergennes, December 17 and 27, 1784, ibid., ms. 550. I have been able to locate these articles in the *Morning Post* of December 11 and 13, 1784, and the *Public Advertiser* of December 17, 1784, but I have found nothing in the *Morning Herald*.

25. Adhémar to Vergennes, December 17, 1784, ibid., ms. 550.

26. Vergennes to Adhémar, December 27, 1784, ibid., ms. 550.

27. *La Mazarinade* in Paul Scarron, *Oeuvres* (Geneva, 1970; Slatkine reprint of the Paris 1786 edition), 1: 295. Personal invective among the mazarinades often took the form of satirical poems and broadsides, just as it did in seventeenth-century England. Lengthier works, printed as pamphlets or tracts, contained surprisingly little libelous material, as far as I can tell by sampling a few dozen of them. They tended to stress ideological issues, and they can be understood as moves in the complex maneuvers of warring factions. See Christian Jouhaud, *Mazarinades: La Fronde des mots* (Paris, 1985), and the selection of mazarinades—which admittedly emphasizes their ideological character—published by Hubert Carrier, *La Fronde: Contestation démocratique et misère paysanne; 52 mazarinades* (Paris, 1982), 2 vols.

28. The following discussion is based on the excellent essay by Gunnar von Proschwitz, "Courrier de l'Europe (1776–1792)," in *Dictionnaire des journaux, 1600–1789*,

ed. Jean Sgard (Oxford, 1991), 1: 267–93, and especially Gunnar von Proschwitz and Mavis von Proschwitz, *Beaumarchais et le "Courier de l'Europe": Documents inédits ou peu connus* (Oxford, 1990), 2 vols. There is also a great deal of information about *Le Courrier de l'Europe* in the memoirs of Brissot: J.-P. Brissot, *Mémoires (1754–1793)*, ed. Claude Perroud (Paris, 1910), 1: 302–97, and in *La Police de Paris dévoilée*, 2: 231–69. Following eighteenth-century usage, the journal's title was spelled as *Courier*. I have modernized it.

29. Brissot, *Mémoires (1754–1793)*, 1: 157.

30. Ibid., 1: 154–79.

31. This information about the staff and wages at the *Courrier de l'Europe* comes from Brissot's interrogations in the Bastille: Archives Nationales, Fonds Brissot 446 AP2. Brissot told the police that he had persuaded La Tour to hire Pelleport "pour travailler à différents articles de sa feuille" at a rate of one louis per week (interrogations of August 3 and 21, 1784).

32. Ibid., interrogation of August 21, 1784. On Saint-Flocel or Flozel, an obscure character whose connection with the *Journal de Bouillon* is unclear, see *Dictionnaire des journalists*, 2: 899; Hatin, *Histoire de la presse en France*, 3: 446–52; *La Police de Paris dévoilée*, 2: 246–47; and Brissot, *Mémoires (1754–1793)*, 1: 329.

33. Interrogation of August 21, 1784, Archives nationales, Fonds Brissot 446 AP2.

34. *La Police de Paris dévoilée*, 2: 248–49.

35. Von Proschwitz and von Proschwitz, *Beaumarchais et le "Courier de l'Europe,"* 2: 1014.

36. The following account is based on Brissot's *Mémoires (1754–1793)*, 1: 302–97; *J.-P. Brissot: Correspondance et papiers*, ed. Claude Perroud (Paris, 1911), 45–80; and Brissot's interrogations in the Bastille, Archives Nationales, Fonds Brissot 446 AP2.

37. Brissot, *Mémoires (1754–1793)*, 1: 377. For Brissot's remarks on translating, see 1: 348–49.

38. Ibid., 1: 378.

39. Interrogations of Brissot, August 3 and 21, 1784, Archives Nationales, Fonds Brissot 446 AP2. I have not been able to locate a copy of *Le Diable dans un ballon*, whose title echoed the most notorious libel by Pelleport, *Le Diable dans un bénitier*. Brissot later proposed a translation of Macaulay's history to Mirabeau, who farmed it out to various hack writers in his entourage. They eventually produced a five-volume work, which appeared after his death: *Histoire d'Angleterre, depuis l'avènement de Jacques I jusqu'à la révolution, par Catherine Macaulay Graham, traduite en français et augmentée d'un discours préliminaire, contenant un précis de l'histoire d'Angleterre jusqu'à l'avènement de Jacques I, et enrichie de notes par Mirabeau* (Paris, 1791–92). See Brissot, *Mémoires*, 1: 348–49.

40. David Williams (anonymously), *Letters on Political Liberty Addressed to a Member of the English House of Commons on His Being Chosen into the Committee of an Associating County* (London, 1782), 40. On the view, which was widespread among the Diggers of 1649 and later English radicals, that the "Norman yoke" had destroyed a variety of popular sovereignty in Anglo-Saxon England, see Christopher Hill, *Puritanism and Revolution: Studies in Interpretation of the English Revolution of the 17th Century* (London, 1958).

41. Williams, *Letters on Political Liberty*, 65.

42. By pretending to translate in the person of a priest—and a Rosecrucian mys-

tic, to boot—Pelleport adopted a burlesque identity, which served as a way to mock the religious foundation of the French monarchy. He also indulged in characteristic allusions to his own past, just as he did throughout *Les Bohémiens*, where he again referred to himself as the author of *Le Boulevard des Chartreux: Les Bohémiens* (Paris, 1790), 1: 129.

43. *Le Boulevard des Chartreux, poème Chrétien* ("à Grenoble, de l'Imprimerie de la Grande Chartreuse," 1779; call number 0.8254, Dauphinois), 21.

44. *Lettres sur la liberté politique, adressées à un membre de la Chambre des Communes d'Angleterre, sur son élection au nombre des membres d'une association de comté; traduites de l'anglais en français, par le R. P. de Roze-Croix, ex-Cordelier. Avec des notes de l'abbé Pacot, auteur de l'Histoire des Pays-Bas, théologien, Conseiller Autique, etc., etc.* ("seconde edition, imprimées à Liège aux depends de la Société, 1783–1789"), 47, 54, 72, 85, 101–2.

45. Ibid., 29.

46. Ibid., 3–4.

47. Ibid., 3.

48. During the interrogation of Brissot in the Bastille on August 21, 1784 (Archives nationales, Fonds Brissot, 446 AP2), the police tried to extract information on the *Lettres sur la liberté politique*, which they characterized as an "ouvrage plein de sarcasmes et d'injures contre le gouvernement de France, ses ministres, etc." Brissot denied having collaborated on it and claimed to have had nothing to do with its distribution, although Pelleport had shipped copies of it, along with two of Brissot's own works, to one of Brissot's key distributors in France: Chopin, a bookseller in Bar-le-Duc who dealt heavily in underground books. When pressed by his interrogators, Brissot admitted that he had advanced the money to Pelleport for the purchase of the manuscript on behalf of the publisher, Virchaux, a book dealer in Hamburg who specialized in illegal French literature and acted as Brissot's distributor in northern Europe. After printing the edition, Virchaux shipped a large proportion of it to Brissot in London. Brissot then turned the books over to a London bookseller named Walter; but they would not sell, so Walter returned them and Brissot finally left them with Pelleport. In the end, according to Brissot's testimony, he never recovered his advance for the manuscript because Virchaux went bankrupt.

49. *Lettres sur la liberté politique*, 25.

50. See Jean-Claude Hauc, *Ange Goudar: Un aventurier des Lumières* (Paris, 2004), and Pelleport's sketch of Goudar in *Le Diable dans un bénitier*, 62.

51. See the essay on Mettra, whose name was often spelled as Metra, in Sgard, *Dictionnaire des journalistes*, 2: 711–13.

52. See *Dictionnaire des journaux*, 1: 255–62. A close reading of issues of the *Correspondance littéraire secrète* from the 1780s (they have no continuous pagination and must be identified by their dates) indicates that it was well informed but very cautious about publishing anything that would offend the French government. As its title announced, it was primarily a literary review, and it was "secret" in the sense that it often discussed forbidden books—though always in a moderate tone. It was far less outspoken than the highly illegal *Mémoires secrets pour servir à l'histoire de la république des lettres en France*. In fact, on December 8, 1784, it condemned the libelous character of the *Mémoires secrets* in a critical review: "Ce recueil littéraire fournira de bons matériaux à l'histoire de ce siècle, mais il conviendrait de le purger d'une infinité de faits

calomnieux que ses différents auteurs ont adoptés avec une légereté bien condamnable."

53. The titles are given here as they appeared in the transcription of Brissot's interrogation of August 3, 1784, Fonds Brissot, Archives nationales 4465 AP2. Different versions of the same titles appeared throughout the correspondence between Vergennes and his agents in London, as recounted in Part 2. The first four probably were made up by the libelers and dangled before Receveur in the hope that he would bid for them. If he did, Pelleport and his collaborators could rapidly cobble together some copy and have it printed. There is no evidence that they were ever published.

54. Interrogation of August 3, 1784, Fonds Brissot, Archives nationales 4465 AP2. Chénon's questions indicated that the police wanted especially to locate the source of the "anecdotes" Mettra received from Versailles and recycled in his *gazette à la main*. Brissot's replies made it clear that he received two kinds of periodicals from Mettra, "l'une imprimée, l'autre à la main," and that the latter contained the "anecdotes."

55. Ibid.

56. Ibid. Brissot emphasized in the interrogation that he knew nothing about "les correspondants de Paris et de Versailles qui fournissent au sieur Mettra les matériaux de ses feuilles."

57. By inserting a hyphen in Bouillon, Pelleport conformed to English usage, which avoided spelling out proper names in full in order to fend off accusations of libel. Although the suicide incident took place at the end of 1778, Pelleport presented the text as if it were a long letter and dated it May 30, 1782.

58. *La Gazette noire*, 169–203.

59. See *Les Petits Soupers et les nuits de l'Hôtel Bouill-n: Lettre de milord comte de ****** à milord ****** au sujet des récréations de M. de C-stri-s, ou de la danse de l'ours; anecdote singulière d'un cocher qui s'est pendu à l'Hôtel Bouill-n, le 31 décembre 1778 à l'occasion de la danse de l'ours* ("à Bouillon," 1783), 60.

60. Ibid., 93.

61. Ibid., 89.

62. Quoted in Brewer, *Party Ideology and Popular Politics*, 139.

Chapter 25. Revolutionary Metamorphoses

1. For example, on p. 29, it reprinted a pasquinade, "Le Prince chiffonnier" (the ragpicker prince), which mocked Orléans for rebuilding the Palais-Royal in order to make money by renting out rooms, a speculation unworthy of a prince. The poem ends with a pun, which dubbed "le prince chiffonnier" as "le prince locques à terre" (i.e., "locataire," a play on the archaic word "locques," meaning rags). This kind of wordplay, typical of light literature in the last years of the Ancien Régime, was anathema to the revolutionaries. The page numbers of citations will be given in the text henceforth. There is an excellent analysis of the literary techniques employed in the text and of its relation to the *Mémoires secrets pour servir à l'histoire de la république des lettres en France* in an unpublished essay, "La *Vie privée . . . du duc de Chartres* et les *Mémoires secrets*" by Olivier Ferret, whom I would like to thank for sending me a copy.

2. *L'Observateur anglais, ou correspondance secrète entre Milord All'Eye et Milord All'Ear* (London, 1777–78).

3. Antoine-Alexandre Barbier in *Dictionnaire des ouvrages anonymes* (Paris, 1872), 4: 968, attributes the book to Morande. Although that seems likely, its style suggests that it could have been written by Pelleport or perhaps by a group of collaborators from the colony of French expatriates in London after Pelleport's arrest in 1784.

4. The book's full title, *Vie de Louis-Philippe-Joseph, duc d'Orléans traduite de l'anglais par M.R.D.W.* ("à Londres, de l'imprimerie du Palais Saint-James, 1789"), suggests that, like the previous libel, it could have originated in London. In an "Avertissement," the anonymous author claimed to be an Englishman who had become intimately acquainted with Orléans as a companion of his debauchery in London and Paris. But in the body of the text he dropped that pretense and addressed the reader as one, plainspoken patriot talking to another. The crude character of the narrative has no similarity to the more sophisticated tone of the pre-revolutionary London libels.

5. Despite his protests about the outrageous price of bread, he noted: "Le peuple est partout un animal que l'on conduit en lui donnant du pain" (46).

6. *Vie de Louis-Philippe-Joseph, duc d'Orléans*, 21.

Chapter 26. Sex and Politics

1. According to a variety of political theology that went back to the Middle Ages, the king of France combined in his sacred person two bodies, that of his individual self, which perished at his death, and that of the monarchy, which never died. He therefore incorporated the public and the private. By exposing his private life and treating him as an ordinary mortal, libels disrupted this ancient view and desacralized the monarchy. They never referred to the concept of the king's two bodies, and it is not possible to know the extent to which that notion persisted into the eighteenth century. But it belonged to the cultural background that libels exploited in order to produce shocking effects. On the long-term view of the king's body as an element in royal ideology, see Ernst H. Kantorowicz, *The King's Two Bodies: A Study in Medieval Political Theology* (1957; Princeton, N.J., 1997); Ralph E. Giesey, *The Royal Funeral Ceremony in Renaissance France* (Geneva, 1960); and Sarah Hanley, *The Lit de Justice of the Kings of France: Constitutional Ideology in Legend, Ritual, and Discourse* (Princeton, N.J., 1983).

2. The following account is based on the edition prepared by Roger Duchêne, which includes the text of Bussy's interrogation in the Bastille and other relevant documents as well as a full introduction and set of notes: Roger de Bussy-Rabutin, *Histoire amoureuse des Gaules* (Paris, 1993).

3. The sequence of the pseudo-Bussy works is difficult to establish because most of them carried no date of publication and named only the notoriously fictitious printer, "Pierre Marteau" of Cologne, on their title pages. For basic information on *La France galante, Histoire amoureuse des Gaules, Amours des dames illustres de notre siècle*, and *Histoire amoureuse de France*, see Antoine-Alexandre Barbier, *Dictionnaire des ouvrages anonymes* (Paris, 1872), 3: columns 639–41.

4. *Histoire amoureuse des Gaules*, 215.

5. According to the documents and commentary in the Duchêne edition of *Histoire amoureuse des Gaules*, it appears that Bussy's original version of his work, in con-

trast to the relatively innocent first edition of the *Histoire amoureuse des Gaules*, contained the "Alleluias," allegedly composed by Bussy and some libertine friends during a bachelor orgy that came to be known as "la débauche de Roissy." During the Easter holiday of 1659, they were said to have met in the village of Roissy, gorged themselves on meat and drink, committed sacrileges such as baptizing a pig, and improvised an obscene song about the most eminent personages in the kingdom. Each verse ended with an "Alleluia!" in parody of Easter rejoicing. The first verse made fun of the king, and the nastiest one of all taunted Mazarin for his supposed affair with the Queen Mother (*Histoire amoureuse des Gaules*, 193). "Le Mazarin est bien lassé / De f. . . un c. . . si bas percé, / Qui sent si fort le faguena. / Alleluia!" This kind of scurrility echoed the grossest satire from the mazarinades. Bussy had rallied to Mazarin and the young king during the Fronde, but he was capable of mocking anyone; and if his authorship of such a poem could have been proven, he might have suffered a more serious punishment than the exile inflicted on him in 1659–60. What provoked Louis's anger in 1665 was the circulation of a text that was more disrespectful of the royal family than the text Bussy claimed to have written and that was the first to appear in print.

6. Ibid., 236, and Marie de Rabutin-Chantal, marquise de Sévigné to Bussy-Rabutin, July 26, 1668, in Mme de Sévigné, *Correspondence,* ed. Roger Duchêne (Paris, 1972), 1: 93.

7. In studying *La France galante, ou histoires amoureuses de la cour* ("Cologne, Pierre Marteau," undated), I have relied on the edition in the Bibliothèque nationale de France, Lb37.3934D, which I have compared with five other editions also catalogued under Lb37.3934. All of them bear the address of Pierre Marteau, and four have dates: 1688, 1695, 1696, and 1709.

8. The text communicates this message most effectively by means of anecdotes, but it also makes it explicit: "Le Grand Alcandre, tout élevé qu'il était par dessus les autres hommes, n'était point d'un autre humeur ni d'un autre tempérament que les hommes du commun" (*La France galante*, 4).

9. The initials stand for M. le comte de Rochefort, as in *Mémoires de M. L. C. D. R.* (1687) by Gatien de Courtilz de Sandras. See Barbier, *Dictionnaire des ouvrages anonymes*, 3: column 204.

10. *Les Amours de Zéokinizul* was printed with its sequel, *L'Asiatique tolérant*, in Crébillon's complete works in 1779, but it does not appear in Barbier's *Dictionnaire des anonymes*, and Crébillon's authorship of it is not accepted in standard works such as *Dictionnaire des lettres françaises: Le XVIIIᵉ siècle*, ed. François Moureau (Paris, 1995), 370. The edition used in the following discussion comes from *Oeuvres complètes de Monsieur de Crébillon, fils* (London, 1779), vol. 12. The first full-length libel about the sex life of Louis XV, *Tanastès*, appeared in August 1745, a year earlier than *Les Amours de Zéokinizul*, but it was a roman à clef in the form of a fairy tale and did not conform to the genre of a "private life." See my study of it and the related literature from the 1740s: "Mlle Bonafon et la vie privée de Louis XV," *Dix-huitième siècle*, no. 35 (2003), 369–91.

11. See also the remarks about kings in general and Louis XIII and Louis XIV in particular on p. 3: "Mais ils travaillent depuis plusieurs siècles à établir le pouvoir arbitraire, et les deux derniers surtout ont frappé de grands coups pour arriver à cet injuste but."

Chapter 27. Decadence and Despotism

1. Reports of inspector Joseph d'Hémery, Bibliothèque nationale de France, nouvelles acquisitions françaises, ms. 10781.

2. The author described her purpose as portraiture, reinforced by anecdotes: "Au reste, on se flatte [de] n'avoir omis aucun trait historique qui puisse servir à faire sortir le vrai caractère de Mme de Pompadour et à donner au lecteur une juste idée de cette fameuse personne. . . . Quant à la sûreté des anecdotes, on s'en rapporte hardiment à ceux qui sont au fait des particularités de sa vie." *L'Histoire de Madame la marquise de Pompadour traduite de l'anglais* ("Londres, aux dépens de S. Hooper, à la tête de César," 1759), 157.

3. Ibid., 132. "Elle prenait l'art de gouverner le roi pour celui de commander son royaume. . . . Les ministres les plus habiles, les plus grands généraux de l'armée étaient tous ou vilement soumis à ses ordres ou injustement sacrifiés à sa vanité et à sa vengeance."

4. Ibid., 178. "Elle joue la femme d'Etat. . . . Elle veut trancher du despote et donner à la machine politique le mouvement qui lui plaît. . . . Des conseils pleins de bassesse et toujours suivis; des changements faits sans rime ni raison; des ministres disgraciés, des généraux congédiés: voilà les tristes preuves qu'elle donne et de son pouvoir et de son vide de pénétration."

5. I have tried to relate antigovernment polemics to politics during the mid-century years in "Public Opinion and Communication Networks in Eighteenth-Century Paris," in *Opinion*, ed. Peter-Eckhard Knabe (Berlin, 2000), 149–230. An excellent study of the political and ideological context of the attacks on Mme de Pompadour is Thomas Kaiser, "Madame de Pompadour and the Theaters of Power," *French Historical Studies* 19 (Autumn 1996), 1025–44.

6. The following account of Montesquieu's political philosophy owes most to Robert Shackleton, *Montesquieu: A Critical Biography* (Oxford, 1961). In addition to Montesquieu's *De l'Esprit des lois*, it draws on his *Lettres persanes* and *Essai sur les causes qui peuvent affecter les esprits et les caractères*.

7. The most important works for identifying the authors of these and related publications are still the two nineteenth-century classics: Antoine-Alexandre Barbier, *Dictionnaire des ouvrages anonymes* (Paris, 1872) and Joseph-Marie Quérard, *Les Supercheries littéraires dévoilées* (Paris, 1869). On the demand for these anonymous tracts, see my *The Forbidden Best-Sellers of Pre-Revolutionary France* (New York, 1995) and its companion volume, *The Corpus of Clandestine Literature in France, 1769–1789* (New York, 1995).

8. The text used here, published under the address of London in 1775, has continuous pagination but is divided into two parts. Judging from a remark on p. 197, the first part was completed in 1772. Part 2 takes du Barry's biography up to her exile after the death of Louis XV.

9. As an example of Mairobert's use of "patriote" to characterize the opposition to the Maupeou government, see p. 268.

10. According to my calculations of the relative importance of the demand for illegal works, *Anecdotes sur Mme la comtesse du Barry* was second in the list of 720 books most ordered by booksellers and *Mémoires de l'abbé Terray* was ninth. See Darnton, *The Corpus of Clandestine Literature*, 194.

11. See, for example, Marcel Marion, *Histoire financière de France* (Paris, 1914); Michel Antoine, *Louis XV* (Paris, 1989), 943–49; and Alfred Cobban, *A History of Modern France* (Baltimore, 1963), 1: 94–97.

12. *Mémoires secrets pour servir à l'histoire de la république des lettres en France* (London, 1777–89), entry for June 10, 1776: "Le héro de l'ouvrage y est peint sous les couleurs les plus odieuses et les plus vraies. . . . Il l'emporte de beaucoup en horreurs et en atrocités sur ses prédécesseurs. . . . C'est un dernier coup porté à sa réputation par l'histoire des faits, qui la rend à jamais exécrable." This reaction is not surprising, since the *Mémoires secrets* expressed the views of the antigovernment forces generally known as patriots. But in emphasizing the convincing character of "différentes anecdotes" recounted in the book, the review suggested that to some readers, at least, the narrative seemed to be strictly factual.

13. See the entry on the book in Barbier, *Dictionnaire des ouvrages anonymes*, 4: 974.

14. On p. 347, *Vie privée du cardinal Dubois, premier minister, archevêque de Cambrai, etc.* ("à Londres," 1789) refers to d'Alembert, who died on October 29, 1783, as if he were still alive. Also, the "Avis des éditeurs" at the beginning of the book claimed that the manuscript on which it was based had come into the editors' possession sixty years after Dubois's death and that they were publishing it immediately. As the cardinal died in 1723, the reference suggests that they had planned to put the book out in 1783 but then delayed publication until 1789.

15. On the repression of 1783, see my *The Literary Underground of the Old Regime* (Cambridge, Mass., 1982), 191–95.

16. In the latest edition, which unfortunately includes only volume 3, the editor, Benedetta Craveri, attributes volumes 1 and 2 to Jean-Benjamin de La Borde, a wealthy tax farmer and friend of Richelieu, and she names Louis-François Faur, a secretary to Richelieu's son, as the probable author of volume 3: *Vie privée du maréchal de Richelieu*, ed. Benedetta Craveri (Paris, 1993), 30–31. This argument seems convincing and corresponds to the conclusions reached by earlier scholars, notably Olga Wormser in *Amours et intrigues du maréchal de Richelieu* (Paris, 1955). See also Olivier Ferret, "Paroles confondantes: L'exemple de la *Vie privée du maréchal de Richelieu*," an excellent, unpublished essay kindly communicated by the author. The quotations that follow come from the Paris 1791 edition.

17. The text frequently referred to key episodes as anecdotes. For example, after recounting some debauchery by the favorites of the Regent, it noted (1: 117), "Vingt anecdotes de ce genre pourraient prouver à quel point leurs moeurs étaient dissolues."

18. The review is reprinted in *Vie privée du maréchal de Richelieu*, ed. Benedetta Craveri, 187. See the similar review by Sébastien-Roch-Nicholas Chamfort in ibid., 188–90.

19. See, for example, the long footnote (3: 120) in which they praise the Revolution's abolition of aristocratic privilege.

Chapter 28. Royal Depravity

1. Maurice Tourneux, *Marie-Antoinette devant l'histoire: Essai bibliographique* (Paris, 1901). It is impossible to arrive at an exact figure because Tourneux listed works

that favored the queen as well as those that attacked her, and he classified them under rubrics that included books published after her death. The total number of publications from the eighteenth and nineteenth centuries listed in his bibliography comes to 459.

2. Jeanne-Louise-Henriette Campan, *Mémoires sur la vie de Marie-Antoinette reine de France et de Navarre* (1823; Paris, 1876). Many books and articles in the enormous literature on Marie-Antoinette emphasize the slanderous attacks on her. The best of them, *La Reine scélérate: Marie-Antoinette dans les pamphlets* (Paris, 1989) by Chantal Thomas, supersedes the older studies. There is little to be gleaned from the popular and inaccurate works of Henri d'Alméras, *Marie-Antoinette et les pamphlets royalistes et révolutionnnaires; avec une bibliographie de ces pamphlets: Les amoureux de la reine* (Paris, 1908) and Hector Fleischmann, *Marie-Antoinette libertine: Bibliographie critique et analytique des pamphlets politiques, galants, et obscènes contre la reine* (Paris, 1911). But there is much to be learned from more general interpretations such as Lynn Hunt, "The Many Bodies of Marie-Antoinette: Political Pornography and the Problem of the Feminine in the French Revolution," in *Eroticism and the Body Politic*, ed. Lynn Hunt (Baltimore, 1991); Antoine de Baecq, *Le Corps de l'histoire: Métaphore et politique (1770–1800)* (Paris, 1993); and Jacques Revel, "Marie-Antoinette dans ses fictions: La mise en scène de la haine," in *De Russie et d'ailleurs: Feux croisés sur l'histoire*, ed. Martine Godet (Paris, 1995), 23–38.

3. Campan, *Mémoires*, 95.

4. Ibid., 157.

5. Pierre Manuel, *La Police de Paris dévoilée* (Paris, 1790), 1: 38.

6. Tourneux, *Marie-Antoinette*, 38, and Jacques Peuchet, *Mémoires tirés des archives de la police de Paris, pour servir à l'histoire de la morale et de la police, depuis Louis XIV jusqu'à nos jours* (Paris, 1838), 3: 31. Peuchet attributed this libel to Beaumarchais, though without citing any evidence. He also claimed that a half-dozen Parisian wits and writers produced libels against the queen.

7. *Les Amours de Charlot et Toinette: Pièce dérobée à V. . . . .* (n.p., 1779), n.p., Bibliothèque nationale de France, Réserve, Enfer 592. This copy contains only photocopies of the copperplate engravings. Another copy, which is dated 1789 and is probably a reprint from the original, has a glossy print showing Lafayette taking an oath with his hand on Marie-Antoinette's genitalia: Bibliothèque nationale de France, Réserve, Enfer 593. A note in a modern hand at the bottom of the print says, "Dessin de Desrais, dont la gravure, maintenant inconnue, était destinée à l'ornement du poème des Amours de Charlot et Toinette."

8. The disabused hedonism of the verse and the connection with Boissière suggests it could have been written by Pelleport, but he did not settle in London until sometime late in 1782, and the contract to suppress *Les Amours de Charlot et Toinette* was signed by Boissière and Goesman on July 31, 1781. Moreover, that date seems oddly late in view of the fact that the title page of the booklet carried the date of 1779. The only explanation for this discrepancy that I can come up with is that the first edition could have been printed in 1779 and kept in stock while the libeler attempted to get the best terms in his blackmail negotiations.

9. Tourneux, *Marie-Antoinette*, 39–44. I have consulted the six editions in the Bibliothèque nationale de France catalogued as LB 39–73, Réserve 8-LB 39–73, and Réserve 8-LB 39–73 (A), (B), (C), (D), and (E). The following discussion of part 1

comes from a private copy entitled *Essais historiques sur la vie de Marie-Antoinette d'Autriche, reine de France; pour servir à l'histoire de cette princesse* ("à Londres, 1789").

10. The text refers to the fall of Necker, which occurred on May 19, 1781, and it notes that the queen was pregnant with her second child, who was born on November 9, 1781: *Essais historiques,* 69–71. The introduction stated on p. vii, "On a voulu racheter à tout prix un manuscrit intitulé *Les Passe-temps d'Antoinette.* Il est vraisemblable que c'est ce que nous donnons sous un titre nouveau."

11. See the critical reference to Orléans (at that time duc de Chartres), in *Essais historiques,* 10, and the note on p. 74 that corrects it with a flattering portrait of the duke: "Ce prince patriote et bon mari, bon père, bon ami; il est généreux, populaire, bienfaisant." The *Essais historiques* could have been part of the Orléanist propaganda produced after the fall of the Bastille.

12. Ibid., 74–75, 90.

13. See, for example, *Antoinette d'Autriche, ou dialogues entre Catherine de Médicis et Frédégonde reine de France, aux Enfers, pour servir de supplément et de suite à tout ce qui a paru sur la vie de cette princesse* (Paris, 1789).

14. See *Essais historiques,* 2–3, and the corrective note on p. 73: "Ces deux femmes ne supportent point le parallèle. L'une avait les faiblesses et la bonhomie d'une fille; l'autre a les ardeurs de Messaline et la cruauté de Frédégonde."

15. Ibid., v.

16. For example, after describing the king's acquiescence in his cuckolding, the libeler remarks, "Le nigaud de mari rentra dans son insouciance et sa nulleté" (*Essais historiques,* 26).

17. Ibid., 54.

18. For example: "Le Parisien accoûtumé à respecter la décence de la majesté et l'éclat qui doit environner ses maîtres, n'a pu voir sans indignation l'abus que cette favorite [Mme Jule] faisait d'un crédit si vilement acquis, ainsi que la profanation que la reine faisait d'elle-même" (*Essais historiques,* 53).

19. The passage that comes closest to a general comment on the meaning of the story goes as follows: "La cour de France est à present une pétaudière" (*Essais historiques,* 69).

20. Ibid., 71.

21. The following account comes from *Essai historique sur la vie de Marie-Antoinette, reine de France et de Navarre, née archiduchesse d'Autriche, le deux novembre 1755: Orné de son portrait, et rédigé sur plusieurs manuscrits de sa main; seconde partie* ("De l'an de la liberté française 1789; A Versailles chez la Montensier, Hôtel des courtisanes"), Bibliothèque nationale de France KB ex: 786 F4. The pages from which the quotations have been taken appear in parentheses in the text that follows.

22. The reference to Vulcan was a standard evocation of cuckoldry. The author made the point explicit on the following page: "Louis XVI sait qu'il est cocu, et il n'en caresse que davantage la malheureuse Bethsabée, qui fait la calamité de ce bel et vaste empire." "Mettre à l'épinette" is to fatten fowl in a wicker cage. Many of the remarks about Louis XVI read like propaganda for the Orléanist cause.

23. The full title of this libel indicated its affinity with many of the other "private lives" about the Bourbons: *Vie privée de Charles-Philippes* [*sic*] *de France, ci-devant comte d'Artois, frère du roi, et sa correspondance avec ses complices, ornée de son portrait, gravé d'après nature, pour servir de clef à la Révolution française et de suite aux vies de*

Marie-Antoinette d'Autriche, reine de France; de Louis-Philippes [sic] d'Orléans; de Louis-François-Joseph de Conti; de Louis-Joseph de Condé; de l'agioteur Necker, ci-devant directeur-général des finances; de Jean-Sylvain Bailly, maire de Paris; et du general Mottier, dit La Fayette, commandant-général des bleuets parisiens. The supposed place of publication, Turin, alluded to the refuge where the royalist émigré leaders were planning to overthrow the Revolution. Although they could be treated as pamphlets, most of these libels were sizable pseudo-biographies, usually about one hundred pages long.

24. See the similar episodes in the *Vie politique et privée de Louis-Joseph de Condé*, 58–59; *Vie privée de Charles-Philippes [sic] de France, ci-devant comte d'Artois*, 39–40; and *Vie privée ou apologie de très-sérénissime prince Monseigneur le duc de Chartres, contre un libel diffamatoire écrit en mil sept cent quatre-vingt-un; mais qui n'a point paru à cause des menaces que nous avons faites à l'auteur de le déceler* ("à cent lieues de la Bastlle," 1784), 60.

25. *Vie privée de Charles-Philippes [sic] de France, ci-devant comte d'Artois*, 48, and *Essai historique sur la vie de Marie-Antoinette*, 57.

26. Georges Lefebvre, *La Grande Peur de 1789* (Paris, 1932).

27. The similarity in the libels against the princes suggests that they could have been written by the same person and commissioned by the same source, but their styles are quite different. I have not found any information about their authors.

28. Tourneux, *Marie-Antoinette*, 46. The circular went on to explain that even if some details were inaccurate and even if they were taken literally, the misinformation would not have any ill effects because the royal family deserved the severest punishment for its attempts to destroy the Revolution by "le complot le plus affreux dont l'histoire nous a transmis le détail."

29. For example, the libeler cited an obscene epitaph, which he said suited the queen: "Ci-gît l'impudique Manon/ Qui, dans le ventre de sa mere,/ Savait si bien placer son c. . ./ Qu'elle f. . . . . avec son père" (1: 7).

30. Messalina, wife of the Emperor Claudius in the first century, was known for her voracious sexual appetite, and Frédégonde, consort of the Merovingian king Chilprec I in the sixth century, was renowned for her monstrous cruelty.

31. As an example of the change of voice, see *Essais historiques* (78): "Je fus diffamée par l'opinion publique" in comparison with *Vie privée libertine* (2: 48): "La reine n'en fut pas moins diffamée dans l'opinion publique." And as an example of plagiarism, see the descriptions of the controller general Calonne in *Essais historiques* (50): "une de ces sangsues publiques dont l'âme de boue, insensible aux cris de la douleur, se fasse un jeu de la misère" and in *Vie privée libertine* (2: 7): "cette impitoyable sangsue, cette âme de boue, insensible aux cris de la douleur et qui se faisait un jeu de la misère publique."

32. The inability of the text to conform to shifts in events shows clearly from a comparison of an earlier printing (Bibliothèque nationale de France, Enfer 793) with a later printing (Bibliothèque nationale de France, Enfer 792). The earlier version contains a five-page denunciation of Marat from the bottom half of page 57 to the bottom half of page 61. The later version eliminates the denunciation and adjusts the phrasing to hide the cut, but the compositor did not redo all the page numbers, which therefore jump from page 57 to page 62. Although the text remains essentially the same, the earlier version can be read as support for the Girondins at the beginning of the Convention and the later version as propaganda for their enemies, the Montagnards, in the

next phase, which led to the purging of the Girondins and the radicalization of the Terror. Curiously, the more moderate, earlier version is the one that looks like a cheap pamphlet, and the radical, later version has all the trappings of an elegant book.

33. Quoted in Frantz Funck-Brentano and Paul d'Estrée, *Les Nouvellistes* (Paris, 1905), 304.

34. Arthur Young, *Travels in France During the Years 1787, 1788 & 1789*, ed. Constantia Maxwell (Cambridge, 1950), 185.

35. Ibid., 189.

36. Ibid., 195.

37. Ibid., 209.

38. In Besançon on July 27, Young noted the "dreadful ignorance of the mass of the people": "At this eventful moment, with no licence, nor even the least restraint on the press, not one paper established at Paris for circulation in the provinces, with the necessary steps taken by *affiche*, or placard, to inform the people in all the towns of its establishment. For what the country knows to the contrary, their deputies are in the Bastille, instead of the Bastille being razed." Ibid., 189.

39. A study of the reception of the libels lies beyond the scope of this book, but the themes of the libels could easily be traced through newspapers, pamphlets, and speeches in revolutionary clubs. When Marie-Antoinette was tried before the Revolutionary Tribunal, the public prosecutor, Antoine Quentin Fouquier-Tinville, opened the case against her with the accusation that she had committed incest with her young son. That was standard fare in the libels against her, but apparently it seemed far-fetched to the public who attended the trial, despite their hostility to her. *Actes du Tribunal révolutionnaire*, ed. Gérard Walter (Paris, 1968), 96.

Chapter 29. Private Lives and Public Affairs

1. This theme appears frequently in Voltaire's correspondence when he is discussing his strategy for making the cause of Enlightenment triumph over its adversaries. See, for example, Voltaire to d'Alembert, May 21, 1760, *Voltaire's Correspondence*, ed. Theodore Besterman (Geneva, 1958), 41: 55; Voltaire to d'Alembert, May 31, 1760, ibid., 78; and d'Alembert to Voltaire, September 6, 1760, ibid., 43: 96.

2. As examples of work on laughter in the eighteenth century, see *Dix-Huitième Siècle: Le Rire*, no. 32 (2000), and the excellent study by Antoine de Baecque, *Les Eclats du rire: La culture des rieurs au XVIIIᵉ siècle* (Paris, 2000).

3. The main sources for locating "vies privées" and "vies secrètes" were the catalogue of the Bibliothèque nationale de France; André Martin and Gérard Walter, *Catalogue de l'histoire de la Révolution française* (Paris, 1936–55), 5 vols.; and Maurice Tourneux, *Bibliographie de l'histoire de Paris pendant la Révolution française* (Paris, 1890–1913), 5 vols. Five private lives, grouped together as short biographies, appeared in *Vie privée des cinq membres du Directoire, ou les puissants tels qu'ils sont* (Paris, 1795). All the others were separate books or pamphlets. The *Histoire de deux célèbres législateurs du dix-huitième siècle, contenant plusieurs anecdotes curieuses et intéressantes* (n.p., n.d.) merely contained reprinted versions of the lives of Pétion and Manuel, which had been published separately. The group LIRE at the Université Lumière Lyon 2 led by Olivier Ferret, A.-M. Mercier-Faivre, and Chantal Thomas is currently preparing a

"Dictionnaire des Vies privées," which will survey the genre from 1789 until well into the nineteenth century, concentrating on the Napoleonic period. I had the opportunity to present my research to that group in 2001 and look forward to the publication of its findings, which should be definitive.

4. "Avis" at the beginning of *Vie sans-pareille, politique et scandaleuse du sangui-naire CARRIER, ex-député à la Convention nationale et envoyé en qualité de représentant du peuple à Nantes, théâtre de ses fureurs, suivie de quelques anecdotes secrètes sur ses complices* ("à Paris, chez Prévost, ci-devant rue Jacques, présentement rue de la Vieille-Bouclerie, vis-à-vis Mâcon, An III de la République française"). See also Prévost's "avis" at the beginning of *Vie criminelle et politique de J.P. Marat, se disant l'Ami du people, adoré, porté en triomphe comme tel, et après sa mort projeté saint par la Jacobi-naille, ou l'homme aux 200,000 têtes, le vampire le plus remarquable de la République française* (Paris, [1795]).

5. *Vie politique de Jérôme Pétion, ci-devant maire de Paris, ex-député à la Conven-tion-nationale et traître à la République française,* (n.p., [1793]), preliminary discourse, unpaginated.

6. *Vie publique et privée de M. le marquis de La Fayette, avec des détails sur l'affaire du 6 octobre, etc.* (n.p., [1791]), 4.

7. Ibid., 52–60. The author asserted that he had uncovered "les ressorts secrets qui le font agir" (4).

8. For example, the authors of *Vie privée et ministérielle de M. Necker, Directeur général des finances, par un citoyen* ("à Genève, chez Pellet, imprimeur, rue des Belles-Filles," 1790), described themselves as "historiens impartiaux. . . . Les faits parleront" (5). But they did not bother much about facts from the period after 1789. Instead, as they emphasized in a preface, "Nous ferons précéder nos observations particulières de notes authentiques sur sa vie privée avant son association à la banque, et afin de rendre cet ouvrage plus piquant, nous le semerons de quelques anecdotes qui ne sont connues que de fort peu de gens" (5–6).

9. *Vie secrète, politique et curieuse de M. J. Maximilien Robespierre, député à l'As-semblée constituante en 1789, et à la Convention nationale jusqu'au 9 thermidor l'an deu-xième de la république, veille de son exécution et de celle de ses complices: Suivie de plusieurs anecdotes sur cette conspiration sans pareille* ("à Paris, chez Prévost, rue Jac-ques, près de la fontaine Séverin, no. 195, An II de la République française"), 23.

10. Ibid., 35.

11. *Vie privée et ministérielle de M. Necker* is attributed in the catalogue of the Bibliothèque nationale de France to Jean-Jacques Rutledge, a hack writer who became a militant partisan of Marat and Hébert. It refers to Rutledge's imprisonment for pro-moting protests against the price of bread in the winter of 1789–90. Judging from its discussion of polemics over the Caisse d'Escompte, it was written in March 1790. As examples of Rutledge's violent rhetoric about Necker's "affreuse conspiration," see pp. 60–64, which concludes with a warning that if the National Assembly fails to limit the power of the king, "Dès ce moment, il [the king] peut disposer de la liberté, de la sûreté, de la fortune, de la vie des citoyens; les décrets de l'Assemblée Nationale seront anéantis, et il ne restera à la nation d'autre fruits de ses longs et pénibles efforts, de ses combats, de ses victoires, que la cruelle nécessité d'obéir en esclave, de gémir en silence et d'être livrée à ses tyrans."

12. In a passage typical of the left-wing libels and their favorite metaphors, the author described the Jacobin Club as the key agency in the revolutionary mission of unmasking: "La Société des Jacobins, prévoyante autant que juste, accueille tout le monde, mais l'hypocrite dans ce séjour sacré, laisse bientôt tomber son masque, les passions y sont bientôt découvertes, des yeux perçants lisent dans le coeur de l'homme corrompu; alors on le chasse, et le perverti devient l'objet de la haine et du mépris public": *Vie secrète et politique de Brissot* (1793), 42. And typically the unmasking exposed financial rather than sexual corruption (40): "Les Jacobins . . . ont perdu ces hommes pervers qui, ne voulant que faire leur fortune ou trouver les moyens de rétablir leurs affaires délabrées sans avoir le moindre amour pour la patrie, avaient pris le masque patriotique. La société populaire le leur arracha, et Brissot et ses semblables sont restés avec leur face hideuse."

13. The *Vie publique et privée de Honoré-Gabriel Riquetti, comte de Mirabeau* claimed that Mirabeau fornicated with Théroigne on the eve of October 5, 1789, then instructed her on how to foment agitation in Paris. Its description of her during the most violent moment of the *journées* is loaded with sexual metaphors: "C'est cette prostituée qui, habillée en amazone, panachée et à cheval, conduisait la bande des femmes. C'est elle qui porta la lance ensanglantée dans les draps de la reine et qui l'y plongea à plusieurs reprises" (89).

14. On the conspiratorial mentality of the revolutionaries, see Richard Cobb, "The Revolutionary Mentality in France," in *A Second Identity: Essays on France and French History* (Oxford, 1969), and Cobb, *The Police and the People: French Popular Protest, 1789–1820* (Oxford, 1970).

15. The concept was formulated most cogently by Jürgen Habermas in *The Transformation of the Public Sphere: An Inquiry into a Category of Bourgeois Society* (Cambridge, Mass., 1991; original German edition, 1962), although it can be traced back to Alexis de Tocqueville, *The Old Regime and the French Revolution* (New York, 1955; original French edition, 1856). For a perceptive discussion of Habermas's theory among current sociologists and historians, see *Habermas and the Public Sphere*, ed. Craig Calhoun (Cambridge, Mass., 1992).

16. On denunciation as an ingredient of the Revolution from its very beginning, see Colin Lucas, "The Theory and Practice of Denunciation in the French Revolution," *Journal of Modern History* 68 (1996), 768–85.

Conclusion

1. See Jeffrey W. Merrick, *The Desacralization of the French Monarchy in the Eighteenth Century* (Baton Rouge, 1990).

Index

Acknowledgments

This book began as the A. S. W. Rosenbach Lectures in Bibliography at the University of Pennsylvania in 2005. It was an honor to give those lectures, and I am grateful for the helpful discussions that accompanied them. But instead of reworking their text as a short book, I decided to draw upon research I had conducted over many years and to write a full-scale study of libelers and libel literature. The starting point went back to my first encounter with Charles Théveneau de Morande in the archives of the Ministry of Foreign Affairs at the Quai d'Orsay in the mid-1960s. Since then, I received funding for many research trips and sabbatical leaves from Princeton University. I would like to express my gratitude to Princeton for making those archival expeditions possible and to my colleagues in Princeton's history department, who included me in a running debate about all aspects of history for nearly four decades. My thanks go especially to the late Lawrence Stone, whose support and friendship sustained me throughout those happy years in Princeton.

I wrote the bulk of this book in 2005 as a fellow of the Carl Friedrich von Siemens Foundation in Munich, which provided generous support in a stimulating setting. Thanks to a fellowship at the National Library of the Netherlands and the Netherlands Institute for Advanced Study in 2006, I was able to complete a first draft and to pursue some related research on the marquis de Pelleport and his extraordinary novel, *Les Bohémiens*. I wish to express my gratitude to Heinrich Meier, Wim Blockmans, Martin Bossenbroek, and the staff of all three institutions.

Several historians and *dix-huitiémistes* read different drafts of the manuscript and offered useful criticism. I would like to thank them and at the same time to absolve them of any responsibility for interpretations I have made that they do not share. They are Olivier Ferret, Renato Pasta, Jeremy Popkin, Jean-François Sené, Will Slauter, and Dale Van Kley. Finally, I want to express my thanks to Jerome Singerman, Yumeko Kawano, and the staff of the University of Pennsylvania Press for their expertise in transforming a complex manuscript into a printed book.

An electronic supplement to this book containing extensive appendices with transcriptions from manuscript sources can be consulted on the Web site of the University of Pennsylvania Press: http://www.upenn.edu/pennpress/darnton supplement.html.